1978
THE COMPLETE HANDBOOK OF
BASEBALL

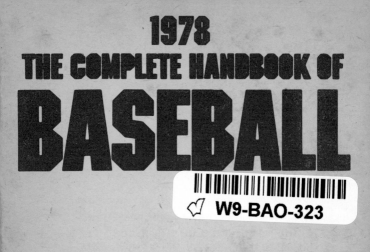

SIGNET Sports Books You'll Enjoy

1978
THE COMPLETE HANDBOOK OF
BASEBALL

EDITED BY ZANDER HOLLANDER

A SIGNET BOOK

NEW AMERICAN LIBRARY

TIMES MIRROR

ACKNOWLEDGMENTS

Good-bye Charlie, hello Marvin and Mile High—at least that's how things stood as THE COMPLETE HANDBOOK OF BASE-BALL went to press. If the anything-can-happen-in-baseball-franchise sweepstakes should produce another turnabout, keep this line ready: Hello Charlie, good-bye Marvin and Mile High. The big question is not really Oakland or Denver, Finley or Davis, but what happens to Charlie's ass. What is more certain is that this is the eighth edition of the handbook, and that it has been made possible through the contributions of the bylined writers and the following all-star lineup: associate editor Jim Poris, Frank Kelly, Lee Stowbridge, Richie Sherwin, Curt Nichols, Steven Danz, Dot Gordineer and Beri Greenwald of Libra Graphics, Seymour Siwoff, Bob Wirz, Bob Fishel, Rick White, Blake Cullen, Katy Feeney, and the publicity directors of the 26 major-league teams.
—*Zander Hollander*

PHOTO CREDITS: Cover—Carl Skalak; back cover—Dorothy Affa. Inside photos: Nancy Hogue, Rich Pilling, Mitch Reibel, George Gojkovich, Mike Valeri, Clifton Boutelle, Ken Regan, William C. Greene, UPI and the major-league teams.

SIGNET TRADEMARK REG. U.S. PAT. OFF. AND FOREIGN COUNTRIES REGISTERED TRADEMARK—MARCA REGISTRADA HECHO EN CHICAGO, U.S.A.

SIGNET, SIGNET CLASSICS, MENTOR, PLUME and MERIDIAN BOOKS are published by The New American Library Inc. 1301 Avenue of the Americas, New York, New York 10019

First Printing, March, 1978

1 2 3 4 5 6 7 8 9

PRINTED IN THE UNITED STATES OF AMERICA

CONTENTS

The Guys Who Killed Carew . . . . By Bob Fowler 6

Bulletin! Howard Cosell
  To Manage the Yankees . . . . By Murray Chass 12

A Tom Seaver Fantasy . . . . By Hal McCoy 18

A Baseball Book of Lists . . . . By Phil Pepe 22

The New Millionaires II 32

Inside the American League . . . . By Phil Pepe 34

New York Yankees 36
Boston Red Sox 47
Baltimore Orioles 57
Milwaukee Brewers 67
Detroit Tigers 77
Cleveland Indians 86
Toronto Blue Jays 96

Texas Rangers 105
California Angels 116
Kansas City Royals . . 126
Chicago White Sox . . 136
Minnesota Twins 147
A's 155
Seattle Mariners 163

Inside the National League . . . . By Pat Calabria 172

Cincinnati Reds 174
Los Angeles Dodgers . 185
Houston Astros 195
San Francisco Giants . 204
San Diego Padres 213
Atlanta Braves 223

Philadelphia Phillies . 231
Pittsburgh Pirates . . . 241
St. Louis Cardinals . . 250
Montreal Expos 260
Chicago Cubs 270
New York Mets 279

Official National League Statistics 294

TV/Radio Roundup 307

Official American League Statistics 310

National League Schedule 328

American League Schedule 332

All-Time Records 336

Editor's Note: The material herein includes trades and rosters up to the final printing deadline.

THE GUYS WHO KILLED CAREW

By BOB FOWLER

Rod Carew believes he can hit .400. He still feels he can become the first major-league baseball player to accomplish that feat since Ted Williams hit .406 in 1941. He thinks he can hit the sport's "magic number" this year. Or, next season. Or the next.

"I don't know when I'll be able to do it," the 32-year-old first baseman of the Minnesota Twins says. "But I think it's possible, if . . ."

If what?

"People don't realize how difficult it is to hit .400," he said. "So much goes into it. You have to avoid getting hurt, and you can't let yourself become tired during the long season, either.

"You can't have any slumps. I have an edge there. When I don't get a hit for a few at-bats, I can beat out a bunt, or try to beat out a bunt.

"Those are the 'ifs.' If I suffer no injuries, don't tire and avoid slumps, I can do it. I can hit .400. Maybe."

"Maybe what?

"Well, in addition to all that, and getting a heckuva lot of hits, you need some luck, too," Carew explained. "I don't mean having bloopers fall in for hits and never having a line drive caught by an infielder. I mean luck fans can't see. For example, if the first pitch is close and the umpire calls it a ball, you get an edge. If it's called a strike, you're in the hole. Well, you need breaks like that, or luck. No one is going to hit .400 when he is constantly hitting from be-

On the beat for the Minneapolis Star, Bob Fowler keeps the count on Rod Carew and his quest for .400.

Rod Carew takes aim anew at the magic .400.

hind in the count. Then, you have to hit the pitcher's pitch and the odds are against you."

It would seem whatever the count, the odds are against Carew, or anyone else, hitting .400. Look at what he accomplished in 1977, for instance:

He hit .388, the highest mark by a major-league player since

Williams hit that in 1957, and the second-highest average since Williams' .406 in 1941. He won an American League batting title by a whopping 52 percentage points over teammate Lyman Bostock, the Twins' outfielder who hit .336 and played out his option to become a free agent.

That was Carew's sixth batting title, and only Ty Cobb (12), Honus Wagner (8), Rogers Hornsby (7) and Stan Musial (7) have won more in big-league history.

In addition, he reached the 100 mark in runs-batted-in for the first time in his illustrious 11-year career, scored a league-leading 128 runs and led the league in triples with 16.

His hit total (239) was the most since Heinie Manush got 241 for the St. Louis Browns in 1928.

Carew set Minnesota club records for runs, hits, batting average, triples and, to prove he was a two-way player, fielding percentage by a first baseman.

For obvious reasons he was named Player of the Year in a poll of major leaguers by *The Sporting News*.

"I can't imagine having a better year," he said. "I can't imagine doing anything more."

Yet, he hit "only" .388. He missed .400 by several hits. Eight to be precise. He batted 616 times and needed 247 hits for a .401 mark instead of the 239 he got.

So why does he believe he still has a chance to reach that ultimate .400 goal?

"In the final analysis, it comes down to the pitchers," he answered. "They're the ones who kept me from hitting .400 last year. And they're the ones I'll have to beat this season, or the next, to hit .400. I don't know why I feel it's a possible goal for me; I'm not optimistic for any particular reason. I just feel I'm 32 years old and reaching the peak of my career. If I have any chance to hit .400, it's going to come in the next few years."

Certainly there were some pitchers who kept Carew from hitting .400 in 1977. Specifically, there were 12 American League rivals who kept him from that plateau. You could call them "The Guys Who Killed Carew." Or, Carew's "Dirty Dozen."

These are 12 pitchers who faced Carew at least six times and were most effective against him. Combined, they limited him to a mere 27 hits in 124 at-bats . . . a .218 average.

But, to be fair about it, we must acknowledge another group, too. This was a collection of 13 pitchers who faced Carew five times or less, but more than twice. And he never got a hit off the members of this group. He was 0-for-47 against them.

They, too, were "The Guys Who Killed Carew." Or, Rod's "Dirty Baker's Dozen."

THE GUYS
WHO KILLED CAREW

(6 or more at-bats)

	AB	H	RBI	AVG.	SO
Ron Guidry, New York	10	1	1	.100	2
Rudy May, Baltimore	9	1	0	.125	4
Dave Rozema, Detroit	12	2	0	.167	0
Moose Haas, Milwaukee	6	1	0	.167	0
Jim Colborn, Kansas City	11	2	1	.182	0
Nolan Ryan, California	14	3	0	.214	4
Paul Hartzell, California	9	2	0	.222	0
Ken Brett, Chicago-California	8	2	0	.250	0
Bill Lee, Boston	11	3	1	.273	1
Andy Hassler, Kansas City	14	4	2	.286	1
Glenn Abbott, Seattle	7	2	3	.286	0
Reggie Cleveland, Boston	7	2	0	.286	0
Dave Lemanczyk, Toronto	7	2	0	.286	0

(5 or less at-bats)

	AB	H	RBI	AVG.	SO
Mike Kekich, Seattle	5	0	2	.000	0
Dave Hamilton, Chicago	4	0	3	.000	0
Dennis Martinez, Baltimore	4	0	0	.000	1
Vincente Romo, Seattle	4	0	0	.000	0
Wayne Simpson, California	4	0	0	.000	0
Dick Tidrow, New York	4	0	0	.000	1
Jim Umbarger, Oakland-Texas	4	0	0	.000	1
Bill Campbell, Boston	3	0	1	.000	1
Steve Hargan, Toronto	3	0	0	.000	0
Dyar Miller, California	3	0	0	.000	0
Rogelio Moret, Texas	3	0	0	.000	1
Marty Pattin, Kansas City	3	0	0	.000	0
Bob Sykes, Detroit	3	0	0	.000	1

After compiling the data to see who had been the most effective in stopping baseball's premiere hitter's bid for a .400 average, it seemed appropriate to ask the man himself who he thought his toughest rivals had been.

"That's hard," Rod admitted. "But I'd say Nolan Ryan was No. 1. He always has given me trouble. He just overpowers hitters.

"Then I'd say Vida Blue, for the same reasons. And No. 3 I'd pick as Sparky Lyle. He has a great slider and, like Ryan and Blue, always challenges you."

Very interesting, Rod. But wrong.

Ryan ranked sixth on the list of pitchers who stopped Carew. Five others, five the Twins' first baseman didn't think of, were more effective than the fastballing right-hander of the California Angels who once again led the American League in strikeouts.

And Vida Blue? Why Carew was 3-for-7 against the Oakland

Yanks' Ron Guidry: toughest on Carew.

THE GUYS
CAREW KILLED

(6 or more at-bats)

	AB	H	RBI	AVG.	SO
Gaylord, Perry Texas	6	5	1	.833	0
Ed Figueroa, New York	12	9	8	.750	0
Jerry Garvin, Toronto	6	4	0	.667	0
Francisco Barrios, Chicago	6	4	0	.667	0
Bob Stanley, Boston	6	4	1	.667	0
Doc Medich, Oakland	10	6	0	.600	0
Paul Lindblad, Texas	7	4	1	.571	1
Larry Sorensen, Milwaukee	9	5	0	.556	0
Paul Splittorff, Kansas City	12	6	0	.500	4
Pat Dobson, Cleveland	6	3	2	.500	0
Catfish Hunter, New York	6	3	0	.500	0

southpaw, making him the 14th "most generous" pitcher for Rod in 1977. Lyle? Carew faced him only four times, but got two hits against the left-hander who eventually won the Cy Young award, becoming the first reliever in American League history to receive it.

But there were other Carew "favorites" last season.

Texas right-hander Gaylord Perry ranked No. 1 on Carew's "hit parade." In six at-bats against Perry, Rod got five hits. Obviously, Perry, who has been accused of throwing "spitters," didn't dampen the ball against Carew.

"I hit the dry spots," Rod said.

Second on this list was New York right-hander Ed Figueroa, who helped his team to win the East Division championship with 17 victories. But in 12 appearances against Carew, he gave up nine hits, including one double, one triple and four home runs. Rod knocked in a whopping eight runs with those nine hits.

"I might have guessed that," Carew said. "He comes at you, he doesn't mess around, and I like that. I knew I wore him out last season, although he's a good pitcher."

Perry and Figueroa weren't alone in being "worn out" by Rod Carew. He compiled .667 averages against Chicago's Francisco Barrios, Boston's Bob Stanley and Toronto rookie Jerry Garvin.

It is interesting to note that Barrios is tied for third on this list.

continued on page 292

BULLETIN

HOWARD COSELL TO MANAGE THE YANKEES

By MURRAY CHASS

The bubbly finally burst for Steinbrenner-Martin.

Believe it or not, stranger than fiction, call it what you will. But remember: the Japanese bombed Pearl Harbor, the Germans blitzed London and the United States dropped an atomic bomb on Hiroshima. It could happen here.

SAN DIEGO, July 10—George Steinbrenner, the irresistible force who owns the Yankees, sits at the bar of the Sheraton Harbor Island Hotel. Next to him is Billy Martin, the immovable object who manages the Yankees. It is the evening before the 1978 All-Star Game and Martin is preparing for his second attempt at managing the American League to victory.

Murray Chass covers the drama of the Yankees for The New York Times and will be pardoned for his flight of fantasy here.

"For Pete's sake, Billy," Steinbrenner is overheard saying to the man who has been his manager for three years now, "why won't you listen to me? If you had listened last year and picked Nolan Ryan from the start instead of making him an afterthought, he could have started for us and the National League wouldn't have scored all those runs in the first inning. Then we would've had a chance to win and it would've been the Yankee brains that turned it around for the American League after all those years of losing.

"And it wasn't just Ryan. If you had put in Nettles and Rice and Scott sooner like I told you, we would have had all those big home-run bats in the game. But just like with Reggie batting cleanup, you wouldn't listen and you wouldn't do it just because I told you to do it. I don't know, Billy. You're just going to have to quit being so stubborn and wake up and do what's right. I won the pennant for you last year and made you look good, didn't I? I mean, we won because Reggie batted cleanup and Piniella played every day. And we won the Series because I got you the right scouting reports, right?

"I would think by now you would realize when to listen to me. But no, you just go on being your stubborn self. You won't be happy until you're managing Peoria in the Three-I League. Now let me tell you for the third time what your lineup should be tomorrow night. First of all, I . . ."

Martin won't let George finish the sentence.

"George," he says, drawling even more than usual, "why don't you shut up? I am sick and tired of hearing what you think I should do with my lineup. I am the manager. THE manager. That means *I* decide who plays and *I* decide who bats where. Me. *I* decide. And *I* don't care what you think. You didn't win the pennant last year. *I* did. In fact, you nearly lost it for us. You had to go and sign Reggie and mess up our nice harmonious team. If you hadn't signed him, we woulda won by 20 games and you coulda given me some of that money because you know I deserved more. I am the best manager in the business, you know. I win wherever I go, or haven't you noticed?"

"With the players I got you, anybody could win," George interrupts, cutting Martin off with a wave of his hand, "Mickey Mouse could win. Mortimer Snerd could win. Why even Howard Cosell could win."

"Cosell!" Martin blurts incredulously. "Cosell! Did you say Cosell? How could you even think such a thing? Cosell do my job? Cosell doesn't know his Astroturf from his toupee. Cosell? You dumb donkey. I'm gonna teach you what you know about baseball. You don't know nuthin' about baseball. You're nuthin' without me and you know it. You and Cosell together couldn't get a man from first to third without having him cut across the pitcher's mound. You #*&%#¢**&#! Cosell, huh. Here's your Howard Cosell!"

SAN DIEGO, July 11—Upon awaking from his night-long sleep, the result of a Billy Martin right to the jaw at a hotel bar, George Steinbrenner announces from his bed at Good Samaritan Hospital that Howard Cosell, the infamous television sports com-

. . . into the hallowed dugout of Miller Huggins and Babe Ruth.

mentator, would replace Martin as manager of the Yankees for the remainder of the season. Or at least for 13 weeks.

"We'll check our ratings—I mean standing—at that time," Steinbrenner mumbles through his wired jaw, "and decide whether or not we want to pick up his option for another 13 weeks. In the meantime, we expect Howard will bring the right touch to the Yankees at this time. From his days on Eastern Parkway in Brooklyn, Howard has possessed an intimate grasp of the game of baseball and this storehouse of knowledge will manifest itself in a preponderance of triumphs for our aggregation the remainder of the season."

NEW YORK, July 13—It is half an hour before the Yankees resume their quest, following the All-Star Game, for a third straight pennant. If they are to win this one, though, they will do it with Happy Howie Cosell as their leader. Howie is about to address his troops for the first time and then send them out to clash with the White Sox of Chicago.

His toupee matted properly on his head, his doubleknit pinstripes hiding his bony legs, the successor to Huggins and McCarthy and Stengel and Martin steps in front of the breathlessly waiting Yankee players.

"Gentlemen," Howie begins in his mellifluous tone, "and I use that word with trepidation, as I said in my book, "Like It Is," which was published in 1974 at $8.95 but I can get it for you wholesale, I have found most baseball players to be afflicted with tobacco-chewing minds. The general run of conversation in the clubhouse and the dugout is a slovenly descent into boastfully profane and vivid recitals of the sexual conquest of the night before. It seems to be almost a psychological compulsion to reestablish one's manhood every day on the ignorant premise that the ability to conquer someone sexually is the all of manhood. No, gentlemen, what we will discourse about from now on in this sanctuary will be, in no particular order of importance, the triumph of our will on the diamond, the importance of the id in our collective effort, the scientific principles behind the propulsion of the spheroid into a state of parabolic fluidity and the deeper meanings of Kantianism as applied to the modern-day work ethic as we know it. And did anybody get 11 down in last Sunday's *New York Times* crossword puzzle?"

KANSAS CITY, July 24—In his first 11 days on the job, Cosell has spent much of his time learning the proper way to put on and wear his uniform. "This isn't as easy as putting on ABC's yellow blazer," he mutters to Pete Sheehy, the Yankees' clubhouse chief who goes back to Babe Ruth's days.

"The Babe would turn in his grave if he could see Cosell in a Yankee uniform," Pete grumbles to himself.

Cosell's sartorial efforts, however, were not enough. Just today he received a note from Steinbrenner telling him his uniform socks were too low; that is, too much blue showed below the bottom of the pants.

"Roone Arledge never complained about my socks," Cosell snorts to his locker.

NEW YORK, Aug. 6—Finally satisfied that his uniform matches his toupee for its impeccable appearance, Cosell feels secure enough to try his hand at some strategy, not dressing strategy but baseball strategy. He calls for a hit-and-run, a run-and-hit, a suicide squeeze bunt, a pitchout, an intentional walk and a five-man infield defense. One problem: the game had been rained out and no one else is on the field.

"Monday night football is never rained out," Happy Howie gripes to the tarpaulin at home plate.

BALTIMORE, Aug. 13—One month after making his debut as Yankee manager, Cosell relieves Dick Howser of his third-base coaching duties and Howser is banished to the dugout to keep a chart on the defensive movements ordered by the Yankees' walkie-talkie brigade. The new third base coach? Who else? Cosell, of course.

"The players," Howie explains at a pre-game news conference, "felt they wanted me to be where they could perceive my visage better, sort of up-close and personal. This way the television cameras can pick up my presence—and I am a presence—with greater facility and the microphone gun can catch my extreme exhortations as I urge my men on in the course of the proceedings."

Howie proves a wizard on the coaching lines. His hands, moving as rapidly as his mouth, flash signals of all varieties to his players. The right hand touches the bill of his cap, the left his thigh. The right hand skims over his left forearm, the left across his letters. He has only one difficulty—he keeps sticking a bony finger in his eye.

He comes through like a drunken sailor doing semaphore. And this gets him into trouble with Mickey Rivers when the fastest Yankee is waved home by a thrashing Cosell. Howard's enthusiasm carries him out of the coaching box and his whirling arm clips Rivers flush on the jaw. Mickey is counted out by both the trainer and the umpire.

continued on page 325

Tom Terrific has a five-year plan.

A TOM SEAVER
FANTASY

By HAL McCOY

A man in a gold jacket, seated between ABC-TV announcers Keith Jackson and Howard Cosell, stuffed a gob of popcorn into his mouth as Game Five of the 1977 World Series droned on down below the booth on the Dodger Stadium grass.

Los Angeles was ripping the Yankees and the outcome of the game was not in doubt.

Suddenly, New York's Reggie Jackson uncoiled that mighty swing he employs and sent the ball spiraling into the right field pavilion for a home run.

The popcorn was no hindrance. Tom Seaver, the third man in the booth, quickly recovered, injecting an incisive and succinct remark about Jackson's home run . . . reacting as a true professional.

Slipping from his red-and-white Cincinnati baseball uniform into the gold blazer of ABC was a smooth operation for Seaver. Critics praised Seaver's work behind the cameras and professional broadcasters liked his work.

"Seaver was refreshing," said veteran Detroit broadcaster Ernie Harwell. "He didn't over-interject himself and he offered real insight when he talked about pitching. His overall discussion of strategy might have been too basic, but when he talked pitching from his own point of view, he was better. As a commentator, he'll have no trouble at all making it."

Hal McCoy has followed the exploits of the Reds in their glory years for the Dayton News, and now he and all of Cincinnati enter the Seaver era.

Partner Keith Jackson was impressed with Seaver's TV delivery, as smooth as the delivery Seaver uses on the mound.

"He worked the broadcast just the way he pitches," said Jackson. "He was not frivolous, He displayed no nonsense and he was completely straight-forward. Tom didn't go within the baseball vernacular, something a lot of jock announcers do.

"Somebody not knowing much about baseball would have been able to understand everything he said. I've known him since he was a pitcher at USC and any time I needed information from him, I've gone to him with my questions and gotten what I wanted. He has the posture and visibility to be a broadcaster if he wants it."

Tom Seaver wants it. It is part of The Tom Seaver Fantasy. Seaver was a journalism major at USC and broadcasting is his No. 2 choice after he finishes dazzling hitters with his fast ball.

"First of all, I'd like to manage," said Seaver. "I'm 33 and I see no reason why I can't pitch five more years, then manage or slip into the broadcasting booth."

Now that Seaver has vacated what he terms "the deterioration of the New York Mets," he can project his future.

"I've joined the best team in baseball," he said. "I love constantly bringing it up, but I can't help but have a better record with the Cincinnati Reds because of their defensive play. People don't realize how much I'm aware of the defense . . . the speed in the outfield and the range in the infield.

"That's why I know, if I remain the consistent pitcher I've always been, I can dream of 300 victories . . . and, yes, 30 victories in one season. Is that so much of a fantasy?

"The trade to Cincinnati is going to help my career. I'm physically capable of winning 300 games, and with the Reds I can do it. If I stay healthy for five years, I can win 300."

Tom went into the 1978 season with 203 victories after achieving a 21-6 mark last year (14-3 for the Reds following his June 15 trade).

"It's like being reborn. There's no telling what I might accomplish now. It's a healthy situation for me . . . I can pitch an entire season for a competitive team and every time out I have a chance to win. That's terrific."

His five-year goals include being in the playoffs and World Series a minimum of three times. "I can envision that. Obviously, with Cincinnati my results will be even better than before. The most important thing—and the most enjoyable—in baseball is to be in the World Series."

When Seaver says, "if I stay healthy for five years . . .," that's no great worry. Taking care of his body is top priority for the 6-1, 205-pounder. Cincinnati manager Sparky Anderson was astound-

Seaver did time on CBS when Jim Bouton (left) was there.

ed when team trainer Larry Starr told him Seaver has never felt a
needle in his pitching arm, has never felt the sting of ice on his
shoulder and that Seaver steps on the scale every day to make sure
the needle stops at 208.

"Seaver's success is no secret," Anderson said. "Body condition-
ing. He works with weights and does nothing to his arm
but stretching exercises. There is a message there for all young
pitchers."

During the World Series, Seaver watched New York's Don
Gullett and immediately determined why Gullett has suffered
arm and shoulder miseries throughout his career. Seaver said Gullett's arm and shoulder must endure all the stress of pitching.
That's not the Seaver method.

"My legs take all the stress of pitching," he said. "That's why I
do so much running and keep my legs in shape. I distribute all the
continued on page 290

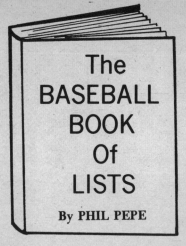

The BASEBALL BOOK Of LISTS

By PHIL PEPE

I must confess, I am an inveterate list-maker. I make lists about anything and everything. I have shopping lists, lists of favorite songs and singers, lists of things to do that never get done, lists of restaurants to try, books to read, movies to see, lists of places to go on vacations I will never take.

I even have a list of my favorite lists.

I once made a list of books I would like to write if I got the time. On it was a Book of Lists. It was 27th on my list. Unfortunately, David Wallechinsky, Irving Wallace and Amy Wallace had it higher on theirs.

The Book of Lists has been on the best seller list, which is a pretty good list to make, speaking of lists. It's also on my list of books to read when I get the time. Trouble is, I never have the time because so much of my time is taken up making lists.

I have been making lists and saving them for years. For no good reason other than it's a lot of fun and a good way to pass the time. I especially enjoy making lists of various baseball teams.

What will I do with these lists? Mostly I keep them for my own amusement, but I have a list of things I can do with them. High on that list is to share them with you, here and now. Excuse me while I make a list of the order in which I present my treasured collection of lists.

The All-Switch-Hitters Team, made up of players who batted

As writers go, Phil Pepe, book author and columnist for the New York Daily News, is at the head of the list.

both right-handed and left-handed for all, or most, of their major league careers:

First base—Ripper Collins

Second base—Red Schoendienst

Shortstop—Maury Wills

Third base—Frank Frisch

Left field—Pete Rose

Center field—Mickey Mantle

Right field—Max Carey

Catcher—Ted Simmons

Pitcher—Robin Roberts

Mickey Mantle: all-time switch-hitter

Readers: If you have your own baseball lists, we'd welcome receiving them. Send to Phil Pepe, Associated Features, 370 Lexington Avenue, New York 10017.

Pete Rose: a swinger from either side

The Seven Commandments of George Steinbrenner, set down by the principal owner of the Yankees when he was asked what he looked for in a manager.

"Actually," Steinbrenner protests, "they are not commandments at all and they aren't even mine. The way this came about, I was talking to Gabe Paul [Yankee president], who has been in baseball for 50 years.

" 'Gabe,' I said, 'what makes a good manager?'

"So Gabe took a piece of his daughter's stationery and wrote on it the seven things he looks for in a manager.

" 'That's good,' I said. 'May I have that?'

"He said I could and so I folded the paper and put it in my jacket pocket. Later that afternoon, I was talking with some newspapermen and they asked me the same question I asked Gabe.

" 'What do you look for in a manager?'

"I pulled out the piece of paper and asked Gabe if I could read it to them and he said I could and that's how this Seven Commandments thing came about."

Nevertheless, they will go down as Steinbrenner's Seven Commandments and he's stuck with them and here they are:

1. Does he win?
2. Does he work hard enough?
3. Is he emotionally equipped to lead men?
4. Is he organized?
5. Does he understand human nature?
6. Is he prepared for each game?
7. Is he honorable?

The best team money can buy.

First base—Norm Cash
Second base—Don Money
Shortstop—Ernie Banks
Third base—Milton Stock
Left field—Art Ruble
Center field—Elmer Pence
Right field—Bobby Bonds
Catcher—Gene Green
Pitcher—Jim Grant

Cash

Banks: an early home-run depositor

This team is for the birds.

First base—Andy Swan
Second base—Johnny Peacock (normally a catcher,
    but played one game at second base
    for Phillies in 1944)
Shortstop—Chicken Stanley
Third base—Jiggs Parrott
Left field—Ducky Medwick
Center field—Goose Goslin
Right field—Bill Eagle
Catcher—Birdie Tebbetts
Pitcher—Robin Roberts or Mark (The Bird) Fidrych.

Goose

Robin

And this one is good in all kinds of weather.

First base—Sunny Jim Bottomley
Second base—Nippy Jones
Shortstop—Gene Freese
Third base—Stormy Weatherly (primarily an out-
    fielder, he played one game at third for
    the 1937 Indians)
Left field—Hurricane Hazle
Center field—Curt Flood
Right field—Icicle Reeder
Catcher—Sun Daly
Pitcher—Windy McCall

Following is a list of major leaguers who are known by the name "Red," even more so than by their real first name, which follows in parentheses.

Red Rolfe (Robert Abial)
Red Ruffing (Charles Herbert)
Red Kress (Ralph)
Red Lucas (Charles Fred)
Red Killefer (Wade)
Red Jones (Maurice Morris)
Red Schoendienst (Albert Fred)
Red Hayworth (Myron Claude)
Red Faber (Urban Clarence)
Red Murff (John Robert)
Red Munger (George David)
Red Barrett (Charles Henry)
Red Embree (Charles Willard)

Red Schoendienst

Following is a similar list of persons known more by their nickname, Whitey, than by their real first name, which follows in parentheses.

Whitey Ford (Edward Charles)
Whitey Kurowski (George John)
Whitey Witt (Lawton Walter)
Whitey Wietelmann (William Frederick)
Whitey Lockman (Carroll Walter)
Whitey Herzog (Dorrel Norman Elvert)

Baseball can discipline itself. Should one of its players step out of line, Bob Dillinger, for instance, or John Crooks or Jimmy Outlaw, that player will quickly be taken to task by one of the following:

Joe Judge
Johnny Bench
Joe Just
Sheriff Robinson
Jim Constable
Marshall Bridges
John Warden
Vernon Law

Law

An order from the Bench in "Mission Impossible"

Then there's the Gamblers Anonymous All-Stars:

First base—Frank Chance
Second base—Lucky Jack Lohrke
Shortstop—John Gamble
Third base—Charlie Deal
Left field—Curt Welch
Center field—Trick McSorley
Right field—Ace Parker
Catcher—Candy LaChance
Pitcher—Tex Hoyle or Shufflin' Phil Douglas

The Women's Lib All-Stars:

First base—She Donahue
Second base—Sadie Houck
Shortstop—Lena Blackburne
Third base—Dolly Stark
Left field—Gail Henley
Center field—Baby Doll Jacobson
Right field—Estel Crabtree
Catcher—Bubbles Hargrave
Pitcher—June Green

Following are lists of batteries (pitcher and catcher) who, unfortunately, never played together. They did, however, play in the major leagues (Source: The Baseball Encyclopedia) and it's a pity we never had the opportunity of hearing the public address announcer say, "The battery for today's game . . ."

East and West
Johnson and Johnson
Holly and Ivie
Barnes and Noble
Hand and Foote
Burns and Allen
Black and White
Butcher and Baker
Nixon and Agnew
Kennedy and Johnson
Lewis and Clark
Rogers and Hart
Gilbert and Sullivan
Franklin and Marshall
Hale and Hardy
Bell and Howell
Mason and Dixon
Masters and Johnson
Black and Decker
More and Moore
Blue and Grey
Queen and King
High and Lowe
Reid and Wright
Short and Long
Stanley and Livingston

Nixon

Agnew

The Church League All-Stars:

First base—Earl Grace
Second base—Johnny Priest
Shortstop—Angel Hermoso
Third base—Frank Bishop
Left field—Dave Pope
Center field—Hi Church
Right field—Maurice Archdeacon
Catcher—Mickey Devine
Pitcher—Howie Nunn or Monk Dubiel, or Tom Parsons and, for the final relief, Digger O'Dell

The Frank Buck "Bring 'Em Back Alive" All-Stars:

First base—Snake Deal
Second base—Nellie Fox
Shortstop—Rabbit Maranville
Third base—Possum Whitted
Left field—Mule Haas
Center field—Goat Anderson
Right field—Ox Echardt
Catcher—Doggie Miller
Pitcher—Old Hoss Radbourne

Fox

Rabbit

The Galloping Gourmet Cook Book All-Stars:

First base—Juice Latham
Second base—Peaches Graham
Shortstop—Joe Bean
Third base—Pie Traynor
Left field—Peanuts Lowrey
Center field—Soupy Campbell
Right field—Oyster Burns
Catcher—Pickles Dillhoefer
Pitcher—Noodles Hahn or Pretzels Pezzullo

This by no means completes my list of lists. I can keep going on, offering you the Alcoholics Anonymous team of Bobby Wine, Jigger Statz, Billy Lush, Half Pint Rye, Brandy Davis and Sherry Robertson.

Or how about the Rand-McNally All-Stars, Germany Schaefer, Frenchy Bordagaray, Chile Gomez, Frank Brazill and the Mad Russian, Lou Novikoff?

Or the Royalty team of King Kelly, Jim King, Mel Queen, Duke Snider, Bris Lord, Earl Averill, Prince Oana, Count Campau and Royal Shaw.

Or the e.e. cummings all-stars, like j.c. martin, j.w. porter, r.c. stevens, i.i. mathison and f.f. mccauley.

I could keep going on and on, an endless list, but then I would have nothing left on my list of things to do and a list with nothing on it is no list at all.

The Duke of Flatbush

Goose Gossage plucked $3.6 million from the Yankees.

The New Millionaires II

It was in Babe Ruth's heyday with the Yankees . . . when he held out for an $80,000 salary. Yankee owner Jacob Ruppert, the beer baron, a hard-nosed bottom-barrel bargainer, told the Babe, "Why the President of the United States (Herbert Hoover) only makes $75,000."

To which the Babe retorted, "I had a better year than he did."

Presidential salaries have changed. And so have those of ballplayers. Jimmy Carter makes $200,000 a year, or $800,000 for a four-year pact as the best softball pitcher ever to take the White House mound. But 11 baseball free agents may well have used Ruth's same line when they went to the bargaining table. Whether they did or didn't have better years than rookie Jimmy Carter, these 11 obtained multiyear contracts ranging from $1,000,000 to $3,600,000.

Except for Ross Grimsley, who had to settle for a little less than $200,000, their annual average exceeds that of the President, with Rich Gossage topping them all at $600,000 per.

Mr. Carter could be pardoned for seeking a new contract for throwing out the first ball on opening day.

PLAYER	TEAM	YEARS	TOTAL
Rich Gossage	Yankees	6	$3,600,000
Larry Hisle	Milwaukee	6	3,200,000
Richie Zisk	Texas	10	2,750,000
Mike Torrez	Boston	7	2,500,000
Oscar Gamble	San Diego	6	2,500,000
Lyman Bostock	California	5	2,400,000
Dave Kingman	Cubs	5	1,400,000
Rawley Eastwick	Yankees	5	1,200,000
Ross Grimsley	Montreal	6	1,100,000
Doc Medich	Texas	4	1,000,000
Elliott Maddox	Mets	5	1,000,000

AMERICAN LEAGUE

By PHIL PEPE
New York News

	East	*West*
PREDICTED	New York Yankees	Texas Rangers
ORDER	Boston Red Sox	California Angels
OF FINISH	Baltimore Orioles	Kansas City Royals
	Milwaukee Brewers	Chicago White Sox
	Detroit Tigers	Minnesota Twins
	Cleveland Indians	Seattle Mariners
	Toronto Blue Jays	A's

Playoff Winner: New York

EAST DIVISION

		Owner		Morning Line Manager
1	**YANKEES** navy blue pin stripe Won last two, trying for three. Class of field.	George M. Steinbrenner	1977 W 100 L 62	**6-5** Billy Martin
2	**RED SOX** navy blue, scarlet & white Early speed, will be in contention to wire.	Mrs. Thomas Yawkey	1977 W 97 L 64	**7-5** Don Zimmer
3	**ORIOLES** black, white & orange Last was perfect; a stayer.	Jerry Hoffberger	1977 W 97 L 64	**4-1** Earl Weaver
4	**BREWERS** white, blue & gold Improving, but still short and in too strong.	Bud Selig	1977 W 67 L 95	**10-1**
5	**TIGERS** white & navy blue Lacks experience in race of older horses.	John Fetzer	1977 W 74 L 88	**20-1** Ralph Houk
6	**INDIANS** scarlet, white & blue Finished badly in last.	Steve O'Neill	1977 W 71 L 90	**30-1** Jeff Torborg
7	**BLUE JAYS** blue, white & red Only one race over track.	Don McDougall	1977 W 54 L 107	**100-1** Roy Hartsfield

Look for the **YANKEES** and **RED SOX** to go to the front, with **ORIOLES** coming on in stretch to challenge. **BREWERS** will make early bid and hang tough until the turn. **TIGERS** could surprise early, but may not handle the distance. **INDIANS** have little to challenge and **BLUE JAYS** in over their heads.

GOOD-BYE CHARLIE O. STAKES

78th Running, American League Race. Distance, 162 games, plus playoff. Purse: $10,000 per winning player, division; $11,000 added, pennant; $7,000 added, World Championship. A field of 14 entered in two divisions.

Track Record 111 Wins—Cleveland 1954

WEST DIVISION		Owner		Morning Line Manager
1	**RANGERS** red, blue & white Stepping up in class. Ready for big effort.	Brad Corbett	1977 W 94 L 68	7-5 Billy Hunter
2	**ANGELS** navy blue, red, gold & white Improving rapidly, but came up lame in last.	Gene Autry	1977 W 74 L 88	8-5 Dave Garcia
3	**ROYALS** royal blue & white Won last two times out. Will be tough to beat.	Ewing Kauffman	1977 W 102 L 60	2-1 Whitey Herzog
4	**WHITE SOX** black & white Last was a surprise. Must be respected.	Bill Veeck	1977 W 90 L 72	10-1 Bob Lemon
5	**TWINS** scarlet, white & blue Not expected to be a factor after poor winter workouts.	Calvin Griffith	1977 W 84 L 77	20-1 Gene Mauch
6	**MARINERS** blue & gold Young and improving, but not ready to challenge.	Danny Kaye-Lester Smith	1977 W 64 L 98	50-1 Darrell Johnson
7	**A's** New stable, same flesh.		1977 W 63 L 98	100-1 Bobby Winkles

Look for a three-horse race, with the **RANGERS, ANGELS** and **ROYALS** battling it out to the wire. **WHITE SOX** will tire after going to front with early speed. **TWINS** will pass tired horses, but will be too far back at turn to challenge. **MARINERS** will be no factor and **A's** will stumble out of gate and go through the motions. **YANKEES**, who have been there, will win match race with **RANGERS.**

NEW YORK YANKEES

TEAM DIRECTORY: Principal Owner: George Steinbrenner III; VP-GM: Cedric Tallis; Exec. VP: Al Rosen; VP-Player Development: Jack Butterfield; Dir. of Minor League Operations: Pat Nugent; Pub. Rel.: Mickey Morabito; Trav. Sec.: Gerry Murphy; Mgr.: Billy Martin. Home: Yankee Stadium (57,131). Field distances: 313, l.f. line; 407, l.f.; 430 l.c.; 419, c.f.; 382, r.c.; 352, r.f. line. Spring training: Ft. Lauderdale, Fla.

SCOUTING REPORT

HITTING: No change here from last year, meaning the Yanks will battle for the league lead in most offensive departments. They won't score as many runs as the Red Sox, perhaps, but they won't need as many, either.

The Yankees tried to add a big bat, but resisted the temptation to acquire Dave Winfield, Dave Parker or Al Oliver. "The price was too high," said owner George Steinbrenner. "I'm not going to break up a championship team for just one man."

So, Billy Martin will have to struggle along with World Series hero Reggie Jackson, Graig Nettles, Thurman Munson, Chris Chambliss and Mickey Rivers, who combined for 116 homers, 476 RBIs. A year under his belt in New York, a sensational second half and the Series showcase could make Jackson even more of a force this year than last. But encroaching age (Nettles 33, Roy White and Lou Piniella, each 34) could be the hidden woe for the world champions.

PITCHING: "I think Catfish is going to come back and have a good year," says Billy Martin.

"We consider Messersmith a good gamble. If his arm is sound, he could be the steal of the year," says George Steinbrenner.

Catfish Hunter (9-9) and Andy Messersmith (5-4) combined for 45 victories just four seasons ago. Even a remote return to that form will set up the Yankee pitching staff, which also includes young sensation Ron Guidry, Don Gullett and Ed Figueroa and three youngsters (Ken Clay, Jim Beattie and Gil Patterson) who will get a long look in spring training.

But the best part is the bullpen—Cy Young winner Sparky Lyle (13 wins, 26 saves), and free agents Rich Gossage (11 wins, 26 saves) and Rawly Eastwick (five wins, 11 saves). With a bullpen like that, Martin can stop the other team in the clubhouse.

FIELDING: Fourth in the league in fielding, the Yankees don't figure to get any worse. "We won last year with pitching and de-

Will Sparky Lyle and Thurman Munson celebrate again in '78?

fense makes your pitching," says Martin. "Especially infield defense."

The Yankees will stack their infield defense with any, especially Gold Glove Graig Nettles at third and their young DP combo of Bucky Dent and Willie Randolph. And don't forget about the man behind the plate. Forget Thurman Munson's 10 errors. Yankee pitchers feel they are better when Thurman is behind the plate and that's why he's not in Cleveland.

OUTLOOK: Still the team to beat until somebody beats them. Just the experience of two straight league titles and the vanity that comes with being world champs makes them better. "We won last year and we improved with Gossage," says Martin. "I don't see any reason why we won't win again."

NEW YORK YANKEES 1978 ROSTER

MANAGER Billy Martin
Coaches—Yogi Berra, Art Fowler, Elston Howard, Dick
       Howser, Gene Michael

PITCHERS

No.	Name	1977 Club	W-L	IP	SO	ERA	B-T	Ht.	Wt.	Born
—	Beattie, Jim	Ft. Lauderdale	1-3	38	28	5.92	R-R	6-6	210	7/4/54 Hampton, VA
		West Haven	2-0	27	20	0.33				
		Syracuse	6-5	80	53	4.15				
50	Clay, Ken	Syracuse	5-1	75	32	1.80	R-R	6-2	194	4/6/54 Lynchburg, VA
		New York(AL)	2-3	56	20	4.34				
—	Eastwick, Rawly	Cin-St. L.	5-9	97	47	3.90	R-R	6-3	180	10/24/50 Camden, NJ
31	Figueroa, Ed	New York(AL)	16-11	239	104	3.58	R-R	6-1	191	10/14/48 Ciales, P.R.
—	Gossage, Rich	Pittsburgh	11-9	133	151	1.62	R-R	6-3	190	7/5/51 Colorado Springs, CO
49	Guidry, Ron	New York(AL)	16-7	211	176	2.82	L-L	5-11	153	8/28/50 Lafayette, LA
35	Gullett, Don	New York(AL)	14-4	158	116	3.59	R-L	6-0	190	1/5/51 Lynn, KY
—	Heinold, Doug	Syracuse	1-2	39	14	2.29	R-R	6-5	167	1/12/55 Victoria, TX
53	Holtzman, Ken	New York(AL)	2-3	72	14	5.75	R-L	6-2	198	11/3/45 St. Louis, MO
29	Hunter, Catfish	New York(AL)	9-9	143	52	4.72	R-R	6-0	205	4/8/46 Hertford, NC
28	Lyle, Sparky	New York(AL)	13-5	137	68	2.17	L-L	6-1	208	7/22/44 DuBois, PA
—	Lysgaard, Jim	Ft. Lauderdale	1-2	22	19	5.73	R-R	6-1	185	6/11/54 Senal, Sask.
		West Haven	13-6	149	102	2.90				
51	McCall, Larry	West Haven	1-1	23	16	2.74	L-R	6-2	182	9/8/52 Candler, NC
		Syracuse	16-7	188	91	3.36				
		New York(AL)	0-1	6	0	7.50				
—	Messersmith, Andy	Atlanta	5-4	102	69	4.41	R-R	6-1	200	8/6/45 Toms River, NJ
22	Patterson, Gil	Syracuse	1-1	28	19	4.88	R-R	6-1	185	9/5/55 Philadelphia, PA
		New York(AL)	1-2	33	29	5.45				
—	Rajsich, Dave	West Haven	8-1	38	38	2.13	L-L	6-5	175	9/21/51 Youngstown, OH
		Syracuse	0-6	57	32	5.88				
19	Tidrow, Dick	New York(AL)	11-4	151	83	3.16	R-R	6-4	213	5/14/47 San Francisco, CA

CATCHERS

No.	Name	1977 Club	H	HR	RBI	Pct.	B-T	Ht.	Wt.	Born
40	Healy, Fran	New York(AL)	17	0	7	.224	R-R	6-5	210	9/6/46 Holyoke, MA
—	Heath, Mike	West Haven	93	8	42	.265	R-R	5-11	175	2/5/55 Tampa, FL
—	Irwin, Dennis	Syracuse	80	14	54	.246	R-R	6-0	170	1/11/54 Tulare, CA
41	Johnson, Cliff	Houston	43	10	23	.299	R-R	6-4	217	7/22/47 San Antonio, TX
		New York(AL)	42	12	31	.296				
15	Munson, Thurman	New York(AL)	183	18	100	.308	R-R	5-11	195	6/7/47 Akron, OH
—	Narron, Jerry	West Haven	132	28	93	.301	L-R	6-3	185	1/15/56 Goldsboro, NC

INFIELDERS

10	Chambliss, Chris	New York(AL)	172	17	90	.287	L-R	6-1	209	12/26/48 Dayton, OH
20	Dent, Bucky	New York(AL)	118	8	49	.247	R-R	5-11	181	11/25/51 Savannah, GA
—	Garcia, Damaso	West Haven	118	0	53	.265	R-R	6-0	155	2/7/57 Moca, D.R.
39	Klutts, Mickey	Syracuse	92	14	66	.288	R-R	5-11	170	9/30/54 Montebello, CA
		New York(AL)	4	1	4	.267				
9	Nettles, Graig	New York(AL)	150	37	107	.255	L-R	6-0	186	8/20/44 San Diego, CA
30	Randolph, Willie	New York(AL)	151	4	40	.274	R-R	5-11	164	7/6/54 Holly Hill, SC
—	Ramos, Domingo	West Haven	106	2	50	.246	R-R	5-10	154	3/29/58 Santiago, D.R.
—	Spencer, Jim	Chicago(AL)	116	18	69	.247	L-L	6-2	195	7/30/47 Hanover, PA
11	Stanley, Fred	New York(AL)	12	1	7	.261	R-R	5-10	166	8/13/47 Farnhamville, IA
25	Zeber, George	New York(AL)	21	3	12	.323	B-R	6-0	181	8/29/50 Ellwood City, PA

OUTFIELDERS

27	Alston, Dell	Syracuse	74	3	21	.298	L-R	6-0	175	9/22/52 Valhalla, NY
		New York(AL)	13	1	4	.325				
2	Blair, Paul	New York(AL)	43	4	25	.262	R-R	6-0	177	2/1/44 Cushing, OK
44	Jackson, Reggie	New York(AL)	150	32	110	.286	L-L	6-0	205	5/18/46 Wyncote, PA
—	Jones, Darryl	Syracuse	118	10	54	.330	R-R	5-10	175	6/5/51 Meadville, PA
14	Piniella, Lou	New York(AL)	112	12	45	.330	R-R	6-2	198	8/28/43 Tampa, FL
17	Rivers, Mickey	New York(AL)	184	12	69	.326	L-L	5-10	165	10/30/48 Miami, FL
6	White, Roy	New York(AL)	139	14	52	.268	B-R	5-10	171	12/27/43 Los Angeles, CA

YANKEE PROFILES

REGGIE JACKSON 31 6-0 205   Bats L Throws L

"This was my toughest year. I'm glad it's over."
. . . Signed for $3 million as a free agent, feuded with manager Billy Martin, criticized for poor fielding, booed in Baltimore, bombarded in Boston with missiles from stands, still he survived, even thrived . . . Moved into cleanup spot on Aug. 10, sparked team with 13 HRs, 49 RBI in last 53 games . . . World Series was his crowning achievement. Record five HRs in six games, including three on three successive swings in climactic sixth game . . . "I can't believe it, I did something even Babe Ruth never did." . . . Born May 18, 1946, in Wyncote, Pa. . . . Three-sport star in HS, went to Arizona State . . . Self-proclaimed superstar, and worthy of name . . . "If I played in New York, they'd name a candy bar after me." . . . They did.

Year	Club	Pos	G	AB	R	H	2B	3B	HR	RBI	SB	Avg.
1967	Kansas City	OF	35	118	13	21	4	4	1	6	1	.178
1968	Oakland	OF	154	553	82	138	13	6	29	74	14	.250
1969	Oakland	OF	152	549	123	151	36	3	47	118	13	.275
1970	Oakland	OF	149	426	57	101	21	2	23	66	26	.237
1971	Oakland	OF	150	567	87	157	29	3	32	80	16	.277
1972	Oakland	OF	135	499	72	132	25	2	25	75	9	.265
1973	Oakland	OF	151	539	99	158	28	2	32	117	22	.293
1974	Oakland	OF	148	506	90	146	25	1	29	93	25	.289
1975	Oakland	OF	157	593	91	150	39	3	36	104	17	.253
1976	Baltimore	OF	134	498	84	138	27	2	27	91	28	.277
1977	New York (AL)	OF	146	525	93	150	39	2	32	110	17	.286
	Totals		1511	5373	891	1442	286	30	313	934	188	.268

THURMAN MUNSON 30 5-11 195   Bats R Throws R

Captain Thurm . . . A huge teddy bear . . . Squatty body . . . Gruff exterior, but warm heart . . . Yankees' indispensable man . . . "One of the greatest players I've seen in 50 years," says president Gabe Paul . . . Grew beard in defiance of club rule as a protest over discontent with contract . . . Born June 7, 1947, in Akron, Ohio . . . Lives in Canton and has hinted he'd like to play closer to home . . . "We're not going to trade Munson unless we can help the Yankees and I don't see how trading him will help the Yankees," says Paul . . . First player in almost 20 years to have three straight years of 100 RBIs,

.300 BA . . . One of most productive catchers of all time . . . A future Hall of Famer.

Year	Club	Pos	G	AB	R	H	2B	3B	HR	RBI	SB	Avg.
1969	New York (AL) ...	C	26	86	6	22	1	2	1	9	0	.256
1970	New York (AL) ...	C	132	453	59	137	25	4	6	53	5	.302
1971	New York (AL) ...	C-OF	125	451	71	113	15	4	10	42	6	.251
1972	New York (AL) ...	C	140	511	54	143	16	3	7	46	6	.280
1973	New York (AL) ...	C	147	519	80	156	29	4	20	74	4	.301
1974	New York (AL) ...	C	144	517	64	135	19	2	13	60	2	.261
1975	New York (AL) ...	C-OF-1B-3B	157	597	83	190	24	3	12	102	3	.318
1976	New York (AL) ...	C-OF	152	616	79	186	27	1	17	105	14	.302
1977	New York (AL) ...	C	149	595	85	183	28	5	18	100	5	.308
	Totals..........		1172	4345	581	1265	184	28	104	591	45	.291

GRAIG NETTLES 33 6-0 186   Bats L Throws L

His finest year; 37 homers (missing second straight title by two), first time over 100 RBIs, finally acknowledged as league's best third baseman with first Gold Glove . . . "A gamer," says Billy Martin. "He plays hurt and he doesn't let his defense suffer when he's not hitting." . . . Has missed only 22 games in five seasons in New York . . . Born Aug. 20, 1944, in San Diego . . . Joined 200 HR club . . . Broke club records for HRs, RBIs by a third baseman . . . "I get as much of a kick out of saving a game with a great play as winning one with a home run." . . . Named all-time Yankee third baseman, but still underpublicized and (he thinks) underpaid. "I guess I'm just not controversial enough."

Year	Club	Pos	G	AB	R	H	2B	3B	HR	RBI	SB	Avg.
1968	Minnesota	OF-3B-1B	22	76	13	17	2	1	5	8	0	.224
1969	Minnesota	OF-3B	96	225	27	50	9	2	7	26	1	.222
1970	Cleveland........	3B-OF	157	549	81	129	13	1	26	62	3	.235
1971	Cleveland........	3B	158	598	78	156	18	1	28	86	7	.261
1972	Cleveland........	3B	150	557	65	141	28	0	17	70	2	.253
1973	New York (AL) ...	3B	160	552	65	129	18	0	22	81	0	.234
1974	New York (AL) ...	3B-SS	155	566	74	139	21	1	22	75	1	.246
1975	New York (AL) ...	3B	157	581	71	155	24	4	21	91	1	.267
1976	New York (AL) ...	3B	158	583	88	148	29	2	32	93	11	.254
1977	New York (AL) ...	3B	158	589	99	150	23	4	37	107	2	.255
	Totals..........		1374	4879	661	1215	186	16	217	699	28	.249

SPARKY LYLE 33 6-1 208   Bats L Throws L

First relief pitcher in AL history (second in majors) to win Cy Young Award . . . "I'm so excited, I can't stand still," when told of award. "If I had to pitch now, I couldn't do it. I'm too nervous." . . . But Mr. Cool on mound . . . "I'm thrilled with this award not only for myself, but for all relief pitchers. Maybe they will get more recognition from now on." . . . Record 621 major-league appearances without start . . . 201 career saves, 160 in six seasons with Yankees . . . Born July 22, 1944, in Dubois, Pa. . . . Notorious practical joker and super flake . . . Married during season and rode from church to reception in fire engine . . . "I've only had a sore arm once in my life and it was in my right arm."

Year	Club	G	IP	W	L	Pct.	SO	BB	H	ERA
1967	Boston	27	43	1	2	.333	42	14	33	2.30
1968	Boston	49	66	6	1	.857	52	14	67	2.73
1969	Boston	71	103	8	3	.727	93	48	91	2.53
1970	Boston	63	67	1	7	.125	51	37	62	3.90
1971	Boston	50	52	6	4	.600	37	23	41	2.77
1972	New York (AL)	59	108	9	5	.643	75	29	84	1.92
1973	New York (AL)	51	82	5	9	.357	63	18	66	2.51
1974	New York (AL)	66	114	9	3	.750	89	43	93	1.66
1975	New York (AL)	49	89	5	7	.417	65	36	94	3.13
1976	New York (AL)	64	104	7	8	.467	61	42	82	2.25
1977	New York (AL)	72	137	13	5	.722	68	33	131	2.17
	Totals	621	965	70	54	.565	696	334	844	2.44

CHRIS CHAMBLISS 29 6-1 209   Bats L Throws L

When Yankees got off to slow start, Martin pulled lineup out of hat and Chambliss was No. 8 . . . Chambliss' bat came alive. "I've got to say he's one of the best eighth-place hitters of all time," said Billy Martin . . . Owner George Steinbrenner calls his two-run homer in second to tie WS game No. 2 at 2-2, "perhaps the biggest hit of the year for us." . . . Born Dec. 26, 1948, in Dayton, Ohio, the son of a Navy chaplain . . . Will always be remembered for sudden-death HR vs. Royals in ninth inning of fifth game of '76 AL playoffs.

Year	Club	Pos	G	AB	R	H	2B	3B	HR	RBI	SB	Avg.
1971	Cleveland	1B	111	415	49	114	20	4	9	48	2	.275
1972	Cleveland	1B	121	466	51	136	27	2	6	44	3	.292
1973	Cleveland	1B	155	572	70	156	30	2	11	53	4	.273
1974	Cleve-N.Y. (AL)	1B	127	467	46	119	20	3	6	50	0	.255
1975	New York (AL)	1B	150	562	66	171	38	4	9	72	0	.304
1976	New York (AL)	1B	156	641	79	188	32	6	17	96	1	.293
1977	New York (AL)	1B	157	600	90	172	32	6	17	90	4	.287
	Totals		977	3723	451	1056	209	27	75	453	14	.284

MICKEY RIVERS 29 5-10 165   Bats L Throws L

Mick The Quick . . . One of most popular Yankees and one of most vocal . . . Fourth-leading hitter in league and covered huge Yankee Stadium center field like a blanket . . . Born October 31, 1948, in Miami . . . Walks like an old man, but runs as if he's being chased . . . "When I go to spring training, I don't work on the bad things, I work on my good things.

You can't improve what's bad." . . . Credits Paul Blair with helping him improve throwing . . . "Do you know how many assists you have?" he was asked in June. "About three," he said. "You have six," he was told. "That's better than three," he decided.

Year	Club	Pos	G	AB	R	H	2B	3B	HR	RBI	SB	Avg.
1970	California	OF	17	25	6	8	2	0	0	3	1	.320
1971	California	OF	78	268	31	71	12	2	1	12	13	.265
1972	California	OF	58	159	18	34	6	2	0	7	4	.214
1973	California	OF	30	129	26	45	6	4	0	16	8	.349
1974	California	OF	118	466	69	133	19	11	3	31	30	.285
1975	California	OF	155	615	70	175	17	13	1	53	70	.285
1976	New York (AL)	OF	137	590	95	184	31	8	8	67	43	.312
1977	New York (AL)	OF	138	565	79	184	18	5	12	69	22	.326
	Totals		731	2817	394	834	111	45	25	258	191	.296

RON GUIDRY 27 5-11 153   Bats L Throws L

After horrible spring training (an ERA over 10), he emerged as Yankees' most consistent starter . . . Could be next pitching superstar of AL . . . Super arm, his fastball timed at 96 mph . . . Remarkable strength for his size . . . Great all-around athlete, helps himself in field and is used as pinch runner . . . Born August 28, 1950, in Lafayette, La. . . . "We always knew he had a great arm," says Billy Martin. "It was just a matter of him gaining the confidence. A lot of people thought he was a seven-inning pitcher and maybe he began believing it, too. He had to learn he could finish games." . . . Completed nine and tied for second in league with five shutouts.

Year	Club	G	IP	W	L	Pct.	SO	BB	H	ERA
1975	New York (AL)	10	16	0	1	.000	15	9	15	3.38
1976	New York (AL)	20	16	0	0	.000	12	4	20	5.63
1977	New York (AL)	31	211	16	7	.696	176	65	174	2.82
	Totals	61	243	16	8	.667	203	78	209	3.04

DON GULLETT 27 6-0 190   Bats R Throws L

After seven years in Cincinnati, left to take Yankees' $1.9 million over six years . . . Continued to be plagued by injuries (shoulder, foot), still had best winning percentage in AL, .778, for career percentage of .686, tops among active pitchers . . . Started opening game of World Series third straight year . . . Born Jan. 5, 1951, in Lynn, Ky. . . . In high school, scored 10 TDs in one game. Also once struck out 20 of 21 batters . . . Quiet, country boy. You can take the boy out of the farm, but you can't take the farm out of the boy . . . "Where I come from, even Cincinnati was a big change. I adjusted to New York."

Year	Club	G	IP	W	L	Pct.	SO	BB	H	ERA
1970	Cincinnati	44	78	5	2	.714	76	44	54	2.42
1971	Cincinnati	35	218	16	6	.727	107	64	196	2.64
1972	Cincinnati	31	135	9	10	.474	96	43	127	3.93
1973	Cincinnati	45	228	18	8	.692	153	69	198	3.51
1974	Cincinnati	36	243	17	11	.607	183	88	201	3.04
1975	Cincinnati	22	160	15	4	.789	98	56	127	2.42
1976	Cincinnati	23	126	11	3	.786	64	48	119	3.00
1977	New York (AL)	22	158	14	4	.778	116	69	137	3.59
	Totals	258	1346	105	48	.686	893	481	1159	3.10

WILLIE RANDOLPH 23 5-11 164   Bats R Throws R

Keeps getting better all the time . . . "He knows how to play the game and he wants to win," says ex-Yankee Gene Michael . . . Serious young man who does charitable work without fanfare or publicity . . . A local product born in Holly Hills, S.C., on July 6, 1954, but raised in Brooklyn . . . Signed with Pirates, but traded to Yankees and figures to be a fixture at second base for years . . . Quick hands make him a whiz at turning double play . . . Knee problem curtailed his running game, but still stole 13 bases in 19 attempts. . . Homered off Don Sutton in World Series opener.

Year	Club	Pos	G	AB	R	H	2B	3B	HR	RBI	SB	Avg.
1975	Pittsburgh	2B-3B	30	61	9	10	1	0	0	3	1	.164
1976	New York (AL)	2B	125	430	59	115	15	4	1	40	37	.267
1977	New York (AL)	2B	147	551	91	151	28	11	4	40	13	.274
	Totals		302	1042	159	276	44	15	5	83	51	.265

JIM HUNTER 31 6-0 205   Bats R Throws R

Catfish . . . First of the free agents . . . Two years left on his $3 million contract and indicates he will pack it in after that. . . Frustrated by recent injuries . . . Bounced back in spring training from last year's shoulder problem and was pitching shutout on opening day when hit in foot with line drive . . . Out for month and never the same. . . Fewest victories since 1966 . . . But one of five active pitchers with 200 victories and fourth pitcher in history (Cy Young, Walter Johnson, Christy Mathewson) to win 200 before 31st birthday . . . Passed Early Wynn as all-time AL champ at giving up home runs . . . Born April 8,

1946, in Hertford, N.C., and still lives there . . . Simple, humble farm boy who has not changed, say friends and neighbors . . . "I think Catfish is going to do a 180 degree turn in 1978 and have a great year," predicts Yankee boss George Steinbrenner.

Year	Club	G	IP	W	L	Pct.	SO	BB	H	ERA
1965	Kansas City	32	133	8	8	.500	82	46	124	4.26
1966	Kansas City	30	177	9	11	.450	103	64	158	4.02
1967	Kansas City	35	260	13	17	.433	196	84	209	2.80
1968	Oakland	36	234	13	13	.500	172	69	210	3.35
1969	Oakland	38	247	12	15	.444	150	85	210	3.35
1970	Oakland	40	262	18	14	.563	178	74	253	3.81
1971	Oakland	37	274	21	11	.656	181	80	225	2.96
1972	Oakland	38	295	21	7	.750	191	70	200	2.04
1973	Oakland	36	256	21	5	.808	124	69	222	3.34
1974	Oakland	41	318	25	12	.676	143	46	268	2.49
1975	New York (AL)	39	328	23	14	.622	177	83	248	2.58
1976	New York (AL)	36	299	17	15	.531	173	68	268	3.52
1977	New York (AL)	22	143	9	9	.500	52	47	137	4.72
	Totals	460	3226	210	151	.582	1922	885	2732	3.18

ANDY MESSERSMITH 32 6-1 200   Bats R Throws R

The Landmark . . . Changed baseball's reserve system by playing out contract with Dodgers and declaring himself a free agent in 1975 . . . That opened the way for free agent market . . . Braves signed him to contract for over $1 million . . . Injuries have checked his career in Atlanta . . . Yanks taking a chance on him . . . Had no-hitter against Montreal broken up in ninth-inning in 1976 . . . Born Aug. 6, 1945, in Toms River, N.J. . . . Has twice won pitcher's Golden Glove award . . . Tied major-league record and set NL mark by striking out the first six Phillies to start a game in 1973 . . . Named to four all-star teams, including one in AL . . . Blows biggest bubble gum bubbles around.

Year	Club	G	IP	W	L	Pct.	SO	BB	H	ERA
1968	California	28	81	4	2	.667	74	35	44	2.22
1969	California	40	250	16	11	.593	211	100	169	2.52
1970	California	37	195	11	10	.524	162	78	144	3.00
1971	California	38	277	20	13	.606	179	121	224	2.99
1972	California	25	170	8	11	.421	142	68	125	2.81
1973	Los Angeles	33	250	14	10	.583	177	77	196	2.70
1974	Los Angeles	39	292	20	6	.769	221	94	227	2.59
1975	Los Angeles	42	322	19	14	.576	213	96	244	2.29
1976	Atlanta	29	207	11	11	.500	135	74	166	3.04
1977	Atlanta	16	102	5	4	.556	69	39	101	4.41
	Totals	327	2146	128	92	.582	1583	782	1640	2.77

RICH GOSSAGE 26 6-3 190   Bats R Throws R

The Goose . . . Found golden egg with Yankees and it's worth $3.6 million . . . Fastball is elusive. . . . With Pirates was second in NL in ERA, had most victories among relievers and was third in league with 26 saves . . . Led Pirates in strikeouts . . . Was starter for White Sox in 1976 after a year in which he had 26 saves and was AL Fireman-of-the-Year . . .

Born July 5, 1951, in Colorado Springs . . . Won first seven major-league decisions, all in relief . . . Purchased a bullpen mascot for Pirates . . . A goose, naturally.

Year	Club	G	IP	W	L	Pct.	SO	BB	H	ERA
1972	Chicago (AL)	36	80	7	1	.875	57	44	72	4.28
1973	Chicago (AL)	20	50	0	4	.000	33	37	57	7.38
1974	Chicago (AL)	39	89	4	6	.400	64	47	92	4.15
1975	Chicago (AL)	62	142	9	8	.529	130	70	99	1.84
1976	Chicago (AL)	31	224	9	17	.346	135	90	214	3.94
1977	Pittsburgh	72	133	11	9	.550	151	49	78	1.62
	Totals	260	718	40	45	.471	570	237	612	3.40

TOP PROSPECTS

MICKEY KLUTTS 23 5-11 170   Bats R Throws R

Suffered tough break when he fractured hand in spring training while competing for regular shortstop job. Returned to Syracuse and was shifted to third base . . . Considered heir apparent to Nettles' third base job . . . Born Sept. 30, 1954, in Montebello, Cal. . . . Almost quit after '75 season, blossomed in '76 with 24 HRs, 80 RBI and shared International League's MVP award.

DELL ALSTON 25 6-0 175   Bats L Throws R

Came up last year and performed well as pinch hitter . . . Missed out on chance to take part in playoffs and World Series when Yankees were disallowed replacement for departed Carlos May . . . Will get full shot as lefty DH this year . . . Born Sept. 22, 1952, in White Plains, N.Y., a stone's throw from Yankee Stadium. Raised in Yonkers, where he was all-county player . . . Great speed and lifetime .300 hitter in minor leagues . . . Works in PR department of college in off season.

MANAGER BILLY MARTIN: "This was my roughest year," he said. "I was fired five times and I fired myself three times." . . . But he survived to win his first world championship and disprove popular theory that he cannot win twice consecutively with a team . . . "This makes it all worthwhile," he said, during victory celebration . . . Born Alfred Manuel Martin, May 16, 1928, in Berkeley, Cal. . . . "As a manager, he borders on genius," says his wife, Gretchen . . . Feuded with owner George Steinbrenner and resisted suggested moves . . . "I have to live and die on my own convictions." . . . His idol is Casey Stengel. Has the only job he ever wanted . . . "When I die, there will be pinstripes on my coffin."

GREATEST MANAGER

There have been three great managers, in three eras, covering three Yankee dynasties. The era of the 20s had Babe Ruth, Murderers' Row and Miller Huggins. In the 30s and 40s, there was Joe DiMaggio and Marse Joe McCarthy. The late 40s and 50s had Mickey Mantle and Casey Stengel . . . and you could look it up.

Picking the greatest Yankee manager of them all is no easy task — each won more than 1,000 games, each dominated the American League in his time. But Huggins' six championships in 11 years and McCarthy's eight championships in 15 years do not compare with Stengel's 10 championships in 12 years.

Clown, syntax scrambler, master of the malaprop, Charles Dillon Stengel was baseball's greatest good-will ambassador. He was 57 years old when he took over as manager of the lordly Yankees, having failed in previous trials in Boston and Brooklyn. In 12 years, he had a winning percentage of .623, failed only twice to win a pennant and finished no lower than third. Nobody ever did it better . . . and you could look that up, too.

ALL-TIME YANKEE LEADERS

BATTING: Babe Ruth, .393, 1923
HRs: Roger Maris, 61, 1961
RBIs: Lou Gehrig, 184, 1931
STEALS: Fred Maisel, 74, 1914
WINS: Jack Chesbro, 41, 1904
STRIKEOUTS: Jack Chesbro, 240, 1904

BOSTON RED SOX

TEAM DIRECTORY: President: Mrs. Thomas A. Yawkey; VP-GM: Haywood Sullivan; VP: Edward "Buddy" LeRoux; Pub. Rel.: Bill Crowley; Trav. Sec.: John Rogers; Mgr.: Don Zimmer. Home: Fenway Park (33,543). Field distances: 315, l.f. line; 390, c.f.; 420, c.f. corner; 380, r.c.; 302, r.f. line. Spring training: Winter Haven, Fla.

SCOUTING REPORT

HITTING: The word is awesome. Second in batting and runs. First in homers and RBIs. The Red Sox intimidate with league

Hank Aaron feels Bosox' Jim Rice may crack his homer mark.

homer and slugging percentage leader Jim Rice, plus Carl Yastrzemski, Butch Hobson, George Scott, Fred Lynn and Carlton Fisk.

Now they've come up with Jerry Remy, who gives them speed and a base-stealing threat, and young Ted Cox, who is ready to step in.

A visit to Fenway Park is something like going into a den of lions armed with a cap pistol.

PITCHING: It was a $2.5 million insurance policy the Red Sox bought when they signed free agent Mike Torrez. Not only did they add his 17 victories to their staff, they took them away from their chief rivals, the Yankees. But the Yankees point out that Torrez was only four games over .500 and he alone cannot carry a staff.

The Sox agree. They are counting on a comeback from Luis Tiant (12-8, 4.52 ERA), the strength and endurance of super reliever Bill Campbell (13-9, 2.96 ERA, 31 saves) and the continued development of youngsters Mike Paxton and Bob Stanley. That's why they traded another young right arm, Don Aase to the Angels. Skeptics insist the Red Sox could not afford to surrender such a pitcher and that pitching remains their main area of vulnerability.

FIELDING: The return to good health of premier right fielder Dwight Evans, the addition of second baseman Jerry Remy and the improvement of third baseman Butch Hobson are the items counted on by the Red Sox to bolster a defense that was fifth best in the league.

Only the Orioles, Twins and Brewers made more DPs and the Sox feel they have improved that part of their game with Remy. George Scott had an off year, his 24 errors letting the Gold Glove slip away. But Fred Lynn was a brilliant center fielder, Rick Burleson his usual steady self at short, Carl Yastrzemski a remarkable ageless magician playing that wall in left and Carlton Fisk outstanding behind the plate.

OUTLOOK: It never changes in Boston. They will win games, 9-8 or lose them, 9-8. They will bludgeon you to death, or go long gaps without scoring. And their pitching will make things as interesting as their bats will make them exciting.

There is no better lineup in the division, but the big question remains: can the hitters continually withstand the burden of having to score six runs a game to win? Last year, they couldn't. And nothing much has changed in Fenway.

BOSTON RED SOX 1978 ROSTER

MANAGER Don Zimmer
Coaches—Walt Hriniak, Al Jackson, John Pesky, Eddie
          Yost

PITCHERS

No.	Name	1977 Club	W-L	IP	SO	ERA	B-T	Ht.	Wt.	Born
43	Burton, Jim	Pawtucket	10-10	160	101	3.78	R-L	6-3	198	4/14/53 Royal Oak, MI
		Boston	0-0	3	3	0.00				
22	Campbell, Bill	Boston	13-9	140	114	2.96	R-R	6-3	190	8/9/48 Highland Park, MI
26	Cleveland, Reggie	Boston	11-8	190	85	4.26	R-R	6-1	205	5/23/48 Swift Current, Sask.
—	Drago, Dick	Cal-Balt	6-4	61	35	3.39	R-R	6-1	200	6/24/45 Toledo, OH
—	Finch, Joel	Bristol	15-6	181	—	3.13	R-R	6-2	175	— South Bend, Ind.
21	Kreuger, Rick	Pawtucket	11-5	96	49	3.19	R-L	6-2	185	11/3/48 Grand Rapids, MI
		Boston	0-1	0	0					
37	Lee, Bill	Boston	9-5	128	31	4.43	L-L	6-3	205	12/28/46 Burbank, CA
—	Paxton, Mike	Pawtucket	5-0	55	—	0.82	R-R	5-11	190	— Memphis, Tenn.
		Boston	10-5	108	58	3.83				
—	Rainey, Chuck	Bristol	4-3	59	—	2.29	R-R	5-11	195	— San Diego, CA
		Pawtucket	5-9	123	60	3.07				
28	Ripley, Allen	Pawtucket	15-4	144	99	4.43	R-R	6-3	180	10/18/52 Norwood, MA
—	Remmerswaal, Win	Bristol	9-11	140	—	3.47	R-R	6-2	160	— Wassenaar, Holland
		Pawtucket	0-0	8	5	4.50				
46	Stanley, Bob	Boston	8-7	151	44	3.99	R-R	6-4	205	11/10/54 Portland, ME
23	Tiant, Luis	Boston	12-8	189	124	4.52	R-R	5-11	190	11/23/40 Havana, Cuba
—	Torrez, Mike	Oak-NY (AL)	17-13	243	102	3.93	R-R	6-5	202	8/28/46 Topeka, KS
—	Waller, Rich	Bristol	4-3	88	—	1.43	R-R	6-2	195	— Clifton, NJ
		Pawtucket	0-0	12	9	4.50				
38	Willoughby, Jim	Boston	6-2	55	33	4.91	R-R	6-2	205	1/31/49 Salinas, CA
40	Wise, Rick	Boston	11-5	128	85	4.78	R-R	6-2	195	9/13/45 Jackson, MI
48	Wright, Jim	Pawtucket	12-8	159	76	2.94	R-R	6-1	165	12/21/50 Reed City, MI

CATCHERS

No.	Name	1977 Club	H	HR	RBI	Pct.	B-T	Ht.	Wt.	Born
39	Diaz, Bo	Pawtucket	81	7	54	.263	R-R	5-11	190	3/23/53 Cua, Venez.
		Boston	0	0	0	.000				
27	Fisk, Carlton	Boston	169	26	102	.315	R-R	6-2	215	12/26/47 Bellows Falls, VT
50	Merchant, Andy	Pawtucket	55	2	32	.239	L-R	5-11	185	8/30/50 Mobile, AL
10	Montgomery, Bob	Boston	12	2	7	.300	R-R	6-1	210	4/16/44 Nashville, TN

INFIELDERS

No.	Name	1977 Club	H	HR	RBI	Pct.	B-T	Ht.	Wt.	Born
11	Aviles, Ramon	Pawtucket	52	1	30	.218	R-R	5-9	155	1/22/52 Manati, P.R.
		Boston	0	0	0	.000				
41	Baker, Jack	Pawtucket	77	14	45	.274	R-R	6-5	218	5/4/50 Birmingham, AL
		Boston	0	0	0	.000				
—	Bailey, Bob	Cincinnati	20	2	11	.253	R-R	6-0	187	10/13/42 Long Beach, CA
		Boston	0	0	0	.000				
—	Brohamer, Jack	Chicago(AL)	39	2	20	.257	L-R	5-9	165	2/26/50 Maywood, CA
7	Burleson, Rick	Boston	194	3	52	.293	R-R	5-10	165	4/29/51 Lynwood, CA
18	Cox, Ted	Pawtucket	114	14	81	.334	R-R	6-3	190	1/24/55 Oklahoma City, OK
		Boston	21	1	6	.362				
3	Dillard, Steve	Boston	34	1	13	.241	R-R	6-1	180	2/8/51 Memphis, TN
5	Doyle, Denny	Boston	109	2	49	.240	L-R	5-9	165	1/17/44 Louisville, KY
—	Helms, Tommy	Pittsburgh	0	0	0	.000	R-R	5-10	177	5/5/41 Charlotte, NC
		Boston	16	1	5	.271				
4	Hobson, Butch	Boston	157	30	112	.265	R-R	6-1	190	8/17/51 Tuscaloosa, AL
—	Remy, Jerry	California	145	4	44	.252	L-R	5-9	160	11/8/52 Fall River, MA
15	Scott, George	Boston	157	33	95	.269	R-R	6-2	210	3/23/44 Greenville, MS

OUTFIELDERS

No.	Name	1977 Club	H	HR	RBI	Pct.	B-T	Ht.	Wt.	Born
—	Bowen, Sam	Pawtucket	96	15	49	.265	R-R	5-9	167	— Brunswick, GA
		Boston	0	0	0	.000				
1	Carbo, Bernie	Boston	66	15	34	.289	L-R	6-0	185	8/5/47 Detroit, MI
24	Evans, Dwight	Boston	66	14	36	.287	R-R	6-3	205	11/3/51 Santa Monica, CA
19	Lynn, Fred	Boston	129	18	76	.260	L-L	6-1	185	2/3/52 Chicago, IL
14	Rice, Jim	Boston	206	39	114	.320	R-R	6-2	200	3/8/53 Anderson, SC
8	Yastrzemski, Carl	Boston	165	28	102	.296	L-R	5-11	190	8/22/39 Southampton, NY

RED SOX PROFILES

CARL YASTRZEMSKI 38 5-11 190   Bats L Throws R

Captain Carl . . . The ageless wonder . . . And one of the game's truly class guys . . . Starting his 18th year and as good as ever . . . "I never get tired. Never. Maybe it's because I enjoy the game and I never let myself get out of shape." . . . Born Aug. 22, 1939, in Southhampton, N.Y. . . . In baseball's all-time top 30 in games, at bats, doubles, homers, RBIs, walks . . . Plays left field wall in Fenway like he was its architect . . . "I haven't set any deadlines on how long I want to play. Nobody is going to have to tell me when it's over. I'll know and I won't hang around."

Year	Club	Pos	G	AB	R	H	2B	3B	HR	RBI	SB	Avg.
1961	Boston	OF	148	583	71	155	31	6	11	80	6	.266
1962	Boston	OF	160	646	99	191	43	6	19	94	7	.296
1963	Boston	OF	151	570	91	183	40	3	14	68	8	.321
1964	Boston	OF-3B	151	567	77	164	29	9	15	67	6	.289
1965	Boston	OF	133	494	78	154	45	3	20	72	7	.312
1966	Boston	OF	160	594	81	165	39	2	16	80	8	.278
1967	Boston	OF	161	579	112	189	31	4	44	121	10	.326
1968	Boston	OF-1B	157	539	90	162	32	2	23	74	13	.301
1969	Boston	OF-1B	162	603	96	154	28	2	40	111	15	.255
1970	Boston	1B-OF	161	566	125	186	29	0	40	102	23	.329
1971	Boston	OF	148	508	75	129	21	2	15	70	8	.254
1972	Boston	OF-1B	125	455	70	120	18	2	12	68	5	.264
1973	Boston	1B-3B-OF	152	540	82	160	25	4	19	95	9	.296
1974	Boston	1B-OF	148	515	93	155	25	2	15	79	12	.301
1975	Boston	1B-OF	149	543	91	146	30	1	14	60	8	.269
1976	Boston	1B-OF	155	546	71	146	23	2	21	102	5	.267
1977	Boston	1B-OF	150	558	99	165	27	3	28	102	11	.296
	Totals		2571	9406	1501	2724	516	53	366	1445	161	.290

CARLTON FISK 30 6-2 215   Bats R Throws R

Had his best year for good reason—he stayed healthy . . . Played over 140 games (152) first time in career and was also first time over 100 in runs, RBIs . . . Developed as excellent handler of pitchers . . . "Mostly it's a matter of confidence," says Mike Paxton. "Pudge has been around the league. He inspires confidence in us and we have confidence in him." . . . Born Dec. 26, 1947, in Bellows Falls, Vt. . . . Lives in New Hampshire and has served as chairman of state's Easter Seals drive . . . Will always be remembered for dramatic game-winning HR, Game 6 of '75 Series, which remains his top thrill.

Year	Club	Pos	G	AB	R	H	2B	3B	HR	RBI	SB	Avg.
1969	Boston	C	2	5	0	0	0	0	0	0	0	.000
1971	Boston	C	14	48	7	15	2	1	2	6	0	.313
1972	Boston	C	131	457	74	134	28	9	22	61	5	.293
1973	Boston	C	135	508	65	125	21	0	26	71	7	.246
1974	Boston	C	52	187	36	56	12	1	11	26	5	.299
1975	Boston	C	79	263	47	87	14	4	10	52	4	.331
1976	Boston	C	134	487	76	124	17	5	17	58	12	.255
1977	Boston	C	152	536	106	169	26	3	26	102	7•	.315
	Totals		699	2491	411	710	120	23	114	376	40	.285

JIM RICE 25 6-2 200   Bats R Throws R

Most devastating hitter in league . . . Led league in HRs and third in RBIs despite month-long slump at end of season . . . "Some day he'll hit 50 homers," says veteran coach Johnny Pesky . . . Maybe this year . . . Tabbed by Hank Aaron as best bet among active players to threaten career HR mark . . . Has hit 79 in three seasons and has short left field to shoot at . . . Born March 8, 1953, in Anderson, S.C. . . . Used primarily as DH, but has played LF and RF . . . Short, smooth swing and should continue to improve with experience . . . Must cut down Ks, 365 in three years.

Year	Club	Pos	G	AB	R	H	2B	3B	HR	RBI	SB	Avg.
1974	Boston	OF	24	67	6	18	2	1	1	13	0	.269
1975	Boston	OF	144	564	92	174	29	4	22	102	10	.309
1976	Boston	OF	153	581	75	164	25	8	25	85	8	.282
1977	Boston	OF	160	644	104	206	29	15	39	114	5	.320
	Totals		481	1856	277	562	85	28	87	314	23	.303

BILL CAMPBELL 29 6-3 190   Bats R Throws R

Hit jackpot playing out option in Minnesota, signing for $1 million with Sox, who are not sorry . . . He kept Boston in race all season . . . Finished with 31 saves, 13 wins, top reliever in AL . . . Appeared in 69 games and tired arm caused late season slump . . . Born August 9, 1948, in Highland Park, Mich. . . . Was turned down by Twins in request for $8,000 raise, enabling him to become "The Millionaire." . . . Was historic first to sign after baseball's first re-entry draft . . . Relies on sinker and screwball as money pitches, obviously worth half a million each.

Year	Club	G	IP	W	L	Pct.	SO	BB	H	ERA
1973	Minnesota	38	52	3	3	.500	42	20	44	3.12
1974	Minnesota	63	120	8	7	.533	89	55	109	2.63
1975	Minnesota	47	121	4	6	.400	76	46	119	3.79
1976	Minnesota	78	168	17	5	.773	115	62	145	3.00
1977	Boston	69	140	13	9	.591	114	60	112	2.96
	Totals	285	601	45	30	.600	436	243	529	3.08

LUIS TIANT 37 5-11 190   Bats R Throws R

Lowest win total since 1971 brought about predictions of his demise . . . But he's been written off before . . . Several times . . . Man of many motions . . . Most popular player in Red Sox history . . . Contract dispute resulted in late reporting to spring training and slow start . . . Heartbroken over death of both parents during winter . . . Born Nov. 11, 1940, in Havana, Cuba . . . Some think he is cheating a few years . . . Tiant resents the insinuation . . . Makes his home in Boston area and plans to remain there . . . Father was Negro League pitching star . . . Released by Minnesota and Atlanta, his is one of game's great all-time comeback stories . . . Now he must prove it again.

Year	Club	G	IP	W	L	Pct.	SO	BB	H	ERA
1964	Cleveland	19	127	10	4	.714	105	47	94	2.83
1965	Cleveland	41	196	11	11	.500	152	66	166	3.54
1966	Cleveland	46	155	12	11	.522	145	50	121	2.79
1967	Cleveland	33	214	12	9	.571	219	67	177	2.73
1968	Cleveland	34	258	21	9	.700	264	73	152	1.60
1969	Cleveland	38	250	9	20	.310	156	129	229	3.71
1970	Minnesota	18	93	7	3	.700	50	41	84	3.39
1971	Boston	21	72	1	7	.125	59	32	73	4.88
1972	Boston	43	179	15	6	.714	123	65	128	1.91
1973	Boston	35	272	20	13	.606	206	78	217	3.34
1974	Boston	38	311	22	13	.629	176	82	281	2.92
1975	Boston	35	260	18	14	.563	142	72	262	4.02
1976	Boston	38	279	21	12	.636	131	64	274	3.06
1977	Boston	32	189	12	8	.600	124	51	210	4.52
	Totals	471	2855	191	140	.577	2052	917	2468	3.15

BUTCH HOBSON 26 6-1 190   Bats R Throws R

Brand new star . . . Remarkable record of hitting in clutch . . . A 112 RBI-man (tied for fourth) in first full season . . . Also much improved defensively . . . Born Aug. 17, 1951, in Tuscaloosa, Ala. . . . Dad, Clell Hobson, was Alabama football great . . . Butch was QB for Bear Bryant in Alabama's 1972 Orange Bowl game vs. Nebraska for national title . . . Real name Clell Lavern, Jr. . . . Knocked Rico Petrocelli into retirement . . . "If I can play him enough to get him 500 at bats, I guarantee he'll hit 20 home runs," predicted Don Zimmer . . . 30 homers in 593 at bats made Zim more than a prophet.

Year	Club	Pos	G	AB	R	H	2B	3B	HR	RBI	SB	Avg.
1975	Boston	3B	2	4	0	1	0	0	0	0	0	.250
1976	Boston	3B	76	269	34	63	7	5	8	34	0	.234
1977	Boston	3B	159	593	77	157	33	5	30	112	5	.265
	Totals		237	866	111	221	40	10	38	146	5	.255

RICK BURLESON 26 5-10 165   Bats R Throws R

Rooster . . . Underrated hero of Red Sox . . . Steady without being flashy and a great competitor . . . "He made himself a good hitter by hard work," says Don Zimmer. "Same when he's taking ground balls in practice. A lot of guys fool around, but Rick's out there working hard." . . . Born April 29, 1951, in Lynwood, Cal. . . . Threatened to play out option in '76, he signed big contract, but did not get complacent . . . Had best year in '77 in BA, at bats, runs, hits, doubles, triples . . . Promoted to leadoff by Zimmer and has responded with his best production over last year and half.

Year	Club	Pos	G	AB	R	H	2B	3B	HR	RBI	SB	Avg.
1974	Boston	SS-2B-3B	114	384	36	109	22	0	4	44	3	.284
1975	Boston	SS	158	580	66	146	25	1	6	62	8	.252
1976	Boston	SS	152	540	75	157	27	1	7	42	14	.291
1977	Boston	SS	154	663	80	194	36	7	3	52	13	.293
	Totals		578	2167	257	606	110	9	20	200	38	.280

GEORGE SCOTT 34 6-2 210   Bats R Throws R

Return to Boston wasn't all Boomer thought it would be . . . Had big year in homers and RBIs, but made staggering total of 24 errors, was criticized widely by press and booed by fans . . . His reaction was to sulk . . . Complained when batted seventh and withdrew into a shell saying "I'm not mentally ready to play." . . . Born March 23, 1944, in Greenville, Miss. . . . "I know I didn't have a good year. I know I have to lose some weight. But I believe you must have faith and all I can do is not worry about it and bounce back next year."

Year	Club	Pos	G	AB	R	H	2B	3B	HR	RBI	SB	Avg.
1966	Boston	1B-3B	162	601	73	147	18	7	27	90	4	.245
1967	Boston	1B-3B	159	565	74	171	21	7	19	82	10	.303
1968	Boston	1B-3B	124	350	23	60	14	0	3	25	3	.171
1969	Boston	3B-1B	152	549	63	139	14	5	16	52	4	.253
1970	Boston	3B-1B	127	480	50	142	24	5	16	63	4	.296
1971	Boston	1B	146	537	72	141	16	4	24	78	0	.263
1972	Milwaukee	1B-3B	152	578	71	154	24	4	20	88	16	.266
1973	Milwaukee	1B	158	604	98	185	30	4	24	107	9	.306
1974	Milwaukee	1B	158	604	74	170	36	2	17	82	9	.281
1975	Milwaukee	1B	158	617	86	176	26	4	36	109	6	.285
1976	Milwaukee	1B	156	606	73	166	21	5	18	77	0	.274
1977	Boston	1B	157	584	103	157	26	5	33	95	1	.269
	Totals		1809	6675	860	1808	260	52	253	948	66	.271

FRED LYNN 26 6-1 185   Bats L Throws L

Riddled by injuries, he has struggled for two years after storybook rookie year . . . But young enough and talented enough to make great comeback . . . One of best center fielders in game, he made miracle catch in Minnesota on national TV . . . Bothered by contract dispute in '76, but signed long-term, $1 million deal and is happy . . . Born Feb. 2, 1952, in Chicago . . . Moved to California and starred at USC . . . Will never duplicate, or forget, night of June 18, 1975, in Detroit. He hit three home runs, triple and single, had 10 RBIs and tied record with 16 total bases.

Year	Club	Pos	G	AB	R	H	2B	3B	HR	RBI	SB	Avg.
1974	Boston	OF	15	43	5	18	2	2	2	10	0	.419
1975	Boston	OF	145	528	103	175	47	7	21	105	10	.331
1976	Boston	OF	132	507	76	159	32	8	10	65	14	.314
1977	Boston	OF	129	497	81	129	29	5	18	76	2	.260
	Totals		421	1575	265	481	110	22	51	256	26	.305

MIKE TORREZ 31 6-5 202   Bats R Throws R

Asked to pitch with three days' rest, he responded with seven straight complete game wins during stretch run . . . Obtained in early trade for Dock Ellis, he was happy in New York and admitted receiving fine offer from Yankees. . . "But I'm curious to see what I can bring on the open market," he said when announcing free agency. "It's my last chance to set up me and my family for life." . . . Red Sox gave him $2.5 million worth of security . . . Born Aug. 28, 1946, in Topeka, Kan. . . . Pitched with one day rest and held Royals scoreless for five innings in relief in fifth playoff game, then won two games in Series, including clincher . . . "Earl Weaver told me he was one of the best competitors in the league," said Billy Martin. "I had to find out for myself."

Year	Club	G	IP	W	L	Pct.	SO	BB	H	ERA
1967	St. Louis	3	6	0	1	.000	5	1	5	3.00
1968	St. Louis	5	19	2	1	.667	6	12	20	2.84
1969	St. Louis	24	108	10	4	.714	61	62	96	3.58
1970	St. Louis	30	179	8	10	.444	100	103	168	4.22
1971	St. L-Montreal	10	39	1	2	.333	10	31	45	5.54
1972	Montreal	34	243	16	12	.571	112	103	215	3.33
1973	Montreal	35	208	9	12	.429	90	115	207	4.46
1974	Montreal	32	186	15	8	.652	92	84	184	3.58
1975	Baltimore	36	271	20	9	.690	119	133	238	3.06
1976	Oakland	39	266	16	12	.571	115	87	231	2.50
1977	Oak-N.Y. (AL)	35	243	17	13	.567	102	86	235	3.93
	Totals	283	1768	114	84	.576	812	817	1644	3.55

BILL LEE 31 6-3 205   Bats L Throws L

Super flake . . . Possessed of quick wit and great intelligence, but known as Space Man . . . Running feud with Yankees' Billy Martin . . . "I don't know if I'm crazy or not. Maybe I'm crazy because I try to buck the system. I know people consider me different." . . . Born Dec. 28, 1946, in Burbank, Cal. . . . Another product of USC, he was picked on 22nd round of 1968 draft . . . "I'm not happy with the commercialization of the game and the players. The economics of it bothers me sometimes. I think the sport should be for the sport's sake." . . . Maybe he's not as flaky as they say.

Year	Club	G	IP	W	L	Pct.	SO	BB	H	ERA
1969	Boston	20	52	1	3	.250	45	28	56	4.50
1970	Boston	11	37	2	2	.500	19	14	48	4.62
1971	Boston	47	102	9	2	.818	74	46	102	2.74
1972	Boston	47	84	7	4	.636	43	32	75	3.21
1973	Boston	38	285	17	11	.607	120	76	275	2.75
1974	Boston	38	282	17	15	.531	95	67	320	3.51
1975	Boston	41	260	17	9	.654	78	69	274	3.95
1976	Boston	24	96	5	7	.417	29	28	124	5.63
1977	Boston	27	128	9	5	.643	31	29	155	4.43
	Totals	293	1326	84	58	.592	534	389	1429	3.67

JERRY REMY 25 5-9 160   Bats L Throws R

Third in league in stolen bases . . . 110 steals in three seasons . . . Jerry Kapstein helped him negotiate five year deal . . . Voted Owner's Trophy (a horse?) as outstanding Angel in '76 . . . "It meant a lot to me because it was voted by my teammates." . . . Born Nov. 8, 1952, in Fall River, Mass. . . . Now back home with Bosox . . . His idol is Pete Rose . . . "He gives baseball everything he's got." . . .

Year	Club	Pos	G	AB	R	H	2B	3B	HR	RBI	SB	Avg.
1975	California	2B	147	569	82	147	17	5	1	46	34	.258
1976	California	2B	143	502	64	132	14	3	0	28	35	.263
1977	California	2B	154	575	74	145	19	10	4	44	41	.252
	Totals		444	1646	220	424	50	18	5	118	110	.258

TOP PROSPECT

TED COX 23 6-3 190   Bats R Throws R

Another in long line of right-handed hitting youngsters promoted by Red Sox in recent years . . . Called up in September, he made sensational debut, hitting safely in first six at bats . . . Born Jan. 24, 1955, in Oklahoma City . . . Signed as shortstop, moved to third base, but with Butch Hobson blocking him there, may wind up as first baseman.

MANAGER DON ZIMMER: Likable skipper whose character is  reflected in wire he sent Billy Martin after Yankees eliminated Red Sox: "Congratulations. It was a great race, but in the stretch we finished like one of the horses I bet on." . . . Born Jan. 17, 1931, in Cincinnati . . . Originally signed with Dodgers, as a hard-hitting shortstop, but career was curtailed by PeeWee Reese playing ahead of him and by two unfortunate beanings . . . Played 12 years for Dodgers, Cubs, Red, Mets and Senators, doing whatever was asked of him, including catching . . . Member in good standing of baseball's tobacco-chewing Hall of Fame.

GREATEST MANAGER

In their long and sometimes glorious history, the Red Sox have won nine championships and they were achieved by seven different managers—James J. Collins, J. Garland Stahl, Bill (Rough) Carrigan, Ed Barrow, Joe Cronin, Dick Williams and Darrell Johnson. Only two—Collins in '03 and '04 and Carrigan in '15 and '16—ever won more than one.

Of Carrigan, Babe Ruth once said: "He was the greatest manager I ever played for."

And, indeed, he might have been one of the greatest of all-time had Carrigan not retired to Maine after three seasons with a promise to "return if the team ever really needs me." It did, in the 20s, and Carrigan returned only to finish seventh, third and fourth in three seasons.

As a rival to Carrigan, there is Joe Cronin, who became manager of the Washington Senators at 26 and moved to the Red Sox two years later. He was at the Red Sox helm longer than any other manager, 13 years, won one pennant, four seconds and a winning percentage of .540. He also holds the distinction of being the only man in baseball history to be a Hall of Fame player, manager, general manager and league president.

ALL-TIME RED SOX LEADERS

BATTING: Ted Williams, .406, 1941
HRs: Jimmy Foxx, 50, 1938
RBIs: Jimmy Foxx, 175, 1938
STEALS: Tommy Harper, 54, 1973
WINS: Joe Wood, 34, 1912
STRIKEOUTS: Joe Wood, 258, 1912

BALTIMORE ORIOLES

TEAM DIRECTORY: Chairman of the Board: Jerold C. Hoffberger; Chairman Exec. Comm. and Treas.: Zanvyl Krieger; VP: Frank Cashen; Exec. VP and Gen. Mgr.: Henry Peters; VP: Jack Dunn III; VP and Sec.: Joseph P. Hamper, Jr.; Pub. Rel.: Bob Brown; Trav. Sec.: Philip Itzoe; Mgr.: Earl Weaver. Home: Memorial Stadium (52,137). Field distances: 309, l.f. line; 385, l.c.; 405, c.f.; 385, r.c.; 309, r.f. line. Spring training: Miami, Fla.

Ken Singleton's .328 average set a new Oriole record.

SCOUTING REPORT

HITTING: Only Earl Weaver predicted the Orioles would hit enough last year to stay in the race, and he was right. Optimistic Earl says the same this year.

"We have Lee May, who drives in 100 runs every year (99 last year) and Eddie Murray, who hit almost as many home runs as Reggie Jackson (27, five fewer) and Ken Singleton, who is one of the best hitters in the league (.328, third behind Rod Carew and Lyman Bostock)," Weaver points out.

With Al Bumbry to get on base ahead of them and Andres Mora expected to improve on last year (.245, 13 homers, 44 RBIs), the Orioles may have just enough bats to keep them in the race.

PITCHING: There's no way, it seems, the Orioles can pick up the 32 wins that departed with Rudy May (traded to Montreal) and Ross Grimsley (free agent). But somehow, the Orioles always find a way.

Fifth in the league in pitching last year, the Orioles are high on their young pitchers—Mike Flanagan, Dennis Martinez and Scott McGregor. They felt they had to shore up their bullpen and they did, getting Don Stanhouse (10 wins, 10 saves) from Montreal to team with Tippy Martinez. And there is always Jim Palmer, with seven 20-game seasons out of the last eight and shooting for an unprecedented fourth Cy Young Award.

FIELDING: It's hard to believe that after seven Gold Glove seasons, the Orioles contemplated trading Mark Belanger, 33. Fortunately, they didn't. "He's the best shortstop in the history of baseball statistically," says Earl Weaver.

And he's better than ever. The Orioles led the AL in fielding and in double plays, and it all starts at shortstop.

Brooks Robinson is gone and so are Bobby Grich and Paul Blair, but the Orioles carry on as the stingiest defense in the league and that kind of leather behind them makes Oriole pitchers tougher than they seem.

OUTLOOK: On paper, the Orioles don't look like they can compete with the Yankees and Red Sox. They didn't last year, either, but they missed the pennant by two-and-a-half games and finished in a tie with the Red Sox for second. They do it with defense, with pitching, with only a handful of key hitters and with mirrors. And they do it with a manager named Earl Weaver, a winner.

BALTIMORE ORIOLES 1978 ROSTER

MANAGER Earl Weaver
Coaches—Jim Frey, Cal Ripken

PITCHERS

No.	Name	1977 Club	W-L	IP	SO	ERA	B-T	Ht.	Wt.	Born
53	Blair, Dennis	Denver	5-4	76	50	5.11	R-R	6-5	182	6/5/54 Middleton, OH
		Rochester	4-3	67	24	3.65				
55	Briles, Nelson	Tex-Balt.	6-4	112	59	4.18	R-R	5-11	205	8/5/43 Dorris, CA
45	Chevez, Tony	Rochester	5-9	123	65	4.46	R-R	5-11	177	6/20/54 Telica, Nicaragua
		Baltimore	0-0	8	7	12.38				
17	Farmer, Ed	Rochester	11-5	131	96	4.47	R-R	6-5	210	10/18/49 Evergreen Park, IL
		Baltimore								
46	Flanagan, Mike	Baltimore	15-10	235	149	3.64	L-L	6-0	185	12/16/51 Manchester, NH
–	Flinn, John	Rochester	10-7	119	80	3.56	R-R	6-1	180	9/2/54 Merced, CA
–	Ford, Dave	Rochester	9-14	176	96	4.81	R-R	6-4	210	12/29/56 Cleveland, OH
–	Kerrigan, Joe	Montreal	3-5	89	43	3.24	R-R	6-5	210	1/30/54 Philadelphia, PA
30	Martinez, Dennis	Baltimore	14-7	167	107	4.10	R-R	6-1	170	5/14/55 Granada, Nicaragua
23	Martinez, Tippy	Baltimore	5-1	50	29	2.70	L-L	5-10	170	5/31/50 LaJunta, CO
39	McGregor, Scott	Baltimore	3-5	114	55	4.42	B-L	6-1	188	1/18/54 Inglewood, CA
–	Pagnozzi, Mike	Charlotte	8-10	152	94	3.73	L-L	6-2	186	8/29/54 Tucson, AZ
22	Palmer, Jim	Baltimore	20-11	319	193	2.91	R-R	6-3	196	10/15/45 New York, NY
–	Rineer, Jeff	Charlotte	8-6	93	48	3.19	L-L	6-4	210	7/3/55 Lancaster, PA
–	Stanhouse, Don	Montreal	10-10	158	89	3.42	R-R	6-2	195	2/12/51 DuQuoin, IL
–	Stewart, Sammy	Rochester	0-5	54	28	6.29	R-R	6-3	207	10/28/54 Asheville, NC
		Charlotte	6-0	117	56	2.08				
–	Stoddard, Tim	Charlotte	10-7	174	94	3.21	R-R	6-7	250	1/24/53 East Chicago, IND

CATCHERS

No.	Name	1977 Club	H	HR	RBI	Pct.	B-T	Ht.	Wt.	Born
24	Dempsey, Rick	Baltimore	61	3	34	.226	R-R	6-0	185	9/13/49 Fayetteville, TN
–	Hendricks, Elrod	New York (AL)	3	1	5	.273	L-R	6-1	185	12/22/40 St. Thomas, V.I.
		Syracuse	38	11	37	.281				
12	Rudolph, Ken	San Francisco	3	0	0	.200	R-R	6-1	190	12/29/46 Rockford, IL
		Baltimore	4	0	2	.286				
8	Skaggs, Dave	Baltimore	62	1	24	.287	R-R	6-1	195	6/12/51 Santa Monica, CA

INFIELDERS

No.	Name	1977 Club	H	HR	RBI	Pct.	B-T	Ht.	Wt.	Born
7	Belanger, Mark	Baltimore	83	2	30	.206	R-R	6-2	170	6/8/44 Pittsfield, MASS
10	Crowley, Terry	Rochester	124	30	80	.308	L-L	6-0	175	2/16/47 Staten Island, NY
		Baltimore	8	1	9	.364				
44	Dauer, Rick	Baltimore	74	5	25	.243	R-R	6-0	180	7/27/52 San Bernardino, CA
11	Decinces, Doug	Baltimore	135	19	69	.259	R-R	6-2	190	8/29/50 Burbank, CA
3	Garcia, Kiko	Baltimore	29	2	10	.221	R-R	5-11	170	10/14/53 Martinez, CA
–	Jarquin, Gersan	Charlotte	32	0	12	.239	R-R	5-7	147	11/26/54 Leon, Nicaragau
		Rochester	37	0	7	.278				
14	May, Lee	Baltimore	148	27	99	.253	R-R	6-3	205	3/23/43 Birmingham, AL
33	Murray, Eddie	Baltimore	173	27	88	.283	B-R	6-2	180	2/24/56 Los Angeles, CA
16	Muser, Tony	Baltimore	27	0	7	.229	L-L	6-1	190	8/1/47 Los Angeles, CA
2	Smith, Billy	Baltimore	79	5	29	.215	B-R	6-2½	185	7/14/53 Hodge, LA

OUTFIELDERS

No.	Name	1977 Club	H	HR	RBI	Pct.	B-T	Ht.	Wt.	Born
1	Bumbry, Al	Baltimore	164	4	41	.317	L-R	5-8	175	4/21/47 Fredericksburg, VA
36	Dimmel, Mike	Charlotte	105	6	22	.288	R-R	6-0	180	10/16/54 Albert Lea, MN
		Miami	40	2	15	.268				
		Baltimore	0	0	0	.000				
34	Harlow, Larry	Baltimore	10	0	8	.208	L-L	6-2	175	11/13/51 Colorado Springs, CO
		Rochester	115	9	50	.335				
18	Kelly, Pat	Baltimore	92	10	49	.256	L-L	6-1	190	7/30/44 Philadelphia, PA
–	Lopez, Carlos	Seattle	84	8	34	.283	R-R	6-1	190	9/27/50 Mazatlan, Mex.
27	Mora, Andres	Rochester	55	11	45	.301	R-R	6-0	170	5/25/55 Saltillo, Coach, Mex.
		Baltimore	57	13	44	.245				
–	Roenicke, Gary	Denver	144	11	72	.321	R-R	6-3	200	12/5/54 Covina, CA
29	Singleton, Ken	Baltimore	176	24	99	.328	B-R	6-4	213	6/10/47 New York, NY

ORIOLE PROFILES

JIM PALMER 32 6-3 196   Bats R Throws R

 Third straight 20-win season, seventh in last eight years . . . Beaten out in bid for fourth Cy Young Award . . . League leader in starts, complete games, innings pitched . . . Outspoken individual . . . Born Oct. 15, 1945, in New York City, but family moved when he was infant . . . Raised in California and Arizona . . . Finished season with seven straight victories after struggling early . . . Came back twice in career from crippling injuries . . . Hit bottom in 1969 when he was sent to minors and not protected in expansion draft. But he bounced back to become the outstanding pitcher in AL.

Year	Club	G	IP	W	L	Pct.	SO	BB	H	ERA
1965	Baltimore	27	92	5	4	.556	75	56	75	3.72
1966	Baltimore	30	208	15	10	.600	147	91	176	3.46
1967	Baltimore	9	49	3	1	.750	23	20	34	2.94
1969	Baltimore	26	181	16	4	.800	123	64	131	2.34
1970	Baltimore	39	305	20	10	.667	199	100	263	2.71
1971	Baltimore	37	282	20	9	.690	184	106	231	2.68
1972	Baltimore	36	274	21	10	.677	184	70	219	2.07
1973	Baltimore	38	296	22	9	.710	158	113	225	2.40
1974	Baltimore	26	179	7	12	.368	84	69	176	3.27
1975	Baltimore	39	323	23	11	.676	193	80	253	2.09
1976	Baltimore	40	315	22	13	.629	159	84	255	2.51
1977	Baltimore	39	319	20	11	.645	193	99	263	2.91
	Totals	386	2823	194	104	.651	1722	952	2301	2.64

KEN SINGLETON 30 6-4 213   Bats S Throws R

 With a brand, new five-year contract worth $750,000, Ken had greatest year of his career, breaking Bob Nieman's club record for batting (.322) and finishing third in league . . . "If you talk about consistency, coming to the ballpark day in and day out and getting the job done, you have to rank Ken right up there with the best of them," says Earl Weaver. "I'd put him in a class with Brooks and Frank (Robinson) as the best I've had play for me." . . . Born June 10, 1947, in New York City . . . A Met fan, he signed with his favorite team, then moved to Montreal and Baltimore . . . "The baseball I knew as a kid, the baseball I enjoy, is playing the game. I know you have to go through contract negotiations, but that's not the part of the game I enjoy."

Year	Club	Pos	G	AB	R	H	2B	3B	HR	RBI	SB	Avg.
1970	New York (NL)...	OF	69	198	22	52	8	0	5	26	1	.263
1971	New York (NL)...	OF	115	298	34	73	5	0	13	46	0	.245
1972	Montreal	OF	142	507	78	139	23	2	14	50	5	.274
1973	Montreal	OF	162	560	100	169	26	2	23	103	2	.302
1974	Montreal	OF	148	511	68	141	20	2	9	74	5	.276
1975	Baltimore........	OF	155	586	88	176	37	4	15	55	3	.300
1976	Baltimore........	OF	154	544	62	151	25	2	13	70	2	.278
1977	Baltimore........	OF	152	536	90	176	24	0	24	99	0	.328
	Totals..........		1097	3740	541	1077	168	12	116	523	18	.288

LEE MAY 35 205   Bats R Throws R

Quiet man . . . A professional hitter who gets paid to drive in runs and does it . . . Joined 300-homer and 1,000-RBI clubs . . . Came back from slow start, two homers, 17 RBIs in first 40 games . . . Born March 23, 1943, in Birmingham, Ala. . . . Not related to teammate Rudy, brother of Carlos . . . They are fourth in history as homer-hitting brothers behind Aarons, DiMaggios and Boyers. . . . Originally signed by Reds, then traded to Houston and an Oriole last three seasons . . . One of best trades ever by Orioles, who have made some good ones.

Year	Club	Pos	G	AB	R	H	2B	3B	HR	RBI	SB	Avg.
1965	Cincinnati	PH	5	4	1	0	0	0	0	0	0	.000
1966	Cincinnati	1B	25	75	14	25	5	1	2	10	0	.333
1967	Cincinnati	1B-OF	127	438	54	116	29	2	12	57	4	.265
1968	Cincinnati	1B-OF	146	559	78	162	32	1	22	80	4	.290
1969	Cincinnati	1B-OF	158	607	85	169	32	3	38	110	5	.278
1970	Cincinnati	1B	153	605	78	153	34	2	34	94	1	.253
1971	Cincinnati	1B	147	553	85	154	17	3	39	98	3	.278
1972	Houston.........	1B	148	592	87	168	31	2	29	98	3	.284
1973	Houston.........	1B	148	545	65	147	24	3	28	105	1	.270
1974	Houston.........	1B	152	556	59	149	26	0	24	85	1	.268
1975	Baltimore........	1B	146	580	67	152	28	3	20	99	1	.262
1976	Baltimore........	1B	148	530	61	137	17	4	25	109	4	.258
1977	Baltimore........	1B	150	585	75	148	15	2	27	99	2	.253
	Totals..........		1653	6229	809	1680	290	26	300	1044	29	.270

DON STANHOUSE 27 6-2 195   Bats R Throws R

Started career as reliever but too good to keep out of starting rotation . . . Could be another gift (remember Singleton) from Expos . . . Only Steve Rogers had a better ERA among Expos . . . Credits strong arm to his time spent playing third base, his original position . . . Was No. 1 draft of Oakland A's in 1969 . . . Was involved in trade that brought Denny McLain from Texas to Oakland . . . Struck out the side in his major-league debut for the Rangers . . . Born Feb. 12, 1951, in DuQuoin, Ill. . . . A good-hitting pitcher who takes batting practice regularly . . . Once beat the Reds with a two-run double in the 16th inning.

Year	Club	G	IP	W	L	Pct.	SO	BB	H	ERA
1972	Texas	24	105	2	9	.182	78	73	83	3.77
1973	Texas	21	70	1	7	.125	42	44	70	4.76
1974	Texas	18	31	1	1	.500	26	17	38	4.94
1975	Montreal	4	13	0	0	.000	5	11	19	8.31
1976	Montreal	34	184	9	12	.429	79	92	182	3.77
1977	Montreal	47	158	10	10	.500	89	84	147	3.42
	Totals	148	561	23	39	.371	319	321	539	3.96

EDDIE MURRAY 22 6-2 180   Bats S Throws R

This rookie was a virtual unknown last year . . . Given chance to play when Birds lost three free agents, he became one of their most dependable hitters . . . Rookie-of-the-Year . . . Five game-winning hits vs. Yanks . . . Born Feb. 24, 1956, in Los Angeles . . . His two older brothers also played pro ball, but not in majors . . . A natural right-hander, he learned to switch hit in 1976 . . . Used mainly as DH, he can play first and OF . . . "There's no telling how good he will be," says Earl Weaver. "From what he has shown so far, you'd have to say he's going to become an excellent hitter with unlimited power."

Year	Club	Pos	G	AB	R	H	2B	3B	HR	RBI	SB	Avg.
1977	Baltimore	OF-1B	160	611	81	173	29	2	27	88	0	.283

MARK BELANGER 33 6-2 170   Bats R Throws R

The peerless shortstop . . . In a class by himself in AL says Red Sox Rick Burleson. . . . "We have the best shortstop in the game," boasts Earl Weaver . . . Fifth straight Gold Glove last year . . . Made only 10 errors and raised career fielding percentage, already highest in major league history for shortstops with 10 years in bigs . . . Born June 8, 1944, in Pittsfield, Mass. . . . A clubhouse and field leader, he was Orioles' player rep and enjoyed teaching and helping young infielders, including Kiko Garcia, his eventual replacement . . . Working with

new partners, Billy Smith and Rich Dauer at second, he helped the
Orioles lead league in DPs.

Year	Club	Pos	G	AB	R	H	2B	3B	HR	RBI	SB	Avg.
1965	Baltimore........	SS	11	3	1	1	0	0	0	0	0	.333
1966	Baltimore........	SS	8	19	2	3	1	0	0	0	0	.158
1967	Baltimore........	SS-2B-3B	69	184	19	32	5	0	1	10	6	.174
1968	Baltimore........	SS	145	472	40	98	13	0	2	21	10	.208
1969	Baltimore........	SS	150	530	76	152	17	4	2	50	14	.287
1970	Baltimore........	SS	145	459	53	100	6	5	1	36	13	.218
1971	Baltimore........	SS	150	500	67	133	19	4	0	35	10	.266
1972	Baltimore........	SS	113	285	36	53	9	1	2	16	6	.186
1973	Baltimore........	SS	154	470	60	106	15	1	0	27	13	.226
1974	Baltimore........	SS	155	493	54	111	14	4	5	36	17	.225
1975	Baltimore........	SS	152	442	44	100	11	1	3	27	16	.226
1976	Baltimore........	SS	153	522	66	141	22	2	1	40	27	.270
1977	Baltimore........	SS	144	402	39	83	13	4	2	30	15	.206
	Totals..........		1549	4781	557	1113	145	26	19	228	147	.233

MIKE FLANAGAN 27 6-0 185 Bats L Throws L

Hard thrower who came fast last year to be
third leading winner on Birds' staff . . . Lost
eight of first 10 decisions, finished with amazing 13-2 . . . Weaver called him "the best 2-8
pitcher in baseball," said he would "sell blue-
chip stocks to bet on that guy's future." . . .
Born Dec. 16, 1951, in Manchester, N.H. . . .
His dad was also pro baseball player . . . Originally drafted by Houston, but decided to attend college (Mass).
. . . "The biggest difference between pitching here and in the
minors is that it's much tougher to go nine innings up here. Down
there, you usually face only two or three good hitters so you can
breeze for a couple of innings."

Year	Club	G	IP	W	L	Pct.	SO	BB	H	ERA
1975	Baltimore...............	2	10	0	1	.000	7	6	9	2.70
1976	Baltimore...............	20	85	3	5	.375	56	33	83	4.13
1977	Baltimore...............	36	235	15	10	.600	149	70	235	3.64
	Totals..................	58	330	18	16	.529	212	109	327	3.74

AL BUMBRY 30 5-8 175 Bats L Throws R

Bumble Bee . . . O's mighty mite . . .
League's seventh leading hitter . . . Now a
fixture as Orioles' leadoff hitter . . . Born
April 21, 1947, in Fredericksburg, Va. . . . A
basketball star in HS, he averaged 32 points per
game in senior year and was awarded basketball scholarship to Virginia State . . . Urged to
play baseball by O's scout, Dick Bowie, who
eventually signed him . . . Signed in 1969, he played 35 games at

Stockton in California League when career was interrupted by military service . . . Spent 11 months in Viet Nam as platoon leader . . . Returned to bat .336 at Aberdeen in '71 and became hot prospect . . . Was named AL Rookie-of-Year in '73.

Year	Club	Pos	G	AB	R	H	2B	3B	HR	RBI	SB	Avg.
1972	Baltimore.	OF	9	11	5	4	0	1	0	0	1	.364
1973	Baltimore.	OF	110	356	73	120	15	11	7	34	23	.337
1974	Baltimore.	OF	94	270	35	63	10	3	1	19	12	.233
1975	Baltimore.	OF-3B	114	349	47	94	19	4	2	32	16	.269
1976	Baltimore.	OF	133	450	71	113	15	7	9	36	42	.251
1977	Baltimore.	OF	133	518	74	164	31	3	4	41	19	.317
	Totals.		593	1954	305	558	90	29	23	162	113	.286

DOUG DE CINCES 27 6-2 190   Bats R Throws R

Will always be remembered as the man who replaced Brooks Robinson, who retired last year . . . But a good third baseman in his own right . . . De-Sin-Say. . . . Has played in more games at third base for Orioles than anybody except Brooks, who was in almost 3,000 . . . Born Aug. 29, 1950, in Burbank, Cal. . . . Attended Pierce Jr. College . . . Originally drafted by Baltimore in 1970 . . . Big night of his career was May 4, 1975 . . . Had four hits, including first major league homer, in first game of doubleheader in Cleveland.

Year	Club	Pos	G	AB	R	H	2B	3B	HR	RBI	SB	Avg.
1973	Baltimore.	3B-2B-SS	10	18	2	2	0	0	0	3	0	.111
1974	Baltimore.	3B	1	1	0	0	0	0	0	0	0	.000
1975	Baltimore.	IFN	61	167	20	42	6	3	4	23	0	.251
1976	Baltimore.	3B-2B-SS-1B	129	440	36	103	17	2	11	42	8	.234
1977	Baltimore.	3B-2B-SS-1B	150	522	63	135	28	3	19	69	8	.259
	Totals.		351	1148	121	282	51	8	34	137	16	.246

CARLOS LOPEZ 27 6-1 190   Bats R Throws R

Impressed rivals with excellent defense and strong arm . . . Hit first big-league homer in Boston on May 8 and explained feeling. "My heart go crazy." . . . Born Sept. 27, 1950, in Mazatlan, Mexico, home town of White Sox' Jorge Orta . . . Served in Mexican Army . . . Impressed Mariners with .350 average, 88 RBIs for Salt Lake City in 1976, and was drafted off roster of Angels . . . After signing contract in spring training, rushed out and bought a green car. "Green like Seattle," he explained. "My name Mariner now." . . . Now his name is Oriole.

Year	Club	Pos	G	AB	R	H	2B	3B	HR	RBI	SB	Avg.
1976	California........	OF	9	10	1	0	0	0	0	0	2	.000
1977	Seattle..........	OF	99	297	39	84	18	1	8	34	16	.283
	Totals...........		108	307	40	84	18	1	8	34	18	.274

TOP PROSPECTS

MIKE PARROTT 23 6-4 205   Bats R Throws R

Orioles' first pick in 1973 draft . . . Nickname "Birdman" for obvious reasons . . . Missed most of 1976 season because of knee injury suffered in basketball game . . . Completely recovered last year, won 15 games for Rochester, one less than league leader . . . Younger brother pitched in Twins' organization last year . . . Born Dec. 6, 1954, in Oxnard, Cal.

GARY ROENICKE 23 6-3 200   Bats R Throws R

Time for him to earn a spot . . . Has chance with Orioles . . . First appeared for Expos in 1976 . . . Went hitless in first nine at-bats but finished with two homers and five RBIs in 29 games . . . Used at third base last season with injuries to Larry Parrish . . . Born Dec. 5, 1954, in Covina, Cal. . . . Converted to outfield in minors . . . Turned down college football scholarships to pursue baseball . . . Younger brother Ron drafted by Oakland and later San Francisco but did not sign.

MANAGER EARL WEAVER: Cocky, feisty, combative, argumentative manager, not the favorite of umpires or rival managers . . . But results speak for themselves . . . Record of 909-605 is third best in major-league history for managers with five years' service . . . Holds AL record of 318 wins in three straight seasons . . . Born Aug. 14, 1930, in St. Louis . . . Never played major-league ball . . . Total optimist who predicted Orioles would win last year despite losing three outstanding players to free agency . . . Came close, 2½ games behind Yankees . . . Rewarded with Manager-of-Year award voted by rival managers and three-year contract.

GREATEST MANAGER

Today's Orioles of Earl Weaver are not descended from the old Orioles of John McGraw, but rather from the Milwaukee club which moved to St. Louis in 1902 and achieved singular failure.

In 52 years, the Browns won just one pennant, that coming during World War II when most teams were depleted of talent. And in 52 years, the Browns finished last 10 times, despite being led on the field by some of the most legendary names in the game— Branch Rickey, George Stovall, George Sisler, Sunny Jim Bottomley, Gabby Street, Fred Haney and Rogers Hornsby, who was one of the game's greatest hitters and poorest managers.

But none of them can compare with the dandy little manager who never played in a major-league game, managed 12 years in the minor leagues, succeeded Hank Bauer in 1968 and is still there. Earl Sidney Weaver has won 909 games in nine seasons and his winning percentage is just a shade under .600, making him the third most successful manager in baseball history. He managed the Orioles into the World Series three consecutive years, winning it all against the Reds in 1970 and losing to the Mets in 1969 and the Pirates in 1971.

ALL-TIME ORIOLE LEADERS

BATTING: Ken Singleton, .328, 1977
HRs: Frank Robinson, 49, 1966
RBIs: Jim Gentile, 141, 1961
STEALS: Luis Aparicio, 57, 1964
WINS: Dave McNally, 24, 1970
          Mike Cuellar, 24, 1970
STRIKEOUTS: Dave McNally, 202, 1968

MILWAUKEE BREWERS

TEAM DIRECTORY: Chairman of the Board: Ed Fitzgerald; Pres.: Allan "Bud" Selig; Exec. VP-GM: Harry Dalton; VP-Marketing: Richard Hackett; VP-Stadium and Broadcast Operations: Gabe Paul Jr.; Farm Dir. and Admin. of Scouting: Tony Siegle; Pub. Rel: Tom Skibosh; Mgr.: Unnamed at press time. Home: Milwaukee County Stadium (49,500). Field distances: 320, l.f. line; 402, c.f.; 315, r.f. line. Spring training: Sun City, Ariz.

SCOUTING REPORT

HITTING: "We're going to try to beef up our offense," said new general manager Harry Dalton. "We've got some young pitchers

Brewers' Robin Yount, 22, is a four-year vet at shortstop.

we think are going to be very good and we think we can coax them along by improving our offense. If we score more runs, we won't have to remove our pitchers too soon."

Toward that end, the Brewers set about to improve their sixth-in-their-division offense through $$$, signing Larry Hisle (.302, 28 HRs, 119 RBI) as a free agent and by trade, swapping pitcher Jim Slaton for Ben Oglivie (.262, 21, 61).

Put them with Sal Bando, Cecil Cooper, Don Money and Sixto Lezcano and the Brewers no longer have to scratch for runs as they did in finishing 33 games out last year.

PITCHING: The young arms Dalton talks about belong to Gary Beare, Jerry Augustine, Barry Cort, Moose Haas, Sam Hinds and Lary Sorensen. Not a household name in the lot, but you have to start somewhere.

With Jim Slaton gone, the veteran of the staff is Bill Travers, 25. He has great stuff and potential, as evidence his 15 wins in 1976. But an arm injury and operation turned him into a 4-12 pitcher last year and a comeback from Travers is a must.

The bullpen, at least, seems well stocked, with Bill Castro, Ed Rodriguez and Bob McClure, who combined to win and save 38 of the Brewers' 67 wins last year.

FIELDING: The Brewers think second baseman Len Sakata can pick it with the best of them and feel their improved offense will permit them to carry his weak stick (.162 in 53 games for the big club last year).

Elsewhere, the defense is good, especially if Larry Hisle can do the job in center and veteran Ray Fosse can bolster a weak catching corps.

At shortstop, 21-year-old Robin Yount continues to improve. Last year, he cut his errors from 31 to 26 and he keeps getting better all the time. Trouble is, by the time he comes all the way, he may be with another team. Yount is indicating he will try for free agent gold next year. But that's a problem the Brewers don't have to face right now.

OUTLOOK: The Brewers may not move up in the standings. They may not even win more games than they did last year. But they will be more exciting, and they will be tougher to beat. That's because they have the best hitting array since Milwaukee returned to the American League. And the White Sox showed what can be done with bats.

MILWAUKEE BREWERS 1978 ROSTER

PITCHERS

No.	Name	1977 Club	W-L	IP	SO	ERA	B-T	Ht.	Wt.	Born
46	Augustine, Jerry	Milwaukee	12-18	209	68	4.48	L-L	6-0	185	7/24/52 Kewaunee, WI
29	Beare, Gary	Milwaukee	3-3	59	32	6.41	R-R	6-3	200	8/22/52 San Diego, CA
		Spokane	5-4	81	58	2.56				
48	Caldwell, Mike	Milwaukee	5-8	94	38	4.60	R-L	6-0	185	1/22/49 Tarboro, NC
		Cincinnati	0-0	25	11	3.96				
35	Castro, Bill	Milwaukee	8-6	69	28	4.17	R-R	170	5-11	12/13/53 Santiago, DR
18	Cort, Barry	Milwaukee	1-1	24	17	3.38	R-R	6-5	195	4/15/56 Toronto, Ont.
		Holyoke	0-0	3	1	9.00				
30	Haas, Moose	Milwaukee	10-12	198	113	4.32	R-R	6-0	170	4/22/56 Baltimore, MD
40	Hinds, Sam	Milwaukee	0-3	72	46	4.75	R-R	6-7	210	7/11/53 Frederick, MD
		Spokane	2-1	53	33	2.89				
10	McClure, Bob	Milwaukee	2-1	71	57	2.54	B-L	5-11	170	4/29/53 Oakland, CA
23	Rodriguez, Ed	Milwaukee	5-6	143	104	4.34	R-R	6-0	185	3/6/52 Barcelonetta, PR
39	Sorenson, Larry	Milwaukee	7-10	142	57	4.37	R-R	6-2	200	10/4/55 Detroit, MI
		Spokane	5-5	72	43	4.63				
25	Travers, Bill	Milwaukee	4-12	122	49	5.24	L-L	6-4	187	10/4/55 Norwood, MA

CATCHERS

No.	Name	1977 Club	H	HR	RBI	Pct.	B-T	Ht.	Wt.	Born
—	Etchebarren, Andy	California	29	0	14	.254	R-R	6-0	200	6/28/43 Whittier, CA
—	Fosse, Ray	Cleve-Seat	75	6	32	.276	R-R	6-2	210	4/4/47 Marion, IL
12	Haney, Larry	Milwaukee	29	0	10	.228	R-R	6-2	195	11/19/42 Charlottesville, VA
—	Martinez, Buck	Kansas City	18	1	9	.225	R-R	5-11	190	11/7/48 Redding, CA
22	Moore, Charlie	Milwaukee	93	5	45	.248	R-R	5-11	180	6/21/53 Birmingham, AL

INFIELDERS

No.	Name	1977 Club	H	HR	RBI	Pct.	B-T	Ht.	Wt.	Born
6	Bando, Sal	Milwaukee	145	17	82	.250	R-R	6-0	195	2/13/44 Cleveland, OH
15	Cooper, Cecil	Milwaukee	193	20	78	.300	L-L	6-2	185	12/20/49 Brenham, TX
31	Gantner, Jim	Milwaukee	14	1	2	.298	L-R	5-11	175	1/5/53 Eden, WI
		Spokane	152	15	80	.281				
1	Johnson, Tim	Milwaukee	2	0	2	.061	L-R	6-1	170	7/22/49 Grand Forks, ND
7	Money, Don	Milwaukee	159	25	83	.279	R-R	6-1	190	6/7/47 Washington, DC
5	Quirk, Jamie	Milwaukee	48	3	13	.217	L-R	6-4	185	10/22/54 Whittier, CA
—	Romero, Ed	Milwaukee	7	0	2	.280	R-R	5-11	150	12/9/57 Santurce, PR
		Holyoke	118	1	38	.258				
21	Sakata, Lenn	Milwaukee	25	2	12	.162	R-R	5-9	160	5/8/53 Honolulu, HI
		Spokane	105	4	73	.308				
19	Yount, Robin	Milwaukee	174	4	49	.288	R-R	6-0	165	9/16/55 Danville, IL

OUTFIELDERS

No.	Name	1977 Club	H	HR	RBI	Pct.	B-T	Ht.	Wt.	Born
11	Brye, Steve	Milwaukee	60	7	28	.249	R-R	6-0	188	2/4/49 Alameda, CA
26	Davis, Dick	Milwaukee	14	0	6	.275	R-R	6-3	195	9/25/43 Long Beach, CA
		Spokane	169	13	74	.355				
9	Hisle, Larry	Minnesota	165	28	119	.302	R-R	6-2	195	5/5/47 Portsmouth, OH
28	Joshua, Von	Milwaukee	140	9	49	.261	L-L	5-10	170	5/1/48 Oakland, CA
3	Kirkpatrick, Ed	TX-Milwaukee	30	0	9	.240	L-R	6-0	202	10/8/44 Spokane, WA
		Pittsburgh	4	1	4	.143				
16	Lezcano, Sixto	Milwaukee	109	21	49	.273	R-R	5-11	172	11/28/53 Arecibo, PR
—	Oglivie, Ben	Detroit	118	21	61	.262	L-L	6-2	170	2/11/49 Colon, Panama
26	Sharp, Bill	Spokane	4	0	3	.211	L-L	5-10	180	1/18/50 Lima, OH
14	Wohlford, Jim	Milwaukee	97	2	36	.248	R-R	5-10	175	2/28/51 Visalia, CA

BREWER PROFILES

SAL BANDO 34 6-0 195   Bats R Throws R

Class and steadiness in infield . . . Escaped Finley's loony bin and signed for $1.5 million . . . But it wasn't all gravy . . . "This is the first time since 1968 that I haven't been going for a pennant," he said in September. "It feels strange." . . . Joined 200-homer club last year . . . Born Feb. 13, 1944, in Cleveland . . . Still lives in Oakland area . . . Attended Arizona State and was MVP in College World Series before being drafted by A's, for whom he was captain and mainstay of three straight world championships . . . Started with A's when they were still in Kansas City.

Year	Club	Pos	G	AB	R	H	2B	3B	HR	RBI	SB	Avg.
1966	Kansas City	3B	11	24	1	7	1	1	0	1	0	.292
1967	Kansas City	3B	47	130	11	25	3	2	0	6	1	.192
1968	Oakland	3B-OF	162	605	67	152	25	5	9	67	13	.251
1969	Oakland	3B	162	609	106	171	25	3	31	113	1	.281
1970	Oakland	3B	155	502	93	132	20	2	20	75	6	.263
1971	Oakland	3B	153	538	75	146	23	1	24	94	3	.271
1972	Oakland	3B	152	535	64	126	20	3	15	77	3	.236
1973	Oakland	3B	162	592	97	170	32	3	29	98	4	.287
1974	Oakland	3B	146	498	84	121	21	2	22	103	2	.243
1975	Oakland	3B	160	562	64	129	24	1	15	78	7	.230
1976	Oakland	SS-3B	158	550	75	132	18	2	27	84	20	.240
1977	Milwaukee	3B-1B	159	580	65	145	27	3	17	82	4	.250
	Totals		1627	5725	802	1456	239	28	209	878	64	.254

CECIL COOPER 28 6-2 185   Bats L Throws L

Under pressure as replacement for George Scott, did not hit HRs like Boomer, but was better all-around hitter and player . . . "I had never played every day. I was happy for the opportunity. If I had to change things, I'd cut down on my strikeouts and step up my run production, but I think I had a good year." . . . Born Dec. 12, 1949, in Brenham, Tex. . . . "He did a great job," said ex-manager Alex Grammas. "He's a very unselfish individual. It's a pleasure to have him on this club." . . . Originally signed by Red Sox, Cooper was drafted by Cardinals, but returned to Sox when Cards had no room for him on major-league roster . . . Batted .452 in 26 games in first season of pro ball.

Year	Club	Pos	G	AB	R	H	2B	3B	HR	RBI	SB	Avg.
1971	Boston	1B	14	42	9	13	4	1	0	3	1	.310
1972	Boston	1B	12	17	0	4	1	0	0	2	0	.235
1973	Boston	1B	30	101	12	24	2	0	3	11	1	.238
1974	Boston	1B	121	414	55	114	24	1	8	43	2	.275
1975	Boston	1B	106	305	49	95	17	6	14	44	1	.311
1976	Boston	1B	123	451	66	127	22	6	15	78	7	.282
1977	Milwaukee	1B	160	643	86	193	31	7	20	78	13	.300
	Totals		566	1973	277	570	101	21	60	259	25	.289

DON MONEY 30 6-1 190   Bats R Throws R

Great veteran pro . . . Outstanding third baseman, moved over to make room for Sal Bando
and excelled at second base . . . Has been assured by club he would play either third or second this year . . . When Bando arrived, Money
accepted his fate . . . After 6½ seasons as a
third baseman, it was hard to move . . . "I
could have sounded off, but that would have
defeated everybody's purpose. I went out to make a second baseman of myself." . . . Born June 7, 1947, in Washington, D.C. . . .
Runs 2½ acre farm in New Jersey . . . Wrote book about teammate Henry Aaron . . . Has had two careers . . . Five years with
Phillies in NL, five with Brewers in AL.

Year	Club	Pos	G	AB	R	H	2B	3B	HR	RBI	SB	Avg.
1968	Philadelphia	SS	4	13	1	3	2	0	0	2	0	.231
1969	Philadelphia	SS	127	450	41	103	22	2	6	42	1	.229
1970	Philadelphia	3B-SS	120	447	66	132	25	4	14	66	4	.295
1971	Philadelphia	3B-2B-OF	121	439	40	98	22	8	7	38	4	.223
1972	Philadelphia	3B-SS	152	536	54	119	16	2	15	52	5	.222
1973	Milwaukee	3B-SS	145	556	75	158	28	2	11	61	22	.284
1974	Milwaukee	3B-2B	159	629	85	178	32	3	15	65	19	.283
1975	Milwaukee	3B-SS	109	405	58	112	16	1	15	43	7	.277
1976	Milwaukee	3B-SS	117	439	51	117	18	4	12	62	6	.267
1977	Milwaukee	3B-SS	152	570	86	159	28	3	25	83	8	.279
	Totals		1206	4484	557	1179	209	29	120	514	76	.263

ROBIN YOUNT 22 6-0 165   Bats R Throws R

Four year major league veteran and not yet 23
. . . Can play out his option and sell himself to
highest bidder after this year . . . Said ex-GM
Jim Baumer, "Robin is one of the most mature
players we have despite his age. He has a mind
of his own and he knows what he wants to do."
. . . Improving every year, he was league's 31st
leading hitter despite second-half slump . . .
Ready to become premier shortstop in league . . . Born Sept. 16,
1955, in Danville, Ill. . . . Moved to California and starred at

Woodland Hills High . . . First round draft in June, 1973, and signed before 18th birthday . . . A year later, he was Brewers' regular shortstop, youngest player in majors.

Year	Club	Pos	G	AB	R	H	2B	3B	HR	RBI	SB	Avg.
1974	Milwaukee.......	SS	107	344	48	86	14	5	3	26	7	.250
1975	Milwaukee.......	SS	147	558	67	149	28	2	8	52	12	.267
1976	Milwaukee.......	SS-OF	161	638	59	161	19	3	2	54	16	.252
1977	Milwaukee.......	SS	154	605	66	174	34	4	4	49	16	.288
	Totals..........		569	2145	240	570	95	14	17	181	51	.266

SIXTO LEXCANO 24 5-11 172   Bats R Throws R

The Sixto Kid . . . "He's going to be the American League's premier right fielder in a year or two," says Alex Grammas . . . Born Nov. 28, 1953, in Arecibo, Puerto Rico . . . In high school, he stood only 5-5, wighed 135 and never thought he'd be big enough for baseball . . . Missed 49 games because of a broken hand when hit by Mike Torrez . . . Excellent fielder with strong arm . . . Patterned his style after boyhood idol, Roberto Clemente . . . Learned to control his temper and should continue to improve, but must cut down on his swing . . . "Stop going for home runs and go for hits and RBIs," suggested Grammas.

Year	Club	Pos	G	AB	R	H	2B	3B	HR	RBI	SB	Avg.
1974	Milwaukee.......	OF	15	54	5	13	2	0	2	9	1	.241
1975	Milwaukee.......	OF	134	429	55	106	19	3	11	43	5	.247
1976	Milwaukee.......	OF	145	513	53	146	19	5	7	56	14	.285
1977	Milwaukee.......	OF	109	400	50	109	21	4	21	49	6	.273
	Totals..........		403	1395	163	374	61	12	41	157	26	.268

LARRY HISLE 30 6-2 195   Bats R Throws R

Season-long negotiations finally ended with Hisle unsigned after he and Twins agreed on $1.25 million for five years. But there was disagreement on deferred payments and Larry decided to play out option and test free agent waters . . . Wound up with $3.2 million from Brewers . . . Led league in RBIs despite missing 21 games with ankle injury . . . Quiet, soft-spoken gentleman who was roommate of late Danny Thompson and has been active in a "Danny Thompson Leukemia Foundation." . . . Born May 5, 1947, in Portsmouth, Ohio . . . Picked by Phillies in first free agent draft and given big buildup as rookie . . . But was unprepared emotionally and failed, getting trials with Dodgers, Cardinals before going to Twins to find success, stardom and wealth.

Year	Club	Pos	G	AB	R	H	2B	3B	HR	RBI	SB	Avg.
1968	Philadelphia......	OF	7	11	1	4	1	0	0	1	0	.364
1969	Philadelphia......	OF	145	482	75	128	23	5	20	56	18	.266
1970	Philadelphia......	OF	126	405	52	83	72	4	10	44	5	.205
1971	Philadelphia......	OF	36	76	7	15	3	0	0	3	1	.197
1973	Minnesota	OF	143	545	88	148	25	6	15	64	11	.272
1974	Minnesota	OF	143	510	68	146	20	7	19	79	12	.286
1975	Minnesota	OF	80	255	37	80	9	2	11	51	17	.314
1976	Minnesota	OF	155	581	81	158	19	5	14	96	31	.272
1977	Minnesota	OF	141	546	95	165	36	3	28	119	21	.302
	Totals..........		976	3411	504	927	158	32	117	515	116	.272

BILL TRAVERS 25 6-4 187   Bats L Throws L

Stork . . . Two straight years of setbacks . . . Recovered from legionnaire's disease in '76 and had sore elbow last year . . . Has stuff to be big winner . . . Challenged Mark Fidrych for ERA lead in '76 with 1.91 at all-star break, when knocked out by flu . . . En route to 20-win season, finished up 5-10 in second half . . . Born Oct. 27, 1952, in Norwood, Mass., just 15 miles from Fenway Park . . . Grew up rooting for Red Sox, played baseball and hockey . . . Slumped off last year and embarrassed when he had to endure 14-run, 18-hit assault in Cleveland because Brewers were short of pitchers.

Year	Club	G	IP	W	L	Pct.	SO	BB	H	ERA
1974	Milwaukee................	23	53	2	3	.400	31	30	59	4.92
1975	Milwaukee................	28	136	6	11	.353	57	60	130	4.30
1976	Milwaukee................	34	240	15	16	.484	120	95	211	2.81
1977	Milwaukee................	19	122	4	12	.250	49	57	140	5.24
	Totals..................	104	551	27	42	.391	257	242	540	3.92

BEN OGLIVIE 29 6-2 170   Bats L Throws L

Excellent run production despite limited service . . . Used as part-time player, averaged one homer ever 20 at bats last two seasons . . . Earned starting job last year with Tigers . . . "One of the most improved players I've seen," said Ralph Houk . . . Born Feb. 11, 1949, in Colon, Panama, was raised in New York City, drafted by Red Sox, traded to Tigers . . . An introspective, intelligent man with a love for learning, he enrolled at Detroit's Wayne State and studied philosophy, among other things . . . Reads Plato, Socrates, Aristotle . . . Also into Zen Buddhism, which he says, "merges into one with sports."

Year	Club	Pos	G	AB	R	H	2B	3B	HR	RBI	SB	Avg.
1971	Boston	OF	14	38	2	10	3	0	0	4	0	.263
1972	Boston	OF	94	253	27	61	10	2	8	30	1	.241
1973	Boston	OF	58	147	16	32	9	1	2	9	1	.218
1974	Detroit	OF-1B	92	252	28	68	11	3	4	29	12	.270
1975	Detroit	OF-1B	100	332	45	95	14	1	9	36	11	.286
1976	Detroit	OF-1B	115	305	36	87	12	3	15	47	9	.285
1977	Detroit	OF-1B	132	450	63	118	24	2	21	61	9	.262
	Totals		605	1777	217	471	83	12	59	216	43	.265

VON JOSHUA 29 5-10 170   Bats L Throws L

After slow start, came on in second half . . . And criticized his teammates for lackluster play . . . "Everybody walks around here in a daze. We're tight. We're not loose. We don't have any sock, no killer instinct. We have great young talent here, but nobody's helping them." . . . Born May 1, 1948, in Oakland, Calif. . . . Originally drafted by Giants, he passed up offer, then was drafted by Dodgers . . . However was purchased by Giants in 1975 and had best year in big leagues . . . Won two minor-league bat titles, Northwest League in 1967, Pacific Coast League in 1972.

Year	Club	Pos	G	AB	R	H	2B	3B	HR	RBI	SB	Avg.
1969	Los Angeles	OF	14	8	2	2	0	0	0	0	1	.250
1970	Los Angeles	OF	72	109	23	29	1	3	1	8	2	.266
1971	Los Angeles	OF	11	7	2	0	0	0	0	0	0	.000
1973	Los Angeles	OF	75	159	19	40	4	1	2	17	7	.252
1974	Los Angeles	OF	81	124	11	29	5	1	1	16	3	.234
1975	San Francisco	OF	129	507	75	161	25	10	7	43	20	.318
1976	San Francisco	OF	42	156	13	41	5	2	0	2	1	.263
1976	Milwaukee	OF	107	423	44	113	13	5	5	28	8	.267
1977	Milwaukee	OF	144	536	58	140	25	7	9	49	12	.261
	Totals		675	2029	247	555	78	29	25	163	54	.274

ED RODRIGUEZ 26 6-0 185   Bats R Throws R

Brilliant as unbeaten reliever in 1975, Rodriguez has vacillated between starting and the bullpen in the last two years with occasional visits to the Brewer doghouse . . . Said former manager Grammas: "When he gets in his pitching groove and stays with the same delivery, he's as good as anybody. It's only when he tries to spoof somebody with different deliveries that he gets in trouble." . . . Those different deliveries earned him name "Edweirdo." . . . Born March 6, 1952, in Barceloneta,

Puerto Rico . . . Still possesses winning record despite never having pitched for a winning team.

Year	Club	G	IP	W	L	Pct.	SO	BB	H	ERA
1973	Milwaukee	30	76	9	7	.563	49	47	71	3.32
1974	Milwaukee	43	112	7	4	.636	58	51	97	3.62
1975	Milwaukee	43	88	7	0	1.000	65	44	77	3.48
1976	Milwaukee	45	136	5	13	277	77	65	124	3.64
1977	Milwaukee	42	143	5	6	.455	104	56	126	4.34
	Totals	203	555	33	30	.524	353	263	495	3.75

JERRY AUGUSTINE 25 6-0 185   Bats L Throws L

Improving rapidly and will be Brewer pitching mainstay this year . . . 21 victories in last two seasons . . . Beat Yankees for first major-league win in '75 and in other major-league decision, pitched complete game victory vs. Tigers . . . Born July 24, 1952, in Kewaunee, Wisc. . . . A local boy, he attended U. of Wisconsin-LaCrosse, graduating with B.S. in phys. ed. . . . Drafted on 15th round of June, 1974 draft . . . Worked as ticket salesman for Brewers in off-season.

Year	Club	G	IP	W	L	Pct.	SO	BB	H	ERA
1975	Milwaukee	5	27	2	0	1.000	8	12	26	3.00
1976	Milwaukee	39	172	9	12	.429	59	56	167	3.30
1977	Milwaukee	33	209	12	18	.400	68	72	222	4.48
	Totals	77	408	23	30	.434	135	140	415	3.88

TOP PROSPECTS

LENN SAKATA 24 5-9 160   Bats R Throws R

After two excellent years in Pacific Coast League (.280 with 70 RBIs in '76, .304 with 73 RBIs last year), he was called up and played 53 games at second base for Brewers . . . Had trouble at bat, but played well in field and could push Don Money elsewhere in time . . . Born May 8, 1953, in Honolulu, and was first choice on secondary phase of January, 1975, draft.

SAM HINDS 24 6-7 210   Bats R Throws R

His size helps him intimidate batters . . . Appeared in 29 games for Brewers without victory after eight games in Spokane . . . Born July 11, 1953, in Frederick, Md. . . . Attended international high school in The Hague, Holland . . . Walked into Brewer training camp in 1974 and asked for a tryout. Got it, impressed scouts and was signed.

GREATEST MANAGER

Perhaps the heading above should read "Greatest Manager?"
Conceived as the Seattle Pilots when the American League expanded in 1969, the team moved to Milwaukee the following year. Any similarity between the old Milwaukee Braves and current Milwaukee Brewers is coincidental—and somewhat embarrassing to the Braves of sainted memory.

The Pilots-Brewers have had four managers, including the recently fired Alex Grammas. Not one of them has been able to get the Brewers to finish above fifth place. Consequently, it would be unfair to each of them to designate any one of them as "Greatest Manager." If you insist, though, you might make a case for Del Crandall. He won 77 games in 1974, the most in the short history of the current Milwaukee club.

ALL-TIME BREWER LEADERS

BATTING: George Scott, .306, 1973
HRs: George Scott, 36, 1975
RBIs: George Scott, 109, 1975
STEALS: Tommy Harper, 73, 1969
WINS: Jim Colborn, 20, 1973
STRIKEOUTS: Marty Pattin, 161, 1971

DETROIT TIGERS

TEAM DIRECTORY: Owner: John Fetzer; Exec. VP and GM: Jim Campbell; Consultant: Richard Ferrell; Sec.-Treas.: Alex Callam; Player Development: Hoot Evers; Player Procurement: Bill Lajoie; Pub. Rel.: Hal Middlesworth; Trav. Sec.: Vince Desmond; Mgr.: Ralph Houk; Home: Tiger Stadium (54,226). Field distances: 340 l.f. line; 365, l.c.; 440, c.f., 370, r.c.; 325, r.f. line. Spring training: Lakeland, Fla.

SCOUTING REPORT

HITTING: Everybody inquired about Jason Thompson at baseball's winter meetings and everybody was told the same thing: he's

Ron LeFlore hit .325, his best ever, and stole 39 bases.

not available. No wonder. In his first full major-league season, Thompson had 31 homers and 105 RBIs. Ralph Houk can hardly wait to see him when he has learned how to hit.

There are some talented bats in the Tiger rack and only one of them can be said to be in the older veteran class. That's the one carried to the plate by Rusty Staub, who learned to like the DH role and produced his second 100-RBI season thanks to a blistering second half.

Ron LeFlore was fifth in the league in hitting and Tito Fuentes, a wonderful free agent pickup, was 12th. But keep your eye on Steve Kemp and a kid catcher with the movie star name, Lance Parrish.

PITCHING: Ralph Houk can only dream about what it would be like to have Mark (The Bird) Fidrych and Dave (The Rose) Rozema together and healthy for a full season. The celebrated Bird suffered from tendinitis and slipped from a 19-game winner and the most talked of player in the game, to a 6-4 pitcher in only 11 games. Rozema looked like a cinch for Rookie-of-the-Year when he hurt his arm and his season stopped dead at 15-7.

With a healthy Fidrych and Rozema, aided by Jim Slaton, relievers Steve Foucault and John Hiller and this year's likely phenom, Jack Morris, the Tigers may be putting together the pitching staff of the future.

FIELDING: Tiger defense wasn't the worst in the league last year, but it wasn't the best, either. In fact, it was right in the middle, as was their pitching, as was their hitting. So it is no surprise that they finished right in the middle of the AL East.

To improve in the standings, the Tigers must improve in all three categories and it's a fact if your defense is better, your pitching will be better. It will take a lot of guts, but the Tigers may go with rookies in the three most critical defensive positions—catch, short, second. In that event, it won't be until mid-season, at least, before we learn if Lance Parrish, Alan Trammell and Sweet Lou Whitaker will make the Tigers better.

OUTLOOK: So many rookies, so many young stars, so many questionable arms make the Tigers the biggest question mark of the AL. They are young and they are talented, but are they ready? And have they been passed by because of a refusal to dip into the free agent pool while their rivals show a willingness to spend?

DETROIT TIGERS 1978 ROSTER

MANAGER Ralph Houk
Coaches—Gates Brown, Fred Gladding, Fred Hatfield, Jim
        Hegan, Dick Tracewski

PITCHERS

No.	Name	1977 Club	W-L	IP	SO	ERA	B-T	Ht.	Wt.	Born
36	Arroyo, Fernando	Detroit	8-18	209	60	4.18	R-R	6-2	180	3/21/52 Sacramento, CA
42	Burnside, Sheldon	Montgomery	10-12	176	100	3.32	R-L	6-5	200	12/22/54 South Bend, IN
28	Crawford, Jim	Detroit	7-8	126	91	4.79	L-L	6-3	200	9/29/50 Chicago,IL
20	Fidrych, Mark	Detroit	6-4	81	42	2.89	R-R	6-3	175	8/14/54 Worcester, MA
—	Folkers, Rich	Milwaukee	0-1	6	6	4.50	L-L	6-2	180	10/17/46 Waterloo, IA
		Spokane	5-7	83	48	4.55				
29	Foucault, Steve	Detroit	7-7	74	58	3.16	L-R	6-0	205	10/3/49 Duluth, MN
48	Glynn, Ed	Evansville	6-8	156	125	4.95	R-L	6-2	180	6/3/53 Flushing, NY
		Detroit	2-1	27	13	5.33				
49	Grilli, Steve	Detroit	1-2	73	49	4.81	R-R	6-2	170	5/2/49 Brooklyn, NY
46	Harrison, Roric	Evansville	9-5	82	75	3.31	R-R	6-3	200	9/20/46 Los Angeles, CA
18	Hiller, John	Detroit	8-14	124	115	3.56	R-L	6-0	165	4/8/43 Scarborough, ONT
47	Morris, Jack	Evansville	6-7	135	95	3.60	R-R	6-3	195	5/16/56 St. Paul, MN
		Detroit	1-1ᴺ	46	28	3.72				
43	Murphy, John	Montgomery	9-3	102	76	3.62	L-L	6-3	185	8/7/57 Brooklyn, NY
19	Rozema, Dave	Detroit	15-7	218	92	3.10	R-R	6-4	185	8/5/56 Grand Rapids, MI
31	Ruhle, Vern	Detroit	3-5	66	27	5.73	R-R	6-1	180	1/25/51 Midland, MI
		Evansville	1-4	21	15	6.86				
—	Slaton, Jim	Milwaukee	10-14	221	104	3.58	R-R	6-0	185	6/19/50 Long Beach, CA
27	Sykes, Bob	Detroit	5-7	133	58	4.40	B-L	6-2	200	12/11/54 Neptune, NJ
32	Taylor, Bruce	Evansville	5-6	77	65	2.21	R-R	6-0	175	4/16/53 Holden, MA
		Detroit	1-0	29	19	3.41				
45	Viefhaus, Steve	Lakeland	1-1	18	12	0.50	R-R	6-3	195	9/28/55 St. Louis, MO
39	Wilcox, Milt	Evansville	9-4	107	69	2.44	R-R	6-2	185	4/20/50 Honolulu, HI
		Detroit	6-2	106	82	3.65				

CATCHERS

No.	Name	1977 Club	H	HR	RBI	Pct.	B-T	Ht.	Wt.	Born
40	Adams, Bob	Evansville	76	10	44	.330	R-R	6-1	195	1/6/52 Pittsburgh, PA
		Detroit	6	2	2	.250				
11	Kimm, Bruce	Rochester	15	0	11	.167	R-R	5-11	170	6/29/51 Cedar Rapids, IA
		Detroit	2	0	1	.080				
12	May, Milt	Detroit	99	12	46	.249	L-R	6-0	190	8/1/50 Gary, IN
13	Parrish, Lance	Evansville	116	25	90	.279	R-R	6-3	195	6/15/56 McKeesport, PA
		Detroit	9	3	7	.196				
14	Wockenfuss, John	Detroit	45	9	25	.274	R-R	6-0	190	2/27/49 Welch, WV

INFIELDERS

No.	Name	1977 Club	H	HR	RBI	Pct.	B-T	Ht.	Wt.	Born
15	Brookens, Tom	Evansville	127	8	52	.289	R-R	5-10	170	8/10/53 Chambersburg, PA
44	Fuentes, Tito	Detroit	190	5	51	.309	B-R	5-11	175	1/4/44 Havana, Cuba
2	Mankowski, Phil	Detroit	79	3	27	.276	L-R	6-0	180	1/9/53 Buffalo, NY
4	Rodriquez, Aurelio	Detroit	67	10	32	.219	R-R	5-11	180	12/28/47 Cananea, Mex
9	Scrivener, Chuck	Detroit	6	0	2	.083	R-R	5-9	170	10/3/47 Alexandria, VA
30	Thompson, Jason	Detroit	158	31	105	.270	L-L	6-4	200	7/6/54 Hollywood, CA
3	Trammell, Alan	Montgomery	132	3	50	.291	R-R	6-0	160	2/21/58 Garden Grove, CA
		Detroit	8	0	0	.186				
5	Wagner, Mark	Evansville	68	3	27	.306	R-R	6-1	175	3/4/54 Conneaut, OH
		Detroit	7	1	3	.146				
1	Whitaker, Lou	Montgomery	111	3	48	.280	R-R	6-1	175	5/12/57 New York, NY
		Detroit	8	0	2	.250				

OUTFIELDERS

No.	Name	1977 Club	H	HR	RBI	Pct.	B-T	Ht.	Wt.	Born
25	Corcoran, Tim	Evansville	47	7	33	.346	L-L	5-11	175	3/19/53 Glendale, CA
		Detroit	29	3	15	.282				
33	Kemp, Steve	Detroit	142	18	88	.257	L-L	6-0	185	8/7/54 San Angelo, TX
8	LeFlore, Ron	Detroit	212	16	57	.325	R-R	6-0	200	6/16/52 Detroit, MI
—	Spikes, Charlie	Toledo	48	7	31	.293	R-R	6-3	220	1/23/51 Bogalusa, LA
		Cleveland	22	3	11	.232				
24	Staub, Mickey	Detroit	51	8	23	.230	R-R	6-1	195	7/20/42 Grand Rapids, MI
10	Staub, Rusty	Detroit	173	22	101	.278	L-R	6-2	205	4/1/44 New Orleans, LA
41	Valle, John	Evansville	78	19	58	.276	R-R	6-0	185	9/8/54 New York, NY

TIGER PROFILES

MARK FIDRYCH 23 6-3 175   Bats R Throws R

The Bird . . . The franchise . . . Averaged 33,000 at home, 26,000 on road, in attendance in games he started in '76 . . . Last year started only 11 games because of knee and arm miseries . . . Tigers are looking for big comeback from tousled-haired young right-hander who was the toast of baseball in '76 . . . Born Aug. 14, 1954, in Worcester, Mass. . . . Burst on scene suddenly and without warning . . . Not even on Tigers' spring roster in '76, when he won 19 . . . Talking to ball, making outrageous statements, he was hero of young and savior of fumbling Tiger franchise.

Year	Club	G	IP	W	L	Pct.	SO	BB	H	ERA
1976	Detroit	31	250	19	9	.679	97	53	217	2.34
1977	Detroit	11	81	6	4	.600	42	12	82	2.89
	Totals	42	331	25	13	.658	139	65	299	2.47

RUSTY STAUB 34 6-2 205   Bats L Throws R

Veteran outfielder, switched to DH, had one of finest seasons after slow start . . . Hit century mark in RBIs only second time in career and combined with Thompson to give Tigers two 100 RBI-men first time since Rocky Colavito and Norm Cash in '61 . . . His 22 homers most since 1970 . . . Fierce competitor who dislikes sitting and had difficult time adjusting to DH role . . . Born April 1, 1944, in New Orleans . . . Still one of baseball's most eligible bachelors . . . A gourmet cook who opened New York restaurant, "Rusty's." . . . "Le Grand Orange" when he played in Montreal.

Year	Club	Pos	G	AB	R	H	2B	3B	HR	RBI	SB	Avg.
1963	Houston	1B-OF	150	513	43	115	17	4	6	45	0	.224
1964	Houston	1B-OF	89	292	26	63	10	2	8	35	1	.216
1965	Houston	OF-1B	131	410	43	105	20	1	14	63	3	.256
1966	Houston	OF-1B	153	554	60	155	28	3	13	81	2	.280
1967	Houston	OF	149	546	71	182	44	1	10	74	0	.333
1968	Houston	1B-OF	161	591	54	172	37	1	6	72	2	.291
1969	Montreal	OF	158	549	89	166	26	5	29	79	3	.302
1970	Montreal	OF	160	569	98	156	23	7	30	94	12	.274
1971	Montreal	OF	162	599	94	186	34	6	19	97	9	.311
1972	New York (NL)	OF	66	239	32	70	11	0	9	38	0	.293
1973	New York (NL)	OF	152	585	77	163	36	1	15	76	1	.279
1974	New York (NL)	OF	151	561	65	145	22	2	19	78	2	.258
1975	New York (NL)	OF	155	574	93	162	30	4	19	105	2	.282
1976	Detroit	OF	161	589	73	176	28	3	15	96	3	.299
1977	Detroit	OF	158	623	84	173	34	3	22	101	1	.278
	Totals		2166	7794	1002	2189	400	43	234	1134	41	.281

RON LEFLORE 29 6-0 200   Bats R Throws R

First Tiger in 22 years (Al Kaline) to get more than 200 hits . . . Also AL's leading right-handed hitter . . . "I always said I could hit." . . . "And I think I could continue at the same pace. I wouldn't say last season was as good as I could hit." . . . Batting .230 on May 30, he pulled average up almost 100 points in four months . . . Born June 16, 1948, in Detroit . . . Learned to play baseball while serving prison term for armed robbery . . . Then Tiger manager Billy Martin visited him behind bars, scouted him, encouraged him . . . Life story released in new book, *"Breakout"* . . . May be fastest player in game.

Year	Club	Pos	G	AB	R	H	2B	3B	HR	RBI	SB	Avg.
1974	Detroit	OF	59	254	37	66	8	1	2	13	23	.260
1975	Detroit	OF	136	550	66	142	13	6	8	37	28	.258
1976	Detroit	OF	135	544	93	172	23	8	4	39	58	.316
1977	Detroit	OF	154	652	100	212	30	10	16	57	39	.325
	Totals		484	2000	296	592	74	25	30	146	148	.296

JASON THOMPSON 23 6-4 200   Bats L Throws L

One of best young sluggers in game . . . Made all-star team last year . . . Tied for sixth in HRs, eighth in RBIs in first full major-league season, third pro season . . . Born July 6, 1954, in Hollywood, Cal. . . . No. 4 pick of Tigers in June, 1975, free agent draft . . . Hit two on Tiger Stadium roof, where few players have hit 'em . . . It took him only 10 months from date of signing to make it to first base for Tigers . . . Played only four games at Evansville when Tigers called him up in 1976 . . . Could be their first baseman for next dozen years.

Year	Club	Pos	G	AB	R	H	2B	3B	HR	RBI	SB	Avg.
1976	Detroit	1B	123	412	45	90	12	1	17	54	2	.218
1977	Detroit	1B	158	585	87	158	24	5	31	105	0	.270
	Totals		281	997	132	248	36	6	48	159	2	.249

DAVE ROZEMA 21 6-4 185   Bats R Throws R

Did history repeat? . . . Like another Tiger right-hander of a year before, Rozey was not on club's roster in spring, was invited to camp and made club . . . Was 15-7 with glittering 3.09 ERA, then was sidelined final month with arm trouble . . . Tigers were not taking chances with this property . . . Was named AL's top rookie pitcher . . . Born August 5,

1956, in Grand Rapids, Mich. . . . Fourth selection in January, 1975, draft, was 14-5 with 2.09 mark for Montgomery with remarkable 1.57 ERA and 15 walks in 126 innings . . . Last year walked only 34 in 218 innings . . . Keeps ball down and has great change . . . "He throws change-up after change-up after change-up," says Brewers' Von Joshua. "He throws slow, slower and slowest."

Year	Club	G	IP	W	L	Pct.	SO	BB	H	ERA
1977	Detroit	28	218	15	7	.682	92	34	222	3.10

TITO FUENTES 34 5-11 175   Bats S Throws R

Veteran infielder starting 13th major-league season . . . Played out option with Padres and signed with Tigers just before deadline for reported $90,000 for one year . . . His .309 was career high . . . And highest average for a Tiger second baseman since Charlie Gehringer in 1940 . . . Signed as stop-gap until youngsters were ready, Fuentes was an asset, especially on offense . . . Self-proclaimed king of baseball's hot dogs, he plays with a flourish . . . His last child is named "Clinch." Why Clinch? "He was born on the day we (the Giants) clinched the pennant."

Year	Club	Pos	G	AB	R	H	2B	3B	HR	RBI	SB	Avg.
1965	San Francisco	SS-2B-3B	26	72	12	15	1	0	0	1	0	.208
1966	San Francisco	SS-2B	133	541	63	141	21	3	9	40	6	.261
1967	San Francisco	2B-SS	133	344	27	72	12	1	5	29	4	.209
1969	San Francisco	3B-SS	67	183	28	54	4	3	1	14	2	.295
1970	San Francisco	2B-SS-3B	123	435	49	116	13	7	2	32	4	.267
1971	San Francisco	2B	152	630	63	172	28	6	4	52	12	.273
1972	San Francisco	2B	152	572	64	151	33	6	7	53	16	.264
1973	San Francisco	2B-3B	160	656	78	182	25	5	6	63	12	.277
1974	San Francisco	2B	108	390	33	97	15	2	0	22	7	.249
1975	San Diego	2B	146	565	57	158	21	3	4	43	8	.280
1976	San Diego	2B	135	520	48	137	18	0	2	36	5	.263
1977	Detroit	2B	151	615	83	190	19	10	5	51	4	.309
	Totals		1486	5523	605	1485	210	46	45	436	80	.269

STEVE KEMP 23 6-0 185   Bats L Throws L

Excellent rookie season in year that produced a number of outstanding rookies in AL, like Murray, Page, Jones, Wills, Bailor . . . "He reminds me so much of Mantle and Murcer," says Ralph Houk. "He's aggressive just like they were. He had the same drive, even makes the same mistakes. He overdoes things sometimes. In a few years, he's going to be something. Just you wait and see." . . . Born Aug. 7, 1954, in San Ange-

lo, Tex. . . . No. 1 pick in nation in January, 1976, free agent draft
. . . Attended USC and followed Fred Lynn as star for Trojans,
but called a better player than Lynn.

Year	Club	Pos	G	AB	R	H	2B	3B	HR	RBI	SB	Avg.
1977	Detroit	OF	151	552	75	142	29	4	18	88	3	.257

JOHN HILLER 35 6-0 165   Bats R Throws L

 One of the great relievers in recent years . . .
May have embarked on new career because of
off-hand remark . . . Talking with pitching
coach Fred Gladding, vet cracked, "Everybody
else has been starting, when am I going to get
my turn?" . . . Gladding mentioned it to manager Ralph Houk and it was done . . . Hiller
started eight times, completing three . . . "If I
can help the club by starting, I'm all for it." . . . Born April 8,
1943, in Scarborough, Ont. . . . 101 saves in nine seasons . . . Rebounded from 1971 heart attack that changed his attitude and his
life style . . . Former roly-poly, trimmed down and became outstanding relief pitcher.

Year	Club	G	IP	W	L	Pct.	SO	BB	H	ERA
1965	Detroit	5	6	0	0	.000	4	1	5	0.00
1966	Detroit	1	2	0	0	.000	1	2	2	9.00
1967	Detroit	23	65	4	3	.571	49	9	57	2.63
1968	Detroit	39	128	9	6	.600	78	51	92	2.39
1969	Detroit	40	99	4	4	.500	74	44	97	4.00
1970	Detroit	47	104	6	6	.500	89	46	82	3.03
1971	Detroit					(Did Not Play)				
1972	Detroit	24	44	1	2	.333	26	13	39	2.05
1973	Detroit	65	125	10	5	.667	124	39	89	1.44
1974	Detroit	59	150	17	14	.548	134	62	127	2.64
1975	Detroit	36	71	2	3	.400	87	36	52	2.15
1976	Detroit	56	121	12	8	.600	117	67	93	2.38
1977	Detroit	45	124	8	14	.364	115	61	120	3.56
	Totals	440	1039	73	65	.529	898	431	855	2.65

JIM SLATON 27 6-0 185   Bats R Throws R

 Called "Pop," by young Brewer pitchers . . . "I
feel like I haven't come into my prime yet and
they're calling me pop." . . . 72 victories in
seven seasons and should get better . . . "He
has to be the guy who leads us," said Alex
Grammas before returning to the Reds as
coach . . . And now Slayton is a Tiger . . .
Born June 19, 1950, in Long Beach, Cal. . . .
Attended Antelope Valley JC . . . Picked by Brewers on 17th
round of June, 1969 draft . . . Pitched minor-league no-hitter . . .
Took correspondence course in self-motivation recommended by

former manager, Del Crandall . . . "I still have it. It's interesting. But you've got to develop confidence by yourself."

Year	Club	G	IP	W	L	Pct.	SO	BB	H	ERA
1971	Milwaukee	26	148	10	8	.556	63	71	140	3.77
1972	Milwaukee	9	44	1	6	.143	17	21	50	5.52
1973	Milwaukee	3B	276	13	15	.464	134	99	266	3.71
1974	Milwaukee	40	250	13	16	.448	126	101	254	3.92
1975	Milwaukee	37	217	11	18	.379	119	90	238	4.52
1976	Milwaukee	38	293	14	15	.483	138	94	287	3.44
1977	Milwaukee	32	221	10	14	.417	104	77	223	3.58
	Totals	220	1449	72	92	.439	701	553	1458	3.86

TOP PROSPECTS

LANCE PARRISH 21 6-3 195   Bats R Throws R

Big strong catcher with home run bat, strong arm and great future . . . Born June 15, 1956, in McKeesport, Pa. . . . Turned down dozens of college football scholarship offers to sign with Tigers, who drafted him first in June, 1974, free agent draft . . . Hit 25 homers, drove in 90 runs in 416 at bats for Evansville before called up to play in 12 games for Tigers.

LOU WHITAKER 20 5-11 160   Bats L Throws R

Got in 11 games at second base for Tigers at end of season and impressed with his bat, range and speed . . . Counted on to be Tiger future second baseman for many years . . . Sweet Lou . . . Born May 12, 1957, in New York City . . . Chosen on fifth round of June, 1975 draft.

ALAN TAMMELL 20 6-0 160   Bats R Throws R

Called up late to team with Sweet Lou Whitaker and give Tiger fans a look at keystone combo of future . . . Excellent fielder with great arm, but must hit more . . . Improved at Montgomery, where he batted .297, third in Southern Assn. . . . Born Feb. 21, 1958, in Garden Grove, Cal. . . . Second pick in June, 1976 draft . . . Only two years of pro ball behind him.

MANAGER RALPH HOUK: The Major . . . Veteran skipper

who broke into pro ball back in 1939 . . . Extremely well-liked by players, but under fire from impatient Tiger fans . . . Great patience with young players, which Tigers have in abundance . . . "The best young players I've ever had all at once," he says . . . Eternal optimist and cigar smoker . . . Also tobacco-chewer, pebble raker during game . . . Born Aug. 9,

1919, in Lawrence, Kan. . . . Played in shadow of Yogi Berra, but succeeded Casey Stengel as Yankee manager and won three straight pennants . . . Unsuccessful attempt at GM's chair . . . Left Yankees and joined Tigers in 1974 . . . When Tigers earned fourth place after defeat of Indians, Houk cracked: "We didn't back into fourth. You don't back in when you win 74 games."

GREATEST MANAGER

No team in baseball has suffered more managerial tragedy than the Tigers, from the manager who took pitching selections from his wife, to the two managers who died on the job in the same year, to the time they traded managers with Cleveland.

Of the 24 men, who have managed the Tigers, Hugh Jennings held the job longest, 14 years. He is also the only Tiger manager to win three pennants. His mistake was winning them in his first three seasons. Had he spread them out, he would have been better off.

Jennings was replaced by Ty Cobb, perhaps the greatest player of all-time . . . but hardly the greatest manager. Talked into taking the job, Cobb managed six years with moderate success. His winning percentage was .519, not much higher than his lifetime batting average.

Few managers in history had the success of Gordon (Mickey) Cochrane, who came from the Philadelphia Athletics in 1934 as a player-manager. He finished first, first, second and second in his first four seasons. Cochrane might have become one of the great manages of all-time. But in May, 1938, he was hit in the head by a pitch at Yankee Stadium. The accident ended his career as a player and seemed to affect his effectiveness as a manager. By August, he was replaced by Del Baker.

ALL-TIME TIGER LEADERS

BATTING: Ty Cobb, .420, 1911
HRs: Hank Greenberg, 58, 1938
RBIs: Hank Greenberg, 183, 1937
STEALS: Ty Cobb, 96, 1915
WINS: Denny McLain, 31, 1968
STRIKEOUTS: Mickey Lolich, 308, 1971

CLEVELAND INDIANS

TEAM DIRECTORY: Principal Owner: Steve O'Neill; Pres.: Gabe Paul; VP-GM: Phillip Seghi; VP-Treasurer: Dudley S. Blossom; VP of Operations: Carl Fazio, Jr.; Dir. of Scouting and Minor League Operations: Bob Quinn; Pub. Dir.: Randy Adamack; Trav. Sec.: Mike Seghi; Mgr.: Jeff Torborg. Home: Cleveland Municipal Stadium (76,713). Field distances: 320, l.f. line; 385, r.c.; 320, r.f. line. Spring training: Tuscon, Ariz.

SCOUTING REPORT

HITTING: Surprisingly, this was the best part of the 1977 Indians, largely because of Andre Thornton, who was almost released in May, caught fire in June and ended up the club leader in homers (28) and runnerup in RBIs (70) to Rico Carty (80).

The Indians batted .269 and they were without the services, at least part of the time, of Buddy Bell, Johnny Grubb, Rick Manning and Duane Kuiper. Nonetheless, the Indians made no significant improvement on offense, while others in their division did, so they are relying on an injury-free season to move up.

PITCHING: What was to have been their forte turned into a bummer for the Indians. The $2 million free agent, Wayne Garland, pitched through a rocky start and finished 13-19. Only one of them, 9-7 Rick Waits, was more than one game over .500. Dennis Eckersley (14-13) pitched a no-hitter and had an ERA of 3.53, but the staff finished with an ERA over four.

Except Jim Kern from criticism because of his eight wins and 18 saves as a stopper, but all other Indian pitchers must improve and carry their end of the load if the Indians are to avoid another drop in the standings.

FIELDING: Third best in the league despite injuries to Bell, Kuiper and Manning and an off year by shortstop Frank Duffy, who has played out his option.

If Alfredo Griffin can handle shortstop and others can stay injury-free, the Indian defense can help make the pitching better which can help make the Indians better.

OUTLOOK: Perhaps the bleakest it's been in years for the immediate future. But the long range looks better than it has in years. There is new ownership and fresh money and Gabe Paul is back to steer the ship. A complete overhaul is needed. Paul did it before, then left. In his absence, the Indians sailed an unsteady course. Now he's back and, in time, the ship may be righted once again.

Tribe needs big season from no-hit ace Dennis Eckersley.

CLEVELAND INDIANS 1978 ROSTER

MANAGER Jeff Torborg
Coaches—Rocky Colavito, Harvey Haddix, Joe Moeller, Joe
          Nossek

PITCHERS

No.	Name	1977 Club	W-L	IP	SO	ERA	B-T	Ht.	Wt.	Born
42	Andersen, Larry	Toledo	5-6	65	40	1.94	R-R	6-3	180	5/6/53 Portland, OR
		Cleveland	0-1	14	8	3.21				
22	Bibby, Jim	Cleveland	12-13	207	141	3.57	R-R	6-5	230	10/29/44 Franklinton, N.C.
35	Buskey, Tom	Cleveland	0-0	34	15	5.29	R-R	6-3	220	2/20/47 Harrisburg, PA
		Toledo	1-3	30	16	4.50				
49	Camper, Cardell	Toledo	11-10	167	86	5.35	R-R	6-2	205	7/6/52 Boley, OK
		Cleveland	1-0	9	9	4.06				
41	Dobson, Pat	Cleveland	3-12	133	81	6.16	R-R	6-3	200	2/12/42 Depew, NY
37	Eckersley, Dennis	Cleveland	14-13	247	191	3.53	R-R	6-2	190	10/3/54 Oakland, CA
39	Fitzmorris, Al	Cleveland	6-10	133	54	5.41	B-R	6-2	200	3/21/46 Buffalo, NY
17	Garland, Wayne	Cleveland	13-19	283	118	3.50	R-R	6-0	195	10/26/50 Nashville, TN
44	Hood, Don	Cleveland	2-1	105	62	3.00	L-L	6-2	180	10/16/49 Florence, SC
34	Kern, Jim	Cleveland	8-10	92	91	3.42	R-R	6-5	205	3/15/49 Gladwin, MI
38	Laxton, Bill	Sea.-CL.	3-2	74	50	4.96	L-L	6-2	190	1/5/48 Camden, NJ
43	Monge, Sid	Cal. CL.	1-3	51	29	5.47	B-L	6-2	195	4/11/51 Agua Prieta, MX
36	Waits, Rick	Cleveland	9-7	135	62	3.99	L-L	6-3	195	5/15/52 Atlanta, GA

CATCHERS

No.	Name	1977 Club	H	HR	RBI	Pct.	B-T	Ht.	Wt.	Born
16	Kendall, Fred	Cleveland	79	3	39	.249	R-R	6-1	185	1/31/49 Torrance, CA
13	Pruitt, Ron	Cleveland	63	2	32	.288	R-R	6-0	185	10/21/51 Flint, MI

INFIELDERS

No.	Name	1977 Club	H	HR	RBI	Pct.	B-T	Ht.	Wt.	Born
25	Bell, Buddy	Cleveland	140	11	64	.292	R-R	6-2	185	8/27/51 Pittsburgh, PA
14	Blanks, Larvell	Cleveland	92	6	38	.286	R-R	5-8	165	1/20/50 Del Rio, TX
9	Carty, Rico	Cleveland	129	5	80	.280	R-R	6-2	190	9/1/40 D.R.
8	Griffin, Alfredo	Toledo	114	1	32	.249	B-R	5-11	160	10/6/57 D.R.
		Cleveland	6	0	3	.146				
18	Kuiper, Duane	Cleveland	169	1	50	.277	L-R	6-0	175	6/19/50 Racine, WI
26	Oliver, Dave	Toledo	134	3	47	.285	L-R	5-11	175	4/7/51 Stockton, CA
		Cleveland	7	0	3	.318				
—	Rosello, Dave	Chicago (NL)	18	1	9	.220	R-R	5-11	160	6/26/50 Mayaquez, PR
29	Thornton, Andre	Cleveland	114	28	70	.263	R-R	6-2	205	8/13/49 Tuskegee, AL
—	Veryzer, Tom	Detroit	69	2	28	.197	R-R	6-1	180	2/11/53 Port Jefferson, NY

OUTFIELDERS

No.	Name	1977 Club	H	HR	RBI	Pct.	B-T	Ht.	Wt.	Born
00	Dade, Paul	Cleveland	134	3	45	.291	R-R	6-0	195	12/7/51 Seattle, WA
52	Gardner, Vassie	Toledo	84	8	40	.220	R-R	6-2	185	9/17/55 Los Angeles, CA
12	Gonzalez, Orlando	Toldeo	145	1	43	.306	L-L	6-2	185	11/15/52 Havana, Cuba
1	Grubb, Johnny	Cleveland	28	2	14	.301	L-R	6-3	180	8/4/48 Richmond, VA
30	Lowenstein, John	Cleveland	36	4	12	.242	L-R	5-11	165	1/27/47 Wolf Point, MO
28	Manning, Rick	Cleveland	57	5	18	.226	L-R	6-1	180	9/2/54 Niagara Falls, NY
27	Norris, Jim	Cleveland	119	2	37	.270	L-L	5-10	190	12/20/48 Brooklyn, NY
—	Speed, Horace	Phoenix	124	10	79	.266	R-R	6-1	180	10/4/51 Los Angeles, CA

INDIAN PROFILES

RICK MANNING 23 6-1 180   Bats L Throws R

Injuries continued to plague this young man, a three-year major-league vet at 23 . . . Still has enormous potential as hitter and center fielder . . . Back injury and broken bone in hand caused him to miss more than half a season . . . Born Sept. 2, 1954, in Niagara Falls, N.Y., his career has been no honeymoon because of injuries . . . Second free agent selection in nation in June, 1972 . . . Won Gold Glove in 1976 at age 21 . . . Worked in Cleveland employment agency in off-season, so should have no trouble finding job when his career ends.

Year	Club	Pos	G	AB	R	H	2B	3B	HR	RBI	SB	Avg.
1975	Cleveland........	OF	120	480	69	137	16	5	3	35	19	.285
1976	Cleveland........	OF	138	552	73	161	24	7	6	43	16	.292
1977	Cleveland........	OF	68	252	33	57	7	3	5	18	9	.226
	Totals...........		326	1284	175	355	47	15	14	96	44	.276

ANDRE THORNTON 28 6-2 205   Bats R Throws R

Thunder . . . Obtained from Expos for Jackie Brown, Thornton was on verge of being released in May . . . Suddenly his bat heated up and he became big man in Indians' lineup . . . Born Aug. 13, 1949, in Tuskeegee, Ala. . . . Raised in Phoenixville, Pa., where he was outstanding three-sport star . . . Played in Babe Ruth World Series in 1965 . . . Originally with Phillies organization, traded to Cubs, Expos before Indians . . . Was third most productive hitter in NL in 1975, then declined in 1976 . . . Was unaware he was playing with broken thumb . . . Traded to Montreal and continued slump until Indians got him . . . Deeply religious, an active member of Fellowship of Christian Athletes.

Year	Club	Pos	G	AB	R	H	2B	3B	HR	RBI	SB	Avg.
1973	Chicago (NL)	1B	17	35	3	7	3	0	0	2	0	.200
1974	Chicago (NL)	1B-3B	107	303	41	79	16	4	10	46	2	.261
1975	Chicago (NL)	1B-3B	120	372	70	109	21	4	18	60	3	.293
1976	Chi(NL) Montreal .	1B-OF	96	268	28	52	11	2	11	38	4	.194
1977	Cleveland........	1B-OF	131	433	77	114	20	5	28	70	3	.263
	Totals...........		471	1411	219	361	71	15	67	216	12	.256

BUDDY BELL 26 6-2 185　　　　　Bats R Throws R

After missing only four games previous year, Bell was hit by Indian injury jinx, suffering stretched ligament in knee that finished him for year on Sept. 4 . . . Developing into one of league's outstanding third baseman . . . Born Aug. 27, 1951, in Pittsburgh, where his dad, Gus, was starring for Pirates . . . Almost overlooked in draft and chosen on 16th round in 1969 as infielder . . . Converted to center field because Indians had Graig Nettles and did superb job . . . Tribe then traded Nettles to make room for Bell.

Year	Club	Pos	G	AB	R	H	2B	3B	HR	RBI	SB	Avg.
1972	Cleveland........	OF-3B	132	466	49	119	21	1	9	36	5	.255
1973	Cleveland........	3B-OF	156	631	86	169	23	7	14	59	7	.268
1974	Cleveland........	3B	116	423	51	111	15	1	7	46	1	.262
1975	Cleveland........	3B-OF	153	553	66	150	20	4	10	59	6	.271
1976	Cleveland........	3B-1B	159	604	75	170	26	2	7	60	3	.281
1977	Cleveland........	3B-1B	129	479	64	140	23	4	11	64	1	.292
	Totals...........		845	3156	391	859	128	19	58	324	23	.272

DENNIS ECKERSLEY 23 6-2 190　　　Bats R Throws R

Outstanding prospect, still young enough to realize great potential . . . 13, 13, 14 wins last three seasons, should do better . . . An inconsistent pitcher who can be awful one day, good enough to throw no-hitter next, as he did on Memorial Day vs. Angels . . . Came two outs away from matching Cy Young's 1904 mark of 23 consecutive hitless innings . . . Awarded $3,000 bonus by owner, Ted Bonda . . . But had poor second half and did not become 20-game winner Indians expected—and still do . . . Born Oct. 3, 1954, in Oakland, Cal.

Year	Club	G	IP	W	L	Pct.	SO	BB	H	ERA
1975	Cleveland................	34	187	13	7	.650	152	90	147	2.60
1976	Cleveland................	36	199	13	12	.520	200	78	155	3.44
1977	Cleveland................	33	247	14	13	.519	191	54	214	3.53
	Totals..................	103	633	40	32	.556	543	222	516	3.23

WAYNE GARLAND 27 6-0 195　　　　Bats R Throws R

Under great pressure to produce when signed for $1.2 million after playing out option with Orioles . . . Stumbled along in first half of season before becoming outstanding pitcher Indians know he is . . . "He's one of the best pitchers in the league," said ex-manager, Frank Robinson. "Maybe the best." . . . Only thing he did to celebrate new wealth was buy

estimated $150,000 house in Cleveland suburb . . . Accused of
lack of loyalty by Orioles' Jim Palmer . . . Snapped back, accus-
ing Palmer of "jealousy." . . . Born Oct. 26, 1950, in Nashville
. . . Signed as free agent by Orioles and hit jackpot by winning 20
for Orioles in 1976 while playing without contract.

Year	Club	G	IP	W	L	Pct.	SO	BB	H	ERA
1973	Baltimore	4	16	0	1	.000	10	7	14	3.94
1974	Baltimore	20	91	5	5	.500	40	26	68	2.97
1975	Baltimore	29	87	2	5	.286	46	31	80	3.72
1976	Baltimore	38	232	20	7	.741	113	64	224	2.68
1977	Cleveland	38	283	13	19	.406	118	88	281	3.59
	Totals	129	709	40	37	.519	327	216	667	3.24

JIM BIBBY 33 6-5 230   Bats R Throws R

Among hardest throwers in baseball, but ball
doesn't always go where he aims it . . . Used as
starter by Frank Robinson, Torborg tried him
as bullpen stopper with success . . . Born Oct.
29, 1944, in Franklinton, N.C. . . . It is source
of amusement that big Jim chose professional
baseball, brother Henry, four inches shorter,
chose pro basketball . . . No-hitter vs. Oak-
land for Texas in 1973 . . . Signed originally with Mets, traded to
Cardinals, then to Rangers . . . "I know I can win if I get the ball
over the plate."

Year	Club	G	IP	W	L	Pct.	SO	BB	H	ERA
1972	St. Louis	6	40	1	3	.250	28	19	29	3.38
1973	St. Louis	6	16	0	2	.000	12	17	19	9.56
1973	Texas	26	180	9	10	.474	155	106	121	3.25
1974	Texas	41	264	19	19	.500	149	113	255	4.74
1975	Tex.-Clev.	36	181	7	15	.318	93	78	172	3.88
1976	Cleveland	34	163	13	7	.650	84	56	162	3.20
1977	Cleveland	37	207	12	13	.480	141	73	197	3.57
	Totals	186	1051	61	69	.469	662	462	955	3.89

JIM KERN 29 6-5 205   Bats R Throws R

Another flame thrower whose talents were
finally recognized when he was chosen to all-
star squad . . . Eight minor-league seasons before making it with Indians in '75 . . . 33 saves
last two seasons . . . Born March 15, 1949, in
Gladwin, Mich. . . . Once fanned 20 in American Legion state tournament . . . Continuing
studies at Michigan State in chemical engineer-
ing . . . Spent one winter trapping in northern Michigan wilder-
ness . . . Estimated he earned total of $80,000 for first 6½ seasons

of pro ball . . . Finally signed three-year pact for estimated $330,000 that runs through 1979 season.

Year	Club	G	IP	W	L	Pct.	SO	BB	H	ERA
1974	Cleveland................	4	15	0	1	.000	11	14	16	4.80
1975	Cleveland................	13	72	1	2	.333	55	45	60	3.75
1976	Cleveland................	50	118	10	7	.588	111	50	91	2.36
1977	Cleveland................	60	92	8	10	.444	91	47	85	3.42
	Totals..................	127	297	19	20	.487	268	156	252	3.15

RICO CARTY 37 6-2 190   Bats R Throws R

"The "Beeg Boy" . . . One of the games' great hitters over the past decade . . . Lifetime .300 hitter for 14 seasons . . . Over 1,400 hits . . . Born Ricardo Adolpho Jacobo Carty on Sept. 1, 1940, in Dominican Republic . . . Boxed professionally in his homeland . . . Three brothers played pro ball . . . His .366 for Atlanta in 1970 was highest in majors since 1957 and until 1977 . . . Had 31-game hit streak in 1970 . . . Suffered several serious setbacks . . . Tuberculosis cost him entire 1968 season, had three shoulder separations and missed entire 1971 with leg injury . . . Feuded with Frank Robinson and might have hastened manager's departure . . . Lost in expansion draft, then recaptured in trade.

Year	Club	Pos	G	AB	R	H	2B	3B	HR	RBI	SB	Avg.
1963	Milwaukee.......	PH	2	2	0	0	0	0	0	0	0	.000
1964	Milwaukee.......	OF	133	455	72	150	28	4	22	88	1	.330
1965	Milwaukee.......	OF	83	271	37	84	18	1	10	35	1	.310
1966	Atlanta..........	OF-C-1B-3B	151	521	73	170	25	2	15	76	4	.326
1967	Atlanta..........	OF-1B	134	444	41	113	16	2	15	64	4	.255
1969	Atlanta..........	OF	104	304	47	104	15	0	16	58	0	.342
1970	Atlanta..........	OF	136	478	84	175	23	3	25	101	1	.366
1972	Atlanta..........	OF	86	271	31	75	12	2	6	29	0	.277
1973	Tex-Oak.........	OF	93	314	25	73	13	0	4	34	2	.232
1973	Chicago(NL).....	OF	22	70	4	15	0	0	1	8	0	.214
1974	Cleveland.......	1B	33	91	6	33	5	0	1	16	0	.363
1975	Cleveland.......	1B-OF	118	383	57	118	19	1	18	64	2	.308
1976	Cleveland.......	1B	152	522	67	171	34	0	13	83	1	.310
1977	Cleveland.......	1B	127	461	50	129	23	1	15	80	1	.280
	Totals..........		1374	4617	594	1410	231	16	161	736	17	.305

DUANE KUIPER 27 6-0 175   Bats L Throws R

Also hit by injury jinx . . . Outstanding young player who has made only 21 errors in two seasons . . . Has become team leader . . . Interceded to save Frank Robinson's job—temporarily . . . "You see so many great plays by Kuiper," said F. Robby, "You come to expect them all the time . . . He is tremendous . . . He is amazing . . . He is fearless." . . . Born

June 19, 1950, in Racine, Wisc. . . . Drafted by Yankees, Pilots, White Sox, Reds, Red Sox before signing with Indians . . . High school team played only 15-game schedule . . . But went to junior college, then to Southern Illinois, reaching finals of 1971 College World Series.

Year	Club	Pos	G	AB	R	H	2B	3B	HR	RBI	SB	Avg.
1974	Cleveland........	2B	10	22	7	11	2	0	0	4	1	.500
1975	Cleveland........	2B	90	346	42	101	11	1	0	25	19	.292
1976	Cleveland........	2B-1B	135	506	47	133	13	6	0	37	10	.263
1977	Cleveland........	2B	148	610	62	169	15	8	1	50	11	.277
	Totals..........		383	1485	158	414	41	15	1	116	41	.279

JIM NORRIS 29 5-10 190   Bats L Throws L

Finally made big leagues after six teams, six seasons in minor leagues . . . Excellent fielder and surprisingly swift runner for size and build . . . Born Dec. 20, 1948, in Brooklyn, N.Y. . . . Family moved to Long Island and he starred at U. of Maryland . . . Once ran 9.8 100, but knee injury has slowed him somewhat . . . Working out with U.S. Pan American team, he threw from center field and suffered six fractures in arm . . . Signed for mere $2,500 bonus . . . Used as player-coach at Toledo in '76 . . . Batted .320 and given shot at Indian job . . . Made starting lineup opening day and debuted with two hits and game-saving catch of Butch Hobson's HR bid.

Year	Club	Pos	G	AB	R	H	2B	3B	HR	RBI	SB	Avg.
1977	Cleveland........	OF-1B	133	440	59	119	23	6	2	37	26	.270

TOP PROSPECTS

ALFREDO GRIFFIN 21 5-11 160   Bats R Throws R

Frank Duffy's decision to become a free agent makes this young speedster an important figure in Indians' plans . . . Has chance to take over as regular shortstop . . . Born Oct. 6, 1957, in Dominican Republic, and attended same high school as Rico Carty . . . While his bat is questionable, he is said to have super range in field.

LARRY ANDERSEN 24 6-3 180   Bats R Throws R

A relief specialist at Toledo last year, Andersen had a 1.94 ERA in 45 games, then was called up to Indians and got in 11 games with a 3.14 ERA . . . Born May 6, 1953, in Bellevue, Wash. . . . A self-admitted flake . . . Works in off-season with juvenile offenders in program called Vision Quest in Arizona . . . "When I go to the mound, there's no question in my mind I'll do the job."

MANAGER JEFF TORBORG: Took over when Frank Robinson was fired on June 19 . . . At 36, is youngest manager in big leagues . . . A man of class, depth and dignity, he graduated from Rutgers University and was NCAA batting champ and All-American catcher in 1963 . . . Born November, 26, 1941, in Westfield, N.J. . . . Signed with Dodgers and caught no-hitters by Sandy Koufax, Bill Singer and Nolan Ryan, one less than major-league record. Also was catcher when Koufax and Ryan set single season strikeout record and when Don Drysdale threw fifth consecutive shutout in '68 . . . Earned masters degree in athletic administration from Montclair State in New Jersey.

GREATEST MANAGER

Despite all the famous names who sat on the Indian dugout as manager—Napoleon Lajoie, Walter Johnson, Roger Peckinpaugh and Frank Robinson, only three can be considered successful managers. The Indians won only three pennants—one each by Tris Speaker, Lou Boudreau and Al Lopez.

Speaker was the famed "Grey Eagle," perhaps the greatest player in Indian history, and no slouch as manger.

Boudreau was the famed "Boy Manager," assuming the job at the tender age of 25.

Lopez was merely "The Senor," a manager good enough to be voted into the Hall of Fame, although winning only two pennants (one in Chicago) in 17 years. However, he is the 10th leading winning manager in history, 1,422 victories and a percentage of .581 at Cleveland and Chicago combined.

His record in Cleveland was even better, a winning percentage of .617. Lopez merely made the mistake of having his job at the wrong time, during one of the Yankees' greatest dynasty. While Lopez was winning enough games to win pennants in most years, the Yankees almost always won more. Five times in six seasons, Lopez' Indians finished second to Casey Stengel's Yankees. The exception was 1954. The Indians, under Lopez, posted a record of 111-43, a percentage of .721. No team—and no manager—ever won more games in one season, before or since.

ALL-TIME INDIAN LEADERS

BATTING: Joe Jackson, .408, 1911
HRs: Al Rosen, 43, 1953
RBIs: Hal Trosky, 162, 1936
STEALS: Ray Chapman, 52, 1917
WINS: Jim Bagby, 31, 1920
STRIKEOUTS: Bob Feller, 348, 1946

Bob Feller's second no-hitter came against Yankees in 1946.

TORONTO BLUE JAYS

TEAM DIRECTORY: Chairman of the Board: R. Howard Webster; Pres.-Chief Oper. Officer: Peter Bavasi; VP-Baseball Operations: Pat Gillick; VP-Business Operations: Paul Beeston; Dir. Pub. Rel.: Howard Starkman; Dir. of Information: Joe Bodolai; Trav. Sec.: Mike Cannon; Mgr.: Roy Hartsfield. Home: Exhibition Stadium (35,000). Field distances: 330, l.f. line; 400, c.f.; 330, r.f. line. Spring training: Dunedin, Fla.

SCOUTING REPORT

HITTING: With a year under their belt, the Blue Jays can look back at what they accomplished and determine what they must do to improve. That's easy. They need to improve their hitting (next to last in the league), their pitching (next to last in the league) and their defense (next to last in the league).

The Jays batted .259 as a team and hit only 100 homers. Ron Fairly, who hit 19 of them, is gone. But he was traded for two young prospects which, the Blue Jays have decided, is the way they must go.

In particular, they are proud of Bob Bailor, whose .310 average was 11th in the league in his first full season. And of Roy Howell, picked up from the Rangers. In 96 games, Howell batted .315 and had 10 homers and 43 RBIs, nine of them coming in one game, a 19-3 rout of the world champion Yankees. Manager Roy Hartsfield has a blowup of that box score in his office in Toronto as a reminder that it can be done, even by an expansion team.

PITCHING: Youth abounds here, too, on a staff that had only three shutouts, the fewest number of saves in the league and yielded more than four-and-one-half runs a game.

Veterans like Jesse Jefferson, Dave Lemanczyk, Tom Murphy and recently-acquired Tom Underwood give the Jays a sense of stability. But Blue Jay brass is excited about the future with youngsters like 10-game winner Jerry Garvin, Dennis DeBarr, Jeff Byrd and Jim Clancy. The latter may be a prize. Only 22, he came up at midseason and impressed the Jays so much, he was the only player they deemed untouchable in trade.

FIELDING: There is much work to be done here, although some of it will be accomplished by experience. Catching and the outfield are the strong points, but it is in the infield where the Jays lost games as the club total of errors (164) was 31 more than their total number of double plays.

OUTLOOK: The Blue Jays are committed to a position of going with kids, building an organization and asking their fans to be patient. They chose not to take the quick way through the signing of free agents. That's their choice and they must live with it, for five years, anyway. If there are no results by then, they will have chosen the wrong road.

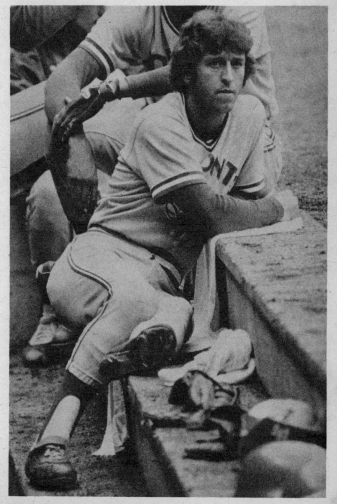

Blue Jays' first pick, Bob Bailor, came through with .310 BA.

TORONTO BLUE JAYS 1978 ROSTER

MANAGER Roy Hartsfield
Coaches—Bobby Doerr, Don Leppert, Bob Miller, Jackie
Moore, Harry Warner

PITCHERS

No.	Name	1977 Club	W-L	IP	SO	ERA	B-T	Ht.	Wt.	Born
21	Bruno, Tom	Toledo	2-4	41	21	5.27	R-R	6-4	205	1/26/53 Chicago, IL
		Toronto	0-1	18	9	8.00				
27	Byrd, Jeff	Jersey City	1-4	69	67	3.13	R-R	6-3	185	11/11/56 La Mesa, CA
		Toronto	2-13	87	40	6.21				
18	Clancy, Jim	Jersey City	5-13	118	99	4.88	R-R	6-5	185	12/18/55 Chicago, IL
		Toronto	4-9	77	44	5.03				
28	Darr, Mike	Jersey City	6-13	132	110	6.14	R-R	6-4	190	3/23/56 Pomona, CA
		Toronto	0-1	1	1	45.00				
22	DeBarr, Dennis	Toledo	2-1	36	17	2.72	L-L	6-2	185	1/16/53 Cheyenne, WY
		Toronto	0-1	21	10	6.00				
17	Edge, Butch	Reno	1-0	13	8	3.46	R-R	6-4	202	7/18/56 Houston, TX
36	Garvin, Jerry	Toronto	10-18	245	127	4.19	L-L	6-3	190	10/21/55 Oakland, CA
32	Henderson, Joe	Indianapolis	5-5	43	21	5.27	L-R	6-2	185	7/4/46 Lake Cormorant, MS
		Cincinnati	0-0	9	8	12.00				
34	Jefferson, Jesse	Toronto	9-17	217	114	4.31	R-R	6-3	195	3/3/49 Midlothian, VA
44	Johnson, Jerry	Toronto	2-4	86	54	4.60	R-R	6-2	190	12/3/43 Miami, FL
23	Lemanczyk, Dave	Toronto	13-16	252	105	4.25	R-R	6-4	230	8/17/50 Syracuse, NY
45	Murphy, Tom	Bost-Toronto	2-2	83	39	4.77	R-R	6-3	205	12/30/45 Cleveland, OH
48	Singer, Bill	Toronto	2-8	60	33	6.75	R-R	6-4	195	4/24/44 Los Angeles, CA
—	Underwood, Tom	Phil-St. L.	9-11	133	86	5.01	R-L	5-11	170	12/22/53 Kokomo, IN
33	Willis, Mike	Toronto	2-6	107	59	3.95	L-L	6-2	210	12/26/50 Oklahoma City, OK

CATCHERS

No.	Name	1977 Club	H	HR	RBI	Pct.	B-T	Ht.	Wt.	Born
8	Ashby, Alan	Toronto	83	2	29	.210	B-R	6-2	190	7/8/51 Long Beach, CA
9	Cerrone, Rick	Charleston	54	6	40	.234	R-R	5-11	190	5/19/54 Newark, NJ
		Toronto	20	1	10	.200				
—	Kelly, Pat	El Paso	99	14	53	.271	R-R	6-3	210	8/27/55 Santa Maria, CA
12	Whitt, Ernie	Charleston	24	0	7	.255	L-R	6-2	200	6/13/52 Detroit, MI
		Toronto	7	0	6	.171				

INFIELDERS

No.	Name	1977 Club	H	HR	RBI	Pct.	B-T	Ht.	Wt.	Born
35	Ault, Doug	Toronto	109	11	64	.245	R-L	6-3	200	3/9/50 Beaumont, TX
4	Gomez, Luis	Minnesota	16	0	11	.246	R-R	5-9	150	8/19/51 Guadalajara, Mex.
13	Howell, Roy	Tex-Toronto	115	10	44	.302	L-R	6-1	190	12/18/53 Lompoc, CA
—	Hutton, Tommy	Philadelphia	25	2	11	.309	L-L	5-11	170	4/20/46 Los Angeles, CA
14	Iorg, Garth	Charleston	77	1	34	.294	R-R	5-11	165	10/12/54 Arcata, CA
39	McKay, Dave	Toronto	54	3	22	.197	B-R	6-1	190	3/14/50 Vancouver, B.C.
6	Nordbrook, Tim	Chi (AL)-Tor	16	0	2	.193	R-R	6-1	170	7/17/49 Baltimore, MD
10	Rader, Doug	San Diego	46	5	27	.271	R-R	6-3	215	7/30/44 Chicago, IL
		Toronto	75	13	40	.240				
2	Staggs, Steve	Okla. City	19	1	9	.279	R-R	5-9	155	5/6/51 Anchorage, AK
		Iowa	73	4	19	.414				
		Toronto	75	2	28	.258				
29	Torres, Hector	Toronto	64	5	26	.240	R-R	6-0	175	9/16/45 Monterrey, Mex.

OUTFIELDERS

No.	Name	1977 Club	H	HR	RBI	Pct.	B-T	Ht.	Wt.	Born
1	Bailor, Bob	Toronto	154	5	32	.310	R-R	5-9	160	7/10/51 Connellsville, PA
3	Bowling, Steve	Toledo	16	3	15	.219	R-R	6-0	185	6/26/52 Tulsa, OK
		Toronto	40	1	13	.206				
5	Ewing, Sam	Toronto	70	4	35	.287	L-R	6-3	195	4/9/49 Lewisburg, TN
19	Velez, Otto	Toronto	92	16	62	.256	R-R	6-0	193	11/29/50 Ponce P.R.
20	Woods, Al	Toronto	125	6	35	.284	L-L	6-3	190	8/8/53 Oakland, CA
35	Woods, Gary	Toledo	85	4	33	.272	R-R	6-2	185	7/20/54 Santa Barbara, CA
		Toronto	49	0	17	.216				

BLUE JAY PROFILES

BOB BAILOR 26 5-9 160   Bats R Throws R

Red Sox' Carlton Fisk called him, "the toughest out in the league for us." . . . League's 11th
leading hitter and one of outstanding batch of
rookies in AL . . . Originally signed as shortstop, switched to outfield because of shoulder
injury . . . Born Oct. 7, 1951, in Connellsville,
Pa. . . . High school basketball star, did not
play baseball . . . Not selected in free agent
draft, signed off sandlots by Orioles . . . Toronto's No. 1 pick in
expansion draft . . . His .310 is highest ever for first year expansion club . . . "A lot of people ask me if I was surprised I hit so
well. How do you know if you can hit major-league pitching until
you get the chance? Next year if somebody asks me if I can hit, I'll
say yes because now I know."

Year	Club	Pos	G	AB	R	H	2B	3B	HR	RBI	SB	Avg.
1975	Baltimore........	SS-2B	5	7	0	1	0	0	0	0	0	.143
1976	Baltimore........	SS	9	6	2	2	0	1	0	0	0	.333
1977	Toronto	SS-OF	122	496	62	154	21	5	5	32	15	.310
	Totals..........		136	509	64	157	21	6	5	32	15	.308

ROY HOWELL 24 6-1 190   Bats L Throws R

Will always remember Saturday afternoon,
Sept. 10, 1977 . . . Scene Yankee Stadium:
Roy had five hits, 13 total bases, two homers,
two doubles, a single and nine RBIs . . . "I just
can't explain a day like this. I don't think I ever
had a nine RBI day before anywhere. A lot of
four or fives, but not a nine. I enjoy playing in
Yankee Stadium. I get psyched up there." . . .
Born Dec. 18, 1953, in Lompoc, Cal. . . . No. 1 choice in nation in
June, 1972 free agent draft. . . . Selected by Rangers, traded to
Blue Jays last year . . . Rangers had given up on him as third
baseman, but he had worked hard to improve and is now better
than adequate at hot corner.

Year	Club	Pos	G	AB	R	H	2B	3B	HR	RBI	SB	Avg.
1974	Texas	3B	13	44	2	11	1	0	1	3	0	.250
1975	Texas	3B	125	383	43	96	15	2	10	51	2	.251
1976	Texas	3B	140	491	55	124	28	2	8	53	1	.253
1977	Texas-Toronto	3B	103	381	41	115	17	1	10	44	4	.302
	Totals...........		381	1299	141	346	61	5	29	151	7	.266

C'mon Elsie! Jays' Sam Ewing in cow-milking contest.

JERRY GARVIN 22 6-3 190   **Bats L Throws L**

Outstanding young pitching prospect who impressed rival batters with his poise and stuff . . . Won first three major-league starts and was 9-6 before suffering through 10-game losing streak . . . It came over a 75-day period and was more the result of bad luck than bad pitching . . . In 13 starts in streak, he never allowed more than three runs . . . "He has more guts than any pitcher I've ever seen," said catcher Rick Cerone . . . "He's just got a good idea of what he's doing out there," said Alan Ashby, another Jay catcher . . . Born Oct. 21, 1955, in Oakland, Cal. . . . Was drafted by Twins and picked on first round of expansion draft . . . Copied Juan Marichal's high kick.

Year	Club	G	IP	W	L	Pct.	SO	BB	H	ERA
1977	Toronto	34	245	10	18	.357	127	85	247	4.19

OTTO VELEZ 27 193   Bats R Throws R

Cooled off after torrid start . . . Hit particularly well vs. Yankees, team from which he came in expansion draft . . . After Otto hit double in Yankee Stadium, Billy Martin went out to change pitcher, then detoured to second base . . . "It wasn't my idea to put you on the expansion list," Martin said. "I always knew you could hit." . . . Had nine hits and eight RBIs in four-game series vs. Yanks. Asked if that was his best series, he replied: "Sure, I never got to play four days in a row before." . . . Born Nov. 29, 1950, in Ponce, Puerto Rico . . . Never lived up to promise with Yankees, but never had real chance . . . Credits Blue Jay batting instructor Bobby Doerr with helping his swing.

Year	Club	Pos	G	AB	R	H	2B	3B	HR	RBI	SB	Avg.
1973	New York (AL) ...	OF	23	77	9	15	4	0	2	7	0	.195
1974	New York (AL) ...	1B-OF-3B	27	67	9	14	1	1	2	10	0	.209
1975	New York (AL) ...	1B	6	8	0	2	0	0	0	1	0	.250
1976	New York (AL) ...	1B-OF-3B	49	94	11	25	6	0	2	10	0	.266
1977	Toronto	1B-OF	120	360	50	92	19	3	16	62	4	.256
	Totals...........		225	606	79	148	30	4	22	90	4	.244

DOUG AULT 28 6-3 200   Bats R Throws L

One of those rarest of birds, a righty hitter, lefty thrower . . . Torrid start made him instant hero in Toronto . . . Hit HRs his first two at bats of season, five in first 18 games . . . Then slumped. Had only two homers in May, June and July, but hit four from Aug. 9 to end of season and pulled average up . . . "I saw some video tapes of my swing and it was awful," he says. "Now I'm concentrating on keeping my hands higher and I've moved four or five inches closer to the plate." . . . Born March 9, 1950, in Beaumont, Tex. . . . Was undrafted and signed as free agent with Rangers . . . Hit 67 homers in four minorleague seasons . . . Has worked as rough-neck on oil rig in North Sea.

Year	Club	Pos	G	AB	R	H	2B	3B	HR	RBI	SB	Avg.
1976	Texas	1B	9	20	0	6	1	0	0	0	0	.300
1977	Toronto	1B	129	445	44	109	22	3	11	64	4	.245
	Totals...........		138	465	44	115	23	3	11	64	4	.248

ALAN ASHBY 26 6-2 190   Bats S Throws R

Still has not fulfilled his potential at bat, although is regarded as one of best defensive catchers in league with excellent arm . . . Born July 8, 1951, in Long Beach, Cal. . . . A Dodger fan as kid, was in stands for two of Sandy Koufax' four no-hitters . . . Pony League and high school teammate of Phillies' Garry Maddox . . . Third selection of Indians in June, 1969 free agent draft . . . Threw out one of every three potential stealers and had only three passed balls for Indians in 1976 . . . Traded to Blue Jays at conclusion of expansion draft.

Year	Club	Pos	G	AB	R	H	2B	3B	HR	RBI	SB	Avg.
1973	Cleveland........	C	11	29	4	5	1	0	1	3	0	.172
1974	Cleveland........	C	10	7	1	1	0	0	0	0	0	.143
1975	Cleveland........	C-1B-3B	90	254	32	57	10	1	5	32	3	.224
1976	Cleveland........	3B-1B-C	89	247	26	59	5	1	4	32	0	.239
1977	Toronto	C	124	396	25	83	16	3	2	29	0	.210
	Totals..........		324	933	88	205	32	5	12	96	3	.220

JESSE JEFFERSON 28 6-3 195   Bats R Throws R

Hard throwing right-hander . . . Delivery reminiscent of Jim Palmer, with whom he played in '73 and '74 . . . Must overcome control problems to be outstanding pitcher . . . Born March 3, 1950, in Midlothian, Va., population 600 . . . Dad played for neighborhood baseball teams . . . Orioles No. 4 pick in June, 1968 free agent draft . . . Traded to White Sox from whom Blue Jays selected him on fourth round of expansion draft . . . Ready to win big in majors.

Year	Club	G	IP	W	L	Pct.	SO	BB	H	ERA
1973	Baltimore................	18	101	6	5	.545	52	46	104	4.10
1974	Baltimore................	20	57	1	0	1.000	31	38	55	4.42
1975	Balt-Chi (AL).............	26	115	5	11	.313	71	102	105	4.93
1976	Chicago (AL).............	19	62	2	5	.286	30	42	86	8.56
1977	Toronto	33	217	9	17	.346	114	83	224	4.31
	Totals...................	116	552	23	38	.377	298	311	574	4.89

DAVE LEMANCZYK 27 6-4 230   Bats R Throws R

Tied record of Gene Brabender, Seattle, 1969—most victories by a pitcher on a first year expansion club (13) . . . Missed by one tying American League record for wild pitches, one season (21), set by legendary Walter Johnson in 1910 . . . His 252 innings more than twice as many as he pitched in any one of five previous pro seasons . . . "I got a lot of miles on my car, but not on my arm." . . . Born Aug. 17, 1950, in Syracuse, but grew up on Long Island . . . Attended Hartwick College, where his athletic director was former Phillies relief great, Jim Konstanty . . . Majored in history, minor in philosophy and religion.

Year	Club	G	IP	W	L	Pct.	SO	BB	H	ERA
1973	Detroit	1	2	0	0	.000	0	0	4	13.50
1974	Detroit	22	79	2	1	.667	52	44	79	3.99
1975	Detroit	26	109	2	7	.222	67	46	120	4.46
1976	Detroit	20	81	4	6	.400	51	34	86	5.11
1977	Toronto	34	252	13	16	.448	105	87	278	4.25
	Totals	103	523	21	30	.412	275	211	567	4.42

DAVE McKAY 28 6-1 190   Bats S Throws R

Started out as third baseman, but switched to second base and impressed there with three DPs in first three games . . . "He makes the double play which we haven't been getting all year long," said manager Roy Hartsfield . . . "And he might have more range than any of our other second basemen. If he hits, he'll stay there.". . . Native Canadian. . . Born March 14, 1950, in Vancouver . . . Attended Creighton U. in Omaha, where he played 2B . . . Signed as free agent by Twins . . . Became 43rd player to hit home run his first at bat in majors . . . Abandoned switch-hitting after 0-17 slump, then reconsidered and went back to switching . . . "He probably works harder than anyone else on the team," says Hartsfield.

Year	Club	Pos	G	AB	R	H	2B	3B	HR	RBI	SB	Avg.
1975	Minnesota	3B	33	125	8	32	4	1	2	16	1	.256
1976	Minnesota	SS-3B	45	138	8	28	2	0	0	8	1	.203
1977	Toronto	SS-3B-2B	95	274	18	54	4	3	3	22	2	.197
	Totals		173	537	34	114	10	4	5	46	4	.212

TOP PROSPECTS

JIM CLANCY 22 6-5 185   Bats R Throws R

Made jump from AA and won four games for Jays at end of season . . . Impressed rivals with his stuff, poise and ability to keep ball down . . . Born Dec. 18, 1955, in Chicago . . . No. 4 pick of Texas in June, 1974 free agent draft . . . Pitching in Texas League in '76, rival manager (Amarillo) was Bob Miller, Blue Jay pitching coach, who recommended his selection.

JEFF BYRD 21 6-3 185   Bats R Throws R

Don't be misled by record with Jays. He's young, throws hard and was up from AA . . . Experience of pitching in big leagues will help him become outstanding pitcher . . . Born Nov. 11, 1956, in LaMesa, Cal. . . . Pitched back-to-back no-hitters in high school . . . Tandem with Clancy . . . Both drafted by Texas in June, 1974 free agent draft, teammates at Sarasota in '74, Anderson in '75, Amarillo in '76, Jersey City '77 and Toronto.

MANAGER ROY HARTSFIELD: Another of many major league managers who came under Branch Rickey's influence . . . Grew up in Dodger organization, as did Sparky Anderson, Tom Lasorda, Gene Mauch, Dick Williams, etc. . . . Great handler of young players . . . Fine southern gentleman and excellent baseball man . . . Played 17 years of pro ball, only three in majors . . . Born Oct. 25, 1925, in Chattahoochee, Ga. . . . Managed 11 years in minors and paid his dues for this chance . . . Feud with Orioles' Earl Weaver over placement of tarp on bullpen mound during rain, resulted in forfeit by Orioles because Weaver feared one of his players would trip over it . . . Said Hartsfield: "Second base has been in the same place for 100 years and I never heard of anybody tripping over it and getting hurt."

ALL-TIME BLUE JAY LEADERS

BATTING: Bob Bailor, .310, 1977
HRs: Ron Fairly, 19, 1977
RBIs: Ron Fairly, 64, 1977
     Doug Ault, 64 1977
STEALS: Bob Bailor, 15, 1977
WINS: Dave Lemanczyk, 13, 1977
STRIKEOUTS: Jerry Garvin, 127, 1977

TEXAS RANGERS

TEAM DIRECTORY: Chairman of the Board: Brad Corbett; Exec. VP: Eddie Robinson; GM: Dan O'Brien; Farm Dir.: Hal Keller; Trav. Sec. and News Media Director: Burton Hawkins; Promotions Dir.: Dan McDonald; Mgr.: Billy Hunter. Home: Arlington Stadium (41,000). Field distances: 330, l.f. line; 400, c.f.; 330, r.f. line. Spring training: Pompano Beach, Fla.

Like father, like son: Bump Wills plays like Maury.

SCOUTING REPORT

HITTING: To a team that finished sixth in the league in batting, seventh in homers and second in their division, add Al Oliver (.308, 19 HRs, 82 RBIs) and Richie Zisk (.290, 30, 101) and you know what the excitement is all about.

The Rangers believe this is their year and, from the looks of their regular lineup, they may be right. They have a bat at every position and a set lineup for the first time since the Alamo fell. To give you an idea of the kind of attack the Rangers will throw into the AL West race, the lowest average last year among the presumed nine starters was Bert Campaneris' .254. And the lowest RBI total was Campy's 46.

PITCHING: Second in the league in ERA, first in shutouts, the Rangers think they have improved their staff, even at the expense of Bert Blyleven. The only thing the Rangers lacked was a powerful left-hander and they got him from the Mets in Jon Matlack. Blyleven will be missed for his second-best 2.72 ERA, 15 complete games and five shutouts. But a pitcher who was only 14-12 should not be difficult to replace with newcomers Matlack, Doc Medich and rookie Len Barker. More difficult to replace may be Adrian Devine, whose 15 saves were tops on a staff that amassed only 31 rescues. Gaylord Perry, Dock Ellis and Fergie Jenkins fill out the corps.

FIELDING: Frank Lucchesi lost his job as Ranger manager, indirectly, over the belief that rookie Bump Wills should replace Lenny Randle as the club's regular second baseman. It won't help him now, but Lucchesi was right. Wills fielded .982, just .006 behind league leader, Frank White.

With Wills at second, Bert Campaneris at short and the continued improvement of Jim Sundberg, the league's top defensive catcher, the Rangers went from ninth in the league in fielding to second.

OUTLOOK: The time is now for the Rangers, bridesmaids twice in the last three years. They did what they had to do, spending money and taking risks in trades, and came away from the winter meetings as the most improved team in the American League. Another plus is that manager Billy Hunter will be there from the bell, instead of joining up at midseason. The KC Royals must look to their laurels.

TEXAS RANGERS 1978 ROSTER

MANAGER Bill Hunter
Coaches—Connie Ryan, Pat Corrales, Fred Koenig, Jim Schaffer

PITCHERS

No.	Name	1977 Club	W-L	IP	SO	ERA	B-T	Ht.	Wt.	Born
33	Alexander, Doyle	Texas	17-11	237	82	3.65	R-R	6-3	190	9/4/50 Cordova, AL
39	Barker, Len	Tucson	9-7	109	93	5.70	R-R	6-4	235	7/7/55 Ft. Knox, KY
		Texas	4-1	47	51	2.68				
24	Cuellar, Bobby	Tucson	10-6	93	66	3.48	R-R	5-11	190	8/20/52 Alice, TX
		Texas	0-0	7	3	1.29				
—	Clyde, David	Tucson	5-7	128	90	5.84	L-L	6-1	185	4/22/55 Kansas City, MO
17	Ellis, Dock	NY (AL)-Oak.								
		Texas	12-12	213	106	3.63	B-R	6-3	195	3/11/45 Los Angeles, CA
25	Jenkins, Ferguson	Boston	10-10	193	105	3.68	R-R	6-5	210	12/13/44 Chatham, Ont.
	Lindblad, Paul	Texas	4-5	99	46	4.18	L-L	6-2	195	8/9/41 Chanute, KA
	Matlack, Jon	N.Y. (NL)	7-15	169	123	4.21	L-L	6-3	205	1/19/50 West Chester, PA
—	Medich, George	N.Y. (NL)	0-1	7	3	3.86	R-R	6-5	227	12/9/48 Aliquippa, PA
		Oak.-Seattle	12-6	170	77	4.55				
29	Moret, Roger	Texas	3-3	72	39	3.75	B-L	6-4	175	9/16/48 Guayama, PR
36	Perry, Gaylord	Texas	15-12	238	177	3.37	R-R	6-4	215	9/15/38 Williamston, NC
27	Poloni, John	Tucson	8-13	187	101	5.15	L-L	6-5	210	2/28/54 Dearborn, MI
		Texas	1-0	7	5	6.43				
49	Umbarger, Jim	San Jose	3-5	56	21	7.71	L-L	6-6	200	2/17/53 Burbank, CA
		Oak.-Texas	2-6	57	29	6.32				

CATCHERS

No.	Name	1977 Club	H	HR	RBI	Pct.	B-T	Ht.	Wt.	Born
9	Ellis, John	Texas	28	4	15	.235	R-R	6-2	215	8/21/48 New London, CT
14	Fahey, Bill	Texas	15	0	5	.221	L-R	6-0	200	6/14/50 Detroit, MI
10	Sundberg, Jim	Texas	132	6	65	.291	R-R	6-0	190	5/18/51 Galesburg, IL

INFIELDERS

No.	Name	1977 Club	H	HR	RBI	Pct.	B-T	Ht.	Wt.	Born
2	Alomar, Sandy	Texas	22	1	11	.265	B-R	5-8	155	10/19/43 Salinas, PR
13	Bevacqua, Kurt	Tucson	126	9	76	.352	R-R	6-1	185	1/23/47 Miami Beach, FL
		Texas	32	5	28	.333				
	Campaneris, Bert	Texas	140	5	46	.254	R-R	5-10	155	3/9/42 Pueblo Neva, Cuba
—	Gray, Gary	Tucson	112	9	88	.310	R-R	6-0	180	9/21/52 New Orleans, LA
		Texas	0	0	0	.000				
21	Hargrove, Mike	Texas	160	18	69	.305	L-L	6-0	195	10/26/49 Perryton, TX
11	Harrah, Toby	Texas	142	27	87	.263	R-R	6-0	180	10/26/48 Sissonville, WV
3	Mason, Jim	Tor.-Texas	25	1	9	.187	L-R	6-2	190	8/14/50 Mobile, AL
—	Norman, Nelson	Shreveport	—	0	23	.251	R-R	6-2	160	5/23/58 San Pedro de Macares, DR
		Columbus	21	0	8	.233				
—	Pinkerton, Wayne	Tucson	97	0	36	.231	B-R	6-0	175	9/16/53 Hollendale, MS
18	Putnam, Pat	Tucson	149	15	102	.301	L-R	6-1	195	12/3/53 Bethel, VT
		Texas	8	0	3	.308				
1	Wills, Bump	Texas	155	9	62	.287	B-R	5-9	170	7/27/52 Washington, DC

OUTFIELDERS

No.	Name	1977 Club	H	HR	RBI	Pct.	B-T	Ht.	Wt.	Born
12	Beniquez, Juan	Texas	114	10	50	.269	R-R	5-11	165	5/13/50 San Sebastian, PR
20	Henderson, Ken	Texas	63	5	23	.258	B-R	6-3	190	6/15/46 Manning, IA
23	Horton, Willie	Det.-Texas	151	15	75	.289	R-R	5-10	205	10/18/42 Arno, VA
16	May, Dave	Texas	82	7	42	.241	L-R	5-11	195	12/23/43 New Castle, DL
	Oliver, Al	Pittsburgh	175	19	82	.308	L-L	6-1	190	10/14/46 Portsmouth, OH
	Rivera, Dave	Asheville	162	24	108	.340	R-R	5-11	175	8/9/57 King City, CA
26	Smith, Keith	Tucson	136	19	77	.323	R-R	5-9	175	5/3/53 Palmetto, FL
		Texas	16	2	6	.239				
—	Thomas, Gorman	Spokane	161	36	114	.322	R-R	6-2	210	12/12/50 Charleston, SC
—	Thompson, Bobby	Tuc-Tol-Rich.	—	8	35	.280	B-R	5-9	175	11/3/53 Mecklenburg City, NC
15	Washington, Claudell	Texas	148	12	68	.284	L-L	6-0	190	8/31/54 Los Angeles, CA
24	Zisk, Richie	Chicago (AL)	154	30	101	.290	R-R	6-1	208	2/6/49 Brooklyn, NY

RANGER PROFILES

RICHIE ZISK 29 6-1 208　　　　　　**Bats R Throws R**

A big winner in re-entry sweepstakes . . . Gambled without contract in Chicago and had big year, 30 HRs, 101 RBIs, then became free agent . . . Signed with Rangers for estimated $2.5 million, a 10-year deal . . . "I think I can provide the long ball they (Rangers) need. I can hit the ball out of any park." . . . Turned down other offers. "I wanted to be with a contending team, I wanted a fair contract to equal my peers and I wanted a town I could bring my family to.". . . Born Feb. 6, 1949, in Brooklyn . . . Moved to Parsipanny, N.J., where he starred in baseball, basketball, soccer . . . Signed with Pirates, then traded to White Sox when he refused to sign Pittsburgh contract . . . Sox gambled one year, then lost.

Year	Club	Pos	G	AB	R	H	2B	3B	HR	RBI	SB	Avg.
1971	Pittsburgh	OF	7	15	2	3	1	0	1	2	0	.200
1972	Pittsburgh	OF	17	37	4	7	3	0	0	4	0	.189
1973	Pittsburgh	OF	103	333	44	108	23	7	10	54	0	.324
1974	Pittsburgh	OF	149	536	75	168	30	3	17	100	1	.313
1975	Pittsburgh	OF	147	504	69	146	27	3	20	75	0	.290
1976	Pittsburgh	OF	155	581	91	168	35	2	21	89	1	.289
1977	Chicago (AL)	OF	141	531	78	154	17	6	30	101	0	.290
	Totals		719	2537	363	754	136	21	99	425	2	.297

JIM SUNDBERG 26 6-0 190　　　　　　**Bats R Throws R**

Already considered best defensive and throwing catcher in league, he became bat man, too, improving average 63 points, almost doubling RBI output . . . "Confidence means more than anything else," he said. "Bill Hunter is partly responsible because he stuck with me in situations I used to be pinch hit for." . . . Only five errors all year . . . Led League's catchers in DPs, assists . . . Born May 18, 1951, in Galesburg, Ill. . . . All-America at U. of Iowa . . . Played in 140 or more games three straight seasons.

Year	Club	Pos	G	AB	R	H	2B	3B	HR	RBI	SB	Avg.
1974	Texas	C	132	368	45	91	13	3	3	36	2	.247
1975	Texas	C	155	472	45	94	9	0	6	36	3	.199
1976	Texas	C	140	448	33	102	24	2	3	34	0	.228
1977	Texas	C	149	453	61	132	20	3	6	65	2	.291
	Totals		576	1741	184	419	66	8	18	171	7	.241

DOC MEDICH 29 6-5 227   Bats R Throws R

Keeps his fastball in a suitcase . . . Much-traveled year began in Pittsburgh, carried him through Oakland and Seattle and ended in New York when Mets claimed him on waivers in September . . . Now a rich Texan . . . Strong, durable and smart . . . Attends U. of Pittsburgh medical school, where he has begun an internship in orthopedics . . . For now, he uses his scapel on the hitters . . . Born Dec. 9, 1948, in Aliquippa, Pa. . . . Real name is George Francis Medich . . . A surprise from 1970 draft when he was chosen by Yankees in 29th round . . . Return to New York presented ironic twist . . . First raised eyebrows when he beat crosstown rival Mets in Mayor's Trophy Game.

Year	Club	G	IP	W	L	Pct.	SO	BB	H	ERA
1972	New York (AL)	1	0	0	0	.000	0	2	2	
1973	New York (AL)	34	235	14	9	.609	145	74	217	2.95
1974	New York (AL)	38	280	19	15	.559	154	91	275	3.60
1975	New York (AL)	38	272	16	16	.500	132	72	271	3.51
1976	Pittsburgh	29	179	8	11	.421	86	48	193	3.52
1977	Oakland-Seattle	29	170	12	6	.667	77	53	181	4.55
1977	New York (NL)	1	7	0	1	.000	3	1	6	3.86
	Totals	170	1143	69	58	.543	597	341	1145	3.59

MIKE HARGROVE 28 6-0 195   Bats L Throws R

Natural hitter . . . Third year over .300 in four big league seasons . . . Lifetime BA over .300 . . . Promoted to lead-off spot by Billy Hunter on recommendation of Orioles' manager, Earl Weaver . . . "I was talking with Earl and said I was looking for a leadoff man," Hunter revealed. "He said, 'What about Hargrove? He's got one of the best on base percentages in the league. Look what Ken Singleton did as a leadoff man.'" . . . Hunter made move and both Hargrove and Rangers benefited . . . Batted every position in the order, from first to ninth . . . "That's got to tie a record, at least." . . . Born Oct. 26, 1949, in Perryton, Tex. . . . Only one season of minor-league ball and never played high school baseball . . . But a good hitter with natural stroke.

Year	Club	Pos	G	AB	R	H	2B	3B	HR	RBI	SB	Avg.
1974	Texas	1B-OF	131	415	57	134	18	6	4	66	0	.323
1975	Texas	1B-OF	145	519	82	157	22	2	11	62	4	.303
1976	Texas	1B-OF	151	541	80	155	30	1	7	58	2	.287
1977	Texas	1B-OF	153	525	98	160	28	4	18	69	2	.305
	Totals		580	2000	317	606	98	13	40	255	8	.303

BERT CAMPANERIS 36 5-10 155　　　Bats R Throws R

Veteran shortstop gave stability to Ranger infield . . . Will pass 600 stolen bases this year, more than any active AL player . . . One of several who escaped Finley's funny farm in Oakland, playing out option and signing with Texas for $900,000 over five years . . . "He got cheated," said Finley . . . Born March 9, 1942, in Pueblo Neuvo, Cuba . . . Once played all nine positions in game for A's . . . Stays in great shape, so age is no handicap . . . Urged by Billy Hunter to bunt more. . .

Year	Club	Pos	G	AB	R	H	2B	3B	HR	RBI	SB	Avg.
1964	Kansas City......	SS-OF-3B	67	269	27	69	14	3	4	22	10	.257
1965	Kansas City......	INF-OF-C-P	144	578	67	156	23	12	6	42	51	.270
1966	Kansas City......	SS	142	573	82	153	29	10	5	42	52	.267
1967	Kansas City......	SS	147	601	85	149	29	6	3	32	55	.243
1968	Oakland.........	SS-OF	159	642	87	177	25	9	4	38	62	.276
1969	Oakland.........	SS	135	547	71	142	15	2	2	25	62	.260
1970	Oakland.........	SS	147	603	97	168	28	4	22	64	42	.279
1971	Oakland.........	SS	134	569	80	143	18	4	5	47	34	.251
1972	Oakland.........	SS	149	625	85	150	25	2	8	32	52	.240
1973	Oakland.........	SS	151	601	89	150	17	6	4	46	34	.250
1974	Oakland.........	SS	134	527	77	153	18	8	2	41	34	.290
1975	Oakland.........	SS	137	509	69	133	15	3	4	46	24	.265
1976	Oakland.........	SS	149	536	67	137	14	1	1	52	54	.256
1977	Texas...........	SS	150	552	77	140	19	7	5	46	27	.254
	Totals...........		1945	7732	1060	2020	289	77	75	575	593	.261

TOBY HARRAH 29 6-0 180　　　Bats R Throws R

Switched from short to third to make room for Campaneris . . . Had some problems in field, but continued to swing potent stick . . . Worked with weights in winter, added 10 pounds and hit career high 27 HRs . . . "I'm thinking more home runs this year than ever before." . . . Credits veep Eddie Robinson with helpful batting tips . . . Rumored trade to Yankees never happened, which pleased Texas fans. Harrah is No. 1 in their hearts . . . Born Oct. 26, 1948, in Sissonville, W. Va., one of nine children . . . Originally signed with Phils . . . He and Bump Wills hit back-to-back inside-the-park HRs in Yankee Stadium, only second time in history it was done.

Year	Club	Pos	G	AB	R	H	2B	3B	HR	RBI	SB	Avg.
1969	Washington	SS	8	1	4	0	0	0	0	0	0	.000
1971	Washington	SS-3B	127	383	45	88	11	3	2	22	10	.230
1972	Texas...........	SS	116	374	47	97	14	3	1	31	16	.259
1973	Texas...........	SS-3B	118	461	64	120	16	1	10	50	10	.260
1974	Texas...........	SS-3B	161	573	79	149	23	2	21	74	15	.260
1975	Texas...........	SS-3B-2B	151	522	81	153	24	1	20	93	23	.293
1976	Texas...........	SS-3B-2B	155	584	64	152	21	1	15	67	8	.260
1977	Texas...........	SS-3B	159	539	90	142	25	5	27	87	27	.263
	Totals...........		995	3437	474	901	134	16	96	424	109	.262

GAYLORD PERRY 39 6-4 215   Bats R Throws R

Does he or doesn't he? Only his druggist knows for sure . . . And Gaylord isn't saying yes or no, but wrote a book, "Me And The Spitter." . . . Leads active pitchers with 48 career shutouts . . . Born Sept. 15, 1938 . . . He and brother Jim have combined for 461 major league victories . . . Joined Cy Young and Jim Bunning as only pitchers with more than 100 wins in both leagues and more than 1,000 strikeouts in both . . . Third on all-time list in strikeouts, could join Young and Bob Gibson as only pitchers with 3,000 Ks this year . . . More records will fall this year.

Year	Club	G	IP	W	L	Pct.	SO	BB	H	ERA
1962	San Francisco	13	43	3	1	.750	20	14	54	5.23
1963	San Francisco	31	76	1	6	.143	52	29	84	4.03
1964	San Francisco	44	206	12	12	.522	155	43	179	2.75
1965	San Francisco	47	196	8	12	.400	170	70	194	4.18
1966	San Francisco	36	256	21	8	.724	201	40	242	2.99
1967	San Francisco	39	293	15	17	.469	230	84	231	2.61
1968	San Francisco	39	291	16	15	.516	173	59	240	2.44
1969	San Francisco	40	325	19	14	.576	233	91	290	2.49
1970	San Francisco	44	329	23	13	.639	214	84	292	3.20
1971	San Francisco	37	280	16	12	.571	158	67	255	2.76
1972	Cleveland	41	343	24	16	.600	234	82	253	1.92
1973	Cleveland	41	344	19	19	.500	238	115	315	3.38
1974	Cleveland	37	322	21	13	.618	216	99	230	2.52
1975	Cleve.-Texas	37	306	18	17	.514	233	70	277	3.24
1976	Texas	32	250	15	14	.517	143	52	232	3.24
1977	Texas	34	238	15	12	.556	177	56	239	3.37
	Totals	589	4098	246	200	.552	2847	1055	3607	2.94

BUMP WILLS 24 5-9 170   Bats S Throws R

Chip off the old block . . . Maury's kid was one of several outstanding AL rookies . . . Innocent bystander in unfortunate story. Bump was given starting 2B job in spring training by then manager Frank Lucchesi, so enraging incumbent Len Randle, he punched out Lucchesi . . . Born July 27, 1952, in Washington, D.C., which is where Rangers came from, too . . . "Bump is a better player than I thought he was," said new manager Billy Hunter . . . Struggling at bat early in season, he telephoned dad who gave him fatherly advice . . . "Not technical stuff," says Bump, "more about the mental aspect of baseball." It worked. Obviously.

Year	Club	Pos	G	AB	R	H	2B	3B	HR	RBI	SB	Avg.
1977	Texas	2B	152	541	87	155	28	6	9	62	28	.287

AL OLIVER 31 6-1 190   Bats L Throws L

Had third best BA on Bucs and was 11th best in
NL . . . A genuine slugger . . . Awesome addition to Rangers' lineup . . . At age 30 he had
more hits (1315) than any active player except
Johnny Bench . . . Plays left field, center field
and first base . . . Good speed and power, too
. . . Range and powerful arm in the outfield
. . . Made only five errors in 1975 . . . Was Pi-
rates' lone representative on all-star team in 1976 . . . Made running catch of shallow fly ball to preserve Candelaria's no-hitter
against Dodgers two years ago . . . Born Oct. 14, 1946, in Portsmouth, Ohio, birthplace of cowboy Roy Rogers.

Year	Club	Pos	G	AB	R	H	2B	3B	HR	RBI	SB	Avg.
1968	Pittsburgh	OF	4	8	1	1	0	0	0	0	0	.125
1969	Pittsburgh	1B-OF	129	463	55	132	19	2	17	70	0	.285
1970	Pittsburgh	OF-1B	151	551	63	149	33	5	12	83	1	.270
1971	Pittsburgh	OF-1B	143	529	69	149	31	7	14	64	4	.282
1972	Pittsburgh	OF-1B	140	565	88	176	27	4	12	89	2	.312
1973	Pittsburgh	OF-1B	158	654	90	191	38	7	20	99	6	.292
1974	Pittsburgh	OF-1B	147	617	96	198	38	12	11	85	10	.321
1975	Pittsburgh	OF-1B	155	628	90	176	39	8	18	84	4	.280
1976	Pittsburgh	OF-1B	121	443	62	143	22	5	12	61	6	.323
1977	Pittsburgh	OF-1B	154	568	75	175	29	6	19	82	13	.308
	Totals		1302	5026	689	1490	276	56	135	717	54	.296

JON MATLACK 28 6-3 205   Bats L Throws L

The big man on campus . . . Handsome, intelligent and talented . . . Only ingredient missing is a big season . . . Lack of support and
shoulder problems have kept him from 20-win
season . . . Move to Rangers might solve that
. . . Was NL Rookie-of-the-Year in 1972 . . .
Allowed only four earned runs in three games
in 1973 Series against Oakland but suffered
two defeats . . . Analytical player who likes to use his head—went
too far in catching line drive by Marty Perez in front of skull in
horrifying 1973 episode . . . Recovered and was back in rotation
in 11 days . . . Born Jan. 19, 1950, in West Chester, Pa. . . . Has
twice led NL in shutouts . . . So careful with pitching arm he
won't even draw blinds with left hand during season.

Year	Club	G	IP	W	L	Pct.	SO	BB	H	ERA
1971	New York (NL)	7	37	0	3	.000	24	15	31	4.14
1972	New York (NL)	34	244	15	10	.600	169	71	215	2.32
1973	New York (NL)	34	242	14	16	.467	205	99	210	3.20
1974	New York (NL)	34	265	13	15	.464	195	76	221	2.41
1975	New York (NL)	33	229	16	12	.571	154	58	224	3.42
1976	New York (NL)	35	262	17	10	.630	153	57	236	2.95
1977	New York (NL)	26	169	7	15	.318	123	43	175	4.21
	Totals	203	1448	82	81	.503	1023	419	1312	3.03

WILLIE HORTON 34 5-10 205   Bats R Throws R

New lease on life in Texas after 14 years in Detroit, where he grew up. Born in Arno, Va., Oct. 18, 1943 . . . Added punch to Rangers as full-time DH . . . Great career hampered somewhat by serious leg injuries . . . Hit one on roof of Tiger Stadium at 16 . . . That was all Tigers had to see to sign him . . . Became instant Texas hero when he took on entire Royals' team in free-for-all . . . "I tried to talk to Willie, to calm him down," said KC manager, Whitey Herzog, "but his eyes were as big as saucers. He was out of his gourd." . . . "He's the strongest man in baseball," says his ex-manager, Ralph Houk . . . Reminds old-timers of Roy Campanella in build and batting style.

Year	Club	Pos	G	AB	R	H	2B	3B	HR	RBI	SB	Avg
1963	Detroit	OF	15	43	6	14	2	1	1	4	2	.326
1964	Detroit	OF	25	80	6	13	1	3	1	10	0	.163
1965	Detroit	OF-3B	143	512	69	140	20	2	29	104	5	.273
1966	Detroit	OF	146	526	72	138	22	6	27	100	1	.262
1967	Detroit	OF	122	401	47	110	20	3	19	67	0	.274
1968	Detroit	OF	143	512	68	146	20	2	36	85	0	.285
1969	Detroit	OF	141	508	66	133	17	1	28	91	3	.262
1970	Detroit	OF	96	371	53	113	18	2	17	69	0	.305
1971	Detroit	OF	119	450	64	130	25	1	22	72	1	.289
1972	Detroit	OF	108	333	44	77	9	5	11	36	0	.231
1973	Detroit	OF	111	411	42	130	19	3	17	53	1	.316
1974	Detroit	OF	72	238	32	71	8	1	15	47	0	.298
1975	Detroit	DH	159	615	62	169	13	1	25	92	1	.275
1976	Detroit	DH	114	401	40	105	17	0	14	56	0	.262
1977	Detroit-Texas	DH-OF	140	523	55	151	23	3	15	75	2	.289
	Totals		1654	5924	726	1640	234	34	277	961	16	.277

DOCK ELLIS 33 6-3 195   Bats R Throws R

Colorful, controversial individual, but extremely likeable . . . Also outspoken and probably talked his way out of New York by suggesting Yankee owner George Steinbrenner "stay out of the clubhouse." . . . Set record of sorts by playing for seven managers in four months— Billy Martin in New York, Jack McKeon and Bobby Winkles in Oakland, Frank Lucchesi, Connie Ryan, Eddie Stanky, Billy Hunter in Texas . . . Born March 11, 1945, in Los Angeles . . . Does excellent imitation of Muhammad Ali . . . Played eight seasons in Pittsburgh, flirting with stardom, before being traded to New York . . . Disagreement with Steinbrenner and inability to come to contract terms, sent him to Oakland, then to Rangers where he was their best pitcher down stretch.

Year	Club	G	IP	W	L	Pct.	SO	BB	H	ERA
1968	Pittsburgh	26	104	6	5	.545	52	38	82	2.51
1969	Pittsburgh	35	219	11	17	.393	173	76	206	3.58
1970	Pittsburgh	30	202	13	10	.565	128	87	194	3.21
1971	Pittsburgh	31	227	19	9	.679	137	63	207	3.05
1972	Pittsburgh	25	163	15	7	.682	96	33	156	2.71
1973	Pittsburgh	28	192	12	14	.462	122	55	176	3.05
1974	Pittsburgh	26	177	12	9	.571	91	41	163	3.15
1975	Pittsburgh	27	140	8	9	.471	69	43	163	3.79
1976	New York (AL)	32	212	17	8	.680	65	76	195	3.18
1977	N.Y. (AL)-Oak-Texas	33	213	12	12	.500	106	64	211	3.63
	Totals	293	1849	125	100	.556	1039	576	1753	3.22

TOP PROSPECT

LEN BARKER 22 6-4 235   Bats R Throws R
Born July 7, 1955, in Ft. Knox, Ky., and considered good as gold by Rangers . . . Impressed with four victories, ERA under 3 and 97 mph fastball . . . Drafted behind highly-publicized schoolboy, David Clyde, but has zoomed past Clyde in Ranger evaluation . . . "I hope I've seen the last of the minor leagues. I'm here to stay."

MANAGER BILLY HUNTER: Finally said yes. Born June 4,  1928, in Punxsutawney, Pa., he stayed underground longer than groundhog . . . Had several opportunities to manage, but kept resisting . . . Was talked to about Cincinnati job before Sparky Anderson . . . "That doesn't mean I would have done what Sparky did," he says. "He's done a terrific job." . . . Chosen to be Rangers' fourth manager of year. First Frank Lucchesi, then Connie Ryan as interim, then Eddie Stanky, who quit after one day . . . Hunter stepped in and brought Rangers into race . . . "If he had been here all year, we might have won it," says Toby Harrah . . . Originally with Dodgers, one of many who withered waiting for Pee Wee Reese to quit . . . Lifetime BA .219 for six seasons . . . Coach with Orioles 1964-77 . . . "That's the job I wanted, but Earl (Weaver) is going to stay there forever."

GREATEST MANAGER

When the original Washington Senators moved to Minnesota in 1961, a new Washington Senators was born through expansion. It was related to the old Senators only in its standing in the American League—at or near the bottom every year.

In 1972, the club moved to Texas and played no better there. Finally, in 1974, the light could be seen at the end of the tunnel and the Rangers finished second, their loftiest perch in 14 years in Washington and Texas.

The manager of that surprise team in the American League was Billy Martin and it earned him designation as "Manager-of-the-year" in the Ameican League and "Greatest Manager" in Ranger history.

It is ironic that Martin gets that honor for finishing second, but not for finishing first in Minnesota, Detroit and twice with the Yankees. But he brought the Rangers home to their highest finish and will remain the best they have had until they win their first championship, which could happen this year.

ALL-TIME RANGER LEADERS

BATTING: Mike Hargrove, .305, 1977
HRs: Jeff Burroughs, 30, 1973
RBIs: Jeff Burroughs, 118, 1974
STEALS: David Nelson, 51, 1972
WINS: Ferguson Jenkins, 25, 1974
STRIKEOUTS: Gaylord Perry, 233, 1975

CALIFORNIA ANGELS

TEAM DIRECTORY: Chairman of the Board-Pres.: Gene Autry; VP-Asst. Chairman of the Board: Red Patterson; VP-GM: Buzzie Bavasi; Dir. of Pub. Rel.: Tom Seeberg; Trav. Sec.: Freddie Federico; Mgr.: Dave Garcia. Home: Anaheim Stadium (43,250). Field distances: 33, l.f. line, 386, l.c.; 404, c.f.; 386, r.c.; 333, r.f. line. Spring training, Holtville and Palm Springs, Cal.

SCOUTING REPORT

HITTING: First came Bobby Grich's back operation. Then Joe Rudi's hand. Injuries racked up the Angels and finished them before Gene Autry's checks (for the purchase of Grich, Rudi and Don Baylor) had cleared the bank. Now Grich and Rudi are supposedly healthy and money continued to burn a hole in Autry's cowboy pants as the Angels spent a couple of million more to add the league's No. 2 hitter, Lyman Bostock. The Angels' jump from last in hitting in '76 to third from last in '77 was not sufficient. What's more, the man mainly responsible for that jump, Bobby Bonds, has gone to Chicago. But the Angels are confident the return of Rudi and Grich will make up for Bonds. To their health!

PITCHING: Desperate for arms to go with their one-two punch of Nolan Ryan and Frank Tanana, the Angels willingly weakened their attack to load up on pitchers—Don Aase from the Red Sox, Chris Knapp and Dave Frost from the White Sox. Tanana and Ryan were one-three in ERA last year, but the former came up with arm trouble and won only 15, and the latter was a workhorse and wound up losing 16. Aase (6-2), Knapp (12-7) and assorted other pitchers may be enough so the Angels won't miss Bonds and Jerry Remy. If your pitching is good, you don't need that much offense anyway.

FIELDING: Maybe more than their bats, the Angels missed the gloves of Grich and Rudi as they finished 11th in the AL in fielding. Grich returns to second base, where he belongs. Rudi moves to first base, where the Angels need help. That leaves the outfield in the capable hands of Bostock, rookie Ken Landreaux and a choice of Rick Miller, Gil Flores or Baylor, with Rudi ready to go back out if needed.

OUTLOOK: Here more than anywhere else, the physical condition of key players is the key. It's never good when two of your best

Sore arm kept ERA king Frank Tanana from 20 victories.

are coming off major injuries. But if all are OK, the Angels can challenge for a pennant because they no longer will be pushovers on the days Tanana and Ryan aren't pitching.

CALIFORNIA ANGELS 1978 ROSTER

MANAGER Dave Garcia
Coaches—Bob Clear, John McNamara, Jimmie Reese

PITCHERS

No.	Name	1977 Club	W-L	IP	SO	ERA	B-T	Ht.	Wt.	Born
—	Aase, Don	Pawtucket	6-6	109	—	5.04	R-R	6-3	185	9/8/54 Orange, CA
		Boston	6-2	92	49	3.13				
33	Barlow, Mike	S. Lake City	3-5	51	38	6.71	R-R	6-6	215	4/30/48 Stamford, NY
		California	4-2	59	25	4.58				
—	Botting, Ralph	Salinas	8-0	53	63	2.04	L-L	6-0	195	5/12/55 Houlton, ME
		El Paso	5-7	101	72	5.06				
34	Brett, Ken	Chi (AL)-Cal	13-14	225	80	4.52	L-L	5-11	195	9/18/48 Brooklyn, NY
39	Caneira, John	S. Lake City	8-4	150	95	4.62	R-R	6-4	200	10/7/52 Naugatuck, CT
		California	2-2	29	17	4.03				
—	Frost, Dave	Iowa	9-8	136	99	4.04	R-R	6-6	225	11/17/52 Long Beach, CA
		Chicago (AL)	1-1	24	15	3.00				
45	Hartzell, Paul	California	8-12	189	79	3.57	R-R	6-5	200	11/2/53 Bloomsburg, PA
—	Knapp, Chris	Iowa	0-4	32	24	1.97	R-R	6-5	195	9/16/53 Cherry Point, NC
		Chicago(AL)	12-7	146	103	4.81				
17	LaRoche, Dave	Clev-Cal	8-7	100	79	3.51	L-L	6-2	195	5/14/48 Colo. Springs, CO
41	Miller, Dyar	Balt-Cal	6-6	115	58	3.52	R-R	6-0	215	5/17/48 Batesville, IN
35	Moore, Balor	S. Lake City	4-4	71	46	3.93	L-L	6-2	185	1/25/51 Smithville, TX
		California	0-2	23	14	3.91				
38	Nolan, Gary	Cincinnati	4-1	39	28	4.85	R-R	6-3	200	5/27/48 Herlong, CA
		California	0-3	18	4	9.00				
—	Overy, Mike	S. Lake City	7-5	131	85	4.33	R-R	6-1	195	1/27/51 Clinton, IL
—	Quintana, Luis	S. Lake City	0-4	42	30	6.00	L-L	6-2	175	11/25/51 VegaBaja, PR
		Syracuse	4-6	90	53	4.00				
47	Ross, Gary	California	2-4	58	30	5.59	R-R	6-0	190	9/16/47 McKeesport, PA
30	Ryan, Nolan	California	19-16	299	341	2.77	R-R	6-2	180	1/31/47 Refugio, TX
40	Tanana, Frank	California	15-9	241	205	2.54	L-L	6-3	180	7/3/53 Detroit, MI

CATCHERS

No.	Name	1977 Club	H	HR	RBI	Pct.	B-T	Ht.	Wt.	Born
—	Cliburn, Stan	Salinas	118	7	54	.311	R-R	6-0	190	12/19/56 Jackson, MS
—	Donohue, Tom	S. Lake City	108	15	67	.273	R-R	6-0	195	11/15/52 Westbury, NY
—	Downing, Brian	Chicago (AL)	48	4	25	.284	R-R	5-10	185	10/9/50 Los Angeles, CA
23	Goodwin, Danny	S. Lake City	85	10	66	.305	L-R	6-1	195	9/2/53 Peoria, IL
		California	19	1	8	.209				
15	Hampton, Ike	California	13	3	9	.295	R-R	6-1	185	8/22/51 Camden, SC
9	Humphrey, Terry	California	69	2	34	.227	R-R	6-3	190	8/4/49 Chickasha, OK

INFIELDERS

No.	Name	1977 Club	H	HR	RBI	Pct.	B-T	Ht.	Wt.	Born
22	Aikens, Willie	S. Lake City	99	14	73	.336	L-R	6-2	220	10/14/54 Seneca, SC
		California	18	0	6	.198				
—	Anderson, Jim	El Paso	119	18	73	.285	R-R	6-0	170	2/23/57 Los Angeles, CA
7	Chalk, Dave	California	144	3	45	.277	R-R	5-10	175	8/30/50 Del Rio, TX
—	Fairly, Ron	Toronto	128	19	64	.279	L-L	5-10	180	7/12/38 Macon, GA
4	Grich, Bobby	California	44	7	23	.243	R-R	6-2	190	1/15/49 Muskegon, MI
16	Jackson, Ron	California	71	8	28	.243	R-R	6-0	205	5/9/53 Birmingham, AL
—	Lansford, Carney	El Paso	147	18	94	.332	R-R	6-2	195	2/7/57 San Jose, CA
18	Mulliniks, Rance	S. Lake City	68	11	51	.309	L-R	6-0	170	1/15/56 Tulare, CA
		California	73	3	21	.269				
—	Rayford, Floyd	Salinas	53	6	39	.259	R-R	5-10	192	7/27/57 Memphis, TN
		El Paso	95	11	60	.297				
27	Solaita, Tony	California	78	14	53	.241	L-L	6-0	215	1/5/47 Nuuuli, Am. Samoa

OUTFIELDERS

No.	Name	1977 Club	H	HR	RBI	Pct.	B-T	Ht.	Wt.	Born
12	Baylor, Don	California	141	25	75	.251	R-R	6-1	190	6/28/49 Austin, TX
—	Bostock, Lyman	Minnesota	199	14	90	.336	L-R	6-1	170	11/22/50 Los Angeles, CA
—	Clark, Bob	Salinas	149	23	88	.284	R-R	6-0	190	6/13/55 Sacramento, CA
28	Flores, Gil	S. Lake City	29	2	8	.333	R-R	6-0	180	10/27/52 Ponce, PR
		California	95	1	26	.278				
—	Kubski, Gil	El Paso	177	9	90	.324	L-R	6-3	185	10/12/54 Longview, TX
19	Landreaux, Ken	El Paso	74	16	59	.354	L-R	5-11	170	12/22/54 Los Angeles, CA
		S. Lake City	92	11	57	.359				
		California	19	0	5	.250				
—	Miller, Rick	Boston	48	0	24	.254	L-L	6-0	180	4/19/48 Grand Rapids, MI
26	Rudi, Joe	California	64	13	53	.264	R-R	6-0	200	9/7/46 Modesto, CA

ANGEL PROFILES

RON FAIRLY 39 5-10 180   Bats L Throws L

Veteran pro beginning 21st year . . . Obtained from Blue Jays during winter . . . Has outside chance of being four decade player . . . Arrived in majors with Dodgers in 1958 . . . Joined 200-home run, 1,000-RBI club last year . . . Also has 300 doubles . . . "I don't have many goals left. I would like to get 2,000 hits." . . . Needs 138 . . . Got first RBI off Robin Roberts . . . Born July 12, 1938, in Macon, Ga. . . . One of first of USC players to make it big in major leagues . . . Eleven years with Dodgers before moving on to Montreal . . . Blue Jays are his second expansion team.

Year	Club	Pos	G	AB	R	H	2B	3B	HR	RBI	SB	Avg.
1958	Los Angeles......	OF	15	53	6	15	1	0	2	8	0	.283
1959	Los Angeles......	OF	118	244	27	58	12	1	4	23	0	.238
1960	Los Angeles......	OF	14	37	6	4	0	3	1	3	0	.108
1961	Los Angeles......	OF-1B	111	245	42	79	15	2	10	48	0	.322
1962	Los Angeles......	1B-OF	147	460	80	128	15	7	14	71	1	.278
1963	Los Angeles......	1B-OF	152	490	62	133	21	0	12	77	5	.271
1964	Los Angeles......	1B	150	454	62	116	19	5	10	74	4	.256
1965	Los Angeles......	OF-1B	158	555	73	152	28	1	9	70	2	.274
1966	Los Angeles......	OF-1B	117	351	53	101	20	0	14	61	3	.288
1967	Los Angeles......	OF-1B	153	486	45	107	19	0	10	55	1	.220
1968	Los Angeles......	OF-1B	141	441	32	103	15	1	4	43	0	.234
1969	L.A.-Montreal	1B-OF	100	317	38	87	16	6	12	47	1	.274
1970	Montreal	1B-OF	119	385	54	111	19	0	15	61	10	.288
1971	Montreal	1B-OF	146	447	58	115	23	0	13	71	1	.257
1972	Montreal	OF-1B	140	446	51	124	15	1	17	68	3	.278
1973	Montreal	OF-1B	142	413	70	123	13	1	17	49	2	.298
1974	Montreal	1B-OF	101	282	35	69	9	1	12	43	2	.245
1975	St. Louis	1B-OF	107	229	32	69	13	2	7	37	0	.301
1976	St. Louis	1B	73	110	13	29	4	0	0	21	0	.264
1976	Oakland.........	1B	15	46	9	11	1	0	3	10	0	.239
1977	Toronto	1B	132	458	60	128	24	2	19	64	0	.279
	Totals...........		2351	6949	908	1862	302	33	205	1004	35	.268

LYMAN BOSTOCK 27 6-1 170   Bats L Throws R

Steady improvement each year . . . Outstanding young hitter, second in league to Rod Carew . . . Over .300 lifetime in only three seasons . . . Moved all around batting order and often asked to be RBI man, which undoubtedly affected his average . . . Announced from start, he would not be back this year . . . Determined to go free agent route to play in better climate, for more money . . . Move to Angels made him $2.4 million rich . . . Born Nov. 22, 1950, in Birmingham,

Ala., birthplace of his idol, Willie Mays . . . His dad was star in Negro Leagues and was invited to play in Twins' old-timer's game . . . A future batting king.

Year	Club	Pos	G	AB	R	H	2B	3B	HR	RBI	SB	Avg.
1975	Minnesota	OF	98	369	52	104	21	5	0	29	2	.282
1976	Minnesota	OF	128	474	75	153	21	9	4	60	12	.323
1977	Minnesota	OF	153	593	104	199	36	12	14	90	16	.336
	Totals..........		379	1436	231	456	78	26	18	179	30	.318

FRANK TANANA 24 6-3 180   Bats L Throws L

ERA champion, but a sorry season, cut short because of arm trouble . . . Started only 31 games, missed more than a month, still led league with seven shutouts . . . Three times predicted shutouts, pitched them, then quit while ahead . . . "If I can keep the ball in the park, my ERA should be 1.00." . . . Said vet Mike Cuellar: "Tanana is the best lefthander in the American League." . . . Born July 3, 1953, in Detroit . . . His father was a cop . . . One of the most refreshing players to come along in years . . . "I honestly don't know what I'm going to say half the time." . . . Interviewed before Super Bowl, he said: "Being with the Angels, this is the closest I've ever come to a championship."

Year	Club	G	IP	W	L	Pct.	SO	BB	H	ERA
1973	California.............	4	26	2	2	.500	22	8	20	3.12
1974	California.............	39	269	14	19	.424	180	77	262	3.11
1975	California.............	34	257	16	9	.640	269	73	211	2.63
1976	California.............	34	288	19	10	.655	261	73	212	2.44
1977	California.............	31	241	15	9	.625	205	61	201	2.54
	Totals..................	242	1081	66	49	.574	937	292	906	2.69

NOLAN RYAN 31 6-2 180   Bats R Throws R

More records for baseball KKKKing . . . First pitcher with more than 300 Ks for five seasons . . . Four 19 strikeout games . . . 10 or more strikeouts in a game 104 times, a record . . . 15th on all-time strikeout list . . . First, third, sixth, seventh and eighth on all-time single season strikeout list . . . Cumulative batting average against him last year was .190 . . . "Any pitcher who walks 200 batters in a season doesn't deserve the Cy Young Award," said Jim Palmer . . . "It doesn't matter how many you walk, just so long as they don't score," retorted Ryan . . . Born Jan. 31, 1947, in Refugio, Tex. . . . Four no-hitters, 34 shutouts, best strikeout per innings pitched ratio in baseball history and this could go on and on and on.

Year	Club	G	IP	W	L	Pct.	SO	BB	H	ERA
1966	New York (NL)	2	3	0	1	.000	6	3	5	15.00
1968	New York (NL)	21	134	6	9	.400	133	75	93	3.09
1969	New York (NL)	25	89	6	3	.667	92	53	60	3.54
1970	New York (NL)	27	132	7	11	.389	125	97	86	3.41
1971	New York (NL)	30	152	10	14	.417	137	116	125	3.97
1972	California	39	284	19	16	.543	329	157	166	2.28
1973	California	41	326	21	16	.568	383	162	238	2.87
1974	California	42	333	22	16	.578	367	202	221	2.89
1975	California	28	198	14	12	.538	186	132	151	3.45
1976	California	39	284	17	18	.486	327	183	193	3.36
1977	California	37	299	19	16	.543	341	204	198	2.77
	Totals	331	2234	141	132	.516	2426	1384	1536	3.07

JOE RUDI 31 6-2 200   Bats R Throws R

Off to sensational start, Rudi had hand broken by pitch from Nelson Briles on July 26 and didn't play again . . . Leading league in RBIs, a 120-pace, when hurt . . . Played out option with Oakland and signed for estimated $2.75 million . . . "Joe Rudi is the most fundamentally sound ballplayer of our generation," said Billy Martin . . . "Joe had a value to our team only his teammates knew," Reggie Jackson . . . Born Sept. 7, 1946, in Modesto, Cal. . . . Generally accepted as best defensive left fielder in league . . . Mr. Nice Guy . . . "I got my values from my parents. I've always been quiet. I don't step on anyone's toes. I try to treat people the way they want to be treated."

Year	Club	Pos	G	AB	R	H	2B	3B	HR	RBI	SB	Avg.
1968	Oakland	OF	68	181	10	32	5	1	1	12	1	.177
1969	Oakland	OF-1B	35	122	10	23	3	1	2	6	1	.189
1970	Oakland	OF-1B	106	350	40	108	23	2	11	42	3	.309
1971	Oakland	OF-1B	127	513	62	137	23	4	10	52	3	.267
1972	Oakland	OF-3B	147	593	94	181	32	9	19	75	3	.305
1973	Oakland	1B-OF	120	437	53	118	25	1	12	66	0	.270
1974	Oakland	1B-OF	158	593	73	174	39	4	22	99	2	.293
1975	Oakland	1B-OF	126	468	66	130	26	6	21	75	2	.278
1976	Oakland	1B-OF	130	500	54	135	32	3	13	94	6	.270
1977	California	1B-OF	64	242	48	64	13	2	13	53	1	.264
	Totals		1100	4042	514	1110	128	33	124	575	22	.275

BOBBY GRICH 29 6-2 180   Bats R Throws R

Another star-crossed Angel millionaire . . . Back problem and eventual disc operation limited him to 52 games after he played out option in Baltimore and signing with Angels for $1.75 million . . . "It hurt so much I had to stand up in the dugout between innings," he said . . . Almost signed with Yankees, who offered more, but wanted to play in California, near home . . . Born Jan. 15, 1949, in Muskegon, Mich. . . . Signed by

Orioles as shortstop, was converted to second and won Gold Glove . . . Angels returned him to short, his preference . . . "I love playing shortstop. It was my original position." But Angels contemplating moving him to first . . . "In my opinion, Bobby Grich is as good as any and probably the best ball player in the American League." That from ex-manager, Earl Weaver.

Year	Club	Pos	G	AB	R	H	2B	3B	HR	RBI	SB	Avg.
1970	Baltimore........	SS-2B-3B	30	95	11	20	1	3	0	8	1	.211
1971	Baltimore........	SS-2B	7	30	3	9	0	0	1	6	1	.300
1972	Baltimore........	SS-2B-1B-3B	133	460	66	128	21	3	12	50	13	.278
1973	Baltimore........	2B	162	581	82	146	29	7	12	50	17	.251
1974	Baltimore........	2B	160	582	92	152	29	6	19	82	17	.261
1975	Baltimore........	2B	150	524	81	136	26	4	13	57	14	.262
1976	Baltimore........	2B	144	518	93	138	31	4	13	54	14	.266
1977	California........	2B-SS	52	181	24	44	6	0	7	23	6	.243
	Totals..........		838	2971	457	773	143	27	77	329	83	.260

DAVE CHALK 27 5-10 175   Bats R Throws R

Moved all over infield, was installed as third baseman in '76 and proved inadequate . . . Threatened with loss of job, he responded, hiking average 60 points, improving HR and RBI totals . . . Always has been good with glove and has won third base job . . . "I learned a lot. The game isn't as easy as I thought it was. I had to prove all over to myself I could play." . . . Born Aug. 30, 1950, in Del Rio, Tex. . . . No. 1 pick in nation in June, 1972 draft . . . "He's the next Brooks Robinson," predicts Royal manager Whitey Herzog.

Year	Club	Pos	G	AB	R	H	2B	3B	HR	RBI	SB	Avg.
1973	California........	SS	24	69	14	16	2	0	0	6	0	.232
1974	California........	SS-3B	133	465	44	117	9	3	5	31	10	.252
1975	California........	3B	149	513	59	140	24	2	3	56	6	.273
1976	California........	SS-3B	142	438	39	95	14	1	0	33	0	.217
1977	California........	SS-3B	149	519	58	144	27	2	3	45	12	.277
	Totals..........		597	2004	214	512	76	8	11	171	28	.255

DON BAYLOR 28 6-1 190   Bats R Throws R

Another instant millionaire . . . Got estimated $2.5 million of Gene Autry's dollars to sign with Angels after playing out option in Oakland . . . Off to terrible start and booed by impatient Angel fans . . . But talent won out and raised average some 40 points in second half . . . On boos: "You just have to remain professional. The best way to eliminate them is to play harder. If you let them get to you, you're in trouble." . . . Resurgence coincided with arrival of Frank Robinson as batting coach . . . Coincidentally, it was Robby who Baylor replaced in regular Orioles' lineup in 1972 . . . Born June 28, 1949, in Austin, Tex. . . . MVP in International League before arriving with Orioles.

Year	Club	Pos	G	AB	R	H	2B	3B	HR	RBI	SB	Avg.
1970	Baltimore........	OF	8	17	4	4	0	0	0	4	1	.235
1971	Baltimore........	OF	1	2	0	0	0	0	0	1	0	.000
1972	Baltimore........	OF-1B	102	319	33	81	13	3	11	38	24	.254
1973	Baltimore........	OF-1B	118	405	64	116	20	4	11	51	32	.286
1974	Baltimore........	OF-1B	137	489	66	133	22	1	10	59	29	.272
1975	Baltimore........	OF	145	524	79	148	21	6	25	76	32	.282
1976	Oakland.........	OF-1B	157	595	85	147	25	1	15	68	52	.247
1977	California........	OF-1B	154	561	87	141	27	0	25	75	26	.251
	Totals...........		842	2913	418	770	128	15	97	372	196	.264

RANCE MULLINIKS 22 6-0 170　　Bats L Throws R

Called up when Bob Grich was placed on disabled list, this youngster accepted the challenge and impressed with glove and bat . . . Only player in big leagues who wears braces on teeth . . . Asked what he likes about Mulliniks, Frank Tanana said, "Everything." . . . "In a couple of years he's going to be the best shortstop in the game," said ex-teammate Jerry Remy . . . Born Jan. 15, 1956, in Tulare, Cal. . . . Dad's pitching career was cut short by sore arm while in Yankees' farm system . . . Turned down college offers to sign with Angels . . . "Making All-America didn't mean anything to me. Making the big leagues did. I've wanted to be a major leaguer since I was six years old."

Year	Club	Pos	G	AB	R	H	2B	3B	HR	RBI	SB	Avg.
1977	California........	SS	78	271	36	73	13	2	3	21	1	.269

GIL FLORES 25 6-0 180　　Bats R Throws R

A promising boxer, his career ended when he was involved in serious auto accident . . . Took a year to recover, then switched to baseball . . . It was a fortunate switch . . . Arrived with big club and took over in center field . . . Single, double, triple in major league debut in Boston, May 8, and hit safely in eight of first nine games . . . Born Oct. 27, 1952, in Ponce, Puerto Rico . . . Nicknamed "Caballo," which is Spanish for horse . . . Runs like one, a 6.3 for 60-yard dash.

Year	Club	Pos	G	AB	R	H	2B	3B	HR	RBI	SB	Avg.
1977	California........	OF	104	342	41	95	19	4	1	26	12	.278

TOP PROSPECTS

CHRIS KNAPP 24 6-5 195   Bats R Throws R
Won 11 games for Sox and can develop into big winner for Angels
. . . Born Sept. 16, 1953, in Cherry Point, N.C., into a sports-
minded family . . . Mom played basketball on girls' team . . . At
Central Michigan College, led Mid-America Conference in
strikeouts . . . Basketball and baseball star in high school . . .
"The longer you're in the major leagues, the more the awe is taken
out of it. You still respect them (hitters), but they're real people,
not just faces on television and bubble gum cards."

DON AASE 23 6-3 185   Bats R Throws R
Called up at midseason, he became one of Red Sox' most dependable starting pitchers . . . Should work into Angels' regular rotation this season . . . All the way back after suffering sore arm . . .
Born Sept. 8, 1954, in Orange, Cal. . . . Considered best righthander developed by Red Sox since Jim Lonborg and expected to win
big for the Angels.

KEN LANDREAUX 23 5-11 170   Bats L Throws R
Hitting .359 at Salt Lake City before call-up by Angels . . . Another product of Arizona State . . . "I always feel I can do better.
I'm never satisfied." . . . May be a year away from cracking Angels' outfield. Born in Los Angeles Dec. 22, 1954.

MANAGER DAVE GARCIA: Is he or isn't he? . . . Kept waiting
weeks while negotiations continued with Twins
to bring Gene Mauch to Angels. When deal fell
through, Garcia was named for '78. . . . Replaced Norm Sherry in midyear . . . Born Sept.
18, 1920, in East St. Louis, Ill. . . . Dedicated,
hard-working baseball man who has 36 years in
game, 15 as player (all in minors), 14 as minor-
league manager, six as coach . . . Managed An-
gels' El Paso club to Texas League pennant in '74, then brought to
Cleveland by Frank Robinson as coach next two years. Left Indians to take coaching job with Angels in '77 to be closer to home
and became manager when Sherry was fired.

GREATEST MANAGER

The California Angels came into the world in 1961, the first expansion year, beating the Kansas City Royals by eight years. But despite the unlimited funds of their owner, cowboy Gene Autry, the Angels have not come close to winning a division title or matching the success of the Royals.

Their first manager was Bill Rigney, bespectacled and much respected, and he did a marvelous job with an expansion team. Rigney was the Angels' only manager for the first eight years of their existence, finally getting the bounce in 1969, when he was replaced after 39 games by Lefty Phillips.

Rigney still holds the record for length of service as an Angel manager and his third place-finish in 1962, the expansion club's second year in existence, was one of the all-time great managing jobs. Significantly, no Angel manager has finished higher.

ALL-TIME ANGEL LEADERS

BATTING: Alex Johnson, .329, 1970
HRs: Leon Wagner, 37, 1962
    Bobby Bonds, 37, 1977
RBIs: Bobby Bonds, 115, 1977
STEALS: Mickey Rivers, 70, 1975
WINS: Clyde Wright, 22, 1970
    Nolan Ryan, 22, 1974
STRIKEOUTS: Nolan Ryan, 383, 1973

KANSAS CITY ROYALS

TEAM DIRECTORY: Pres.: Ewing Kaufman; Exec. VP-GM: Joe Burke; VP-Operations: Operations: Spencer Robinson; Pub. Rel.: Dean Vogelaar; Dir. Player Development: John Schuerholz; Trav. Sec.: Bill Beck; Mgr.: Whitey Herzog. Home: Royals Stadium (40,762). Field distances: 330, l.f. line; 385, l.c.; 410, c.f.; 385, r.c.; 330, r.f. line. Spring training: Fort Myers, Fla.

SCOUTING REPORT

HITTING: The Royals raised their team BA eight points and still fell from third to fifth in team batting during a hitter's year. There are no new bats in the Royals' rack except for a few young players coming along, but there is nothing wrong with their old bats . . . and those youngsters may be something special. The Royals must find a place for rookie Clint Hurdle to play, and they would also like to find room for Willie Wilson. Even without them, there is still a hitter at every position and the likelihood that Al Cowens, "the most improved player in the league," according to Birdie Tebbetts, will keep getting better.

PITCHING: First in the league in pitching with only 41 complete games tells you one thing—that the Royals excelled in the bullpen. They led the AL with 42 saves and have added Al "The Mad Hungarian" Hrabosky to team with Doug Bird and give the Royals a one-two bullpen punch that is almost the equal of the Yankees'. For starters, there is Dennis Leonard, who was one of five 20-game winners in the AL, and the same cast of characters who brought the Royals their second straight division title and led the league in ERA—Jim Colborn (18 wins, 3.62 ERA), Paul Splittorff (16 wins, 3.69 ERA) and part-timers Marty Pattin (10 wins) and Larry Gura (eight wins)—is back again.

FIELDING: This may be the Royals' strength, the key to the success of their pitching. They had defensive leaders at first (John Mayberry), second (Frank White) and center field (Amos Otis) and a Gold Glove in right in Al Cowens. The right side of the Royals' infield, Mayberry and White, made only 15 errors between them, which may be a testimonial to artificial surface, but makes the Royals tough, nonetheless.

OUTLOOK: The Royals will get their sternest challenge from the improved Rangers and maybe from the Angels. They hope to combat that challenge with improvement from their young players and with the experience they have gained as champions of their division two straight years. It will make for an interesting race in the AL West and, no doubt, a close one.

No one plays harder than gritty Royal leader Freddie Patek.

KANSAS CITY ROYALS 1978 ROSTER

MANAGER Whitey Herzog
Coaches—Steve Boros, Galen Cisco, Chuck Hiller, Charley
        Lau

PITCHERS

No.	Name	1977 Club	W-L	IP	SO	ERA	B-T	Ht.	Wt.	Born
29	Bird, Doug	Kansas City	11-4	118	83	3.89	R-R	6-4	180	3/5/50 Corona, CA
40	Busby, Steve	Daytona Bch.	0-1	3	2	15.00	R-R	6-2	190	9/29/49 Burbank, CA
48	Colborn, Jim	Kansas City	18-14	239	103	3.62	R-R	6-0	191	5/22/46 Santa Paula, CA
38	Gale, Rich	Jacksonville	6-5	80	68	3.60	R-R	6-7	225	1/19/54 Littleton, NH
		Omaha	6-2	71	62	3.69				
37	Gura, Larry	Kansas City	8-5	106	46	3.14	L-L	6-1	185	11/26/47 Joliet, IL
16	Hassler, Andy	Kansas City	9-6	156	83	4.21	L-L	6-5	215	10/18/51 Texas City, TX
—	Hrabosky, Al	St. Louis	6-5	86	68	4.40	R-L	5-11	180	7/21/49 Oakland, CA
39	Lance, Gary	Omaha	16-7	204	113	3.18	B-R	6-3	200	9/21/48 Greenville, SC
		Kansas City	0-1	2	0	4.50				
22	Leonard, Dennis	Kansas City	20-12	293	244	3.04	R-R	6-1	190	5/8/51 Brooklyn, NY
31	McGilberry, Randy	Jacksonville	3-3	54	50	2.17	R-R	6-1	195	10/29/53 Mobile, AL
		Omaha	2-0	18	19	2.50				
		Kansas City	0-1	7	1	5.14				
23	Mingori, Steve	Kansas City	2-4	64	19	3.09	L-L	5-10	170	2/29/44 Kansas City, MO
33	Pattin, Marty	Kansas City	10-3	128	55	3.59	R-R	5-10	180	4/6/43 Charleston, IL
34	Splittorff, Paul	Kansas City	16-6	229	99	3.69	L-L	6-3	210	10/8/46 Evansville, IN
35	Throop, George	Omaha	0-0	14	11	4.50	R-R	6-7	205	11/24/50 Pasadena, CA
		Jacksonville	6-6	106	64	2.46				
		Kansas City	0-0	5	1	3.60				

CATCHERS

No.	Name	1977 Club	H	HR	RBI	Pct.	B-T	Ht.	Wt.	Born
15	Porter, Darrell	Kansas City	117	16	60	.275	L-R	6-0	193	1/17/52 Joplin, MO
12	Wathan, John	Kansas City	39	2	21	.328	R-R	6-2	205	10/4/49 Cedar Rapids, IA

INFIELDERS

No.	Name	1977 Club	H	HR	RBI	Pct.	B-T	Ht.	Wt.	Born
42	Barranca, German	Jacksonville	98	0	31	.263	L-R	6-1	160	10/19/56 Veracruz, Mex.
5	Brett, George	Kansas City	176	22	88	.312	L-R	6-0	200	5/15/53 Shawnee Mission, KS
6	Heise, Bob	Kansas City	16	0	5	.258	R-R	5-11	175	5/12/47 San Antonio, TX
8	LaCock, Pete	Kansas City	66	3	29	.303	L-L	6-3	210	1/17/52 Burbank, CA
7	Mayberry, John	Kansas City	125	23	82	.230	L-L	6-3	220	2/18/50 Detroit, MI
3	Nelson, Dave	Kansas City	9	0	4	.188	R-R	5-10	165	6/20/44 Fort Sill, OK
2	Patek, Fred	Kansas City	130	5	60	.262	R-R	5-4	140	10/9/44 Oklahoma City, OK
—	Terrell, Jerry	Minnesota	48	1	20	.224	R-R	6-0	170	7/13/46 Waseca, MN
30	Washington, U. L.	Omaha	131	2	37	.255	B-R	5-11	175	10/27/53 Otoka, OK
		Kansas City	4	0	1	.200				
20	White, Frank	Kansas City	116	5	50	.245	R-R	5-11	170	9/4/50 Greenville, MS

OUTFIELDERS

No.	Name	1977 Club	H	HR	RBI	Pct.	B-T	Ht.	Wt.	Born
18	Cowens, Al	Kansas City	189	23	112	.312	R-R	6-2	200	10/25/51 Los Angeles, CA
9	Hurdle, Clint	Omaha	145	16	66	.328	L-R	6-3	195	7/30/57 Big Rapids, MI
		Kansas City	8	2	7	.308				
10	Lahoud, Joe	Omaha	90	19	69	.317	L-L	6-2	190	4/14/47 Danbury, CT
		Kansas City	17	2	8	.262				
11	McRae, Hal	Kansas City	191	21	92	.298	R-R	5-11	180	7/10/46 Avon Park, FL
26	Otis, Amos	Kansas City	120	17	78	.251	R-R	5-11	166	4/26/47 Mobile, AL
25	Poquette, Tom	Kansas City	100	2	33	.292	L-R	5-11	175	10/30/51 Eau Claire, WI
43	Silverio, Luis	Jacksonville	75	7	42	.243	R-R	5-11	150	10/23/56 Villa Gonzalez, D. R.
32	Wilson, Willie	Omaha	139	4	47	.281	B-R	6-3	195	7/9/55 Montgomery, AL
		Kansas City	11	0	1	.324				
19	Zdeb, Joe	Kansas City	58	2	23	.297	R-R	5-11	185	6/27/53 Medota, IL

ROYAL PROFILES

AL COWENS 26 6-2 200   Bats R Throws R

"The most improved player in the league," according to former manager Birdie Tebbetts, who scouted Royals for Yankees . . . Took several giant leaps both offensively and defensively and surpassed Dwight Evans of Red Sox as premier right fielder in league . . . Also filled in expertly in center when Otis was out . . . "The ideal player," says Whitey Herzog . . . "Our most valuable player, no doubt about it," says John Mayberry . . . Born Oct. 25, 1951, in Los Angeles . . . High school football star . . . A.C. to teammates . . . Signed as infielder . . . Passed over several times when in minors, contemplated quitting baseball . . . Quiet, soft-spoken, almost bashful and modest about his accomplishments . . . Should continue to improve and be star for years.

Year	Club	Pos	G	AB	R	H	2B	3B	HR	RBI	SB	Avg.
1974	Kansas City	OF-3B	110	269	28	65	7	1	1	25	5	.242
1975	Kansas City	OF	120	328	44	91	13	8	4	42	12	.277
1976	Kansas City	OF	152	581	71	154	23	6	3	59	23	.265
1977	Kansas City	OF	162	606	98	189	32	14	23	112	16	.312
	Totals		544	1784	241	499	75	29	31	238	56	.280

DENNIS LEONARD 26 6-1 190   Bats R Throws R

Came into his own last year as one of three ALers to win 20 . . . Steady improvement each year in big leagues . . . Born May 18, 1951, in Brooklyn, raised on Long Island, attended college in Westchester County . . . A Yankee fan, his big thrill was beating Yankees, 6-2, in Game 3 of AL playoffs last year . . . Has won almost 65 percent of decisions over last three years . . . Hard thrower with slider and newly-acquired curveball to make him tougher . . . Threw eight no-hitters in six years in sandlot, high school, college and minor league ball . . . "He's just reaching the point, experience-wise, where he will be even more effective," says Herzog.

Year	Club	G	IP	W	L	Pct.	SO	BB	H	ERA
1974	Kansas City	5	22	0	4	.000	8	12	28	5.32
1975	Kansas City	32	212	15	7	.682	146	90	212	3.78
1976	Kansas City	35	259	17	10	.630	150	70	247	3.51
1977	Kansas City	38	293	20	12	.625	244	79	246	3.04
	Totals	110	786	52	33	.612	548	251	733	3.46

AL HRABOSKY 28 5-11 180   Bats R Throws L

The Mad Hungarian . . . Has blazing fastball with pysche to match . . . They call him a flake, but his stuff isn't fake . . . Goes through prolonged, frenzied routine before he'll deliver pitch . . . All part of the act . . . Had second straight disappointing season, with save total falling from 13 to 10 . . . Was Fireman-of-the-Year in 1975 after gaining 22 saves . . . Appeared in 68 games two years ago, setting club record . . . Born July 21, 1949, in Oakland, Cal. . . . Said early-season trouble last year was because Card manager Vern Rapp made him shave his beard . . . Believe it . . . Rapp relented, Hrabosky grew beard again and was much better the second half . . . Success prompted bumper stickers in St. Louis, which read "I Hlove Hraboky."

Year	Club	G	IP	W	L	Pct.	SO	BB	H	ERA
1970	St. Louis	16	19	2	1	.667	12	7	22	4.74
1971	St. Louis	1	2	0	0	.000	2	0	2	0.00
1972	St. Louis	5	7	1	0	1.000	9	3	2	0.00
1973	St. Louis	44	56	2	4	.333	57	21	45	2.09
1974	St. Louis	65	88	8	1	.889	82	38	71	2.97
1975	St. Louis	65	97	13	3	.813	82	33	72	1.67
1976	St. Louis	68	95	8	6	.571	73	39	89	3.32
1977	St. Louis	65	86	6	5	.545	68	41	82	4.40
	Totals	329	450	40	20	.667	385	182	385	2.94

GEORGE BRETT 24 6-0 200   Bats L Throws R

Slumped off 21 points in BA, but tripled home run production and improved RBIs by one-third . . . Fiery player who does not believe in safety first . . . Battled Yankees' Graig Nettles in fight at third base in fifth game of playoff . . . Heartbroken over second straight defeat to Yanks for pennant . . . Born May 15, 1953, in Glendale, W. Va. . . . Younger brother of Ken Brett and the two are very close . . . One of baseball's most eligible bachelors . . . Signed five-year contract worth $1.5 million last year . . . Received over three million votes and was starting third baseman on all-star team second straight year . . . "George Brett can hit snowballs on Christmas Day," says Whitey Herzog.

Year	Club	Pos	G	AB	R	H	2B	3B	HR	RBI	SB	Avg.
1973	Kansas City	3B	13	40	2	5	2	0	0	0	0	.125
1974	Kansas City	3B-SS	133	457	49	129	21	5	2	47	8	.282
1975	Kansas City	3B-SS	159	634	84	195	35	13	11	89	13	.308
1976	Kansas City	3B	159	645	94	215	34	14	7	67	21	.333
1977	Kansas City	3B	139	564	105	176	32	13	22	88	14	.312
	Totals		603	2340	334	720	124	45	42	291	56	.308

HAL McRAE 31 5-11 180   Bats R Throws R

One of hardest players in game . . . Took Willie Randolph out of play at second base in first game of AL playoffs that almost set off free-for-all with Yankees . . . Asked to sacrifice average for run production, he slipped off 34 points, but raised HR total by 13, RBIs by 19 . . . Led league with 54 doubles, most in baseball in 27 years . . . Born July 10, 1946, in Avon Park, Fla. . . . Signed by Reds, but was expendable in midst of so many hitters . . . Three straight years over .300 for Royals until last . . . "My emphasis shifted from being a good hitter to being a strong hitter." . . . Better defensively than given credit.

Year	Club	Pos	G	AB	R	H	2B	3B	HR	RBI	SB	Avg.
1968	Cincinnati	2B	17	51	1	10	1	0	0	2	1	.196
1970	Cincinnati	OF-3B-2B	70	165	18	41	6	1	8	23	0	.248
1971	Cincinnati	OF	99	337	39	89	24	2	9	34	3	.264
1972	Cincinnati	OF-3B	62	97	9	27	4	0	5	26	0	.278
1973	Kansas City......	OF-3B	106	338	36	79	18	3	9	50	2	.234
1974	Kansas City......	OF-3B	148	539	71	167	36	4	15	88	11	.310
1975	Kansas City......	OF-3B	126	480	58	147	38	6	5	71	11	.306
1976	Kansas City......	OF	149	527	75	175	34	5	8	73	22	.332
1977	Kansas City......	OF	162	641	104	191	54	11	21	92	18	.298
	Totals...........		938	3175	411	926	215	32	80	457	68	.292

JOHN MAYBERRY 28 6-3 220   Bats L Throws L

Came back slightly from poor '76, but still has not bounced back to 1975 34-homer, 106-RBI form . . . Roger Maris worked with him in spring training at invitation of Whitey Herzog . . . Has more than paid back Royals, who got him from Houston for pitcher Jim York in 1972 . . . All-time Royals' home run leader . . . One of most feared hitters in league, many clubs overshift on him . . . Born Feb. 18, 1950, in Detroit . . . Attended same high school as Willie Horton and Alex Johnson . . . Missed final game of playoffs with toothache.

Year	Club	Pos	G	AB	R	H	2B	3B	HR	RBI	SB	Avg.
1968	Houston	1B	4	9	0	0	0	0	0	0	0	.000
1969	Houston	PH	5	4	0	0	0	0	0	0	0	.000
1970	Houston	1B	50	148	23	32	3	2	5	14	1	.216
1971	Houston	1B	46	137	16	25	0	1	7	14	0	.182
1972	Kansas City......	1B	149	503	65	150	24	3	25	100	0	.298
1973	Kansas City......	1B	152	510	87	142	20	2	26	100	3	.278
1974	Kansas City......	1B	126	427	63	100	13	1	22	69	4	.234
1975	Kansas City......	1B	156	554	95	161	38	1	34	106	5	.291
1976	Kansas City......	1B	161	594	76	138	22	2	13	95	3	.232
1977	Kansas City......	1B	153	543	73	125	22	1	23	82	1	.230
	Totals...........		1002	3429	498	873	142	13	155	580	17	.255

FRED PATEK 33 5-4 140　　　　　Bats R Throws R

Smallest man in majors, but stands 10 feet tall in desire, competitiveness and class . . . Best player in playoffs for Royals . . . Hit in nine straight league championship games, finally stopped in fifth game last year . . . League leader in stolen bases . . . 287 thefts in seven years . . . Three-year contract relaxed him . . "They gave me security, I want to give them production.". . . Born Oct. 9, 1944, raised in Sequin, Texas, proving not eveything in Lone Star State is big . . . Signed with Pirates, but traded to Royals in '70 and has been their shortstop ever since with no sign of slowing . . . Collected 1,000th hit last year and got standing ovation, which he calls his biggest baseball thrill.

Year	Club	Pos	G	AB	R	H	2B	3B	HR	RBI	SB	Avg.
1968	Pittsburgh	SS-OF-3B	61	208	31	53	4	2	2	18	18	.255
1969	Pittsburgh	SS	147	460	48	110	9	1	5	32	15	.239
1970	Pittsburgh	SS	84	237	42	58	10	5	1	19	8	.245
1971	Kansas City	SS	147	591	86	158	21	11	6	36	49	.267
1972	Kansas City	SS	136	518	59	110	25	4	0	32	33	.212
1973	Kansas City	SS	135	501	82	117	19	5	5	45	36	.234
1974	Kansas City	SS	149	537	72	121	18	6	3	38	33	.225
1975	Kansas City	SS	136	483	58	110	14	5	5	45	32	.228
1976	Kansas City	SS	144	432	58	104	19	3	1	43	51	.241
1977	Kansas City	SS	154	497	72	130	26	6	5	60	53	.262
	Totals		1293	4464	608	1071	165	48	33	368	328	.240

PAUL SPLITTORFF 31 6-3 210　　　　Bats L Throws L

Beat Yankees in opening game of playoff, perhaps his biggest major league victory . . . Frequent injuries have hampered his career . . . First 20-game winner in Royals history, but injuries limited him to 33 wins next three years . . . Missed no-hitter last year on Charlie Moore's single with two out in eighth . . . Born Oct. 8, 1946, in Evansville, Ind. . . . Studious looking on mound with glasses . . . "I feel I'm a better pitcher now than ever." . . . First player originally signed by expansion Royals to make it to big leagues . . . Sells real estate during off season.

Year	Club	G	IP	W	L	Pct.	SO	BB	H	ERA
1970	Kansas City	2	9	0	1	.000	10	5	16	7.00
1971	Kansas City	22	144	8	9	.471	80	35	129	2.69
1972	Kansas City	35	216	12	12	.500	140	67	189	3.12
1973	Kansas City	38	262	20	11	.645	110	78	279	3.98
1974	Kansas City	36	226	13	19	.406	90	75	252	4.10
1975	Kansas City	35	159	9	10	.474	76	56	156	3.17
1976	Kansas City	26	159	11	8	.578	59	59	169	3.96
1977	Kansas City	37	229	16	6	.727	99	83	243	3.69
	Totals	231	1404	89	76	.539	664	458	1433	3.62

AMOS OTIS 30 5-11 166   Bats R Throws R

Royals all-time leader in every offensive category save homers and steals . . . Frequently rumored on trading block, but has been KC's center fielder last seven years since traded from Mets, who tried to convert him to third base . . . Moody, sometimes uncommunicative, but one of best fielders in AL, specializing in one-hand catches . . . Born April 26, 1947, in Mobile, Ala., same area that produced Willie Mays, Willie McCovey, Henry Aaron, Cleon Jones, Tommie Agee . . . Famous Amos . . . Was traded to Pirates with Cookie Rojas for Al Oliver before 1976 season, but Rojas invoked veteran status to veto deal.

Year	Club	Pos	G	AB	R	H	2B	3B	HR	RBI	SB	Avg.
1967	New York (NL)...	OF-3B	19	59	6	13	2	0	0	1	0	.220
1969	New York (NL)...	OF-3B	48	93	6	14	3	1	0	4	1	.151
1970	Kansas City......	OF	159	620	91	176	36	9	11	58	33	.284
1971	Kansas City......	OF	147	555	80	167	26	4	15	79	52	.301
1972	Kansas City......	OF	143	540	75	158	28	2	11	54	28	.293
1973	Kansas City......	OF	148	583	89	175	21	4	26	93	13	.300
1974	Kansas City......	OF	146	552	87	157	31	9	12	73	18	.284
1975	Kansas City......	OF	132	470	87	116	26	6	9	46	39	.247
1976	Kansas City......	OF	153	592	93	165	40	2	18	86	26	.279
1977	Kansas City......	OF	142	478	85	120	20	8	17	78	23	.251
	Totals..........		1237	4542	699	1261	233	45	119	572	233	.279

DARRELL PORTER 26 6-0 193   Bats L Throws R

Great addition to Royals . . . Found a home after six tough years in Milwaukee . . . "I decided I had to go to spring training and prove everything all over. First I had to prove it to myself." . . . Born Jan. 17, 1952, in Joplin, Mo. . . . High school All-America in football, chose baseball when picked No. 1 in June, 1970 free agent draft . . . Regular catcher at Milwaukee at age 21 . . . "It's not easy to play on a losing team." . . . Chose to sign one year contract with Royals, but not so he could play out option. "I like playing here," he said. "It's near my home and I'd like to finish my career here. I just didn't want to sign a multi-year contract on the basis of what I did in '76. I want to have a good season and then sign a better contract."

Year	Club	Pos	G	AB	R	H	2B	3B	HR	RBI	SB	Avg.
1971	Milwaukee.......	C	22	70	4	15	2	0	2	9	2	.214
1972	Milwaukee.......	C	18	56	2	7	1	0	1	2	0	.125
1973	Milwaukee.......	C	117	350	50	89	19	2	16	67	5	.254
1974	Milwaukee.......	C	131	432	59	104	15	4	12	56	8	.241
1975	Milwaukee.......	C	130	409	66	95	12	5	18	60	2	.232
1976	Milwaukee.......	C	119	389	43	81	14	1	5	32	2	.208
1977	Kansas City......	C	130	425	61	117	21	3	16	60	1	.275
	Totals..........		667	2131	285	508	84	15	70	286	20	.238

DOUG BIRD 28 6-4 180   Bats R Throws R

Emerged last year as Royals' top reliever . . . Born March 5, 1950, in Corona, Cal. . . . Was three-sport star at Pomona HS . . . Selected in third round of secondary phase of June, 1969 free agent draft . . . Solid man when Royals hit pitching shorts . . . Has been used as starter and reliever, but used almost exclusively in relief last year (he started five games) and with 11 wins, 14 saves, should continue as the top bull in the Royals' pen . . . Attended Mt. San Antonio JC and Mesa (Ariz.) CC.

Year	Club	G	IP	W	L	Pct.	SO	BB	H	ERA
1973	Kansas City..............	54	102	4	4	.500	83	30	81	3.00
1974	Kansas City..............	55	92	7	6	.538	62	27	100	2.74
1975	Kansas City..............	51	105	9	6	.600	81	40	100	3.26
1976	Kansas City..............	39	198	12	10	.545	107	31	191	3.36
1977	Kansas City..............	53	118	11	4	.733	83	29	120	3.89
	Totals..................	252	615	43	30	.589	416	157	592	3.29

TOP PROSPECTS

CLINT HURDLE 20 6-3 195   Bats L Throws R
Super prospect who can do it all—hit, hit with power, run and throw . . . His arm is so strong, he was heavily recruited as college QB, but chose baseball after being No. 1 pick of Royals in June, 1976 free agent draft . . . Born June 30, 1957, in Big Rapids, Mich. . . . Called up after .328, 16 HRs, 66 RBIs in 442 at bats at Omaha, batted .308 in nine games with Royals . . . "If he stays healthy, he's going to make more money than anybody has," said vet Joe Lahoud after seeing him in minors.

WILLIE WILSON 22 6-3 195   Bats R Throws R
One day, he will take over as Royals' center fielder. Only a matter of time . . . Improved bat at Omaha and impressed in late season trial in KC, could be ready . . . Born July 9, 1955, in Montgomery, Ala., but grew up in Summit, N.J., where he was all-state in baseball, basketball, football . . . Turned down football scholarship at U. of Maryland to sign with Royals . . . Lightning speed his greatest asset.

MANAGER WHITEY HERZOG: Frustrated by two straight playoff defeats to Yankees . . . Outspoken and frank, he criticized Yankees when they called off game in July, forcing Royals to return to New York in August . . . "The don't deserve to win anything," he said. "Win, win, win, that's all that interests them." . . . Became hero in KC because he won, won, won, and awarded with fat contract as a result . . . Openly critical of AL president Lee MacPhail for allowing Yankee replay . . . Born Dorrel Norman Elvert Herzog, Nov. 9, 1931, in New Athens, Ill. . . . Lives in Independence, Mo.

GREATEST MANAGER

Conceived in 1969 when the American League expanded, no expansion team has met with such success as the Royals, winners of the American League West for the past two years.

In that time, the Royals have had five managers as they built a team from the ground floor until today it is one of the powers in the American League. Indeed, second-place finishes by Bob Lemon in 1971 and by Jack McKeon in 1973 were great accomplishments. But neither was really around long enough to benefit from the building job done in Kansas City.

Chief beneficiary and, consequently, the Royals' greatest manager, is the man who still holds the job, Dorrel Norman Elvert Herzog, better known as Whitey.

ALL-TIME ROYAL LEADERS

BATTING: George Brett, .333, 1976
HRs: John Mayberry, 34, 1975
RBIs: Al Cowens, 112, 1977
STEALS: Fred Patek, 53, 1977
WINS: Steve Busby, 22, 1974
STRIKEOUTS: Dennis Leonard, 244, 1977

CHICAGO WHITE SOX

TEAM DIRECTORY: President: Bill Veeck; VP-Roland Hemond; Business Mgr: Rudy Schaffer; Dir. of Player Development: Paul Richards; Pub. Rel.: Don Unferth; Trav. Sec.: Glen Rosenbaum; Mgr.: Bob Lemon. Home: Comiskey Park (44,492). Field distances: 352, l.f. line; 375, l.c.; 445, c.f.; 375, r.c.; 352, r.f. line. Spring training: Sarasota, Fla.

SCOUTING REPORT

HITTING: "We lost 61 home runs (Oscar Gamble, 31, and Richie Zisk, 30 became free agents)" says GM Roland Hemond in announcing the Sox had traded for Bobby Bonds. "With Bonds and (free agent) Ron Blomberg, we have now offset that loss and added speed (Bonds and outfielder Thad Bosley)."

"We got where we did last year with offense," says manager Bob Lemon.

Where the Sox got was a surprising third, thanks to a team BA of .278 and a club high 192 homers. At one point, in late August, the White Sox were in first place despite a team ERA over four. That's supposed to be impossible. But the White Sox did it and, flushed with that success, Bill Veeck will try to do it the same way again—with hitting and by Rent-a-Player. This year it's Bonds, who will play one year in Chicago, then be a free man.

PITCHING: The prospects are no better this year than they were last, when the White Sox were 10th in the league in pitching. They got lucky with free agent Steve Stone (15-12) and hope to do the same this year with free agents Ron Schueler and Jim Hughes. Lerrin LaGrow, picked up from the Cardinals, was a life saver . . . and a game saver (25). The Sox also hope Francisco Barrios (14-7) will continue to improve and Wilbur Wood, his injuries behind him, will once again float his baffling knuckleball past enemy bats.

FIELDING: Not the best part of the White Sox' game. They finished 12th in fielding and last in double plays. The Sox are strong at third (Eric Soderholm was the league leader), behind the plate with Jim Essian and in center (Chet Lemon). But Alan Bannister made 40 errors at short and Jorge Orta kicked in 19 more at second. "You can't keep giving the other team four outs an inning," says Lemon. "That's what we did and we've got to put an end to that."

OUTLOOK: "If a fighter is a slugger, he can't become a Jim Corbett overnight," says Bob Lemon. "We're not going to change, but I hope we'll be better on defense." The White Sox won 90 games last year, but will be hard pressed to do as well this year. "We'll have 55 men in camp," says Lemon. "Get there early. I'm planning to."

Ralph Garr hit exactly .300 for second straight year.

CHICAGO WHITE SOX 1978 ROSTER

MANAGER Bob Lemon
Coaches—Orestes Minoso, Larry Doby, Bobby Knoop,
        Stan Williams

PITCHERS

No.	Name	1977 Club	W-L	IP	SO	ERA	B-T	Ht.	Wt.	Born
46	Barrios, Francisco	Chicago (AL)	14-7	231	119	4.13	R-R	6-3	195	6/10/53 Hermosillo, MX
34	Carroll, Clay	St. Louis	4-2	90	34	2.50	R-R	6-1	205	5/2/41 Clanton, AL
		Chicago (AL)	1-3	11	4	4.91				
24	Johnson, Bart	Chicago (AL)	4-5	92	46	4.01	R-R	215	6-5	1/3/50 Torrance, CA
33	Kirkwood, Don	CA-Chi. (AL)	2-1	58	34	5.12	R-R	6-3	192	9/24/49 Pontiac, MI
35	Hughes, Jim	Minnesota	0-0	4	1	2.25	R-R	6-3	190	7/2/51 Los Angeles, CA
		Tacoma	9-10	159	76	5.15				
27	Kravec, Ken	Iowa	4-4	59	62	2.59	L-L	6-2	185	7/29/51 Cleveland, OH
		Chicago (AL)	11-8	167	125	4.10				
55	Kucek, Jack	Iowa	6-8	117	83	2.54	R-R	6-2	200	6/8/53 Newton Falls, OH
		Chicago (AL)	0-1	35	25	3.60				
36	LaGrow, Lerrin	Chicago, (AL)	7-3	99	63	2.45	R-R	6-5	230	7/8/48 Phoenix, AZ
50	Renko, Steve	Chicago (NL)	2-2	51	34	4.59	R-R	6-6	226	12/10/44 Kansas City, MO
		Chicago (AL)	5-0	53	36	3.57				
52	Schueler, Ron	Minnesota	8-7	135	77	4.40	R-R	6-4	205	4/18/48 Hays, KS
32	Stone, Steve	Chicago (AL)	15-12	207	124	4.52	R-R	5-10	175	7/14/47 Cleveland, OH
—	Thomas, Stan	Seattle-NY (AL)	3-6	65	15	6.09	R-R	6-1	185	7/11/49 Rumford, ME
		Syracuse	2-2	35	15	5.09				
51	Verhoeven, John	Salt Lake City	4-1	33	26	4.91	R-R	6-5	200	7/3/53 Long Beach, CA
		CA-Chi. (AL)	0-2	15	9	3.00				
28	Wood, Wilbur	Chicago (AL)	7-8	123	42	4.98	R-L	6-0	200	10/22/41 Cambridge, MA

CATCHERS

No.	Name	1977 Club	H	HR	RBI	Pct.	B-T	Ht.	Wt.	Born
11	Essian, Jim	Chicago (AL)	88	10	44	.273	R-R	6-1	187	1/2/52 Detroit, MI
54	Foley, Marvis	Knoxville	66	6	41	.306	L-R	6-0	195	8/29/53 Stanford, KY
20	Nahorodny, Wm.	Oklahoma City	101	17	69	.262	R-R	6-2	190	8/31/53 Detroit, MI

INFIELDERS

No.	Name	1977 Club	H	HR	RBI	Pct.	B-T	Ht.	Wt.	Born
7	Bannister, Alan	Chicago (AL)	154	3	57	.275	R-R	5-11	175	9/3/51 Buena Park, CA
8	Bell, Kevin	Chicago (AL)	5	1	6	.179	R-R	6-0	185	7/13/55 Los Angeles, CA
		Iowa	56	14	39	.306				
1	Flannery, John	Salinas	56	1	25	.287	R-R	6-3	170	1/25/57 Long Beach, CA
		Iowa	58	0	22	.249				
		Chicago (AL)	0	0	0	.000				
23	Johnson, Lamar	Chicago (AL)	113	18	65	.302	R-R	6-2	207	9/2/50 Bessemer, AL
30	Kessinger, Don	St. Louis	32	0	7	.239	B-R	6-1	170	12/17/42 Forrest City, AR
		Chicago (AL)	28	0	11	.235				
6	Orta, Jorge	Chicago (AL)	159	11	84	.282	L-R	5-10	170	11/26/50 Mazatlan, MX
—	Pryor, Greg	Syracuse	125	7	52	.271	R-R	6-0	175	10/2/49 Marietta, OH
12	Soderholm, Eric	Chicago (AL)	129	25	67	.280	R-R	5-11	187	9/24/48 Cortland, NY
19	Squires, Mike	Iowa	134	1	45	.323	L-L	5-11	185	3/5/52 Kalamazoo, MI
		Chicago (AL)	0	0	0	.000				

OUTFIELDERS

No.	Name	1977 Club	H	HR	RBI	Pct.	B-T	Ht.	Wt.	Born
10	Blomberg, Ron	New York (AL)	On Disabled List				L-R	6-1	200	8/23/48 Atlanta, GA
—	Bonds, Bobby	California	156	37	115	.264	R-R	6-1	190	3/15/46 Riverside, CA
—	Bosley, Thad	Salt Lake City	97	2	38	.326	L-L	6-3	165	9/17/56 Oceanside, CA
		California	63	0	19	.297				
5	Coluccio, Bob	Charleston	95	11	53	.249	R-R	5-11	180	10/2/51 Centralia, WA
		Iowa	3	0	0	.300				
		Chicago (AL)	10	0	7	.270				
38	Cruz, Henry	Albuquerque	174	18	88	.353	L-L	6-0	175	2/27/52 St. Croix, VI
		Chicago (AL)	6	2	5	.286				
48	Garr, Ralph	Chicago (AL)	163	10	54	.300	L-R	5-11	185	12/12/45 Ruston, AL
44	Lemon, Chet	Chicago (AL)	151	19	67	.273	R-R	6-0	182	2/12/55 Jackson, MI
53	Milinaro, Bob	Evansville	138	17	91	.303	L-R	6-0	180	5/21/50 Newark, NJ
		Chicago (AL)	2	0	0	.333				
—	Moore, Alvin	Atlanta	94	5	34	.260	R-R	5-11	183	1/25/53 Waskom, TX
15	Nordhagen, Wayne	Chicago (AL)	39	4	22	.315	R-R	6-2	200	7/4/48 Thief River Falls, MN
18	Stillman, Royle	Chicago (AL)	25	3	13	.210	L-L	5-11	180	1/2/51 Santa Monica, CA

WHITE SOX PROFILES

JORGE ORTA 27 5-10 170   Bats L Throws R

No position in field, but what a bat . . . Consistent and productive . . . Says former hitting instructor, Deacon Jones: "His bat is as quick as a Joe Louis punch." . . . Played 40 consecutive errorless games at second base in '75, but inability to make double play and lack of range forced Sox to switch him to oufield . . . That experiment failed, they tried him at third. That failed, too. Back to second . . . Born Nov. 26, 1950, in Mazatlan, Mexico . . . Father called "Babe Ruth of Cuba," and taught Jorge the game . . . However, his father forbade him from playing in HS so he could concentrate on studies . . . Played basketball and so well, he was recruited by UCLA.

Year	Club	Pos	G	AB	R	H	2B	3B	HR	RBI	SB	Avg.
1972	Chicago (AL).....	SS-2B-3B	51	124	20	25	3	1	3	11	1	.202
1973	Chicago (AL).....	–2B-SS	128	425	46	113	9	10	6	40	8	.266
1974	Chicago (AL).....	2B-SS	139	525	73	166	31	2	10	67	9	.316
1975	Chicago (AL).....	2B	140	542	64	165	26	10	11	83	16	.304
1976	Chicago (AL).....	OF-2B	158	636	74	174	29	8	14	72	24	.274
1977	Chicago (AL).....	OF-2B	144	564	71	159	27	8	11	84	4	.282
	Totals...........		760	2816	348	802	125	39	55	357	62	.285

Bobby Bonds brings 37 HRs, 114 RBIs to White Sox lineup.

BOBBY BONDS 32 6-1 190   Bats R Throws R

Fabulous year, but on the road again . . . Missed by three HRs becoming first 40-40 player in history—40 homers, 40 stolen bases . . . Already member of exclusive 30-30 club. With 140 Ks, closing in on Mickey Mantle's all-time strikeout record . . . Can do it in four years . . . "People don't realize what an accomplishment it is to steal and hit home runs. It takes a lot out of you. I could steal a lot more, but I only steal in certain situations." . . . Born March 15, 1946, in Riverside, Cal. . . . Has one goal. "I'd like to win a home run title. I've never won one, not even in the minors." Missed last year by two.

Year	Club	Pos	G	AB	R	H	2B	3B	HR	RBI	SB	Avg.
1968	San Francisco	OF	81	307	55	78	10	5	9	35	16	.254
1969	San Francisco	OF	158	622	120	161	25	6	32	90	45	.259
1970	San Francisco	OF	157	663	134	200	36	10	26	78	48	.302
1971	San Francisco	OF	155	619	110	178	32	4	33	102	26	.288
1972	San Francisco	OF	153	626	118	162	29	5	26	80	44	.259
1973	San Francisco	OF	160	643	131	182	34	4	39	96	43	.283
1974	San Francisco	OF	150	567	97	145	22	8	21	71	41	.256
1975	New York (AL) ...	OF	145	529	93	143	26	3	32	85	30	.270
1976	California........	OF	99	378	48	100	10	3	10	54	30	.265
1977	California........	OF	158	592	103	156	23	9	37	115	41	.264
	Totals...........		1416	5546	1009	1505	247	57	265	776	364	.271

ERIC SODERHOLM 29 5-11 187   Bats R Throws R

Great comeback story . . . Spent entire 1976 on injured list with cartilage damage in left knee . . . Rehabilitated himself with weight program and considered one of strongest men in baseball . . . Played out option in Minnesota and signed as free agent with Sox for bargain basement price . . . Proved to be best buy . . . Signed conditional contract and paid off . . . "It was a fantastic year," he said . . . The Bionic Man . . . Born Sept. 24, 1948, in Miami, Fla. . . . Brother Dale is shortstop in Twins' organization . . . "Bill (Veeck) and I were both in the depths of despair last year. Bill was going broke and I didn't know if I had a career. But we both made it."

Year	Club	Pos	G	AB	R	H	2B	3B	HR	RBI	SB	Avg.
1971	Minnesota	3B	21	64	9	10	4	0	1	4	0	.156
1972	Minnesota	3B	93	287	28	54	10	0	13	39	3	.188
1973	Minnesota	3B-SS	35	111	22	33	7	2	1	9	1	.297
1974	Minnesota	3B-SS	141	464	63	128	18	3	10	51	7	.276
1975	Minnesota	3B	117	419	62	120	17	2	11	58	3	.286
1976	Minnesota		(Did Not Play)									
1977	Chicago (AL).....	3B	130	460	77	129	20	3	25	67	7	.280
	Totals...........		537	1805	261	474	76	10	61	228	16	.263

ALAN BANNISTER 26 5-11 175   Bats R Throws R

Inherited shortstop job when Bucky Dent was traded to NY . . . Made alarming 40 errors, but showed good bat . . . And never stopped hustling . . . "Bobby Winkles taught me to hustle at Arizona State." . . . All-America there and drafted on first round by Phillies in January, 1973 . . . Has played both infield and outfield . . . Set NCAA records for hits, RBIs and total bases . . . Born Sept. 9, 1951, in Buena Park, Cal. . . . Drafted out of high school by Angels, but decided to go to college first.

Year	Club	Pos	G	AB	R	H	2B	3B	HR	RBI	SB	Avg.
1974	Philadelphia......	OF-SS	26	25	4	3	0	0	0	1	0	.120
1975	Philadelphia......	OF-SS-2B	24	61	10	16	3	1	0	0	2	.262
1976	Chicago (AL).....	OF-SS-2B-3B	73	145	19	36	6	2	0	8	12	.248
1977	Chicago (AL).....	SS-3B-2B	139	560	87	154	20	3	3	57	4	.275
	Totals...........		262	791	120	209	29	6	3	66	18	.264

CHET LEMON 23 6-0 182   Bats R Throws R

Converted from infield to become one of top center fielders in game . . . Excellent speed and arm . . . Plays extremely shallow . . . Credits Larry Doby with helping his hitting . . . "It's a big field out there," advised Doby. "Don't be afraid to use it all." . . . Says baseball has become fun . . . Very modest, he calls sportswriters "Mister" . . . Born Feb. 12, 1955, in Jackson, Miss. . . . Moved to Los Angeles and was outstanding high school athlete . . . Played against Anthony Davis in high school football . . . Oakland's No. 1 pick in June, 1972 draft, he was traded to Sox for pitcher Stan Bahnsen . . . One of few bad deals made by Charles O. Finley.

Year	Club	Pos	G	AB	R	H	2B	3B	HR	RBI	SB	Avg.
1975	Chicago (AL).....	3B-OF	9	35	2	9	2	0	0	1	1	.257
1976	Chicago (AL).....	OF	132	451	46	111	15	5	4	38	13	.246
1977	Chicago (AL).....	OF	150	553	99	151	38	4	19	67	8	.273
	Totals...........		291	1039	147	271	55	9	23	106	22	.261

LAMAR JOHNSON 27 6-2 207   Bats R Throws R

Second straight year over .300 . . . "He's the second best hitter in the league, next to Rod Carew," said Bill Veeck . . . Sang National Anthem before Father's Day doubleheader, then hit two homers in 2-1 opening game victory . . . "He sang, he picked it, he hit it, he did everything," said manager Bob Lemon . . . Born Sept. 2, 1950, in Bessemer, Ala. . . .

Seven seasons in minor leagues before sticking with big club . . .
Caught in high school and was defensive end in football . . . Platooned with Spencer at first, but slated for full time duty this
season.

Year	Club	Pos	G	AB	R	H	2B	3B	HR	RBI	SB	Avg.
1974	Chicago (AL).....	1B	10	29	1	10	0	0	0	2	0	.345
1975	Chicago (AL).....	1B	8	30	2	6	3	0	1	1	0	.200
1976	Chicago (AL).....	1B-OF	82	222	29	71	11	1	4	33	2	.320
1977	Chicago (AL).....	1B-OF	118	374	52	113	12	5	18	65	1	.302
	Totals..........		218	655	84	200	26	6	23	101	3	.305

RALPH GARR 32 5-11 185   Bats L Throws R

After 10 years, his bat is still magic . . . Second
straight year at .300 on the nose . . . Fifth time
at .300 or better . . . The Road Runner . . .
Notorious bad ball hitter . . . "I swing at anything. People say I'm a lousy looking hitter.
That doesn't bother me. I'd rather have a pretty
average." . . . He does . . . Became something
of elder statesman on Sox . . . Turned on by
White Sox fans . . . Says his hero is Pete Rose . . . "I just love the
way that man plays." . . . Says teammate Chet Lemon: "Ralph
Garr is more than a great player, he's a great human being." . . .
Born Oct. 12, 1945, in Ruston, La. . . . Graduate of Grambling
College.

Year	Club	Pos	G	AB	R	H	2B	3B	HR	RBI	SB	Avg.
1968	Atlanta..........	PH	11	7	3	2	0	0	0	0	1	.286
1969	Atlanta..........	OF	22	27	6	6	1	0	0	2	1	.222
1970	Atlanta..........	OF	37	96	18	27	3	0	0	8	5	.281
1971	Atlanta..........	OF	154	639	101	219	24	6	9	44	30	.343
1972	Atlanta..........	OF	134	554	87	180	22	0	12	53	25	.325
1973	Atlanta..........	OF	148	668	94	200	32	6	11	55	35	.299
1974	Atlanta..........	OF	143	606	87	214	24	17	11	54	26	.353
1975	Atlanta..........	OF	151	625	74	174	26	11	6	31	14	.278
1976	Chicago (AL).....	OF	136	527	63	158	22	6	4	36	14	.300
1977	Chicago (AL).....	OF	134	543	78	163	29	7	10	54	12	.300
	Totals..........		1070	4292	611	1343	183	53	63	337	163	.313

LERRIN LaGROW 29 6-5 230   Bats R Throws R

A checkered career as starter, blossomed into
outstanding relief pitcher . . . Ace of White
Sox' pen, his 25 saves were third best in league
. . . Won seven games in relief. As starter, his
high win total was eight for Tigers . . . Previously best known as pitcher who had bat
thrown at him by Bert Campaneris in 1972
playoffs . . . Another great deal by Bill Veeck,
getting him from Cardinals for Clay Carroll, who wound up back

with Sox . . . Born July 8, 1948, in Phoenix . . . Considered quitting until traded to Sox . . . "I wasn't getting anywhere . . . But now my temperament has changed. I finally realized baseball is not the only thing in my life. I learned to leave my disappointments and frustrations in the clubhouse."

Year	Club	G	IP	W	L	Pct.	SO	BB	H	ERA
1970	Detroit.................	10	12	0	1	.000	7	6	16	7.50
1972	Detroit.................	16	27	0	1	.000	9	6	22	1.33
1973	Detroit.................	21	54	1	5	.167	33	23	54	4.33
1974	Detroit.................	37	216	8	19	.296	85	80	245	4.67
1975	Detroit.................	32	164	7	14	.333	75	66	183	4.39
1976	St. Louis..............	8	24	0	1	.000	10	7	21	1.50
1977	Chicago (AL)...........	66	99	7	3	.700	63	35	81	2.45
	Totals.................	190	596	23	44	.343	282	223	622	3.97

JUNIOR MOORE 25 5-11 183   Bats R Throws R

Gave Braves Moore than they expected . . . Had fifth-best BA on club in first full season . . . Earned 1976 trial after finishing with a .329 mark in International League . . . Began career as outfielder but Braves converted him to infielder to fill hole . . . Was International League all-star second baseman in 1975 . . . Was Western Carolina League all-star third baseman in 1972 . . . A line drive hitter with good speed . . . Born Jan. 25, 1953, in Waskom, Tex. . . . An 11th-round draft pick in 1971 . . . Real name is Alvin Earl Moore . . . Attended College of Alameda in California.

Year	Club	Pos	G	AB	R	H	2B	3B	HR	RBI	SB	Avg.
1976	Atlanta..........	3B-2B-OF	20	26	1	7	1	0	0	2	0	.269
1977	Atlanta..........	OF-3B-2B	112	361	41	94	9	3	5	34	4	.260
	Totals..........		132	387	42	101	10	3	5	36	4	.261

STEVE STONE 30 5-10 175   Bats R Throws R

Has bounced back and forth between north and south side of Chicago . . . Born June 14, 1947, in Cleveland . . . Originally signed by Giants, was traded to White Sox and spent 1973 season with them . . . Traded to city rival Cubs in Ron Santo deal . . . Spent three seasons there, then opted for free-agency and returned to Sox . . . "They made me feel from the start that they were really interested in me." . . . He and footballer Bobby Douglass are part of group called "Lettuce Entertain You," which has interest in Chicago night clubs and restaurants . . . Among them is famed Pump Room, where Stone worked as

manager. It was there, wearing a tuxedo, that Stone was signed
. . . Interested in poetry and has had his work published in LA,
Cleveland, San Francisco papers and National Jewish Monthly.

Year	Club	G	IP	W	L	Pct.	SO	BB	H	ERA
1971	San Francisco	24	111	5	9	.357	63	55	110	4.14
1972	San Francisco	27	124	6	8	.429	85	49	97	2.98
1973	Chicago (AL)	36	176	6	11	.353	138	82	163	4.24
1974	Chicago (NL)	38	170	8	6	.571	90	64	185	4.13
1975	Chicago (NL)	33	214	12	8	.600	139	80	198	3.95
1976	Chicago (NL)	17	75	3	6	.333	33	21	70	4.08
1977	Chicago (AL)	31	207	15	12	.556	124	80	228	4.52
	Totals	206	1077	55	60	.478	672	431	1051	4.05

RON BLOMBERG 29 6-1 200   Bats L Throws R

Injury-prone Boomer has managed the equiva-
lent of two full seasons in seven years . . . Only
two at-bats since July, 1975, because of shoulder and knee injuries . . . Played out option
and accepted a four-year no-cut, no-trade contract from Sox worth $650,000 . . . "I wanted
to stay in New York (Mets also bid), but Bill
Veeck sold me. He is a beautiful person." . . .
Born Aug. 23, 1948, in Atlanta . . . Nation's No. 1 pick in June,
1967, free agent draft . . . Enormous strength and great potential,
never fulfilled, but looks forward to a new start. "I respect the
Yankee pinstripes. I wore them with great honor. I'm going to save
my uniform so that my son (one-year-old Adam Lance) will know
I was a Yankee."

Year	Club	Pos	G	AB	R	H	2B	3B	HR	RBI	SB	Avg.
1969	New York (AL)	OF	4	6	0	3	0	0	0	0	0	.500
1971	New York (AL)	OF	64	199	30	64	6	2	7	31	2	.322
1972	New York (AL)	1B	107	299	36	80	22	1	14	49	0	.268
1973	New York (AL)	1B	100	301	45	99	13	1	12	57	2	.329
1974	New York (AL)	OF	90	264	39	82	11	2	10	48	2	.311
1975	New York (AL)	OF	34	105	18	27	8	2	4	17	0	.255
1976	New York (AL)	DH	1	2	0	0	0	0	0	0	0	.000
1977	New York (AL)					(Did Not Play)						
	Totals		400	1177	168	355	60	8	47	202	6	.302

TOP PROSPECTS

THAD BOSLEY 21 6-3 165   Bats L Throws L

Was called Angels' center fielder of future . . . Came to Sox with
Bobby Bonds . . . Long and lean, built like greyhound and runs
like one . . . 90 stolen bases in 1976, a California League record
. . . "I think he has a chance to be a star," said Del Crandall, his
minor-league manager . . . Born Sept. 17, 1956, in Oceanside,
Cal. . . . An accomplished pianist.

RICH WORTHAM 24 6-0 185   Bats R Throws L

Won 50 games at U. of Texas, an NCAA record, and drafted on first round in January, 1976 draft . . . Born Oct. 22, 1953, in Odessa, Tex. . . . Only two seasons of pro ball behind him, and still may be a year or two away, but this is one to watch . . . In first try at pro ball, fanned 56 in 68 innings at Knoxville.

MANAGER BOB LEMON: Fired in Kansas City because he was too old, he came close to being manager of year with Sox at 57 . . . Extremely patient . . . Did masterful job taking team picked for last and finishing third with 90 victories . . . Flew in from California to be interviewed by Bill Veeck, in a Chicago hospital. "Do you want the job," asked Veeck. "Yes," said Lemon. "OK, it's yours," said Veeck . . . "It took me five hours to fly there and two minutes to get the job . . . Born Sept. 22, 1920, in San Bernardino, Cal. . . . Originally signed as outfielder, played CF opening day, 1946, for Indians and made great catch that saved Bob Feller's no-hitter . . . Converted to pitcher, had seven 20-win seasons and elected to Hall of Fame . . . "I never took a defeat home with me. I left it in the bar on the way home."

GREATEST MANAGER

Can one man be the greatest manager for two different teams?

Consider the case of Al Lopez, already designated at the greatest manager in Cleveland Indian history in a narrow victory over Tris Speaker and Lou Boudreau. Is it wrong to call him the greatest manager in the history of the Chicago White Sox as well?

Only five managers in Chicago history have won pennants—one apiece—and Lopez won one of them. He also finished second five times in nine seasons, the secon longest tenure of any White Sox manager.

Clark Griffith won the first White Sox pennant in 1901, but finished fourth the next year then moved on to the New York Knickerbockers (now Yankees).

Fielder Jones won in 1906, finished third the next two seasons, then moved on to St. Louis.

Clarence (Pants) Rowland won in 1917, finished sixth the next year and was let go.

Then came William (Kid) Gleason, who won in 1919, an ill-fated year in White Sox history. The following year he finished second, but when it was discovered eight members of the White Sox had conspired to throw the 1919 World Series and were suspended, Kid Gleason, as a manager, could never be the same again.

ALL-TIME WHITE SOX LEADERS

BATTING: Luke Appling, .388, 1936
HRs: Dick Allen, 37, 1972
RBIs: Zeke Bonura, 138, 1936
STEALS: Wally Moses, 56, 1943
         Luis Aparicio, 56, 1959
WINS: Ed Walsh, 40, 1908
STRIKEOUTS: Ed Walsh, 269, 1908

Al Lopez gave White Sox first pennant in 40 years in 1959.

MINNESOTA TWINS

TEAM DIRECTORY: Chairman of the Board and Pres.: Calvin R. Griffith; VP/Asst. Treas.: Mrs. Thelma Griffith Haynes; VP-Sec. Treas.: Clark Griffith; VP: George Brophy; Pub. Rel.: Tom Mee; VP and Trav. Sec.: Howard T. Fox Jr.; Mgr.: Gene Mauch. Home: Metropolitan Stadium, Bloomington, Minn. (45,919). Field distances: 343, l.f. line; 402, c.f.; 330, r.f. line. Spring training: Orlando, Fla.

Rod Carew, fielder, had best average of AL first basemen.

SCOUTING REPORT

HITTING: Tops in the league in hitting last year, but how long can the Twins go on losing players and remain competitive? Thank heaven for Rod Carew, whose bat magic keeps the Twins competitive and interesting. Except for him, the cupboard is practically bare now that Lyman Bostock (the league's No. 2 hitter at .336) and Larry Hisle (RBI king with 119) have flown the coop.

The Twins are looking for youngsters like Willie Norwood, Rich Chiles, Randy Bass and Craig Kusick to pick up the slack. Never before has a farm system been entrusted with such a difficult task.

PITCHING: Gene Mauch found a way to replace reliever Bill Campbell, coming up with the bandaid twins, Johnson and Johnson. Tom Johnson had 15 saves, while Dave Johnson was 6-0. Dave Goltz was the most under-publicized 20-game winner in baseball and the Twins have high hopes for Paul Thormodsgard, Gary Serum, Jeff Holly and Pete Redfern to improve and bolster a staff that had the third highest ERA in the American League and gave up 151 home runs, 28 more than the Twins hit.

FIELDING: For all his batting titles and records, the thing that pleased Rod Carew most was his play at first base. He made only 10 errors in 1,590 chances and had a fielding average of .994. Unfortunately, the Twins didn't have many more like that and finished in the lower half of the AL in team fielding. There was inconsistency at short, where Roy Smalley made 33 errors, and no regular second baseman or third baseman, lending an air of instability.

In losing Hisle and Bostock, the Twins must replace two outfielders who combined for 21 assists and held down left field and center. On the plus side, young Butch Wynegar is fast becoming one of the finest defensive catchers in the league. But all in all, it's a mess and the Twins have a lot of patching up to do.

OUTLOOK: The tip-off on the Twins' prospects came from the manager, himself. With one year remaining on his contract, Gene Mauch asked for permission to talk to the Angels about managing there. The Twins declined and Mauch is stuck with a team that has had more defectors than East Germany. Mauch is a miracle worker as a manager and he will get his biggest test this year.

MINNESOTA TWINS 1978 ROSTER

MANAGER Gene Mauch
Coaches—Karl Kuehl, Tony Oliva, Jerry Zimmerman

PITCHERS

No.	Name	1977 Club	W-L	IP	SO	ERA	B-T	Ht.	Wt.	Born
18	Carrithers, Don	Minnesota	0-1	14	3	7.07	R-R	6-3	195	9/15/49 San Mateo, CA
–	Field, Greg	Orlando	14-7	162	103	2.78	R-R	6-4	175	1/6/57 West Palm Beach, FL
30	Goltz, Dave	Minnesota	20-11	303	186	3.36	R-R	6-4	210	6/23/49 Pelican Rapids, MN
36	Holly, Jeff	Tacoma	4-3	55	32	3.76	L-L	6-5	210	3/1/53 Torrance, CA
		Minnesota	2-3	48	32	6.94				
27	Johnson, Dave	San Jose	2-0	15	12	0.60	R-R	6-1	183	10/4/49 Abilebe, TX
		Minnesota	2-5	73	33	4.56				
21	Johnson, Tom	Minnesota	16-7	147	87	3.12	R-R	6-1	185	4/2/51 St. Paul, MN
–	May, Davis	Tacoma	4-6	102	43	5.65	R-R	6-0	175	10/16/51 Covington, KY
17	Redfern, Pete	Minnesota	6-9	137	73	5.19	R-R	6-2	195	8/25/54 Glendale, CA
20	Serum, Gary	Orlando	2-3	–	16	4.09	R-R	6-1	160	10/24/56 Alexandria, MN
		Minnesota	0-0	23	14	4.30				
		Tacoma	4-0	30	18	1.80				
–	Scarce, Mac	Indianapolis	1-3	13	15	4.05	L-L	6-3	190	8/8/49 Danville, VA
–	Sutton, John	New Orleans	5-4	95	55	3.32	R-R	5-11	185	11/13/52 Dallas, TX
		St. Louis	2.1	24	9	2.63				
–	Thayer, Greg	Orlando	8-1	–	89	3.14	R-R	5-11	180	10/23/49 St. Cloud, MN
23	Thormodsgard, Paul	Minnesota	11-15	218	94	4.62	R-R	6-2	190	11/10/53 San Francisco, CA
38	Zahn, Geoff	Minnesota	12-14	198	88	4.68	L-L	6-1	175	12/19/46 Baltimore, MD

CATCHERS

No.	Name	1977 Club	H	HR	RBI	Pct.	B-T	Ht.	Wt.	Born
14	Borgmann, Glenn	Minnesota	11	2	7	.164	R-R	6-2	210	5/25/50 Paterson, NJ
40	Bulling, Terry	Orlando	–	5	36	.285	R-R	6-0	200	12/15/52 Westminster, CA
		Minnesota	5	0	5	.156				
8	Lonchar, John	Tacoma	85	4	36	.263	R-R	6-4	207	9/10/52 Euclid, OH
16	Wynegar, Butch	Minnesota	139	10	79	.261	B-R	6-0	185	3/14/56 York, PA

INFIELDERS

No.	Name	1977 Club	H	HR	RBI	Pct.	B-T	Ht.	Wt.	Born
2	Bass, Randy	Tacoma	146	25	117	.321	L-R	6-1	225	3/13/54 Lawton, OK
		Minnesota	2	0	0	.105				
29	Carew, Rod	Minnesota	239	14	100	.388	L-R	6-0	182	10/1/45 Gatun, Panama
26	Cubbage, Mike	Minnesota	110	9	55	.264	L-R	6-0	180	7/21/50 Charlottesville, VA
–	Graham, Dan	Tacoma	79	12	51	.258	L-R	6-1	205	7/19/54 Phoenix, AZ
		Orlando	–	8	36	.284				
22	Kusick, Craig	Minnesota	68	12	45	.254	R-R	6-3	203	9/30/48 Milwaukee, WI
36	Perlozzo, Sam	Tacoma	110	0	26	.310	R-R	5-9	174	3/4/51 Cumberland, MD
		Minnesota	7	0	0	.292				
–	Pittman, John	Orlando	–	14	60	.263	R-R	6-1	180	5/10/56 Dawson, GA
32	Randall, Bob	Minnesota	73	0	22	.239	R-S	6-0	180	6/10/48 Norton, KS
5	Smalley, Roy	Minnesota	135	6	56	.231	B-R	6-2	195	10/25/52 Los Angeles, CA
–	Soderholm, Dale	Orlando	–	8	47	.241	R-R	6-2	181	7/13/52 Miami, FL
7	Wilfong, Rob	Tacoma	40	2	17	.325	L-R	6-1	177	9/1/53 Pasadena, CA
		Minnesota	42	1	13	.246				
–	Wolfe, Larry	Charleston	–	9	77	.304	R-R	5-11	170	3/2/53 Rancho Cordova, CA
		Minnesota	6	0	6	.240				

OUTFIELDERS

No.	Name	1977 Club	H	HR	RBI	Pct.	B-T	Ht.	Wt.	Born
43	Adams, Glenn	Minnesota	91	6	49	.338	L-R	6-0	185	10/4/47 Northbridge, MASS
12	Chiles, Rich	Minnesota	69	3	36	.264	L-L	6-0	175	11/22/49 Sacramento, CA
38	Edwards, Dave	Tacoma	122	11	80	.269	R-R	6-0	166	2/24/54 Los Angeles, CA
15	Ford, Dan	Minnesota	121	11	60	.267	R-R	6-1	185	5/19/52 Los Angeles, CA
39	Gorinski, Bob	Minnesota	23	3	22	.195	R-R	6-2	220	1/7/52 Calumet, PA
24	Norwood, Willie	Tacoma	82	8	33	.412	R-R	6-0	185	11/7/50 Long Beach, CA
		Minnesota	19	3	9	.229				
–	Powell, Hosken	Tacoma	154	5	51	.326	L-L	6-1	180	5/14/55 Pensacola, FL
–	Rivera, Bombo	Denver	133	17	95	.302	R-R	5-10	186	8/2/52 Ponce, PR
–	Sofield, Rick	Visalia	132	27	107	.328	L-R	6-1	185	12/16/56 Morris Plains, NJ
		Tacoma	3	0	1	.250				
–	Youngbauer, Jeff	Orlando	–	6	49	.292	L-R	6-1	180	8/30/53 Alma, WS

TWIN PROFILES

ROD CAREW 32 6-0 182   Bats L Throws R

The incredible hitting machine . . . Challenged .400 barrier and fell only 12 points short, unbelievable in these days . . . Highest average in majors in 20 years . . . Became sixth player to win more than five bat titles . . . More amazing, won title by margin of 52 points . . . Ultimate team player . . . "What I'd really like to do this year is win a Gold Glove," he said in midst of .400 try. "I'm proud of my defense." . . . Born Oct. 1, 1945, in Gatun, Panama, but raised in New York City . . . "The tough thing about hitting .400 is that it's a long season and toward the end your arms get tired and that affects your swing." . . . Still, he raised average in final weeks.

Year	Club	Pos	G	AB	R	H	2B	3B	HR	RBI	SB	Avg.
1967	Minnesota.......	2B	137	514	66	150	22	7	8	51	5	.292
1968	Minnesota.......	2B-SS	127	461	46	126	27	2	1	42	12	.273
1969	Minnesota.......	2B	123	458	79	152	30	4	8	56	19	.332
1970	Minnesota.......	2B-1B	51	191	27	70	12	3	4	28	4	.366
1971	Minnesota.......	2B-3B	147	577	88	177	16	10	2	48	6	.307
1972	Minnesota.......	2B	142	535	61	170	21	6	0	51	12	.318
1973	Minnesota.......	2B	149	580	98	203	30	11	6	62	41	.350
1974	Minnesota.......	2B	153	599	86	218	30	5	3	55	38	.364
1975	Minnesota.......	2B-1B	143	535	89	192	-24	4	14	80	35	.359
1976	Minnesota.......	1B	156	605	97	200	29	12	9	90	49	.331
1977	Minnesota.......	1B	155	616	128	239	38	16	14	100	23	.388
	Totals..........		1483	5671	865	1897	279	80	69	663	244	.335

BUTCH WYNEGAR 22 6-0 185   Bats S Throws R

Super kid . . . What sophomore jinx? . . . Because of his age, position and being a switch hitter, perhaps the most valuable property in baseball . . . Says Gene Mauch: "It's not easy to catch for me. I demand a lot. But Butch never complained. He's a beautiful kid." . . . Says Butch: "Baseball is my entire life. I do nothing but sleep, eat, watch television and go to the park." . . . Born March 14, 1956, in York, Pa. . . . Harold Delano, but aunt nicknamed him "Butch." . . . A Yankee fan as a kid, his favorite player was Mickey Mantle and started switch-hitting at age nine "because Mantle hit that way."

Year	Club	Pos	G	AB	R	H	2B	3B	HR	RBI	SB	Avg.
1976	Minnesota.......	C	149	534	58	139	21	2	10	69	0	.260
1977	Minnesota.......	C	144	532	76	139	22	3	10	79	2	.261
	Totals..........		293	1066	134	278	43	5	20	148	2	.261

DAVE GOLTZ 28 6-4 210   Bats R Throws R

Hail the arrival. After three years at .500, was one of three AL pitchers to win 20 . . . Working on three-year contract which makes him safe for two more years, Twin fans . . . With Blyleven gone, Twins looked to him for pitching leadership and he met challenge . . . Born June 23, 1949, in Pelican Rapids, Minn. . . . First time over 300 innings, second in league . . . Excellent strikeout-walk ratio of 2-1 . . . An old-fashioned story in these days of central scouting and the free agent draft . . . Was spotted throwing baseball in backyard by Twins' scout.

Year	Club	G	IP	W	L	Pct.	SO	BB	H	ERA
1972	Minnesota	15	91	3	3	.500	38	26	75	2.67
1973	Minnesota	32	106	6	4	.600	65	32	138	5.26
1974	Minnesota	28	174	10	10	.500	89	45	192	3.26
1975	Minnesota	32	243	14	14	.500	128	72	235	3.67
1976	Minnesota	36	249	14	14	.500	133	91	239	3.36
1977	Minnesota	39	303	20	11	.645	186	91	284	3.36
	Totals	182	1166	67	56	.545	639	357	1163	3.53

ROY SMALLEY 25 6-2 195   Bats S Throws R

Trade from Rangers was big break for him. It gave him chance to be regular shortstop . . . "I feel my most valuable asset was as a shortstop, that I was being wasted playing another position." . . . It also gave him chance to play for his uncle, Gene Mauch, brother of Roy's mother . . . Lifted weights in off season and improved HR and RBI production at expense of average . . . Born Oct. 25, 1952, in Los Angeles . . . Dad, Roy, Sr., played 11 years at shortstop for Cubs, Braves, Phillies . . . Starred at USC and drafted No. 1 in country in January, 1973.

Year	Club	Pos	G	AB	R	H	2B	3B	HR	RBI	SB	Avg.
1975	Texas	SS-2B-C	78	250	22	57	8	0	3	33	4	.228
1976	Texas-Minnesota	SS-3B-2B	144	513	61	133	18	3	3	44	2	.259
1977	Minnesota	SS-3B-2B	150	584	93	135	21	5	6	56	5	.231
	Totals		372	1347	176	325	47	8	12	133	11	.241

MIKE CUBBAGE 27 6-0 180   Bats L Throws R

Part of big deal with Texas that brought Smalley to Twins . . . Bounced around infield by Rangers, has settled at third where he is most comfortable . . . "I felt he could play third base when I saw him in Texas," says Gene Mauch . . . Always noted more for his bat, which keeps getting better . . . "I feel I have matured as a hitter." . . . Born July 21, 1950, in

Charlottesville, Va. . . . Outstanding high school quarterback for school that won 53 straight games . . . Chosen high school All-America in football . . . Went to U. of Virginia . . . Also all ACC shortstop and drafted by the then Washington Senators.

Year	Club	Pos	G	AB	R	H	2B	3B	HR	RBI	SB	Avg.
1974	Texas	2B-3B	9	15	0	0	0	0	0	0	0	.000
1975	Texas	2B-3B	58	143	12	32	6	0	4	21	0	.224
1976	Tex.-Min.	3B-2B	118	374	42	96	19	5	3	49	1	.257
1977	Minnesota	2B-3B	129	417	60	110	16	5	9	55	1	.264
	Totals		314	949	114	238	41	10	16	125	2	.251

BOB RANDALL 29 6-3 180   Bats R Throws R

Tall for middle infielder . . . Spent seven years in minors and finally made it as 26-year old rookie . . . Owes his opportunity to switch of Carew from second base to first . . . "I've learned the fundamentals you use in the minors are used in the majors, too." . . . Expert at turning double play and Twins finished first in '76 and second in '77 in double plays with Randall at second . . . Born June 10, 1948, in Norton, Kan. . . . Signed by Dodgers and obtained by Twins in minor-league deal . . . Not on Twins' roster in 1976 but impressed Mauch enough to win job . . . Graduate of Kansas State, has taught school in off-season.

Year	Club	Pos	G	AB	R	H	2B	3B	HR	RBI	SB	Avg.
1976	Minnesota	2B	153	475	55	127	18	4	1	34	3	.267
1977	Minnesota	2B	103	306	36	73	13	2	0	22	1	.239
	Totals		256	781	91	200	31	6	1	56	4	.256

DAN FORD 25 6-1 185   Bats R Throws R

Cut down on strikeouts from 118 to 79, but mysteriously, this didn't have the customary effect as he fell off in all offensive categories . . . Hit first home run in renovated Yankee Stadium . . . Had six-RBI day in '76 . . . Born Darnell Glenn Ford on May 19, 1952, in Los Angeles . . . Drafted by Oakland and traded to Twins . . . Center of one of most amusing stories of year. Oriole manager Earl Weaver, making mistake, ordered Ford walked thinking it was Larry Hisle, on deck . . . Hisle then hit game-winning single.

Year	Club	Pos	G	AB	R	H	2B	3B	HR	RBI	SB	Avg.
1975	Minnesota	OF	130	440	72	123	21	1	15	59	6	.280
1976	Minnesota	OF	145	514	87	137	24	7	20	86	17	.267
1977	Minnesota	OF	144	453	66	121	25	7	11	60	6	.267
	Totals		419	1407	225	381	70	15	46	205	29	.271

TOM JOHNSON 26 6-1 185   Bats R Throws R

Came out of nowhere to fill big shoes vacated by Bill Campbell . . . Seventh in league in saves . . . Teamed with Dave Johnson to form "Band Aid Kids." Johnson and Johnson, get it? . . . "A relief pitcher needs a good arm, a good head and guts," says Gene Mauch. "Johnson has those qualities." . . . Born April 2, 1951, in St. Paul, Minn. . . . A local boy who made good . . . "In the spring of '76, we didn't know how good Campbell would be," Mauch said in the spring of '77. "Maybe this year somebody will come along like Campbell did last year." . . . Enter Johnson.

Year	Club	G	IP	W	L	Pct.	SO	BB	H	ERA
1974	Minnesota	4	7	2	0	1.000	4	0	4	0.00
1975	Minnesota	18	39	1	2	.333	17	21	40	4.15
1976	Minnesota	18	48	3	1	.750	37	8	44	2.63
1977	Minnesota	71	147	16	7	.696	87	47	152	3.12
	Totals	111	241	22	10	.688	145	76	240	3.10

TOP PROSPECTS

ROB WILFONG 24 6-1 177   Bats L Throws R

Came fast and was surprise of Twins' camp, challenging Randall for second base job and hitting over .300 in first 35 games . . . Born Sept. 1, 1953, in Pasadena . . . Played on Pony League World Series finalist in '68, Colt League world champion in '70, American Legion national champ in '71 . . . Won Silver Glove as outstanding defensive second baseman with Orlando in '74.

WILLIE NORWOOD 27 6-0 185   Bats R Throws R

Loss of Hisle and Bostock should give this speedster another opportunity to make it in Twins' outfield . . . Batted .412 in 199 at-bats for Tacoma before moving up to big club . . . Born Nov. 7, 1950, in Green County, Ala. . . . Helped lead LaVerne College to NAIA championship in '72 and was MVP of NAIA tournament . . . Named son Aaron Mays Norwood after his two idols.

JOHNNY SUTTON 25 5-11 185   Bats R Throws R

Chance to make it this year as reliever . . . Won 12 games first pro season at Gastonia . . . Won 10 games with 12 saves for Sacramento in 1976 . . . Rangers No. 3 pick in 1974 draft . . . Born Nov. 13, 1952, in Dallas . . . Obtained from Texas for Mike Wallace . . . Acquirred by Twins during winter . . . Was member of Connie Mack team that won national championship in 1970.

MANAGER GENE MAUCH: Extremely confident and long regarded as dugout genius and most innovative manager in game . . . Angels wanted him to manage this season, but Calvin Griffith refused to let him out of contract . . . "I never realized how smart he was," says Roy Smalley, his nephew . . . Born Nov. 18, 1925, in Salina, Kan. . . . Undistinguished major-league career, playing in 304 games in eight seasons with .239 BA and five HRs . . . Begins 19th consecutive years as major league manager for three teams—Philadelphia, Montreal, Minnesota . . . Leg surgery after season . . . "I don't want a contending team, I want to win."

GREATEST MANAGER

Stanley Raymond (Bucky) Harris was only 27 years old when he became "The Boy Manager" of the Washington Senators in 1924, a choice that was a surprising one to fans and a reluctant one by club owner Clark Griffith.

Harris, the Senators' shortstop, had incurred Griffith's wrath by playing semipro basketball in the off-season against club rules. But when Donie Bush was fired as manager, Griffith realized Harris was the logical choice and he called Harris in Florida to offer him the job.

Harris wired back, "I'll take that job and win Washington's first American League pennant." Then he tipped a Western Union clerk $20 to send the same message every hour for the next four hours.

True to his word, Harris not only won Washington's first AL pennant in 1924, he beat the New York Giants in seven games for Washington's first world championship, then followed up by winning the AL pennant the next year.

Since then the Senators, who moved to Minnesota in 1961, have had four first-place finishes and still have not won another world championship.

ALL-TIME TWIN LEADERS

BATTING: Rod Carew, .388, 1977
HRs: Harmon Killebrew, 49, 1964, 1969
RBIs: Harmon Killebrew, 140, 1969
STEALS: Rod Carew, 49, 1976
WINS: Jim Kaat, 25, 1966
STRIKEOUTS: Bert Blyleven, 258, 1973

A's

(Editor's Note: At the time this book went to press, sale and shift of the Oakland A's to Marvin Davis and Denver had not been formally approved.)

When not bailing out, rookie slugger Wayne Gross hit 22 HRs.

SCOUTING REPORT

HITTING: Money can't hit home runs, it can't steal bases, it can't win games. That's what Charlie Finley found out. He let all those players get away and paid the price last year with a last-place finish. He was last in batting, too, 12 points less than an expansion team.

There were only two bright spots—rookie Wayne Gross, who made the all-star team after a blistering start, then slacked off; and Mitchell Page, who came in a deal with the Pirates and just missed being Rookie-of-the-Year because he missed 17 games with a leg injury. But Gross crashed 22 homers and drove in 63 runs and Page did it all, a .307 average, 21 HRs, 75 RBIs and 42 stolen bases. What the A's need are a few more like them, but they don't have them.

PITCHING: A disaster. The A's won only 63 games last year, had only 32 complete games and four shutouts. Vida Blue accounted for 14 of the wins, half of the complete games, one-fourth of the shutouts and now he's gone, too, another victim of greed. In his place the cupboard is bare, except for a few youngsters who are unproven and inexperienced. The best of these are Rick Langford and Doug Bair, both of whom came in the same deal that brought Page, and rookie Matt Keough.

FIELDING: Another disaster area. The A's were last in fielding, made the most number of errors (190), and fewer double plays than any AL team except the White Sox and Blue Jays. There are new players at almost every position and even Wayne Gross, who made the all-star team at third last year, will be shifted to first to make room for Taylor Duncan, obtained in the major-league draft.

OUTLOOK: As bleak as it ever has been. There is no way the A's can rise above the cellar of the AL West, no matter how sky-high they get. They can't even beat an expansion team. Only one player (Bill North) remains from the glory days and he played in only 56 games last year because of injury. What did Charlie Finley have against North to keep him? Having traded or sold all his players, Finley left the new owner with very little with which to build.

A's 1978 ROSTER

MANAGER Bobby Winkles
Coaches—Cal Ermer, Red Schoendienst, Lee Stange

PITCHERS

No.	Name	1977 Club	W-L	IP	SO	ERA	B-T	Ht.	Wt.	Born
17	Bair, Doug	San Jose	5-2	33	49	2.18	R-R	6-1	170	8/22/49 Defiance, OH
		Oakland	4-6	83	68	3.47				
46	Bell, Ron	Chattanooga	8-9	131	93	2.75	L-R	6-4	198	3/3/53 Long Beach, CA
		San Jose	0-2	20	9	9.45				
15	Coleman, Joe	Oakland	4-4	128	55	2.95	R-R	6-3	195	2/3/47 Boston, MA
24	Dunning, Steve	New Orleans	8-13	179	127	3.93	R-R	6-2	200	5/15/49 Denver, CO
		Oakland	1-0	18	4	4.00				
27	Keough, Matt	Chattanooga	9-12	175	153	3.81	R-R	6-3	190	7/3/55 Pomona, CA
		Oakland	1-3	43	23	4.81				
47	Kingman, Brian	San Jose	3-6	60	47	7.35	R-R	6-1	190	7/27/54 Los Angeles, CA
34	Lacey, Bob	San Jose	2-0	16	9	0.00	R-L	6-4	190	8/25/53 Fredericksburg, VA
		Oakland	6-8	122	69	3.02				
22	Langford, Rick	Oakland	8-19	208	141	4.02	R-R	6-0	180	3/20/52 Farmville, VA
54	McCatty, Steve	Chattanooga	4-2	56	39	1.93	R-R	6-3	195	3/20/54 Detroit, MI
		San Jose	7-8	146	78	5.73				
		Oakland	0-0	14	9	5.14				
29	Mitchell, Craig	San Jose	10-11	189	118	4.48	R-R	6-3	190	4/14/54 Santa Rosa, CA
		Oakland	0-1	6	1	7.50				
16	Norris, Mike	San Jose	3-2	46	35	3.52	R-R	6-2	172	3/19/55 San Francisco, CA
		Oakland	2-7	77	35	4.79				
28	Torrealba, Pablo	Oakland	4-6	117	51	2.62	L-L	5-9	159	4/28/48 Estado Lara, Ven.
23	Tronerud, Rick	Modesto	0-0	7	3	5.14	R-R	6-2	200	9/18/53 Minneapolis, MN

CATCHERS

No.	Name	1977 Club	H	HR	RBI	Pct.	B-T	Ht.	Wt.	Born
40	Haines, Dennis	San Jose	79	5	52	.276	L-R	6-2	210	1/24/52 McCloud, CA
25	Hosley, Tim	San Jose	79	9	54	.321	R-R	5-10	195	5/10/47 Spartanburg, SC
		Oakland	15	1	10	.192				
5	Newman, Jeff	Oakland	36	4	15	.222	R-R	6-2	218	9/11/48 Fort Worth, TX
48	Robinson, Bruce	Chattanooga	53	3	24	.275	L-R	6-2	195	4/16/54 La Jolla, CA
		San Jose	41	5	21	.229				
35	Sanguillen, Manny	Oakland	157	6	58	.275	R-R	6-0	189	3/21/44 Colon, Panama
32	Williams, Earl	Oakland	84	13	38	.241	R-R	6-3	220	7/14/48 Newark, NJ

INFIELDERS

No.	Name	1977 Club	H	HR	RBI	Pct.	B-T	Ht.	Wt.	Born
—	Duncan, Taylor	Rochester	148	27	76	.301	R-R	6-0	170	5/12/53 Memphis, TN
		St. Louis	4	1	2	.333				
10	Gross, Wayne	Oakland	113	22	63	.233	L-R	6-2	205	1/14/52 Riverside, CA
21	Lintz, Larry	San Jose	33	0	15	.270	B-R	5-10	150	10/10/49 Martinez, CA
		Oakland	4	0	0	.133				
9	McKinney, Rich	San Jose	11	3	9	.239	R-R	5-11	188	11/22/46 Piqua, OH
		Oakland	35	6	21	.177				
8	Picciolo, Rob	San Jose	8	1	4	.211	R-R	6-2	185	2/4/53 Santa Monica, CA
		Oakland	84	2	22	.200				
—	Revering, Dave	Indianapolis	133	29	110	.300	L-R	6-4	205	2/12/53 Roseville, CA
3	Scott, Rodney	Oakland	95	0	20	.261	B-R	6-0	160	10/16/53 Indianapolis, IN
12	Tabb, Jerry	San Jose	98	11	45	.344	L-R	6-2	195	3/17/52 Altus, OK
		Oakland	32	6	19	.222				

OUTFIELDERS

No.	Name	1977 Club	H	HR	RBI	Pct.	B-T	Ht.	Wt.	Born
2	Alexander, Matt	Oakland	10	0	2	.238	B-R	5-11	170	1/30/47 Shreveport, LA
11	Armas, Tony	Oakland	87	13	53	.240	R-R	6-1	182	7/12/53 Anzoategui, Ven.
30	Cosey, Ray	Chatanooga	101	8	49	.255	L-L	5-11	185	12/5/56 San Rafael, CA
19	Mallory, Sheldon	San Jose	17	1	17	.262	L-L	6-2	165	7/16/53 Argo, IL
		Oakland	27	0	5	.214				
36	Murphy, Dwayne	Chattanooga	104	5	53	.256	L-R	6-1	180	3/18/55 Merced, CA
20	Murray, Larry	San Jose	32	1	12	.364	B-R	5-11	180	3/1/53 Chicago, IL
		Oakland	29	1	9	.179				
4	North, Bill	Oakland	48	1	9	.261	B-R	5-11	185	5/15/48 Seattle, WA
6	Page, Mitchell	Oakland	154	21	75	.307	L-R	6-2	205	10/15/51 Compton, CA
26	Tyrone, Jim	San Jose	34	6	20	.347	R-R	6-1	185	1/29/49 Alice, TX
		Oakland	72	5	26	.245				
31	Williams, Mark	San Jose	135	9	88	.277	L-L	6-0	180	7/28/53 Elmira, NY
		Oakland	0	0	1	.000				

A's PROFILES

MANNY SANGUILLEN 34 6-0 189   **Bats R Throws R**

Perpetual smile . . . Traded to A's from Pirates for manager Chuck Tanner . . . "I'll trade a manager for a player any time," said Charles O. Finley . . . One of best hitters in majors for years, but reluctant walker, only 209 in 10 seasons . . . Born March 21, 1944, in Colon, Panama . . . Played basketball, soccer, ran track in HS . . . No baseball . . . Helped start baseball program at Pan American Bible School . . . Four times a .300 hitter, rare for catcher.

Year	Club	Pos	G	AB	R	H	2B	3B	HR	RBI	SB	Avg.
1967	Pittsburgh	C	30	96	6	26	4	0	0	8	0	.271
1969	Pittsburgh	C	129	459	62	139	21	6	5	57	8	.303
1970	Pittsburgh	C	128	486	63	158	19	9	7	61	2	.325
1971	Pittsburgh	C	138	533	60	170	26	5	7	81	6	.319
1972	Pittsburgh	C-OF	136	520	55	155	18	8	7	71	1	.298
1973	Pittsburgh	C-OF	149	589	64	166	26	7	12	65	2	.282
1974	Pittsburgh	C	151	596	77	171	21	4	7	68	2	.287
1975	Pittsburgh	C	133	481	60	158	24	4	9	58	5	.328
1976	Pittsburgh	C	114	389	52	113	16	6	2	36	2	.290
1977	Oakland	C-OF	152	571	42	157	17	5	6	58	2	.275
	Totals		1260	4720	541	1413	192	54	62	563	30	.299

BILL NORTH 29 5-11 185   **Bats S Throws R**

Series of nagging injuries caused him to miss more than 100 games and lose chance at second consecutive stolen base title . . . First time under 140 games since coming to A's . . . "Every time I came back and got going, I got injured." . . . Hurt hand, foot, ankle . . . Also problems with Finley . . . Punished when he called A's "inept." . . . "It's been a long year, but I can see the light at the end of the tunnel. It's called October," said North . . . Finley responded: "Yes and until October comes, Bill, I'll have someone playing center field who can do the job as well as you." . . . Born May 15, 1948, in Seattle . . . Signed by Cubs and traded to A's in one of many excellent deals by Finley.

Year	Club	Pos	G	AB	R	H	2B	3B	HR	RBI	SB	Avg.
1971	Chicago (NL)	OF	8	16	3	6	0	0	0	0	1	.375
1972	Chicago (NL)	OF	66	127	22	23	2	3	0	4	6	.181
1973	Oakland	OF	146	554	98	158	10	5	5	34	53	.285
1974	Oakland	OF	149	543	79	141	20	5	4	33	54	.260
1975	Oakland	OF	140	524	74	143	17	5	1	43	30	.273
1976	Oakland	OF	154	590	91	163	20	5	2	31	75	.276
1977	Oakland	OF	56	184	32	48	3	3	1	9	17	.261
	Totals		719	2538	399	682	72	26	13	154	246	.269

WAYNE GROSS 26 6-2 205   Bats L Throws R

Cooled off after explosive start put him among league's RBI and HR leaders and earned him All-Star Game selection . . . Still a highly regarded prospect who should get better . . . 52 homers in three minor league seasons before coming up . . . Born Jan. 14, 1952, in Riverside, Cal. . . . All-America honorable mention in football while in high school . . . Attended Cal Poly and was all-coast in football, third in nation in punting in 1972 with 42.1 average . . . But chose baseball and was A's sixth selection in June, 1973 free agent draft . . . Also hit by injury jinx that plagued A's last year.

Year	Club	Pos	G	AB	R	H	2B	3B	HR	RBI	SB	Avg.
1976	Oakland	1B-OF	10	18	0	4	0	0	0	1	0	.222
1977	Oakland	3B-1B-OF	146	485	66	113	21	1	22	63	5	.233
	Totals		156	503	66	117	21	1	22	64	5	.233

RICK LANGFORD 26 6-0 180   Bats R Throws R

Also obtained in Phil Garner deal . . . Got reprieve from being farmed out when ex-manager Jack McKeon changed his mind two days before season opener . . . Won first three games and earned $10,000 raise from Charles O. Finley . . . Helped as reliever by vet Dave Giusti . . . "If he keeps pitching like that, he won't need any more schooling," said Giusti . . . Born March 20, 1952, in Farmville, Va. . . . Balding, which makes him appear older than his years . . . Almost quit baseball at 21 because of two deaths in family . . . Talked back by late Danny Murtaugh.

Year	Club	G	IP	W	L	Pct.	SO	BB	H	ERA
1976	Pittsburgh	12	23	0	1	.000	17	14	27	6.26
1977	Oakland	37	208	8	19	.296	141	73	223	4.02
	Totals	49	231	8	20	.286	158	87	250	4.29

EARL WILLIAMS 29 6-3 220   Bats R Throws R

Much-traveled players . . . A's were his fourth team in last six years . . . Was National League Rookie-of-Year for Braves in '72, but indicated he disliked catching and traded after two seasons . . . 138 homers in eight seasons . . . Born July 14, 1948, in Newark, N.J. . . . Also hit by injury jinx that ran rampant through A's, suffering fractured wrist . . . Stole his first base

in major league career after 824 games vs. Thurman Munson . . .
He had held major-league record streak for no steals and question
is, with a record like that, what made A's even let him attempt
steal?

Year	Club	Pos	G	AB	R	H	2B	3B	HR	RBI	SB	Avg.
1970	Atlanta..........	1B-3B	10	19	4	7	4	0	0	5	0	.368
1971	Atlanta..........	C-3B-1B	145	497	64	129	14	1	33	87	0	.260
1972	Atlanta..........	C-3B-1B	151	565	72	146	24	2	28	87	0	.258
1973	Baltimore........	C-1B	132	459	58	109	18	1	22	83	0	.237
1974	Baltimore........	C-1B	118	413	47	105	16	0	14	52	0	.254
1975	Atlanta..........	1B-C	111	383	42	92	13	0	11	50	0	.240
1976	Atl.-Mtl.........	1B-C	122	374	35	84	13	2	17	55	0	.225
1977	Oakland.........	1B-C	100	348	39	84	13	0	13	38	2	.241
	Totals..........		889	3058	361	756	115	6	138	457	2	.247

JOE COLEMAN 31 6-3 195   Bats R Throws R

"Junior." . . . Suddenly a veteran pitcher hoping for comeback with Denver's depleted A's . . . Born Feb. 3, 1947, in Boston . . . Dad, Joe, Sr., pitched 10 years in American League in Philadelphia, Baltimore, Detroit . . . Drafted by Senators, Joe, Jr., was part of big deal that sent Denny McLain to Senators, Joe to Tigers . . . Deal was announced by commissioner Bowie Kuhn . . . Won 20 games twice for Tigers and pitched game that tied 1972 AL playoffs at 2-2, easily his biggest win of career.

Year	Club	G	IP	W	L	Pct.	SO	BB	H	ERA
1965	Washington	2	18	2	0	1.000	7	8	9	1.50
1966	Washington	1	9	1	0	1.000	4	2	6	2.00
1967	Washington	28	134	8	9	.471	77	47	154	4.63
1968	Washington	33	223	12	16	.429	139	51	212	3.27
1969	Washington	40	248	12	13	.480	182	100	222	3.27
1970	Washington	39	219	8	12	.400	152	89	190	3.58
1971	Detroit..................	39	286	20	9	.690	236	96	241	3.15
1972	Detroit..................	40	280	19	14	.576	222	110	216	2.80
1973	Detroit..................	40	288	23	15	.605	202	93	283	3.53
1974	Detroit..................	41	286	14	12	.538	177	158	272	4.31
1975	Detroit..................	31	201	10	18	.357	125	85	234	5.55
1976	Detroit..................	12	67	2	5	.286	38	34	80	4.84
1976	Chicago (NL)	39	79	2	8	.200	66	35	72	4.10
1977	Oakland.................	43	128	4	4	.500	55	49	114	2.95
	Totals..................	428	2466	137	135	.504	1682	957	2305	3.67

MITCHELL PAGE 26 6-2 205   Bats L Throws L

The Rage . . . Another fantastic Charlie Finley deal . . . Got him in return for Phil Garner and Mitch tore up league from start . . . Played with hand injury that caused mid-season slump, finally forced to miss 17 games . . . Still finished with impressive stats . . . Set AL record with 27 consecutive steals . . . "They told me I could get him out with off speed pitches," said Catfish Hunter after Page drove an off-speed pitch out of sight . . . When a sportswriter said he would not win Rookie-of-Year because his low HR total, Page hit three in two days and told writer, "That was for you."

Year	Club	Pos	G	AB	R	H	2B	3B	HR	RBI	SB	Avg.
1977	Oakland.........	OF	145	501	85	154	28	8	21	75	42	.307

TOP PROSPECTS

MATT KEOUGH 22 6-3 190   **Bats R Throws R**
Signed as outfielder, he had one outstanding year, 1975, with 81 RBIs, .303 average . . . But slumped in '76 and converted to pitcher because of great arm . . . Led Southern League in Strikeouts . . . Born July 3, 1955, in Westwood, Cal. . . . His dad, Marty, played OF for six major-league clubs . . . Majoring in pre-law at UCLA in off-season.

DAVE REVERING 25 6-4 205   **Bats L Throws R**
Another promising slugger who was buried in Reds' organization . . . Will get chance with A's . . . Batted .300 with 29 homers and 110 RBIs for Indianapolis . . . Plays first base . . . Big and strong and a pull hitter . . . Born Feb. 12, 1953, in Roseville, Cal. . . . Has had at least 20 homers his last three minor-league seasons . . . A No. 7 pick in 1971.

MANAGER BOBBY WINKLES: Probably the most successful college baseball coach of all-time . . . His alumni from Arizona State would make a Who's Who list . . . Reggie Jackson, Sal Bando, Duffy Dyer, Rick Monday, Gary Gentry . . . NCAA championship three times . . . College record 524-173 . . . Played in minor leagues seven seasons as infielder, getting as high as Tulsa in Texas League . . . Left college to become Angels coach 1972 . . . Named manager in '73 and held job two seasons . . . Coached at Oakland and San Francisco, where he was when Jack McKeon was fired . . . Became Charlie Finley's 14th manager in 17 years.

GREATEST MANAGER

It is one of the great ironies of baseball that today's A's, who have changed managers like Charlie Finley changes shirts, are descendants of the old Philadelphia Athletics, who changed managers like Jack Benny changed $10 bills.

Finley had 14 managers in 17 years in Kansas City and Oakland and two of them, Alvin Dark and Hank Bauer, served two terms.

By contrast, the Philadelphia Athletics had only three mangers in 54 years, one of them serving in the job for 50 years. As part owner of the club, Connie Mack (his real name was Cornelius Alexander McGillicuddy), never had to worry about job security. He managed until he was 88 years old, finally giving way to a younger man, 54-year-old Jimmie Dykes, midway in the 1950 season.

With his business suit and starched collar, his flat top straw hat and the inevitable rolled-up scorecard with which he used to position fielders with an almost imperceptible wave, Mr. Mack was a familiar figure in the Philadelphia dugout for five decades. And having been there so long, he set records that, undoubtedly, will never be approached for games managed (7,878), won (3,776) and lots (4,025).

ALL-TIME A's LEADERS

BATTING: Napoleon Lajoie, .422, 1901
HRs: Jimmy Foxx, 58, 1932
RBIs: Jimmy Foxx, 169, 1932
STEALS: Eddie Collins, 81, 1910
WINS: John Coombs, 31, 1910
       Lefty Grove, 31, 1931
STRIKEOUTS: Rube Waddell, 349, 1904

SEATTLE MARINERS

TEAM DIRECTORY: General Partners: Stanley Golub, Danny Kaye, Walter Schoenfeld, Lester M. Smith, James Stillwell, James A. Walsh; Exec. Dir.-GM: Dick Vertlieb; Dir. of Baseball Operations: Lou Gorman; Dir. of Farm System and Scouting: Mel Didier; Dir. Pub. Rel.: Hal Childs; Mgr.: Darrell Johnson; Home: Kingdome (59,059). Field distances: 316, l.f. line; 405, c.f.; 316, r.f. line. Spring Training: Tempe, Ariz.

Mariners' All-Star Game rep Ruppert Jones socked 24 homers.

SCOUTING REPORT

HITTING: Opportunity knocked with expansion and people like Lee Stanton, Ruppert Jones, Bill Stein and Dan Meyer answered. They never would have had a chance with their old clubs. As a result, the Mariners finished ahead of three other teams in batting and six others in home runs, not bad for a new club. And they figure to improve, with experience and with the addition of proven hitters, Bruce Bochte (free agent), Leon Roberts (trade) and John Hale (purchase). The Mariners were particularly tough at home and, when you think about an expansion team, the Mariners were lucky to come up with four players—Jones, Stein, Meyer and Stanton—who combined for 86 homers and 343 RBIs.

PITCHING: The weak link for the Mariners, who were dead last in the league with a team ERA of 4.83. But the arms are young and the hope is that Glenn Abbott, Rick Honeycutt, Rick Jones, Paul Mitchell, John Montague and Gary Wheelock will some day form a respectable staff. In addition to those mentioned, the Mariners added Steve Hamrick, Jim Todd, Rick Baldwin and Mike Parrott. And they still have ageless Enrique Romo, a great find with his eight wins and 16 saves.

FIELDING: Playing on artificial turf gave the expansion Mariners an advantage at home where visiting clubs had trouble adjusting. The Mariners finished ahead of four clubs in defense and only three topped their 162 double plays. Craig Reynolds, obtained from the Pirates, took over at shortstop and did a creditable job, teaming with a variety of second baseman for an effective DP combination. In only his rookie season, Ruppert Jones was a skillful player, both at bat and in the field. He made only nine errors in 485 chances, took part in three double plays, had 11 assists and should be an outstanding center fielder for the Mariners for years.

OUTLOOK: The Mariners did extemely well in their first major-league season. They avoided losing 100 games and won 10 more than their expansion cousins, the Blue Jays. They also avoided the cellar of the AL West, but then they were fortunate to be in the same division as the Oakland Nobodies. And the way the Twins are losing players, the Mariners have an outside chance to move up another notch this year.

SEATTLE MARINERS 1978 ROSTER

MANAGER Darrell Johnson

Coaches—Don Bryant, Jim Busby, Vada Pinson, Wes Stock

PITCHERS

No.	Name	1977 Club	W-L	IP	SO	ERA	B-T	Ht.	Wt.	Born
17	Abbott, Glenn	Seattle	12-13	204	100	4.46	R-R	6-6	200	2/16/51 Little Rock, AR
—	Baldwin, Rick	Tidewater	4-1	—	—	2.25	L-R	6-3	180	6/1/53 Fresno, CA
		N.Y. (NL)	1-2	63	23	4.43				
39	Burke, Steve	Jacksonville	6-6	95	—	3.22	R-R	6-2	200	3/5/55 Stockton, CA
		Seattle	0-1	16	6	2.81				
35	Erardi, Greg	W. Haven-Holyoke	10-9	97	—	2.66	R-R	6-1	190	5/31/54 Syracuse, NY
		Spokane	0-0	6	—	28.50				
		Seattle	0-1	9	5	6.00				
19	Galasso, Bob	Toledo	4-4	60	—	3.45	L-R	6-0	205	1/13/52 Connellsville, PA
		New Orleans	1-2	20	—	2.70				
		Seattle	0-6	35	21	9.00				
—	Hamrick, Steve	Wichita	6-11	135	96	4.87	R-L	6-1	195	4/17/52 Cleveland, OH
40	Honeycutt, Rick	Shreveport	10-6	135	—	2.47	L-L	6-1	190	6/29/52 Chattanooga, TN
		Seattle	0-1	29	17	4.34				
29	House, Tom	Boston-Seattle	5-5	97	45	4.64	L-L	5-10	175	4/29/47 Seattle, WA
46	Jones, Rick	Wichita	0-2	11	—	6.75	L-L	6-5	195	4/16/55 Jacksonville, FL
		Seattle	1-4	42	16	5.14				
37	Kekich, Mike	Seattle	5-4	90	55	5.60	L-L	6-2	205	4/2/45 San Diego, CA
24	MacCormack, Frank	Bellingham	3-2	27	—	8.33	R-R	6-4	210	9/21/54 Jersey City, NJ
		Seattle	0-0	7	4	3.86				
30	McLaughlin, Byron	Nuevo Lardo	18-13	244	—	1.84	R-R	6-1	175	9/29/55 Van Nuys, CA
		Seattle	0-0	1	1	36.00				
34	Mitchell, Paul	Oak-Seattle	3-6	53	25	6.45	R-R	6-1	195	8/19/50 Worcester, MA
25	Montague, John	Seattle	8-12	182	98	4.30	R-R	6-2	205	9/12/47 Newport News, VA
—	Parrott, Mike	Rochester	15-7	184	146	3.42	R-R	6-4	205	12/6/54 Oxnard, CA
		Baltimore	0-0	4	2	2.25				
45	Pole, Dick	Seattle	7-12	122	51	5.16	R-R	6-3	215	10/13/50 Trout Creek, MI
—	Rawley, Shane	Den-Ind	6-10	152	92	4.75	L-R	6-0	170	7/27/55 Racine, WI
43	Romo, Enrique	Seattle	8-10	114	105	2.84	R-R	5-11	185	7/15/47 Baja Calif., Mex.
—	Todd, Jim	Wichita	3-0	27	—	1.33	L-R	6-2	195	9/21/47 Lancaster, PA
		Chicago(NL)	1-1	31	17	9.00				
16	Wheelock, Gary	Seattle	6-9	88	47	4.91	R-R	6-3	210	11/29/51 Bakersfield, CA

CATCHERS

No.	Name	1977 Club	H	HR	RBI	Pct.	B-T	Ht.	Wt.	Born
3	Jutze, Skip	Seattle	24	3	15	.200	R-R	5-11	190	5/28/47 Bayside, NY
18	Pasley, Kevin	Los Angeles	1	0	0	.333	R-R	6-0	185	7/22/53 Bronx, NY
		Albuquerque	109	1	58	.304				
		Seattle	5	0	2	.385				
15	Stinson, Bob	Seattle	80	8	32	.269	B-R	5-11	185	10/11/45 Elkin, NC

INFIELDERS

No.	Name	1977 Club	H	HR	RBI	Pct.	B-T	Ht.	Wt.	Born
14	Baez, Jose	Seattle	79	1	17	.259	R-R	5-9	150	12/31/53 San Cristobal, D.R.
—	Bochte, Bruce	Cal-Cleve	148	7	51	.301	L-L	6-3	195	11/12/50 Pasadena, CA
—	Beamon, Charlie	Omaha	43	2	22	.246	L-L	6-0	170	12/4/53 Oakland, CA
		San Jose	47	2	25	.229				
26	Bernhardt, Juan	Seattle	74	7	30	.243	R-R	6-0	175	8/31/53 San Pedro de Macoris, D.R.
2	Cruz, Julio	Hawaii	111	0	33	.366	B-R	5-9	160	12/2/54 Brooklyn, NY
		Seattle	51	1	7	.256				
21	McMillan, Tom	Rochester	26	0	12	.274	R-R	5-10	165	9/13/51 Richmond, VA
		New Orleans	10	0	2	.238				
		Seattle	0	0	0	.000				
7	Meyer, Dan	Seattle	159	22	90	.273	L-R	5-11	180	8/3/52 Hamilton, Ont.
10	Milbourne, Larry	Seattle	53	2	21	.219	B-R	6-0	155	2/14/51 Port Norris, NJ
12	Reynolds, Craig	Seattle	104	4	28	.248	L-R	6-1	175	12/27/52 Houston, TX
—	Robertson, Bob		Did Not Play				R-R	6-1	210	10/2/46 Frostburg, MD
1	Stein, Bill	Seattle	144	13	67	.259	R-R	5-10	170	1/21/47 Battle Creek, MI

OUTFIELDERS

No.	Name	1977 Club	H	HR	RBI	Pct.	B-T	Ht.	Wt.	Born
4	Braun, Steve	Seattle	106	5	31	.235	L-R	5-10	175	5/8/48 Trenton, NJ
5	Collins, Dave	Seattle	96	5	28	.239	B-L	6-0	175	10/20/52 Rapid City, SD
23	Delgado, Luis	Pawtucket	132	7	53	.281	R-L	5-11	170	2/2/54 Hatillo, P.R.
		Seattle	4	0	2	.182				
—	Hale, John	Los Angeles	26	2	11	.241	L-R	6-2	195	8/5/53 Fresno, CA
		Albuquerque	16	0	12	.340				
9	Jones, Ruppert	Seattle	157	24	76	.263	L-L	5-10	170	3/12/55 Dallas, TX
—	Roberts, Leon	Charleston	79	2	34	.299	R-R	6-3	200	1/22/51 Kalamazoo, MI
		Houston	2	0	2	.074				
36	Stanton, Lee	Seattle	125	27	90	.275	R-R	6-1	200	4/10/46 Latta, SC

MARINER PROFILES

RUPPERT JONES 23 5-10 170   Bats L Throws L

No. 1 pick in expansion draft, he more than vindicated the choice . . . Outstanding rookie season . . . Center field fans are "Rupe's Troops." . . . His HR broke Dennis Eckersley's consecutive hitless inning streak and chance at Cy Young's record . . . "Roop, Roop, Roop" roared crowd . . . Born March 12, 1955, in Dallas, but moved to California at young age and batted .457 his senior year at Berkeley High, alma mater of Yankee manager Billy Martin . . . Chosen off roster of Royals, who were loaded with young players . . . "With Kansas City, I probably would have been sent back to the minors and I wouldn't have reported. I'm happy here."

Year	Club	Pos	G	AB	R	H	2B	3B	HR	RBI	SB	Avg.
1976	Kansas City	OF	28	51	9	11	1	1	1	7	0	.216
1977	Seattle	OF	160	597	85	157	26	8	24	76	13	.263
	Totals		188	648	94	168	27	9	25	83	13	.259

DAN MEYER 25 5-11 180   Bats L Throws R

Disappointment in Detroit, he showed bat potential in Seattle . . . Second on club in HRs, tied for first in RBIs . . . Found a home at first base after unhappy tour in left field for Tigers . . . Steady play and confidence made him a hitter . . . Born Aug. 3, 1952, in Hamilton, Ohio . . . 10 for 10 in steals in '76, although not known for speed . . . Batted over .400 in three straight seasons in high school . . . Attended U. of Arizona and Santa Ana Junior College before signing with Tigers.

Year	Club	Pos	G	AB	R	H	2B	3B	HR	RBI	SB	Avg.
1974	Detroit	OF	13	50	5	10	1	1	3	7	1	.200
1975	Detroit	OF-1B	122	470	56	111	17	3	8	47	8	.236
1976	Detroit	OF-1B	105	294	37	74	8	4	2	16	10	.252
1977	Seattle	OF-1B	159	582	75	159	24	4	22	90	11	.273
	Totals		399	1396	173	354	50	12	35	160	30	.254

LEE STANTON 32 6-1 200   Bats R Throws R

Comeback year . . . Led Mariners in HRs, tied with Meyer in RBIs . . . Won pre-game homer hitting contest against Royals . . . "Last year with the Angels, I didn't play regularly. I was platooned and I got down. Here I'm playing every day and I'm happy." . . . Born April 10, 1946, in Latta, S.C. . . . Originally property of Mets, but sent to Angels with Nolan Ryan in

Jim Fregosi deal . . . Quiet, soft-spoken individual with great faith in others, and himself.

Year	Club	Pos	G	AB	R	H	2B	3B	HR	RBI	SB	Avg.
1970	New York (NL)...	OF	4	4	0	1	0	1	0	0	0	.250
1971	New York (NL)...	OF	5	21	2	4	1	0	0	2	0	.190
1972	California........	OF	127	402	44	101	15	3	12	39	2	.251
1973	California........	OF	119	306	41	72	9	2	8	34	3	.235
1974	California........	OF	118	415	48	111	21	2	11	62	10	.267
1975	California........	OF	137	440	67	115	20	3	14	82	18	.261
1976	California........	OF	93	231	12	44	13	1	2	25	2	.190
1977	Seattle..........	OF	133	454	56	125	24	1	27	90	0	.275
	Totals...........		736	2273	270	573	103	13	74	334	35	.252

ENRIQUE ROMO 30 5-11 185   Bats R Throws R

Spent 11 years in Mexican League before coming to Mariners . . . Purchased for $75,000 after 20-4, 1.89 ERA and 239 Ks in 233 innings for Mexico City Reds in 1976 . . . His eight wins and 16 saves are remarkable for team that won only 64 games . . . "Enrique Romo is the best reliever in the American League," said manager Darrell Johnson . . . Born July 15, 1947, in Santa Rosalia, Mexico . . . Brother Vicente pitched for Indians and Red Sox . . . Converted from starter to reliever to fill Mariner need and because he is a veteran pitcher.

Year	Club	G	IP	W	L	Pct.	SO	BB	H	ERA
1977	Seattle.................	58	114	8	10	.444	105	39	93	2.84

GLENN ABBOTT 27 6-6 200   Bats R Throws R

Always considered outstanding prospect, may have acquired experience he needed with Mariners last year . . . Had seven-game win streak and finished one victory below all-time record for wins by pitcher on first year expansion club . . . Born Feb. 16, 1951, in Little Rock, Ark., spent entire career in Oakland system until taken by Mariners in expansion draft . . . Won 18 for Tucson in 1973 . . . Pitched one perfect inning in relief of Vida Blue in game in which four Oakland pitchers shared no-hitter on final day of 1975 season.

Year	Club	G	IP	W	L	Pct.	SO	BB	H	ERA
1973	Oakland.................	5	19	1	0	1.000	6	7	16	3.79
1974	Oakland.................	19	96	5	7	.417	38	34	89	3.00
1975	Oakland.................	30	114	5	5	.500	51	50	109	4.26
1976	Oakland.................	19	62	2	4	.333	27	16	87	5.52
1977	Seattle.................	36	204	12	13	.480	100	56	212	4.46
	Totals.................	109	495	25	29	.463	222	163	513	4.22

CRAIG REYNOLDS 25 6-1 175   Bats R Throws R

Obtained for Grant Jackson one day after expansion draft . . . Became Mariners regular shortstop . . . Highly touted by Pirates, who had no room for him with Frank Taveras at short and Rennie Stennett at second . . . Drafted and signed as outfielder, was converted to shortstop in 1971 . . . Was International League all-star shortstop in 1975, teaming with Yankees' Willie Randolph for all-star double play combo . . . Born Dec. 27, 1952, in Houston . . . All-city and all-district in baseball and basketball, also school president in high school.

Year	Club	Pos	G	AB	R	H	2B	3B	HR	RBI	SB	Avg.
1975	Pittsburgh	SS	31	76	8	17	3	0	0	4	0	.224
1976	Pittsburgh	SS-2B	7	4	1	1	0	0	1	1	0	.250
1977	Seattle	SS-2B	135	420	41	104	12	3	4	28	6	.248
	Totals		173	500	50	122	15	3	5	33	6	.244

JUAN BERNHARDT 24 6-0 175   Bats R Throws R

Blistering start put him among league leaders, until the freeze came . . . Always hits well early in season, according to Brave manager Bobby Cox, who managed him in minors . . . "In the spring, Juan can hit in the league above this one," said Cox . . . Born Aug. 31, 1953, in San Pedro, Dominican Republic . . . Represented homeland in 1971 Pan American games . . . Always a good hitter, batted over .300 in four minor-league seasons in Yankee chain . . . Trouble was always finding a place for him to play . . . Was tried at first, second, third and outfield and wound up DH.

Year	Club	Pos	G	AB	R	H	2B	3B	HR	RBI	SB	Avg.
1976	New York (AL)	OF	10	21	1	4	1	0	0	1	0	.190
1977	Seattle	OF-DH	89	305	32	74	9	2	7	30	2	.243
	Totals		99	326	33	78	10	2	7	31	2	.239

STEVE BRAUN 29 5-10 175   Bats L Throws R

He had the opportunity, the desire and the attitude, but still came up with poorest year of very productive seven-year career . . . Looked forward to playing for Mariners. Even agreed to sign one-year contract with Twins in '76 if he was guaranteed he'd be exposed to expansion draft . . . "My second career," he called playing in Seattle . . . His only child was also born day he was selected by Mariners . . . Born May 8, 1948, in Trenton, N.J. . . . Always an excellent hitter without a position, must now aim for comeback.

Year	Club	Pos	G	AB	R	H	2B	3B	HR	RBI	SB	Avg.
1971	Minnesota	3B-2B-SS-Of	128	343	51	87	12	2	5	35	8	.254
1972	Minnesota	3B-2B-SS-OF	121	402	40	116	21	0	2	50	4	.289
1973	Minnesota	3B-OF	115	361	46	102	28	5	6	42	4	.283
1974	Minnesota	OF-3B	129	453	53	127	12	1	8	40	4	.280
1975	Minnesota	OF-3B	136	453	70	137	18	3	11	45	0	.302
1976	Minnesota	OF-3B	122	417	73	120	12	3	3	61	12	.288
1977	Seattle	OF	139	451	51	106	19	1	5	31	8	.235
	Totals		890	2880	384	795	122	15	40	304	40	.276

BILL STEIN 31 5-10 170   Bats R Throws R

Played five different positions for White Sox in 1976, but was Mariner third baseman all season and responded with best year . . . Born Jan. 21, 1947, in Battle Creek, Mich., moved to Cocoa, Fla., as youngster . . . All-county, all-state in basketball, baseball . . . Collegiate All-America at Southern Illinois University . . . Originally property of Cardinals and played in 46 games for them . . . Pitched one game in Tulsa in 1971, going six innings with no decision.

Year	Club	Pos	G	AB	R	H	2B	3B	HR	RBI	SB	Avg.
1972	St. Louis	3B-OF	14	35	2	11	0	1	2	3	1	.314
1973	St. Louis	1B-3B-OF	32	55	4	12	2	0	0	2	0	.218
1974	Chicago (AL)	3B	13	43	5	12	1	0	0	5	0	.279
1975	Chicago (AL)	2B-3B-OF	76	226	23	61	7	1	3	21	2	.270
1976	Chicago (AL)	INF-OF	117	392	32	105	15	2	4	36	4	.268
1977	Seattle	2B-3B-OF	151	556	53	144	26	5	13	67	3	.259
	Totals		403	1307	119	345	51	9	22	134	10	.264

BRUCE BOCHTE 27 6-3 200   Bats L Throws L

Went to Indians in early 1977 deal with California and came to Mariners as a free agent in December . . . Angels' top hitter in 1975, but fell off in 1976 . . . His .301 average led the Tribe, and he did it mostly on singles . . . Born Nov. 11, 1950, in Pasadena, Cal. . . . Holds finance degree from Santa Clara U., where he played basketball and baseball . . . Angels' second selection in June, 1972 free agent draft . . . Spent part of

'75 winter on a goodwill tour of Japan . . . Never hit lower than
.319 in minors, with top of .355 at Salt Lake City.

Year	Club	Pos	G	AB	R	H	2B	3B	HR	RBI	SB	Avg.
1974	California........	OF-1B	57	196	24	53	4	1	5	26	6	.270
1975	California........	1B	107	375	41	107	19	3	3	48	3	.285
1976	California........	OF-DH-1B	146	466	53	120	17	1	2	49	4	.258
1977	Cal.-Cle..........	OF-DH-1B	137	492	64	148	23	1	7	51	6	.301
	Totals..........		447	1529	182	428	63	6	17	174	19	.280

TOP PROSPECT

CHARLIE BEAMON 24 6-0 170   **Bats L Throws L**
Drafted on minor-league level, but may prove to be steal . . . Out
of KC organization, where Lou Gorman worked before going to
Mariners . . . Born Dec. 4, 1953, in Oakland, Cal. . . . His dad
pitched for Orioles in 50s . . . Attended famed McClymonds
High, alma mater of basketball Hall of Famer Bill Russell . . .
Batted .500, .589, .607 in three years there.

MANAGER DARRELL JOHNSON: Proved to be perfect manager for expansion team . . . Patient, hard-working . . . Why are so many managers ex-catch-
ers? And back-up catchers at that? . . . Played
in big leagues six years and appeared in only
134 games . . . Third stringer to Yogi Berra . . .
Also played with St. Louis Browns, Cardinals,
Phillies, Reds, Orioles . . . Born Aug. 25, 1927,
in Fort Ord, Neb. . . . Once involved in 17-
player trade between Orioles and Yankees . . . Living example of
the hell of managing . . . In 1975, he was toast of baseball world,
Manager of Year for having brought Red Sox into World Series,
beaten in seventh game . . . Halfway into next season, he was
fired.

ALL-TIME MARINER LEADERS

BATTING: Carlos Lopez, .283, 1977
HRs: Lee Stanton 27, 1977
RBIs: Dan Meyer, 90, 1977
        Lee Stanton, 90, 1977
STEALS: Dave Collins, 25, 1977
WINS: Glenn Abbott, 12, 1977
STRIKEOUTS: Enrique Romo 105, 1977

High-flying Jose Baez helped turn 54 double plays for Mariners.

NATIONAL LEAGUE

By PAT CALABRIA
Newsday

	West	East
PREDICTED	Cincinnati Reds	Philadelphia Phillies
ORDER	Los Angeles Dodgers	Pittsburgh Pirates
OF FINISH	Houston Astros	St. Louis Cardinals
	San Diego Padres	Montreal Expos
	San Francisco Giants	Chicago Cubs
	Atlanta Braves	New York Mets

Playoff Winner: Cincinnati

FREEDOM STAKES

102nd Running, National League race. Distance, 162 games, plus playoff. Purse, $10,000 per winning player, division; $11,000 added, pennant; $7,000 added, World Championship. A field of 12 entered in two divisions.

Track Record 116 wins—Chicago 1906

WEST DIVISION	Owner		Morning Line / Manager
1 REDS red & white A big stakes winner.	Lou Nippert	1977 W 88 L 74	**2-5** Sparky Anderson
2 DODGERS royal blue & white Experienced horse. Knows course.	Walter O'Malley	1977 W 98 L 64	**3-2** Tom Lasorda
3 ASTROS orange & white Lacks strength for stretch drive.	T.H. Neyland	1977 W 81 L 81	**9-1** Bill Virdon
4 PADRES brown, gold & white Improving, could surprise.	Ray A. Kroc	1977 W 69 L 93	**15-1** Alvin Dark
5 GIANTS white, black & red Fades early and dies.	Robert Lurie	1977 W 75 L 87	**30-1** Joe Altobelli
6 BRAVES royal blue & white Owner can't sail with this horse.	Ted Turner	1977 W 61 L 101	**75-1** Bobby Cox

REDS have the endurance for tough race. **DODGERS** must break out quickly and take big lead. **ASTROS** could be in it until final turn. **PADRES** and **GIANTS** can't last in tough field. **BRAVES** may not get out of the gate. In match race: **REDS** unbeatable.

Cheer up, Sparky, we'll win this year, says Joe Morgan.

EAST DIVISION	Owner		Morning Line Manager
1 PHILLIES crimson & white Strong winner in last two starts.	R.R.M. Carpenter	1977 W 101 L 61	**6-5** Danny Ozark
2 PIRATES old gold, black & white Top challenger. Always in money.	John Galbreath	1977 W 96 L 66	**8-5** Chuck Tanner
3 CARDINALS red & white Could close fast in tight race.	August A. Busch	1977 W 83 L 79	**4-1** Vern Rapp
4 EXPOS scarlet, white & royal blue Moving up in class. Not quite ready.	Charles Bronfman	1977 W 75 L 87	**12-1** Dick Williams
5 CUBS royal-blue & white Quick starter. Fades easily.	Phillip K. Wrigley	1977 W 81 L 81	**25-1** Herman Franks
6 METS orange & blue Strictly a long shot.	Mrs. Vincent de Roulet	1977 W 64 L 98	**100-1** Joe Torre

PHILLIES need to get out of gate quickly. **PIRATES** should stay close into stretch. **CARDINALS** could go to the wire, but **EXPOS** will wither under the pace. **CUBS** and **METS** will be out of it by the first turn.

CINCINNATI REDS

TEAM DIRECTORY: Chairman of the Board: Louis Nippert; Pres.: Bob Howsam; Scouting Director: Joe Bowen; Publicity: Jim Ferguson; Trav. Sec.: Doug Bureman; Mgr.: Sparky Anderson. Home: Riverfront Stadium (51,963). Field distances: 330, l.f. line; 404, c.f.; 330, r.f. line. Spring training: Tampa, Fla.

SCOUTING REPORT

HITTING: Of course, the Reds invented the long ball—or, at least, seemed to have. The lineup is, and has been, so top-heavy with sluggers that opposing teams joke the Reds' lineup card bends over from all the weight. Only Philadelphia had a higher team BA than Cincinnati's .274 last season. Hitting isn't just the cornerstone of the Reds' attack. It's the entire foundation.

George Foster, Ken Griffey and Pete Rose all have the ability to lead the NL in hitting. All were in the top ten last season. And for those who say they would like to see MVP Foster hit 52 home runs again—well, he just might. The discouraging word for pitching staffs around the rest of the league is the Reds can expect more help from Joe Morgan. He slumped below .300 last year and doesn't expect to repeat.

Besides being heavy-handed, the Reds are even-handed. Morgan, Griffey and Dan Driessen from the left side and Johnny Bench and Foster from the right side. And Rose, who goes from both sides. About the worst thing that can be said of the Reds—who slugged 181 homers last season—is that nobody has been added to that rich lineup. A good thing.

PITCHING: The addition of Bill Bonham should help a little. Having Tom Seaver for a full season should help even more. And the acquisition of Vida Blue will help a lot. Over the winter, the ability of the staff grew from a question mark to an exclamation point. For once, the Reds may have the best pitching in the league. Surprise!

Jack Billingham, a workhorse, and gutty Fred Norman round out the rotation. Other candidates for starting jobs, should someone falter, are Doug Capilla and Paul Moskau. The need the Reds themselves see is for a left-handed relief pitcher. They don't call manager Sparky Anderson "Captain Hook" for nothing. The right-handers in the bullpen are Pedro Borbon and Dale Murray, who won 17 games between them last season. The Reds' 4.22 ERA was better than those of only Atlanta and San Diego—not very good company. This season, the rest of the league looks at the Reds' pitching and grows Blue with envy.

FIELDING: Speed, defense, strong arms. Is there anything the Reds don't have? Apparently not. A Gold Glove infield that hinges on Morgan and Dave Concepcion. Rose battles grounders at third and Driessen battles grounders at first, but both get the job done. Griffey is an antelope in right, Geronimo a cannon in center and Foster everything you could ask for in left. Which leaves catching. Isn't Bench still the best? Of course, the Reds do have one major flaw here. The manager has been known to boot a grounder in batting practice.

OUTLOOK: There is no reason the Reds shouldn't win this year. Then again, there is no reason they shouldn't have won last season. A better start is in order, so the team won't have to snap at the Dodgers' heels again. The Reds played Los Angeles even after the acquisition of Seaver in June and, if anything, the pitching is stronger. Very interesting.

MVP George Foster takes aim at Triple Crown and 60 HRs.

CINCINNATI REDS 1978 ROSTER

MANAGER Sparky Anderson
Coaches—Alex Grammas, Ted Kluszewski, Russ Nixon,
    Ron Plaza, George Scherger, Larry Shepard

PITCHERS

No.	Name	1977 Club	W-L	IP	SO	ERA	B-T	Ht.	Wt.	Born
43	Billingham, Jack	Cincinnati	10-10	162	76	5.22	R-R	6-4	215	2/21/43 Winter Park, FL
—	Blue, Vida	Oakland	14-19	280	157	3.83	B-L	6-0	192	7/28/49 Mansfield, LA
42	Bonham, Bill	Chicago (NL)	10-13	215	134	4.35	R-R	6-3	195	10/1/48 Glendale, CA
34	Borbon, Pedro	Cincinnati	10-5	127	48	3.19	R-R	6-2	190	12/2/46 Valverde, DR
44	Capilla, Doug	New Orleans	3-4	—	—	4.50	L-L	5-8	175	1/7/52 Honolulu, HI
		Cincinnati	7-8	109	75	4.46				
50	Dumoulin, Dan	Indianapolis	1-2	47	28	2.87	R-R	6-0	178	8/20/53 Kokomo, IN
		Cincinnati	0-0	5	5	14.40				
46	Ferreyra, Raul	Indianapolis	4-3	82	39	3.73	R-R	6-2	180	10/10/55 Jima Abajo, DR
47	Hume, Tom	Indianapolis	5-6	106	76	2.80	R-R	6-1	180	3/29/53 Cincinnati, OH
		Cincinnati	3-3	43	22	7.12				
51	LaCoss, Mike	Indianapolis	11-13	186	104	3.87	R-R	6-4	186	5/30/56 Glendale, CA
54	Moore, David	Three Rivers	10-2	—	—	3.69	R-R	6-2	185	9/19/54 Lexington, KY
		Indianapolis	8-4	86	54	3.56				
31	Moskau, Paul	Indianapolis	7-1	—	—	3.54	R-R	6-2	210	12/20/53 St. Joseph, MO
		Cincinnati	6-6	108	71	4.00				
37	Murray, Dale	Cincinnati	7-2	102	42	4.94	R-R	6-4	205	2/2/50 Cuero, TX
32	Norman, Fred	Cincinnati	14-13	221	160	3.38	R-L	5-8	170	8/20/42 San Antonio, TX
52	O'Keeffe, Rick	Holyoke-Three Rivers	9-10	—	—	4.05	L-L	6-6	210	7/26/57 Bronx, NY
53	Pastore, Frank	Tampa	4-5	—	—	2.27	R-R	6-2	205	8/21/57 Alhambra, CA
		Three Rivers	6-6	—	—	3.64				
45	Sarmiento, Manny	Indianapolis	3-4	35	35	6.69	R-R	5-11	155	2/2/56 Cagua, VZ
		Cincinnati	0-0	40	23	2.48				
41	Seaver, Tom	NY (NL)-Cin.	21-6	261	196	2.59	R-R	6-1	206	11/17/44 Fresno, CA
36	Soto, Mario	Indianapolis	11-5	—	—	3.08	R-R	6-0	165	7/12/56 Bani, DR
		Cincinnati	2-6	61	44	5.31				
88	Torres, Angel	Three Rivers	2-2	—	—	3.52	L-L	5-11	165	10/24/52 Azua, DR
		Denver-Ind.	2-2	30	25	6.90				
		Cincinnati	0-0	8	7	2.25				

CATCHERS

No.	Name	1977 Club	H	HR	RBI	Pct.	B-T	Ht.	Wt.	Born
5	Bench, Johnny	Cincinnati	136	31	109	.275	R-R	6-1	215	12/7/47 Oklahoma City, OK
9	Plummer, Bill	Cincinnati	16	1	7	.137	R-R	6-1	210	3/21/47 Oakland, CA
7	Werner, Don	Indianapolis	20	5	13	.213	R-R	6-1	185	3/8/53 Appleton, WI
		Cincinnati	4	2	4	.174				

INFIELDERS

No.	Name	1977 Club	H	HR	RBI	Pct.	B-T	Ht.	Wt.	Born
23	Auerbach, Rick	Tidewater	19	0	7	.235	R-R	6-0	165	2/15/50 Glendale, CA
		Cincinnati	7	0	3	.156				
13	Concepcion, Dave	Cincinnati	155	8	64	.271	R-R	6-2	175	6/17/48 Aragua, VZ
22	Driessen, Dan	Cincinnati	161	17	91	.300	L-R	5-11	187	7/29/51 Hilton Head, SC
17	Grace, Mike	Indianapolis	66	1	30	.218	R-R	5-11	170	6/14/56 Pontiac, MI
26	Kennedy, Junior	Phoenix	152	0	76	.316	R-R	6-0	180	8/9/50 Fort Gibson, OK
25	Knight, Ray	Cincinnati	24	1	13	.261	R-R	6-2	185	12/28/52 Albany, GA
8	Morgan, Joe	Cincinnati	150	22	78	.288	L-R	5-7	165	9/19/43 Bonham, TX
16	Oester, Ron	Indianapolis	116	3	33	.255	B-R	6-1	175	5/5/56 Cincinnati, OH
14	Rose, Pete	Cincinnati	204	9	64	.311	B-R	5-11	200	4/14/41 Cincinnati, OH
57	Santo Domingo, Rafael	Three Rivers	—	2	45	.281	B-R	6-0	160	11/24/55 Orocovis, PR
56	Spilman, Harry	Three Rivers	174	16	75	.385	L-R	6-1	180	7/18/54 Albany, GA

OUTFIELDERS

No.	Name	1977 Club	H	HR	RBI	Pct.	B-T	Ht.	Wt.	Born
33	Armbrister, Ed	Cincinnati	20	1	5	.256	R-R	6-1	175	7/4/48 Nassau, Bahamas
15	Foster, George	Cincinnati	197	52	149	.320	R-R	6-1	185	12/1/48 Tuscaloosa, AL
20	Gerohimo, Cesar	Cincinnati	131	10	52	.266	L-L	6-2	180	1/31/48 El Seibo, DR
30	Griffey, Ken	Cincinnati	186	12	57	.318	L-L	5-11	200	4/10/50 Donora, PA
21	Lum, Mike	Cincinnati	20	5	16	.160	L-L	6-0	180	10/27/45 Honolulu, HI
28	Summers, Champ	Cincinnati	13	3	6	.171	L-R	6-1	205	6/15/48 Bremerton, WA

RED PROFILES

PETE ROSE 36 5-11 200   Bats S Throws R

Doesn't have the crewcut anymore but is still the symbol of the Reds . . . Overcame salary squabble to bat .300 for 12th time . . . Had 200 hits for ninth time, tying Ty Cobb's major-league record . . . Prides himself on being a singles hitter but gets a lot of extra-base hits . . . A 10-time all-star whose next goal is 3,000 hits . . . Already has more hits than any switch-hitter in history, surpassing Frank Frisch last season . . . Born April 14, 1941, in Cincinnati and still lives there, naturally . . . Broke in as a second baseman, moved to outfield and then shifted to third base three years ago . . . Has a .378 average over five NL championship series . . . Son, Pete III, once came to dinner in Steve Garvey T-shirt and was sent back to put on a Pete Rose T-shirt.

Year	Club	Pos	G	AB	R	H	2B	3B	HR	RBI	SB	Avg.
1963	Cincinnati	2B-OF	157	623	101	170	25	9	6	41	13	.273
1964	Cincinnati	2B	136	516	64	139	13	2	4	34	4	.269
1965	Cincinnati	2B	162	670	117	209	35	11	11	81	8	.312
1966	Cincinnati	2B-3B	156	654	97	205	38	5	16	70	4	.313
1967	Cincinnati	OF-2B	148	585	86	176	32	8	12	76	11	.301
1968	Cincinnati	OF-2B-1B	149	626	94	210	42	6	10	49	3	.335
1969	Cincinnati	OF-2B	156	627	120	218	33	11	16	82	7	.348
1970	Cincinnati	OF	159	649	120	205	37	9	15	52	12	.316
1971	Cincinnati	OF	160	632	86	192	27	4	13	44	13	.304
1972	Cincinnati	OF	154	645	107	198	31	11	6	57	10	.307
1973	Cincinnati	OF	160	680	115	230	36	8	5	64	10	.338
1974	Cincinnati	OF	163	652	110	185	45	7	3	51	2	.284
1975	Cincinnati	3B-OF	162	662	112	210	47	4	7	74	0	.317
1976	Cincinnati	3B-OF	162	665	130	215	42	6	10	63	9	.323
1977	Cincinnati	3B-OF	162	655	95	204	38	7	9	64	16	.311
	Totals		2346	9541	1554	2966	521	108	143	902	122	.311

TOM SEAVER 33 6-1 206   Bats R Throws R

Principal in one of most publicized trades in history . . . Sent to Reds June 15, 1976 for Pat Zachry, Steve Henderson, Dan Norman and Doug Flynn . . . Mets' refusal to improve club through free agent draft plus contract disagreement led to end of fabulous 10-season career in New York . . . A three-time Cy Young Award winner . . . Holds major-league record with nine consecutive years of striking out at least 200 batters . . . Failed by a handful to extend that streak last season . . . Born George Thomas Seaver Nov. 17, 1944, in Fresno, Cal. . . . Has best stuff in league and head to match . . . Holds major-league record of 10 consecutive strikeouts . . . Literally picked out of hat by Mets in special 1966 drawing after contract with Braves was voided.

Year	Club	G	IP	W	L	Pct.	SO	BB	H	ERA
1967	New York (NL)..........	35	251	16	13	.552	170	78	224	2.76
1968	New York (NL)..........	36	278	16	12	.571	205	48	224	2.20
1969	New York (NL)..........	36	273	25	7	.781	208	82	202	2.21
1970	New York (NL)..........	37	291	18	12	.600	283	83	230	2.81
1971	New York (NL)..........	36	286	20	10	.667	289	61	210	1.76
1972	New York (NL)..........	35	262	21	12	.636	249	77	215	2.92
1973	New York (NL)..........	36	290	19	10	.655	251	64	219	2.07
1974	New York (NL)..........	32	236	11	11	.500	201	75	199	3.20
1975	New York (NL)..........	36	280	22	9	.710	243	88	217	2.38
1976	New York (NL)..........	35	271	14	11	.560	235	77	211	2.59
1977	New York (NL)-Cincinnati ..	33	261	21	6	.778	196	66	199	2.59
	Totals...................	387	2979	203	113	.642	2530	799	2350	2.48

BILL BONHAM 29 6-3 195   Bats R Throws R

The Doctor . . . Majored in psychology at UCLA . . . Could use some on hitters . . . Whip-like motion and good arm, but has trouble getting hitters out . . . Hasn't been the same since 1974 when he led NL in games lost and tied a major-league record with eight balks . . . That also was year he led Cubs in strikeouts, managing four in one inning to tie a record . . . Born Oct. 1, 1948 in Glendale, Cal. . . . A good fielding pitcher who once led NL pitchers in assists.

Year	Club	G	IP	W	L	Pct.	SO	BB	H	ERA
1971	Chicago (NL)	33	60	2	1	.667	41	36	38	4.65
1972	Chicago (NL)	19	58	1	1	.500	49	25	56	3.10
1973	Chicago (NL)	44	152	7	5	.583	121	64	126	3.02
1974	Chicago (NL)	44	243	11	22	.333	191	109	246	3.85
1975	Chicago (NL)	38	229	13	15	.464	165	109	254	4.72
1976	Chicago (NL)	32	196	9	13	.409	110	96	215	4.27
1977	Chicago (NL)	34	215	10	13	.435	134	82	207	4.35
	Totals...................	244	1153	53	70	.431	811	521	1167	4.08

GEORGE FOSTER 29 6-1 185   Bats R Throws R

Sprouted as the most dangerous hitter around two years ago when teammate Joe Morgan beat him out for MVP award . . . This time, he's the MVP . . . Led NL in homers last season with 52 . . . That was the highest homer total since Willie Mays hit that number in 1965 . . . Has led the league in RBIs the last two seasons . . . Uses a black hickory bat to drive in all those runs . . . A threat to win the triple crown . . . Offensive ability overshadows fine defense . . . Plays left field but was moved to center in last year's All-Star Game . . . Born Dec. 1, 1948, in Tuscaloosa, Ala. . . . Deeply religious . . . Broke in with Giants, but was given chance to play regularly by Sparky Anderson . . . Has size 30 waist and broadest shoulders on team.

Year	Club	Pos	G	AB	R	H	2B	3B	HR	RBI	SB	Avg.
1969	San Francisco	OF	9	5	1	2	0	0	0	1	0	.400
1970	San Francisco	OF	9	19	2	6	1	1	1	4	0	.316
1971	S.F.-Cin.	OF	140	473	50	114	23	4	13	58	7	.241
1972	Cincinnati	OF	59	145	15	29	4	1	2	12	2	.200
1973	Cincinnati	OF	17	39	6	11	3	0	4	9	0	.282
1974	Cincinnati	OF	106	276	31	73	18	0	7	41	3	.264
1975	Cincinnati	OF-1B	134	463	71	139	24	4	23	78	2	.300
1976	Cincinnati	OF	144	562	86	172	21	9	29	121	17	.306
1977	Cincinnati	OF	158	615	124	197	31	2	52	149	6	.320
	Totals...........		776	2597	386	743	125	21	131	473	37	.286

JOE MORGAN 34 5-7 165

Bats L Throws R

May be the greatest all-around player today . . . Excellent offensive player who also fields his position well . . . Had slow start last year but finished strong . . . Was MVP in 1975 and '76 . . . Those were the first back-to-back awards since Ernie Banks, 1958-59 . . . A pudgy second-baseman who has a lot of power for a little guy . . . Flapping arm is his trademark . . . Born in Beham, Tex., Sept. 19, 1943 . . . Started career in Houston but delivered to Reds in eight-player trade in 1971 . . . Good speed and ability to steal bases make him a triple threat . . . Only fifth second baseman in history to drive in 100 runs in a season . . . Legend has it Casey Stengel wanted him for early Mets but couldn't swing trade with Astros.

Year	Club	Pos	G	AB	R	H	2B	3B	HR	RBI	SB	Avg.
1963	Houston.........	2B	8	25	5	6	0	1	0	3	1	.240
1964	Houston.........	2B	10	37	4	7	0	0	0	0	0	.189
1965	Houston.........	2B	157	601	100	163	22	12	14	40	20	.271
1966	Houston.........	2B	122	425	60	121	14	8	5	42	11	.285
1967	Houston.........	2B-OF	133	494	73	136	27	11	6	42	29	.275
1968	Houston.........	2B-OF	10	20	6	5	0	1	0	0	3	.250
1969	Houston.........	2B-OF	147	535	94	126	18	5	15	43	49	.236
1970	Houston.........	2B	144	548	102	147	28	9	8	52	42	.268
1971	Houston.........	2B	160	583	87	149	27	11	13	56	40	.256
1972	Cincinnati	2B	149	552	122	161	23	4	16	73	58	.292
1973	Cincinnati	2B	157	576	116	167	35	2	26	82	67	.290
1974	Cincinnati	2B	149	512	107	150	31	3	22	67	58	.293
1975	Cincinnati	2B	146	498	107	163	27	6	17	94	67	.327
1976	Cincinnati	2B	141	472	113	151	30	5	27	111	60	.320
1977	Cincinnati	2B	153	521	113	150	21	6	22	78	49	.288
	Totals		1786	6399	1209	1802	303	84	191	783	554	.282

JOHNNY BENCH 30 6-1 215   Bats R Throws R

Considered one of the greatest catchers in history . . . A defensive gem and brilliant hitter . . . Shoulder surgery slowed him two years ago but he rebounded with fine offensive year last season . . . Selected for all-star team last 10 seasons . . . Joined Frank Robinson and Tony Perez as only third player in club history to reach 1,000 career RBI mark . . . Twice the NL MVP . . . Also won World Series MVP in 1976 with .533 average, fourth highest in WS history . . . Born Dec. 7, 1947, in Oklahoma City . . . Has overcome problems resulting from breakup of brief marriage to a New York model . . . Expects to move to outfield to prolong career . . . Has also played first base and third base.

Year	Club	Pos	G	AB	R	H	2B	3B	HR	RBI	SB	Avg.
1967	Cincinnati	C	26	86	7	14	3	1	1	6	0	.163
1968	Cincinnati	C	154	564	67	155	40	2	15	82	1	.275
1969	Cincinnati	C	148	532	83	156	23	1	26	90	6	.293
1970	Cincinnati	C-OF-1B-3B	158	605	97	177	35	4	45	148	5	.293
1971	Cincinnati	C-1B-OF-3B	149	562	80	134	19	2	27	61	2	.238
1972	Cincinnati	C-OF-1B-3B	147	538	87	145	22	2	40	125	6	.270
1973	Cincinnati	C-OF-1B-3B	152	557	83	141	17	3	25	104	4	.253
1974	Cincinnati	C-3B-1B	160	621	108	174	38	2	33	129	5	.280
1975	Cincinnati	C-OF-1B	142	530	83	150	39	1	28	110	11	.283
1976	Cincinnati	C-OF-1B	135	465	62	109	24	1	16	74	13	.234
1977	Cincinnati	C-OF-1B	142	494	67	136	34	2	31	109	2	.275
	Totals		1513	5554	824	1491	294	21	287	1038	55	.268

KEN GRIFFEY 27 5-11 200   Bats L Throws L

Exceptional all-around player with speed, defense and ability to hit for high average . . . Coveted by Mets in trade for Tom Seaver but Reds wouldn't let go . . . Doesn't have much power but doesn't need it . . . Beats out a lot of infield hits . . . Good bunter despite AstroTurf in home park . . . Born April 19, 1950, in Donora, Pa., Stan Musial's hometown . . . Selected on 29th round of 1969 free agent draft and had outstanding minor-league career before promotion in 1973 . . . Had highest batting average going into final day of 1976 season but was overtaken by Bill Madlock for crown.

Year	Club	Pos	G	AB	R	H	2B	3B	HR	RBI	SB	Avg.
1974	Cincinnati	OF	88	227	24	57	9	5	2	19	9	.251
1975	Cincinnati	OF	132	463	95	141	15	9	4	46	16	.305
1976	Cincinnati	OF	148	562	111	189	28	9	6	74	34	.336
1977	Cincinnati	OF	154	585	117	186	35	8	12	57	17	.318
	Totals		547	1923	366	606	92	32	27	210	80	.315

CESAR GERONIMO 30 6-2 170   Bats L Throws L

Extraordinary center fielder with a magnet for a glove and a mortar for an arm . . . Fleet and graceful . . . Has had good seasons at the plate but his batting average dropped 40 points last season after first .300 year of career . . . Called the Chief but born March 11, 1948, in El Seibo, Dominican Republic . . . Perennial Golden Glove winner who has added stolen base to offensive arsenal . . . Originally signed by Yankees and obtained by Reds from Houston . . . "I always wanted to play in Yankee Stadium," he says . . . He did, in 1976 World Series, when he batted .308.

Year	Club	Pos	G	AB	R	H	2B	3B	HR	RBI	SB	Avg.
1969	Houston	OF	28	8	8	2	1	0	0	0	0	.250
1970	Houston	OF	47	37	5	9	0	0	0	2	0	.243
1971	Houston	OF	94	82	13	18	2	2	1	6	2	.220
1972	Cincinnati	OF	120	255	32	70	9	7	4	29	2	.275
1973	Cincinnati	OF	139	324	35	68	14	3	4	33	5	.210
1974	Cincinnati	OF	150	474	73	133	17	8	7	54	9	.281
1975	Cincinnati	OF	148	501	69	129	25	5	6	53	13	.257
1976	Cincinnati	OF	149	486	59	149	24	11	2	49	22	.307
1977	Cincinnati	OF	149	492	54	131	22	4	10	52	10	.266
	Totals		1024	2659	348	709	114	40	34	278	63	.267

JACK BILLINGHAM 35 6-4 215   Bats R Throws R

Dependable pitcher now in his sixth year with the club . . . Had disappointing season last year but believes he can recover to form of pennant-winning years when he was leading righthander on the team . . . Has started three World Series games, winning two and compiling an 0.35 ERA . . . Nagging injuries, including muscle spasms in right bicep, have slowed his recovery . . . Born Feb. 21, 1943, in Winter Park, Fla. . . . Another product of Houston organization traded to Reds in 1971.

Year	Club	G	IP	W	L	Pct.	SO	BB	H	ERA
1968	Los Angeles	50	71	3	0	1.000	46	30	54	2.15
1969	Houston	52	83	6	7	.462	71	29	92	4.23
1970	Houston	46	188	13	9	.591	134	63	190	3.97
1971	Houston	33	228	10	16	.385	139	68	205	3.39
1972	Cincinnati	36	218	12	12	.500	137	64	197	3.18
1973	Cincinnati	40	293	19	10	.655	155	95	257	3.04
1974	Cincinnati	36	212	19	11	.633	103	64	233	3.95
1975	Cincinnati	33	208	15	10	.600	79	76	222	4.11
1976	Cincinnati	34	177	12	10	.545	76	62	190	4.32
1977	Cincinnati	36	162	10	10	.500	76	56	195	5.22
	Totals	396	1840	119	95	.556	1016	607	1835	3.76

DAVE CONCEPCION 29 6-2 175   Bats R Throws R

Standout shortstop with good range and arm . . . One of the leading offensive players at his position . . . Has hit .270 or better the last five seasons . . . Played in third straight All-Star Game last year . . . Also a threat to steal, ranking 10th on club's all-time list . . . Born June 17, 1948 in Aragua, Venezuela . . . Buried in Reds' lineup but would bat sixth or better for a lot of teams . . . Occasional power usually displayed in clutch situations . . . Likeable fellow who is popular with teammates.

Year	Club	Pos	G	AB	R	H	2B	3B	HR	RBI	SB	Avg.
1970	Cincinnati	SS-2B	101	265	38	69	6	3	1	19	10	.260
1971	Cincinnati	SS-2B-3B-OF	130	327	24	67	4	4	1	20	9	.205
1972	Cincinnati	SS	119	378	40	79	13	2	2	29	13	.209
1973	Cincinnati	SS-OF	89	328	39	94	18	3	8	46	22	.287
1974	Cincinnati	SS-OF	160	594	70	167	25	1	14	82	41	.281
1975	Cincinnati	SS-3B	140	507	62	139	23	1	5	49	33	.274
1976	Cincinnati	SS	152	576	74	162	28	7	9	69	21	.281
1977	Cincinnati	SS	156	572	59	155	26	3	8	64	29	.271
	Totals		1047	3547	406	932	143	24	48	378	178	.263

VIDA BLUE 28 6-0 192   Bats S Throws L

Unhappy, frustrated, disgruntled . . . While all his teammates got out of Finley's Funny Farm, Vida was stuck . . . His sale to Yankees for $1.5 million in '76 was voided by Commissioner . . . Contending fraud, bad faith, Vida sued Finley . . . "I'm going home and pray I don't have to come back," he said . . . Two years later, his prayers were answered by Reds . . . Still one of premier pitchers in league despite record . . . With 19 defeats, A's manager Bob Winkles scratched him from last start . . . "I don't want a guy of Vida's class losing 20," he explained . . . Born July 28, 1949, in Mansfield, La. . . . Secret dream was to be lefty QB in NFL . . . Purchased 3,500 acre ranch in nothern California, will raise cattle.

Year	Club	G	IP	W	L	Pct.	SO	BB	H	ERA
1970	Oakland	6	39	2	0	1.000	35	12	20	2.08
1971	Oakland	39	312	24	8	.750	301	88	209	1.82
1972	Oakland	25	151	6	10	.375	111	48	117	2.80
1973	Oakland	37	264	20	9	.690	158	105	214	3.27
1974	Oakland	40	282	17	15	.531	174	98	246	3.26
1975	Oakland	39	278	22	11	.667	189	99	243	3.01
1976	Oakland	37	298	18	13	.581	166	63	268	2.39
1977	Oakland	38	280	14	19	.424	157	86	284	3.83
	Totals	273	1946	124	86	.590	1315	617	1650	2.95

DAN DRIESSEN 26 5-11 187   Bats L Throws R

Got first chance to play every day and responded with a .300 average and 16 homers . . . Reds had enough faith in him to trade longtime favorite Tony Perez to Montreal before 1977 season . . . Succeeded Perez at first base but previously played third base and the outfield . . . Got recognition as hitter after being inserted as DH in lineup during 1976 World Series and batting .357 . . . Born July 29, 1951, in Hilton Head, S.C. . . . Not an outstanding fielder, but won't hurt you either . . . Says he doesn't want fans to forget Perez, but wants them to remember Driessen.

Year	Club	Pos	G	AB	R	H	2B	3B	HR	RBI	SB	Avg.
1973	Cincinnati	3B-1B	102	366	49	110	15	2	4	47	8	.301
1974	Cincinnati	3B-1B-OF	150	470	63	132	23	6	7	56	10	.281
1975	Cincinnati	1B-OF	88	210	38	59	8	1	7	38	10	.281
1976	Cincinnati	1B-OF	98	219	32	54	11	1	7	44	14	.247
1977	Cincinnati	1B-OF	151	536	75	161	31	4	17	91	31	.300
	Totals		589	1801	257	516	88	14	42	276	73	.287

TOP PROSPECT

RON OESTER 21 6-1 175   Bats S Throws R

Considered an outstanding defensive shortstop but kept out of majors by presence of Dave Concepcion . . . Won't hit a lot but may not have to in Reds' powerful lineup . . . Batted .255 for Indianapolis last season with 33 RBIs . . . Also had 33 stolen bases . . . Born May 5, 1956, in Cincinnati . . . Was an all-city school star and club's ninth pick in '74 draft.

MANAGER SPARKY ANDERSON:

An old-fashioned, honest gentleman who is well-liked by players despite traditional rules and mottos . . . Gave his players the credit when team won five division titles, four NL pennants and two World Championships, then took blame when club straggled behind Dodgers last year . . . Has great lineup to work with but still does his homework and handles a weakened pitching staff . . . Called "Captain Hook" because of his quickness in resorting to bullpen . . . Born Feb. 22, 1934, in Brightwater, S.D. . . . Was undistinguished in brief major-league career as player but has grown into a top manager . . . Coached in San Diego and had signed to coach with Angels when Reds offered him managing job in 1970 . . . Angels released him and Anderson has gone on to win Manager-of-the-Year Award twice.

GREATEST MANAGER

You don't have to go very far back to find the Reds' greatest manager. He's still there. What Sparky Anderson has done has exceeded all the achievements of other Red managers. Fred Hutchinson took the Reds from sixth in 1960 to the NL pennant in 1961, their first league championship in 21 years. And Bill McKechnie won back-to-back pennants in 1939-40 and had seven winning records in nine years.

But no Reds' manager has to his credit 773 victories like Anderson. And no other Reds' manager has five first-place finishes like Anderson. And Anderson is the leading active manager in winning percentage, which means he still is the greatest.

ALL-TIME RED LEADERS

BATTING: Cy Seymour, .377, 1905
HRs: George Foster, 52, 1977
RBIs: George Foster, 149, 1977
STEALS: Bob Bescher, 80, 1911
WINS: Adolpho Luque, 27, 1923
        Bucky Walters, 27, 1939
STRIKEOUTS: Jim Maloney, 265, 1963

LOS ANGELES DODGERS

TEAM DIRECTORY: Chairman: Walter O'Malley; Pres.: Peter O'Malley; Vice-Pres., Player Personnel: Al Campanis; Vice-Pres., Public Relations: Fred Claire; Vice-Pres., Minor Leagues: Bill Schweppe; Publicity: Steve Brener; Trav. Sec.: Lee Scott; Mgr.: Tom Lasorda. Home: Dodger Stadium (56,000). Field distances: 330 l.f. line; 400, c.f.; 330, r.f. line. Spring training: Vero Beach, Fla.

SCOUTING REPORT

HITTING: This was how Walter O'Malley planned it: a lineup of all-stars from first to last. You have to go to the bench to find a weakness in the batting, and even then ace pinch-hitter Manny Mota still occupies a place in the dugout. The Dodgers crashed 191 homers last season, the most in the NL, and they have line-drive hitters and speed to complement the power. Manager Tom Lasorda's trick is to make the Dodgers believe they are better than

Spirit of the Dodgers, Steve Garvey soared to 33 HRs, 115 RBIs.

they really are. Last year, he succeeded. The fact is, no matter how much Lasorda goes overboard, the Dodgers do have a fine lineup.

Davey Lopes has deceiving power for a leadoff man, and excellent speed. Ron Cey almost never leaves a runner in scoring position and Steve Garvey turned from line drives to home runs and added power to the batting order. He's handsome, too. Steve Yeager hits and Dusty Baker found a home in Chavez Ravine after being let go in Atlanta. Want more? Rick Monday should be better after suffering back problems. And, saving the best for last, Reggie Smith is the consummate switch-hitter in the game today—power, speed and always a hit at the right time. And he's a nice man , too.

PITCHING: It's almost a crime to have such an accomplished pitching staff. Don Sutton is reliable, though he does not have gaudy figures, and Burt Hooton is bewildering. Tommy John still has 20,000 miles left on his bionic arm, so his 20-win season was not a fluke. No wonder the Dodgers led the NL with a 3.22 ERA last season.

Also, there is Rick Rhoden and Doug Rau, who won 30 games between them. It's almost a flawless rotation. In the bullpen, Charlie Hough pronounces his name like tough and pitches the same way. The question marks are Mike Garman, who was in-and-out, though he had a fine ERA, and Elias Sosa, who had the best ERA of his life and probably won't match it again. The lefty relievers are Lance Rautzhan, who is inexperienced, and free agent Terry Forster, who won six last year for the Pirates.

FIELDING: Take the outfield—who wouldn't? Dusty Baker can catch, Monday was born in center field and Smith does anything and everything. Right now, there's a movement underway to outlaw his arm. Garvey is the golden boy with the Gold Glove at first base and Lopes is sooooo good at second base and what a right side that is. Lasorda spent the entire season last year telling shortstop Bill Russell he was the greatest thing since pocket-formed gloves. Maybe Russell believed. He was not erratic as he had been. Cey is an all-star at third. Yeager is a fine catcher. Now you know why the Dodgers made only 124 errors last year, third best in the league.

OUTLOOK: The Dodgers won last season, so why shouldn't they do it again? The need for a lefty reliever may seem like a picayune point, but it's there. If that problem is solved, the Dodgers have enough hitting and enough pitching and enough defense. They'll need a good start, which they got last year.

LOS ANGELES DODGERS 1978 ROSTER

MANAGER Tom Lasorda
Coaches—Red Adams, Monty Basgall, Jim Gilliam,
          Preston Gomez

PITCHERS

No.	Name	1977 Club	W-L	IP	SO	ERA	B-T	Ht.	Wt.	Born
41	Castillo, Robert	Los Angeles	1-0	11	7	4.09	R-R	5-10	170	4/18/55 Los Angeles, CA
		Monterrey	19-11	255	199	2.22				
—	Forster, Terry	Pittsburgh	6-4	87	58	4.45	L-L	6-3	210	1/14/52 Sioux Falls, SD
29	Garman, Mike	Los Angeles	4-4	63	29	2.71	R-R	6-3	200	9/16/49 Caldwell, ID
46	Hooton, Burt	Los Angeles	12-7	223	153	2.62	R-R	6-1	200	2/7/50 Greenville, TX
49	Hough, Charlie	Los Angeles	6-12	127	105	3.33	R-R	6-2	190	1/5/48 Honolulu, HI
25	John, Tommy	Los Angeles	20-7	220	123	2.78	R-L	6-3	185	5/22/43 Terre Haute, IN
35	Lewallyn, Dennis	Los Angeles	3-1	17	8	4.24	R-R	6-4	200	8/11/53 Pensacola, FL
		Albuquerque	13-12	175	59	6.22				
31	Rau, Doug	Los Angeles	14-8	212	126	3.44	L-L	6-2	175	12/15/48 Columbus, TX
38	Rautzhan, Lance	Los Angeles	4-1	21	13	4.29	R-L	6-1	203	8/20/52 Pottsville, PA
		Albuquerque	4-4	74	45	4.86				
36	Rhoden, Rick	Los Angeles	16-10	216	122	3.75	R-R	6-3	195	5/16/53 Boynton Beach, FL
59	Shirley, Steve	Lodi	8-3	120	125	3.90	L-L	6-0	170	10/12/56 San Francisco, CA
		San Antonio	1-2	27	18	8.23				
27	Sosa, Elias	Los Angeles	2-2	64	47	1.97	R-R	6-2	190	6/10/50 La Vega, DR
48	Stewart, Dave	Clinton	17-4	176	144	2.15	R-R	6-2	200	2/19/57 Oakland, CA
		Albuquerque	1-0	6	3	4.50				
43	Sutcliffe, Rick	Albuquerque	3-10	77	48	6.43	R-R	6-6	200	6/21/56 Independence, MO
20	Sutton, Don	Los Angeles	14-8	240	150	3.19	R-R	6-2	185	4/2/45 Clio, AL
51	Tennant, Mike	Lodi	12-6	158	143	4.16	R-R	6-3	190	10/14/55 Humansville, MO
37	Webb, Hank	Los Angeles	0-0	8	2	2.25	R-R	6-2	180	5/21/50 Amityville, NY
		Albuquerque	10-9	155	88	4.70				

CATCHERS

No.	Name	1977 Club	H	HR	RBI	Pct.	B-T	Ht.	Wt.	Born
9	Grote, Jerry	NY (NL)-LA	38	0	11	.268	R-R	5-11	190	10/6/42 San Antonio, TX
40	Gulden, Brad	Lodi	127	15	86	.300	L-R	5-10	175	6/10/56 New Ulm, MN
5	Oates, Johnny	Los Angeles	42	3	11	.269	L-R	6-0	185	1/21/46 Sylva, NC
7	Yeager, Steve	Los Angeles	99	12	57	.256	R-R	6-0	190	11/24/48 Huntington, WV

INFIELDERS

No.	Name	1977 Club	H	HR	RBI	Pct.	B-T	Ht.	Wt.	Born
10	Cey, Ron	Los Angeles	136	30	110	.241	R-R	5-10	185	2/15/48 Tacoma, WA
6	Garvey, Steve	Los Angeles	192	33	115	.297	R-R	5-10	190	12/22/48 Tampa, FL
21	Goodson, Ed	Los Angeles	11	1	5	.167	L-R	6-2	185	1/25/48 Pulaski, VA
57	Guerrero, Pedro	Albuquerque	52	4	39	.403	R-R	5-11	176	6/29/56 San Pedro de Macoris, DR
34	Lacy, Lee	Los Angeles	45	6	21	.266	R-R	6-1	175	4/10/48 Longview, TX
56	Landestoy, Rafael	Los Angeles	5	0	0	.278	B-R	5-10	163	5/28/53 Bani, DR
		Albuquerque	154	0	41	.276				
15	Lopes, Davey	Los Angeles	142	11	53	.283	R-R	5-10	170	5/3/46 E. Providence, RI
23	Martinez, Teddy	Los Angeles	41	1	10	.299	R-R	6-0	160	12/10/47 Central Barahona, DR
18	Russell, Bill	Los Angeles	176	4	51	.278	R-R	6-0	180	10/21/48 Pittsburg, KA
44	Washington, Ron	Los Angeles	7	0	1	.368	R-R	5-11	155	4/29/52 New Orleans, LA
		San Antonio	44	0	13	.278				
		Albuquerque	116	8	59	.323				

OUTFIELDERS

No.	Name	1977 Club	H	HR	RBI	Pct.	B-T	Ht.	Wt.	Born
12	Baker, Dusty	Los Angeles	155	30	86	.291	R-R	6-2	195	6/15/49 Riverside, CA
55	Bradley, Mark	Lodi	160	16	87	.329	R-R	6-1	180	12/3/56 Elizabethtown, KY
3	Burke, Glenn	Los Angeles	43	1	13	.254	R-R	6-0	205	11/16/52 Oakland, CA
		Albuquerque	58	6	47	.309				
33	Davalillo, Vic	Los Angeles	15	0	4	.313	L-L	5-8	155	7/31/39 Cabimas, Estado Zulia, VZ
		Aguascalientes	198	6	78	.384				
22	Leonard, Jeff	Los Angeles	19	0	2	.300	R-R	6-2	200	9/22/55 Philadelphia, PA
		San Antonio	147	12	70	.314				
16	Monday, Rick	Los Angeles	90	15	48	.230	L-L	6-3	200	11/20/45 Batesville, AZ
11	Mota, Manny	Los Angeles	15	1	4	.395	R-R	5-11	168	2/18/38 Santo Domingo, DR
17	Simpson, Joe	Los Angeles	4	0	1	.174	L-L	6-3	175	12/31/51 Purcell, OK
		Albuquerque	152	2	74	.349				
8	Smith, Reggie	Los Angeles	150	32	87	.307	B-R	6-0	195	4/2/45 Shreveport, LA
52	White, Myron	Lodi	100	14	65	.258	L-L	5-10	180	8/1/57 Long Beach, CA

DODGER PROFILES

RON CEY 30 5-10 185   Bats R Throws R

The Penguin . . . Walks funny, but watch him hit . . . Set major league record with 29 RBIs in April . . . Holds club record for RBIs in one game (8) set in 1974 against San Diego . . . Has most homers in one season by a Dodger third baseman . . . A four-time all-star . . . Series disappointment with one home run and .190 BA against Yankees . . . Not smooth in the field but gets job done . . . Has record for highest fielding average by a Dodger third baseman (.965) . . . Born Feb. 15, 1948, in Tacoma, Wash . . . Once recorded songs for Long Ball Records, naturally . . . Titles were "Third Base Bag" and "One Game At A Time," naturally . . . A better player than singer.

Year	Club	Pos	G	AB	R	H	2B	3B	HR	RBI	SB	Avg.
1971	Los Angeles......	PH	2	2	0	0	0	0	0	0	0	.000
1972	Los Angeles......	3B	11	37	3	10	1	0	1	3	0	.270
1973	Los Angeles......	3B	152	507	60	124	18	4	15	80	1	.245
1974	Los Angeles......	3B	159	577	88	151	20	2	18	97	1	.262
1975	Los Angeles......	3B	158	566	72	160	29	2	25	101	5	.283
1976	Los Angeles......	3B	145	502	69	139	18	3	23	80	0	.277
1977	Los Angeles......	3B	153	564	77	136	22	3	30	110	3	.241
	Totals..........		780	2755	369	720	108	14	112	471	10	.261

STEVE GARVEY 29 5-10 190   Bats R Throws R

The bluest Dodger of them all . . . Grew up eyeing Pee Wee Reese, Duke Snider, Gil Hodges and the other summer boys when his father drove team bus in spring training . . . Strong and handsome like the boy next door . . . Wife Cyndy is stunning ex-model . . . Most invited sports couple on TV quiz shows . . . Led Dodgers with .375 BA in Series . . . The all-star first baseman for fourth straight year . . . Was write-in candidate in 1974 and was game's MVP . . . Born Dec. 22, 1948, in Tampa, Fla. . . . First Dodger to have three straight 200-hit seasons . . . Has NL record for fewest errors by first baseman (3) with 1500 or more chances . . . His eyes are blue, too . . . Actually applauded Reggie Jackson after Jackson's third homer in sixth Series game.

Year	Club	Pos	G	AB	R	H	2B	3B	HR	RBI	SB	Avg.
1969	Los Angeles......	3B	3	3	0	1	0	0	0	0	0	.333
1970	Los Angeles......	3B-2B	34	93	8	25	5	0	1	6	1	.269
1971	Los Angeles......	3B	81	225	27	51	12	1	7	26	1	.227
1972	Los Angeles......	3B-1B	96	294	36	79	14	2	9	30	4	.269
1973	Los Angeles......	1B-OF	114	349	37	106	17	3	8	50	0	.304
1974	Los Angeles......	1B	156	642	95	200	32	3	21	111	5	.312
1975	Los Angeles......	1B	160	659	85	210	38	6	18	95	11	.319
1976	Los Angeles......	1B	162	631	85	200	37	4	13	80	19	.317
1977	Los Angeles......	1B	162	646	91	192	25	3	33	115	9	.297
	Totals..........		968	3542	464	1064	180	22	110	513	50	.300

REGGIE SMITH 33 6-0 195   Bats S Throws R

There isn't anything he can't do . . . Plays seven musical instruments, scuba dives, flies airplanes, trains quarter horses, cooks, plays tennis, dabbles in real estate and has been a lab assistant in a morgue . . . Also plays baseball . . . Outstanding all-around player . . . Can hit ball over a building . . . Can throw ball over a building . . . Had three homers against Yankees in Series . . . Only Mickey Mantle has more career homers among switch-hitters . . . Born April 2, 1945, in Shreveport, La. . . . A gifted right fielder with flair for circus catches . . . Has played some third base . . . As high school senior he had pre-game tryout with Astros and nearly beaned Sandy Koufax, who was warming up on sidelines.

Year	Club	Pos	G	AB	R	H	2B	3B	HR	RBI	SB	Avg.
1966	Boston..........	OF	6	26	1	4	1	0	0	0	0	.154
1967	Boston..........	OF-2B	158	565	78	139	24	6	15	61	16	.246
1968	Boston..........	OF	155	558	78	148	37	5	15	69	22	.265
1969	Boston..........	OF	143	543	87	168	29	7	25	93	7	.309
1970	Boston..........	OF	147	580	109	176	32	7	22	74	10	.303
1971	Boston..........	OF	159	618	85	175	33	2	30	96	11	.283
1972	Boston..........	OF	131	467	75	126	25	4	21	74	15	.270
1973	Boston..........	OF-1B	115	423	79	128	23	2	21	69	3	.303
1974	St. Louis	OF-1B	143	517	79	160	26	9	23	100	4	.309
1975	St. Louis	OF-1B-3B	135	477	67	144	26	3	19	76	9	.302
1976	St. L.-L.A.	OF-1B-3B	112	395	55	100	15	5	18	49	3	.253
1977	Los Angeles......	OF	148	488	104	150	27	4	32	87	7	.307
	Totals..........		1552	5657	897	1618	298	54	241	848	107	.286

DAVE LOPES 31 5-10 170   Bats R Throws R

A pesty runner, hitter and fielder . . . Second most steals in NL last season after leading league for previous two years . . . Once stole five bases in one game, tying a 70-year-old record . . . Set record by stealing 38 straight bases without being caught . . . Deceptive power . . . Hit three homers in one game at Wrigley Field Aug. 20, 1974 . . . Originally an outfielder, but a minor-league manager named Tom Lasorda converted him to a second baseman . . . Born May 3, 1946, in East Providence, R.I. . . . Comes from family of 12 . . . Has taught elementary school . . . Received telephone death threat during Series . . . Skeptics would say it came from Yankees, who were impressed by him.

Year	Club	Pos	G	AB	R	H	2B	3B	HR	RBI	SB	Avg.
1972	Los Angeles......	2B	11	42	6	9	4	0	0	1	4	.214
1973	Los Angeles......	2B-OF-SS-3B	142	535	77	147	13	5	6	37	36	.275
1974	Los Angeles......	2B	145	530	95	141	26	3	10	35	59	.266
1975	Los Angeles......	2B-OF-SS	155	618	108	162	24	6	8	41	77	.262
1976	Los Angeles......	2B-OF	117	427	72	103	17	7	4	20	63	.241
1977	Los Angeles......	2B	134	502	85	142	19	5	11	53	47	.283
	Totals..........		704	2654	443	704	103	26	39	187	286	.265

DUSTY BAKER 28 6-2 195   Bats R Throws R

No butcher, this Baker, and a home run maker . . . Hit the homer on last day of the season that made the Dodgers the first team in history to have four hitters with 30 homers . . . That blast completed recovery from knee operation which sidelined him the year before . . . Knocked in five runs in Series, tying Steve Yeager and Reggie Smith for team high . . . Born June 15, 1949, in Riverside, Calif. . . . Skilled outfielder with strong arm . . . Wears No. 12, worn by boyhood idol Tommy Davis . . . Real name is Johnnie Baker . . . Hit a home run in his first Dodger at-bat after trade from Atlanta.

Year	Club	Pos	G	AB	R	H	2B	3B	HR	RBI	SB	Avg.
1968	Atlanta..........	OF	6	5	0	2	0	0	0	0	0	.400
1969	Atlanta..........	OF	3	7	0	0	0	0	0	0	0	.000
1970	Atlanta..........	OF	13	24	3	7	0	0	0	4	0	.292
1971	Atlanta..........	OF	29	62	2	14	2	0	0	4	0	.226
1972	Atlanta..........	OF	127	446	62	143	27	2	17	76	4	.321
1973	Atlanta..........	OF	159	604	101	174	29	4	21	99	24	.288
1974	Atlanta..........	OF	149	574	80	147	35	0	20	69	18	.256
1975	Atlanta..........	OF	142	494	63	129	18	2	19	72	12	.261
1976	Los Angeles......	OF	112	384	36	93	13	0	4	39	2	.242
1977	Los Angeles......	OF	153	533	86	155	26	1	30	86	2	.291
	Totals..........		893	3133	433	864	150	9	111	449	62	.276

TOMMY JOHN 34 6-3 185   Bats R Throws L

The Bionic Man . . . Delicate operation restored pitching life after career was doomed . . . Underwent surgery Sept. 25, 1974 for ligament damage and Dr. Frank Jobe used tendon from right forearm to reconstruct left elbow . . . Was NL Comeback player of the Year the following season . . . Second in Cy Young vote to Steve Carlton . . . Sparkling sense of humor

. . . Says, "Ever since the operation I've been a messy eater. I just can't keep the peas on my knife" . . . Born May 22, 1943, in Terre Haute, Ind. . . . Led Dodgers in victories and ERA last season . . . A control pitcher with remarkable strikeout-to walk-ratio throughout career . . . An avid reader.

Year	Club	G	IP	W	L	Pct.	SO	BB	H	ERA
1963	Cleveland	6	20	0	2	.000	9	6	23	2.25
1964	Cleveland	25	94	2	9	.182	65	35	97	3.93
1965	Chicago (A.L.)	39	184	14	7	.667	126	58	162	3.03
1966	Chicago (A.L.)	34	223	14	11	.560	138	57	195	2.62
1967	Chicago (A.L.)	31	178	10	13	.435	110	47	143	2.48
1968	Chicago (A.L.)	25	177	10	5	.667	117	49	135	1.98
1969	Chicago (A.L.)	33	232	9	11	.450	128	90	230	3.26
1970	Chicago (A.L.)	37	269	12	17	.414	138	101	253	3.28
1971	Chicago (A.L.)	38	229	13	16	.448	131	58	244	3.62
1972	Los Angeles	29	187	11	5	.688	117	40	172	2.89
1973	Los Angeles	36	218	16	7	.696	116	50	202	3.10
1974	Los Angeles	22	153	13	3	.813	78	42	133	2.59
1975	Los Angeles			Did Not Play						
1976	Los Angeles	31	207	10	10	.500	91	61	207	3.09
1977	Los Angeles	31	220	20	7	.741	123	50	225	2.78
	Totals	417	2591	154	123	.556	1487	744	2421	2.97

DON SUTTON 33 6-2 185   Bats R Throws R

Steady, reliable pitcher whose totals are among the best in club history . . . Only Don Drysdale and Sandy Koufax have more strikeouts . . . Only Drysdale has more victories . . . Was only starter not defeated by Yankeees in Series, winning once in two appearances . . . Has pitched four one-hitters . . . Has a special interest in records . . . He plays them as part-time disc jockey . . . Born May 2, 1945, in Clio, Ala. . . . Vetoed a proposed trade to Mets in 1975 and club is glad he did . . . He had first 20-win season the next year . . . Finished third in Cy Young voting that year behind Randy Jones and Jerry Koosman.

Year	Club	G	IP	W	L	Pct.	SO	BB	H	ERA
1966	Los Angeles	37	226	12	12	.500	209	52	192	2.99
1967	Los Angeles	37	233	11	15	.423	169	57	223	3.94
1968	Los Angeles	35	208	11	15	.423	162	59	179	2.60
1969	Los Angeles	41	293	17	18	.486	217	91	269	3.47
1970	Los Angeles	38	260	15	13	.536	201	78	251	4.08
1971	Los Angeles	38	265	17	12	.586	194	55	231	2.55
1972	Los Angeles	33	273	19	9	.679	207	63	186	2.08
1973	Los Angeles	33	256	18	10	.643	200	56	196	2.43
1974	Los Angeles	40	276	19	9	.679	179	80	241	3.23
1975	Los Angeles	35	254	16	13	.552	175	62	202	2.87
1976	Los Angeles	35	268	21	10	.677	161	82	231	3.06
1977	Los Angeles	33	240	14	8	.636	150	69	207	3.19
	Totals	435	3052	190	144	.569	2224	804	2608	3.04

RICK MONDAY 32 6-3 200 Bats L Throws L

Never makes an error . . . Never hits into double plays . . . Never on Monday . . . Once led NL center fielders with .992 percentage . . . Hit into only four double plays in 1974, best in league . . . Broke in with Kansas City A's in 1966 and in April 1967 had at least one RBI in 10 straight games . . . Met his future wife the same night streak ended . . . Was third leading home run hitter in NL two years ago but was bothered by chronic back problem last season . . . Born Nov. 20, 1945, in Batesville, Ark. . . . No. 1 draft in entire country in 1965 . . . Does marvelous impersonation of an English butler.

Year	Club	Pos	G	AB	R	H	2B	3B	HR	RBI	SB	Avg.
1966	Kansas City	OF	17	41	4	4	1	1	0	2	1	.098
1967	Kansas City	OF	124	406	52	102	14	6	14	58	3	.251
1968	Oakland	OF	148	482	56	132	24	7	8	49	14	.274
1969	Oakland	OF	122	399	57	108	17	4	12	54	12	.271
1970	Oakland	OF	112	376	63	109	19	7	10	37	17	.290
1971	Oakland	OF	116	355	53	87	9	3	18	56	6	.245
1972	Chicago (NL)	OF	138	434	68	108	22	5	11	42	12	.249
1973	Chicago (NL)	OF	149	554	93	148	24	5	26	56	5	.267
1974	Chicago (NL)	OF	142	538	84	158	19	7	20	58	7	.294
1975	Chicago (NL)	OF	136	491	89	131	29	4	17	60	8	.267
1976	Chicago (NL)	OF-1B	137	534	107	145	20	5	32	77	5	.272
1977	Los Angeles	OF	118	392	47	90	13	1	15	48	1	.230
	Totals		1459	5002	773	1322	211	55	183	597	91	.264

BILL RUSSELL 29 6-0 180 Bats R Throws R

Call him "Ropes" . . . Doesn't hit them but does catch them . . . Erratic, but good . . . Can steal a base or overthrow one . . . Will hold his own at plate . . . Strong arm is no secret . . . He broke in as an oufielder and gunned down runner at plate in first pro game . . . Converted to shortstop and hit for cycle in first major-league game . . . Born Oct. 21, 1948, in Pittsburg, Kan. . . . Tinkered with switch-hitting but gave it up . . . Career has been checkered by injuries . . . Bone chips in left elbow sidelined him two years ago . . ..A real nut . . . Has pecan business with former Dodger Jim Brewer.

Year	Club	Pos	G	AB	R	H	2B	3B	HR	RBI	SB	Avg.
1969	Los Angeles	OF	98	212	35	48	6	2	5	15	4	.226
1970	Los Angeles	OF-SS	81	278	30	72	11	9	0	28	9	.259
1971	Los Angeles	2B-OF-SS	91	211	29	48	7	4	2	15	6	.227
1972	Los Angeles	SS-OF	129	434	47	118	19	5	4	34	14	.272
1973	Los Angeles	SS	162	615	55	163	26	3	4	56	15	.265
1974	Los Angeles	SS-OF	160	553	61	149	18	6	5	65	14	.269
1975	Los Angeles	SS	84	252	24	52	9	2	0	14	5	.206
1976	Los Angeles	SS	149	544	53	152	17	3	5	65	15	.274
1977	Los Angeles	SS	153	634	84	176	28	6	4	51	16	.278
	Totals		1107	3743	388	978	141	40	29	343	98	.261

STEVE YEAGER 29 6-0 190   Bats R Throws R

Competitive, crusty player who still isn't con-
vinced Dodgers weren't better than Yankees
. . . Opponents are convinced he is one of the
best catchers around . . . Had five RBIs in
Series and hit two home runs . . . Survived
freak accident two years ago when splinters
from batter Bill Russell's bat lodged in his neck
while Steve was crouched in on-deck circle . . .
Incident nearly repeated last season when part of bat flew into his
shoulder, causing only a bruise . . . Born Nov. 24, 1948, in Hun-
tington, W. Va. . . . Once stole home plate, first Dodger catcher to
do that since Roy Campanella . . . Nephew of Chuck Yeager, the
Air Force captain who became the first man to break the sound
barrier.

Year	Club	Pos	G	AB	R	H	2B	3B	HR	RBI	SB	Avg.
1972	Los Angeles......	C	35	106	18	29	0	1	4	15	0	.274
1973	Los Angeles......	C	54	134	18	34	5	0	2	10	1	.254
1974	Los Angeles......	C	94	316	41	84	16	1	12	41	2	.266
1975	Los Angeles......	C	135	452	34	103	16	1	12	54	2	.228
1976	Los Angeles......	C	117	359	42	77	11	3	11	35	3	.214
1977	Los Angeles......	C	125	387	53	99	21	2	16	55	1	.256
	Totals..........		560	1754	206	426	69	8	57	210	9	.243

TOP PROSPECTS

PEDRO GUERRERO 21 5-11 176   Bats R Throws R
Fits the Dodger mold perfectly . . . Slick fielder who runs the
bases well . . . Has made minor-league all-star teams at both first
base and third base . . . Born June 29, 1956 in the Dominican Republic . . . Could be useful in utility role . . . Led Waterbury
farm club with 66 RBIs and 30 doubles . . . Originally signed by
Cleveland after an eye-popping .438 BA in American Legion ball
. . . Hit .345 for Danville in third minor-league season.

DENNIS LEWALLYN 24 6-4 200   Bats R Throws R
Getting one more shot . . . Has been late-season addition the last
three years . . . Dodgers figure he should be ready . . . Born Aug.
11, 1953, in Pensacola, Fla. . . . Signed as Dodgers No. 1 draft in
1972 after 7-1 record and 86 strikeouts in 66 innings at Chipola Junior College . . . Could be used either as starter or in relief. . . . A
strikeout pitcher with good control.

MANAGER TOM LASORDA: Mr. Dodger . . . Eats a lot of lasa-

gna but many think he's full of baloney . . .
Says he bleeds Dodger-blue . . . Also says he
wants a Dodger schedule pinned to his tomb-
stone so visitors will know whether the team is
home or away . . . A member of the organization for 28 years who turned down other managerial offers to wait for the one he really wanted
. . . Players like him enough to tolerate his tall
tails . . . Once convinced outfielder Joe Ferguson he could become a great catcher by telling him Mickey Cochrane and Bill
Dickey had started out as outfielders . . . They hadn't, of course,
but Ferguson believed and became a catcher . . . Born Sept. 22,
1927, in Norristown, Pa. . . . Never stops telling his players how
good they are until they believe it . . . Fluent in Spanish . . .
Friend of Frank Sinatra and Don Rickles . . . Toiled in Dodger
farm system as pitcher for 16 years and played briefly in majors.

GREATEST MANAGER

Managers come and go, but Walter Alston came and stayed. He
stayed, in fact, for 23 years before retiring as Dodger manager and
only two men—Connie Mack and John J. McGraw—managed a
team longer, and they were from a different baseball era.

By the time Alston left at nearly 65 years old, he had become the
most victorious manager in Dodger history. His 2,042 wins rank
him fifth on the all-time list. He managed all four of the Dodger
world championship teams (1955, 1959, 1963, 1965) and won
seven pennants. Eight times he managed the NL all-star team and
seven times he won. All that from a man who played in his only
major-league game and had his only major-league at-bat with St.
Louis in 1936. And that was a strikeout.

Before the 1954 season, Charlie Dressen demanded a long-term
contract before he would continue to manage the Dodgers. He
didn't get that long-term contract and neither did Alston, his replacement. Instead, Alston happily received one-year contracts
for the next 23 years. And he stayed and stayed.

ALL-TIME DODGER LEADERS

BATTING: Babe Herman, .393, 1930
HRs: Duke Snider, 43, 1956
RBIs: Tommy Davis, 153, 1962
STEALS: Maury Wills, 104, 1962
WINS: Joe McGinnity, 29, 1900
STRIKEOUTS: Sandy Koufax, 382, 1965

HOUSTON ASTROS

TEAM DIRECTORY: Pres.-Chief Exec. Off. (Astrodomain): T.H. Neyland; VP-Chief Oper. Officer: Martin Kelly; Pres.-GM (Houston Sports Assoc.): Tal Smith; Admin. Asst.: Donald Davidson; Dir. of Scouting; Lynwood Stallings; Dir. Pub. Rel.: Art Perkins; Trav. Sec.: Carlos Alfonso; Mgr.: Bill Virdon. Home: Astrodome (45,000). Field distances: 340, l.f. line; 460, c.f.; 340, r.f. line. Spring training: Cocoa Beach, Fla.

SCOUTING REPORT

HITTING: The Astros have some rising stars, some falling stars and some stars that are simply burned out. The lineup still flickers, but there are not quite enough stars to light up anyone's hopes. Cesar Cedeno is and has been a superstar. He should improve on last season, when he slumped early, then rallied to bat .279. In this

Veteran Bob Watson raised Astro RBI record to 110.

batting order, he is still the brightest star of all. Bob Watson is an intelligent, hard-working hitter, who can knock in runs. There is no reason to believe he won't hit to form this season.

Jose Cruz appears on his way up after a year in which he nearly batted .300. Another season like that and the Astros are going to have a solid middle lineup. But there are some dimming stars, as well. Danny Walton will get a shot after having hit 42 home runs in the minor leagues last season. It might be his last chance in the majors. Enos Cabell is a streaky hitter, but more than capable. After that, there is Joe Ferguson, who has some power. None of the infielders except Cabell will hit. Ed Herrmann batted .291 in a reserve role. He is the slowest runner in baseball.

PITCHING: The club's redeeming quality. The best young staff in the league with an improved bullpen to go along with it. J.R. Richard is big, strong and fast and can strike out anybody. Joe Niekro is coming off the best season of his career, and it's been a long career. Joaquin Andujar has only two years experience but already is top notch. Mark Lemongello doesn't deserve another season like last year, when he lost 14 games despite an acceptable 3.47 ERA. The team ERA, in fact, was 3.54 and second in the NL to the Dodgers.

In the bullpen, Joe Sambito turned in a 2.33 ERA in his first year in the league. He's the only lefty reliever, but a good one. More is expected of Dan Larson, who won only one game coming out of the bullpen. Ken Forsch is capable. If the Astros get in trouble, Floyd Bannister may be able to help. He's a lefty and may also start. If not, look for Gene Pentz. He was 5-2 in relief last year.

FIELDING: There's an infield that would do any pitcher in and an outfield that is anchored by Cedeno, who is among the best. The Astros made 142 errors last season, too many for a team that hopes to remain in third place or go higher. Cabell is on and off at third and has an erratic arm. Art Howe is the second baseman and Roger Metzger the shortstop. Metzger is among the best at his position. Howe is not. Watson is shaky at first base, but he tries. Cedeno will go far to catch a long ball. Cruz is an adequate fielder with an adequate arm. Wilbur Howard is deficient. Joe Ferguson was an outfielder before he became a catcher and will do both.

OUTLOOK: Another good year from the pitching staff would mean another good year. The Astros don't have enough talent to supplant either the Dodgers or the Reds. In the race for third place, the Astros look strong. If the defense falls apart again, even some strong hitting may not make up the difference.

HOUSTON ASTROS 1978 ROSTER

MANAGER Bill Virdon
Coaches—Deacon Jones, Bob Lillis, Tony Pacheco, Mel Wright

PITCHERS

No.	Name	1977 Club	W-L	IP	SO	ERA	B-T	Ht.	Wt.	Born
47	Andujar, Joaquin	Houston	11-8	159	69	3.68	B-R	6-0	175	12/21/52 San Pedro de Macoris, DR
38	Bannister, Floyd	Houston	8-9	143	112	4.03	L-L	6-1	188	6/10/55 Pierre, SD
37	Dixon, Tom	Charleston	13-4	140	44	2.25	R-R	6-0	183	4/23/55 Orlando, FL
		Houston	1-0	30	15	3.30				
43	Forsch, Ken	Houston	5-8	86	45	2.72	R-R	6-4	205	9/8/46 Sacramento, CA
34	Larson, Dan	Houston	1-7	98	44	5.79	R-R	6-0	180	7/4/54 Los Angeles, CA
42	Lemongello, Mark	Houston	9-14	215	83	3.47	R-R	6-1	180	7/21/55 Jersey City, NJ
39	McLaughlin, Bo	Houston	4-7	85	59	4.24	R-R	6-5	205	10/23/53 Oakland, CA
54	Mendoza, Mike	Columbus	8-7	134	93	3.36	R-R	6-5	215	11/26/55 Inglewood, CA
36	Niekro, Joe	Houston	13-8	181	101	3.03	R-R	6-1	190	11/7/44 Lansing, OH
30	Pentz, Gene	Charleston	1-2	18	10	5.00	R-R	6-0	215	6/21/53 Johnstown, PA
		Houston	5-2	87	51	3.83				
50	Richard, J.R.	Houston	18-12	267	214	2.97	R-R	6-8	220	3/7/50 Vienna, LA
35	Sambito, Joe	Houston	5-5	89	67	2.33	L-L	6-1	190	6/28/52 Brooklyn, NY
41	Selak, Ron	Charleston	15-6	184	93	4.20	R-R	6-2	170	3/25/55 Berkeley, CA
48	Stanton, Mike	Charleston	8-7	116	81	3.40	R-R	6-2	205	9/25/52 St. Louis, MO
45	Thomas, Roy	Charleston	11-6	168	71	3.16	R-R	6-5	215	6/22/53 Quantico, VA
—	Zamora, Oscar	Wichita	7-2	80	42	4.37	R-R	5-10	175	9/23/44 Camaguey, Cuba

CATCHERS

No.	Name	1977 Club	H	HR	RBI	Pct.	B-T	Ht.	Wt.	Born
13	Ferguson, Joe	Houston	108	16	61	.257	R-R	6-2	215	9/19/46 San Francisco, CA
8	Herrmann, Ed	Houston	46	1	17	.291	L-R	6-1	210	8/27/46 San Diego, CA
53	Pujols, Luis	Charleston	41	1	19	.228	R-R	6-1	195	11/18/55 Santiago, DR
		Houston	1	0	0	.067				

INFIELDERS

No.	Name	1977 Club	H	HR	RBI	Pct.	B-T	Ht.	Wt.	Born
23	Cabell, Enos	Houston	176	16	68	.282	R-R	6-4	185	10/8/49 Fort Riley, KS
19	Cacek, Craig	Charleston	127	13	77	.307	R-R	6-2	200	9/10/54 Hollywood, CA
		Houston	1	0	1	.050				
10	Fischlin, Mike	Ft. Lauderdale	59	0	20	.294	R-R	6-1	165	9/13/55 Sacramento, CA
		Columbus	50	1	16	.242				
		Houston	3	0	0	.200				
9	Gonzalez, Julio	Houston	94	1	27	.245	R-R	5-11	162	12/25/53 Caguas, PR
18	Howe, Art	Houston	109	8	58	.264	R-R	6-2	185	12/15/46 Pittsburgh, PA
14	Metzger, Roger	Houston	50	0	16	.186	B-R	6-0	165	10/10/47 Fredricksburg, TX
—	Sexton, Jimmy	San Jose	78	2	23	.258	R-R	5-9	160	12/12/51 Mobile, AL
		Seattle	8	1	3	.216				
11	Sperring, Rob	Houston	24	1	9	.186	R-R	6-1	183	10/10/49 San Francisco, CA
27	Watson, Bob	Houston	160	22	110	.289	R-R	6-2	205	4/10/46 Los Angeles, CA

OUTFIELDERS

No.	Name	1977 Club	H	HR	RBI	Pct.	B-T	Ht.	Wt.	Born
—	Bergman, Dave	Syracuse	146	16	59	.312	L-L	6-2	191	6/6/53 Evansville, IL
		N.Y.(AL)	1	0	1	.250				
20	Cannon, Joe	Charleston	132	10	60	.306	L-R	6-2	185	7/13/53 Jacksonville, NC
		Houston	2	0	1	.118				
28	Cedeno, Cesar	Houston	148	14	71	.279	R-R	6-2	190	2/25/51 Santo Domingo, DR
25	Cruz, Jose	Houston	173	17	87	.299	L-L	6-0	175	8/8/48 Arroyo, PR
51	Drake, Kevin	Columbus	62	5	32	.201	R-R	6-3	195	7/12/56 Nagoya, Japan
26	Howard, Wilbur	Charleston	9	0	3	.200	B-R	6-2	175	1/8/49 Lowell, NC
		Houston	48	2	13	.257				
55	Pisker, Don	Columbus	110	7	42	.288	L-L	6-2	180	12/29/53 Camden, NJ
21	Puhl, Terry	Charleston	86	4	33	.302	L-R	6-1	170	7/8/56 Melville, Sask.
		Houston	69	0	10	.301				
29	Walling, Dennis	San Jose	3	0	4	.300	L-R	6-0	183	4/17/54 Neptune, NJ
		Charleston	31	4	14	.348				
		Houston	6	0	6	.286				
31	Walton, Danny	Albuquerque	142	42	122	.289	B-R	6-0	210	7/14/47 Los Angeles, CA
		Houston	4	0	1	.190				

ASTRO PROFILES

CESAR CEDENO 27 6-2 190   Bats R Throws R

Emperor of outfielders . . . Ruler of the Astrodome . . . Troubled last season by slow start . . . Still maintains superstar tag due to live bat and powerful arm . . . Fleet, graceful and exciting . . . Explosive speed makes him a good base-stealer . . . Once burdened by extraordinary talent and withdrew from clubhouse tomfoolery . . . More outgoing now . . . Has hit for cycle twice and no other Astro has done it once . . . Born Feb. 25, 1951, in Santa Domingo . . . Has put off-season gun accident in which woman companion was killed behind him . . . Manager Bill Virdon compares him favorably to any outfielder he's ever seen, including Bill Virdon.

Year	Club	Pos	G	AB	R	H	2B	3B	HR	RBI	SB	Avg.
1970	Houston	OF	90	355	46	110	21	4	7	42	17	.310
1971	Houston	OF-1B	161	611	85	161	40	6	10	81	20	.264
1972	Houston	OF	139	559	103	179	39	8	22	82	55	.320
1973	Houston	OF	139	525	86	168	35	2	25	70	56	.320
1974	Houston	OF	160	610	95	164	29	5	26	102	57	.269
1975	Houston	OF	131	500	93	144	31	3	13	63	50	.288
1976	Houston	OF	150	575	89	171	26	5	18	83	58	.297
1977	Houston	OF	141	530	92	148	36	8	14	71	61	.279
	Totals		1111	4265	689	1245	257	41	135	594	374	.292

MARK LEMONGELLO 22 6-1 180   Bats R Throws R

Mr. Hard Luck . . . Could use a rabbitt's foot instead of a resin bag . . . Lost first 11 decisions last season but was a constant victim of non-support . . . Rebounded in second half of season when he approached lightheartedly the early misfortune . . . Maybe that's because he was a minor-league roommate of Mark Fidrych when both broke in with Detroit . . . Born July 21, 1955, in Jersey City, N.J. . . . Strikes seem to run in the family—his cousin is pro bowler Mike Lemongello . . . Beat Randy Jones in his second major-league start . . . A throw-in in 1975 trade with Tigers.

Year	Club	G	IP	W	L	Pct.	SO	BB	H	ERA
1976	Houston	4	29	3	1	.750	9	7	26	2.79
1977	Houston	34	215	9	14	.391	83	52	237	3.47
	Totals	38	244	12	15	.444	92	59	263	3.39

J.R. RICHARD 28 6-8 220   Bats R Throws R

His name is James Rodney, but call him Sir . . . Frightens batters with his size and speed . . . Fastball is one of the best around . . . Two years ago became only the second pitcher in club history, after Larry Dierker, to win 20 games . . . Led club in victories again last season . . . Credits positive thinking and faithful reading of the Bible for his success . . . Born March 7, 1950, in Vienna, La. . . . A high school basketball player who refused 100 college offers to pursue baseball at Arizona State . . . Struck out 15 Giants in first major league start, tying Karl Spooner's rookie record . . . Only Phil Niekro had more NL strikeouts last season.

Year	Club	G	IP	W	L	Pct.	SO	BB	H	ERA
1971	Houston	4	21	2	1	.667	29	16	17	3.43
1972	Houston	4	6	1	0	1.000	8	8	10	13.50
1973	Houston	16	72	6	2	.750	75	38	54	4.00
1974	Houston	15	65	2	3	.400	42	36	58	4.15
1975	Houston	33	203	12	10	.545	176	138	178	4.34
1976	Houston	39	291	20	15	.571	214	151	221	2.75
1977	Houston	36	267	18	12	.600	214	104	212	2.97
	Totals	147	925	61	43	.587	758	491	750	3.45

JOSE CRUZ 30 6-0 175   Bats L Throws L

Now considered a legitimate hitter after second straight impressive season . . . Had second-best career average and a career high in homers . . . Purchased from St. Louis after he failed to attain predicted stardom there . . . Oldest of three baseball-playing Cruz brothers . . . Born Aug. 8, 1947, in Arroyo, Puerto Rico . . . Excellent speed has helped offensive production and inflated stolen base total . . . A spray hitter who always tests outfielders arms . . . Credits Astro coach Deacon Jones for improving his hitting . . . Led NL outfielders with five double plays in 1973.

Year	Club	Pos	G	AB	R	H	2B	3B	HR	RBI	SB	Avg.
1970	St. Louis	OF	6	17	2	6	1	0	0	1	0	.353
1971	St. Louis	OF	83	292	46	80	13	2	9	27	6	.274
1972	St. Louis	OF	117	332	33	78	14	4	2	23	9	.235
1973	St. Louis	OF	132	406	51	92	22	5	10	57	10	.227
1974	St. Louis	OF-1B	107	161	24	42	4	3	5	20	4	.261
1975	Houston	OF	120	315	44	81	15	2	9	49	6	.257
1976	Houston	OF	133	439	49	133	21	5	4	61	28	.303
1977	Houston	OF	157	579	87	173	31	10	17	87	44	.299
	Totals		855	2541	336	685	121	31	56	325	107	.270

BOB WATSON 32 6-2 205   Bats R Throws R

Grandpa. . .One of the oldest Astros with career in Houston dating back 12 years . . . A legitimate slugger and leading RBI man . . . Does not strike out often which is unusual for a player with his strength and power . . . Used mostly at first base but also plays the outfield . . . An underrated player but pitchers respect him . . . Born April 10, 1946, in Los Angeles . . . Scored the millionth run in baseball history when he belted a three-run homer at San Francisco May 4, 1975 . . . He sprinted around bases that time to assure himself of the honor. . . A high school teammate of Bobby Tolan and Willie Crawford . . . Enjoys listening to music and wears headphones as often as his uniform.

Year	Club	Pos	G	AB	R	H	2B	3B	HR	RBI	SB	Avg.
1966	Houston	PH	1	1	0	0	0	0	0	0	0	.000
1967	Houston	1B	6	14	1	3	0	0	1	2	0	.214
1968	Houston	OF	45	140	13	32	7	0	2	8	1	.229
1969	Houston	OF-1B-C	20	40	3	11	3	0	0	3	0	.275
1970	Houston	1B-C-OF	97	327	48	80	19	2	11	61	1	.272
1971	Houston	OF-1B	129	468	49	135	17	3	9	67	0	.288
1972	Houston	OF-1B	147	548	74	171	27	4	16	86	1	.312
1973	Houston	OF-1B-C	158	573	97	179	24	3	16	94	1	.312
1974	Houston	OF-1B	150	524	69	156	19	4	11	67	3	.298
1975	Houston	1B-OF	132	485	67	157	27	1	18	85	3	.324
1976	Houston	1B	157	585	76	183	31	3	16	102	3	.313
1977	Houston	1B	151	554	77	160	38	6	22	110	5	.289
	Totals		1193	4259	574	1276	212	26	122	685	18	.300

ROGER METZGER 30 6-0 165   Bats R Throws R

Doesn't hit his weight and isn't asked to . . . One of the smoothest gloves in baseball makes him an outstanding shortstop . . . Has been a starter for seven seasons, one of the logest tenures on the team . . . Set an NL record for consecutive errorless games by a shortstop (59) ,– 1976 . . . Born Oct. 10, 1947, in Fredericksburg, Tex. . . . Hit 14 triples in 1973, a club record . . . Holds mathematics degree from St. Edwards U. in Austin . . . Durable player who doesn't like to be kept out of lineup.

Year	Club	Pos	G	AB	R	H	2B	3B	HR	RBI	SB	Avg.
1970	Chicago (NL.)	SS	1	2	0	0	0	0	0	0	0	.000
1971	Houston	SS	150	562	64	132	14	11	0	26	15	.235
1972	Houston	SS	153	641	84	142	12	3	2	38	23	.222
1973	Houston	SS	154	580	67	145	11	14	1	35	10	.250
1974	Houston	SS	143	572	66	145	18	10	0	30	9	.253
1975	Houston	SS	127	450	54	102	7	9	2	26	4	.227
1976	Houston	SS-2B	152	481	37	101	13	8	0	29	1	.210
1977	Houston	SS-2B	97	269	24	50	9	6	0	16	2	.186
	Totals		977	3557	396	817	84	58	5	200	64	.230

JOE NIEKRO 33 6-1 190   Bats R Throws R

The senior statesman . . . Crafty veteran who had his best season in 12 years and the lowest ERA of his career . . . Refuses to fade away . . . Thought to be washed up when purchased from Atlanta three years ago but has been effective both as starter and reliever . . . Once pitched against brother Phil of the Braves and beat him, hitting a home run . . . Came within two outs of no-hitter for Detroit in 1970 when Yankee second baseman Horace Clarke singled . . . Born Nov. 7, 1944, in Martin's Ferry, Ohio . . . No gray hairs but can give the hitters plenty . . . Broke in with Cubs and was their opening day pitcher in 1968.

Year	Club	G	IP	W	L	Pct.	SO	BB	H	ERA
1967	Chicago (N.L.)	35	170	10	7	.588	77	32	171	3.34
1968	Chicago (N.L.)	34	177	14	10	.583	65	59	204	4.32
1969	Chi. (N.L.) S.D.	41	221	8	18	.308	62	51	237	3.71
1970	Detroit	38	213	12	13	.480	101	72	221	4.06
1971	Detroit	31	122	6	7	.462	43	49	136	4.50
1972	Detroit	18	47	3	2	.600	24	8	62	3.83
1973	Atlanta	20	24	2	4	.333	12	11	23	4.13
1974	Atlanta	27	43	3	2	.600	31	18	36	3.56
1975	Houston	40	88	6	4	.600	54	39	79	3.07
1976	Houston	36	118	4	8	.333	77	56	107	3.36
1977	Houston	44	181	13	8	.619	101	64	155	3.03
	Totals	365	1404	81	83	.494	647	459	1431	3.71

ENOS CABELL 28 6-4 185   Bats R Throws R

Fine offensive player who has also begun to master third base . . . Worked on erratic arm and unsure glove and had another productive season at plate . . . Improved BA to a career high . . . Has played first, second and the outfield but was handed starting third base job when Astros traded Doug Rader before 1976 season . . . Overcame some defensive problems and went 42 games without an error that year . . . Born Oct. 8, 1949, in Fort Riley, Kan. . . . Has good speed and runs bases well . . . Has no power but gets a lot of hits . . . Arrived in trade that sent Lee May to Baltimore . . . Twice a batting champion in minor leagues.

Year	Club	Pos	G	AB	R	H	2B	3B	HR	RBI	SB	Avg.
1972	Baltimore	1B	3	5	0	0	0	0	0	1	0	.000
1973	Baltimore	1B-3B	32	47	12	10	2	0	1	3	1	.213
1974	Baltimore	1B-OF-3B-2B	80	174	24	42	4	2	3	17	5	.241
1975	Houston	OF-1B-3B	117	348	43	92	17	6	2	43	12	.264
1976	Houston	3B-1B	144	586	85	160	13	7	2	43	35	.273
1977	Houston	3B	150	625	101	176	36	7	16	68	42	.282
	Totals		526	1785	265	480	72	22	24	175	95	.269

JOAQUIN ANDUJAR 25 6-0 175   Bats R Throws R

Diamond in the rough . . . Polished edges last season and emerged as a valuable starter . . . Credits permanent move into rotation for last year's success . . . Suffocated for years in farm system of talent-rich Cincinnati . . . Don't blink or you'll miss his fastball . . . Still battling control problems . . . Born Dec. 21, 1952, in San Pedro De Macoris, Dominican Republic . . . Had nine CG after being promoted to Astros in 1976 . . . Has played professionally since he was 17 . . . Opponents still can't spell his name, but they know who he is now.

Year	Club	G	IP	W	L	Pct.	SO	BB	H	ERA
1976	Houston	28	172	9	10	.474	59	75	163	3.61
1977	Houston	26	159	11	8	.579	69	64	149	3.68
	Totals	54	331	20	18	.526	128	139	312	3.64

JOE FERGUSON 31 6-2 215   Bats R Throws R

Filled glaring hole at catcher after joining team in off-season trade that sent Larry Dierker to St. Louis . . . Had highest average in five years and displayed good power . . . Has not come close to matching career-high 25 homers with Dodgers in 1973, but still a feared long-ball hitter . . . Shifted between outfield and catcher with Los Angeles and made memorable 1974 Series throw from right field, nailing Sal Bando at home plate . . . Born Sept. 19, 1946, in San Francisco . . . Finally seems to have recovered from fractured right arm suffered in 1975.

Year	Club	Pos	G	AB	R	H	2B	3B	HR	RBI	SB	Avg.
1970	Los Angeles	C	5	4	0	1	0	0	0	1	0	.250
1971	Los Angeles	C	36	102	13	22	3	0	2	7	1	.216
1972	Los Angeles	C-OF	8	24	2	7	3	0	1	5	0	.292
1973	Los Angeles	C-OF	136	487	84	128	26	0	25	88	1	.263
1974	Los Angeles	C-OF	111	349	54	88	14	1	16	57	2	.252
1975	Los Angeles	C-OF	66	202	15	42	2	1	5	23	2	.208
1976	L.A.-St. L.	C-OF	125	374	46	79	15	4	10	39	6	.211
1977	Houston	C-OF	132	421	59	108	21	3	16	61	6	.257
	Totals		619	1963	273	475	84	9	75	281	18	.242

TOP PROSPECTS

JOE CANNON 24 6-2 185   Bats L Throws L-R

Astros gave him good look last season and feel this might be his year . . . An outfielder with good speed and a proven bat . . . Hit .297 for Columbus farm club two years ago and was named to Southern League all-star team . . . Also had 39 stolen bases . . . Born July 13, 1953, in Jacksonville, N.C.

TERRY PUHL 21 6-1 190   Bats L Throws L

A scrappy outfielder who has been threatening to break into line-up for two years . . . Has little power but battles even the toughest pitchers . . . Born July 8, 1956, in Melville, Sask. . . . Earned half-season trial with Astros after rapid progression in minors . . . First two professional homers were grand slams.

MANAGER BILL VIRDON: Coaxed second straight third-place finish out of Astros . . . Even challenged Cincinnati for second place in September rush . . . A gentleman who speaks softly and is patient with players . . . Honest, and doesn't make excuses . . . Least quoted and one of most-liked managers . . . Fired from first job with Pirates with team in second place . . . Was Manager-of-the-Year after guiding Yankees to surprise second-place finish in 1974 . . . Bounced the next season by owner George Steinbrenner in fit of pique . . . Astros grabbed him a few weeks later on advice of Tal Smith, club VP who was Virdon's neighbor on Long Island when both were in Yankee organization . . . Born June 9, 1931 in Hazel Park, Mich. . . . NL Rookie of the Year with St. Louis in 1955 . . . Had long, successful career as Pirate center fielder.

GREATEST MANAGER

Not only is Bill Virdon the current Astro manager, he also is the greatest. In two seasons he has managed the club to two third-place finishes, the best back-to-back seasons it has had in its 16 years. Only one Astro team had a better finish and that was the team of 1972 which finished second after Leo Durocher replaced Harry Walker. But Durocher could finish no better than fourth after that and Preston Gomez had the club in sixth-place before Virdon replaced him at the end of the 1975 season. The first three Astro managers—Harry Craft, Luman Harris and Grady Hatton—could do no better than one eight-place finish.

ALL-TIME ASTRO LEADERS

BATTING: Rusty Staub, .333, 1967
HRs: Jimmy Wynn, 37, 1967
RBIS: Bob Watson, 110, 1977
STEALS: Cesar Cedeno, 61, 1977
WINS: Larry Dierker, 20, 1969
         J.R. Richard, 20, 1976
STRIKEOUTS: Mike Cuellar, 235, 1967
            Don Wilson, 235, 1969

SAN FRANCISCO GIANTS

TEAM DIRECTORY: Co-Chairmen: Bud Herseth and Robert Lurie; GM: Spec Richardson; Dir. of Scouting and Minor League Operations: Jack Schwarz; Dir. of Player Development: Carl Hubbell; Trav. Sec.: Frank Bergonzi; Marketing Director: Pat Gallagher; Pub. Dir.: Stu Smith; Mgr.: Joe Altobelli. Home: Candlestick Park (58,000). Field distances: 335, l.f. line; 410, c.f.; 335 r.f. line. Spring training: Phoenix, Arizona.

SCOUTING REPORT

HITTING: One of the Giants' best hitters, who came back to the team after being traded away three years ago, can barely stand up some days because of a chronic knee problem and is 40 years old. That Willie McCovey can still hit the ball should not be thought of as indicative of most of the players on this team. Of course, there is

Comeback kid Willie McCovey, 40, returned to SF with 28 HRs.

Bill Madlock, a polished hitter, but the Giants lack bats at both ends of the lineup.

Terry Whitfield did emerge as a good hitter after starting out on a part-time basis. He could begin to make a difference in a team that is only one or two hitters away from being average. Darrell Evans supplies some power, but not enough. Gary Thomasson supplies some power, but not enough. Vic Harris has not yet sprouted into the hitter the Giants hoped he would be. Larry Herndon is coming off a season shortened by injuries. The Giants expect more from Jack Clark and may get it. They expect more from Derrel Thomas and may not get it.

PITCHING: A fine young pitching staff which rises and falls with its fine young pitchers. With a comeback from John Montefusco, sidelined much of last season, the Giants could even improve on their 3.75 ERA, which was fifth best in the NL. The Count can be counted on to double last year's victory total of seven. Ed Halicki is a workhorse and throws hard, too. One of the question marks is Lynn McGlothen. He pitched in only 80 innings and had only two victories. He could be valuable if he returns to form. The other starters are veteran Jim Barr and Bob Knepper, the only lefty.

Gary Lavelle had an outstanding season as the team's No. 1 man in the bullpen. He'll have to do it again. After Lavelle, it's Randy Moffitt, who slumped, and Dave Heaverlo, who was 5-1 in relief. John Curtis has experience, Charlie Williams has experience and Greg Minton doesn't have experience, but he is a switch-hitter and you don't find that too often.

FIELDING: There is a need for a shortstop since the trade of Tim Foli. The Giants expect Johnnie LeMaster will fill that spot. He's called Bones and hit a home run in his first major-league at-bat. Madlock battles ground balls at third, but handles most of them. Thomas is erratic at second base. McCovey doesn't play first like he used to. The Giants made 179 errors last season, which is no surprise. The best of the outfielders is Herndon, who has speed and a glove and is built like Bobby Bonds. Jack Clark has speed in the outfield, Thomasson doesn't. The Giants won't beat you with defense.

OUTLOOK: It is going to be a long, hard climb for the Giants. The pitchers will be able to shoulder the burden only so long and another quality hitter is needed in the lineup. Even then, the Giants are likely to give up as many runs as they score just on their defense alone. The Count may be reduced to predicting the dates of victories, instead of shutouts.

SAN FRANCISCO GIANTS 1978 ROSTER

MANAGER Joe Altobelli
Coaches—Jim Davenport, Tom Haller, Herm Starrette

PITCHERS

No.	Name	1977 Club	W-L	IP	SO	ERA	B-T	Ht.	Wt.	Born
33	Barr, Jim	San Francisco	12-16	234	97	4.77	R-R	6-3	205	2/10/48 Lynwood, CA
34	Cornutt, Terry	San Francisco	1-2	44	23	3.89	R-R	6-2	195	10/2/52 Roseburg, OR
		Phoenix	2-1	33	19	4.36				
40	Curtis, John	San Francisco	3-3	77	47	5.49	L-L	6-1½	190	3/9/48 Foster City, CA
25	Dressler, Rob	Phoenix	10-10	199	75	5.29	R-R	6-3	195	2/2/54 Portland, OR
28	Halicki, Ed	San Francisco	16-12	257	168	3.31	R-R	6-7	220	10/4/50 Newark, NJ
60	Heaverlo, Dave	Phoenix	1-0	11	10	4.09	R-R	6-1	195	8/25/50 Ellensburg, WA
		San Francisco	5-1	98	58	2.55				
—	Johnson, John	Fresno	14-2	149	155	3.38	L-L	6-2	185	8/21/56 Houston, TX
38	Knepper, Bob	Phoenix	3-6	51	24	7.41	L-L	6-2	180	5/25/54 Akron, OH
		San Francisco	11-9	166	100	3.36				
46	Lavelle, Gary	San Francisco	7-7	118	93	2.06	S-L	6-1	190	1/3/49 Scranton, OH
47	McGlothen, Lynn	San Francisco	2-9	80	42	5.63	L-R	6-2	210	3/27/50 Monroe, LA
—	Minton, Greg	San Francisco	1-1	14	5	4.50	S-R	6-2	190	7/29/51 Lubbock, TX
		Phoenix	14-6	161	77	4.86				
17	Moffitt, Randy	San Francisco	4-9	87	68	3.58	R-R	6-3	190	10/13/48 Long Beach, CA
26	Montefusco, John	San Francisco	7-12	157	110	3.50	R-R	6-1	180	5/25/50 Keansburg, NJ
43	Plank, Ed	Phoenix	14-7	186	74	4.55	R-R	6-1	195	4/9/52 Chicago, IL
51	Toms, Tommy	San Francisco	0-1	4	2	2.25	R-R	6-4	195	10/15/51 Charlottesville, VA
		Phoenix	2-1	77	67	2.81				
49	Williams, Charlie	San Francisco	6-5	119	41	4.01	R-R	6-2	200	10/11/47 Flushing, NY
48	Wirth, Alan	Waterbury	15-5	210	149	2.87	R-R	6-5	190	12/8/56 Mesa, AZ

CATCHERS

No.	Name	1977 Club	H	HR	RBI	Pct.	B-T	Ht.	Wt.	Born
42	Alexander, Gary	Phoenix	72	7	55	.341	R-R	6-2	200	3/27/53 Los Angeles, CA
		San Francisco	36	5	20	.303				
2	Hill, Marc	San Francisco	80	9	50	.250	R-R	6-3	210	2/18/52 Louisiana, MO
3	Sadek, Mike	San Francisco	29	1	15	.230	R-R	5-10	170	5/30/46 Minneapolis, MN

INFIELDERS

No.	Name	1977 Club	H	HR	RBI	Pct.	B-T	Ht.	Wt.	Born
21	Andrews, Rob	San Francisco	115	0	25	.264	R-R	5-11	180	12/11/52 Santa Monica, CA
41	Evans, Darrell	San Francisco	117	17	72	.254	L-R	6-2	200	5/26/47 Pasadena, CA
20	Harris, Vic	Phoenix	37	1	18	.266	S-R	6-0	170	3/27/50 Los Angeles, CA
		San Francisco	43	2	13	.261				
36	James, Skip	Phoenix	149	14	97	.308	L-L	6-0	190	10/21/49 Elmhurst, IL
		San Francisco	4	0	3	.267				
10	LeMaster, Johnnie	San Francisco	20	0	8	.149	R-R	6-2	160	6/19/54 Portsmouth, OH
		Phoenix	22	0	13	.314				
18	Madlock, Bill	San Francisco	161	12	46	.302	R-R	5-11	180	1/12/51 Memphis, TN
44	McCovey, Willie	San Francisco	134	28	86	.280	L-L	6-4	210	1/10/38 Mobile, AL
—	Murray, Richard	Cedar Rapids	132	21	93	.275	R-R	6-4	195	7/6/57 Los Angeles, CA
30	Thomas, Derrell	San Francisco	135	8	45	.267	S-R	6-0	160	1/14/51 Los Angeles, CA

OUTFIELDERS

No.	Name	1977 Club	H	HR	RBI	Pct.	B-T	Ht.	Wt.	Born
22	Clark, Jack	San Francisco	104	13	51	.252	R-R	6-1	170	11/10/55 Brighton, PA
16	Elliott, Randy	San Francisco	40	7	26	.240	R-R	6-2	195	6/5/51 Camarillo, CA
31	Herndon, Larry	San Francisco	26	1	5	.239	R-R	6-3	190	11/3/53 Sunflower, MS
12	Thomasson, Gary	San Francisco	114	17	71	.256	L-L	6-1	180	7/29/51 San Diego, CA
45	Whitfield, Terry	San Francisco	93	7	36	.285	L-R	6-1	197	1/12/53 Blythe, CA

GIANT PROFILES

JOHN MONTEFUSCO 27 6-1 180   **Bats R Throws R**

Call him the Count . . . Has a lot of talent and knows it . . . Friendly, talkative and controversial . . . Was quieted only a little by broken ankle which kept him out much of last season . . . Still the cog in a young staff . . . Likes to predict shutouts . . . Was NL Rookie-of-the-year three years ago and said; "I deserved it." . . . His 215 strikeouts that season were the most by a rookie pitcher since Grover Cleveland Alexander in 1911 . . . Born May 25, 1950, in Keansburg, N.J. . . . Discovered while playing in an industrial league . . . Pitched a no-hitter against Atlanta Sept. 29, 1976 . . . That was his biggest thrill, ahead of homering in first major-league at-bat . . . Works in public relations at race track during off-season.

Year	Club	G	IP	W	L	Pct.	SO	BB	H	ERA
1974	San Francisco	7	39	3	2	.600	34	19	41	4.85
1975	San Francisco	35	244	15	9	.625	215	86	210	2.88
1976	San Francisco	37	253	16	14	.533	172	74	224	2.85
1977	San Francisco	26	157	7	12	.368	110	46	170	3.50
	Totals	105	693	41	37	.526	531	215	645	3.12

ED HALICKI 27 6-7 220   **Bats R Throws R**

Teammates call him "Ho-ho," but batters don't laugh . . . Nickname comes from Jolly Green Giant, who is only slightly bigger than Ed . . . Doesn't throw anything fancy but try to hit that fastball . . . A lion on mound, a mouse in the locker room . . . When he no-hit Mets in August, 1975 he celebrated with a few cans of beer . . . Born Oct. 4, 1950, in Newark, N.J. . . . Has good strikeout to walk ratio . . . Gets tougher as game gets longer . . . Led team in victories last year despite nagging arm and back injuries . . . A backgammon player.

Year	Club	G	IP	W	L	Pct.	SO	BB	H	ERA
1974	San Francisco	16	74	1	8	.111	40	31	84	4.26
1975	San Francisco	24	160	9	13	.409	153	59	143	3.49
1976	San Francisco	32	186	12	14	.462	130	61	171	3.63
1977	San Francisco	37	258	16	12	.571	168	70	241	3.31
	Totals	109	678	38	47	.447	491	221	639	3.54

WILLIE McCOVEY 40 6-4 210   Bats L Throws L

They'll make movie out of last season . . . Was Comeback-Player-of-the-Year after returning to city where he began a long, loud career . . . Invited to spring training as non-roster player and made the club . . . Led team in both homers and RBIs . . . Also hit two grand slams for an NL career record of 18 . . . Moved into 12th place on all-time homer list and went over 2,000 hit mark . . . Was Rookie-of-the-Year in 1959 and MVP 10 years later . . . Traded by Giants to San Diego in 1973 and played briefly with Oakland before going back to the other side of the bay . . . Born Jan. 10, 1938, in Mobile, Ala. . . . Can still play first, but wears heavy brace on knee . . . An institution at Candlestick, where he said, "I saw a whole generation grow up."

Year	Club	Pos	G	AB	R	H	2B	3B	HR	RBI	SB	Avg.
1959	San Francisco	1B	52	192	32	68	9	5	13	38	2	.354
1960	San Francisco	1B	101	260	37	62	15	3	13	51	1	.238
1961	San Francisco	1B	106	328	59	89	12	3	18	50	1	.271
1962	San Francisco	OF-1B	91	229	41	67	6	1	20	54	3	.293
1963	San Francisco	OF-1B	152	564	103	158	19	5	44	102	1	.280
1964	San Francisco	OF-1B	130	364	55	80	14	1	18	54	2	.220
1965	San Francisco	1B	160	540	93	149	17	4	39	92	0	.276
1966	San Francisco	1B	150	502	85	148	26	6	36	96	2	.295
1967	San Francisco	1B	135	456	73	126	17	4	31	91	3	.276
1968	San Francisco	1B	148	523	81	153	16	4	36	105	4	.293
1969	San Francisco	1B	149	491	101	157	26	2	45	126	0	.320
1970	San Francisco	1B	152	495	98	143	39	2	39	126	0	.289
1971	San Francisco	1B	105	329	45	91	13	0	18	70	0	.277
1972	San Francisco	1B	81	263	30	56	8	0	14	35	0	.213
1973	San Francisco	1B	130	383	52	102	14	3	29	75	1	.266
1974	San Diego	1B	128	344	53	87	19	1	22	63	1	.253
1975	San Diego	1B	122	413	43	104	17	0	23	68	1	.252
1976	San Diego	1B	71	202	20	41	9	0	7	36	0	.203
1976	Oakland	DH	11	24	0	5	0	0	0	0	0	.208
1977	San Francisco	1B	141	478	54	134	21	0	28	86	3	.280
	Totals		2315	7380	1155	2020	317	44	493	1418	25	.274

BILL MADLOCK 27 5-11 180   Bats R Throws R

Nicknamed "Mad" and he hits like it . . . Was only 24 when he won his first NL batting title, the second-youngest player to win crown since Tommy Davis in 1963 . . . Repeated as batting champ in 1976, but contract dispute led to his trade to Giants before start of last season . . . Has never hit below .300 in more than four major-league seasons . . . Not a smooth third baseman but he battles grounders and gets the job done . . . Born Jan. 12, 1951, in Memphis . . . A tough strikeout due to short, compact stroke . . . Can muscle a pitch out if he has to . . .

Biggest surprise of 1968 draft when chosen No. 268 by Washington Senators.

Year	Club	Pos	G	AB	R	H	2B	3B	HR	RBI	SB	Avg.
1973	Texas	3B	21	77	16	27	5	3	1	5	3	.351
1974	Chicago (NL)	3B	128	453	65	142	21	5	9	54	11	.313
1975	Chicago (NL)	3B	130	514	77	182	29	7	7	64	9	.354
1976	Chicago (NL)	3B	142	514	68	174	36	1	15	84	15	.339
1977	San Francisco	3B	140	533	70	161	28	1	12	46	13	.302
	Totals		561	2091	296	686	119	17	44	253	51	.328

GARY LAVELLE 29 6-1 190   Bats S Throws L

The tortoise that beat the hare . . . Made sure, steady progress and then exploded onto scene last year . . . Went from 12 saves in 1976 to 20 last year . . . Originally a starter but much too useful a reliever to move out of bullpen now . . . His ERA was second in NL only to Rich Gossage . . . Teammates call him "Pudge" but batters can't say that about his pitches . . . Born Jan. 3, 1949, in Scranton, Pa. . . . Tinkers with switch-hitting, rare for a pitcher . . . Pitched a minor-league no-hitter for Decatur after returning from stint in Marine Corps.

Year	Club	G	IP	W	L	Pct.	SO	BB	H	ERA
1974	San Francisco	10	17	0	3	.000	12	10	14	2.12
1975	San Francisco	65	82	6	3	.667	51	48	80	2.96
1976	San Francisco	65	110	10	6	.625	71	52	102	2.70
1977	San Francisco	73	118	7	7	.500	93	37	106	2.06
	Totals	213	327	23	19	.548	227	147	302	2.50

RANDY MOFFITT 29 6-3 190   Bats R Throws R

Suffered setback last season after leading club in saves four straight years . . . Again used in short relief . . . Sinker must work for him to be effective but also has good slider . . . Was a starter in first pro season at Fresno but has made only one major-league start . . . Born Oct. 13, 1948, in Long Beach, Cal. . . . If name sounds familiar it's because he is brother of tennis star Billie Jean (Moffitt) King . . . Club figures a return to form will give them good righty-lefty combo with Gary Lavelle . . . A college star at Long Beach State and first-round draft pick in 1970.

Year	Club	G	IP	W	L	Pct.	SO	BB	H	ERA
1972	San Francisco	40	71	1	5	.167	37	30	72	3.68
1973	San Francisco	60	100	4	4	.500	65	31	86	2.43
1974	San Francisco	61	102	5	7	.417	49	29	99	4.50
1975	San Francisco	55	74	4	5	.444	39	32	73	3.89
1976	San Francisco	58	103	6	6	.500	50	35	92	2.27
1977	San Francisco	64	88	4	9	.308	68	39	91	3.58
	Totals	338	538	24	36	.400	308	196	513	3.35

JACK CLARK 22 6-1 170   Bats R Throws R

A Jack-of-all-trades . . . Handed right field job in spring training and didn't lose it . . . Can also play third base, which he handled in minors . . . Originally signed as a pitcher but bat was too good . . . Giants had enough confidence in him to trade Bobby Murcer . . . Good speed helped account for 16 triples for Phoenix farm team . . . Born Nov. 10, 1955, in New Brighton, Pa. . . . Needs to make more contact . . . Has occasional power . . . Another graduate of Little League and American Legion ball . . . could move up to leadoff spot.

Year	Club	Pos	G	AB	R	H	2B	3B	HR	RBI	SB	Avg.
1975	San Francisco	OF-3B	8	17	3	4	0	0	0	2	1	.235
1976	San Francisco	OF	26	102	14	23	6	2	2	10	6	.225
1977	San Francisco	OF	136	413	64	104	17	4	13	51	12	.252
	Totals..........		170	532	81	131	23	6	15	63	19	.246

BOB KNEPPER 23 6-2 180   Bats L Throws L

Made his first full season a good one, finishing third on club in wins . . . Got chance to move into rotation through injury to John Montefusco . . . Among starters, only Ed Halicki had a better ERA . . . Still walks too many . . . Flip side is he twice led minor leagues in strikeouts . . . Had September trial two years ago and Giants scored only two runs in his two defeats . . . Born May 25, 1954, in Akron, Ohio . . . Curveball is his out pitch . . . A second-round choice in 1972 free agent draft . . . Was California League's first 20-game winner in 15 years . . . Won a minor-league playoff game in his first start after getting married.

Year	Club	G	IP	W	L	Pct.	SO	BB	H	ERA
1976	San Francisco	4	25	1	2	.333	11	7	26	3.24
1977	San Francisco	27	166	11	9	.550	100	72	151	3.36
	Totals..................	31	191	12	11	.522	111	79	177	3.35

TERRY WHITFIELD 25 6-1 197   Bats L Throws R

Arrived last season after waiting years for his chance in Yankee organization . . . The Yanks' No. 1 draft choice in 1971 and twice an International League all-star . . . Giants used him both at first base and in outfield . . . Only Bill Madlock and Willie McCovey had higher averages on Giants last season . . . Excellent base runner with side-to-side motion popularized by Jackie Robinson . . . Winner of two minor-league home run titles but concentrates on just making contact now . . . Born Jan. 12, 1953, in Blythe, Cal. . . . Outstanding all-around athlete who also played football, basketball and ran track in high school.

Year	Club	Pos	G	AB	R	H	2B	3B	HR	RBI	SB	Avg.
1974	New York (AL) ...	OF	2	5	0	1	0	0	0	0	0	.200
1975	New York (AL) ...	OF	28	81	9	22	1	1	0	7	1	.272
1976	New York (AL) ...	OF	1	0	0	0	0	0	0	0	0	.000
1977	San Francisco	OF	114	326	41	93	21	3	7	36	2	.285
	Totals..........		145	412	50	116	22	4	7	43	3	.282

TOP PROSPECTS

SKIP JAMES 28 6-0 190　　　　　　Bats L Throws L
A spray hitter with several good minor-league seasons behind him . . . Might be useful as a utility player . . . Outstanding glove at first base and also has played outfield . . . Once hit 32 home runs for Fresno but has not displayed much power the last five years . . . Born Oct. 21, 1949, in Elmhurst, Ill. . . . Attended U. of Kansas where he was an All-Big Eight outfielder and a member of 1969 Orange Bowl team . . . The California League MVP in 1972.

GREG MINTON 26 6-2 190　　　　　　Bats S Throws R
Has been battling for spot in rotation the last two years . . . Used both as a starter and reliever in minors . . . All-around athlete who is a good fielder . . . Born July 29, 1951, in Lubbock, Tex. . . . Won 10 games in relief for Phoenix farm team in 1975 . . . Played American Legion ball with football's Tom Dempsey . . . Orginally signed by Kansas City Royals and acquired in 1973 for catcher Fran Healy.

MANAGER JOE ALTOBELLI: Friendly, no-nonsense guy who always makes his point . . . Brought club home fourth last season, his first as major-league manager . . . Enforces dress code and curfews but somehow players don't mind . . . Had great success as minor-league pilot of Baltimore's farm team in Rochester . . . Finished first four times and fourth once . . . Got tired of waiting for Earl Weaver to quit and quickly accepted

Giants' offer . . . Born May 26, 1932, in Detroit . . . A first baseman for 17 seasons, most of them in the minors . . . Played briefly with Cleveland and Minnesota, compiling a .210 average in 166 games . . . Committed to young players and tolerant of their mistakes . . . Instructs without reprimanding.

GREATEST MANAGER

He was called "Little Napoleon" because he was one of baseball's first emperors. He reigned over the New York Giants as manager for 31 straight seasons, a feat of longevity surpassed only by Connie Mack. He was John J. McGraw, not very tall, but a Giant.

McGraw began his managing career with Baltimore in 1899 and took over the New York Giants in 1902. When his rule ended in 1932 the Giants had won ten pennants and won the Series in 1905, 1921 and 1922. And McGraw had managed Christy Matthewson, Bill Terry and Mel Ott among other great players of the era. His 4,879 games and 2,840 victories are second only to Mack. Twice McGraw's Giants won pennants in three straight seasons.

Even the salty, tempestuous Leo Durocher, who managed the Giants to pennants in 1951 and 1954, can't displace McGraw as the greatest Giant manager. In eight seasons with the Giants, Durocher never finished lower than fifth. And the miracle of 1951, when the Giants sliced the Dodgers' 13-game August lead and won the playoff on Bobby Thomson's home run is still one of the most memorable feats in baseball history.

It was Durocher who said, "Nice guys finish last." No Giant manager ever finished first more than John J. McGraw.

ALL-TIME GIANT LEADERS

BATTING: Bill Terry, .401, 1930
HRs: Willie Mays, 52, 1965
RBIs: Mel Ott, 151, 1929
STEALS: George Burns, 62, 1914
WINS: Christy Mathewson, 37, 1908
STRIKEOUTS: Christy Mathewson, 267, 1903

SAN DIEGO PADRES

TEAM DIRECTORY: Board Chairman-President: Ray Kroc; VP-GM: Bob Fontaine; Minor League Admin.: Mike Port; Trav. Sec.: John Mattei; Pub. Rel.: Mike Ryan; Mgr.: Alvin Dark. Home: San Diego Stadium (48,460). Field distances: 330 l.f. line, 410 c.f., 330 r.f. line. Spring training: Yuma, Ariz.

SCOUTING REPORT

HITTING: Harshest critics of the Padres claim the team has the worst offense in the NL. That's totally false. Last year, the Padres were only second worst. Their .250 team BA was better than that

Dave Winfield had a career-high 25 HRs, 92 RBIs.

of the Mets, so of course the Padres added some punch to the line-up over the winter, right? Right. Owner Ray Kroc will have to sell a lot more Big Macs to pay free agent Oscar Gamble's whopper of a contract—$2,500,000. But Gamble comes equipped with other figures, like 31 HRs, 83 RBIs, and a .297 BA.

There is triple-threat Dave Winfield, who can hit, hit for power, run, throw and flash a very bright smile for photographers. He's San Diego's natural resource. And there is the sullen George Hendrick, who responded with a fine season last year. He still doesn't talk much, though his bat can be loud. Gene Tenace suffered through last season and Mike Ivie runs hot and cold, but Gene Richards was a surprise. Even with Gamble, the team will need an even bigger surprise this season. If not, pray for the Padres.

PITCHING: Talking about second worsts, guess which team in the NL was next-to-last in ERA? The Padres? How did you guess? The numbers were 4.43 and the only redeeming quality was Rollie Fingers. He led the league in saves, which is the biggest indication of how much trouble the staff is in. Of course, Randy Jones should be better after having had more time to recover from surgery. A good year from him could make a difference between a surprising season and another disappointing one.

And some trivia: Who led the Padres with 12 victories last season? Dave Freisleben? No. Brent Strom? No. How about Bob Shirley? How'd you guess? Shirley was a surprise last season. So was an injury to Strom, which also hampered the staff. If Freisleben can put together a good season, along with Strom, the staff would be acceptable. If not, manager Alvin Dark will have to go to the bullpen—where Fingers lives, it seems, alone.

FIELDING: The excuse last year was the Padres were young. They'll need a better excuse this season. The team's 189 errors was the most in the NL and an astonishing total besides. The double-play combo of Mike Champion and Bill Almon, a rookie duo last year, will have to do better. So will Ivie and Tucker Ashford at the corners. And so will almost everyone else. Hendrick can be a top flight outfielder when the mood strikes him. For a catcher, Tenace is a good first baseman. But he'll play both positions. Winfield will be conspicuous by his ability in the outfield.

OUTLOOK: People have stopped expecting too much of what once was a promising young team. This is not time to resume the optimism. The Padres will have to get more hitting, get more pitching and get more defense to any progress. Besides that, everything's fine.

SAN DIEGO PADRES 1978 ROSTER

MANAGER Alvin Dark
Coaches—Roger Craig, Bob Skinner, Whitey Wietelmann, Don Williams

PITCHERS

No.	Name	1977 Club	W-L	IP	SO	ERA	B-T	Ht.	Wt.	Born
—	Alfano, Don	Amarillo	4-3	—	—	5.52	L-L	6-2	195	10/1/55 Visalia, CA
—	Bernal, Vic	San Diego	1-1	20	6	5.40	R-R	6-0	175	10/6/53 Los Angeles, CA
		Hawaii	5-6	58	32	3.72				
—	D'Acquisto, John	St. Louis-S.D.	1-2	52	54	6.58	R-R	6-2	195	12/24/51 San Diego, CA
		Hawaii	4-3	60	47	3.75				
43	Dupree, Mike	Hawaii	3-7	97	39	4.27	R-R	6-0	175	5/29/53 Kansas City, KS
—	Eichelberger, Juan									
		Amarillo	12-7	—	—	4.10	R-R	6-2	195	10/21/53
—	Fierbaugh, Randy	Amarillo	2-9	—	—	5.21	L-R	6-3	205	10/16/52
—	Finger, Rollie	San Diego	8-9	132	113	3.00	R-R	6-3	195	8/25/46 Steubenville, OH
12	Freisleben, Dave	Hawaii	4-4	64	29	3.94	R-R	5-11	205	10/31/51 Coroapolis, CA
		San Diego	7-9	139	72	4.60				
35	Jones, Randy	San Diego	6-12	147	44	4.59	R-L	6-0	180	1/12/50 Brea, CA
—	Owchinko, Bob	Hawaii	5-1	44	30	1.43	L-L	6-2	185	1/1/55 Detroit, MI
		San Diego	9-12	170	101	4.45				
—	Shirley, Bob	San Diego	12-18	214	146	3.70	R-L	5-11	185	6/25/54 Oklahoma City, OK
48	Spillner, San	Hawaii	1-1	—	—	3.38	R-R	6-1	190	11/27/51 Casper, WY
		San Diego	7-6	123	74	3.73				
22	Strom, Brent	San Diego	0-2	17	8	12.18	R-L	6-3	190	10/14/48 San Diego, CA
		Hawaii	1-1	34	20	3.97				
37	Tomlin, Dave	San Diego	4-4	102	55	3.00	L-L	6-3	175	6/22/49 Maysville, KY
24	Wehremeister, Dave	Hawaii	2-2	39	23	2.54	R-R	6-4	195	11/9/52 Berwyn, IL
		San Diego	1-3	70	32	6.04				
—	Wiley, Mark	Hawaii	16-7	214	93	4.33	R-R	6-1	190	2/28/49 San Diego, CA

CATCHERS

No.	Name	1977 Club	H	HR	RBI	Pct.	B-T	Ht.	Wt.	Born
—	Castillo, Tony	Amarillo	—	5	45	.261	R-R	6-2	185	6/14/57 Santo Domingo, DR
—	Davis, Bob	San Diego	17	1	10	.181	R-R	6-0	180	3/1/52 Pryor, OK
—	Roberts, Dave	San Diego	41	1	23	.220	R-R	6-3	200	2/17/51 Lebanon, OR
—	Sweet, Rick	Hawaii	146	11	67	.323	B-R	6-0	190	9/7/52
—	Tenace, Gene	San Diego	102	15	61	.233	R-R	6-0	190	10/10/46 Russellton, PA

INFIELDERS

No.	Name	1977 Club	H	HR	RBI	Pct.	B-T	Ht.	Wt.	Born
5	Almon, Bill	San Diego	160	2	43	.261	R-R	6-3	170	11/21/52 Providence, RI
—	Ashford, Tucker	Hawaii	79	7	45	.281	R-R	6-1	190	12/4/54 Memphis, TN
		San Diego	54	3	24	.217				
—	Baker, Chuck	Hawaii	119	11	68	.243	R-R	5-11	175	12/6/52
18	Champion, Mike	San Diego	116	1	43	.229	R-R	6-0	180	2/10/55 Montgomery, AL
11	Hernandez, Enzo	San Diego	0	0	0	.000	R-R	5-8	150	2/12/49 Valle de Guanape, VZ
15	Ivie, Mike	San Diego	133	9	66	.272	R-R	6-3	205	8/8/52 Decatur, GA
—	Scanlon, Pat	New Orleans	33	6	22	.363	L-R	6-0	180	9/23/52 Minneapolis, MN
		Hawaii	17	0	12	.378				
		San Diego	15	1	11	.190				
—	Sutherland, Gary	San Diego	25	1	11	.243	R-R	6-0	185	9/27/44 Glendale, CA

OUTFIELDERS

No.	Name	1977 Club	H	HR	RBI	Pct.	B-T	Ht.	Wt.	Born
—	Derryberry, Tim	Reno	147	25	87	.333	L-R	6-1	185	4/21/58
—	Gamble, Oscar	Chicago (AL)	121	31	83	.297	L-R	5-11	170	12/20/46 Ramer, AL
—	Greer, Brian	Walla Walla	—	7	27	.183	R-R	6-3	210	5/13/59
		San Diego	0	0	0	.000				
20	Hendrick, George	San Diego	168	23	81	.311	R-R	6-3	195	10/18/49 Los Angeles, CA
—	Reynolds, Don	Hawaii	56	1	31	.368	R-R	5-8	180	4/16/53
—	Richards, Gene	San Diego	152	5	32	.290	L-L	6-0	175	9/29/53
42	Turner, Jerry	San Diego	71	10	48	.246	L-L	5-9	180	1/7/54 Texarkana, AR
—	Wilhelm, Jim	Hawaii	117	5	51	.246	R-R	6-3	190	9/20/52 Greenbrae, CA
31	Winfield, Dave	San Diego	169	25	92	.275	R-R	6-6	220	10/3/51 St. Paul, MN

PADRE PROFILES

DAVE WINFIELD 26 6-6 220   Bats R Throws R

Dangerous hitter with power to all fields . . . Steady improvement made him an all-star for first time last season . . . Good speed and knows when to use it . . . Not a great judge of fly balls, but has range and one of the strongest arms in league . . . Wants to hit .300 badly . . .Spurned free agent market to sign long-term contract for $1.5 million with Padres . . . Born Oct. 3, 1951, in St. Paul Minn. . . . Played basketball at U. of Minnesota and was drafted by NBA and ABA . . . Played outfield and pitched for college baseball team . . . Has never played in the minor leagues . . . Says, "I think I can get even better," and means it.

Year	Club	Pos	G	AB	R	H	2B	3B	HR	RBI	SB	Avg.
1973	San Diego	OF-1B	56	141	9	39	4	1	3	12	0	.277
1974	San Diego	OF	145	498	57	132	18	4	20	75	9	.265
1975	San Diego	OF	143	509	74	136	20	2	15	76	23	.267
1976	San Diego	OF	137	492	81	139	26	4	13	69	26	.283
1977	San Diego	OF	157	615	104	169	29	7	25	92	16	.275
	Totals		638	2255	325	615	97	18	76	324	74	.273

OSCAR GAMBLE 28 5-11 170   Bats L Throws R

Lefty slugger with remarkable ratio of one homer per 13 at bats last year . . . Known for magnificent afro haircut, which he was forced to trim when traded to Yankees . . . Did so with flourish, as his wife cried . . . Born Dec. 20, 1949, in Ramer, Ala. . . . Originally signed by Phillies . . . Has bounced around with several clubs . . . "When I first got traded I was disappointed. After the first trade, it doesn't bother you any more. And I enjoy going to new places, meeting different guys." . . . Used to bristle at being platooned. Now, it doesn't bother him . . . "If you're angry, you just hurt yourself." . . . Unable to come to terms with White Sox, became free agent, looking for the jackpot . . . Found it with Padres.

Year	Club	Pos	G	AB	R	H	2B	3B	HR	RBI	SB	Avg.
1969	Chicago (NL)	OF	24	71	6	16	1	1	1	5	0	.225
1970	Philadelphia	OF	88	275	31	72	12	4	1	19	5	.262
1971	Philadelphia	OF	92	280	24	62	11	1	6	23	5	.221
1972	Philadelphia	OF-1B	74	135	17	32	5	2	1	13	0	.237
1973	Cleveland	OF	113	390	56	104	11	3	20	44	3	.267
1974	Cleveland	OF	135	454	74	132	16	4	19	59	5	.291
1975	Cleveland	OF	121	348	60	91	16	3	15	45	11	.261
1976	New York (AL)	OF	110	340	43	79	13	1	17	57	5	.232
1977	Chicago (AL)	OF	137	408	75	121	22	2	31	83	1	.297
	Totals		894	2701	386	709	107	21	111	348	35	.262

GENE TENACE 31 6-0 190   Bats R Throws R

Had disappointing season, first with club after signing as free agent . . . Commanded multi-year contract in excess of $1 million . . . Benched for several weeks and didn't like it . . . Good power hitter who has never hit for average . . . Had four homers vs. Reds in '72 World Series . . . Had two homers first two WS at-bats, a record . . . Fled Oakland after '76 season . . . Born Oct. 10, 1946, in Russelton, Pa. . . . Doesn't really have a position, but better at first base . . . Broke in as catcher but more useful as backup now . . . A durable player who will play anywhere to get into lineup.

Year	Club	Pos	G	AB	R	H	2B	3B	HR	RBI	SB	Avg.
1969	Oakland	C	16	38	1	6	0	0	1	2	0	.158
1970	Oakland	C	38	105	19	32	6	0	7	20	0	.305
1971	Oakland	C-OF	65	179	26	49	7	0	7	25	2	.274
1972	Oakland	C-OF-INF	82	227	22	51	5	3	5	32	0	.225
1973	Oakland	1B-C-2B	160	510	83	132	18	2	24	84	2	.259
1974	Oakland	1B-C	158	484	71	102	17	1	26	73	2	.211
1975	Oakland	1B-C	158	498	83	127	17	0	29	87	7	.255
1976	Oakland	1B-C	128	417	64	104	19	1	22	66	5	.249
1977	San Diego	C-1B	147	437	66	102	24	4	15	61	5	.233
	Totals		952	2895	435	705	113	11	136	450	23	.244

ROLLIE FINGERS 31 6-3 195   Bats R Throws R

His 35 saves were only three off the major-league mark set by John Hiller in 1973 and the most in either league last season . . . Signed as a free agent after years of success in the AL . . . Still has handlebar moustache left over from days with Oakland . . . Participated in unusual four-pitcher no-hitter vs. California Sept. 28, 1975 . . . Has had at least 20 saves in each of the last six years . . . A real stopper with excellent control . . . Born Aug. 25, 1946, in Steubenville, Ohio . . . Won World Series MVP in '74 after one win, two saves and 1.93 ERA against Dodgers . . . Played out option with A's in '76, after the commissioner voided his sale from Oakland to Boston for $1 million.

Year	Club	G	IP	W	L	Pct.	SO	BB	H	ERA
1968	Oakland	1	1	0	0	.000	0	1	4	36.00
1969	Oakland	60	119	6	7	.462	61	41	116	3.71
1970	Oakland	45	148	7	9	.438	79	48	137	3.65
1971	Oakland	48	129	4	6	.400	98	30	94	3.00
1972	Oakland	65	111	11	9	.550	113	33	85	2.51
1973	Oakland	62	127	7	8	.467	110	39	107	1.92
1974	Oakland	76	119	9	5	.643	95	29	104	2.65
1975	Oakland	75	127	10	6	.625	115	33	95	2.98
1976	Oakland	70	135	13	11	.542	113	40	118	2.53
1977	San Diego	78	132	8	9	.471	113	36	123	3.00
	Totals	580	1148	75	70	.517	897	329	973	2.92

MIKE IVIE 25 6-3 205   Bats R Throws R

Broke in as a catcher as club's No. 1 draft choice in 1970 . . . Converted to first base and now prefers that position . . . Angered by shift to third base in middle of last season and jumped team for several days . . . Occasional power but mostly a line-drive hitter . . . Still learning how to field but improving . . . Opposing pitchers call him Poison Ivie . . . Born Aug. 8, 1952, in Decatur, Ga. . . . Batting coach Dick Sisler credited with making him a major-league hitter . . . Does not strike out much, but could walk more.

Year	Club	Pos	G	AB	R	H	2B	3B	HR	RBI	SB	Avg.
1971	San Diego	C	6	17	0	8	0	0	0	3	0	.471
1974	San Diego	1B	12	34	1	3	0	0	1	3	0	.088
1975	San Diego	3B-1B-C	111	377	36	94	16	2	8	46	4	.249
1976	San Diego	3B-1B-C	140	405	51	118	19	5	7	70	6	.291
1977	San Diego	1B-3B-C	134	489	66	133	29	2	9	66	3	.272
	Totals		403	1322	154	356	64	9	25	188	13	.269

MIKE CHAMPION 23 6-0 180   Bats R Throws R

Good defensive second baseman, but still learning the hitters . . . Won position in spring training last year after becoming one of top prospects in organization . . . Teamed with shortstop Bill Almon for only rookie keystone combination in league . . . Inexperience shows, but give him time . . . Displays occasional power, though he is not a threat as a hitter . . . Born Feb. 10, 1955, in Montgomery, Ala. . . . A second-round draft choice in 1973 . . . Good minor-league seasons earned him first invitation to spring training two years later . . . Overmatched against best pitchers but doesn't give up easily.

Year	Club	Pos	G	AB	R	H	2B	3B	HR	RBI	SB	Avg.
1976	San Diego	2B	11	38	4	9	2	0	1	2	0	.237
1977	San Diego	2B	150	507	35	116	14	6	1	43	3	.229
	Totals		161	545	39	125	16	6	2	45	3	.229

RANDY JONES 28 6-0 180   Bats R Throws L

Off-season operation for nerve damage in left elbow hurt chance to repeat as Cy Young winner . . . Finished second in voting for that award to Tom Seaver three years ago before winning it the following season . . . One of the best lefthanders in baseball when healthy . . . Sinker is his "out" pitch . . . Had career high 25-complete games and second 20-win season in '76 . . . Hopes to bounce back into that form and doctors say his recovery should be complete . . . Born Jan. 12, 1950, in Fullerton, Cal. . . . Holder of nine club records . . . Just quick enough to keep the hitters off balance . . . "You get a good look at his sinker and then it disappears," batters complain.

Year	Club	G	IP	W	L	Pct.	SO	BB	H	ERA
1973	San Diego	20	140	7	6	.538	77	37	129	3.15
1974	San Diego	40	208	8	22	.267	124	78	217	4.46
1975	San Diego	37	285	20	12	.625	103	56	242	2.24
1976	San Diego	40	315	22	14	.611	93	50	274	2.74
1977	San Diego	27	147	6	12	.333	44	36	173	4.59
	Totals	164	1095	63	66	.488	441	257	1035	3.24

GEORGE HENDRICK 28 6-3 195   Bats R Throws R

Superstar potential blunted by reputation as a loafer . . . Good hitter with power to all fields . . . Hit for high average for first time last season . . . Has good speed but never has had a lot of stolen bases . . . Started career in Oakland but was later dealt to Cleveland . . . Padres obtained him for Johnny Grubb, Fred Kendall and Hector Torres . . . Born Oct. 18, 1949, in Los Angeles . . . Can play all three outfield positions but used mostly in center . . . Tutored by Joe Rudi when both played with A's . . . A moody player who does not want to be reminded of mistakes.

Year	Club	Pos	G	AB	R	H	2B	3B	HR	RBI	SB	Avg.
1971	Oakland	OF	42	114	8	27	4	1	0	8	0	.237
1972	Oakland	OF	58	121	10	22	1	1	4	15	3	.182
1973	Cleveland	OF	113	440	64	118	18	0	21	61	7	.268
1974	Cleveland	OF	139	495	65	138	23	1	19	67	6	.279
1975	Cleveland	OF	145	561	82	145	21	2	24	86	6	.258
1976	Cleveland	OF	149	551	72	146	20	3	25	81	4	.265
1977	San Diego	OF	152	541	75	168	25	2	23	81	11	.311
	Totals		798	2823	376	764	112	10	115	399	37	.271

BILL ALMON 25 6-3 170   Bats R Throws R

Outstanding shortstop prone to rookie mistakes . . . Will make impossible play one inning, boot an easy grounder the next . . . No. 1 draft choice in country in 1974 . . . Could grow into an all-star if club is patient . . . No power, but no automatic out, either . . . Hit .291 last minor-league season . . . Born Nov. 21, 1952, in Providence, R.I. . . . Drafted by Padres out of high school but chose to go to Brown instead . . . Signed after his junior year . . . *Sporting News'* College Player of the Year in

1974 . . . Can steal a base and would be even better if he had more chances . . . A good one and club knows it.

Year	Club	Pos	G	AB	R	H	2B	3B	HR	RBI	SB	Avg.
1974	San Diego	SS	16	38	4	12	1	0	0	3	1	.316
1975	San Diego	SS	6	10	0	4	0	0	0	0	0	.400
1976	San Diego	SS	14	57	6	14	3	0	1	6	3	.246
1977	San Diego	SS	155	613	75	160	18	11	2	43	20	.261
	Totals		191	718	85	190	22	11	3	52	24	.265

GENE RICHARDS 24 6-0 175   Bats L Throws L

Arrived last season as polished hitter after two outstanding minor-league seasons . . . Gives club dependable lefty hitter in middle of right-handed lineup . . . Batted .381 for Reno after being chosen in first round of 1975 free-agent draft . . . Hit .331 for Hawaii the next year . . . Once stole 85 bases in minors and displayed good speed last season as well . . . Hits lefties as well as righties . . . Born September 29, 1953, in Monticello, S.C. . . . Wanted to hit .300 in first season and missed, tailing off at end of year . . . Padres' general manager, Bob Fontaine: "He's got that little bit of daring in him that makes a good baserunner."

Year	Club	Pos	G	AB	R	H	2B	3B	HR	RBI	SB	Avg.
1977	San Diego	1B-OF	146	525	79	152	16	11	5	32	56	.290

DAN SPILLNER 26 6-1 190   Bats R Throws R

May be ready to blossom after struggling for several seasons . . . Improved record and ERA encouraged Padres . . . Still walks too many batters . . . Back surgery cut short 1976 season . . . Tied for club wins (9) as rookie in 1974 but has not matched that total since . . . One-hit the Cubs June 19, 1974, when Rick Monday singled off his leg in third inning . . . Also used in relief . . . Born Nov. 27, 1951, in Casper, Wyo. . . . Needs a good season to restore confidence . . . Could wind up in bullpen if he stumbles at start . . . Club thinks he might be effective in long relief.

Year	Club	G	IP	W	L	Pct.	SO	BB	H	ERA
1974	San Diego	30	148	9	11	.450	95	70	153	4.01
1975	San Diego	37	167	5	13	.278	104	63	194	4.26
1976	San Diego	32	107	2	11	.154	57	55	120	5.05
1977	San Diego	76	123	7	6	.538	74	60	130	3.73
	Totals	175	545	23	41	.359	330	248	597	4.23

TOP PROSPECTS

RICK SWEET 25 6-0 187   **Bats L Throws R**
Will get a long look after an impressive season at Hawaii . . . A
top flight catcher who can swing a bat . . . Hit .323 last year, his
third in minor leagues . . . Also had club record 34 doubles, 11
homers and 67 RBIs . . . Born Sept. 7, 1952, in Longview, Wash.
. . . Drafted by Padres out of Gonzaga U. . . . Batted .350 his first
year of pro ball at Walla Walla.

STEVE MURA 23 6-12 188   **Bats R Throws R**
A hard thrower who totaled 123 strikeouts in 165 innings at
Hawaii last season . . . Padres liked his 12-10 record and his size
. . . Raised eyebrows with a 7-0 mark and 1.37 ERA at Walla
Walla in 1976 . . . Born Feb. 12, 1955, in New Orleans . . . Draft-
ed by Padres out of Tulane . . . Has never had a losing season in
three years of pro ball.

MANAGER ALVIN DARK: A hard-bitten veteran who took over
for John McNamara after club's disappointing
start last season . . . Owner Ray Kroc liked his
reputation as a tough disciplinarian . . . Immediately banned beer from team flights and required jackets and ties on road, leading to
much-publicized unhappiness among players
. . . Born Jan. 7, 1922 in Comanche, Okla. . . .
Knows the game but can be harsh with young
players . . . Was the manager when Giants won NL pennant in
'62 . . . Moved on to Kansas City and then Cleveland and returned to A's in '74, leading them to World Championship . . .
Also got A's into '75 playoffs, but was defeated by Boston . . .
Batted .289 in 14 seasons as a major-league shortstop.

GREATEST MANAGER

The success was modest, but John McNamara presided over the
most marked improvements in the history of the San Diego
Padres. The team had finished sixth in each of its six previous seasons, but in his second year as manager, in 1975, McNamara
moved the team into fourth place. In his 3½ years, McNamara
won more games than each of his predecessors, Preston Gomez
and Don Zimmer. His 60 wins in 1974 were the best for a first-year

manager with the club. No Padres' manager has matched his 73 victories in 1976. They called the Padres "McNamara's Band" and he orchestrated the team's gradual progress.

ALL-TIME PADRE LEADERS

BATTING: Clarence Gaston, .318, 1970
HRs: Nate Colbert, 38, 1970
RBIs: Nate Colbert, 111, 1972
STEALS: Gene Richards, 56, 1977
WINS: Randy Jones, 22, 1976
STRIKEOUTS: Clay Kirby, 231, 1971

Randy Jones hopes to rebound and top his 22-win club record.

ATLANTA BRAVES

TEAM DIRECTORY: Chairman of the Board: Bill Bartholomay; Pres.: Ted Turner; Dir. Player Personnel: Bill Lucas; Dir Player Development: Hank Aaron; Trav. Sec.: Pete Van Wieren; Pub. Rel.: Bob Hope; Mgr.: Bobby Cox. Home: Atlanta Stadium (52,870). Field distances: 330, l.f. line; 400, c.f.; 330, r.f. line. Spring training: West Palm Beach, Fla.

SCOUTING REPORT

HITTING: It can honestly be said that the state of the Braves' offense is such that the team can't afford to lose a good hitter. The trouble is, the Braves can't afford to keep a good hitter, either, In fact, the best hitter the club had—Willie Montanez—was traded away in an economy move. And flamboyant owner Ted Turner would have dealt Gary Matthews, too, if he could have convinced someone to assume the burden of Matthews' $400,000 a year salary.

But it is a good thing from the players' point of view that Matt-

Braves' barren order still boasts Jeff Burroughs' 41 homers.

hews is still around. He is one of the few established sluggers on the team and the Braves' .254 BA last season hardly woke up Chief Noc-A-Homa in his left field teepee in Atlanta Stadium. The Braves also have Jeff Burroughs, who swatted 41 homers, and Barry Bonnell, who batted .300. After that, the cupboard is bare. Biff Pocoroba shows signs of being a hitter, but Rowland Office lost his job over an unexciting batting average. Jerry Royster has been a disappointment. Chances are, the Chief won't be doing too much dancing this year, either.

PITCHING: Only one thing could be worse than the Braves' listless lineup—a listless pitching staff. Andy Messersmith, who might have been of some help after being injured most of last season, was discarded, along with his millions. Phil Niekro is the sole dependable member of the staff, a shrewd pitcher with a winning knack. He has a sense of humor, too. With this team, he needs it. Other starters are likely to be Buzz Capra, Dick Ruthven and Steve Hargan. Together, they combined for all of 15 wins last season. No wonder the Braves were last in the NL with a 4.85 ERA.

Max Leon is also available as a spot starter and has the enviable status of being one of the team's few .500 pitchers (he was 4-4). The rest of the staff is getting its first chance. Jamie Easterly and Preston Hanna will be in the bullpen. Or, rather, they will be out of it, quite often. It may be indicative that one of the players who has been promoted from the Richmond farm team is Larry McWilliams. Last season, in the minors, he was 8-9.

FIELDING: More trouble here, too. Montanez was the only Gold Glove in the infield. Rod Gilbreath has been around the block. Tom Paciorek is a useful utility player, but may find himself starting. Craig Robinson, Pat Rockett, Royster and Rob Belloir are the others. Office, who probably is the best outfielder on the team, sat much of last season because he didn't hit. Matthews is merely adequate. Bonnell can catch a fly ball too. No one here will make the unexpected play. Some won't even make the expected one. The Braves made 175 errors last season and only two teams made more. This year, the team has a chance to lead the league in something.

OUTLOOK: You need a flashlight, it's so dim. The Braves needed more hitting, so they lost a hitter. They needed more pitching, so they lost a pitcher. The infield is bad news. They call Atlanta Stadium the Launching Pad. This year, it's likely to be the Yawning Pad.

ATLANTA BRAVES 1978 ROSTER

MANAGER Bobby Cox

Coaches—Cloyd Boyer, Pete Ward, Tom Burgess, Chris
        Cannizzaro

PITCHERS

No.	Name	1977 Club	W-L	IP	SO	ERA	B-T	Ht.	Wt.	Born
—	Boggs, Tommy	Tucson	5-10	97	70	8.54	R-R	6-2	197	10/25/55 Poughkeepsie, NY
		Texas	0-3	27	15	6.00				
—	Bradford, Larry	Savannah	5-6	81	45	3.00	R-L	6-1	200	12/21/51 Chicago, IL
		Richmond	6-5	89	54	3.34				
		Atlanta	0-0	3	1	3.00				
33	Camp, Rick	Atlanta	6-3	79	51	3.99	R-R	6-1	198	6/10/53 Trion, GA
32	Campbell, David	Richmond	2-0	6	5	0.00	R-R	6-3	210	9/3/51 Princeton, IN
		Atlanta	0-6	89	42	3.03				
47	Capra, Buzz	Atlanta	6-11	139	100	5.37	R-R	5-10	168	10/1/47 Chicago, IL
42	Collins, Don	Richmond	1-0	19	7	3.32	R-L	6-2	195	9/15/52 Lyons, GA
		Atlanta	3-9	71	27	5.07				
39	Davey, Mike	Richmond	3-3	78	45	2.31	R-L	6-2	190	6/2/52 Spokane, WA
		Atlanta	0-0	16	7	5.06				
—	Devine, Adrian	Texas	11-6	106	67	3.57	R-R	6-4	205	12/2/51 Galveston, TX
45	Easterly, Jamie	Atlanta	2-4	59	37	6.10	L-L	5-9	170	2/17/53 Houston, TX
38	Hanna, Preston	Savannah	2-1	31	20	1.16	R-R	6-1	180	9/10/54 Pensacola, FL
50	Hargan, Steve	Tor-TX	2-3	42	21	6.21	R-R	6-3	195	9/8/42 Ft. Wayne, IN
		Atlanta	0-3	37	18	6.81				
26	LaCorte, Frank	Atlanta	1-8	37	28	11.68	R-R	6-1	180	10/13/51 San Jose, CA
		Richmond	2-3	37	40	6.08				
31	Leon, Max	Atlanta	4-4	82	44	3.95	R-R	6-0	170	2/4/50 Villa Acula, MX
	Mahler, Mickey	Richmond	13-10	217	145	3.53	B-L	6-3	189	7/30/52 Montgomery, AL
		Atlanta	1-2	23	14	6.26				
—	McLaughlin, Joey	Richmond	9-10	179	70	3.82	R-R	6-2	192	7/11/56 Tulsa, OK
		Atlanta	0-0	9	0	15.00				
—	McWilliams, Larry	Savannah	8-9	158	139	3.36	L-L	6-5	175	2/10/54 Wichita, KS
35	Niekro, Phil	Atlanta	16-20	330	262	4.04	R-R	6-1	180	4/1/39 Blaine, OH
40	Ruthven, Dick	Atlanta	7-13	151	84	4.23	R-R	6-2	195	3/27/51 Sacramento, CA
37	Solomon, Eddie	New Orleans	4-2	45	30	4.23	R-R	6-3	190	2/9/51 Perry, GA
		Richmond	5-1	52	34	2.77				
		Atlanta	6-6	89	54	4.55				
34	Theiss, Duane	Savannah	6-1	61	50	1.18	R-R	6-3	185	11/20/53 Zanesville, OH
		Atlanta	1-1	21	7	6.43				

CATCHERS

No.	Name	1977 Club	H	HR	RBI	Pct.	B-T	Ht.	Wt.	Born
29	Correll, Vic	Atlanta	30	7	16	.208	R-R	5-10	180	2/5/46 Florence, SC
3	Murphy, Dale	Richmond	142	22	90	.305	R-R	6-4	190	3/12/56 Portland, OR
		Atlanta	24	2	14	.316				
11	Nolan, Joe	Atlanta	23	3	9	.280	L-R	5-11	175	5/12/51 St. Louis, MO
4	Pocoroba, Biff	Atlanta	93	8	44	.290	B-R	5-10	180	7/25/53 Los Angeles, CA

INFIELDERS

10	Belloir, Rob	Richmond	130	5	54	.263	R-R	5-10	170	7/13/48 Heidelberg, Germany
		Atlanta	0	0	0	.000				
15	Chaney, Darrel	Atlanta	42	3	15	.201	B-R	6-1	190	3/9/48 Hammond, IN
19	Gilbreath, Rod	Atlanta	99	8	43	.243	R-R	6-2	170	9/24/52 Laurel, MS
—	Hubbard, Glenn	Greenwood	70	5	44	.385	R-R	5-9	150	9/25/57 Hann AFB, Germany
		Savannah	67	6	32	.225				
12	Paciorek, Tom	Atlanta	37	3	15	.239	R-R	6-4	210	11/2/46 Detroit, MI
16	Robinson, Craig	Atlanta	6	0	1	.207	R-R	5-9	165	8/21/48 Abingdon, PA
9	Rockett, Pat	Atlanta	67	1	24	.254	R-R	5-10	165	1/9/55 San Antonio, TX
13	Royster, Jerry	Atlanta	96	6	28	.216	R-R	6-0	165	10/18/52 Sacramento, CA

OUTFIELDERS

18	Asselstine, Brian	Richmond	27	0	13	.276	L-R	6-1	170	9/23/53 Santa Barbera, CA
		Atlanta	26	4	17	.210				
2	Bonnell, Barry	Richmond	19	0	10	.380	R-R	6-3	190	10/27/53 Milford, OH
		Atlanta	108	1	45	.300				
7	Burroughs, Jeff	Atlanta	157	41	114	.271	R-R	6-2	193	3/7/51 Long Beach, CA
—	Cooper, Gary	Greenwood	127	12	62	.277	R-R	6-0	175	12/22/56 Savannah, GA
43	Gaston, Cito	Atlanta	23	3	21	.271	R-R	6-4	210	3/17/44 San Antonio, TX
36	Matthews, Gary	Atlanta	157	17	64	.283	R-R	6-3	190	7/5/50 San Fernando, CA
—	Miller, Eddie	Tulsa	110	1	37	.294	L-R	5-9	165	6/29/57 San Pablo, CA
		Texas	2	0	1	.333				
22	Office, Rowland	Atlanta	103	5	39	.241	L-L	6-0	170	10/25/52 Sacramento, CA
—	Whisenton, Larry	Savannah	84	4	36	.302	L-L	6-1	190	7/3/56 St. Louis, MO
		Richmond	40	0	11	.235				
		Atlanta	1	0	1	.250				

BRAVE PROFILES

BARRY BONNELL 24 6-3 190   Bats R Throws R

Same story happens every spring . . . Player gets invited to Florida expecting to be sent to minors . . . Instead, he makes club . . . Then he makes headlines by leading club in hitting . . . With Bonnell, that shouldn't have been a surprise . . . He led the Western Carolina League with a .324 BA in 1975 . . . Obtained by Braves in compensation for allowing Phillies to sign Dick Allen . . . Born Oct. 27, 1953, in Cincinnati . . . Attended Ohio State . . . Brother Glenn is an infielder in Reds' organization . . . Has pilot's license . . . Also dabbles in photography and amateur radio.

Year	Club	Pos	G	AB	R	H	2B	3B	HR	RBI	SB	Avg.
1977	Atlanta..........	3B	100	360	41	108	11	0	1	45	7	.300

PHIL NIEKRO 39 6-1 180   Bats R Throws R

Really knuckles down . . . Has best soft stuff in league . . . Led NL in strikeouts and led club in victories . . . Just one win short of Lew Burdette's second-best Braves' total . . . Only original Atlanta Brave left . . . No-hit Padres Aug. 5, 1973 . . . Nearly had second no-hitter in 1976 . . . On next to last day of season he came within two outs before Cesar Geronimo of Reds doubled . . . Born April 1, 1939, in Blaine, Ohio . . . Asked to manage Braves after Dave Bristol was fired in October . . . Once had 12 RBIs in one season . . . Brother Joe pitches for Astros . . . Grew up with Boston Celtic star John Havlicek . . . Active in March of Dimes fund drive . . . Holds 22 club pitching records.

Year	Club	G	IP	W	L	Pct.	SO	BB	H	ERA
1964	Milwaukee................	10	15	0	0	.000	8	7	15	4.80
1965	Milwaukee................	41	75	2	3	.400	40	26	73	2.88
1966	Atlanta................	28	50	4	3	.571	17	23	48	4.14
1967	Atlanta................	46	207	11	9	.550	129	55	164	1.87
1968	Atlanta................	37	257	14	12	.538	140	45	228	2.50
1969	Atlanta................	40	284	23	13	.639	193	57	235	2.57
1970	Atlanta................	34	230	12	18	.400	168	68	222	4.27
1971	Atlanta................	42	269	15	14	.517	173	70	248	2.98
1972	Atlanta................	38	282	16	12	.571	164	53	254	3.06
1973	Atlanta................	42	245	13	10	.565	131	89	214	3.31
1974	Atlanta................	41	302	20	13	.606	195	88	249	2.38
1975	Atlanta................	39	276	15	15	.500	144	72	285	3.20
1976	Atlanta................	38	271	17	11	.607	173	101	249	3.29
1977	Atlanta................	44	330	16	20	.444	262	164	315	4.04
	Totals................	520	3093	178	153	.538	1946	918	2799	3.09

JEFF BURROUGHS 27 6-2 193   Bats R Throws R

Most successful rocket on the "Launching Pad" . . . Second only to George Foster in homers . . . Fourth in NL in RBIs . . . Was AL MVP for Texas Rangers in 1974 . . . Was Senators' and country's No. 1 draft in 1969 . . . Once hit three grand slams in 10 days for Texas . . . Also had at least one RBI in 10 straight games in 1974 . . . Born March 7, 1951, in Long Beach, Cal. . . . Braves gave up Adrian Devine, Roger Moret, Carl Morton, Dave May and Ken Henderson to get him . . . Also gave up an estimated $225,000 . . . A good arm . . . He led AL outfielders in double plays in 1974 . . . A camper in the off-season.

Year	Club	Pos	G	AB	R	H	2B	3B	HR	RBI	SB	Avg.
1970	Washington	OF	6	12	1	2	0	0	0	1	0	.167
1971	Washington	OF	59	181	20	42	9	0	5	25	1	.232
1972	Texas	OF-1B	22	65	4	12	1	0	1	3	0	.185
1973	Texas	OF-1B	151	526	71	147	17	1	30	85	0	.279
1974	Texas	OF	152	554	84	167	33	2	25	118	2	.301
1975	Texas	OF	152	585	81	132	20	0	29	94	4	.226
1976	Texas	OF	158	604	71	143	22	2	18	86	0	.237
1977	Atlanta	OF	154	579	91	157	19	1	41	114	4	.271
	Totals		854	3106	423	802	121	6	129	526	11	.258

DICK RUTHVEN 27 6-2 195   Bats R Throws R

Growing into dependable pitcher . . . Poor support ruined his bid for statistical success last season . . . Still was second on club in ERA . . . Was only Brave named to all-star team in 1976, leading Braves with four shutouts . . . Traded twice within three days at winter meetings in 1975 . . . Phillies sent him to White Sox, who shipped him to Atlanta . . . Born March 27, 1951, in Sacramento . . . Had two unusual statistics two years ago . . . Got a decision in each of his first 18 appearances and did not allow an unearned run all season . . . Married to twin sister of former Phillie teammate Tommy Hutton.

Year	Club	G	IP	W	L	Pct.	SO	BB	H	ERA
1973	Philadelphia	25	128	6	9	.400	98	75	125	4.22
1974	Philadelphia	35	213	9	13	.409	153	116	182	4.01
1975	Philadelphia	11	41	2	2	.500	26	22	37	4.17
1976	Atlanta	36	240	14	17	.452	142	90	255	4.20
1977	Atlanta	25	151	7	13	.350	84	62	158	4.23
	Totals	132	773	38	54	.413	503	365	757	4.16

ROWLAND OFFICE 25 6-0 170   Bats L Throws L

Held the office in center field but running for re-election . . . Slumped last season, with knee injury suffered season before cited as reason . . . Received injury while making patented, diving catch against Pittsburgh . . . Holds club record of five consecutive pinch-hits . . . Once walked intentionally three times in one game, tying a record . . . Had longest hitting streak in two years by Brave in 1976, hitting in 29 straight . . . Born Oct. 25, 1952, in Sacramento . . . A high school opponent of teammate Jerry Royster . . . When he pinch-runs, it's an Office running for a man.

Year	Club	Pos	G	AB	R	H	2B	3B	HR	RBI	SB	Avg.
1972	Atlanta..........	OF	2	5	1	2	0	0	0	0	0	.400
1974	Atlanta..........	OF	131	248	20	61	16	1	3	31	5	.246
1975	Atlanta..........	OF	126	355	30	103	14	1	3	30	2	.290
1976	Atlanta..........	OF	99	359	51	101	17	1	4	34	2	.281
1977	Atlanta..........	OF	124	428	42	103	13	1	5	39	2	.241
	Totals..........		482	1395	144	370	60	4	15	134	11	.265

BIFF POCOROBA 24 5-10 180   Bats R Throws R

Can boff the ball . . . Was surprise in finishing second on club in hitting . . . Suffered knee injury in home plate collision with Mike Sadek that jeopardized his 1976 season . . . Won job again in next spring training . . . First noticed in 1975 when he threw out 11 straight runners in spring . . . Made jump from AA to major leagues that year . . . Born July 25, 1953, in Burbank, Cal. . . . Was a 17th round pick by Braves in 1971 . . . Led two minor leagues in fielding to earn shot . . . Biff is his real name.

Year	Club	Pos	G	AB	R	H	2B	3B	HR	RBI	SB	Avg.
1975	Atlanta..........	C	67	188	15	48	7	1	1	22	0	.255
1976	Atlanta..........	C	54	174	16	42	7	0	0	14	1	.241
1977	Atlanta..........	C	113	321	46	93	24	1	8	44	3	.290
	Totals..........		234	683	77	183	38	2	9	80	4	.268

GARY MATTHEWS 27 6-3 190   Bats R Throws R

Hits hard, throws hard and runs hard . . . Was fourth on club in hitting, his first season after joining Braves as free agent . . . Had played out contract with Giants and was claimed by maximum 12 teams in free agent draft . . . Owner Ted Turner was so eager to get him, he was fined and suspended by commissioner for tampering . . . Was NL Rookie-of-the-Year in

1973 . . . Born July 5, 1950, in San Fernando, Cal. . . . No. 1 draft by Giants in 1968 . . . Holds Phoenix club record of 108 hits in 1972 . . . Give him a lead and he'll steal a base . . . May be the best disco dancer in the league.

Year	Club	Pos	G	AB	R	H	2B	3B	HR	RBI	SB	Avg.
1972	San Francisco	OF	20	62	11	18	1	1	4	14	0	.290
1973	San Francisco	OF	148	540	74	162	22	10	12	58	17	.300
1974	San Francisco	OF	154	561	87	161	27	6	16	82	11	.287
1975	San Francisco	OF	116	425	67	119	22	3	12	58	13	.280
1976	San Francisco	OF	156	587	79	164	28	4	20	84	12	.279
1977	Atlanta	OF	148	555	89	157	25	5	17	64	22	.283
	Totals		742	2730	407	781	125	29	81	360	75	.286

TOP PROSPECTS

DALE MURPHY 22 6-4 185   **Bats R Throws R**
A superb defensive catcher with strong, accurate arm . . . Has displayed some power . . . Hit 16 homers when he split 1976 minor-league season in Savannah and Richmond . . . Has had two September trials since and has impressed . . . Born March 12, 1956, in Portland, Ore. . . . Twice a minor-league all-star . . . Could make club as backup this season . . . A high school star in baseball and basketball.

BRIAN ASSELSTINE 24 6-1 170   **Bats R Throws R**
Fine defensive outfielder who can play all three outfield positions . . . Hit first major-league home run after just seven games in late-season appearance two years ago . . . Good base stealer . . . Braves No. 1 choice and No. 15 overall in 1973 draft . . . Born Sept. 23, 1953, in Santa Barbara, Cal. . . . An International League all-star on basis of .293 BA.

TOM BOGGS 22 6-2 197   **Bats R Throws R**
Did not live up to expectations last year with Rangers, but still young enough to make it on Braves' staff . . . Impressed Billy Martin and Frank Robinson with his stuff . . . Must gain confidence, which will come with experience . . . Born Oct. 25, 1955, in Poughkeepsie, N.Y. . . . His dad worked for IBM and moved family first to Kentucky before settling in Austin, Tex. . . . No. 1 draft of Rangers (No. 2 in country) in June, 1974 free agent draft.

MANAGER BOBBY COX: Replaces Dave Bristol, who was fired at the end of last season . . . Comes to Atlanta after championship year with the Yankees, with whom he was a first-year coach, at first base . . . Born May 21, 1941, in Tulsa, Okla. . . . Was a third baseman, over two seasons, with the Yankees, batting .225 in total of 225 games for his only major league team . . . Managed five years in Yankee farm system—with one first-place finish (Syracuse in the International League, 1976), two seconds, a third and a fourth . . . No relation to ex-Dodger Billy Cox . . . Has five children, 10,11,12,13,14.

GREATEST MANAGER

It was a brief tenure, but also one of the most successful of any Braves' manager. The team, then in Milwaukee, had not won the Series since 1914, when it was still in Boston. And when Fred Haney arrived in 1956, the team had not won a pennant in eight years. In his first season, Haney got the club into second place, only one game out of first.

But 1957 was the season as the Braves won the pennant and then, with Lew Burdette getting three victories, went on to defeat the Yankees in seven games in the Series. In 1958, the Braves repeated as National League champions, but the Yankees rallied to win the Series rematch in seven games after trailing three games to one. The next season, Haney's last, the Braves finished in a first-place tie with the Dodgers but lost a three-game pennant playoff.

Still, no other manager in the club's history had as much success as Haney. Truly, it was short and also sweet.

ALL-TIME BRAVE LEADERS

BATTING: Rogers Hornsby, .387, 1928
HRs: Eddie Mathews, 47, 1953
    Hank Aaron, 47, 1971
RBIs: Eddie Mathews, 135, 1953
STEALS: Ralph Meyers, 57, 1913
WINS: Vic Willis, 27, 1902
    Charles Pittinger, 27, 1902
    Dick Rudolph, 27, 1914
STRIKEOUTS: Phil Niekro, 262, 1977

PHILADELPHIA PHILLIES

TEAM DIRECTORY: Chairman of the Board: R.R.M. Carpenter, Jr.; Pres.: R.R.M. Carpenter III; Exec. VP: William Y. Giles; VP and Director of Player Personnel: Paul Owens; VP and Director of Finances: George F.H. Harrison; Director of Minor Leagues and Scouting: Dallas Green; Pub. Rel.: Larry Shenk; Trav. Sec.: Ed Ferenz; Mgr.: Danny Ozark. Home: Veterans Stadium (56,581) Field distances: 330 l.f. line; 408, c.f.; 330, r.f. line. Spring training: Clearwater, Fla.

SCOUTING REPORT

HITTING: About the biggest weakness that can be found in the lineup of the East Division champions is the departure of Tommy Hutton, who made a career of hitting against Tom Seaver. But Hutton rarely hit against anyone else. Be assured, the rest of the Phillies don't have that problem. Greg Luzinski was second in the MVP voting and also wrested the club homer title from the dangerous Mike Schmidt. That one-two punch can deliver a knockout. Only the Dodgers hit more homers last season and no team had a better BA than the Phillies .279. Problems? In this batting order, they don't exist.

From top to bottom—that's Garry Maddox to Ted Sizemore—

Fourth 20-win year gave Steve Carlton second Cy Young.

the Phils will hit. In between, there is Bake McBride, who was obtained from the Cardinals a year ago. And Richie Hebner, who came from the Pirates a year ago. The batters may not always be home-grown, but they feel very comfortable, anyway. Opposing pitchers, of course, do not.

Even the little guys, such as Larry Bowa, will hit and then make a nuisance of themselves once they reach base. The bench is sagging from all the heavy hitters that have to wait for their chance—the experienced veterans, such as Davey Johnson and Jay Johnstone and Tim McCarver and Jose Cardenal.

PITCHING: Start with Steve Carlton—that's a good start. He was merely voted the best pitcher in the league last season. Larry Christenson is just beginning to ripen as a major talent. And, yes, Jim Lonborg is still around and doing the job. The real need here is for another capable starter who can hold the opposition to, say, five or six runs long enough for the Phillies to erupt in their half of the inning.

That person could be Barry Lerch, who won 10 games last season despite an ERA that grew faster than inflation. If the Phils don't develop another starter, there is always the bullpen. Manager Danny Ozark calls it his "first resort." And why not? Gene Garber, Tug McGraw and Ron Reed make a trio grande. And despite all the notions about the Philadelphia lineup, it is a fact that the pitching staff compiled a 3.71 ERA last season, which was simply the fourth best in the league.

FIELDING: The Phillies made the fewest errors (95) of any team except Cincinnati last season. The team lives by the creed, the best offense is sometimes a good defense. During the rare moments when the Phillies won't hit or their pitchers won't get anyone out, an all-star infield and outfield will help. Bowa at short and Schmidt at third probably are the best left side in either league. In the outfield, Maddox and McBride supply grace and speed. Luzinski is weak in left, but then you can't have everything. If you want to include pitchers, there is even Jim Kaat, who has won several Gold Gloves.

OUTLOOK: There isn't anything the Phillies need, except maybe better weather in October when they participate in the playoffs. The cold seems to sting the hands of the batters—or something like that. Anyway, there is no reason the team can't win the pennant, just as there was no reason they couldn't last year. In Philadelphia, the biggest crack is still located in the Liberty Bell and not in this team.

PHILADELPHIA PHILLIES 1978 ROSTER

MANAGER Danny Ozark
Coaches—Carroll Beringer, Billy DeMars, Ray Rippelmeyer, Bobby Wine, Tony Taylor

PITCHERS

No.	Name	1977 Club	W-L	IP	SO	ERA	B-T	Ht.	Wt.	Born
46	Boitano, Dan	Okla. City	4-8	102	66	5.75	R-R	6-0	185	3/22/53 Sacramento, CA
		Reading	2-2	19	8	2.84				
40	Brusstar, Warren	Okla. City	0-1	6	5	1.50	R-R	6-3	200	2/2/52 Oakland, CA
		Philadelphia	7-2	71	46	2.66				
32	Carlton, Steve	Philadelphia	23-10	283	198	2.64	L-L	6-5	210	12/22/44 Miami, FL
38	Christenson, Larry	Philadelphia	19-6	219	118	4.07	R-R	6-2	210	11/10/53 Everett, WA
26	Garber, Gene	Philadelphia	8-6	103	78	2.36	R-R	5-10	175	11/13/47 Lancaster, Pa.
39	Kaat, Jim	Philadelphia	6-11	160	55	5.40	L-L	6-5	215	11/7/38 Zeeland, MI
47	Lerch, Randy	Philadelphia	10-6	169	81	5.06	L-L	6-3	195	10/9/54 Sacramento, CA
41	Lonborg, Jim	Philadelphia	11-4	158	76	4.10	R-R	6-5	202	4/16/43 Santa Maria, CA
45	McGraw, Tug	Philadelphia	7-3	79	58	2.62	R-L	6-0	185	8/30/44 Martinez, CA
42	Reed, Ron	Philadelphia	7-5	124	84	2.76	R-R	6-6	215	11/2/42 LaPorte, IN
33	Warthen, Dan	Mont.-Phil.	2-4	39	27	7.15	B-L	6-0	200	12/1/52 Omaha, NB
		Okla. City	1-1	16	23	8.82				
—	Waterbury, Steve	N.O.-Okl. City	6-3	68	37	3.16	R-R	6-5	180	4/6/52 Carbondale, IL
24	Wright, Jim	Okla. City	14-6	161	118	3.13	R-R	6-5	205	3/3/55 St. Joseph, MO.

CATCHERS

No.	Name	1977 Club	H	HR	RBI	Pct.	B-T	Ht.	Wt.	Born
8	Boone, Bob	Philadelphia	125	11	66	.284	R-R	6-2	208	11/19/47 San Diego, CA
9	Foote, Barry	Mont.-Phil.	19	3	11	.235	R-R	6-3	210	2/16/52 Smithfield, N.C.
11	McCarver, Tim	Philadelphia	54	6	30	.320	L-R	6-0	195	10/16/41 Memphis, TN
—	Moreland, Bobby	Reading	131	8	55	.327	R-R	6-0	186	5/2/54 Dallas, TX
		Okla. City	1	0	1	.077				

INFIELDERS

No.	Name	1977 Club	H	HR	RBI	Pct.	B-T	Ht.	Wt.	Born
16	Andrews, Fred	Okla. City	113	7	51	.290	R-R	5-8	153	5/4/52 Lafayette, LA.
		Philadelphia	4	0	2	.174				
10	Bowa, Larry	Philadelphia	175	4	41	.280	B-R	5-10	155	12/6/45 Sacramento, CA
43	Buskey, Mike	Okla. City	109	8	54	.234	R-R	5-11	175	1/13/49 San Francisco, CA
		Philadelphia	2	0	1	.286				
48	Cruz, Todd	Reading	98	2	51	.218	R-R	6-0	170	11/23/55 Highland Park, MI
17	Harmon, Terry	Philadelphia	11	2	5	.183	R-R	6-2	185	4/12/44 Toledo, OH
18	Hebner, Rich	Philadelphia	113	18	62	.285	L-R	6-1	197	11/26/47 Boston, MA
15	Johnson, Dave	Philadelphia	50	8	36	.321	R-R	6-0	182	1/30/43 Orlando, FL
—	Jones, Joe	Spartanburg	98	17	71	.309	R-R	6-2	193	12/15/56 Phoenix, AZ
—	Moreno, Jose	Reading	133	5	49	.267	B-R	6-0	175	11/2/57 Santo Domingo, D.R.
30	Morrison, Jim	Okla. City	133	12	71	.294	R-R	5-11	175	9/23/52 Pensacola, FL
		Philadelphia	3	0	1	.429				
—	Poff, John	Reading	61	11	31	.284	L-L	6-2	190	10/23/52 Chillicothe, OH
		Okla. City	69	5	36	.307				
20	Schmidt, Mike	Philadelphia	149	38	101	.274	R-R	6-2	198	9/27/49 Dayton, OH
6	Sizemore, Ted	Philadelphia	146	4	47	.281	R-R	5-10	165	4/15/45 Gadsden, AL

OUTFIELDERS

No.	Name	1977 Club	H	HR	RBI	Pct.	B-T	Ht.	Wt.	Born
23	Brown, Bobby	Reading	69	5	28	.290	L-R	6-1	190	5/24/54 Norfolk, VA
		Okla. City	98	4	22	.314				
—	Cardenal, Jose	Chicago (NL)	54	3	18	.239	R-R	5-10	150	10/7/43 Matanzas, Cuba
—	Isales, Orlando	Peninsula	107	9	46	.240	R-R	5-9	174	12/22/59 Santurce, P.R.
21	Johnstone, Jay	Philadelphia	103	15	59	.284	L-R	6-1	185	11/20/46 Manchester, CT
19	Luzinski, Greg	Philadelphia	171	39	130	.309	R-R	6-1	225	11/22/50 Chicago, IL
31	Maddox, Garry	Philadelphia	167	14	74	.292	R-R	6-3	175	9/1/49 Cincinnati, OH
25	Martin, Jerry	Philadelphia	56	6	28	.260	R-R	6-1	195	5/11/49 Columbia, S.C.
22	McBride, Bake	St. L-Phil.	127	15	61	.316	L-R	6-2	190	2/3/49 Fulton, MO.
27	Smith, Lonnie	Okla. City	132	4	41	.277	R-R	5-9	170	12/22/55 Chicago, IL

PHILLIE PROFILES

STEVE CARLTON 33 6-5 210   Bats L Throws L

Cy Young winner . . . Had most victories in either league last season and was third among NL starters in ERA . . . Big and strong and can whiff anybody . . . Took Cy Young in 1972, his first year with Phillies after trade from St. Louis . . . Only Jim Kaat, Tom Seaver and Don Sutton have more victories among active NL pitchers . . . Only Sutton and Seaver have more shutouts . . . Born Dec. 22, 1944, in Miami . . . Shares major-league record with Seaver for 19 strikeouts in a nine-inning game . . . He lost that 1969 game to Mets when Ron Swoboda beat him with two home runs . . . Always pitches to Tim McCarver, his first receiver with Cardinals . . . With four other southpaws on team, Carlton is the one called "Lefty."

Year	Club	G	IP	W	L	Pct.	SO	BB	H	ERA
1965	St. Louis	15	25	0	0	.000	21	8	27	2.52
1966	St. Louis	9	52	3	3	.500	25	18	56	3.12
1967	St. Louis	30	193	14	9	.609	168	62	173	2.98
1968	St. Louis	34	232	13	11	.542	162	61	214	2.99
1969	St. Louis	31	236	17	11	.607	210	93	185	2.17
1970	St. Louis	34	254	10	19	.345	193	109	239	3.72
1971	St. Louis	37	273	20	9	.690	172	98	275	3.56
1972	Philadelphia	41	346	27	10	.730	310	87	257	1.98
1973	Philadelphia	40	293	13	20	.394	223	113	293	3.90
1974	Philadelphia	39	291	16	13	.552	240	136	249	3.22
1975	Philadelphia	37	225	15	14	.517	192	104	217	3.56
1976	Philadelphia	35	253	20	7	.741	195	72	224	3.13
1977	Philadelphia	36	283	23	10	.697	198	89	229	2.64
	Totals	418	2986	191	136	.584	2309	1050	2638	3.06

MIKE SCHMIDT 28 6-2 198   Bats R Throws R

Invented the tape-measure . . . Home runs are not only numerous but very long . . . An awesome slugger who once conked a speaker suspended from roof of the Astrodome . . . Failed to lead NL in home runs for the first time in four years last season . . . Also runs well and is one of top third baseman in the game . . . No wonder he is believed to be highest paid player in baseball with long-term contract worth over $3 million . . . Born Sept. 27, 1949 in West Berlin, N.J. . . . Hit four homers in one game April 11, 1976 against Cubs . . . Has worked hard to reduce strikeouts after a club record 180 in 1976 . . . Wife

Donna is a professional singer who has made several television appearances.

Year	Club	Pos	G	AB	R	H	2B	3B	HR	RBI	SB	Avg.
1972	Philadelphia......	3B-2B	13	34	2	7	0	0	1	3	0	.206
1973	Philadelphia......	3B-2B-1B-SS	132	367	43	72	11	0	18	52	8	.196
1974	Philadelphia......	3B	162	568	108	160	28	7	36	116	23	.282
1975	Philadelphia......	3B-SS	158	562	93	140	34	3	38	95	29	.249
1976	Philadelphia......	3B	160	584	112	153	31	4	38	107	14	.262
1977	Philadelphia......	3B	154	544	114	149	27	11	38	101	15	.274
	Totals..........		779	2659	472	681	131	25	169	474	89	.256

LARRY BOWA 32 5-10 155   Bats S Throws R

A hard-nosed player who gets maximum performance from his talents . . . A battler at the plate and equally effective from both sides . . . An expert bunter . . . Also a smooth fielder, especially on home AstroTurf . . . Set major-league fielding record for shortstops with more than 1,000 games (.979) . . . Born Dec. 6, 1945, in Sacramento . . . Hard to throw out on bases due to clever slides . . . Stole home twice in 1970 . . . Has reduced a quick temper which once got him suspended for three games after run-in with an umpire . . . Signed by club as free agent after being overlooked in 1965 draft.

Year	Club	Pos	G	AB	R	H	2B	3B	HR	RBI	SB	Avg.
1970	Philadelphia......	2B	145	547	50	137	17	6	0	34	24	.250
1971	Philadelphia......	SS	159	650	74	162	18	5	0	25	28	.249
1972	Philadelphia......	SS	152	579	67	145	11	13	1	31	17	.250
1973	Philadelphia......	SS	122	446	42	94	11	3	0	23	10	.211
1974	Philadelphia......	SS	162	669	97	184	19	10	1	36	39	.275
1975	Philadelphia......	SS	136	583	79	178	18	9	2	38	24	.305
1976	Philadelphia......	SS	156	624	71	155	15	9	0	49	30	.248
1977	Philadelphia......	SS	154	624	93	175	19	3	4	41	32	.280
	Totals..........		1186	4722	573	1230	128	48	8	277	204	.260

GREG LUZINSKI 27 6-1 225   Bats R Throws R

The Bull . . . Paul Bunyan in a major-league uniform . . . Coming off best all-around season of career . . . Wrestled club homer lead away from Schmidt . . . His long homers are called Bulls-eyes, naturally . . . Plays left field but chronic bad knees make it difficult for him . . . A quiet guy who teammates know to leave alone when he's mad . . . Born Nov. 22, 1950, in Chicago . . . Got his nickname when local butcher sent him bull horns to put on top of his locker . . . They're still there . . . Was a top football prospect headed for Kansas State before

Phillies drafted him first in 1968 . . . He's the Polish baseball player in airline television commercial.

Year	Club	Pos	G	AB	R	H	2B	3B	HR	RBI	SB	Avg.
1970	Philadelphia......	1B	8	12	0	2	0	0	0	0	0	.167
1971	Philadelphia......	1B	28	100	13	30	8	0	3	15	2	.300
1972	Philadelphia......	OF-1B	150	563	66	158	33	5	18	68	0	.281
1973	Philadelphia......	OF	161	610	76	174	26	4	29	97	3	.285
1974	Philadelphia......	OF	85	302	29	82	14	1	7	48	3	.272
1975	Philadelphia......	OF	161	596	85	179	35	3	34	120	3	.300
1976	Philadelphia......	OF	149	533	74	162	28	1	21	95	1	.304
1977	Philadelphia......	OF	149	544	99	171	35	3	39	130	3	.309
	Totals...........		891	3260	442	958	179	17	151	573	15	.294

GARRY MADDOX 28 6-3 175   Bats R Throws R

If he can't catch it, no one can . . . Fleet, graceful center fielder considered the best in league at his position . . . Won first Golden Glove ever awarded to a Phillies outfielder after 1975 trade from Giants . . . Contract dispute in San Francisco had helped sink his average to .159 . . . He batted over .300 for Phils the rest of season . . . Sorely missed in last year's playoffs against Dodgers when bad knee kept him out of first two games . . . Born Sept. 1, 1949, in Cincinnati . . . Runs singles into doubles and doubles into triples . . . Deceptive power forces outfielders to play him deeper than they want to . . . Served two-year Army hitch in Vietnam.

Year	Club	Pos	G	AB	R	H	2B	3B	HR	RBI	SB	Avg.
1972	San Francisco	OF	125	458	62	122	26	7	12	58	13	.266
1973	San Francisco	OF	144	587	81	187	30	10	11	76	24	.319
1974	San Francisco	OF	135	538	74	153	31	3	8	50	21	.284
1975	S.F.-Phil.........	OF	116	426	54	116	26	4	5	50	25	.272
1976	Philadelphia......	OF	146	531	75	175	37	6	6	68	29	.330
1977	Philadelphia......	OF	139	571	85	167	27	10	14	74	22	.292
	Totals...........		805	3111	431	920	177	44	56	376	134	.296

TUG McGRAW 33 6-0 185   Bats R Throws L

One of baseball's best screwballs on the mound, too . . . Friendly and flaky . . . Likes to wear Frankenstein mask around clubhouse . . . His screwball scares batters . . . Has twice overcome arm and shoulder miseries which threatened distinguished career as relief pitcher . . . Came off disabled list last season and contributed seven saves . . . Born Aug. 30, 1944, in Martinez, Cal. . . . Popular Met for many years and author of comic strip "Scroogie" . . . A three-time all-star . . . Real name is Frank Edwin McGraw . . . After signing a $90,000 contract with Mets he once said, "I'll spend $80,000 of it on fast cars, loose women and good Irish whiskey—and the rest of the money I'll waste."

Year	Club	G	IP	W	L	Pct.	SO	BB	H	ERA
1965	New York	37	98	2	7	.222	57	48	88	3.31
1966	New York	15	62	2	9	.182	34	25	72	5.37
1967	New York	4	17	0	3	.000	18	13	13	7.94
1969	New York	42	100	9	3	.750	92	47	89	2.25
1970	New York	57	91	4	6	.400	81	49	77	3.26
1971	New York	51	111	11	4	.733	109	41	73	1.70
1972	New York	54	106	8	6	.571	92	40	71	1.70
1973	New York	60	119	5	6	.455	81	55	106	3.86
1974	New York	41	89	6	11	.353	54	32	96	4.15
1975	Philadelphia	56	103	9	6	.600	55	36	84	2.97
1976	Philadelphia	58	97	7	6	.538	76	42	81	2.51
1977	Philadelphia	45	79	7	3	.700	58	24	62	2.62
	Totals	520	1072	70	70	.500	807	452	912	3.05

BAKE McBRIDE 29 6-2 190   Bats L Throws R

Shake and Bake . . . Speedy right fielder who led club in hitting after mid-season trade from St. Louis . . . Can't steal first but doesn't have to . . . Hits through holes or over them . . . Also a good bunter . . . Gets good jump on pitchers and makes life miserable for catchers . . . Was first Cardinal chosen Rookie-of-the-Year since Bill Virdon in 1955 . . . Born Feb. 3, 1949, in Fulton, Mo. . . . Outruns a lot of fly balls and doesn't make many errors . . . Teammates say they needed him to outlast Pirates in division race last season . . . Real name is Arnold Ray McBride . . . A tough out and a tougher strikeout.

Year	Club	Pos	G	AB	R	H	2B	3B	HR	RBI	SB	Avg.
1973	St. Louis	OF	40	63	8	19	3	0	0	5	0	.300
1974	St. Louis	OF	150	559	81	173	19	5	6	56	30	.309
1975	St. Louis	OF	116	413	70	124	10	9	5	36	26	.300
1976	St. Louis	OF	72	272	40	91	13	4	3	24	10	.335
1977	St. L-Phil.	OF	128	402	76	127	25	6	15	61	36	.316
	Totals		506	1709	275	534	70	24	29	182	102	.312

TED SIZEMORE 32 5-10 165   Bats R Throws R

Ring out the new, ring in the old . . . Did excellent job filling spot vacated by second baseman Dave Cash . . . Irony is he played in playoffs against Dodgers, who traded him to Phils because they thought he was finished . . . Was NL Rookie-of-the-Year for Los Angeles in 1969, was later dealt to St. Louis and returned to Dodgers in 1976 . . . Capable fielder who can really make pivot . . . Born April 15, 1945, in Gadsden,

Ala. . . . Don't expect a homerun but don't expect a strikeout, either . . . Dodgers converted him from catcher because they thought he was too small . . . Plays chess, which has no height requirements.

Year	Club	Pos	G	AB	R	H	2B	3B	HR	RBI	SB	Avg.
1969	Los Angeles	2B-SS-OF	159	590	69	160	20	5	4	46	5	.271
1970	Los Angeles	2B-OF-SS	96	340	40	104	10	1	1	34	5	.306
1971	St. Louis	2B-SS-OF-3B	135	478	53	126	14	5	3	42	4	.264
1972	St. Louis	2B	120	439	53	116	17	4	2	38	8	.264
1973	St. Louis	3B-2B	142	521	69	147	22	1	1	54	6	.282
1974	St. Louis	2B-SS-OF	129	504	68	126	17	0	2	47	8	.250
1975	St. Louis	2B	153	562	56	135	23	1	3	49	1	.240
1976	Los Angeles	2B-3B-C	84	266	18	64	8	1	0	18	2	.241
1977	Philadelphia	2B	152	519	64	146	20	3	4	47	8	.281
	Totals		1170	4219	490	1124	151	21	20	375	47	.266

LARRY CHRISTENSON 24 6-2 210   Bats R Throws R

Arrived last season after years of promise . . . His 19 wins were second-best on staff to Steve Carlton . . . Injuries have kept him from blossoming sooner . . . Suffered pulled back muscle in 1976 after good start . . . Had impressive spring in 1975 but started season in minors after pulling muscle in rib cage . . . Has real live fastball . . . Beat the Mets in his first major-league start in 1973 at the age of 19 . . . Born Nov. 10, 1953, in Everett, Wash. . . . Phils' No. 1 selection in 1972 draft . . . A good-hitting pitcher who hit first major-league grand slam last season.

Year	Club	G	IP	W	L	Pct.	SO	BB	H	ERA
1973	Philadelphia	10	34	1	4	.200	11	20	53	6.62
1974	Philadelphia	10	23	1	1	.500	18	15	20	4.30
1975	Philadelphia	29	172	11	6	.647	88	45	149	3.66
1976	Philadelphia	32	169	13	8	.619	54	42	199	3.67
1977	Philadelphia	34	219	19	6	.760	118	69	229	4.07
	Totals	115	617	45	25	.643	289	191	650	4.00

RICHIE HEBNER 30 6-1 197   Bats L Throws R

Fine third baseman for years with Pirates, but converted to first base after joining Phils . . . One of those who played out option in first free agent draft . . . Has always been a slugger but found himself buried in Pittsburgh's top-heavy lineup . . . Had best average and most homers in four years last season . . . Born Nov. 26, 1947, in Boston . . . Won scholastic All-American honors in hockey and was offered a minor-league contract by Boston Bruins . . . Had publicized run-in with manager Bill

Virdon when both were in Pittsburgh . . . A grave-digger in the off-season.

Year	Club	Pos	G	AB	R	H	2B	3B	HR	RBI	SB	Avg.
1968	Pittsburgh	PH	2	1	0	0	0	0	0	0	0	.000
1969	Pittsburgh	3B-1B	129	459	72	138	23	4	8	47	4	.301
1970	Pittsburgh	3B	120	420	60	122	24	8	11	46	2	.290
1971	Pittsburgh	3B	112	388	50	105	17	8	17	67	2	.271
1972	Pittsburgh	3B	124	427	63	128	24	4	19	72	0	.300
1973	Pittsburgh	3B	144	509	73	138	28	1	25	74	0	.271
1974	Pittsburgh	3B	146	550	97	160	21	6	18	68	0	.291
1975	Pittsburgh	3B	128	472	65	116	16	4	15	57	0	.246
1976	Pittsburgh	3B	132	434	60	108	21	3	8	51	1	.249
1977	Philadelphia	1B-3B	118	397	67	113	17	4	18	62	7	.285
	Totals...........		1155	4057	607	1128	191	42	139	544	16	.278

TOP PROSPECTS

LONNIE SMITH 22 5-9 170   **Bats R Throws R**
Has hit on every minor-league level, but finds it hard to crack Phils' outfield . . . Team's first selection in 1974 draft . . . A Richie Ashburn copy, who sprays hits and plays well defensively . . . Born Dec. 22, 1955, in Chicago . . . Player-of-the-Year in the Western Carolina League in 1975 after a .323 average and 56 stolen bases . . . Likes to bowl, which is where he gets most of his strikes.

JIM WRIGHT 23 6-5 205   **Bats R Throws R**
A big, hard thrower in the mode of Steve Carlton . . . Won seven games over his first two minor-league seasons, but has been in double figures every year since . . . Born March 3, 1955, in St. Joseph, Mo. . . . Had an eye-opening 2.39 ERA for Reading in 1976 . . . Was non-roster player in spring training last year but will have chance to make the club this season.

MANAGER DANNY OZARK: Has won NL East last two years with best talent around . . . His critics say no one would have lost with those teams . . . Second-guessed in playoffs when he left Greg Luzinski in left field with Phils trying to preserve a two-run lead in ninth inning of pivotal third game . . . Luzinski did not catch a fly ball a defensive sub might have and Dodgers went on to win . . . Still, only Gene Mauch has more wins as a Phillies' manager since 1900 and he never made it to first-place . . . Has amusing habit of confusing his words, like comic Norm Crosby . . . Never played in major leagues but spent 17 years trying to get there . . . Coached Dodgers before moving to Phils and replacing Frank Lucchesi in 1973.

GREATEST MANAGER

They were still laughing at the Philadelphia Phillies when Eddie Sawyer took over as manager for Ben Chapman during the 1948 season. The team had finished last or next-to-last in 24 of the previous 29 years. Not since 1915 had the Phillies finished first. But Sawyer moved the team into sixth place that first half-season. And in 1949 the team finished third, its best finish in 32 years.

But 1950 was the astounding year that made Sawyer the manager generations of Phillies' fans would remember. That was the year the "Whiz Kids" of Philadelphia won the pennant, the year Cinderella finally fit into the glass slipper. The Phillies went on to be swept by the Yankees in the Series. But still it was a surprising performance by the "Whiz Kids" and it was Sawyer who was the "Whizzard."

ALL-TIME PHILLIE LEADERS

BATTING: Frank O'Doul, .398, 1929
HRs: Chuck Klein, 43, 1929
RBIs: Chuck Klein, 170, 1930
STEALS: Sherry Magee, 55, 1906
WINS: Grover Alexander, 33, 1916
STRIKEOUTS: Steve Carlton, 310, 1972

PITTSBURGH PIRATES

TEAM DIRECTORY: Chairman: John Galbreath; Pres.: Daniel Galbreath; VP-Player Personnel: Harding Peterson; VP-Business Administration: Joseph O'Toole; Minor Leagues/Scouting: Murray Cook; Trav. Sec.: Charlie Muse; Pub. Rel.: Bill Guilfoile; Mgr.: Chuck Tanner. Home: Three Rivers Stadium (50,364). Field distances: 335, l.f. line; 400, c.f.; 335, r.f. line. Spring training: Bradenton, Fla.

SCOUTING REPORT

HITTING: The Pirates did not invent hitting, they just copyrighted it. The biggest tribute to the punch of the lineup is the Pirates were able to trade slugger Al Oliver without damaging the batting order much at all. Only Philadelphia and Cincinnati had a better team BA than Pittsburgh's .273. This season, there is every reason to believe that figure could be even better.

The Pirates are hoping they can reclaim John Milner, once a promising power hitter, who they received in a complicated series of deals that led to Oliver's departure. In addition, there is the aging, but valuable, Willie Stargell. And, of course, Dave Parker, who was the NL batting champion and the wrecker of more than

NL batting king Dave Parker led outfielders with 26 assists.

one pitching staff. Bill Robinson, who waited years for his chance, got it and didn't fumble it. He proved himself a capable hitter who fit right in with the club's mold of a slugger.

In Pittsburgh, batting practice lasts for hours. Even second baseman Rennie Stennett is dangerous. If the Pirates need any replacement, it may be the outfield wall which will have to endure all those searing line drives.

PITCHING: The Pirates' staff used to be a laughing stock. Last year, it began to laugh back. This year, it may erupt into guffaws. The team lost Rich Gossage in the free agent draft, but did obtain Bert Blyleven, who is merely one of the most effective pitchers around. Of course, there is John Candelaria, who can beat anyone and has. The burden of the staff will lie mostly with them, but there will be help from others. Jerry Reuss has teetered on the edge of superstardom for years, but probably has resigned himself to being simply good enough. Jim Rooker, coming off a fine season, rounds out a very capable staff.

The bullpen may need some help, with the absence of Gossage, but there seems to be enough to weather most stormy innings. Kent Tekulve emerged as a top reliever last season after having toiled in lopsided games to gain experience. He will be helped by Grant Jackson, the left-hander, who has been dependable, if overshadowed, by the other big-name relief pitchers with whom he has shared the bullpen. With no Gossage or Sparky Lyle-type around, Jackson may really prove himself. Bruce Kison, Larry Demery are the incumbent candidates for an extra starting position and Dave Pagan has the best fastball on the staff.

FIELDING: The blemish on the Pirates' creamy complexion. The team made 145 errors last season, 25 more than the Phillies, their chief rivals. The defense will do the job. It won't do an outstanding job, however. Frank Taveras is a quick shortstop, but erratic. Stennett is a fine second baseman, but Phil Garner at third base and Milner at first are just adequate. In the outfield, Parker can catch and throw and Omar Moreno is swift, but hesitant. Robinson, who plays the outfield as well as third base, is adequate. The Pirates' best defensive player is Duffy Dyer, the reserve catcher behind Ed Ott.

OUTLOOK: The Pirates have enough hitting and they have enough pitching. What they lack is the very fine touches—a star in the bullpen, a Gold Glove in the outfield. But if the Pirates aren't tired of chasing the Phillies, as they have the last two seasons, they could find themselves alone down the stretch.

PITTSBURGH PIRATES 1978 ROSTER

MANAGER Chuck Tanner
Coaches—Joe Lonnett, Al Monchak, Jose Pagan, Larry Sherry

PITCHERS

No.	Name	1977 Club	W-L	IP	SO	ERA	B-T	Ht.	Wt.	Born
—	Blyleven, Bert	Texas	14-12	235	182	2.72	R-R	6-3	200	4/6/51 Zeist, Holland
45	Candelaria, John	Pittsburgh	20-5	231	133	2.34	L-L	6-7	215	11/6/53 New York, NY
44	Demery, Larry	Pittsburgh	6-5	90	35	5.10	R-R	6-0	169	6/4/53 Bakersfield, CA
—	Holland, Al	Shreveport	4-1	36	—	1.25	R-L	5-11	215	8/16/52 Roanoke, VA
		Columbus	6-3	86	73	3.57				
		Pittsburgh	0-0	2	1	9.00				
—	Jackson, Grant	Pittsburgh	5-3	91	41	3.86	L-L	6-0	198	9/28/42 Fostoria, OH
50	Jones, Odell	Pittsburgh	3-7	108	66	5.08	R-R	6-3	174	1/13/53 Tulare, CA
51	Jones, Tim	Columbus	15-6	190	91	4.12	R-R	6-4	210	1/24/54 Sacramento, CA
		Pittsburgh	1-0	10	5	0.00				
25	Kison, Bruce	Pittsburgh	9-10	193	122	4.90	R-R	6-4	176	2/18/50 Pasco, WA
—	Pagan, Dave	Seattle	1-1	66	30	6.14	R-R	6-2	184	9/15/49 Nipawin, Sask.
		Spokane	0-3	25	—	7.56				
		Columbus	2-1	38	17	3.79				
		Pittsburgh	0-0	3	4	0.00				
41	Reuss, Jerry	Pittsburgh	10-13	208	116	4.11	L-L	6-5	219	6/19/49 St. Louis, MO
19	Rooker, Jim	Pittsburgh	14-9	204	89	3.09	R-L	6-0	195	9/23/42 Lakeview, OR
—	Robinson, Don	Shreveport	7-6	114	—	4.08	R-R	6-4	225	6/8/57 Ashland, KY
		Columbus	1-0	5	3	0.00				
—	Scurry, Rod	Shreveport	3-11	113	—	2.87	L-L	6-2	180	3/17/56 Sacramento, CA
		Columbus	2-2	37	39	4.58				
27	Tekulve, Kent	Pittsburgh	10-1	103	59	3.06	R-R	6-4	167	3/5/47 Cincinnati, OH
—	Whitson, Ed	Columbus	7-13	175	120	3.34	R-R	6-3	194	5/19/55 Johnson City, TN
		Pittsburgh	1-0	16	10	3.38				

CATCHERS

No.	Name	1977 Club	H	HR	RBI	Pct.	B-T	Ht.	Wt.	Born
5	Dyer, Duffy	Pittsburgh	65	3	19	.241	R-R	6-0	198	8/15/45 Dayton, OH
—	Nicosia, Steve	Columbus	18	4	12	.212	R-R	5-10	183	8/6/55 Paterson, NJ
32	Ott, Ed	Pittsburgh	82	7	38	.264	L-R	5-10	196	7/11/51 Muncy, PA

INFIELDERS

No.	Name	1977 Club	H	HR	RBI	Pct.	B-T	Ht.	Wt.	Born
—	Berra, Dale	Columbus	127	18	54	.290	R-R	6-0	180	12/13/56 Ridgewood, NJ
		Pittsburgh	7	0	3	.175				
—	Edwards, Mike	Columbus	157	4	61	.296	R-R	5-10	152	8/27/52 Ft. Lewis, WA
		Pittsburgh	0	0	0	.000				
—	Fregosi, Jim	Texas	7	1	5	.250	R-R	6-2	205	4/4/42 San Francisco, CA
		Pittsburgh	16	3	16	.286				
3	Garner, Phil	Pittsburgh	152	17	77	.260	R-R	5-10	176	4/30/50 Jefferson City, TN
—	Gonzalez, Fernando	Pittsburgh	50	4	27	.276	R-R	5-10	178	6/19/50 Utuado, P.R.
—	Hargis, Gary	Columbus	88	4	52	.252	R-R	5-11	155	11/2/56 Minneapolis, MN
—	Macha, Ken	Columbus	85	11	64	.335	R-R	6-2	205	9/29/50 Wilkinsburg, PA
		Pittsburgh	26	0	11	.274				
11	Mendoza, Mario	Pittsburgh	16	0	4	.198	R-R	5-11	187	12/26/50 Chihuahua, Mexico
—	Milner, John	N.Y. (NL)	99	12	57	.255	L-L	6-0	185	12/28/49 Fort Wayne, IN
8	Stargell, Willie	Pittsburgh	51	13	35	.274	L-L	6-2½	228	3/6/41 Earlsboro, OK
6	Stennett, Rennie	Pittsburgh	152	5	51	.336	R-R	5-11	175	4/5/51 Colon, Panama
10	Taveras, Frank	Pittsburgh	137	1	29	.252	R-R	6-0	170	12/24/50 Villa Vasquez, D.R.

OUTFIELDERS

No.	Name	1977 Club	H	HR	RBI	Pct.	B-T	Ht.	Wt.	Born
37	Dilone, Miguel	Columbus	31	0	7	.215	B-R	6-0	161	11/1/54 Santiago, D.R.
		Pittsburgh	6	0	0	.136				
—	Easler, Mike	Columbus	136	18	75	.302	L-R	6-0	192	11/29/50 Cleveland, OH
		Pittsburgh	8	1	5	.444				
—	Louis, Alberto	Columbus	40	4	17	.282	R-R	5-9	175	5/6/56 Hato Mayor, D.R.
48	Moreno, Omar	Pittsburgh	118	7	34	.240	L-L	6-3	175	10/24/52 Puerto Armuelles, Panama
—	Olivares, Oswaldo	Salem	—	6	79	.370	L-L	5-11	154	9/15/53 Caracas, Venez.
		Columbus	6	0	1	.400				
39	Parker, Dave	Pittsburgh	215	21	88	.338	L-R	6-5	220	6/9/51 Cincinnati OH
28	Robinson, Bill	Pittsburgh	154	26	104	.304	R-R	6-3	200	6/26/43 Elizabeth, PA
—	Tolan, Bobby	Phil-Pitts.	17	2	10	.189	L-L	5-11	174	11/19/45 Los Angeles, CA

PIRATE PROFILES

WILLIE STARGELL 37 6-2 1/2 228   Bats L Throws L

You need "Star" to spell Stargell . . . Chief officer on the Pirate ship . . . Club's career home run leader . . . Hit eight homers out of old Forbes Field, more than anybody . . . Has hit four upper deck homers at Three Rivers, more than anybody . . . A first baseman now after years in the outfield . . . Winner of 1974 Roberto Clemente Award for setting an example off the field . . . Winner of the 1975 Lou Gehrig Award for typifying character and ability of Hall of Famer . . . Active in Sickle Cell Anemia foundation . . . Born March 6, 1941, in Earlsboro, Okla. . . . Has missed parts of last two seasons due to serious brain illness to wife Dolores . . . Holds NL record of four extra-base-hits in one game four times.

Year	Club	Pos	G	AB	R	H	2B	3B	HR	RBI	SB	Avg.
1962	Pittsburgh	OF	10	31	1	9	3	1	0	4	0	.290
1963	Pittsburgh	OF-1B	108	304	34	74	11	6	11	47	0	.243
1964	Pittsburgh	OF-1B	117	421	53	115	19	7	21	78	1	.273
1965	Pittsburgh	OF-1B	144	533	68	145	25	8	27	107	1	.272
1966	Pittsburgh	OF-1B	140	485	84	153	30	0	33	102	2	.315
1967	Pittsburgh	OF-1B	134	462	54	125	18	6	20	73	1	.271
1968	Pittsburgh	OF-1B	128	435	57	103	15	1	24	67	5	.237
1969	Pittsburgh	OF-1B	145	522	89	160	31	6	29	92	1	.307
1970	Pittsburgh	OF-1B	136	474	70	125	18	3	31	85	0	.264
1971	Pittsburgh	OF	141	511	104	151	26	0	48	125	0	.295
1972	Pittsburgh	1B-OF	138	495	75	145	28	2	33	112	1	.293
1973	Pittsburgh	OF	148	522	106	156	43	3	44	119	0	.299
1974	Pittsburgh	OF	140	508	90	153	37	4	25	96	0	.301
1975	Pittsburgh	1B	124	461	71	136	32	2	22	90	0	.295
1976	Pittsburgh	1B	117	428	54	110	20	3	20	65	2	.257
1977	Pittsburgh	1B	63	186	29	51	12	0	13	35	0	.274
	Totals		1933	6778	1039	1911	368	52	401	1297	14	.282

DAVE PARKER 26 6-5 220   Bats L Throws R

The Slasher . . . Won his first NL batting title . . . Also led league in hits and led club in runs . . . A line drive hitter who also has long-ball power . . . Selected for first all-star team last season . . . A strong arm in right field and no wonder . . . Used to be a flame-throwing pitcher in high school . . . Passed over in amateur draft because of knee injury until Pirates took him on 14th round . . . Born June 9, 1951, in Cincinnati . . . Led NL in slugging percentage (.541) in 1975 . . . Likes to steal and runs well . . . He also was a fullback on high school football team.

Year	Club	Pos	G	AB	R	H	2B	3B	HR	RBI	SB	Avg.
1973	Pittsburgh.......	OF	54	139	17	40	9	1	4	14	1	.288
1974	Pittsburgh.......	OF-1B	73	220	27	62	10	3	4	29	3	.282
1975	Pittsburgh.......	OF	148	558	75	172	35	10	25	101	8	.308
1976	Pittsburgh.......	OF	138	537	82	168	28	10	13	90	19	.313
1977	Pittsburgh.......	OF	159	637	107	215	44	8	21	88	17	.338
	Totals..........		572	2091	308	657	126	32	67	322	48	.314

BERT BLYLEVEN 27 6-3 200   Bats R Throws R

Always on the brink, may be ready to come into his own . . . Pirates think so. They took him for Al Oliver . . . 122 big league wins and not yet 28 . . . But only nine games over .500 in big league career, curious because hitters say he has best stuff in the AL . . . No-hitter vs. Angels on Sept. 22, first of career, although pitching with groin injury . . . Born Rik Aalbert Blyleven in Zeist, Holland, on April 6, 1951. Grew up in California . . . Four career one-hitters . . . Twins tired of waiting for him to realize potential, traded him to Rangers, who expected him to be pitching mainstay in pennant bid last year.

Year	Club	G	IP	W	L	Pct.	SO	BB	H	ERA
1970	Minnesota	27	164	10	9	.526	135	47	143	3.18
1971	Minnesota	38	278	16	15	.516	224	59	267	2.82
1972	Minnesota	39	287	17	17	.500	228	69	247	2.73
1973	Minnesota	40	325	20	17	.541	258	67	296	2.52
1974	Minnesota	37	281	17	17	.500	249	77	244	2.66
1975	Minnesota	35	276	15	10	.600	233	84	219	3.00
1976	Minnesota-Tex	36	298	13	16	.448	219	81	283	2.87
1977	Texas...................	30	235	14	12	.538	182	69	181	2.72
	Totals..................	282	2144	122	113	.519	1728	553	1880	2.79

JOHN CANDELARIA 24 6-7 215   Bats L Throws L

The Candy Man . . . Coming off real sweet season . . . Fifth in NL in ERA and first among starting pitchers . . . First gained wide attention when he struck out 14 Reds in third game start of 1975 playoffs . . . Became first Pirate to throw a no-hitter in Pittsburgh since Nicholas Maddox in 1907 when he blanked Dodgers Aug. 8, 1976 . . . Last year led team in victories and innings pitched for second straight season . . . Born Nov. 6, 1953, in New York City . . . A high school basketball star who is second only to a fellow named Kareem Abdul-Jabbar in

Catholic League rebounding records . . . Did not play baseball last two years of high school when program was eliminated due to lack of facilities.

Year	Club	G	IP	W	L	Pct.	SO	BB	H	ERA
1975	Pittsburgh	18	121	8	6	.571	95	36	95	2.75
1976	Pittsburgh	32	220	16	7	.696	138	60	173	3.15
1977	Pittsburgh	33	231	20	5	.800	133	50	197	2.34
	Totals...................	83	572	44	18	.710	366	146	465	2.74

BILL ROBINSON 34 6-3 200   Bats R Throws R

No Brooks at third . . . No Frank at bat . . . Gets the job done when given the chance, though . . . Worked way into starting lineup in 1976 and led club in homers and RBIs . . . Was super sub in infield and outfield before getting chance to play every day . . . Hit three homers in one game June 5, 1976 against San Diego . . . Pirate teammates voted him player of the year that season . . . Born June 26, 1943, in Elizabeth, Pa. . . . Had sensational minor-league career and was touted as another Hank Aaron by Braves' organization . . . Dealt to Yankees for Clete Boyer and later traded to Phillies.

Year	Club	Pos	G	AB	R	H	2B	3B	HR	RBI	SB	Avg.
1966	Atlanta..........	OF	6	11	1	3	0	1	0	3	0	.273
1967	New York (A.L.)..	OF	116	342	31	67	6	1	7	29	2	.196
1968	New York (A.L.)..	OF	107	342	34	82	16	7	6	40	7	.240
1969	New York (A.L.)..	OF-1B	87	222	23	38	11	2	3	21	3	.171
1972	Philadelphia......	OF	82	188	19	45	9	1	8	21	2	.239
1973	Philadelphia......	3B-OF	124	452	62	130	32	1	25	65	5	.288
1974	Philadelphia......	OF	100	280	32	66	14	1	5	29	5	.236
1975	Pittsburgh.......	OF	92	200	26	56	12	2	6	33	3	.280
1976	Pittsburgh.......	OF-3B-1B	122	393	55	119	22	3	21	64	2	.303
1977	Pittsburgh.......	1B-OF-3B	137	507	74	154	32	1	26	104	12	.304
	Totals		973	2937	357	760	154	20	107	409	41	.259

RENNIE STENNETT 27 5-11 175   Bats R Throws R

The Bridesmaid . . . Finished second in NL batting race, two points behind teammate Dave Parker . . . Makes for a marriage of two splendid hitters in middle of lineup . . . Remarkable player who hits, steals, fields well and rarely strikes out . . . Set modern major-league record with 7-for-7 performance against Cubs . . . That was first perfect seven-hit effort since Wilbert Robinson of Baltimore in 1892 . . . Born April 5, 1951, in Colon, Panama . . . Range and strong arm make him one of best second basemen around . . . In 1974 came within eight chances of Ken Hubbs' record of 418 chances without an error . . . Holds record for most hits in one season by Pirate second baseman.

Year	Club	Pos	G	AB	R	H	2B	3B	HR	RBI	SB	Avg.
1971	Pittsburgh	2B	50	153	24	54	5	4	1	15	1	.353
1972	Pittsburgh	2B-OF-SS	109	370	43	106	14	5	3	30	4	.286
1973	Pittsburgh	2B-OF-SS	128	466	45	113	18	3	10	55	2	.242
1974	Pittsburgh	2B-OF	157	673	84	196	29	3	7	56	8	.291
1975	Pittsburgh	2B	148	616	89	176	25	7	7	62	5	.286
1976	Pittsburgh	2B-SS	157	654	59	168	31	9	2	60	18	.257
1977	Pittsburgh	2B	116	453	53	152	20	4	5	51	28	.336
	Totals..........		865	3385	397	965	142	35	35	329	66	.285

FRANK TAVERAS 27 6-0 170   Bats R Throws R

The Three Rivers Run . . . Led major leagues with 70 stolen bases . . . Was caught only 18 times . . . Finished third in NL with 58 stolen bases two years ago, behind only Joe Morgan and Davey Lopes . . . String of 27 straight stolen bases two years ago ended when he was nabbed on a pitchout . . . Was tutored in base stealing art by former Dodger and Pirate Maury Wills. . . Improving at shortstop, too . . . Born Dec. 24, 1950, in Villa Vasquez, Dominican Republic . . . Batted .300 in first NL playoff appearance in 1974.

Year	Club	Pos	G	AB	R	H	2B	3B	HR	RBI	SB	Avg.
1971	Pittsburgh	PR	1	0	0	0	0	0	0	0	0	.000
1972	Pittsburgh	SS	4	3	0	0	0	0	0	0	0	.000
1974	Pittsburgh	SS	126	333	33	82	4	2	0	26	13	.246
1975	Pittsburgh	SS	134	378	44	80	9	4	0	23	17	.212
1976	Pittsburgh	SS	144	519	76	134	8	6	0	24	58	.258
1977	Pittsburgh	SS	147	544	72	137	20	10	1	29	70	.252
	Totals..........		556	1777	225	433	41	22	1	102	158	.244

BRUCE KISON 28 6-4 176   Bats R Throws R

Coming off worst major-league season . . . Still maintained good walk-to-strikeout ratio . . . Had highest ERA among starters reversing 1976 form when he led club in that department . . . Got first national recognition when he beat Baltimore in fourth game of 1971 Series, allowing only one hit in 6⅓ innings of relief . . . Set a Series record that same night by hitting three batters . . . Born Feb. 18, 1950, in Pasco, Wash. . . . Has 3-0 record in NL playoffs . . . Has allowed only one run in 22 innings of post-season play.

Year	Club	G	IP	W	L	Pct.	SO	BB	H	ERA
1971	Pittsburgh	18	95	6	5	.545	60	36	93	3.41
1972	Pittsburgh	32	152	9	7	.563	102	69	123	3.26
1973	Pittsburgh	7	44	3	0	1.000	26	24	36	3.07
1974	Pittsburgh	40	129	9	8	.529	71	57	123	3.49
1975	Pittsburgh	33	192	12	11	.522	89	92	160	3.23
1976	Pittsburgh	31	193	14	9	.609	98	52	180	3.08
1977	Pittsburgh	33	193	9	10	.474	122	55	209	4.90
	Totals.................	194	998	62	50	.554	568	385	924	3.57

JERRY REUSS 28 6-5 219   Bats L Throws L

Club once thought he'd be Rolls Reuss of staff . . . Had disappointing season last year, though he was second among Pirates in innings pitched . . . Started the 1975 All-Star Game for NL . . . Has attended three different colleges, majoring in math . . . Would like to improve his own numbers . . . Had 1972 no-hitter against Philadelphia broken up in ninth inning . . . Born June 19, 1949, in St. Louis . . . Demand to be allowed to bring wife on road trips led to trade from St. Louis to Houston . . . Now divorced . . . Plays guitar and sings . . . Shares club record of 16 hits by pitcher in one season.

Year	Club	G	IP	W	L	Pct.	SO	BB	H	ERA
1969	St. Louis	1	7	1	0	1.000	3	3	2	0.00
1970	St. Louis	20	127	7	8	.467	74	49	132	4.11
1971	St. Louis	36	211	14	14	.500	131	109	228	4.78
1972	Houston	33	192	9	13	.409	174	83	177	4.17
1973	Houston	41	279	16	13	.552	177	*117	271	3.74
1974	Pittsburgh	35	260	16	11	.593	105	101	259	3.50
1975	Pittsburgh	32	237	18	11	.621	131	78	224	2.54
1976	Pittsburgh	31	209	14	9	.609	108	51	209	3.53
1977	Pittsburgh	33	208	10	13	.435	116	71	225	4.11
	Totals	262	1730	105	92	.533	1019	662	1727	3.75

TOP PROSPECT

DALE BERRA 21 6-0 180   Bats R Throws R

Yogi's son . . . Has more to him than just the family name . . . Fine third baseman who will get good look this year . . . First major league hit was extra-inning, game-winning single . . . Chosen to Western Carolina all-star team in 1976 after .298 BA and 16 homers . . . Born Dec. 13, 1956, in Ridgewood, N.J. . . . Could provide infield backup for Phil Garner and Rennie Stennett . . . All-around scholastic athlete who captained football and hockey teams.

MANAGER CHUCK TANNER: Came home to Pittsburgh after

seven seasons in AL . . . Grew up only 60 miles from Three Rivers . . . Became manager after rare trade for player . . . Oakland owner Charlie Finley demanded catcher Manny Sanguillen and $100,000 in return for letting Tanner go . . . Before that, managed Chicago White Sox . . . A Yankee Doodle Dandy . . . Born July 4, 1929 in New Castle, Pa. . . . Homered on the first pitch of his first major-league at-bat April 5, 1955, the second player to accomplish that feat . . . Played eight seasons as outfielder for Braves, Cubs, Indians and Angels with career .261 BA.

GREATEST MANAGER

They called him "Irish" and Danny Murtaugh was that, raised in the coal fields of Pennsylvania and, it seemed, brought up to be manager of the Pittsburgh Pirates. He was foxy and ingenious and he could spin tall stories. And Danny Murtaugh could win.

He transformed the Pirates from patsies to powerhouses in his long, though interrupted, career as manager. In 1958, his first full season in Pittsburgh, the Pirates finished an astonishing second. In 1960, the team won the pennant and its first Series championship since 1925. When bad health made him give up the job in 1965, Murtaugh took a position as a Pirate scout, but only two years later he was asked to serve as interim manager.

And in 1970 Murtaugh returned as manager again and the Pirates won the East Division. In 1971, they did it again and added their second Series victory under Murtaugh in two tries. And that's no tall story.

ALL-TIME PIRATE LEADERS

BATTING: Arky Vaughan, .385, 1935
HRs: Ralph Kiner, 54, 1949
RBIs: Paul Waner, 131, 1927
STEALS: Frank Taveras, 70, 1977
WINS: Jack Chesbro, 28, 1902
STRIKEOUTS: Bob Veale, 276, 1965

ST. LOUIS CARDINALS

TEAM DIRECTORY: Chairman of the Board and Pres.: August A. Busch Jr.; Exec. VP-GM: Bing Devine; Senior VP: Stan Musial; Director of Player Personnel: Jim Bayens; Pub. Rel.: Jerry Lovelace; Trav. Sec.: Lee Thomas; Mgr.: Vern Rapp. Home: Busch Memorial Stadium (50,100). Field Distances: 330, l.f. line; 404, c.f.; 330, r.f. line. Spring training: St. Petersburg, Fla.

SCOUTING REPORT

HITTING: Promises, promises. What do the Cardinals promise this season? Maybe another surprise. The team had a surprising .269 BA last season, for one thing. And with Ken Reitz supplying some power, it no longer took the Cards three hits to score a run. The lineup may not be as fearsome as some others, but the Cardinals may double you to death, which can also be effective.

Young Garry Templeton sprouted into a solid .300 hitter.

The addition of all-star Jerry Morales will help take some of the longball burden off Reitz. Ted Simmons doesn't have much power, but he is the toughest out in the league and a threat to win the batting title. And if Simmons doesn't have the best average, Garry Templeton just might. Obviously, the top of the lineup is going to be tough for opposing pitchers to get through. If Keith Hernandez continues to improve, it could even be tougher.

There is the graceful Lou Brock, who can still hit and still run. Jerry Mumphrey is coming off a fine sophomore season in which he won a job. About the only player who won't be expected to hit is Mike Tyson. True, it is a lineup of middleweights, but middleweights punch hard, too.

PITCHING: The Mad Hungarian is gone and that's too bad. Al Hrabosky was lively and entertaining and talented. His place in the bullpen will be taken by Mark Littell, who is quiet and reserved and talented. The starters began to come around last season, but the biggest question mark still is here. Bob Forsch won 20 games for the first time. The doubters say, "Let's see him do it again." John Urrea was helpful. He'll have to be helpful again. John Denny has been in-and-out for three seasons now. He'll have to be in this season.

The Cards also will have to replace Tom Underwood, who was traded, and Rawly Eastwick, who played out his option and wound up a Yankee. Larry Dierker is still around and likely to be a starter again. And there is Pete Falcone, who last season slumped to 4-8 with a gaudy 5.44 ERA. Butch Metzger also is a capable starter, but Littell will need help in the bullpen. He may or may not get it.

FIELDING: A solid infield, but watery elsewhere. Tyson, at second base, is a skilled glove man. Templeton is a superior shortstop. That's about as good a keystone as there is. And, at third base, Reitz can catch any ball and make any play. But Morales is just adequate in center field and Mumphrey's biggest asset in right field is his speed. Brock can still catch a fly ball in left. Simmons has trouble throwing and fielding behind the plate. Hernandez is improved at first, but still has a way to go.

OUTLOOK: The Cardinals could be the surprise of the division. They also could be the biggest disappointment. So much depends on the pitching, which looked promising last season. The Cards will score enough, won't make too many errors in the outfield, won't make many in the infield and will be in most games. The question is, how many can they win?

ST. LOUIS CARDINALS 1978 ROSTER

MANAGER Vern Rapp
Coaches—Jack Krol, Mo Mozzali, Claude Osteen, Dave
        Ricketts, Sonny Ruberto

PITCHERS

No.	Name	1977 Club	W-L	IP	SO	ERA	B-T	Ht.	Wt.	Born
—	Bass, Earl	New Orleans	10-10	134	96	3.55	R-R	6-1	170	11/26/52 Columbia, SC
36	Denny, John	St. Louis	8-8	150	60	4.50	R-R	6-3	185	11/8/52 Prescott, AZ
49	Dierker, Larry	St. Louis	2-6	39	6	4.62	R-R	6-4	210	9/22/46 Hollywood, CA
—	Edelen, Joe	St. Petersburg	6-3	97	58	1.58	R-R	6-0	165	9/16/55 Durant, OK
		Arkansas	6-3	80	62	3.36				
41	Falcone, Pete	St. Louis	4-8	124	75	5.44	L-L	6-2	185	10/1/53 Brooklyn, N.Y.
31	Forsch, Bob	St. Louis	20-7	217	95	3.48	R-R	6-4	200	1/13/50 Sacramento, CA
—	Hamilton, Dave	Chicago (AL)	4-5	67	45	3.63	L-L	6-0	190	12/13/47 Seattle, WA
—	Littell, Mark	Kansas City	8-4	105	106	3.60	L-R	6-3	210	1/17/53 Cape Girardeau, MO
—	Lopez, Aurelio	Mexico City	19-8	157	165	2.01	R-R	6-0	200	9/21/48 Puebla, Mex
34	Metzger, Butch	SD-St. Louis	4-2	115	54	3.68	R-R	6-1	185	5/23/52 Lafayette, IN
42	Rasmussen, Eric	St. Louis	11-17	233	120	3.48	R-R	6-3	205	3/22/52 Racine, WI
—	Riccelli, Frank	Phoenix	8-9	163	135	6.35	L-L	6-3	205	2/24/53 Syracuse, NY
22	Schultz, Buddy	St. Louis	6-1	85	66	2.33	R-L	6-0	175	9/19/50 Cleveland, OH
		New Orleans	1-0	15	25	3.07				
38	Urrea, John	St. Louis	7-6	140	81	3.15	R-R	6-3	195	2/9/55 Los Angeles, CA
—	Vuckovich, Pete	Toronto	7-7	148	123	3.47	R-R	6-4	220	10/27/52 Johnstown, Pa.

CATCHERS

No.	Name	1977 Club	H	HR	RBI	Pct.	B-T	Ht.	Wt.	Born
—	Kennedy, Terry	Johnson City	23	3	15	.590	L-R	6-4	220	6/4/56 Mesa, AZ
		St. Petersburg	41	4	22	.247				
23	Simmons, Ted	St. Louis	164	21	95	.318	B-R	6-0	200	8/9/49 Highland Park, MI
—	Swisher, Steve	Chicago (NL)	39	5	15	.190	R-R	6-2	205	8/9/51 Parkersburg, WV
12	Tamargo, John	New Orleans	119	10	42	.254	B-R	5-10	180	11/7/51 Tampa, FL
		St. Louis	0	0	0	.000				

INFIELDERS

No.	Name	1977 Club	H	HR	RBI	Pct.	B-T	Ht.	Wt.	Born
—	Castillo, Manny	Arkansas	128	0	43	.298	B-R	5-9	160	4/1/57 Santo Domingo, DR
—	Farkas, Ron	Arkansas	59	2	19	.343	R-R	6-0	180	7/30/53 Cleveland, OH
		New Orleans	12	1	4	.158				
7	Freed, Roger	St. Louis	33	5	21	.398	R-R	6-0	205	6/2/46 Los Angeles, CA
37	Hernandez, Keith	St. Louis	163	15	91	.291	L-L	6-0	185	10/20/53 San Francisco, CA
—	Herr, Tom	St. Petersburg	156	1	53	.303	B-R	6-0	175	4/4/56 Lancaster, PA
24	Oberkfell, Ken	St. Louis	105	4	32	.251	L-R	6-0	175	5/4/56 Maryville, IL
		St. Louis	1	0	1	.111				
5	Phillips, Mike	NY(NL)-St. L.	39	1	12	.225	L-R	6-0	180	8/19/50 Beaumont, TX
—	Ramsey, Mike	Arkansas	121	1	28	.250	B-R	6-1	170	3/29/54 Roanoke, VA
44	Reitz, Ken	St. Louis	153	17	79	.261	R-R	6-0	185	6/24/51 San Francisco, CA
1	Templeton, Garry	St. Louis	200	8	79	.322	B-R	5-11	170	3/24/56 Lockey, TX
10	Tyson, Mike	St. Louis	103	7	57	.246	R-R	5-9	170	1/13/50 Rocky Mount, NC

OUTFIELDERS

No.	Name	1977 Club	H	HR	RBI	Pct.	B-T	Ht.	Wt.	Born
27	Anderson, Mike	St. Louis	34	4	17	.221	R-R	6-2	190	6/22/51 Florence, SC
21	Bosetti, Rick	Oklahoma City	56	3	10	.280	R-R	5-11	175	8/5/53 Redding, CA
		New Orleans	54	4	11	.340				
		St. Louis	16	0	3	.232				
20	Brock, Lou	St. Louis	133	2	46	.272	L-L	5-11	170	6/18/39 El Dorado, ARK
—	Dwyer, Jim	Wichita	154	18	70	.332	L-L	5-10	175	1/3/50 Evergreen Park, IL
		St. Louis	7	0	2	.226				
19	Iorg, Dane	Phil-St. Louis	15	0	6	.242	L-R	6-0	180	5/11/50 Eureka, CA
		Oklahoma City	72	5	24	.354				
		New Orleans	44	4	24	.308				
—	Morales, Jerry	Chicago (NL)	142	11	69	.290	R-R	6-1	175	2/18/49 Yabucoa, PR
29	Mumphrey, Jerry	St. Louis	133	2	38	.287	B-R	6-2	185	9/9/52 Tyler, TX
43	Potter, Mike	New Orleans	113	15	87	.263	R-R	6-1	195	5/16/51 Montebello, CA
		St. Louis	0	0	0	.000				
—	Scott, John	Toronto	56	2	15	.240	R-R	6-2	165	1/24/52 Jackson, MS
30	Scott, Tony	St. Louis	85	3	41	.291	B-R	6-0	175	9/18/51 Cinti, OH

CARD PROFILES

BOB FORSCH 28 6-4 200   Bats R Throws R

The Turnaround . . . Led club in victories after depressing season the year before . . . Was Cards' first 20-game winner since Steve Carlton in 1971 . . . In 1976, had just one decision in first 10 starts . . . Led Cards in winning percentage and ERA in 1975 . . . Originally a reliever . . . Actually began pro career as third baseman but didn't have the bat . . . Born Jan. 13, 1950, in Sacramento . . . A good-hitting pitcher . . . Second major-league homer came off John Candelaria . . . Younger brother of Houston's Ken Forsch . . . Caught Cards' attention after minor-league no-hitter at Tulsa.

Year	Club	G	IP	W	L	Pct.	SO	BB	H	ERA
1974	St. Louis	19	100	7	4	.636	39	34	84	2.97
1975	St. Louis	34	230	15	10	.600	108	70	213	2.86
1976	St. Louis	33	194	8	10	.444	76	71	209	3.94
1977	St. Louis	35	217	20	7	.741	95	69	210	3.48
	Totals	121	741	50	31	.617	318	244	716	3.34

JERRY MORALES 29 6-1 175   Bats R Throws R

The Latin Glover . . . Speed and strong arm plus ability to play all three outfield positions made him valuable addition to Cards . . . Obtained from Cubs in four-player deal . . . Career-high average was third best on club last season . . . Had five straight hits at Wrigley Field Aug. 27 and 28, 1976 . . . Led Cubs in RBIs each of his first two seasons . . . Born Feb. 18, 1949, in Yabucoa, Puerto Rico . . . One of toughest strikeouts in the league . . . Originally signed by Mets but taken by Padres in 1968 expansion draft . . . Played a little third base in San Diego.

Year	Club	Pos	G	AB	R	H	2B	3B	HR	RBI	SB	Avg.
1969	San Diego	OF	19	41	5	8	2	0	1	6	0	.195
1970	San Diego	OF	28	58	6	9	0	1	1	4	0	.155
1971	San Diego	OF	12	17	1	2	0	0	0	1	1	.118
1972	San Diego	OF-3B	115	347	38	83	15	7	4	18	4	.239
1973	San Diego	OF	122	388	47	109	23	2	9	34	6	.281
1974	Chicago (NL)	OF	151	534	70	146	21	7	15	82	2	.273
1975	Chicago (NL)	OF	153	578	62	156	21	0	12	91	3	.270
1976	Chicago (NL)	OF	140	537	66	147	17	0	16	67	3	.274
1977	Chicago (NL)	OF	136	490	56	142	34	5	11	69	0	.290
	Totals		876	2990	351	802	133	22	69	372	19	.268

TED SIMMONS 28 6-0 200   Bats S Throws R

Terrible Ted . . . One of the best hitting catchers of his generation . . . Finished in fifth-place tie in NL batting race last season, regaining all-star form . . . Led club in homers and RBIs . . . Doesn't strike out often . . . In 1975, he finished third in NL in hitting and set NL record for hits by catcher with 188 . . . That was just three off Yogi Berra's major-league mark . . . Remaining five hits by Ted that year came while he played first base or the outfield . . . Born Aug. 9, 1949, in Highland Park, Mich. . . . Caught Bob Gibson's 1971 no-hitter . . . Had longest hair in majors but cut it two years ago after it caught fire while he burned leaves in his backyard . . . Holds club record for home runs by a catcher.

Year	Club	Pos	G	AB	R	H	2B	3B	HR	RBI	SB	Avg.
1968	St. Louis	C	2	3	0	1	0	0	0	0	0	.333
1969	St. Louis	C	5	14	0	3	0	1	0	3	0	.214
1970	St. Louis	C	82	284	29	69	8	2	3	24	2	.243
1971	St. Louis	C	133	510	64	155	32	4	7	77	1	.304
1972	St. Louis	C-1B	152	594	70	180	36	6	16	96	1	.303
1973	St. Louis	C-1B-OF	161	619	62	192	36	2	13	91	2	.310
1974	St. Louis	C-1B	152	599	66	163	33	6	20	103	0	.272
1975	St. Louis	C-1B-OF	157	581	80	193	32	3	18	100	1	.332
1976	St. Louis	C-1B-OF-3B	150	546	60	159	35	3	5	75	0	.291
1977	St. Louis	C-1B	150	516	82	164	25	3	21	95	2	3.18
	Totals		1144	4266	513	1279	237	30	103	664	9	.300

KEITH HERNANDEZ 24 6-0 185   Bats L Throws L

Finally got to first base . . . Established himself at position with third best BA on club . . . Only Ted Simmons had more RBIs . . . Cards thought all along he could play, but watched him flop in 1975 . . . Given first base job, he hit only .203 and was sent down . . . Returned to salvage season and maybe career . . . Steady improvement in field, too . . . Born Oct. 20, 1953, in San Francisco . . . Remembers sneaking into Candlestick to watch boyhood idol Willie McCovey . . . Attended San Mateo JC and had outstanding scholastic career as well . . . His .500 BA in high school was a league record.

Year	Club	Pos	G	AB	R	H	2B	3B	HR	RBI	SB	Avg.
1974	St. Louis	1B	14	34	3	10	1	2	0	2	0	.294
1975	St. Louis	1B	64	188	20	47	8	2	3	20	0	.250
1976	St. Louis	1B	129	374	54	108	21	5	7	46	4	.289
1977	St. Louis	1B	161	560	90	163	41	4	15	91	7	.291
	Totals		368	1156	167	328	71	13	25	159	11	.284

GARRY TEMPLETON 22 5-11 170   Bats S Throws R

Ace of the Cards . . . Finished with third best BA in NL in first full season . . . Voted to all-star team . . . RBI total was just four short of Doc Lavan's 1921 club record by a shortstop . . . Has enough power to threaten Solly Hemus' record 15 homers by Cardinal shortstop . . . Good arm, good range and a fleet runner besides . . . Singled in first major-league game the same night his contract was purchased from Tulsa by Cards . . . Born March 24, 1956, in Lockey, Tex. . . . His father, Spiavia, played for Kansas City Monarchs of old Negro League . . . Scored five runs in one game last season at Chicago.

Year	Club	Pos	G	AB	R	H	2B	3B	HR	RBI	SB	Avg.
1976	St. Louis	SS	53	213	32	62	8	2	1	17	11	.291
1977	St. Louis	SS	153	621	94	200	19	18	8	79	28	.322
	Totals		206	834	126	262	27	20	9	96	39	.314

JERRY MUMPHREY 25 6-2 185   Bats S Throws R

His rapid development allowed Cards to trade Bake McBride . . . Speed makes him a natural center fielder, but has played all three outfield positions . . . Big surprise was fourth-best BA on club . . . His 14-game hitting streak in 1976 was second longest on team to Lou Brock's 15-game stretch . . . Also stole 22 bases that season, again second to Brock . . . Born Sept. 9, 1952, in Tyler, Tex. . . . Elevated to major leagues after just two years in minors . . . Stole 40 bases for Arkansas farm club . . . First major-league hit was a pinch-single off Ray Burris that scored a run.

Year	Club	Pos	G	AB	R	H	2B	3B	HR	RBI	SB	Avg.
1974	St. Louis	OF	5	2	2	0	0	0	0	0	0	.000
1975	St. Louis	OF	11	16	2	6	2	0	0	1	0	.375
1976	St. Louis	OF	112	384	51	99	15	5	1	26	22	.258
1977	St. Louis	OF	145	463	73	133	20	10	2	38	22	.287
	Totals		273	865	128	238	37	15	3	65	44	.275

LOU BROCK 38 5-11 170   Bats L Throws L

Larcenous Lou . . . Cards got him from Cubs in 1964 and what a steal . . . Broke Ty Cobb's major-league stolen base record of 892 last season . . . His 118 steals in 1974 broke Maury Wills' season record of 104 . . . Finished second that season to Steve Garvey in MVP voting . . . In 1968, led NL in doubles, triples and stolen bases . . . Was first to do that since

Honus Wagner in 1908 . . . Tied Series mark of 13 hits against Tigers in 1968 . . . Also stole seven bases to tie Series mark he set a year earlier against Boston . . . Born June 18, 1939, in El Dorado, Ark. . . . Once hit ball into center field seats of Polo Grounds in game against Mets . . . That's more than 500 feet away . . . Active in community work . . . A cousin, Dale Brock, is in Cards' farm system.

Year	Club	Pos	G	AB	R	H	2B	3B	HR	RBI	SB	Avg.
1961	Chicago (NL)	OF	4	11	1	1	0	0	0	0	0	.091
1962	Chicago (NL)	OF	123	434	73	114	24	7	9	35	16	.263
1963	Chicago (NL)	OF	148	547	79	141	19	11	9	37	24	.258
1964	Chi. (NL)-St.L....	OF	155	634	111	200	20	11	14	58	43	.315
1965	St. Louis	OF	155	631	107	182	35	8	16	69	63	.288
1966	St. Louis	OF	156	643	94	183	24	12	15	46	74	.285
1967	St. Louis	OF	159	689	113	206	32	12	21	76	52	.299
1968	St. Louis	OF	159	660	92	184	46	14	6	51	62	.279
1969	St. Louis	OF	157	655	97	195	33	10	12	47	53	.298
1970	St. Louis	OF	155	664	114	202	29	5	13	57	51	.304
1971	St. Louis	OF	157	640	126	200	37	7	7	61	64	.313
1972	St. Louis	OF	153	621	81	193	26	8	3	42	63	.311
1973	St. Louis	OF	160	650	110	193	29	8	7	63	70	.297
1974	St. Louis	OF	153	635	105	194	25	7	3	48	118	.306
1975	St. Louis	OF	136	528	78	163	27	6	3	47	56	.309
1976	St. Louis	OF	133	498	73	150	24	5	4	67	56	.301
1977	St. Louis	OF	141	489	69	133	22	6	2	46	35	.272
	Totals...........		2404	9629	1523	2834	462	137	144	850	900	.294

KEN REITZ 26 6-0 185   Bats R Throws R

The Zamboni Machine . . . Scoops up anything that gets in his way . . . Led NL third baseman for two straight years in fielding percentage before winning Golden Glove in 1975 . . . Returned to Cards last season after one year with Giants . . . Was second on club in homers . . . Was third in RBIs . . . Born June 24, 1951, in San Francisco . . . First major-league home run was hit at Candlestick Park, a mile from where he grew up . . . Passed up until 11th round of 1969 draft . . . Wife Kathy was usherette at Tulsa ballpark when Ken played for Oilers . . . Hit the ninth-inning homer that gave Cards a tie with Mets in 1974 . . . Teams then went on to play 25 innings.

Year	Club	Pos	G	AB	R	H	2B	3B	HR	RBI	SB	Avg.
1972	St. Louis	3B	21	78	5	28	4	0	0	10	0	.359
1973	St. Louis	SS-3B	147	426	40	100	20	2	6	42	0	.235
1974	St. Louis	3B-SS-2B	154	579	48	157	28	2	7	54	0	.271
1975	St. Louis	3B	161	592	43	159	25	1	5	63	1	.269
1976	San Francisco	3B-SS	155	577	40	154	21	1	5	66	5	.267
1977	St. Louis	3B	157	587	58	153	36	1	17	79	2	.261
	Totals...........		795	2839	234	751	134	7	40	314	8	.265

JOHN DENNY 25 6-3 185   **Bats R Throws R**

Had high expectations . . . Met them with low output . . . Slipped to fifth-best ERA on club after leading NL in 1976 at age 23 . . . That tied him with three others as youngest righthander to win ERA title . . . Previous one was Lon Warneke in 1932 . . . Was youngest ERA winner since lefty Mike McCormick, then 22, won for Giants in 1960 . . . Encountered control problems last season . . . Born Nov. 8, 1952, in Prescott, Ariz. . . . Had 1.29 ERA in first pro season at Sarasota in 1970 . . . Pitched only no-hitter in Texas League in 1973 . . . One of the best-hitting pitchers around . . . Cards 29th pick in 1970 draft.

Year	Club	G	IP	W	L	Pct.	SO	BB	H	ERA
1974	St. Louis	2	2	0	0	.000	1	0	3	0.00
1975	St. Louis	25	136	10	7	.588	72	51	149	3.97
1976	St. Louis	30	207	11	9	.550	74	74	189	2.52
1977	St. Louis	26	150	8	8	.500	60	62	165	4.50
	Totals	83	495	29	24	.547	207	187	506	3.51

MIKE TYSON 28 5-9 170   **Bats R Throws R**

Dal Maxvill reincarnated . . . Moved to second base but didn't lose his glove . . . Like Maxvill, a weak hitter who performs in clutch . . . First major-league homer gave cards a 1-0 win . . . Outstanding range and arm better suited for second than shortstop . . . Came back last season after 1976 season was marked by injury . . . Suffered thigh bruise in base path collision with Bill Madlock . . . Suffered broken finger making tag on Jim Barr . . . Born Jan. 13, 1950, in Rocky Mount, N.C. . . . Once stole home as part of double steal with Jerry Mumphrey . . . Was first steal of home by Cardinal since Jose Cardenal's in 1971.

Year	Club	Pos	G	AB	R	H	2B	3B	HR	RBI	SB	Avg.
1972	St. Louis	2B-SS	13	37	1	7	1	0	0	0	0	.189
1973	St. Louis	SS-2B	144	469	48	114	15	4	1	33	2	.243
1974	St. Louis	SS-2B	151	422	35	94	14	5	1	37	4	.223
1975	St. Louis	SS-2B-3B	122	368	45	98	16	3	2	37	5	.266
1976	St. Louis	2B	76	245	26	70	12	9	3	28	3	.286
1977	St. Louis	2B	138	418	42	103	15	2	7	57	3	.246
	Totals		644	1959	197	486	73	23	14	192	17	.248

TOP PROSPECT

RICK BOSETTI 24 5-11 175   **Bats R Throws R**

Hard-hitting outfielder with good speed . . . Stole 47 and 42 bases

in back-to-back minor-league seasons . . . Originally signed by
Phillies . . . Has made two minor-league all-star teams . . .
Couldn't crack Phils' outfield . . . Might serve as utility player for
Cards . . . Born Aug. 5, 1953, in Redding, Cal. . . . Describes
himself as "a free spirit" . . . Likes to water ski . . . Attended
Shasta JC in his hometown.

MANAGER VERN RAPP: The rap on Rapp—he has a rule for

everything . . . A stickler for grooming . . .
Doesn't like high stirrups . . . Ban on beards
and long hair led to confrontation with Al Hrabosky last season . . . Owner Gussie Busch was
called in to mediate . . . Rapp relaxed rules and
Hrabosky won more games . . . And Rapp kept
his job . . . Credited with having knack for developing pitchers . . . Had two first-place fin-
ishes and two second-place finishes in last four years as a minor-
league manger in Indianapolis and Denver . . . Got first managing job in Charleston in 1955, succeeding Danny Murtaugh . . .
Born May 11, 1928, in St. Louis, a fly ball away from Busch Stadium . . . Was minor-league catcher in Cardinal chain for 15 years
. . . Has worked in public relations and in radio . . . An off-
season plumber and heating salesman.

GREATEST MANAGER

He was a crusty, crafty little guy, but Billy Southworth holds one
of the most startling achievements in the history of major-league
managers. The Cardinals were a good, but struggling team when
Southworth became the club's third manager in one year in 1940.
The next year, in his first full season, the Cardinals finished sec-
ond—the lowest standing they would ever have under Southworth.
The team finished in first place the next three seasons, winning the
Series in 1942 and again in 1944.

In those three years, the Cardinals won 316 games. Even in
1945, Southworth's last season in St. Louis, the club finished in
second place and won 95 games. In the five years under Southworth, the Cardinals were 508-261, the third-best five-year stretch
in history.

Southworth went on to manage the Boston Braves and only one
manager, Frank Chance, has won more games in his first seven

years as a manager. Southworth brought the Braves a pennant and he gave them something else, too. In later years, he scouted and recommended a player named Hank Aaron.

ALL-TIME CARDINAL LEADERS

BATTING: Rogers Hornsby, .424, 1924
HRs: Johnny Mize, 43, 1940
RBIs: Joe Medwick, 154, 1937
STEALS: Lou Brock, 118, 1974
WINS: Dizzy Dean, 30, 1934
STRIKEOUTS: Bob Gibson, 274, 1970

No Card has matched Dizzy Dean's 30 wins or style.

MONTREAL EXPOS

TEAM DIRECTORY: Chairman of the Board: Charles Bronfman; Pres.: John McHale; VP, Baseball Operations: Charlie Fox; VP, Player Development: Jim Fanning; VP, Marketing: Roger Landry; VP, Sec.-Treas.: Harry Renaud; Pub. Rel.: Larry Chiasson; Trav. Sec.: Rodger Brulotte; Mgr.: Dick Williams. Home: Olympic Stadium (59,789). Spring training: Daytona Beach, Fla.

SCOUTING REPORT

HITTING: The most enchanting thing about the Expos is no longer the French ambiance or the tricolored insignia or even the modern, spacious stadium on the outskirts of Montreal. This season, those who have to pitch against the Expos will be occupied by other things—the lineup, for instance. The Expos will hit to all distances and to all fields. Only the high half-roof of the Olympic Stadium may go untouched.

For beginners, there are Ellis Valentine and Warren Cromartie and Andre Dawson, who are barely over being beginners. Dawson was the best young talent in the league last season and has power. Valentine won a lot of hearts. He has power, too. Cromartie does not have power, only a quick bat and a good eye. Dave Cash is an excellent leadoff hitter and Gary Carter has a nasty habit of bashing down fences with line drives.

And then there is Tony Perez, who is aging gracefully and can still drive in a run. Larry Parrish is a fine young talent who should have a better season than he did last year. Chris Speier is no automatic out, either. And how do you say home run in French, anyway? The rest of the league may soon learn.

PITCHING: And how do you say pitching staff in French? No one had to learn to say it before. It always consisted of two words: Steve Rogers. That's changed. The Expos signed free agent Ross Grimsley, who has a curly hairdo which makes him look rather innocent. Batters know better. Then, the Expos traded for Rudy May, another lefty, which so angered Baltimore manager Earl Weaver (he was not consulted on the deal) he nearly quit. Obviously, May has something. And Rogers has been a premier pitcher for years, though he has toiled without much support.

The other places in the rotation will be filled by Stan Bahnsen, Jackie Brown, or Tom Underwood. That's where the Expos may have some trouble. The bullpen has Will McEnaney, the lefty, and Bill Atkinson, the righty. After that, manager Dick Williams takes his chances with Rick Sawyer, Don DeMola or Santo Alcala. But

Cannon-armed Ellis Valentine batted .293 and hit 25 HRs.

make no mistake, the pitching is improved. Rogers may have to get used to all the company. So will the opposing hitters.

FIELDING: The Expos made 129 errors last season and only three teams made fewer. Dawson, Cromartie and Valentine are easily the best trio of outfielders in the league. Cash is a superb second baseman and Speier is capable, if somewhat erratic, at short. The Expos may need defensive help at the corners, where Parrish is still learning and Perez is suffering a little. Carter is not fancy behind the plate, but can get the job done when he has to. Del Unser is a useful utility outfielder.

OUTLOOK: The Expos are much improved, but it would take more than a lot of improvement for them to surpass anyone but the Cubs and Mets. The pitching staff suddenly is a plus and the hitting is there. What the Expos need more than anything is a little time. They are still dark horses in a tough field.

MONTREAL EXPOS 1978 ROSTER

MANAGER Dick Williams

Coaches—Jim Brewer, Billy Gardner, Norm Sherry, Mickey Vernon, Ozzie Virgil

PITCHERS

No.	Name	1977 Club	W-L	IP	SO	ERA	B-T	Ht.	Wt.	Born
32	Alcala, Santo	Cin-Mont.	3-7	117	73	4.85	R-R	6-6	210	12/23/52 San Pedro de Macoris, D.R.
42	Atkinson, Bill	Montreal	7-2	83	56	3.36	R-R	5-8	165	10/4/54 Chatham, Ontario
22	Bahnsen, Stan	Oakland	1-2	22	21	6.14	R-R	6-3	198	12/15/44 Council Bluffs, IA
		Montreal	8-9	127	58	4.82				
31	Brown, Jackie	Montreal	9-12	186	89	4.50	R-R	6-1	185	5/31/43 Holdenville, OK
13	DeMola, Don	Denver	5-3	61	48	3.81	R-R	6-2	185	7/5/52 Glen Cove, N.Y.
28	Dues, Hal	Quebec	6-6	96	56	3.75	R-R	6-3	190	9/22/54 LaMarque, TX
		Montreal	1-1	23	9	4.30				
—	Grimsley, Ross	Baltimore	14-10	218	53	3.96	L-L	6-3	200	1/7/50 Topeka, KS
35	Hannahs, Gerald	Montreal	1-5	37	21	4.86	L-L	6-3	200	3/6/52 Binghamton, N.Y.
		Denver	6-2	82	60	3.83				
16	Holdsworth, Fred	Baltimore	0-1	14	4	6.43	R-R	6-1	190	5/29/52 Detroit, MI
		Montreal	3-3	42	21	3.21				
—	Horn, Larry	W. Palm Bch.	6-0	54	50	1.67	R-R	6-2	200	11/24/56 Dallas, TX
		Quebec	6-8	125	59	3.89				
—	Keener, Joe	Denver	7-8	134	60	4.65	R-R	6-2	189	4/21/53 San Pedro, CA
—	Knowles, Darold	Texas	5-2	50	14	3.24	L-L	6-0	190	12/9/41 Brunswick, MO
21	Landreth, Larry	Denver	10-10	195	134	4.15	R-R	6-1	173	3/11/55 Stratford, Ont.
		Montreal	0-2	9	5	10.00				
—	May, Rudy	Baltimore	18-14	252	105	3.61	L-L	6-3	198	7/18/44 Coffeysville, KS
20	McEnaney, Will	Montreal	3-5	87	38	3.93	L-L	6-0	180	2/14/52 Springfield, OH
—	Miller, Randy	Rochester	2-5	94	72	3.54	R-R	6-1	180	3/18/53 Oxnard, CA
		Baltimore	0-0	1	0	27.00				
45	Rogers, Steve	Montreal	17-16	302	206	3.10	R-R	6-1	177	10/26/49 Jefferson City, MO
27	Sawyer, Rick	San Diego	7-6	111	45	5.84	R-R	6-2	200	4/7/48 Bakersfield, CA
43	Schatzeder, Dan	Quebec	5-3	62	59	2.76	L-L	6-0	195	12/1/54 Elmhurst, IL
		Denver	2-2	36	28	6.00				
		Montreal	2-1	22	14	2.45				
33	Twitchell, Wayne	Phil-Mont.	6-10	185	130	4.28	R-R	6-6	225	3/10/48 Portland, OR

CATCHERS

No.	Name	1977 Club	H	HR	RBI	Pct.	B-T	Ht.	Wt.	Born
44	Blackwell, Tim	Reading	7	0	2	.500	B-R	5-11	185	8/19/52 San Diego, CA
		Phil-Mont.	2	0	0	.091				
8	Carter, Gary	Montreal	148	31	84	.284	R-R	6-2	210	4/8/54 Culver City, CA
34	Morales, Jose	Montreal	15	1	9	.203	R-R	6-0	195	12/30/44 St. Croix, V.I.
—	Ramos, Roberto	W. Palm Bch.	99	5	58	.309	R-R	5-11	190	11/5/55 Havana, Cuba.
—	Reece, Bob	Denver	74	3	26	.285	R-R	6-1	190	1/5/51 Sacramento, CA

INFIELDERS

No.	Name	1977 Club	H	HR	RBI	Pct.	B-T	Ht.	Wt.	Born
30	Cash, Dave	Montreal	188	0	43	.289	R-R	5-11	170	6/11/48 Utica, N.Y.
38	Frias, Pepe	Montreal	180	0	5	.257	B-R	5-11	160	7/14/48 San Pedro De Macoris, D.R.
11	Garrett, Wayne	Montreal	43	2	22	.270	L-R	5-11	185	12/3/47 Brooksville, FL
5	Mackanin, Pete	Montreal	19	1	6	.224	R-R	6-2	190	8/1/51 Chicago, IL
—	Ortenzio, Frank	Denver	147	40	126	.311	R-R	6-2	215	2/24/51 Fresno, CA
12	Papi, Stan	Denver	134	13	80	.296	R-R	6-0	178	2/4/51 Fresno, CA
		Montreal	10	0	4	.233				
15	Parrish, Larry	Montreal	99	11	46	.246	R-R	6-3	200	11/10/53 Winter Haven, FL
24	Perez, Tony	Montreal	158	19	91	.283	R-R	6-2	215	5/14/42 Camaguey, Cuba
4	Speier, Chris	SF-Mont.	128	5	38	.234	R-R	6-1	182	6/28/50 Alameda, CA

OUTFIELDERS

No.	Name	1977 Club	H	HR	RBI	Pct.	B-T	Ht.	Wt.	Born
49	Cromartie, Warren	Montreal	175	5	50	.282	L-L	6-0	190	9/23/53 Miami, FL
10	Dawson, Andre	Montreal	148	19	65	.282	R-R	6-3	180	7/10/54 Miami, FL
14	Mejias, Sam	Montreal	23	3	8	.228	R-R	6-0	168	5/9/52 Santiago, D.R.
25	Unser, Del	Montreal	79	12	40	.273	L-L	5-11	180	12/9/44 Decatur, IL
17	Valentine, Ellis	Montreal	149	25	76	.293	R-R	6-4	205	7/30/54 Helena, AR
37	White, Jerry	Denver	145	14	57	.313	B-R	5-11	165	8/23/52 Shirley, MA
		Montreal	4	0	1	.190				

EXPO PROFILES

ELLIS VALENTINE 23 6-4 205   Bats R Throws R

Has won a lot of hearts . . . Also has won a lot of games . . . Runs hard, throws hard and hits hard . . . Expos' only representative at All-Star Game last year . . . Led club in hitting . . . No sweetheart to pitchers or catchers . . . Once had 14 straight stolen bases including three in one game . . . Team's best threat to Rusty Staub's club record for RBIs . . . Born July 30, 1954, in Helena, Ark. . . . Opponents call his arm "Cupid's Arrow" . . . He's straight and true and even more effective . . . Expos' No. 2 draft choice in 1972 . . . Unbeatable at chess and pretty good at billiards, too . . . To friends, he's "Bubba" . . . To pitchers, he's trouble.

Year	Club	Pos	G	AB	R	H	2B	3B	HR	RBI	SB	Avg.
1975	Montreal	OF	12	33	2	12	4	0	1	3	0	.364
1976	Montreal	OF	94	305	36	85	15	2	7	39	14	.279
1977	Montreal	OF	127	508	63	149	28	2	25	76	13	.293
	Totals..........		233	846	101	246	47	4	33	118	27	.291

RUDY MAY 33 6-3 198   Bats L Throws L

Getting better as he get older . . . 47-36 over last three seasons leaving him eight games under .500 for career . . . Much traveled player, has been with seven major-league organizations . . . Came to Expos as part of six-player swap with Orioles . . . Nicknamed "Dude" . . . Born July 18, 1944, in Coffeyville, Kan., but raised in Oakland . . . Lettered in baseball, football, basketball, track in high school, where classmate was Joe Morgan . . . Attended San Francisco State on baseball scholarship . . . Originally signed by Minnesota, but lost in first-year draft . . . Has commercial scuba diving license.

Year	Club	G	IP	W	L	Pct.	SO	BB	H	ERA
1965	California.............	30	124	4	9	.308	76	78	111	3.92
1969	California................	43	180	10	13	.435	133	66	142	3.45
1970	California..............	38	209	7	13	.350	154	81	190	4.00
1971	California..............	32	208	11	12	.478	156	87	160	3.03
1972	California..............	35	205	12	11	.522	169	82	162	2.94
1973	California..............	34	185	7	17	.292	134	80	177	4.38
1974	Calif-New York (AL)........	35	141	8	5	.615	102	58	104	3.19
1975	New York (AL).......	32	212	14	12	.538	145	99	179	3.06
1976	New York (AL)-Balt........	35	220	15	10	.600	109	70	205	3.72
1977	Baltimore................	37	252	18	14	.563	105	78	243	3.61
	Totals..................	351	1936	106	116	.477	1293	779	1673	3.52

ROSS GRIMSLEY 28 6-3 200   Bats L Throws L

Rebounded from so-so 1976 to be one of Orioles' most reliable starters in '77 . . . Often accused of throwing greaseball (rivals says he gets it from hair), which he denies, of course . . . Decided to test free agent waters and got $1.1 million from Expos . . . Born Jan. 7, 1950, in Topeka, Kan. . . . Was Cincinnati's first choice in 1969 draft . . . Traded to Orioles for Merv Rettenmund in 1974 and won 18 games . . . Pitched for Memphis American Legion team that won national title in 1968 . . . His father, Ross, Sr., pitched in seven games for White Sox in 1951.

Year	Club	G	IP	W	L	Pct.	SO	BB	H	ERA
1971	Cincinnati	26	161	10	7	.588	67	43	151	3.58
1972	Cincinnati	30	198	14	8	.636	79	50	194	3.05
1973	Cincinnati	38	242	13	10	.565	90	68	245	3.24
1974	Baltimore	40	296	18	13	.581	158	76	267	3.07
1975	Baltimore	35	197	10	13	.435	89	47	210	4.07
1976	Baltimore	28	137	8	7	.533	41	35	143	3.94
1977	Baltimore	34	218	14	10	.583	53	74	230	3.96
	Totals	231	1449	87	68	.561	577	393	1440	3.50

DAVE CASH 29 5-11 170   Bats R Throws R

Money in the bank when he's in lineup . . . Also money in his bank . . . Left Phillies to sign as free agent for more than $1 million . . . Exciting player who hits, steals and fields his position well . . . Also durable, playing in 496 straight games until sitting out second game of a doubleheader after Phillies clinched 1976 division title . . . Doesn't have any power but doesn't need it . . . Born June 11, 1948, in Utica, N.Y. . . . Set a major league record with 699 at-bats in 1975 . . . One of toughest strikeouts around . . . Fans only once every 51 times up . . . Quiet and serious guy who has dabbled in transcendental meditation.

Year	Club	Pos	G	AB	R	H	2B	3B	HR	RBI	SB	Avg.
1970	Pittsburgh	2B	64	210	30	66	7	6	1	28	5	.314
1971	Pittsburgh	2B-3B-SS	123	478	79	138	17	4	2	34	13	.289
1972	Pittsburgh	2B	99	425	58	120	22	4	3	30	9	.282
1973	Pittsburgh	2B-3B	116	436	59	118	21	2	2	31	2	.271
1974	Philadelphia	2B	162	687	89	206	26	11	2	58	20	.300
1975	Philadelphia	2B	162	699	111	213	40	3	4	57	13	.305
1976	Philadelphia	2B	160	666	92	189	14	12	1	56	10	.284
1977	Montreal	2B	153	650	91	188	42	7	0	43	21	.289
	Totals		1057	4312	617	1255	192	50	15	341	95	.291

TONY PEREZ 35 6-2 215   Bats R Throws R

The Ageless Wonder . . . Has driven in 90 or more runs 11 straight years . . . Has 1,119 RBIs over that span, more than any other active player . . . Aging gracefully . . . Plays a smooth first base, though he started career as third baseman with Reds . . . Did not have to accept 1976 trade to Expos, but said he wanted to play every day . . . He has, delivering experience to Montreal's young lineup . . . Born May 14, 1942, in Camaguey, Cuba . . . Friendly, talkative guy whose conversation is spiced with Latin humor . . . A clutch performer who had game-winning single off Catfish Hunter in 1976 Series and three homers in 1975 Series.

Year	Club	Pos	G	AB	R	H	2B	3B	HR	RBI	SB	Avg.
1964	Cincinnati	1B	12	25	1	2	1	0	0	1	0	.080
1965	Cincinnati	1B	104	281	40	73	14	4	12	47	0	.260
1966	Cincinnati	1B	99	257	25	68	10	4	4	39	1	.265
1967	Cincinnati	3B-1B-2B	156	600	78	174	28	7	26	102	0	.290
1968	Cincinnati	3B	160	625	93	176	25	7	18	92	3	.282
1969	Cincinnati	3B	160	629	103	185	31	2	37	122	4	.294
1970	Cincinnati	3B-1B	158	587	107	186	28	6	40	129	8	.317
1971	Cincinnati	3B-1B	158	609	72	164	22	3	25	91	4	.269
1972	Cincinnati	1B	136	515	64	146	33	7	21	90	4	.283
1973	Cincinnati	1B	151	564	73	177	33	3	27	101	3	.314
1974	Cincinnati	1B	158	596	81	158	28	2	28	101	1	.265
1975	Cincinnati	1B	137	511	74	144	28	3	20	109	1	.282
1976	Cincinnati	1B	139	527	77	137	32	6	19	91	10	.260
1977	Montreal	1B	154	559	71	158	32	6	19	91	4	.283
	Totals		1882	6885	959	1948	345	60	296	1206	43	.283

GARY CARTER 24 6-2 210   Bats R Throws R

Rebounded from injury-plagued season to break Rusty Staub's seven-year-old club homer mark . . . Broke left thumb and later right pinky, forcing him to miss 55 games the year before . . . Useful both in outfield and as catcher . . . A strong arm is his ace at both positions . . . Was NL Rookie-of-the-Year in 1975 and named to the all-star team that year . . . Broke in with a flair . . . His first major-league hit was off Jon Matlack . . . His first homer was off Steve Carlton . . . Older brother Gordon played in California and San Francisco farm systems.

Year	Club	Pos	G	AB	R	H	2B	3B	HR	RBI	SB	Avg.
1974	Montreal	C-OF	9	27	5	11	0	1	1	6	2	.407
1975	Montreal	OF-C-3B	144	503	58	136	20	1	17	68	5	.270
1976	Montreal	C-OF	91	311	31	68	8	1	6	38	0	.219
1977	Montreal	C-OF	154	522	86	148	29	2	31	84	5	.284
	Totals		398	1363	180	363	57	5	55	196	12	.266

WARREN CROMARTIE 24 6-0 190   Bats L Throws L

The Cro flies . . . Outstanding rookie year, finishing fourth on club in hitting . . . A No. 1 draft choice in 1973 who was promoted to major-league roster only a year later . . . Had late-season trial with Expos in 1976 and had two hits in first four at-bats . . . A contact hitter and a rare strikeout . . . Will steal a base if you give him a lead . . . Born Sept. 29, 1953, in Miami . . . Shares the outfield and the pool table with Ellis Valentine . . . His 175 hits led the team and were only nine short of Rusty Staub's club record . . . Wife Carole is a native Canadian.

Year	Club	Pos	G	AB	R	H	2B	3B	HR	RBI	SB	Avg.
1974	Montreal	OF	8	17	2	3	0	0	0	0	1	.176
1976	Montreal	OF	33	81	8	17	1	0	0	2	1	.210
1977	Montreal	OF	155	620	64	175	41	7	5	50	10	.282
	Totals		196	718	74	195	42	7	5	52	12	.272

ANDRE DAWSON 23 6-3 180   Bats R Throws R

The third Musketeer . . . Joins Valentine and Cromartie in youngest outfield in league . . . Rookie-of-the-year . . . A storybook career . . . Reported to Venezuelan winter-league team as spare outfielder but quickly moved into lineup . . . Homered in his second AA at-bat and had seven homers in first six games . . . Singled off Steve Carlton for first major-league hit . . . All that from someone who wasn't chosen until the 11th round of the 1975 draft . . . Born July 10, 1954, in Miami . . . Played high school ball against Cromartie . . . Attended Florida A&M, where he also played football . . . Enough speed to steal a base or stretch a single.

Year	Club	Pos	G	AB	R	H	2B	3B	HR	RBI	SB	Avg.
1976	Montreal	OF	24	85	9	20	4	1	0	7	1	.235
1977	Montreal	OF	139	525	64	148	26	9	19	65	21	.282
	Totals		163	610	73	168	30	10	19	72	22	.275

LARRY PARRISH 24 6-3 200   Bats R Throws R

Still learning third base . . . Still learning to hit . . . Big and rugged with good power . . . Playing time cut by injuries last season after leading club in games played the year before . . . Signed as a free agent after a .455 BA as collegian at Seminole JC in Sanford, Fla. . . . Enrolled after being ignored in 1971 draft . . . Originally an outfielder but Expos converted him in to third baseman . . . Also has played some shortstop and second base . . . Born Nov. 10, 1953, in Winter Haven, Fla. . . . Leaped from AA to major leagues.

Year	Club	Pos	G	AB	R	H	2B	3B	HR	RBI	SB	Avg.
1974	Montreal	3B	25	69	9	14	5	0	0	4	0	.203
1975	Montreal	3B-2B-SS	145	532	50	146	32	5	10	65	4	.274
1976	Montreal	3B	154	543	65	126	28	5	11	61	2	.232
1977	Montreal	3B-2B	123	402	50	99	19	2	11	46	2	.246
	Totals		447	1546	174	385	84	12	32	176	8	.249

STEVE ROGERS 28 6-1 177   Bats R Throws R

A hard thrower and hard worker . . . Again the ace of the staff . . . Led club in victories, strikeouts and ERA . . . Holds several club records . . . Has had little support through most of his career . . . Expos scored only 27 runs in his 17 defeats two years ago . . . Was named the top NL rookie pitcher in 1973, his third season of pro ball . . . Originally drafted by Yankees in 1967, but went to U. of Tulsa instead . . . Born Oct. 27, 1949, in Jefferson City, Mo. . . . Named to all-star team in 1974 . . . Doesn't walk many and doesn't throw gophers, either . . . Holds a degree in petroleum engineering . . . Expos have struck it rich with him.

Year	Club	G	IP	W	L	Pct.	SO	BB	H	ERA
1973	Montreal	17	134	10	5	.667	64	49	93	1.54
1974	Montreal	38	254	15	22	.405	154	80	255	4.46
1975	Montreal	35	252	11	12	.478	137	88	248	3.29
1976	Montreal	33	230	7	17	.292	150	69	212	3.21
1977	Montreal	40	302	17	16	.515	206	81	272	3.10
	Totals	163	1172	60	72	.455	711	367	1080	3.28

WILL McENANEY 26 6-0 180   Bats L Throws L

Where there's Will, there's a way . . . Was Reds' outstanding reliever for two seasons and upset by trade after third year with Cincinnati . . . Managed only three saves for Expos . . . Humble guy who saw baseball as way out of the coal mines . . . Once went 12 straight appearances before he was scored on . . . Once went 68 innings before allowing a home run . . . Born Feb. 14, 1952, in Springfield, Ohio . . . Had 15 saves his first full season in majors, making second-most appearances in NL . . . Throws strikes . . . Pitched the final inning in the clinching games of Cincinnati's Series triumphs in 1975 and 1976.

Year	Club	G	IP	W	L	Pct.	SO	BB	H	ERA
1974	Cincinnati	24	27	2	1	.667	13	9	24	4.33
1975	Cincinnati	70	91	5	2	.714	48	23	92	2.47
1976	Cincinnati	55	72	2	6	.250	28	23	97	4.88
1977	Montreal	69	87	3	5	.375	38	22	92	3.93
	Totals	218	277	12	14	.462	127	77	305	3.74

TOP PROSPECT

DAN SCHATZEDER 23 6-0 195   Bats L Throws L
A Dandy Dan . . . Has knuckle curve, patterned after Burt Hooton's . . . Also has slider and good fastball . . . Was 5-3 with 2.76 ERA for Quebec City last season despite missing eight weeks with arm injury . . . Born Dec. 1, 1954, in Elmhurst, Ill. . . . Club's No. 3 draft choice out of the U. of Denver . . . Had 2-2 record in late-season stint with Triple-A Denver team.

MANAGER DICK WILLIAMS: A miracle worker in need of a  miracle . . . Rose to prominence after guiding Cinderella Boston team into 1967 Series . . . Was at the helm of Oakland dynasty, getting the team home first three times and winning the Series twice . . . Failed to turn corner with California, finishing last twice before being fired in mid-season of third year . . . A tough guy who can be tough on young players . . . Born May 7, 1929, in St. Louis . . . signed to manage Yankees after leaving A's but Charlie Finley had contract voided in court battle . . . A gritty manager . . . A gritty player . . . A gritty person . . . Compiled .260 BA in 14 years as infielder-outfielder with Brooklyn, Baltimore, Cleveland, Kansas City and Boston.

GREATEST MANAGER

Not only was Gene Mauch the greatest manager of the Expos, but for the first seven years of the expansion club's existence he was its only manager.

In Montreal, they called Mauch a genius and he didn't protest. Casey Stengel once said of Mauch, "He thinks he invented the game." Perhaps, but Mauch's accomplishments in Montreal were something. The first Expo team won 52 games, but from then on the Expos never failed to win at least 70 games. In 1973, the team won 79 games and even challenged for the East Division lead in September before folding.

Mauch will be most remembered as the man who managed the Philadelphia Phillies when they lost 10 straight games at the end of the season to blow the 1964 pennant. It may not be as memorable, but it's possible that no Montreal manager may ever win as many games as Mauch did, or last as long, either.

ALL-TIME EXPO LEADERS

BATTING: Rusty Staub, .311, 1971
HRS: Gary Carter, 31, 1977
RBIs: Ken Singleton, 103, 1973
STEALS: Lary Lintz, 50, 1974
WINS: Carl Morton, 18, 1970
STRIKEOUTS: Bill Stoneman, 251, 1971

Expos' pitchers will shoot for Carl Morton's 18-win club mark.

CHICAGO CUBS

TEAM DIRECTORY: Pres.: Philip K. Wrigley; VP-Operations: Bob Kennedy; VP: Charles J. Grimm; Dir. of Player Development: C.V. Davis; Dir. of Scouting: Vedie Himsl; Pub. Rel.: Buck Peden; Dir. Park Operations: E.R. Saltwell; Mgr.: Herman Franks. Home: Wrigley Field (37,471). Field distances: 355, l.f. line; 400, c.f.; 353, r.f. line. Spring training: Scottsdale, Ariz.

SCOUTING REPORT

HITTING: All along Waveland Avenue, beyond the left field fence in Wrigley Field, the owners of the old, brown apartments are preparing for a long, hot summer. Armoured shields are being constructed in front of their homes and small children are being kept indoors during the days that the Cubs play. This in response to Dave Kingman, who has been known to shower home runs to the farthest precincts of Wrigley, across Waveland and even on to Kenmore Street—as he did with one 620-foot blast two years ago.

But then Kingman was playing against the Cubs. Now he is a Cub, his fifth uniform in less than a year, but he says he is happy. So are the Cubs. So heady were the Cubs with the signing of a

Rick Reuschel fashioned first 20-game season with 2.79 ERA.

power hitter such as Kingman, they traded all-star Jerry Morales for line-drive hitter Hector Cruz. Bobby Murcer is an accomplished hitter, who should do better this season and Steve Ontiveros is expected to continue his comeback after having been given up for dead by the Giants two years ago.

Bill Buckner can be a valuable hitter, though he is coming off injuries. Larry Biittner has a sweet swing. Manny Trillo emerged as a hitter last season. It could be a terrible summer for the apartments along Waveland Avenue.

PITCHING: The people along Waveland may also have to protect themselves against the long balls of opposing batters. Among starters, the Cubs have 20-game winner Rick Reuschel and 14-game winner Ray Burris and then a lot of trouble. Nobody else won in double figures for a team that was in first place half of the season. Dave Roberts, a late-season addition from Detroit, should help a little. Woodie Fryman retired briefly when he was with the Reds last season, though he probably will be given a spot in the rotation.

Mike Krukow also will start and his best asset right now is a year's experience. If the starters need help—and they are bound to need plenty—manager Herman Franks can call on reliever Bruce Sutter, he of the split-finger curve. Sutter is one of the best firemen around. It was no coincidence that the Cubs took a dive when Sutter was injured last season. Willie Hernandez is the left-hander in the bullpen and is coming off a mediocre season. Righty reliever Paul Reuschel is coming off a bad one.

FIELDING: The first order of business is to find a place for Kingman to play. His best position is first base, where the Cubs already have Biittner and Buckner. His worst position is the outfield, where the Cubs have a vacancy. Kingman has no other position, which makes things a bit difficult. Manny Trillo and Ivan DeJesus are far from the best double-play combination around and one reason the Cubs made 153 errors last season, the fourth worst total in the NL.

Murcer has made himself into a skilled outfielder, but Ontiveros struggles at third base. George Mitterwald does the job behind home plate.

OUTLOOK: The Cubs needed to get off to a tremendous start to finish fourth last season. They need even a better start to do that well again. The team will hit—but Kingman strikes out a lot, too. And if he hits 50 homers, which is not out of the question, the pitching staff is likely to give up at least twice that many.

CHICAGO CUBS 1978 ROSTER

MANAGER Herman Franks
Coaches—Joe Amalfitano, Jack Bloomfield, Harry Lowrey,
      Mike Roarke, Cookie Rojas

PITCHERS

No.	Name	1977 Club	W-L	IP	SO	ERA	B-T	Ht.	Wt.	Born
40	Broberg, Pete	Chicago (NL)	1-2	36	20	4.75	R-R	6-3	205	3/2/50 West Palm Beach, FL
		Wichita	6-5	87	64	5.46				
34	Burris, Ray	Chicago (NL)	14-16	221	105	4.72	R-R	6-5	195	8/22/50 Idabel, OK
–	Fryman, Woodie	Cincinnati	5-5	75	57	5.40	R-L	6-2	205	4/12/40 Ewing, KY
38	Hernandez, Willie	Chicago (NL)	8-7	110	78	3.03	L-L	6-2	180	11/14/55 Aquada, PR
39	Krukow, Mike	Chicago (NL)	8-14	172	106	4.40	R-R	6-4	195	1/21/52 Long Beach, CA
47	Lamp, Dennis	Wichita	11-4	129	52	2.94	R-R	6-3	190	9/23/52 Los Angeles, CA
		Chicago (NL)	0-2	30	12	6.30				
49	Moore, Donnie	Wichita	4-4	66	34	4.93	L-R	6-0	170	2/13/54 Lubbock, TX
		Chicago (NL)	4-2	49	34	4.04				
43	Reuschel, Paul	Chicago (NL)	5-6	107	62	4.37	R-R	6-4	210	1/12/47 Quincy, IL
48	Reuschel, Rick	Chicago (NL)	20-10	252	166	2.79	R-R	6-3	230	5/16/49 Quincy, IL
41	Roberts, Dave	Detroit	4-10	129	46	5.15	L-L	6-3	192	9/11/44 Gallipolis, OH
		Chicago (NL)	1-1	53	23	3.23				
–	Seoane, Manny	Oklahoma City	11-8	156	100	3.87	R-R	6-3	187	6/26/55 Tampa, FL
		Philadelphia	0-0	6	4	6.00				
42	Sutter, Bruce	Chicago (NL)	7-3	107	129	1.35	R-R	6-2	190	1/8/53 Lancaster, PA
–	Caudill, Bill	Indianapolis	2-2	44	25	3.65	R-R	6-1	190	7/13/56 Santa Monica, CA

CATCHERS

No.	Name	1977 Club	H	HR	RBI	Pct.	B-T	Ht.	Wt.	Born
–	Cox, Larry	Seattle	23	2	6	.247	R-R	5-11	190	9/11/47 Bluffton, OH
23	Gordon, Mike	Wichita	77	9	54	.228	S-R	6-3	216	9/11/53 Leominster, MA
		Chicago (NL)	1	0	2	.043				
15	Mitterwald, George	Chicago (NL)	83	9	43	.238	R-R	6-2	205	6/7/45 Berkeley, CA
–	Rader, Dave	St. Louis	30	1	6	.263	L-R	6-0	175	12/26/48 Claremore OK

INFIELDERS

No.	Name	1977 Club	H	HR	RBI	Pct.	B-T	Ht.	Wt.	Born
30	Adams, Mike	Wichita	119	23	91	.321	R-R	6-2	200	7/22/48 Cincinnati, OH
		Chicago (NL)	0	0	0	.000				
26	Biittner, Larry	Chicago (NL)	147	12	62	.298	L-L	6-2	200	7/27/47 Pocahonatas, LA
22	Buckner, Bill	Chicago (NL)	121	11	60	.284	L-L	6-1	185	12/14/49 Vallejo, CA
11	DeJesus, Ivan	Chicago (NL)	166	3	40	.266	R-R	5-11	165	1/9/53 Santurce, PR
20	Kelleher, Mick	Chicago (NL)	28	0	11	.230	R-R	5-9	175	7/25/47 Seattle, WA
–	Meoli, Rudy	Indianapolis	124	7	48	.286	L-R	5-9	160	5/1/51 Troy, NY
16	Ontiveros, Steve	Chicago (NL)	163	10	68	.299	R-R	6-0	185	10/26/51 Bakersfield, CA
10	Sember, Mike	Wichita	79	6	27	.245	R-R	6-0	185	2/24/53 Hammond, IN
		Chicago (NL)	1	0	0	.250				
19	Trillo, Manny	Chicago (NL)	141	7	57	.280	R-R	6-1	160	12/25/50 Caritito, VZ

OUTFIELDERS

No.	Name	1977 Club	H	HR	RBI	Pct.	B-T	Ht.	Wt.	Born
18	Clines, Gene	Chicago (NL)	70	3	41	.293	R-R	5-9	170	10/6/46 San Pablo, CA
–	Cruz, Hector	St. Louis	80	6	42	.236	R-R	5-11	175	4/2/53 Arroyo, PR
21	Gross, Greg	Chicago (NL)	77	5	32	.322	L-L	5-11	170	8/1/52 York, PA
–	Kingman, Dave	NY (NL)-SD	84	20	67	.222	R-R	6-6	210	12/21/48 Pendleton, OR
		Cal-NY (AL)	13	6	11	.217				
7	Murcer, Bobby	Chicago (NL)	147	27	89	.265	L-R	6-1	180	5/20/46 Oklahoma City, OK
27	Wallis, Joe	Chicago (NL)	20	2	8	.250	B-R	5-11	180	1/9/52 East St. Louis, IL

CUB PROFILES

BOBBY MURCER 31 6-1 180   Bats L Throws L

Once nicknamed "Lemon" because he was in a sour mood . . . Actually, one of the nicest guys in baseball with good, ol' country humor . . . When he's in lineup, it's "Lemon-aid" . . . Steady hitter who has regained home run stroke . . . Made himself into good outfielder after breaking in as shortstop with Yankees . . . Was signed by Tom Greenwade, scout that also signed Mickey Mantle . . . Like Mantle, he's from Oklahoma . . . Born May 20, 1946, in Oklahoma City . . . Traded to Giants even-up for Bobby Bonds in one of the biggest exchanges of stars in history . . . Traded to Cubs in Bill Madlock deal . . . Hit four homers in consecutive at-bats spanning two games of doubleheader June 24, 1970 . . . Has hit for cycle . . . Likes to pass the hours in clubhouse sitting in homemade rocking chair.

Year	Club	Pos	G	AB	R	H	2B	3B	HR	RBI	SB	Avg.
1965	New York (AL) ...	SS	11	37	2	9	0	1	1	4	0	.243
1966	New York (AL) ...	SS	21	69	3	12	1	1	0	5	2	.174
1967	New York (AL)		In Military Service									
1968	New York (AL)		In Military Service									
1969	New York (AL) ...	OF-3B	152	564	82	146	24	4	26	82	7	.259
1970	New York (AL) ...	OF	159	581	95	146	23	3	23	78	15	.251
1971	New York (AL) ...	OF	146	529	94	175	25	6	25	94	14	.331
1972	New York (AL) ...	OF	153	585	102	171	30	7	33	96	11	.292
1973	New York (AL) ...	OF	160	616	83	187	29	2	22	95	6	.304
1974	New York (AL) ...	OF	156	606	69	166	25	4	10	88	14	.274
1975	San Francisco	OF	147	526	80	157	29	4	11	91	9	.298
1976	San Francisco	OF	147	533	73	138	20	2	23	90	12	.259
1977	Chicago (NL)	OF	154	554	90	147	18	3	27	89	16	.265
	Totals..........		1406	5200	773	1454	224	37	201	812	104	.280

BRUCE SUTTER 25 6-2 190   Bats R Throws R

Sprouted as top reliever in only second season . . . Had lowest ERA in NL . . . Also had 31 saves, second best in NL . . . Led club with 10 saves the year before . . . Throws split-finger curve, similar to forkball used by Elroy Face . . . Excellent strikeout-to-walk ratio . . . Named to all-star team but injury prevented his appearance . . . Has started only two games, both in low minors . . . Born Jan. 8, 1953, in Lancaster, Pa., home of the Pennsylvania Dutch . . . Lives in a place called Mt. Joy . . . Had best month of career in May when he notched 11 saves . . . Of Cubs first 48 wins, he was responsible for half with three victories and 21 saves.

Year	Club	G	IP	W	L	Pct.	SO	BB	H	ERA
1976	Chicago (NL)	52	83	6	3	.667	73	26	63	2.71
1977	Chicago (NL)	62	107	7	3	.700	129	23	69	1.35
	Totals...................	114	190	13	6	.684	202	49	132	1.94

MANNY TRILLO 27 6-1 160   Bats R Throws R

Led NL in hitting first half of season, batting over .320 into June . . . That earned him his first selection to all-star team . . . Originally signed as catcher, but speed and range make him ideal second baseman . . . Born Dec. 25, 1950, in Caripito, Venezuela . . . First major-league hit was game-winning single for Oakland A's . . . Gained exposure during 1973 Series and didn't even play . . . Charlie Finley tried to dump Mike Andrews from roster and add Manny . . . Finley was fined $5,000 by Commissioner . . . Once had streak of 42 straight errorless games . . . Has emerged as base-stealer.

Year	Club	Pos	G	AB	R	H	2B	3B	HR	RBI	SB	Avg.
1973	Oakland.........	2B	17	12	0	3	2	0	0	3	0	.250
1974	Oakland.........	2B	21	33	3	5	0	0	0	2	0	.152
1975	Chicago (NL)	2B-SS	154	545	55	135	12	2	7	70	1	.248
1976	Chicago (NL)	2B-SS	158	582	42	139	24	3	4	59	17	.239
1977	Chicago (NL)	2B-SS	152	504	51	141	18	5	7	57	3	.280
	Totals..........		502	1676	151	423	56	10	18	191	21	.252

RICK REUSCHEL 28 6-3 230   Bats R Throws R

Quick Rick . . . Has come on fast and strong . . . Had fifth best ERA among NL starters and best by a Cub starter since Fergy Jenkins' 2.62 ERA in 1968 . . . Had most victories by a Cub pitcher in six years . . . Led club in strike-outs for second straight season . . . Younger brother by nearly two years of Cub reliever Paul Reuschel . . . Born May 16, 1949, in Quincy, Ill. . . . An excellent fielder who shared 1975 fielding mark with Phil Niekro, handling 62 chances without an error . . . In first major-league game he struck out the only man he faced, Bobby Bonds . . . Combined with brother Paul for shutout over Dodgers Aug. 21, 1976 . . . Rick got the win and Paul got the save.

Year	Club	G	IP	W	L	Pct.	SO	BB	H	ERA
1972	Chicago (NL)	21	129	10	8	.556	87	29	127	2.93
1973	Chicago (NL)	36	237	14	15	.483	168	62	244	3.00
1974	Chicago (NL)	41	241	13	12	.520	160	83	262	4.29
1975	Chicago (NL)	38	234	11	17	.393	155	67	244	3.73
1976	Chicago (NL)	38	260	14	12	.538	146	64	260	3.46
1977	Chicago (NL)	39	252	20	10	.667	166	74	233	2.79
	Totals...................	313	1353	82	74	.526	882	379	1370	3.40

LARRY BIITTNER 30 6-2 200   Bats L Throws L

That's two 'i's and no hands . . . Not smooth in the field, but what a hitter . . . Sprays line drives, using all of the ballpark . . . Ted Williams said of Biittner, "He has the sweetest swing I've ever seen." . . . A tough strikeout . . . Added power to his arsenal last season, almost doubling previous home run output . . . Born July 27, 1947, in Pocahontas, Iowa . . . Enrolled at Drake on basketball scholarship but transferred to, Buena Vista College in Storm Lake, Iowa . . . Also transferred sports . . . A teacher in the off-season . . . Has settled into first base, but occasionally used in outfield.

Year	Club	Pos	G	AB	R	H	2B	3B	HR	RBI	SB	Avg.
1970	Washington	PH	2	2	0	0	0	0	0	0	0	.000
1971	Washington	OF-1B	66	171	12	44	4	1	0	16	1	.257
1972	Texas	OF-1B	137	382	34	99	18	1	3	31	1	.259
1973	Texas	1B-OF	83	258	19	65	8	2	1	12	1	.252
1974	Montreal	OF	18	26	2	7	1	0	0	3	0	.269
1975	Montreal	OF	121	346	34	109	13	5	3	28	2	.315
1976	Mtl.-Chi. (NL)	OF-1B	89	224	23	53	14	1	0	18	0	.237
1977	Chicago (NL)	1B-OF-P	138	493	74	147	28	1	12	62	2	.298
	Totals		654	1902	198	524	86	11	19	170	7	.275

BILL BUCKNER 28 6-1 185   Bats L Throws L

Dollar Bill . . . A money player . . . Proven hitter who finished with fourth best BA on club last season . . . That continued a revival from injury-riddled 1975 season—a sprained ankle that year eventually required surgery . . . Re-bounded next year but Dodgers had enough depth to let him go . . . One of the hardest batters to strike out with one whiff every 26 times up . . . Born Dec. 14, 1949, in Vallejo, Cal. . . . A spray hitter who makes contact . . . Used mostly at first base by Cubs but has played the outfield . . . An outstanding scholastic football star who was named to Northern California Football Hall of Fame.

Year	Club	Pos	G	AB	R	H	2B	3B	HR	RBI	SB	Avg.
1969	Los Angeles	PH	1	1	0	0	0	0	0	0	0	.000
1970	Los Angeles	OF-1B	28	68	6	13	3	1	0	4	0	.191
1971	Los Angeles	OF-1B	108	358	37	99	15	1	5	41	4	.277
1972	Los Angeles	OF-1B	105	383	47	122	14	3	5	37	10	.319
1973	Los Angeles	1B-OF	140	575	68	158	20	0	8	46	12	.275
1974	Los Angeles	1B-OF	145	580	83	182	30	3	7	58	31	.314
1975	Los Angeles	OF	92	288	30	70	11	2	6	31	8	.243
1976	Los Angeles	1B-OF	154	642	76	193	28	4	7	60	28	.301
1977	Chicago (NL)	1B-OF	122	426	40	121	27	0	11	60	7	.284
	Totals		895	3321	387	958	148	14	49	337	100	.288

STEVE ONTIVEROS 26 6-0 185   Bats S Throws R

Resurrected in Wrigley . . . Led club in hitting after miserable season as part-time player with Giants . . . Hit home run in first pro game . . . Saved no-hitter for Ed Halicki, making diving catch of John Milner's line drive Aug. 24, 1975 . . . Arrived with Bobby Murcer in trade for Bill Madlock . . . Born Oct. 26, 1951, in Bakersfield, Cal. . . . Used mostly at third but can play outfield . . . Good glove and strong arm . . . Led the PCL with a .357 BA, the highest in 17 years . . . Best ping-pong player in clubhouse.

Year	Club	Pos	G	AB	R	H	2B	3B	HR	RBI	SB	Avg.
1973	San Francisco	1B-OF	24	33	3	8	0	0	1	5	0	.242
1974	San Francisco	1B-3B-OF	120	343	45	91	15	1	4	33	0	.265
1975	San Francisco	3B-OF-1B	108	325	21	94	16	0	3	31	2	.289
1976	San Francisco	OF-3B-1B	59	74	8	13	3	0	0	5	0	.176
1977	Chicago (NL)	3B-OF	156	546	54	163	32	3	10	68	3	.299
	Totals..........		467	1321	131	369	66	4	18	142	5	.279

RAY BURRIS 27 6-5 195   Bats R Throws R

Won first six decisions last season but got caught up in club's second half slump . . . Hard thrower who still is looking for home plate . . . Was second on club in victories after leading team the two previous seasons . . . Got off to slow start in 1976, losing three of first 14 decisions . . . Reversed field and won 12 games in second half . . . Born Aug. 22, 1950, in Idabel, Okla. . . . Has motion and delivery reminiscent of Bob Gibson . . . Has Gibson-like fastball, too . . . A 17th-round draft choice who took only one year to make it to major leagues.

Year	Club	G	IP	W	L	Pct.	SO	BB	H	ERA
1973	Chicago (NL)	31	65	1	1	.500	57	27	65	2.91
1974	Chicago (NL)	40	75	3	5	.375	40	26	91	6.60
1975	Chicago (NL)	36	238	15	10	.600	108	73	259	4.12
1976	Chicago (NL)	37	249	15	13	.536	112	70	251	3.11
1977	Chicago (NL)	39	221	14	16	.467	105	67	270	4.72
	Totals..................	183	848	48	45	.516	422	263	936	4.11

DAVE KINGMAN 29 6-6 210   Bats R Throws R

Is he worth it? . . . Movie remake of "King Kong" was a financial flop, but maybe $1.4 million can remake this King Kong . . . Wrigley Field just the place for his big home-run swing . . . Shuffled from Mets to Padres to Yankees but still skied 26 HRs into space . . . Born Dec. 21, 1948, in Pendleton, Ore. . . . Went to high school in Chicago suburb of

Mount Prospect . . . Not graceful in the field or at the plate, but don't tell him that . . . Once destroyed Mets' locker room . . . With his uncontrolled swing he is a sure bet to either strike out or hit a homer . . . Knows how to bunt, knows how to run, but that's not what he's paid for.

Year	Club	Pos	G	AB	R	H	2B	3B	HR	RBI	SB	Avg.
1971	San Francisco	1B-OF	41	115	17	32	10	2	6	24	5	.278
1972	San Francisco	3B-1B-OF	135	472	65	106	17	4	29	83	16	.225
1973	San Francisco	3B-1B-P	112	305	54	62	10	1	24	55	8	.203
1974	San Francisco	1B-3B-OF	121	350	41	78	18	2	18	55	8	.223
1975	New York (NL) ...	OF-1B-3B	134	502	65	116	22	1	36	88	7	.231
1976	New York (NL) ...	OF-1B	123	474	70	113	14	1	37	86	7	.238
1977	NY (NL)-SD	OF-1B	114	379	38	84	16	0	20	67	5	.222
1977	Calif.-NY (AL)	1B-DH-OF	18	60	9	13	4	0	6	11	0	.217
	Totals..........		798	2657	359	604	111	11	176	469	56	.227

TOP PROSPECTS

DENNIS LAMP 25 6-3 190　　　　　**Bats R Throws R**
Could move into starting rotation . . . Had 7-2 record and 1.93 ERA in 1972, only his second year in pro ball . . . Had 1.74 ERA for Key West in 1974 . . . Tied for team lead with eight wins at Wichita in 1976 . . . Born Sept. 23, 1952, in Los Angeles . . . Split last season with Wichita and Cubs . . . A good fielder . . . Once led the Texas League pitchers with six doubleplays.

DONNIE MOORE 24 6-0 170　　　　　**Bats L Throws R**
Cubs' No. 1 choice in 1973 draft . . . Hard thrower with good minor league seasons behind him . . . Got first taste of major leagues with September start in 1975 . . . That fall he pitched in Arizona Instructional League, getting in 15 games with 0.90 ERA . . . Born Feb. 13, 1954, in Lubbock, Tex. . . . Won 11 games in second pro season . . . Won 14 games in third . . . Won 18 of 19 decisions at Ranger JC.

MANAGER HERMAN FRANKS: Crusty and irritable . . . Almost never smiles . . . Said, "I told you so," a lot during Cubs' first-half surge last season . . . Didn't say much when team plummeted in second half . . . Returned to managing for first time since bringing Giants home second four straight years, 1965-68 . . . First rule as manager is he's the boss . . . Second rule is the boss is never wrong . . . Born Jan. 4, 1915, at Price,

Utah . . . Started career in baseball as 17-year-old minor league catcher . . . When he retired in 1949 he had spent six years in majors with the New York Giants, Brooklyn, St. Louis and the Philadelphia Athletics . . . A millionaire who made his money in real estate . . . Investment counselor for friend and former employee Willie Mays . . . Was general manager of Salt Lake City farm team when he gave Bob Kennedy his first managerial job . . . It was Kennedy who offered Cubs' job to Franks afer assuming post of vice-president.

GREATEST MANAGER

You have to go back to 1907 and 1908 to find the only Series ever won by the Cubs. Although they have not won a pennant since 1945, the Cubs were one of the earliest dynasties in the National League. Frank Chance, the Tinker-to Evers-to Chance first baseman, was the Cub manager then. In seven full seasons under Chance, the Cubs finished first four times, second twice and third once. From 1906-1910 Chance complied the best five-year stretch in the history of the game, with a record of 530-235 for a percentage of .693.

The Cubs won the pennant in each of Chance's first three seasons with back-to-back Series championships. Chance finished with the best record for the first seven years of any manager in history—a mark of 713-356, a percentage of .667. And it is said that during the rare slumps the Cubs encountered in those years, the players were advised to leave everything to Chance.

ALL-TIME CUB LEADERS

BATTING: Rogers Hornsby, .380, 1929
HRs: Hack Wilson, 56, 1930
RBIs: Hack Wilson, 190, 1930
STEALS: Frank Chance, 67, 1903
WINS: Mordecai Brown, 29, 1908
STRIKEOUTS: Ferguson Jenkins, 274, 1970

NEW YORK METS

TEAM DIRECTORY: Pres.: Mrs. Vincent de Roulet; Chairman
of the Board: M. Donald Grant; GM: Joe McDonald; Pub. Rel.:
Arthur Richman; Trav. Sec.: Lou Niss; Mgr.: Joe Torre. Home:
Shea Stadium (55,300). Field distances: 341, l.f. line; 410, c.f.; 341,
r.f. line. Spring training: St. Petersburg, Fla.

SCOUTING REPORT

HITTING: The Mets have one of the most dependable sluggers in
the history of the game, a former MVP who still is in remarkable
shape. Unfortunately, his name is Joe Torre. He is the manager.
Torre's first priority after taking over last season was to make
more batting practice time available. The team needed it. The
Mets were dead last in the NL with a .243 BA and they've lost as
many bats as they've added.

The Mets hit only 88 homers—also last in the league—and don't

Lenny Randle parlayed chance with Mets into a .305 BA.

have Dave Kingman anymore. They also don't have John Milner. They do have Willie Montanez, who is expected to be the sole source of left-handed power. Steve Henderson is exciting and talented, but it may become easy to pitch around him. Mike Vail, a legitimate hitter, may or may not make the starting lineup because of the addition of free agent Elliot Maddox. Lenny Randle hustles, which couldn't always be said of the others.

It was Torre who said for years the Mets were thought of as "pitchers and other people." He intends to change that, but it may take time for the rust to dissolve from the batting machines.

PITCHING: Once the forte of the club, the staff now is being reconstructed. Tom Seaver is gone. Jon Matlack is gone. Jerry Koosman is a good soldier. The team still is waiting for Craig Swan and Nino Espinosa. Pat Zachry was co-Rookie-of-the-Year two years ago, but is coming off a disappointing season. At least, he doesn't throw up before starts like he used to. The bullpen? It accounted for only 28 saves last season and no other team had fewer.

And if the Mets have decided to sink or swim with their young staff, they may need a life preserver early. Bob Myrick is capable either as a starter or in relief, but Jackson Todd did not overwhelm anyone last year in his rookie season. The Mets did sign free agent Tom Hausman, who pitched in Milwaukee the year before last.

Even Koosman, the likeable veteran, could become unruffled if he is expected to assume the burden of the staff while the Mets rock the cradle. The Mets will be fortunate if they don't drown in their own ERA.

FIELDING: Lee Mazzilli in center uses the basket catch like Willie Mays, sprints after long fly balls like Curt Flood and runs into walls like Pete Reiser. He needs a stronger arm. Henderson, in left, can catch a fly ball. He needs a stronger arm. Maddox already can throw. He needs a stronger right knee. Maddox didn't play a whole lot last season, having an operation on damaged cartilage. What's new is the infield. Montanez is good and flashy, too, and there is Doug Flynn at second and Tim Foli, acquired from the Giants, at shortstop. Flynn will be getting his first shot, Foli his fourth. John Stearns is a fine catcher.

OUTLOOK: Torre, a bright guy and a nice man, can win only so many games from the bench. The Mets won't hit a lot of homers. They won't score a lot of runs. They probably won't win a lot of games. Defense and pitching was once the foundation of the team, but the foundation has crumbled. For the Mets, it will be either a long season, or a longer one.

NEW YORK METS 1978 ROSTER

MANAGER Joe Torre
Coaches—Phil Cavarretta, Dal Maxvill, Willie Mays, Joe Pignatano, Denny Sommers, Rube Walker

PITCHERS

No.	Name	1977 Club	W-L	IP	SO	ERA	B-T	Ht.	Wt.	Born
34	Apodaca, Bob	New York (NL)	4-8	84	53	3.43	R-R	5-11	175	1/31/50 Los Angeles, CA
48	Berenguer, Juan	Jackson	9-8	–	–	3.42	R-R	5-11	186	11/30/54 unavailable
39	Espinosa, Nino	New York (NL)	10-13	200	105	3.42	R-R	6-0	184	8/15/53 Villa Altagracia, DR
–	Hausman, Tom	Spokane	13-6	207	88	4.22	R-R	6-4	190	3/31/53 Mobridge, SD
31	Jackson, Roy Lee	Tidewater	13-7	168	110	3.69	R-R	6-2	200	5/1/54 unavailable
		New York (NL)	0-2	24	13	6.00				
36	Koosman, Jerry	New York (NL)	8-20	227	192	3.49	R-L	6-2	208	12/23/43 Appleton, MN
38	Lockwood, Skip	New York (NL)	4-8	104	84	3.38	R-R	6-0	186	8/17/46 Boston, MA
44	Myrick, Bob	New York (NL)	2-2	87	49	3.62	R-L	6-1	200	10/1/52 Hattiesburg, MS
20	Pacella, John	Jackson	3-4	–	–	4.07	R-R	6-2	184	9/15/56 Brooklyn, NY
		Tidewater	6-5	93	46	3.95				
		New York (NL)	0-0	4	1	0.00				
43	Siebert, Paul	Hawaii	4-2	50	20	3.60	L-L	6-2	195	6/3/53 Minneapolis, MN
		Tidewater	0-2	–	–	5.40				
		SD-NY (NL)	2-1	32	21	3.66				
27	Swan, Craig	New York (NL)	9-10	147	71	4.22	R-R	6-3	225	11/30/50 Van Nuys, CA
30	Todd, Jackson	Tidewater	2-3	63	47	4.02	R-R	6-2	195	11/20/51 Lancaster, PA
		New York (NL)	3-6	72	39	4.75				
40	Zachry, Pat	Cin-NY (NL)	10-13	195	99	4.25	R-R	6-5	175	4/24/52 Richmond, TX

CATCHERS

No.	Name	1977 Club	H	HR	RBI	Pct.	B-T	Ht.	Wt.	Born
42	Hodges, Ron	New York (NL)	31	1	5	.265	L-R	6-1	185	6/22/49 Rocky Mount, VA
35	Rosado, Luis	Tidewater	112	8	59	.273	R-R	6-0	180	12/6/55 unavailable
		New York (NL)	5	0	3	.208				
12	Stearns, John	New York (NL)	108	12	55	.251	R-R	6-0	185	8/21/51 Denver, CO

INFIELDERS

No.	Name	1977 Club	H	HR	RBI	Pct.	B-T	Ht.	Wt.	Born
22	Brant, Marshall	Jackson	–	17	84	.288	R-R	6-5	215	9/17/55 Unavailable
23	Flynn, Doug	Cin-NY (NL)	62	0	19	.197	R-R	5-11	160	4/18/51 Lexington, KY
–	Foli, Tim	Mont-SF	94	4	30	.221	R-R	6-0	176	12/8/50 Culver City, CA
19	Foster, Leo	Tidewater	40	1	24	.274	R-R	5-11	165	2/2/51 Covington, KY
		New York (NL)	17	0	6	.227				
3	Harrelson, Bud	New York (NL)	48	1	12	.178	B-R	5-11	160	6/6/44 Niles, CA
17	Millan, Felix	New York (NL)	78	2	21	.248	R-R	5-11	172	8/21/43 Yabucoa, PR
–	Montanez, Willie	Atlanta	156	20	68	.287	L-L	6-1	193	4/1/48 Catano, PR
11	Randle, Len	New York (NL)	156	5	27	.304	B-R	5-10	169	2/12/49 Long Beach, CA
2	Staiger, Roy	Tidewater	71	15	57	.287	R-R	6-0	195	1/6/50 Tulsa, OK
		New York (NL)	31	2	11	.252				
1	Valentine, Bobby	SD-NY (NL)	23	2	13	.153	R-R	5-10	185	5/13/50 Stamford, CT
18	Youngblood, Joel	St.L-NY (NL)	51	0	12	.244	R-R	5-11	175	8/28/51 Houston, TX

OUTFIELDERS

No.	Name	1977 Club	H	HR	RBI	Pct.	B-T	Ht.	Wt.	Born
4	Boisclair, Bruce	New York (NL)	90	4	44	.293	L-L	6-2	200	12/9/52 Putnam, CT
55	Cipot, Ed	Jackson	–	9	53	.271	L-L	5-11	180	1/10/56 unavailable
–	Grieve, Tom	Texas	53	7	30	.225	R-R	6-2	190	4/4/48 Pittsfield, MA
5	Henderson, Steve	Indianapolis	76	7	25	.326	R-R	6-1	197	11/18/52 Houston, TX
		New York (NL)	104	12	65	.297				
7	Kranepool, Ed	New York (NL)	79	10	40	.281	L-L	6-3	215	11/8/44 New York, NY
21	Maddox, Elliott	Baltimore	28	2	9	.262	R-R	5-11	174	12/21/48 East Orange, NJ
–	Mangual, Pepe	Tidewater	120	20	62	.252	R-R	5-9	165	5/23/52 Ponce, PR
		New York (NL)	1	0	2	.143				
16	Mazzilli, Lee	New York (NL)	134	6	46	.250	B-R	6-1	180	3/25/55 New York, NY
33	Norman, Dan	Indianapolis	52	5	33	.249	R-R	6-2	196	1/11/55 Los Angeles, CA
		Tidewater	73	10	30	.264				
		New York (NL)	4	0	0	.250				
6	Vail, Mike	New York (NL)	73	8	35	.262	R-R	6-1	180	11/10/51 San Francisco, CA

MET PROFILES

STEVE HENDERSON 25 6-1 197   Bats R Throws R

Stevie Wonder . . . Signed, sealed and delivered in controversial trade for Tom Seaver . . . Mets insisted on his inclusion before they would make deal . . . Led club in RBIs, though he didn't arrive until June . . . Of first five home runs, four were game-winners and another tied a game . . . Ordinary arm in left field but he can catch a fly ball . . . Born Nov. 18, 1952, in Houston . . . Was Reds' top minor-league prospect but couldn't crack established outfield . . . Can steal a base . . . Had clubhouse bet with teammate Jerry Koosman to buy beer for one another when either one had a good game . . . Koosman bought a lot of beer . . . Manager Joe Torre intended to work him into lineup slowly but never figured on his immediate success.

Year	Club	Pos	G	AB	R	H	2B	3B	HR	RBI	SB	Avg.
1977	New York (NL)...	OF	99	350	67	104	16	6	12	65	6	.297

WILLIE MONTANEZ 30 6-1 193   Bats L Throws L

The Hotdog . . . Specializes in one-hand catches . . . A crowd-pleaser . . . Braves' only representative in All-Star Game last year . . . Finished third on club in hitting . . . Finished second in NL in hits in 1976, splitting season with Braves and Giants . . . Sent from St. Louis to Philadelphia as part of famous Curt Flood case . . . Finished second in 1971 Rookie-of-the-Year balloting after setting Phillie rookie record of 30 homers . . . Born April 1, 1948, in Catano, Puerto Rico . . . Has regained home run stroke while reducing strikeouts . . . Has led NL first baseman in total chances and double plays . . . Led NL in sacrifice flies with 13 in 1971.

Year	Club	Pos	G	AB	R	H	2B	3B	HR	RBI	SB	Avg.
1966	California........	1B	8	2	2	0	0	0	0	0	1	.000
1970	Philadelphia......	OF-1B	18	25	3	6	0	0	0	3	0	.240
1971	Philadelphia......	OF-1B	158	599	78	153	27	6	30	99	4	.255
1972	Philadelphia......	OF-1B	147	531	60	131	39	3	13	64	1	.247
1973	Philadelphia......	1B-OF	146	552	69	145	16	5	11	65	2	.263
1974	Philadelphia......	1B-OF	143	527	55	160	33	1	7	79	3	.304
1975	Phil.-San Fran. ...	1B	156	602	61	182	34	2	10	101	6	.302
1976	San Fran.-Atl.	1B	163	650	74	206	29	2	11	84	2	.317
1977	Atlanta.........	1B	136	544	70	156	31	1	20	68	1	.287
	Totals..........		1075	4032	472	1139	209	20	102	563	20	.282

LEE MAZZILLI 23 6-1 180   Bats S Throws R

Mazz . . . Brought the basket catch back to New York . . . Exciting and handsome . . . Has a Lee-gion of teenaged fans . . . Made jump from AA and struggled early in season . . . Gained confidence and batted over .290 the second half . . . Fastest man on club . . . Specializes in circus catches . . . Tutored by Willie Mays, a Met coach . . . Has the build of a weight lifter and the grace of a ballet dancer . . . Born March 25, 1955, in Brooklyn, N.Y. . . . Grew up just a subway ride away from Shea Stadium . . . Doesn't have strong arm . . . Was a switch-thrower and switch-hitter in high school . . . Hit three-run pinch-homer in second major-league at-bat . . . A favorite of manager Joe Torre, also Brooklyn born.

Year	Club	Pos	G	AB	R	H	2B	3B	HR	RBI	SB	Avg.
1976	New York (NL)...	OF	24	77	9	15	2	0	2	7	5	.195
1977	New York (NL)...	OF	159	537	66	134	24	3	6	46	22	.250
	Totals..........		183	614	75	149	26	3	8	53	27	.243

PAT ZACHRY 25 6-5 175   Bats R Throws R

The Thin Man . . . Has slight build but is strong on the mound . . . NL's co-Rookie of the Year with Reds in 1976 . . . Experienced elbow trouble last season . . . Trade to Mets came at bad time . . . He was scheduled to be married in Cincinnati that week . . . Postponed wedding until move to New York . . . A nervous type who only recently overcame habit of vomiting before each start . . . Beat Phillies in 1976 playoffs, then beat Yankees in first Series start . . . Born April 24, 1952, in Richmond, Tex. . . . Won five of last six decisions last season to salvage year.

Year	Club	G	IP	W	L	Pct.	SO	BB	H	ERA
1976	Cincinnati	38	204	14	7	.667	143	83	170	2.74
1977	Cincinnati-N.Y. (NL).......	31	195	10	13	.435	99	77	207	4.25
	Totals..................	69	399	24	20	.545	242	160	377	3.47

TIM FOLI 27 6-0 176   Bats R Throws R

Gutty, scrappy shortstop out of the Billy Martin mold . . . Will beat you with his bat, glove, spikes or fists . . . Came up with Mets and once had shoving match with coach Joe Pignatano over rights to free hockey tickets . . . That led to his trade to Montreal Expos, where he was a fan favorite . . . Arrived in San Francisco last season in mid-year trade for Chris

Speier . . . Has never hit for high average but is still a tough out
. . . Born in Culver City, Cal., Dec. 8, 1950 . . . Mainly a shortstop last few seasons but has also played second, third and the outfield . . . Once suffered broken jaw in basepath collision with Bob
Watson in play characteristic of Foli's hard-nosed style . . . A
high school quarterback who turned down several college offers.

Year	Club	Pos	G	AB	R	H	2B	3B	HR	RBI	SB	Avg.
1970	New York (NL)...	3B-SS	5	11	0	4	0	0	0	1	0	.364
1971	New York........	2B-3B-SS-OF	97	288	32	65	12	2	6	24	5	.226
1972	Montreal	SS-2B	149	540	45	130	12	2	2	35	11	.241
1973	Montreal	SS-2B-OF	126	458	37	110	11	0	2	36	6	.240
1974	Montreal	SS-3B	121	441	41	112	10	3	0	39	8	.254
1975	Montreal	SS-2B	152	572	64	136	25	2	1	29	13	.238
1976	Montreal	SS	149	546	41	144	36	1	6	54	6	.264
1977	Mont.-S.F.	SS-2B-3B	117	425	32	94	22	4	4	30	2	.221
	Totals...........		916	3281	292	795	128	14	15	248	51	.242

JOHN STEARNS 26 6-0-185   Bats R Throws R

Bad Dude . . . Don't get him mad . . . A gung-
ho type who doesn't take losing lightly . . .
Took over as first-string catcher with Jerry
Grote acting as his instructor . . . Requested to
be sent down to minors the year before so he
could play every day . . . Returned more confident . . . Cocky and hyper . . . Was Mets'
only representative in All-Star game last year
. . . Born Aug. 21, 1951, in Denver . . . Earned his nickname
playing defense for Colorado football team . . . Was 17th round
draft choice of Buffalo Bills . . . Was second in nationwide baseball draft in 1973 to fellow named David Clyde.

Year	Club	Pos	G	AB	R	H	2B	3B	HR	RBI	SB	Avg.
1974	Philadelphia......	C	2	2	0	1	0	0	0	0	0	.500
1975	New York (NL)...	C	59	169	25	32	5	1	3	10	4	.189
1976	New York (NL)...	C-3B	32	103	13	27	6	0	2	10	1	.262
1977	New York (NL)...	C-1B	139	431	52	108	25	1	12	55	9	.251
	Totals...........		230	705	90	168	37	2	17	75	14	.238

JERRY KOOSMAN 34 6-2 208   Bats R Throws L

Riches to rags . . . Finished second in Cy
Young voting two years ago then had almost
complete reversal of record last year . . . Lost
last 10 decisions of season for worst stretch of
major-league career . . . ERA was still one of
best on club . . . Lost nine games by a total 14
runs . . . In first seven defeats of season his
teammates scored just 10 runs . . . Finished
fifth in NL strikeouts . . . Born Dec. 23, 1943, in Appleton, Minn.
. . . Takes pride in his hitting and had annual bet with former
teammate Tom Seaver for most hits . . . Said his most discourag-

ing moment was when old pal Seaver doubled off him in first meeting after Tom's trade.

Year	Club	G	IP	W	L	Pct.	SO	BB	H	ERA
1967	New York (NL)...........	9	22	0	2	.000	11	19	22	6.14
1968	New York (NL)...........	35	264	19	12	.613	178	69	221	2.08
1969	New York (NL)...........	32	241	17	9	.654	180	68	187	2.28
1970	New York (NL)...........	30	212	12	7	.632	118	71	189	3.14
1971	New York (NL)...........	26	166	6	11	.353	96	51	160	3.04
1972	New York (NL)...........	34	163	11	12	.478	147	52	155	4.14
1973	New York (NL)...........	35	263	14	15	.483	156	76	234	2.84
1974	New York (NL)...........	35	265	15	11	.577	188	85	258	3.36
1975	New York (NL)...........	36	240	14	13	.519	173	98	234	3.41
1976	New York (NL)...........	34	247	21	10	.677	200	66	205	2.70
1977	New York (NL)...........	32	227	8	20	.286	192	81	195	3.49
	Totals...................	338	2310	137	122	.529	1639	736	2060	3.03

ELLIOTT MADDOX 29 5-11 181   Bats R Throws R

Nearly $1 million brought him back to the scene of the crime—the Shea Stadium outfield . . . Ripped apart right knee with Yanks in '75 when he slipped on grass . . . Has suit pending against New York City for not maintaining outfield . . . Injury has kept him virtually inactive for two years . . . Played only 49 games last year for Baltimore, but Mets think he's worth the risk . . . Born Dec. 21, 1948, in East Orange, N.J. . . . Solid .300 hitter . . . Excellent center fielder, but may move to right . . . Likes NY fans . . . Intelligent and well-spoken . . . Has running feud with Billy Martin from their days in Texas . . . Big Ten batting champion while attending U. of Michigan.

Year	Club	Pos	G	AB	R	H	2B	3B	HR	RBI	SB	Avg.
1970	Detroit............	3B-OF-SS-2B	109	258	30	64	13	4	3	24	2	.248
1971	Washington	OF-3B	128	258	38	56	8	2	1	18	10	.217
1972	Texas............	OF	98	294	40	74	7	2	0	10	20	.252
1973	Texas............	OF-3B	100	172	24	41	1	0	1	17	5	.238
1974	New York........	OF-2B-3B	137	466	75	141	26	2	3	45	6	.303
1975	New York (AL) ...	OF-2B	55	218	36	67	10	3	1	23	9	.307
1976	New York (AL) ...	OF	18	46	4	10	2	0	0	3	0	.217
1977	Baltimore........	OF	49	107	14	28	7	0	2	9	2	.262
	Totals...........		694	1819	261	481	74	13	11	149	54	.264

LENNY RANDLE 29 5-10 169   Bats S Throws R

Speaks softly and carries a big stick . . . Quiet, polite guy whose publicized punchout of former Texas manager Frank Lucchesi last spring was described as uncharacteristic by Ranger teammates . . . Louder on field, where energetic style made him favorite of New York fans . . . Led club in hitting . . . Moved from second base to third when Joe Torre took over as manager . . . Has also played the outfield and was shortstop on NCAA champion Arizona State team in 1969 . . . Born Feb. 12, 1949, in Long Beach, Cal. . . . Not a smooth fielder but he has a big chest . . . Holds a social science degree . . . Head-first slides give him the dirtiest uniform on team.

Year	Club	Pos	G	AB	R	H	2B	3B	HR	RBI	SB	Avg.
1971	Washington	2B	75	215	27	47	11	0	2	13	1	.219
1972	Texas	2B-SS-OF	74	249	23	48	13	0	2	21	4	.193
1973	Texas	2B-OF	10	29	3	6	1	1	1	1	0	.207
1974	Texas	3B-2B-OF-SS	151	520	65	157	17	4	1	49	26	.302
1975	Texas	2B-OF-3B-SS-C	156	601	85	166	24	7	4	57	16	.276
1976	Texas	2B-OF-3B	142	539	53	121	11	6	1	51	30	.224
1977	New York (NL)	3B-OF-2B	136	513	78	156	22	7	5	27	33	.304
	Totals		744	2666	334	701	99	25	16	219	110	.263

MIKE VAIL 26 6-1 180   Bats R Throws R

Broke in with an exclaimation point, but now a question mark . . . Compiled a 23-game hitting streak after reporting to Mets in 1975 that tied the NL rookie record and equalled the club record . . . His bright star fell the following season after winter basketball accident in which right foot was dislocated . . . Was part-time player again last season and didn't like it . . . Strong arm but he has to catch ball first . . . Born Nov. 10, 1951, in San Francisco . . . Married to ballgirl he met at minor-league club in Tidewater . . . Originally signed by Cardinals as infielder.

Year	Club	Pos	G	AB	R	H	2B	3B	HR	RBI	SB	Avg.
1975	New York (NL)	OF	38	162	17	49	8	1	3	17	0	.302
1976	New York (NL)	OF	53	143	8	31	5	1	0	9	0	.217
1977	New York (NL)	OF	108	279	29	73	12	1	8	35	0	.262
	Totals		199	584	54	153	25	3	11	61	0	.262

CRAIG SWAN 27 6-3 225   Bats R Throws R

The Swan Dive . . . Good start again wasted by mid-season slump . . . Has all the tools but still learning to be a mechanic . . . Has been ready for good season for years . . . Hampered by physical problems, including elbow fracture and appendectomy . . . Prodigious eater who dieted last season . . . A teammate once said of him, "He's the only guy I know who leaves a wake-up call with room service." . . . Born Nov. 30, 1950, in Van Nuys, Cal. . . . Has motion and delivery similar to Tom Seaver's . . . Also has a slider Seaver helped teach him . . . Another Arizona State alumnus.

Year	Club	G	IP	W	L	Pct.	SO	BB	H	ERA
1973	New York (NL)	3	8	0	1	.000	4	2	16	9.00
1974	New York (NL)	7	30	1	3	.250	10	21	28	4.50
1975	New York (NL)	6	31	1	3	.250	19	13	38	6.39
1976	New York (NL)	23	132	6	9	.400	89	44	129	3.55
1977	New York (NL)	26	147	9	10	.474	71	56	153	4.22
	Totals	65	348	17	26	.395	193	136	364	4.29

TOP PROSPECTS

DAN NORMAN 23 6-2 196   Bats R Throws R

A year away . . . Hard-hitting, swift outfielder who was part of trade for Tom Seaver . . . Tied club record of 17 home runs for Reds' farm team at Three Rivers . . . Also stole 33 bases . . . Born Jan. 11, 1955, in Los Angeles . . . Mets sent him to Tidewater and promoted him in late-season trial . . . Could be moved up ahead of schedule if need develops . . . A minor league teammate of Steve Henderson.

ROY JACKSON 23 6-2 200   Bats R Throws R

Called "Big Daddy" . . . One look and it's easy to see why . . . A hard thrower who had 5-1 record and 50 strikeouts in 56 innings in Venezuelan League stint . . . Also was second in Texas League with 3.00 ERA . . . Born May 1, 1954, in Opelika, Ala. . . . Once recorded 21 strikeouts in seven-inning high school game . . . Has three speeds: fast, faster and fastest . . . Thinks a change is something you do after a game.

MANAGER JOE TORRE: The Godfather . . . Players say he can kill you with one glance from his dark eyes . . . On the inside he's warm, friendly and the king of one-liners . . . Replaced Joe Frazier last May and club immediately showed signs of life . . . Stays on top of the game . . . Thinks innings ahead . . . Street-smart kid from Brooklyn who returned to New York as player and was used at first base on part-time basis . . . Was first player-manager in NL since Solly Hemus in 1960 . . . Honest to a fault . . . Says, "I figure I should always tell the truth. That way, I don't have to remember what I said." . . . One of the best hitters of his generation during years with Atlanta and St. Louis . . . Was NL MVP for Cards in 1971 . . . Lifetime batting average of .298.

GREATEST MANAGER

It was described as a miracle and the manager of the "Miracle Mets" of 1969 was Gil Hodges. The Mets had finished ninth under Hodges the year before and in the six previous seasons were last five times and next-to-last once. They were the "Amazin' Mets" because of the amazin' ways they fumbled games away. They were baseball's bumbling clowns, laughingstocks of the league.

In 1969, Hodges relied on a system of platooning, and it worked. And he relied on a young pitching staff, and it worked. And the Mets—surprise—finished first. That was truly amazin', of course, but then the Mets swept Atlanta in the first NL playoff and then stunned the seasoned and favored Baltimore Orioles in the Series, winning in five games. No team and no manager has been able to duplicate that feat. Hodges gave the Mets the strength so that for once they could laugh at all the other teams. It was a miracle and Hodges managed it.

ALL-TIME MET LEADERS

BATTING: Cleon Jones, .340, 1969
HRs: Dave Kingman, 37, 1976
RBIs: Rusty Staub, 105, 1975
STEALS: Len Randle, 33, 1977
WINS: Tom Seaver, 25, 1969
STRIKEOUTS: Tom Seaver, 289, 1971

Gil Hodges directed '69 Met Miracle. Yogi won flag in '73.

Cleon Jones led Mets with club mark .340 in miracle '69.

SEAVER continued from page 21

energy, power and stress of pitching through my legs so my arm and shoulder don't take it."

That's why Seaver's right uniform knee is caked with dirt after he pitches. Seaver dips so low to transfer the weight, his knee drags the pitching mound.

Though his career may endure many more seasons, Seaver's name already is etched alongside some of baseball's great pitching names.

He struck out 196 batters in 1977, falling four short of attaining his 10th straight season of striking out 200 or more. Nine straight seasons was already a major league record, "so since it was already my own record, I'm not too unhappy about not making it."

Bob Gibson is the only other man to strike out 200 hitters in nine seasons, but his weren't consecutively and Seaver figures to move ahead of him with his 10th 200-strikeout season in one or more of his next few years.

Seaver's earned-run average for his career is 2.48, lowest for any active major leaguer with more than 2,000 innings, and he stands 26th on the all-time list.

"Of course, there's no way I can catch Cy Young's 511 career victories, but 300 would put me in some select company," Seaver said. An even 300 victories would place him tied for 13th on the all-time charts with Hall of Famers Lefty Grove and Early Wynn, plus move him ahead of such notables as Robin Roberts (286), Red Ruffing (273), Burleigh Grimes (270), Eppa Rixey (266) and Bob Feller (266). Only 14 pitchers have won 300 games.

Seaver's 2,530 career strikeouts place him 10th on the all-time list behind Walter Johnson (3,508), Bob Gibson (3,117), Jim Bunning (2,855), Gaylord Perry (2,847), Cy Young (2,819), Mickey Lolich (2,679), Warren Spahn (2,583), Bob Feller (2,581) and Tim Keefe (2,533).

Some thought Seaver's move from Gotham to the midwest hinterlands would be a traumatic experience for a man in love with New York. It wasn't.

"The adjustment was very simple," he said. "The people here in Cincinnati were very, very warm and open and they accepted me very readily . . . and that's exactly what I expected. They are good baseball fans and they have always recognized effort. They know every time I came here with the Mets that I gave them a good performance. The move didn't bother me at all."

Seaver purchased a condominium at Kings Island on the fringes of a large amusement park and alongside the fairway of a golf course designed by Jack Nicklaus. The complex runs alongside Interstate 71, which empties into Riverfront Stadium, 25 miles from Seaver's residence. He retained his home in Greenwich, Conn., where wife, Nancy, and the two girls remained most of last summer.

Anxious to become part of the Cincinnati community, Seaver bought a restaurant called the Edwards Manufacturing Company, a few blocks from Riverfront. It quickly became Tom Seaver's Edwards Manufacturing Company.

Anderson immediately put Seaver to work helping Cincinnati's young pitching staff, mostly rookies Paul Moskau, Mario Soto and Doug Capilla. "There's no question I can help each of them. If they don't come to me for help, I go to them if I see a couple of things blatantly wrong."

One of Anderson's pet projects was to mold 23-year-old Moskau in Seaver's image. Every time Anderson saw Seaver do something constructive, which seemingly is always, Sparky would grab Moskau by the sleeve and say, "See. See that? Now that's a professional. Do that and you'll never go wrong."

Says Anderson, "I'm convinced there are a lot of Tom Seavers walking around, guys with the ability who never grasp it, never make the most of it."

Seaver's attention to Moskau hasn't been a waste of time. Moskau is looking forward to the day his salary escalates from his 1977 paycheck of $19,500 to the vicinity of Seaver's $225,000 for 1977.

"It's so good to be able to talk to Seaver," Moskau said. He is so fundamentally sound and in total control of the game when he is out there. You know he'll be a success in whatever he does because, even with his baseball success, he is not hard-nosed. He takes time for everybody, gives them all what they need."

For Seaver's part, he says, "I love pitching and everything about it. I have some knowledge to impart and can help anybody who asks. I came over here to win, not finish second."

Anderson wasn't kidding when he penciled in 30 victories for Seaver in 1978 and team captain Pete Rose agreed, understating, "it is certainly nice to have baseball's best pitcher with the Cincinnati Reds."

CAREW continued from page 11

He last faced Carew on September 13 in Chicago and got the Twins' first baseman on a called third strike in the first inning. After Carew singled in the third, the pitcher started yelling at him. "You'll never get another hit off me," he said. "The next time up, I'm throwing it at your head."

This was in Spanish and Carew, a native of Panama, answered in Spanish which translates as, "I don't care what you throw, or where you throw it, I'll hit it."

In the sixth, Carew lined a single past Barrios into center field and repeated with another in the eighth. Again, while he was standing at first base, the pitcher, who ended up winning with a complete game, shouted toward the hitter.

"Forget it, Barrios," Carew yelled back. "I'm the best hitter you'll ever face."

Certainly Barrios, Perry and Figueroa might be willing to admit that. But there are some other pitchers in the league who while respecting Carew as a super hitter, were not awed by him.

They are "The Guys Who Killed Carew."

No. 1 in this group is Ron Guidry, the Yankees' 5-foot-11, 150-pound left-hander who was so spectacular during the regular season, playoffs and World Series. He faced the league's top hitter 10 times and allowed only one hit, a single.

"He may look skinny, like a guy who can't throw hard, but he has a good live arm," Carew said. "I don't know if he's that good, though. I mean, 1-for-10. Maybe it's just that he's new to the league. It was his first full season. I often have trouble at first against new pitchers. It takes me a while to catch up to some of them. Maybe he's one of those."

Well, No. 2 on this list certainly can't be placed in that category. Baltimore left-hander Rudy May has been in the league for 10 years.

"So what's new?" Carew asked when informed that May ranked second among his "stoppers." "Rudy has been tough on me throughout my career."

And 1977 was no exception. The bespectacled southpaw faced Carew eight times and gave up only one hit, a single. And he struck Rod out four times.

"He was in the Twins' minor league system and they let him go," Carew said. "I've always wanted him back. To me, he is the toughest pitcher in our league. I mean, this guy has great stuff. Sometimes, he's just unhittable.

"And you know what? He has a losing record. You figure it out. I can't."

That wasn't all the Twins couldn't figure out last year.

Detroit had a rookie right-hander named Dave Rozema, who started against Minnesota three times and won two decisions. He should have won a third, but he collapsed in the ninth inning and blew a 5-2 lead.

After watching his team lose to the Tiger rookie, Twins' manager Gene Mauch said he had "high school stuff."

"My guys are all trying to kill him," Mauch explained. "If they would just remember how they hit when they were 18 years old, they'd kill him because all he throws is a little sinking fastball."

Well, Carew was one of those who couldn't remember how he hit in high school. Carew faced Rozema 12 times and managed just two hits off him, both singles. And the rookie's ball must have been sinking—of the 10 outs Rod made against him, six were on infield grounders.

"He was new and I didn't know much about him," Carew said. "I guess, looking at the record, I didn't learn much, either."

Another rookie who could rank in that category is Milwaukee right-hander Moose Haas. Carew was 1-for-6 against him.

But it was a veteran, Jim Colborn of Kansas City, who was the fifth pitcher to hold Carew under .200. In 11 at-bats against Colborn, Rod got only two hits.

Then came Nolan Ryan, who faced Carew 14 times and gave up only three hits while striking out the league batting champion four times.

Among those who faced Carew five times or less, Seattle's left-handed reliever, Mike Kekich, was the most successful. He opposed Rod five times and retired him each time. Since Kekich, Guidry and May are left-handed, does this indicate Carew has more difficulty hitting southpaws than right-handers?

Well, yes.

In 1977, against right-handed pitchers, Carew hit .400 with 158 hits in 395 at-bats. Against left-handers, he was 81 for 221, a .367 average.

"That's not bad," Carew said.

True. But it's not .400.

And that's the "magic number" we're talking about here.

Can he hit that in 1978? In 1979?

If so, he'll have to hit left-handed pitchers better than he did in 1977. Or, he'll have to hit right-handers at a .420 clip to offset his "weakness" against southpaws.

He'll also have to improve against the likes of Guidry, May, Rozema, Haas, Colborn and Kekich.

They were "The Guys Who Killed Carew" in 1977.

And they'll be back in 1978 as they again try to stop him from becoming the first .400 hitter since Ted Williams.

1977 Official
National League Records

(Compiled by Elias Sports Bureau, New York)

STANDINGS AT CLOSE OF SEASON, 1977

EASTERN DIVISION

Club	WON	LOST	PCT	GB	PHIL	PITT	STL	CHI	MTL	N Y	ATL	CIN	HOU	L A	S D	S F	EAST W-L	WEST W-L
Philadelphia	101	61	.623	--		8	11	12	11	13	10	4	8	6	9	9	55-35	46-26
Pittsburgh ..	96	66	.593	5	10	--	9	11	11	14	9	9	8	3	10	2	55-35	41-31
St. Louis ...	83	79	.512	18	7	9	--	11	6	10	11	7	7	6	4	5	43-47	40-32
Chicago	81	81	.500	20	6	7	7	--	10	9	7	6	6	7	9	4	39-51	42-30
Montreal	75	87	.463	26	7	7	12	8	--	10	6	5	4	5	6	6	44-46	31-41
New York	64	98	.395	37	5	4	8	9	8	--	5	2	6	4	6	7	34-56	30-42

WESTERN DIVISION

Club	WON	LOST	PCT	GB	L A	CIN	HOU	S F	S D	ATL	CHI	MTL	N Y	PHIL	PITT	STL	WEST W-L	EAST W-L
Los Angeles .	98	64	.605	--		8	9	14	12	13	6	7	8	6	9	8	56-34	42-30
Cincinnati ..	88	74	.543	10	10	--	5	10	11	14	5	7	10	8	3	5	50-40	38-34
Houston	81	81	.500	17	9	13	--	9	8	9	6	8	6	4	4	5	48-42	33-39
San Francisco	75	87	.463	23	4	8	9	--	10	10	3	6	5	3	10	7	41-49	34-38
San Diego ...	69	93	.426	29	6	7	10	8	--	7	5	7	6	3	2	8	38-52	31-41
Atlanta	61	101	.377	37	5	4	9	8	11	--	5	6	7	2	3	1	37-53	24-48

CHAMPIONSHIP SERIES: Los Angeles defeated Philadelphia 3 games to 1

Batting

INDIVIDUAL BATTING LEADERS

Percentage	:	.338	Parker, Pitt.
Games	:	162	Garvey, L.A. & Rose, Cin.
			(only players in all of team's games)
At Bats	:	655	Rose, Cin.
Runs	:	124	Foster, Cin.
Hits	:	215	Parker, Pitt.
Total Bases	:	388	Foster, Cin.
Singles	:	155	Templeton, St.L.
Doubles	:	44	Parker, Pitt.
Triples	:	18	Templeton, St.L.
Home Runs	:	52	Foster, Cin.
Runs Batted In	:	149	Foster, Cin.
Sacrifice Hits	:	20	Almon, S.D.
Sacrifice Flies	:	10	Cruz, Hou. & Murcer, Chi.
Stolen Bases	:	70	Taveras, Pitt.
Caught Stealing	:	24	Brock & Templeton, St.L.
Longest Batting Streak	:	22	Parker, Pitt. Apr. 15 - May 11
			Parker, Pitt. July 17 2g - Aug. 11
			Cedeno, Hou. Aug. 25 - Sept. 21

During the 1977 season 421 players participated in regular season games.

INDIVIDUAL BATTING

TOP FIFTEEN QUALIFIERS FOR BATTING CHAMPIONSHIP
(*Bats Lefthanded #Switch Hitter)

Player & Club	PCT	G	AB	R	H	TB	2B	3B	HR	RBI	SH	SF	SB	CS
Parker, David, Pitt.*	.338	159	637	107	215	338	44	8	21	88	0	4	17	19
Templeton, Garry, St.L.#	.322	153	621	94	200	279	19	18	8	79	2	5	28	24
Foster, George, Cin.	.320	158	615	124	197	388	31	2	52	149	0	8	6	4
Griffey, G. Kenneth, Cin.*	.318	154	585	117	186	273	35	8	12	57	1	2	17	8
Simmons, Ted, St.L.#	.318	150	516	82	164	258	25	3	21	95	0	4	2	6
Rose, Peter, Cin.#	.311	162	655	95	204	283	38	7	9	64	1	4	16	4
Hendrick, George, S.D.	.311	152	541	75	168	266	25	2	23	81	1	2	11	6
Luzinski, Gregory, Phil.	.309	149	554	99	171	329	35	3	39	130	0	8	3	2
Oliver, Albert, Pitt.*	.308	154	568	75	175	273	29	6	19	82	2	8	13	16
Smith, C. Reginald, L.A.#	.307	148	488	104	150	281	27	4	32	87	1	7	7	5
Randle, Leonard, N.Y.#	.304	136	513	78	156	207	22	7	5	27	3	2	33	21
Robinson, William, Pitt.	.304	137	507	74	154	266	32	1	26	104	4	5	12	6
Madlock, Bill, S.F.	.302	140	533	70	161	227	28	1	12	46	1	2	13	10
Driessen, Daniel, Cin.*	.300	151	536	75	161	251	31	4	17	91	0	5	31	13
Cruz, Jose, Hou.*	.299	157	579	87	173	275	31	10	17	87	3	10	44	23

ALL PLAYERS LISTED ALPHABETICALLY

Player & Club	PCT	G	AB	R	H	TB	2B	3B	HR	RBI	SH	SF	SB	CS
Adams, R. Michael, Chi.	.000	2	2	0	0	0	0	0	0	0	0	0	0	0
Alcala, Santo, 7-Cin.;31-Mtl.	.071	38	28	1	2	5	0	0	1	2	2	0	0	0
Alexander, Gary, S.F.	.303	51	119	17	36	59	4	2	5	20	0	2	3	1
Almon, William, S.D.	.261	135	613	75	160	206	18	11	2	43	20	0	20	9
Alvarado, Luis, N.Y.	.000	1	2	0	0	0	0	0	0	0	0	0	0	0
Anderson, Michael, St.L.	.221	94	154	18	34	52	4	1	4	17	1	0	2	3
Andrews, Fred, Phil.	.174	12	23	3	4	6	0	1	0	2	0	1	1	0
Andrews, Robert, S.F.	.264	127	436	60	115	132	11	3	0	25	5	3	5	6
Andujar, Joaquin, Hou.#	.189	26	53	6	10	12	2	0	0	2	4	0	0	0
Apodaca, Robert, N.Y.	.167	59	6	0	1	1	0	0	0	1	1	0	0	0
Armbrister, Edison, Cin.	.256	65	78	12	20	33	4	3	1	5	2	1	5	6
Ashford, Thomas, S.D.	.217	81	249	25	54	81	18	0	3	24	4	2	2	3
Asselstine, Brian, Atl.*	.210	83	124	12	26	44	6	0	4	17	1	0	1	1
Atkinson, William, Mtl.*	.200	56	5	0	1	1	0	0	0	0	1	0	0	0
Auerbach, Frederick, Cin.	.156	33	45	5	7	9	2	0	0	3	1	2	0	0
Ayala, Benigno, St.L.	.333	1	3	0	1	1	0	0	0	0	0	0	0	0
Bahnsen, Stanley, Mtl.	.119	23	42	0	5	7	2	0	0	7	4	0	0	0
Bailey, Robert, Cin.	.253	49	79	9	20	30	2	1	2	11	0	1	1	1
Baker, Johnnie, L.A.	.291	153	533	86	155	273	26	1	30	86	2	5	2	6
Baldwin, Rick, N.Y.*	.500	40	4	1	2	2	0	0	0	0	0	0	0	0
Bannister, Floyd, Hou.*	.188	24	48	4	9	9	0	0	0	1	6	0	0	0
Barr, James, S.F.	.132	44	76	2	10	12	2	0	0	9	13	0	0	0
Beard, Michael, Atl.*	—	4	0	0	0	0	0	0	0	0	0	0	0	0
Belloir, Robert, Atl.	.000	6	1	2	0	0	0	0	0	0	0	0	0	0
Bench, Johnny, Cin.	.275	142	494	67	136	267	34	2	31	109	0	7	2	4
Bernal, Victor, S.D.	.000	15	1	0	0	0	0	0	0	0	0	0	0	0
Berra, Dale, Pitt.	.175	17	40	0	7	8	1	0	0	3	0	0	0	0
Biittner, Larry, Chi.#	.298	138	493	74	147	213	28	1	12	62	1	2	2	1
Billingham, John, Cin.	.161	36	56	3	9	10	1	0	0	3	6	0	0	0
Blackwell, Timothy, 1-Phil;16-Mtl.#	.091	17	22	4	2	3	1	0	0	1	0	0	0	0
Boisclair, Bruce, N.Y.*	.293	127	307	41	90	125	21	1	4	44	7	1	6	4
Bonham, William, Chi.	.231	35	65	3	15	18	3	0	0	3	11	0	0	0
Bonnell, R. Barry, Atl.	.300	100	360	41	108	122	11	0	1	45	3	1	7	5
Boone, Robert, Phil.	.284	132	440	55	125	192	26	4	11	66	3	8	5	5
Borbon, Pedro, Cin.	.182	73	22	0	4	5	1	0	0	2	0	0	0	0
Bosetti, Richard, St.L.	.232	41	69	12	16	16	0	0	0	3	0	0	4	0
Boswell, Kenneth, Hou.*	.216	72	97	7	21	24	1	1	0	12	0	1	0	0

Greg Luzinski's 130 RBIs, 39 HRs led Phils to NL East flag.

Player & Club	PCT	G	AB	R	H	TB	2B	3B	HR	RBI	SH	SH	SB	CS
Bowa, Lawrence, Phil.#	.280	156	624	93	175	212	19	3	4	41	13	6	32	3
Bradford, Larry, Atl.*	---	2	0	0	0	0	0	0	0	0	0	0	0	0
Broberg, Peter, Chi.	.000	22	6	0	0	0	0	0	0	0	0	0	0	0
Brock, Louis, St.L.*	.272	141	489	69	133	173	22	6	2	46	0	0	35	24
Brown, Jackie, Mtl.	.125	42	56	2	7	7	0	0	0	1	4	0	0	0
Brown, Ollie, Phil.	.243	53	70	5	17	25	3	1	1	13	0	1	1	1
Brusstar, Warren, Phil.	.000	46	6	0	0	0	0	0	0	0	1	0	0	0
Buckner, William, Chi.*	.284	122	426	40	121	181	27	0	11	60	2	7	5	5
Burke, Glenn, L.A.	.254	83	169	16	43	54	8	0	1	13	0	0	13	5
Burris, B. Ray, Chi.	.174	40	69	4	12	19	2	1	1	8	9	0	0	0
Burroughs, Jeffrey, Atl.	.271	154	579	91	157	301	19	1	41	114	0	6	4	1
Buskey, Michael, Phil.	.286	6	7	1	2	4	0	1	0	1	0	0	0	0
Cabell, Enos, Hou.	.282	150	625	101	176	274	36	7	16	68	2	3	42	22
Cacek, Craig, Hou.	.050	7	20	0	1	1	0	0	0	1	0	0	0	0
Caldwell, R. Michael, Cin.	.500	14	4	1	2	4	2	0	0	0	0	0	0	0
Camp, Rick, Atl.	.000	54	6	0	0	0	0	0	0	0	0	0	0	0
Campbell, David, Atl.	.083	65	12	1	1	1	0	0	0	1	2	0	0	0
Candelaria, John, Pitt.*	.225	33	80	5	18	25	3	2	0	11	4	0	0	1
Cannon, Joseph, Hou.*	.118	9	17	3	2	4	2	0	0	1	0	0	1	1
Capilla, Douglas, 2-St.L.;22-Cin.*	.059	24	34	1	2	2	0	0	0	2	3	1	0	0
Capra, Lee, Atl.	.111	45	36	1	4	4	0	0	0	2	3	1	0	0
Cardenal, Jose, Chi.	.239	100	226	33	54	77	12	1	3	18	2	1	5	4
Carlton, Steven, Phil.*	.268	36	97	7	26	39	4	0	3	15	7	3	0	0
Carroll, Clay, St.L.	.091	51	11	0	1	1	0	0	0	3	0	0	0	0
Carter, Gary, Mtl.	.284	154	522	86	148	274	29	2	31	84	3	7	5	5
Cash, David, Mtl.	.289	153	650	91	188	244	42	7	0	43	4	1	21	12
Castillo, Robert, L.A.	.000	6	1	0	0	0	0	0	0	0	0	0	0	0
Cedeno, Cesar, Hou.	.279	141	530	92	148	242	36	8	14	71	2	8	61	14
Cey, Ronald, L.A.	.241	153	564	77	136	254	22	3	30	110	3	7	3	3
Champion, R. Michael, S.D.	.229	150	507	35	116	145	14	6	1	43	10	3	3	3
Chaney, Darrell, Atl.#	.201	74	209	22	42	62	7	2	3	15	4	1	0	0
Christenson, Larry, Phil.	.135	34	74	4	10	19	0	0	3	13	10	0	0	0
Clark, Jack, S.F.	.252	136	413	64	104	168	17	4	13	51	1	3	12	4
Clines, Eugene, Chi.	.293	101	239	27	70	95	12	2	3	41	1	3	1	2
Collins, Donald, Atl.	.000	40	11	0	0	0	0	0	0	1	0	0	0	0
Concepcion, David, Cin.	.271	156	572	59	155	211	26	9	8	64	6	6	29	7
Cornutt, Terry, S.F.	.000	28	1	0	0	0	0	0	0	0	1	0	0	0
Correll, Victor, Atl.	.208	54	144	16	30	58	7	0	7	16	1	2	2	3
Crawford, Willie, Hou.*	.254	42	114	14	29	38	3	0	2	18	0	2	0	0
Cromartie, Warren, Mtl.*	.282	155	620	64	175	245	41	7	5	50	2	3	10	3
Cruz, Hector, St.L.	.236	118	339	50	80	121	19	2	6	42	2	3	4	3
Cruz, Jose, Hou.*	.299	157	579	87	173	275	31	10	17	87	3	10	44	23
Curtis, John, S.F.*	.231	44	13	4	3	5	0	1	0	0	3	0	0	0
D'Acquisto, John, 3-St.L.;17-S.D.	.000	20	8	0	0	0	0	0	0	0	2	0	0	0
Darwin, A. Bobby, Chi.	.167	11	12	2	2	3	1	0	0	0	0	0	0	0
Davalillo, Victor, L.A.*	.313	24	48	3	15	17	2	0	0	4	0	1	0	0
DaVanon, F. Gerald, St.L.	.000	9	8	2	0	0	0	0	0	0	0	0	0	0
Davey, Michael, Atl.	.000	16	1	0	0	0	0	0	0	0	0	0	0	0
Davis, Robert, S.D.	.181	48	94	9	17	22	2	0	1	10	2	1	0	0
Dawson, Andre, Mtl.	.282	139	525	64	148	249	26	9	19	65	1	4	21	7
DeJesus, Ivan, Chi.	.266	155	624	91	166	220	31	7	3	40	7	4	24	12
Demery, Lawrence, Pitt.	.150	47	20	4	3	5	2	0	0	3	3	0	0	0
Denny, John, St.L.	.098	26	51	4	5	5	0	0	0	2	5	0	1	0
Dierker, Lawrence, Hou.	.000	11	8	0	0	0	0	0	0	0	3	0	0	0
Dilone, Miguel, Pitt.#	.136	29	44	5	6	6	0	0	0	3	0	0	12	0
Dixon, Thomas, Hou.	.000	9	7	0	0	0	0	0	0	0	1	0	0	0
Downing, Alphonso, L.A.	.000	12	1	0	0	0	0	0	0	0	0	0	0	0
Driessen, Daniel, Cin.*	.300	151	536	75	161	251	31	4	17	91	0	5	31	13
Dues, Hal, Mtl.	.000	5	1	0	0	0	0	0	0	0	0	0	0	0
Dumoulin, Daniel, Cin.	.000	5	0	0	0	0	0	0	0	0	0	0	0	0
Duncan, Taylor, St.L.	.333	8	12	2	4	7	0	0	1	2	0	1	0	0
Dwyer, James, St.L.*	.226	13	31	3	7	8	1	0	0	2	0	0	0	0
Dyer, Donald, Pitt.	.241	94	270	27	65	87	11	1	3	19	1	3	6	0
Easler, Michael, Pitt.*	.444	10	18	3	8	13	2	0	1	5	0	1	0	0
Easterly, James, Atl.*	.267	23	15	0	4	6	2	0	0	1	2	0	0	0
Eastwick, Rawlins, 23-Cin.;41-St.L.	.273	64	11	0	3	3	0	0	0	1	3	0	0	0
Edwards, Michael, Pitt.	.000	7	6	1	0	0	0	0	0	0	2	0	0	2
Elliott, Randy, S.F.*	.240	73	167	7	40	68	5	1	7	26	0	2	2	2
Espinosa, Arnulfo, N.Y.	.129	32	62	1	8	9	1	0	0	5	7	0	0	0
Evans, Darrell, S.F.*	.254	144	461	64	117	192	18	3	17	72	1	5	9	6
Falcone, Peter, St.L.*	.244	27	41	3	10	12	0	1	0	2	1	0	0	0
Ferguson, Joe, Hou.	.257	132	421	59	108	183	21	3	16	61	2	3	6	2
Fingers, Roland, S.D.	.050	78	20	0	1	1	0	0	0	0	1	0	0	0
Fischlin, Michael, Hou.	.200	13	15	0	3	5	2	0	0	3	0	0	0	0
Flynn, R. Douglas, 36-Cin.;90-N.Y.	.197	126	314	46	62	73	7	2	0	19	5	1	3	0
Foli, Timothy, 13-Mtl.;104-S.F.	.221	117	425	32	94	136	22	4	4	30	3	6	2	4
Foote, Barry, 15-Mtl.;18-Phil.	.235	33	81	7	19	34	4	1	3	11	0	0	0	0
Forsch, Kenneth, Hou.	.077	42	13	1	1	1	0	0	0	1	3	0	0	0
Forsch, Robert, St.L.	.167	35	72	6	12	16	4	0	0	4	12	0	0	0
Forster, Terry, Pitt.*	.346	36	26	2	9	12	1	1	0	1	1	0	0	0
Foster, George, Cin.	.320	158	615	124	197	388	31	2	52	149	0	8	6	4
Foster, Leonard, N.Y.	.227	36	75	6	17	20	3	0	0	6	0	0	3	1
Freed, Roger, St.L.	.398	49	83	10	33	52	2	1	5	24	0	3	0	0
Fregosi, James, Pitt.	.286	36	56	10	16	28	1	1	3	16	0	2	2	0
Freisleben, David, S.D.	.135	33	37	4	5	6	1	0	0	3	3	0	0	0
Frias, Jesus, Mtl.#	.257	53	70	10	18	19	1	0	0	5	2	0	1	0
Fryman, Woodrow, Cin.	.318	17	22	1	7	9	2	0	0	4	0	0	0	0
Fuller, James, Hou.	.160	34	100	5	16	28	6	0	2	11	0	0	0	0
Garber, H. Eugene, Phil.	.000	64	16	0	0	0	0	0	0	0	2	0	0	0
Gardner, Arthur, Hou.*	.154	66	65	7	10	10	0	0	0	3	1	0	0	0
Garman, Michael, L.A.	.000	49	7	0	0	0	0	0	0	0	0	0	0	0
Garner, Philip, Pitt.	.260	153	585	99	152	258	35	10	17	77	7	2	32	9
Garrett, R. Wayne, Mtl.*	.270	68	159	17	43	57	6	1	2	22	1	2	2	3
Garvey, Steven, L.A.	.297	162	646	91	192	322	25	3	33	115	7	4	9	6
Gaston, Clarence, Atl.	.271	56	85	6	23	36	4	0	3	21	0	3	1	0
Geronimo, Cesar, Cin.*	.266	149	492	54	131	191	22	4	10	52	5	1	10	4

Player & Club	PCT	G	AB	R	H	TB	2B	3B	HR	RBI	SH	SF	SB	CS
Gilbreath, Rodney, Atl.	.243	128	407	47	99	142	15	2	8	43	7	2	3	9
Giusti, David, Chi.	.000	20	2	0	0	0	0	0	0	0	0	0	0	0
Gonzalez, J. Fernando, Pitt.	.276	80	181	17	50	72	10	0	4	27	0	3	3	3
Gonzalez, Julio, Hou.	.245	110	383	34	94	121	18	3	1	27	5	2	3	3
Goodson, J. Edward, L.A.*	.167	61	66	3	11	15	1	0	1	5	0	0	0	1
Gordon, Michael, Chi.#	.043	8	23	0	1	1	0	0	0	0	1	0	0	0
Gossage, Richard, Pitt.	.217	72	23	0	5	6	1	0	0	2	1	0	0	0
Greer, Brian, S.D.	.000	1	1	0	0	0	0	0	0	0	0	0	0	0
Griffey, G. Kenneth, Cin.*	.318	154	585	117	186	273	35	8	12	57	1	2	17	8
Griffin, Thomas, S.D.	.133	39	45	2	6	15	3	0	2	4	3	1	0	0
Gross, Gregory, Chi.*	.322	115	239	43	77	110	10	4	5	32	3	5	0	1
Grote, Gerald, 42-N.Y.; 18-L.A.	.268	60	142	11	38	43	3	1	0	11	3	0	0	1
Hairston, Jerry, Pitt.#	.192	51	52	5	10	18	2	0	2	6	0	1	0	0
Hale, John, L.A.*	.241	79	108	10	26	38	4	1	2	6	0	1	0	0
Halicki, Edward, S.F.	.176	37	85	7	15	25	4	0	2	5	5	1	0	0
Hanna, Preston, Atl.	.071	17	14	2	1	1	0	0	0	1	1	0	0	0
Hannahs, Gerald, Mtl.*	.000	8	7	1	0	0	0	0	0	0	2	0	0	0
Hargan, Steven, Atl.	.000	16	6	0	0	0	0	0	0	0	0	0	0	0
Harmon, Terry, Phil.	.183	46	60	13	11	18	1	0	2	5	0	1	0	2
Harrelson, Derrel, N.Y.#	.178	107	269	25	48	61	6	2	1	24	7	1	5	4
Harris, Victor, S.F.#	.261	69	165	28	43	61	12	0	2	14	2	3	2	1
Heaverlo, David, S.F.	.000	56	5	0	0	0	0	0	0	0	3	0	0	0
Hebner, Richard, Phil.*	.285	118	397	67	113	192	17	4	18	62	1	4	7	8
Heintzelman, Thomas, S.F.	.000	2	2	0	0	0	0	0	0	0	0	0	0	0
Helms, Tommy, Pitt.	.000	15	12	0	0	0	0	0	0	0	0	0	0	0
Henderson, Joseph, Cin.*	.000	7	1	0	0	0	0	0	0	0	0	0	0	0
Henderson, Stephen, N.Y.	.297	99	350	67	104	168	16	6	12	65	0	4	6	3
Hendrick, George, S.D.	.311	152	541	75	168	266	25	2	23	81	1	2	11	6
Hernandez, Enzo, S.D.	.000	7	3	1	0	0	0	0	0	0	0	0	0	0
Hernandez, Guillermo, Chi.*	.063	67	16	0	1	1	0	0	0	0	0	0	0	0
Hernandez, Keith, St.L.*	.291	161	560	90	163	257	41	4	15	91	3	2	7	7
Hernandez, Ramon, Chi.#	.000	6	1	0	0	0	0	0	0	0	0	0	0	0
Herndon, Larry, S.F.	.239	49	109	13	26	39	4	3	1	5	2	0	4	2
Herrmann, Edward, Hou.*	.291	56	158	7	46	56	7	0	1	17	3	2	1	1
Hill, Marc, S.F.	.250	108	320	28	80	117	10	0	9	43	5	3	7	0
Hodges, Ronald, N.Y.*	.265	66	117	6	31	38	4	0	1	5	0	0	0	2
Hoerner, Joseph, Cin.	.000	4	0	0	0	0	0	0	0	0	0	0	0	0
Holdsworth, Fredrick, Mtl.	.000	14	10	0	0	0	0	0	0	0	1	0	0	0
Holland, Alfred, Pitt.	---	2	0	0	0	0	0	0	0	0	0	0	0	0
Hooton, Burt, L.A.	.164	32	67	1	11	13	2	0	0	3	14	0	0	0
Hough, Charles, L.A.	.182	70	22	1	4	7	0	0	1	2	0	0	0	0
Howard, Wilbur, Hou.#	.257	87	187	22	48	60	6	0	2	13	7	0	11	1
Howe, Arthur, Hou.	.264	125	413	44	109	170	23	7	8	58	2	2	0	1
Hrabosky, Alan, St.L.	.000	65	8	0	0	0	0	0	0	0	2	0	0	0
Hume, Thomas, Cin.	.200	14	10	1	2	5	0	0	1	1	2	0	0	0
Hundley, C. Randolph, Chi.	.000	2	4	0	0	0	0	0	0	0	0	0	0	0
Hutton, Thomas, Phil.*	.309	107	81	12	25	34	3	0	2	11	1	1	1	1
Iorg, Dane, 12-Phil.; 30-St.L.*	.242	42	62	5	15	17	2	0	0	5	0	1	0	0
Ivie, Michael, S.D.	.272	134	489	66	133	193	29	2	9	66	1	4	3	2
Jackson, Grant, Pitt.*	.333	49	18	1	6	7	1	0	0	1	6	0	0	0
Jackson, Roy, N.Y.	.000	4	6	0	0	0	0	0	0	0	0	0	0	0
James, Philip, S.F.*	.067	10	15	3	1	4	1	0	0	3	0	0	0	0
John, Thomas, L.A.	.177	31	79	3	14	18	1	0	1	4	6	1	0	0
Johnson, Clifford, Hou.	.299	51	144	22	43	81	8	0	10	23	0	0	1	0
Johnson, David, Phil.	.321	78	156	23	50	85	9	1	8	36	2	3	1	1
Johnson, Robert, Atl.*	.333	15	3	0	1	1	0	0	0	0	1	0	0	0
Johnstone, John, Phil.*	.284	112	363	64	103	174	18	4	15	59	1	7	5	3
Jones, Odell, Pitt.	.143	34	28	2	4	4	0	0	0	1	4	0	0	0
Jones, Randall, S.D.	.116	28	43	2	5	6	1	0	0	3	6	0	0	0
Jones, Timothy, Pitt.#	.000	3	2	0	0	0	0	0	0	0	0	0	0	0
Jorgensen, Michael, Mtl.*	.200	19	20	3	4	5	1	0	0	0	0	0	0	0
Kaat, James, Phil.*	.189	36	53	4	10	13	3	0	0	2	1	0	0	0
Kelleher, Michael, Chi.	.230	63	122	14	28	37	5	2	0	11	1	0	0	0
Kerrigan, Joseph, Mtl.	.000	66	8	0	0	0	0	0	0	0	1	0	0	0
Kessinger, Donald, St.L.#	.239	59	134	14	32	36	4	0	0	7	1	0	1	0
Kingman, David, 58-N.Y.; 56-S.D.* .	.222	114	379	38	84	160	16	0	20	67	2	4	5	5
Kirkpatrick, Edgar, Pitt.*	.143	21	28	5	4	9	2	0	1	1	0	1	0	0
Kison, Bruce, Pitt.	.261	35	69	8	18	25	4	0	1	7	3	0	1	2
Kline, Steven, Atl.	---	16	0	0	0	0	0	0	0	0	0	0	0	0
Knepper, Robert, S.F.*	.182	27	55	4	10	11	1	0	0	4	5	0	0	0
Knight, C. Ray, Cin.	.261	80	92	8	24	34	5	1	1	13	1	1	1	0
Konieczny, Douglas, Hou.	.143	4	7	0	1	1	0	0	0	0	1	0	0	0
Kooyman, Jerry, N.Y.	.111	32	72	2	8	11	0	0	1	5	7	1	0	0
Kranepool, Edward, N.Y.*	.281	108	281	28	79	126	17	0	10	40	0	5	1	4
Krukow, Michael, Chi.	.200	34	55	4	11	12	1	0	0	2	7	0	0	0
LaCorte, Frank, Atl.	.200	14	10	1	2	2	0	0	0	0	2	0	0	0
Lacy, Leondaus, L.A.	.266	75	169	28	45	70	7	0	6	21	0	1	4	0
Lamp, Dennis, Chi.	.375	11	8	0	3	3	0	0	0	0	0	0	0	0
Landestoy, Rafael, L.A.	.278	15	18	6	5	5	0	0	0	0	1	0	2	0
Landreth, Larry, Mtl.	.000	4	2	0	0	0	0	0	0	0	0	0	0	0
Larsen, Daniel, Hou.	.214	33	28	1	6	6	0	0	0	1	3	1	0	0
Lavelle, Gary, S.F.#	.000	73	14	0	0	0	0	0	0	0	0	0	0	0
LeMaster, Johnnie, S.F.	.149	68	134	13	20	27	5	1	0	8	4	1	2	1
Lemongello, Mark, Hou.	.087	35	69	2	6	8	0	1	0	1	5	0	0	0
Leon, Maximino, Atl.	.316	33	19	3	6	6	0	0	0	3	3	1	1	0
Leonard, Jeffrey, L.A.	.300	11	10	1	3	5	0	1	0	1	1	0	1	0
Lerch, Randy, Phil.*	.167	33	54	2	9	11	2	0	0	5	5	2	0	0
Lewallyn, Dennis, L.A.	.000	7	2	0	0	0	0	0	0	0	0	0	0	0
Lockwood, Claude, N.Y.	.200	63	15	1	3	3	0	0	0	1	0	0	0	0
Lonborg, James, Phil.	.104	35	48	1	5	5	0	0	0	1	9	0	0	0
Lopes, David, L.A.	.283	134	502	85	142	204	19	5	11	53	6	4	47	12
Lum, Michael, Cin.*	.160	81	125	14	20	36	1	0	5	16	0	1	2	0
Luzinski, Gregory, Phil.	.309	149	554	99	171	329	35	3	39	130	0	8	3	5
Macha, Kenneth, Pitt.	.274	35	95	2	26	30	4	0	0	10	2	0	0	1
Mackanin, Peter, Mtl.	.224	55	85	9	19	28	2	1	1	6	0	0	0	0
Maddox, Garry, Phil.	.292	139	571	85	167	256	27	10	14	74	0	4	22	6

Player & Club	PCT	G	AB	R	H	TB	2B	3B	HR	RBI	SH	SF	SB	CS
Madlock, Bill, S.F.	.302	140	533	70	161	227	28	1	12	46	1	0	13	10
Mahler, Michael, Atl.	.500	5	6	1	3	4	1	0	0	0	1	0	0	0
Mangual, Jose, N.Y.	.143	8	7	1	1	1	0	0	0	2	0	0	0	0
Marshall, Michael, Atl.	1.000	4	1	0	1	1	0	0	0	1	0	0	0	0
Martin, Jerry, Phil.	.260	116	215	34	56	96	16	1	6	28	0	1	6	4
Martinez, Teodoro, L.A.	.299	67	137	21	41	52	6	1	1	10	4	0	3	4
Matlack, Jonathan, N.Y.*	.060	26	50	1	3	4	1	0	0	0	1	0	0	0
Matthews, Gary, Atl.	.283	148	555	89	157	243	25	5	17	64	2	1	22	8
Mazzilli, Lee, N.Y.#	.250	159	537	66	134	182	24	3	6	46	4	2	22	15
McBride, Arnold, 43-St.L.;85-Phil.*	.316	128	402	76	127	209	25	6	15	61	1	8	36	7
McCarver, J. Timothy, Phil.*	.320	93	169	28	54	89	13	2	6	30	0	6	3	5
McCovey, Willie, S.F.*	.280	141	478	54	134	239	21	0	28	86	0	3	3	0
McKinney, William, Mtl.*	.000	69	8	0	0	0	0	0	0	0	0	0	0	0
McGlothen, Lynn, S.F.*	.105	21	19	1	2	3	1	0	0	2	1	0	0	0
McGraw, Frank, Phil.	.400	45	10	1	4	4	0	0	0	1	3	0	0	0
McLaughlin, Joey, Atl.	.000	3	1	0	0	0	0	0	0	0	0	0	0	0
McLaughlin, Michael, Hou.	.000	46	9	0	0	0	0	0	0	0	2	0	0	0
Medich, George, N.Y.	.000	1	2	0	0	0	0	0	0	0	0	0	0	0
Mejias, Samuel, Mtl.	.228	74	101	14	23	38	4	1	3	8	1	0	1	0
Melendez, Luis, S.D.	.000	8	3	1	0	0	0	0	0	0	0	0	0	0
Mendoza, Mario, Pitt.	.198	70	81	5	16	19	3	0	0	4	2	0	0	0
Messersmith, John, Atl.	.118	16	34	2	4	9	2	0	1	3	2	0	0	0
Metzger, Clarence, 17-S.D.;58-St.L.	.000	75	7	0	0	0	0	0	0	0	0	0	0	0
Metzger, Roger, Hou.#	.186	97	269	24	50	71	9	6	0	16	5	1	2	0
Millan, Felix, N.Y.	.248	91	314	40	78	99	11	2	2	21	3	2	1	1
Milner, John, N.Y.*	.255	131	388	43	99	161	20	3	12	57	0	4	6	2
Minton, Gregory, S.F.#	.333	3	3	0	1	1	0	0	0	0	0	1	0	0
Mitterwald, George, Chi.	.238	110	349	40	83	132	22	0	9	43	2	2	3	1
Moffitt, Randall, S.F.	.000	64	3	0	0	0	0	0	0	0	0	1	0	0
Monday, Robert, L.A.*	.230	118	392	47	90	150	13	1	15	48	2	2	1	4
Montanez, Guillermo, Atl.*	.287	136	544	70	156	249	31	1	20	68	0	3	1	2
Montefusco, John, S.F.	.122	26	49	1	6	9	0	0	1	4	4	0	0	0
Moore, Alvin, Atl.	.260	112	361	41	94	124	9	3	5	34	12	1	4	5
Moore, Donnie, Chi.*	.300	27	10	0	3	5	1	0	0	1	0	0	0	0
Morales, Jose, Mtl.	.203	65	74	3	15	24	4	1	1	9	0	2	0	0
Morales, Julio, Chi.	.290	136	490	56	142	219	34	5	11	69	0	3	0	3
Moreno, Omar, Pitt.*	.240	150	492	69	118	176	19	9	7	34	0	2	53	16
Morgan, Joe, Cin.*	.288	153	521	113	150	249	21	6	22	78	0	5	49	10
Morrison, James, Phil.	.429	5	7	3	3	3	0	0	0	1	0	0	0	0
Moskau, Paul, Cin.	.184	22	38	3	7	11	1	0	1	2	1	0	0	0
Mota, Manuel, L.A.	.395	49	38	5	15	19	1	0	1	4	2	0	1	1
Humphrey, Jerry, St.L.#	.287	145	463	73	133	179	20	10	2	38	1	0	22	15
Murcer, Bobby, Chi.*	.265	154	554	90	147	252	18	3	27	89	2	0	16	7
Murphy, Dale, Atl.	.316	18	76	5	24	40	8	1	2	14	0	0	0	1
Murray, Dale, Cin.	.167	61	12	1	2	2	0	0	0	0	0	0	0	0
Myrick, Robert, N.Y.	.182	44	11	0	2	2	0	0	0	0	0	0	0	0
Niekro, Joseph, Hou.	.140	44	50	2	7	7	0	0	0	2	3	0	0	0
Niekro, Philip, Atl.	.174	44	109	2	19	20	1	0	0	7	12	1	0	0
Nolan, Gary, Cin.	.067	8	15	1	1	1	0	0	0	0	0	0	0	0
Nolan, Joseph, Atl.*	.280	62	82	13	23	35	3	0	3	9	0	1	1	0
Norman, Daniel, N.Y.	.250	7	16	2	4	5	1	0	0	0	0	0	0	0
Norman, Fredie, Cin.#	.110	35	73	4	8	9	1	0	0	2	6	0	0	0
Oates, Johnny, L.A.*	.269	60	156	18	42	55	4	0	3	11	2	2	1	0
Oberkfell, Kenneth, St.L.*	.111	9	9	0	1	1	0	0	0	0	0	0	2	0
Office, Rowland, Atl.*	.241	124	428	42	103	133	13	1	5	39	4	3	2	4
Oliver, Albert, Pitt.*	.308	154	568	75	175	273	29	6	19	82	2	8	13	16
Ontiveros, Steven, Chi.#	.299	156	546	54	163	231	32	3	10	68	2	4	3	3
Ott, N. Edward, Pitt.*	.264	104	311	40	82	123	14	3	7	38	0	2	7	7
Owchinko, Robert, S.D.*	.082	30	49	2	4	6	0	0	0	1	11	0	0	0
Pacella, John, N.Y.	.000	3	0	0	0	0	0	0	0	0	0	0	0	0
Paciorek, Thomas, Atl.	.239	72	155	20	37	54	8	0	3	15	0	3	1	0
Pagan, David, Pitt.	---	1	0	0	0	0	0	0	0	0	0	0	0	0
Papi, Stanley, Mtl.	.233	13	43	5	10	14	2	1	0	4	0	0	3	0
Parker, David, Pitt.*	.338	159	637	107	215	338	44	8	21	88	0	4	17	19
Parrish, Larry, Mtl.	.246	123	402	50	99	155	19	2	11	46	3	3	3	4
Pasley, Kevin, L.A.	.333	2	3	0	1	1	0	0	0	0	0	0	0	0
Pentz, Eugene, Hou.	.000	41	13	0	0	0	0	0	0	0	0	0	0	0
Perez, Atanasio, Mtl.	.283	154	559	71	158	259	32	6	19	91	0	9	4	3
Phillips, Michael, 38-N.Y.;48-St.L.*	.225	86	173	22	39	53	5	3	1	12	0	0	1	1
Plummer, William, Cin.	.137	51	117	10	16	24	5	0	1	7	0	1	1	1
Pocoroba, Biff, Atl.#	.290	113	321	46	93	143	24	1	8	44	4	3	4	0
Potter, Michael, St.L.	.000	5	7	0	0	0	0	0	0	0	0	0	0	0
Powell, John, L.A.*	.244	50	41	0	10	10	0	0	0	5	0	0	0	0
Puhl, Terry, Hou.*	.301	60	229	40	69	92	13	5	0	10	5	0	10	1
Pujols, Luis, Hou.	.067	6	15	0	1	1	0	0	0	0	0	0	0	0
Rader, David, St.L.*	.263	66	114	15	30	42	7	1	1	16	3	3	1	0
Rader, Douglas, S.D.	.271	52	170	19	46	75	8	3	5	27	1	0	0	1
Randle, Leonard, N.Y.#	.304	136	513	78	156	207	22	7	5	27	3	2	33	21
Rasmussen, Eric, St.L.	.139	34	72	4	10	15	5	0	0	3	6	0	0	0
Rau, Douglas, L.A.*	.141	32	71	4	10	11	1	0	0	2	3	1	0	0
Rautzhan, Clarence, L.A.	.000	25	1	0	0	0	0	0	0	0	0	0	0	0
Reed, Ronald, Phil.	.111	60	18	2	2	3	1	0	0	2	1	0	0	0
Reitz, Kenneth, St.L.	.261	157	587	58	153	242	36	1	17	79	5	2	2	6
Renko, Steve, Chi.	.167	13	12	0	2	2	0	0	0	0	0	0	0	0
Rettenmund, Mervin, S.D.	.286	107	126	23	36	56	6	1	4	17	4	2	1	2
Reuschel, Paul, Chi.	.000	69	11	0	0	0	0	0	0	0	0	0	0	0
Reuschel, Ricky, Chi.	.207	41	87	9	18	26	3	1	1	6	1	0	0	0
Reuss, Jerry, Pitt.*	.171	35	70	3	12	14	2	0	0	4	2	0	0	0
Rhoden, Richard, L.A.	.231	32	78	8	18	30	3	3	1	12	6	0	0	0
Richard, James, Hou.	.230	36	87	10	20	30	0	2	2	7	11	0	1	0
Richards, Clarence, L.A.	.290	146	525	79	152	205	16	11	5	32	2	2	56	12
Roberts, David A., Chi.*	.059	17	17	0	1	1	0	0	0	0	0	0	0	0
Roberts, David W., S.D.	.220	82	186	15	41	60	14	1	1	23	4	0	2	1
Roberts, Leon, Hou.	.074	19	27	1	2	2	0	0	0	1	0	0	0	0
Robinson, Craig, Atl.	.207	27	29	4	6	7	1	0	0	3	0	0	1	0
Robinson, William, Pitt.	.304	137	507	74	154	266	32	1	26	104	4	5	12	6

Player & Club	PCT	G	AB	R	H	TB	2B	3B	HR	RBI	SH	SF	SB	CS
Rockett, Patrick, Atl.	.254	93	264	27	67	80	10	0	1	24	3	0	1	2
Rogers, Stephen, Mtl.	.104	40	96	1	10	10	0	0	0	3	12	0	1	0
Rooker, James, Pitt.	.186	30	70	4	13	14	1	0	0	5	1	0	1	0
Rosado, Luis, N.Y.	.208	9	24	1	5	6	1	0	0	3	0	2	0	0
Rose, Peter, Cin.#	.311	162	655	95	204	283	38	7	9	64	1	4	16	4
Rosello, David, Chi.	.220	56	82	18	18	25	2	1	1	9	1	0	0	0
Royster, Jeron, Atl.	.216	140	445	64	96	128	10	2	6	28	6	1	28	10
Rudolph, Kenneth, S.F.	.200	11	15	1	3	3	0	0	0	3	0	0	0	0
Russell, William, L.A.	.278	153	634	84	176	228	28	6	4	51	9	4	16	7
Ruthven, Richard, Atl.	.267	25	45	4	12	18	1	1	1	3	5	0	0	0
Sadecki, Raymond, N.Y.*	----	4	0	0	0	0	0	0	0	0	0	0	0	0
Sadek, Michael, S.F.	.230	61	126	12	29	39	7	0	1	15	3	0	2	1
Sambito, Joseph, Hou.*	.154	54	13	1	2	2	0	0	0	1	0	0	0	0
Sarmiento, Manuel, Cin.	.000	24	1	0	0	0	0	0	0	0	1	0	0	0
Sawyer, Richard, S.D.	.150	56	20	2	3	3	0	0	0	2	2	0	0	0
Scanlon, J. Patrick, S.D.*	.190	47	79	9	15	21	3	0	1	11	0	0	0	0
Schatzeder, Daniel, Mtl.*	.333	6	6	0	2	2	0	0	0	1	0	0	0	0
Schmidt, Michael, Phil.	.274	154	544	114	149	312	27	11	38	101	1	9	15	8
Schultz, C. Budd, St.L.	.167	41	12	1	2	2	0	0	0	2	0	0	0	0
Scott, Anthony, St.L.#	.291	95	292	38	85	116	16	3	3	41	2	1	13	10
Seaver, G. Thomas, 13-N.Y.;20-Cin. .	.198	33	86	11	17	27	1	0	3	9	13	1	0	0
Sember, Michael, Chi.	.250	3	4	0	1	1	0	0	0	0	0	0	0	0
Seoane, Manuel, Phil.	.500	2	2	0	1	1	0	0	0	0	0	0	0	0
Shirley, Robert, S.D.	.122	39	74	5	9	11	2	0	0	2	4	0	0	0
Siebert, Paul, 4-S.D.;25-N.Y.*	.000	29	1	1	0	0	0	0	0	0	0	0	0	0
Simmons, Ted, St.L.#	.318	150	516	82	164	258	25	3	21	95	0	4	2	6
Simpson, Joe, L.A.*	.174	29	23	2	4	4	0	0	0	1	0	0	1	1
Sizemore, Ted, Phil.	.281	152	519	64	146	184	20	3	4	47	5	4	8	11
Smith, C. Reginald, L.A.#	.307	148	488	104	150	281	27	4	32	87	1	7	7	5
Solomon, Eddie, Atl.	.129	18	31	2	4	4	0	0	0	1	1	0	0	0
Sosa, Elias, L.A.	.250	45	4	1	1	1	0	0	0	0	1	0	0	0
Soto, Mario, Cin.	.077	12	13	0	1	1	0	0	0	1	1	1	0	0
Speier, Chris, 6-S.F.;139-Mtl.	.234	145	548	59	128	186	31	6	5	38	3	2	1	2
Sperring, Robert, Hou.	.186	58	129	8	24	30	3	0	1	9	1	1	3	0
Spillner, Daniel, S.D.	.118	76	17	1	2	2	0	0	0	1	0	0	0	0
Staiger, Roy, N.Y.	.252	40	123	16	31	46	9	0	2	11	2	0	1	0
Stanhouse, Donald, Mtl.	.191	47	47	2	9	12	0	0	1	5	4	1	0	0
Stargell, Wilver, Pitt.*	.274	63	186	29	51	102	12	0	13	35	0	2	0	1
Stearns, John, N.Y.	.251	139	431	52	108	171	25	1	12	55	1	4	9	8
Stennett, Renaldo, Pitt.	.336	116	453	53	152	195	20	4	5	51	3	3	28	18
Strom, Brent, S.D.	.333	4	3	0	1	1	0	0	0	0	1	0	0	0
Summers, John, Cin.*	.171	59	76	11	13	26	4	0	3	6	0	1	0	0
Sutherland, Gary, S.D.	.243	80	103	5	25	31	3	0	1	11	3	0	0	0
Sutter, H. Bruce, Chi.	.150	62	20	4	3	3	0	0	0	0	6	0	0	0
Sutton, Donald, L.A.	.151	33	73	3	11	13	2	0	0	8	10	0	0	0
Sutton, Johnny, St.L.	.000	14	1	0	0	0	0	0	0	0	0	0	0	0
Swan, Craig, N.Y.	.188	26	48	3	9	9	0	0	0	6	6	0	0	0
Swisher, Steven, Chi.	.190	74	205	21	39	61	7	0	5	15	2	2	0	0
Tamargo, John, St.L.#	.000	4	4	0	0	0	0	0	0	0	0	0	0	0
Taveras, Franklin, Pitt.	.252	147	544	72	137	180	20	10	1	29	9	3	70	18
Tekulve, Kenton, Pitt.	.250	72	12	0	3	3	0	0	0	0	2	0	0	0
Templeton, Garry, St.L.#	.322	153	621	94	200	279	19	18	8	79	2	5	28	24
Tenace, F. Gene, S.D.	.233	147	437	66	102	179	24	4	15	61	2	4	5	3
Terpko, Jeffrey, Mtl.	.000	13	1	0	0	0	0	0	0	0	0	0	0	0
Theis, Duane, Atl.	.000	17	1	0	0	0	0	0	0	0	0	0	0	0
Thomas, Derrel, S.F.#	.267	148	506	75	135	192	13	10	8	44	10	4	15	13
Thomas, Roy, Hou.	----	4	0	0	0	0	0	0	0	0	0	0	0	0
Thomasson, Gary, S.F.*	.256	145	446	63	114	201	24	6	17	71	4	8	16	4
Todd, Jackson, N.Y.	.059	19	17	0	1	1	0	0	0	0	0	0	0	0
Todd, James, Chi.*	.000	20	1	0	0	0	0	0	0	0	1	0	0	0
Tolan, Robert, 15-Phil.;49-Pitt.*	.189	64	90	8	17	27	4	0	2	10	1	1	1	1
Tomlin, David, S.D.*	.286	76	7	1	2	2	0	0	0	0	1	0	0	0
Toms, Thomas, S.F.	----	4	0	0	0	0	0	0	0	0	0	0	0	0
Torre, Joseph, N.Y.	.176	26	51	2	9	15	3	0	1	9	0	1	0	0
Torres, Angel, Cin.*	----	5	0	0	0	0	0	0	0	0	0	0	0	0
Trillo, J. Manuel, Chi. ..../......	.280	152	504	51	141	190	18	5	7	57	4	8	3	5
Turner, John, S.D.*	.246	118	289	43	71	119	16	1	10	48	0	3	12	4
Twitchell, Wayne, 12-Phil.;22-Mtl. .	.180	34	50	2	9	11	2	0	0	5	5	0	0	0
Tyson, Michael, St.L.	.246	138	418	42	103	143	15	2	7	57	5	2	3	4
Underwood, Thomas, 14-Phil.;19-St.L.	.121	33	33	4	4	5	1	0	0	3	2	0	0	0
Unser, Delbert, Mtl.*	.273	113	289	33	79	131	14	1	12	40	7	2	2	5
Urrea, John, St.L.	.138	41	29	2	4	4	0	0	0	3	0	0	0	0
Vail, Michael, N.Y.	.262	108	279	29	73	111	12	1	8	35	0	3	0	7
Valentine, Ellis, Mtl.	.293	127	508	63	149	256	28	2	25	76	1	2	13	5
Valentine, Robert, 44-S.D.;42-N.Y. .	.153	86	150	13	23	33	4	0	2	13	1	1	0	0
Vukovich, John, Phil.	.000	2	2	0	0	0	0	0	0	0	0	0	0	0
Walker, R. Thomas, Mtl.	.000	11	2	0	0	0	0	0	0	0	2	0	0	0
Wall, Stanley, L.A.*	.000	25	1	0	0	0	0	0	0	0	0	0	0	0
Walling, Dennis, Hou.*	.286	6	21	1	6	8	0	1	0	6	0	0	1	1
Wallis, H. Joe, Chi.*	.250	56	80	14	20	29	3	0	2	8	0	0	0	1
Walton, Daniel, Hou.#	.190	13	21	0	4	4	0	0	0	1	0	0	0	0
Warthen, Daniel, 12-Mtl.;3-Phil.#	.111	15	9	1	1	1	0	0	0	0	1	0	0	0
Washington, Ronald, L.A.	.368	10	19	4	7	7	0	0	0	1	0	0	1	1
Watson, Robert, Hou.	.289	151	554	77	160	276	38	6	22	110	1	4	0	0
Webb, Henry, L.A.	.000	5	2	0	0	0	0	0	0	0	0	0	0	0
Wehrmeister, David, S.D.	.167	30	12	2	2	3	1	0	0	2	0	0	0	0
Werner, Donald, Cin.	.174	10	23	3	4	10	0	0	2	4	0	1	0	1
Whisenton, Larry, Atl.*	.250	4	4	1	1	1	0	0	0	1	0	0	0	0
White, Jerome, Mtl.#	.190	16	21	4	4	6	2	0	0	0	0	0	0	0
Whitfield, Terry, S.F.*	.285	114	326	41	93	141	21	3	7	36	2	2	2	2
Whitson, Edward, Pitt.	.000	5	1	0	0	0	0	0	0	0	0	0	0	0
Williams, Charles, S.F.	.222	55	18	0	4	4	0	0	0	3	1	0	0	0
Winfield, David, S.D.	.275	157	615	104	169	287	29	7	25	92	0	5	16	7
Yeager, Stephen, L.A.	.256	125	387	53	99	172	21	2	16	55	1	3	3	3
Youngblood, Joel, 25-St.L.;70-N.Y. .	.244	95	209	17	51	66	13	1	0	12	1	1	5	5
Zachry, Patrick, 12-Cin.;19-N.Y.	.141	31	64	3	9	9	0	0	0	1	5	0	0	0

Pitching

INDIVIDUAL PITCHING LEADERS

Earned Run Average	:	2.34	Candelaria, Pitt.
Won & Lost Percentage	:	.800	Candelaria, Pitt. (20-5)
Games Won	:	23	Carlton, Phil.
Games Lost	:	20	Koosman, N.Y. & Niekro, Atl.
Games	:	78	Fingers, S.D.
Games Started	:	43	Niekro, Atl.
Complete Games	:	20	Niekro, Atl.
Games Finished	:	69	Fingers, S.D.
Saves	:	35	Fingers, S.D.
Shutouts	:	7	Seaver, N.Y.-Cin.
Innings	:	330	Niekro, Atl.
Hits	:	315	Niekro, Atl.
Batsmen Faced	:	1428	Niekro, Atl.
Runs	:	166	Niekro, Atl.
Earned Runs	:	148	Niekro, Atl.
Home Runs	:	29	Burris, Chi. & Candelaria, Pitt.
Sacrifice Hits	:	18	Rogers, Mtl.
Sacrifice Flies	:	10	Kison, Pitt. & Montefusco, S.F.
Bases on Balls	:	164	Niekro, Atl.
Bases on Balls Intentional	:	18	Lavelle, S.F.
Hit Batsmen	:	10	Billingham, Cin.
Strikeouts	:	262	Niekro, Atl.
Wild Pitches	:	17	Niekro, Atl.
Balks	:	7	Carlton, Phil.
Longest Winning Streak (games):		8	John, L.A. June 18 - Aug. 13
			Christenson, Phil. June 6 - Aug. 19
			Seaver, Cin. July 9 - Aug. 31
			Lonborg, Phil. July 15 - Sept. 2

During the 1977 season 178 pitchers participated in regular season games.

Pirates' John Candelaria had NL's best ERA at 2.34.

PITCHERS' RECORDS

NATIONAL LEAGUE PITCHING AVERAGES
(Top Fifteen Qualifiers for Earned Run Leadership)
* Throws Lefthanded

Pitcher & Club	ERA	W	L	PCT	G	GS	CG	GF	SV	SHO	IP	H	BFP	R	ER	HR	SH	SF	TBB	IBB	HB	SO	WP	BK
Candelaria, John, Pitt.*	2.34	20	5	.800	33	33	6	0	0	0	231	197	920	64	60	29	9	6	50	2	0	133	1	2
Seaver, G.Thomas, N.Y.–Cin.	2.59	21	6	.778	33	33	19	0	0	7	261	199	1031	78	75	19	5	6	66	6	5	196	7	1
Hooton, Burt, L.A.	2.62	12	7	.632	32	31	6	1	1	2	223	184	897	74	65	14	13	4	60	5	3	153	5	1
Carlton, Steven, Phil.*	2.64	23	10	.697	36	36	17	0	0	1	283	229	1135	99	83	25	4	4	89	5	3	198	3	7
John, Thomas, L.A.*	2.78	20	7	.741	31	31	11	0	0	3	220	225	906	82	68	12	10	1	50	3	3	123	6	0
Reuschel, Ricky, Chi.	2.79	20	10	.667	39	37	8	2	1	4	252	233	1030	84	78	13	3	4	74	11	5	166	9	1
Richard, James, Hou.	2.97	18	12	.600	36	36	13	0	0	3	267	212	1092	94	88	18	9	5	104	3	5	214	6	0
Niekro, Joseph, Hou.	3.03	13	8	.619	44	14	9	12	5	2	181	155	737	66	61	14	13	6	64	3	1	101	6	1
Rooker, James, Pitt.*	3.09	14	9	.609	30	30	7	0	0	2	204	196	854	87	70	24	10	6	64	4	0	89	8	2
Rogers, Stephen, Mtl.	3.10	17	16	.515	40	40	17	0	0	3	302	272	1235	122	104	16	18	9	81	2	3	206	14	1
Sutton, Donald, L.A.	3.19	14	8	.636	33	33	12	0	0	0	240	207	979	93	85	23	12	7	69	2	3	150	5	1
Halicki, Edward, S.F.	3.31	16	12	.571	37	37	7	0	0	2	258	241	1076	105	95	27	9	1	70	5	7	168	1	3
Knepper, Robert, S.F.*	3.36	11	9	.550	27	27	6	0	0	3	166	151	710	73	62	18	11	4	72	5	5	100	6	0
Norman, Fredie, Cin.*	3.38	14	13	.519	35	34	8	0	0	1	221	200	945	97	84	28	11	4	98	9	3	160	11	1
Espinosa, Arnulfo, N.Y.	3.42	10	13	.435	32	29	7	2	0	1	200	188	825	82	76	17	8	2	55	5	5	105	2	2

ALL PITCHERS LISTED ALPHABETICALLY
* Throws Lefthanded

Pitcher & Club	ERA	W	L	PCT	G	GS	CG	GF	SV	SHO	IP	H	BFP	R	ER	HR	SH	SF	TBB	IBB	HB	SO	WP	BK
Alcala, Santo, Cin.–Mtl.	4.85	3	7	.300	38	12	0	8	1	0	117	126	520	66	63	13	2	2	54	6	3	73	6	3
Andujar, Joaquin, Hou.	3.68	11	8	.579	26	25	4	1	0	1	159	149	678	80	65	11	10	6	64	3	4	69	2	2
Apodaca, Robert, N.Y.	3.43	4	8	.333	59	0	0	37	7	0	84	83	367	38	32	7	8	2	30	11	0	53	5	1
Atkinson, William, Mtl.	3.36	7	2	.778	55	0	0	30	5	0	83	72	346	38	31	12	5	4	29	11	0	56	2	0
Bahnsen, Stanley, Mtl.	4.82	8	9	.471	23	22	3	0	0	0	127	142	547	76	68	14	5	2	38	2	5	58	4	0
Baldwin, Rick, N.Y.	4.43	1	2	.333	40	0	0	13	1	0	63	62	274	32	31	6	2	2	31	9	5	23	2	1

Pitcher & Club	ERA	W	L	PCT	G	GS	CG	GF	SV	SHO	IP	H	BFP	R	ER	HR	SH	SF	TBB	IBB	HB	SO	WP	BK
Bannister, Floyd, Hou.*	4.03	8	9	.471	24	23	4	0	0	0	143	138	622	70	64	11	4	6	68	1	4	112	6	2
Barr, James, S.F.	4.77	12	16	.429	38	38	6	0	0	2	234	286	1011	130	124	18	10	6	56	4	3	97	2	2
Beard, Michael, Atl.*	9.00	0	1	.000	4	0	0	0	0	0	5	14	33	11	5	3	0	0	2	1	0	1	0	0
Bernal, Victor, S.D.	5.40	1	1	.500	15	0	0	6	0	0	20	23	89	13	12	4	0	0	9	2	0	6	0	0
Blittner, Larry, Chi.*	54.00	0	0	.000	1	0	0	1	0	0	1	5	10	6	6	0	0	0	0	0	0	3	0	0
Billingham, John, Cin.	5.22	10	10	.500	36	23	3	8	0	2	162	195	724	105	94	16	14	6	56	9	0	76	7	0
Bonham, William, Chi.	4.35	10	13	.435	34	34	1	0	0	0	215	207	915	111	104	15	13	1	82	16	3	134	2	0
Borbon, Pedro, Cin.	3.19	10	5	.667	73	0	0	54	18	0	127	131	525	48	45	7	6	1	24	4	0	48	0	0
Bradford, Larry, Atl.*	3.00	0	0	.000	2	0	0	2	0	0	3	3	11	1	1	0	1	0	0	0	0	1	0	0
Broberg, Peter, Chi.	4.75	1	2	.333	22	0	0	2	0	0	36	34	158	22	19	8	5	4	18	0	4	20	0	0
Brown, Jackie, Mtl.	4.50	9	12	.429	42	25	6	3	0	2	186	189	804	99	93	15	9	5	71	5	5	89	2	0
Brusstar, Warren, Phil.	2.66	7	3	.778	46	0	0	8	3	0	71	64	285	26	21	1	6	3	24	1	3	46	3	0
Burris, B.Ray, Chi.	4.72	14	16	.467	39	39	5	0	0	1	221	270	970	132	116	29	11	9	67	9	3	105	8	3
Caldwell, R.Michael, Cin.*	3.96	0	0	.000	14	0	0	5	1	0	25	25	105	11	11	1	5	1	8	1	0	11	0	0
Camp, Rick, Atl.	3.99	6	3	.667	54	0	0	34	10	0	79	89	374	47	35	6	7	9	47	13	1	51	8	2
Campbell, David, Atl.	3.03	0	6	.000	65	0	0	31	13	0	89	78	375	32	30	7	7	6	33	6	3	42	3	0
Candelaria, John, Pitt.*	2.34	20	5	.800	33	33	6	0	0	1	231	197	920	64	60	29	6	9	50	2	2	133	1	2
Capilla, Douglas, St.L.-Cin.*	4.46	7	8	.467	24	16	1	3	0	0	109	96	472	57	54	10	3	6	61	4	4	75	8	0
Capra, Lee, Atl.	5.37	6	11	.353	45	16	0	7	0	2	139	142	633	88	83	28	8	3	80	12	4	100	7	1
Carlton, Steven, Phil.*	2.64	23	10	.697	36	36	17	0	0	2	283	229	1135	99	83	25	17	5	89	5	4	198	7	1
Carroll, Clay, St.L.	2.50	4	2	.667	51	1	0	16	4	0	90	77	357	28	25	8	3	4	24	8	0	34	0	0
Castillo, Robert, L.A.	4.09	1	0	1.000	6	1	0	3	0	0	11	12	46	5	5	2	1	0	2	0	1	7	0	1
Christenson, Larry, Phil.	4.07	19	6	.760	34	34	5	0	0	1	219	229	945	113	99	21	5	8	69	1	7	118	6	0
Collins, Donald, Atl.*	5.07	3	9	.250	40	6	0	8	2	0	71	82	324	42	40	4	5	1	41	8	1	27	3	6
Cornutt, Terry, S.F.	3.89	1	3	.250	28	1	0	12	0	0	44	38	191	24	19	4	1	2	22	5	0	23	3	3
Curtis, John, S.F.*	5.49	3	3	.500	43	9	0	13	1	1	77	95	360	48	47	5	5	3	48	9	0	47	4	0
D'Acquisto, John, St.L.-S.D.	6.58	4	7	.333	20	14	0	7	0	0	52	54	259	45	38	5	3	0	57	4	1	54	7	1
Davey, Michael, Atl.*	5.06	0	0	.000	16	0	0	2	0	0	16	19	75	19	9	1	1	3	9	4	0	7	1	1
Demery, Lawrence, Pitt.	5.10	6	5	.545	39	8	0	8	1	0	90	100	409	59	51	13	7	1	47	3	0	35	6	6
Denny, John, St.L.	4.50	8	8	.500	26	26	3	0	0	1	150	165	664	85	75	7	9	7	62	5	0	60	6	1
Dierker, Lawrence, St.L.	4.62	2	6	.250	11	9	1	0	0	0	39	40	191	21	20	7	0	1	16	2	5	6	2	1
Dixon, Thomas, Hou.	3.30	1	0	1.000	9	4	1	0	0	0	30	40	135	12	11	0	4	0	7	0	2	15	1	0
Downing, Alphonso, L.A.*	6.75	0	1	.000	12	1	0	2	0	0	20	22	99	15	15	4	2	0	16	0	1	23	1	1
Dues, Hal, Mtl.	4.30	1	1	.500	6	4	0	0	0	0	23	26	108	14	11	2	1	0	9	1	0	9	1	1

Name	ERA	W	L	PCT	SV	G	GS	CG	IP	H	R	ER	BB	SO	HR	HB	WP
Dumoulin, Daniel, Cin.	14.40	0	0	.000	0	5	0	0	5	12	32	8	8	3	1	4	0
Easterly, James, Atl.*	6.10	2	4	.333	2	22	5	0	59	72	275	40	40	37	5	1	0
Eastwick, Rawlins, Cin.-St.L.	3.90	5	9	.357	11	64	1	0	97	114	420	48	42	47	0	1	2
Espinosa, Arnulfo, N.Y.	3.42	10	13	.435	38	32	29	7	200	188	825	82	76	105	4	2	2
Falcone, Peter, St.L.*	5.44	4	8	.333	1	27	22	1	124	130	553	79	75	75	3	0	1
Fingers, Roland, S.D.	3.00	8	9	.471	35	78	0	0	132	123	543	47	44	113	4	0	0
Forsch, Kenneth, Hou.	2.72	5	8	.385	0	42	5	2	86	80	364	32	26	45	2	3	0
Forsch, Robert, St.L.	3.48	20	7	.741	0	35	35	8	217	210	915	97	84	95	6	9	0
Forster, Terry, Pitt.*	4.45	6	4	.600	3	33	6	0	87	90	378	45	43	58	3	6	1
Freisleben, David, S.D.	4.60	5	7	.438	0	33	23	1	139	140	608	86	71	72	9	6	0
Fryman, Woodrow, Cin.*	5.40	5	5	.500	17	12	0	0	87	83	343	45	45	57	2	3	1
Garber, H.Eugene, Phil.	2.36	8	6	.571	44	64	0	0	103	82	406	30	27	78	7	6	0
Garman, Michael, L.A.	2.71	4	4	.500	19	49	0	0	63	60	264	20	19	29	8	0	0
Giusti, David, Chi.	6.12	0	0	.000	0	20	0	0	25	30	116	17	17	15	5	1	0
Gossage, Richard, Pitt	1.62	11	9	.550	26	72	0	0	133	78	523	29	24	151	2	9	6
Griffin, Thomas, S.D.	4.47	6	9	.400	4	38	20	1	151	144	672	88	75	79	6	8	5
Halicki, Edward, S.F.	3.31	16	12	.571	0	37	37	7	258	241	1082	105	95	168	5	3	3
Hanna, Preston, Atl.	4.95	2	6	.250	2	17	9	1	60	69	282	40	33	37	3	1	1
Hannahs, Gerald, Mtl.*	4.86	0	3	.167	0	8	7	0	37	43	170	27	20	21	1	0	6
Hargan, Steven, Atl.	6.81	0	5	.000	3	16	5	0	37	49	172	31	28	37	0	3	1
Heaverlo, David, S.F.	2.55	5	1	.833	12	56	0	0	99	92	398	36	28	58	8	3	0
Henderson, Joseph, Cin.	12.00	0	0	.000	0	7	1	0	7	17	50	13	12	8	0	0	0
Hernandez, Guillermo, Chi.* .	3.03	8	7	.533	4	67	1	0	110	94	437	42	37	28	9	0	0
Hernandez, Ramon, Chi.*	7.88	0	0	.000	1	23	0	0	8	11	39	9	7	6	0	3	0
Hoerner, Joseph, Cin.*	12.00	0	0	.000	0	6	4	0	9	32	8	8	2	1	1	0	0
Holdsworth, Fredrick, Mtl ...	3.21	3	3	.500	1	14	6	0	42	35	173	17	15	21	3	3	0
Holland, Alfred, Pitt.*	9.00	0	0	.000	0	2	0	0	4	10	32	6	4	1	0	0	0
Hooton, Burt, L.A.	2.62	12	7	.632	6	32	31	6	223	184	897	74	65	60	14	13	3
Hough, Charles, L.A.	3.33	6	12	.333	22	70	1	0	127	98	551	53	47	105	10	10	7
Hrabosky, Alan, St.L.*	4.40	6	5	.545	10	65	0	0	86	82	374	44	42	68	4	12	3
Hume, Thomas, Cin.	7.12	3	3	.500	0	14	5	0	43	54	197	36	34	22	1	0	3
Jackson, Grant, Pitt.*	3.86	5	3	.625	4	49	2	0	91	81	385	44	39	41	3	2	0
Jackson, Roy, N.Y.	6.00	0	2	.000	0	4	4	0	24	25	116	16	16	13	1	2	1
John, Thomas, L.A.*	2.78	20	7	.741	31	31	11	0	220	225	906	82	68	123	13	12	6
Johnson, Robert, Atl.	7.36	0	1	.000	0	15	0	0	22	24	106	18	18	7	2	0	1

Pitcher & Club	ERA	W	L	PCT	G	GS	CG	GF	SV	SHO	IP	H	BFP	R	ER	HR	SH	SF	TBB	IBB	HB	SO	WP	BK
Jones, Odell, Pitt.	5.08	3	7	.300	34	15	1	9	0	0	108	118	466	63	61	14	5	5	31	2	3	66	4	2
Jones, Randall, S.D.*	4.59	6	12	.333	27	25	1	1	0	0	147	173	642	85	75	12	5	7	36	10	0	44	1	3
Jones, Timothy, Pitt.	0.00	1	0	1.000	3	0	0	2	0	0	10	4	37	0	0	0	0	0	3	0	1	5	0	1
Kaat, James, Phil.*	5.40	6	11	.353	35	27	2	3	0	0	160	211	709	100	96	20	6	2	40	6	0	55	2	0
Kerrigan, Joseph, Mtl.	3.24	3	5	.375	66	0	0	36	11	0	89	80	379	37	32	4	6	3	33	3	2	43	1	0
Kison, Bruce, Pitt.	4.90	9	10	.474	33	32	3	0	0	0	193	209	830	113	105	25	8	0	55	6	1	122	6	1
Kline, Steven, N.Y.	6.75	0	0	.000	16	0	0	7	1	0	20	21	93	15	15	3	0	0	12	3	0	10	1	0
Knepper, Robert, S.F.*	3.36	11	9	.550	27	27	6	0	0	2	166	151	710	73	62	14	7	4	72	2	3	100	6	0
Konieczny, Douglas, Hou.	6.00	1	1	.500	4	4	0	0	0	0	21	26	97	15	14	1	9	0	8	0	4	7	0	2
Koosman, Jerry, N.Y.*	3.49	8	20	.286	32	32	6	0	0	1	227	195	940	102	88	17	9	1	81	8	3	192	2	4
Krukow, Michael, Chi.	4.40	8	14	.364	34	33	1	0	0	1	172	195	767	96	84	16	5	3	61	8	3	106	6	4
LaCorte, Frank, Atl.	11.68	0	2	.000	14	7	0	4	0	0	37	67	205	51	48	10	3	1	29	1	2	28	0	0
Lamp, Dennis, Chi.	6.30	0	2	.000	11	3	0	1	0	0	30	43	137	21	21	3	1	0	8	4	1	12	0	1
Landreth, Larry, Mtl.	10.00	0	0	.000	4	1	0	0	0	0	9	16	51	11	10	0	0	0	5	1	0	5	0	0
Larson, Daniel, Hou.	5.79	1	7	.125	32	10	1	5	1	0	98	108	443	72	63	13	6	4	45	1	2	44	9	0
Lavelle, Gary, S.F.*	2.06	7	7	.500	73	0	0	49	20	0	118	106	485	35	27	4	1	4	37	18	0	93	2	0
Lemongello, Mark, Hou.	3.47	9	14	.391	34	30	5	1	0	1	215	237	910	88	83	20	7	5	52	4	3	83	0	3
Leon, Maximino, Atl.	3.95	4	4	.500	31	9	0	11	6	0	82	89	359	42	36	9	0	0	25	3	1	44	8	1
Lerch, Randy, Phil.*	5.06	10	6	.625	32	28	3	1	1	0	169	207	761	102	95	20	14	8	75	3	3	81	8	0
Lewallyn, Dennis, L.A.	4.24	3	1	.750	5	1	0	2	1	0	17	22	76	8	8	1	0	4	4	0	1	8	1	0
Lockwood, Claude, N.Y.	3.38	4	8	.333	63	0	0	50	20	0	104	87	427	40	39	5	4	0	31	11	5	84	2	2
Lonborg, James, Phil.	4.10	11	4	.733	25	25	4	0	0	1	158	157	666	77	72	15	5	5	50	5	5	76	6	2
Mahler, Michael, Atl.*	6.26	1	2	.333	5	5	0	0	0	0	23	31	109	19	16	4	1	0	9	0	0	14	1	0
Marshall, Michael, Atl.	9.00	1	0	1.000	4	0	0	3	0	0	6	12	32	6	6	1	5	1	3	0	0	6	0	0
Matlack, Jonathan, N.Y.*	4.21	7	15	.318	26	26	5	0	0	0	169	175	702	86	79	19	8	6	43	7	2	123	2	2
McEnaney, William, Mtl.*	3.93	3	5	.375	69	0	0	32	3	0	87	92	372	39	38	6	2	6	22	4	2	38	2	0
McGlothen, Lynn, S.F.	5.63	2	9	.182	21	15	0	3	0	0	80	94	373	62	50	9	3	3	52	5	1	42	3	0
McGraw, Frank, Phil.*	2.62	7	3	.700	45	0	0	31	9	0	79	62	311	25	23	6	3	2	24	5	1	58	1	0
McLaughlin, Joey, Atl.	15.00	0	0	.000	3	2	0	0	0	0	6	10	31	10	10	3	0	0	3	0	0	0	1	0
McLaughlin, Michael, Hou.	4.24	4	7	.364	46	6	0	29	5	0	85	81	359	44	40	4	0	3	34	6	0	59	3	0
Medich, George, N.Y.	3.86	0	1	.000	1	1	0	0	0	0	7	6	25	3	3	0	0	0	1	0	0	3	0	1
Mendoza, Mario, Pitt.	13.50	0	0	.000	1	0	0	1	0	0	2	3	10	3	3	1	0	0	2	0	0	0	0	0
Messersmith, John, Atl.	4.41	5	4	.556	16	16	0	0	0	0	102	101	447	54	50	12	8	0	39	5	2	69	5	0
Metzger, Clarence, S.D.-St.L.	3.60	4	2	.667	75	1	0	32	7	0	115	105	494	52	46	13	8	4	50	6	2	54	2	0

Player																								
Minton, Gregory, S.F.	2	1	0	0	5	0	4	0	0	4	7	8	14	14	0	0	0	2	2	.500	1	1	4.50
Moffitt, Randall, S.F.	1	0	3	3	68	13	39	6	4	35	41	57	91	0	0	0	0	64	0	.308	9	4	3.58
Montefusco, John, S.F.	0	1	6	6	110	7	46	7	10	61	82	388	170	0	11	0	25	26	2	.368	7	12	3.50
Moore, Donnie, Chi.	4	0	3	1	34	8	18	10	5	22	27	689	51	0	0	4	1	27	0	.667	4	2	4.04
Moskau, Paul, Cin.	2	0	1	0	71	7	40	5	8	48	51	207	116	2	0	0	19	20	1	.500	6	6	4.00
Murray, Dale, Cin.	1	2	0	2	42	6	46	4	10	10	60	467	125	0	4	20	0	61	0	.778	7	2	4.94
Myrick, Robert, N.Y.*	4	2	0	2	49	5	33	7	3	56	39	457	86	0	2	0	0	44	0	.500	2	2	3.62
Niekro, Joseph, Hou.	0	0	5	1	101	11	64	6	7	35	367	155	0	4	0	19	4	44	9	.619	13	8	3.03
Niekro, Philip, Atl.	3	0	3	8	262	12	164	8	14	61	66	737	155	2	0	12	2	14	20	.444	16	20	4.04
Nolan, Gary, Cin.	1	1	0	0	28	0	12	1	13	14	148	166	1428	315	0	0	0	8	0	.800	4	1	4.85
Norman, Fredie, Cin.*	1	0	9	3	160	9	98	5	4	26	21	179	53	0	0	0	0	35	0	.519	14	13	3.38
Owchinko, Robert, S.D.*	1	0	0	1	101	5	67	8	11	11	5	945	200	3	0	0	8	34	0	.429	9	12	4.45
Pacella, John, N.Y.	0	0	0	0	1	0	0	0	4	2	97	191	1	2	0	0	28	30	0	.000	0	0	0.00
Pagan, David, Pitt.	0	0	0	0	4	0	2	0	0	0	84	744	0	0	0	3	0	3	0	.000	0	0	0.00
Pentz, Eugene, Hou.	0	0	1	0	51	5	44	6	6	37	0	17	0	0	0	0	4	0	0	.714	5	2	3.83
Rasmussen, Eric, St.L.	1	0	9	1	120	7	63	8	2	90	41	375	76	0	3	16	2	41	4	.393	11	17	3.48
Rau, Douglas, L.A.*	2	2	2	5	126	5	49	5	4	81	103	962	223	0	11	0	0	34	0	.636	14	8	3.44
Rautzhan, Clarence, L.A.*	0	1	3	0	13	2	7	0	0	15	87	896	232	3	0	0	2	32	1	.800	4	1	4.29
Reed, Ronald, Phil.	1	0	2	2	84	2	37	1	1	7	10	89	25	0	0	5	0	25	0	.583	7	5	2.76
Renko, Steve, Chi.	0	0	7	0	34	1	21	1	2	38	10	498	101	2	0	0	3	60	0	.500	9	2	4.59
Reuschel, Paul, Chi.	2	0	6	0	62	6	40	4	7	26	41	452	51	0	2	26	0	13	0	.455	5	6	4.37
Reuschel, Ricky, Chi.	1	1	0	5	166	8	74	4	9	78	32	1030	105	4	4	4	0	39	0	.667	20	10	2.79
Reuss, Jerry, Pitt.*	1	3	9	1	122	11	116	9	7	13	58	452	233	0	1	2	0	37	8	.435	10	13	4.11
Rhoden, Richard, L.A.	0	2	1	5	122	5	71	2	10	95	84	1030	208	1	0	0	8	31	1	.615	16	10	3.75
Richard, James, Hou.	1	1	6	2	214	8	104	4	10	11	109	894	225	3	0	0	0	33	3	.600	18	12	2.97
Roberts, David, Chi.*	0	0	3	1	89	4	12	9	6	88	98	906	223	4	0	1	0	36	0	.500	1	1	3.23
Rogers, Stephen, Mtl.	1	0	5	3	206	1	81	3	18	104	94	1092	212	0	3	5	5	40	13	.515	17	16	3.10
Rooker, James, Pitt.*	4	2	0	0	89	0	64	6	10	16	22	854	196	0	1	0	1	30	0	.609	14	9	3.09
Ruthven, Richard, Atl.	2	0	1	3	84	3	62	3	11	70	87	1235	158	2	0	0	0	30	7	.350	7	13	4.23
Sadecki, Raymond, N.Y.*	5	1	1	0	0	2	3	2	1	71	86	666	3	0	0	2	6	4	0	.000	0	1	6.00
Sambito, Joseph, Hou.*	1	0	2	0	67	0	24	3	6	23	14	357	77	0	32	0	0	54	0	.500	5	0	2.33
Sarmiento, Manuel, Cin.	0	0	2	0	23	2	11	2	0	6	34	357	28	0	7	11	2	1	0	.000	0	0	2.48
Sawyer, Richard, S.D.	1	1	5	0	45	0	55	4	8	72	13	158	136	0	0	0	0	24	9	.538	7	6	5.84
Schatzeder, Daniel, Mtl.*	0	0	10	0	14	2	13	0	2	15	50	507	93	1	1	15	3	6	3	.667	2	1	2.45
Schultz, C.Budd, St.L.*	1	3	5	0	66	0	24	7	0	22	77	93	76	0	0	0	6	40	0	.857	6	1	2.33

Pitcher & Club	ERA	W	L	PCT	G	GS	CG	GF	SV	SHO	IP	H	BFP	R	ER	HR	SH	SF	TBB	IBB	HB	SO	WP	BK
Seaver, G.Thomas, N.Y.-Cin.	2.59	21	6	.778	33	33	19	0	0	7	261	199	1031	78	75	19	5	6	66	6	0	196	7	1
Seoane, Manuel, Phil.	6.00	0	0	.000	2	1	0	0	0	0	6	11	30	4	4	1	0	0	3	0	0	4	1	0
Shirley, Robert, S.D.*	3.70	12	18	.400	39	35	1	1	0	0	214	215	948	107	88	22	8	8	100	14	4	146	5	6
Siebert, Paul, S.D.-N.Y.*	3.66	1	2	.667	29	0	0	14	0	0	32	30	142	16	13	1	3	1	17	5	1	21	1	0
Solomon, Eddie, Atl.	4.55	6	6	.500	18	16	0	0	0	0	89	110	403	64	45	10	1	3	34	5	2	54	5	0
Sosa, Elias, L.A.	1.97	2	2	.500	44	0	0	20	1	0	64	42	239	15	14	7	3	3	12	3	1	47	4	0
Soto, Mario, Cin.	5.31	2	6	.250	12	10	0	1	0	0	61	60	266	38	36	12	2	0	26	1	1	44	4	0
Spillner, Daniel, S.D.	3.73	7	6	.538	76	0	0	30	6	0	130	130	542	61	51	12	10	6	60	13	3	74	5	0
Stanhouse, Donald, Mtl.	3.42	10	10	.500	47	16	1	17	10	0	158	147	689	72	60	12	10	2	84	9	4	89	0	1
Strom, Brent, S.D.*	12.18	0	2	.000	8	3	0	1	0	0	17	23	85	25	23	5	1	2	12	2	0	8	0	0
Sutter, H.Bruce, Chi.	1.35	7	3	.700	62	0	0	48	31	0	107	69	411	21	16	5	9	1	23	7	1	129	0	1
Sutton, Donald, L.A.	3.19	14	8	.636	33	33	9	0	0	3	240	207	979	93	85	23	12	7	69	2	3	150	5	0
Sutton, Johnny, St.L.	2.63	2	1	.667	14	0	0	5	0	0	24	28	101	10	7	0	5	2	9	1	0	9	1	0
Swan, Craig, N.Y.	4.22	9	10	.474	29	24	2	2	0	0	147	153	638	76	69	10	5	6	56	3	1	71	2	0
Tekulve, Kenton, Pitt.	3.06	10	1	.909	72	0	0	35	7	0	103	89	419	41	35	6	5	5	33	6	1	59	1	0
Terpko, Jeffrey, Mtl.	5.57	1	1	.500	13	0	0	7	0	0	21	28	99	13	13	4	1	0	15	5	0	14	1	0
Theiss, Duane, Atl.	6.43	1	1	.500	17	0	0	7	0	0	21	26	102	16	15	1	4	1	16	5	0	7	0	0
Thomas, Roy, Hou.	3.00	0	0	.000	4	0	0	1	0	0	6	5	27	2	2	0	4	0	3	0	0	4	0	0
Todd, Jackson, N.Y.	4.75	3	6	.333	19	10	0	2	0	0	72	78	312	41	38	8	2	4	20	0	2	39	2	1
Todd, James, Chi.	9.00	0	1	.000	20	0	0	11	0	0	31	47	161	37	31	4	1	0	19	5	2	17	0	0
Tomlin, David, S.D.*	3.00	4	4	.500	76	0	0	22	3	0	102	98	424	38	34	8	3	2	32	11	2	55	2	0
Toms, Thomas, S.F.	2.25	0	0	.000	4	0	0	1	0	0	8	7	23	5	2	1	0	0	2	0	0	2	0	0
Torres, Angel, Cin.*	2.25	0	0	.000	5	0	0	0	0	0	8	7	39	5	2	2	1	0	8	0	2	8	0	0
Twitchell, Wayne, Phil.-Mtl.	4.28	6	10	.375	34	30	2	3	0	0	185	166	776	98	88	21	13	4	74	4	5	130	7	0
Underwood, Thomas, Phil.-St.L.*	5.01	9	11	.450	33	17	1	2	1	0	133	148	601	82	74	14	9	2	75	6	3	86	7	1
Urrea, John, St.L.	3.15	7	6	.538	33	12	2	15	0	0	140	126	560	56	49	13	11	2	35	6	0	81	5	0
Walker, R.Thomas, Mtl.	4.74	1	1	.500	11	0	0	4	0	0	19	15	75	10	10	3	2	0	7	0	0	10	0	0
Wall, Stanley, L.A.*	5.34	2	3	.400	25	0	0	9	0	0	32	36	145	20	19	7	1	0	13	2	0	22	0	0
Warthen, Daniel, Mtl.-Phil.*	7.15	2	4	.333	23	6	1	3	0	0	39	37	193	37	31	7	8	1	43	1	0	27	3	0
Webb, Henry, L.A.	2.25	0	0	.000	5	0	0	3	0	0	8	5	29	2	2	1	0	0	2	0	0	3	0	0
Wehrmeister, David, S.D.	6.04	1	3	.250	30	6	0	10	0	0	70	81	329	53	47	8	4	4	44	4	3	32	2	0
Whitson, Edward, Pitt.	3.38	1	0	1.000	6	2	0	1	0	0	16	11	66	8	6	0	1	2	9	1	0	10	0	0
Williams, Charles, S.F.	4.01	6	5	.545	55	8	0	33	3	0	119	116	512	62	53	9	9	3	60	16	3	41	3	0
Zachry, Patrick, Cin.-N.Y.	4.25	10	13	.435	31	31	5	0	0	1	195	207	845	104	92	21	5	7	77	5	4	99	0	1

TV/RADIO ROUNDUP

NETWORK COVERAGE

ABC-TV: ABC will televise the American and National League playoff games and the All-Star Game. In addition, the network will televise Monday night games.

NBC-TV: The World Series will be televised by NBC. The network will also cover the Saturday Game of the Week.

NATIONAL LEAGUE

ATLANTA BRAVES: WSB (750) and WTCG (Channel 17) are the flagship stations for networks covering the South. Ernie Johnson, Pete Van Wieren and Skip Caray provide the coverage on both TV and radio.

CINCINNATI REDS: Joe Nuxhall and Marty Brennaman call the action over WLW (700). Ken Coleman and Bill Brown handle the TV coverage on WLWT (Channel 5).

CHICAGO CUBS: Jack Brickhouse, Vince Lloyd and Lou Boudreau are at the mikes for WGN (720) and WGN (Channel 9) and a 13-station network.

HOUSTON ASTROS: KPRC (Channel 2) heads the TV network and KPRC (950) the radio network. Gene Elston and DeWayne Staats do the play-by-play for both radio and television.

LOS ANGELES DODGERS: Vin Scully, Ross Porter and Jerry Doggett broadcast over KABC (790) and KTTV (Channel 11). Spanish coverage is done by Jaime Jarrin and Rudy Hoyos on XEGM (950).

MONTREAL EXPOS: Dave Van Horne and Duke Snider provide English coverage on CFCF (600) and the CBC-TV network. Jacques Doucet and Claude Raymond do French broadcasts on CKAC (730) and 16 other provincial stations, and Guy Ferron and Jean-Pierre Roy provide the French play-by-play on CBC-TV (French) network.

NEW YORK METS: Lindsey Nelson, Ralph Kiner and Bob Murphy handle TV originating at WOR-TV (Channel 9) and radio over WNEW (1130). Weekday afternoon games are on WNYC (830).

PHILADELPHIA PHILLIES: WPHL (Channel 17) originates telecasts while KYW (1060) heads up the radio network. Andy Musser, Richie Ashburn and Harry Kalas do the announcing.

PITTSBURGH PIRATES: Milo Hamilton and Larry Frattare are the broadcasters over KDKA (1020) and KDKA-TV (Channel 2).

SAN DIEGO PADRES: Jerry Coleman and Bob Chandler handle the play-by-play on radio KOGO (600).

SAN FRANCISCO GIANTS: Lon Simmons and Gary Park broadcast over KTVU (Channel 2) and Simmons and Joe Angel announce for the Golden West radio network over KSFO (560).

ST. LOUIS CARDINALS: Bob Starr, Mike Shannon and Jack Buck are on KMOX radio (1120); Starr, Shannon, Jay Randolph and Buck handle TV on KSD (Channel 5).

AMERICAN LEAGUE

BALTIMORE ORIOLES: Chuck Thompson and Bill O'Donnell call the action over radio station WBAL (1090) and WJZ-TV (Channel 13).

BOSTON RED SOX: Ned Martin and Jim Woods are at the mike for radio WMEX (1510) while television coverage originates over WSKB-TV (Channel 38) with Dick Stockton and Ken Harrelson.

CALIFORNIA ANGELS: Dick Enberg, Don Drysdale and Al Wisk broadcast on radio KMPC (710) and KTLA-TV (Channel 5).

CHICAGO WHITE SOX: Harry Caray, Jimmy Piersall, and Lorn Brown provide the coverage over WMAQ (670) and WSNS-TV (Channel 44).

CLEVELAND INDIANS: Joe Tait and Herb Score describe the action on three-state radio network with WWWE (1100) as flagship. Announcers will be named this spring for WJKW-TV (Channel 8) television broadcasts.

DENVER A's: Broadcast arrangements were unsettled at press time.

DETROIT TIGERS: Ernie Harwell and Paul Carey are the Tiger broadcasters on a 50-station radio network originating on WJR (760). WWJ-TV (Channel 4) and a seven-station network have George Kell, Al Kaline and Larry Osterman behind the mikes.

KANSAS CITY ROYALS: Five-state TV network originates with KBMA (Channel 41). Radio network headed by KMBZ (980) in K.C. and WIBW (580) in Topeka with Fred White and Denny Matthews.

MILWAUKEE BREWERS: WTMJ (620) and WTMJ-TV (Channel 4) head radio and TV networks covering five states. Merle Harmon, Ray Scott and Bob Uecker describe the action.

MINNESOTA TWINS: Joe Boyle and Harmon Killebrew broadcast for WCCO (Channel 4). Frank Quilici and Herb Carneal call the plays on a 5-station radio network headed by WCCO (830).

NEW YORK YANKEES: Frank Messer, Phil Rizzuto and Bill White share duties on networks headed by WPIX-TV (Channel 11) and radio station WMCA (570).

SEATTLE MARINERS: The Mariners can be heard over radio station KVI (570) and seen on Channel 5, KING-TV. Dave Niehaus and Ken Wilson describe the action.

TEXAS RANGERS: Dick Risenhoover and Bill Merrill broadcast over WBAP (820) and KXAS-TV (Channel 5).

TORONTO BLUE JAYS: Tom Cheek is the play-by-play man for a network headed by radio station CKFH.

OFFICIAL 1977 AMERICAN LEAGUE AVERAGES

compiled by

SPORTS INFORMATION CENTER

STANDING OF CLUBS AT CLOSE OF SEASON

AMERICAN LEAGUE EAST

	Won	Lost	Pct.	Games Behind
New York	100	62	.617	
Baltimore	97	64	.602	2½
Boston	97	64	.602	2½
Detroit	74	88	.457	26
Cleveland	71	90	.441	28½
Milwaukee	67	95	.414	33
Toronto	54	107	.335	45½

AMERICAN LEAGUE WEST

	Won	Lost	Pct.	Games Behind
Kansas City	102	60	.630	
Texas	94	68	.580	8
Chicago	90	72	.556	12
Minnesota	84	77	.522	17½
California	74	88	.457	28
Seattle	64	98	.395	38
Oakland	63	98	.391	38½

TOP FIFTEEN QUALIFIERS FOR BATTING CHAMPIONSHIP
(Rankings Based on 502 Plate Appearances)

*Bats Lefthanded   †Switch Hitter

Batter and Club	PCT	G	AB	R	H	TB	2B	3B	HR	RBI	SH	SF	SB	CS	SLG	TBB	IBB	HP	SO	GIDP
Carew, Rod, Minn.*	.388	155	616	128	239	351	38	16	14	100	2	6	23	13	.570	69	15	3	55	6
Bostock, Lyman, Minn.*	.336	153	593	104	199	301	36	12	14	90	2	8	16	7	.508	51	5	6	59	16
Singleton, Ken, Balt.†	.328	152	536	90	176	272	24	4	24	99	5	6	2	1	.507	107	13	4	101	15
Rivers, Mickey, N.Y.*	.326	138	565	79	184	248	18	5	12	69	1	6	22	14	.439	18	1	4	45	2
LeFlore, Ron, Det.	.325	154	652	100	212	310	30	10	16	57	7	4	39	19	.475	37	4	4	121	11
Rice, Jim, Bos.	.320	160	644	104	206	382	29	15	39	114	1	5	7	6	.593	53	10	8	120	21
Bumbry, Al, Balt.*	.317	133	518	74	164	213	31	3	4	41	2	4	19	7	.411	45	4	2	88	6
Fisk, Carlton, Bos.	.315	152	536	106	169	279	26	3	26	102	2	10	7	6	.521	75	4	9	85	9
Brett, George, K.C.*	.312	139	564	105	176	300	32	13	22	88	3	5	14	12	.532	55	9	2	24	12
Cowens, Al, K.C.*	.312	162	606	98	189	318	32	14	23	112	3	5	16	12	.525	41	4	8	64	14
Bailor, Bob, Tor.	.310	122	496	62	154	200	21	5	5	32	6	2	15	6	.403	17	1	2	26	5
Fuentes, Tito, Det.†	.309	151	615	83	190	244	19	10	5	51	13	5	5	4	.397	38	2	2	61	11
Munson, Thurman, N.Y.	.308	149	595	85	183	275	28	1	18	100	4	3	5	6	.462	39	1	6	55	18
Page, Mitchell, Oak.*	.307	145	501	85	154	261	28	8	21	75	4	3	42	5	.521	78	8	6	95	7
Hargrove, Mike, Tex.*	.305	153	525	98	160	250	28	4	18	69	8	6	2	5	.476	103	7	6	59	13

INDIVIDUAL BATTING
(All Players — Listed Alphabetically)

*Bats Lefthanded   †Switch Hitter

Batter and Club	PCT	G	AB	R	H	TB	2B	3B	HR	RBI	SH	SF	SB	CS	SLG	TBB	IBB	HP	SO	GIDP
Adams, Bob, Det.	.250	15	24	2	6	13	1	0	0	2	0	0	0	2	.542	18	0	0	5	0
Adams, Glenn, Minn.*	.338	95	269	32	91	126	17	4	0	49	3	0	0	2	.468	18	3	0	30	5
Aikens, Willie, Calif.*	.198	42	91	5	18	22	4	0	0	6	1	1	0	2	.242	10	2	0	23	1
Alexander, Matt, Oak.†	.238	90	42	42	10	11	1	0	0	2	0	4	26	14	.262	4	0	0	6	0
Allen, Dick, Oak.	.240	54	171	19	41	60	4	3	5	31	0	4	1	3	.351	24	1	3	36	4
Alomar, Sandy, Tex.†	.265	69	83	21	22	28	3	0	1	11	4	3	4	3	.337	8	0	1	13	0
Alston, Dell, N.Y.*	.325	22	40	10	13	20	4	0	1	4	0	0	3	3	.500	3	0	0	4	0
Alvarado, Luis, Det.	.000	2	1	0	0	0	0	0	0	0	0	0	0	0	.000	0	0	0	0	2
Armas, Tony, Oak.	.240	118	363	26	87	138	8	2	13	53	1	8	1	2	.380	20	2	4	99	8
Ashby, Alan, Tor.†	.210	124	396	25	83	111	16	3	2	29	10	1	2	2	.280-	50	5	2	50	14
Ault, Doug, Tor.	.245	129	445	44	109	170	22	3	11	64	1	3	0	4	.382	39	4	6	68	20
Aviles, Ramon, Bos.	.000	1	0	0	0	0	0	0	0	0	0	0	0	0	.000	0	0	0	0	0

*Bats Lefthanded †Switch Hitter

Batter and Club	PCT	G	AB	R	H	TB	2B	3B	HR	RBI	SH	SF	SB	CS	SLG	TBB	IBB	HP	SO	GIDP
Baez, Jose, Sea.	.259	91	305	39	79	98	14	1	1	17	8	2	6	1	.321	19	1	0	20	6
Bailey, Bob, Bos.	.000	2	2	0	0	0	0	0	0	0	0	0	0	0	.000	0	1	0	1	0
Bailor, Bob, Tor.	.310	122	496	62	154	200	21	5	0	32	6	2	15	6	.403	17	1	0	26	7
Baker, Jack, Bos.	.000	2	3	0	0	0	0	0	0	0	0	0	0	0	.000	0	0	0	1	0
Bando, Sal, Milw.	.250	159	580	65	145	229	27	3	17	82	3	5	4	2	.395	75	3	3	89	10
Bannister, Alan, Chgo.	.275	139	560	87	154	189	20	3	3	57	1	11	0	3	.338	54	1	2	49	11
Bass, Randy, Minn.*	.105	9	19	0	2	2	0	0	0	0	0	0	0	1	.105	0	0	0	5	0
Baylor, Don, Calif.	.251	154	561	87	141	243	27	1	25	75	2	8	26	12	.433	62	7	1	76	16
Beasley, Lew, Tex.*	.219	25	32	5	7	8	1	0	0	3	2	1	15	8	.250	2	1	0	2	0
Belanger, Mark, Balt.	.206	144	402	39	83	110	13	4	2	30	8	1	8	7	.274	43	0	1	68	7
Bell, Buddy, Clev	.292	129	479	64	140	204	23	4	11	64	5	5	1	8	.426	45	5	1	63	14
Bell, Kevin, Chgo	.179	9	28	4	5	9	1	0	1	6	0	0	1	0	.321	3	0	1	8	0
Beniquez, Juan, Tex.	.269	123	424	56	114	175	19	6	10	50	8	2	26	18	.413	43	0	2	43	13
Bergman, Dave, N.Y.*	.250	5	4	1	1	1	0	0	0	1	0	1	0	0	.250	0	0	0	0	0
Bernhardt, Juan, Sea.	.243	89	305	32	74	108	7	2	7	30	4	2	1	2	.354	6	1	0	26	9
Bevacqua, Kurt, Tex.	.333	39	96	13	32	58	7	1	5	28	0	5	0	3	.604	6	0	1	13	6
Blair, Paul, N.Y.	.262	83	164	20	43	65	4	0	6	38	5	3	3	0	.396	9	0	1	16	7
Blanks, Larvell, Clev.	.286	105	322	43	92	128	10	0	4	38	8	2	3	0	.398	19	1	1	37	7
Blue, Vida, Oak.†	.000	38	1	0	0	0	0	0	0	0	0	0	0	0	.000	0	0	0	1	0
Bochte, Bruce, Ca. 25, Cl. 112*	.301	137	492	64	148	194	23	0	7	51	3	5	6	4	.394	47	3	1	42	20
Bonds, Bobby, Calif.	.264	158	592	103	156	308	23	3	37	115	0	10	41	18	.520	74	5	2	141	9
Borgmann, Glenn, Minn.	.256	17	43	12	11	18	1	0	2	7	2	0	0	4	.419	11	0	0	9	2
Bosley, Thad, Calif.*	.297	58	212	19	63	77	10	2	0	19	4	2	5	0	.363	16	0	1	32	4
Bostock, Lyman, Minn.*	.336	153	593	104	199	301	36	12	14	90	3	8	16	7	.508	51	5	6	59	16
Bowen, Rich, Bos.	.000	5	16	0	0	0	0	0	0	0	0	0	0	0	.000	0	0	0	1	0
Bowling, Steve, Tor.	.206	89	194	19	40	53	8	1	1	13	3	0	2	3	.273	37	1	2	41	8
Braun, Steve, Sea.*	.235	139	451	51	106	142	19	1	5	31	8	3	2	3	.315	80	2	2	59	14
Brett, George, K.C.*	.312	139	564	105	176	300	32	13	22	88	3	1	14	12	.532	55	9	2	24	12
Briggs, Dan, Calif.*	.162	59	74	6	12	17	2	0	1	4	1	1	0	0	.230	8	1	1	14	3
Brohamer, John, Chgo.*	.257	59	152	26	39	61	10	0	3	20	3	2	2	0	.401	21	0	0	8	1
Brye, Steve, Milw.	.249	94	241	27	60	101	14	3	7	28	2	0	0	0	.419	16	1	0	39	5
Bulling, Terry, Minn.	.156	15	32	2	5	6	1	0	0	5	2	0	1	0	.188	5	0	1	5	2
Bumbry, Al, Balt.*	.317	133	518	74	164	213	31	3	4	41	3	4	19	8	.411	45	4	2	88	4
Burleson, Rick, Bos.	.293	154	663	80	194	253	36	7	3	52	8	6	13	12	.382	47	1	2	69	15
Campaneris, Bert, Tex.*	.254	150	552	77	140	188	19	1	5	46	40	5	27	20	.341	47	1	2	86	12
Carbo, Bernie, Bos.*	.289	86	228	36	66	119	6	1	15	34	0	1	2	2	.522	47	3	0	72	4

Carew, Rod, Minn.*	.388	155	616	128	239	351	38	16	14	100	1	5	23	13	.570	69	15	3	55	6
Carty, Rico, Clev.	.280	127	461	50	129	199	23	1	15	80	0	4	1	2	.432	56	6	0	51	17
Cerone, Rick, Tor.	.200	31	100	7	20	27	4	0	1	10	1	0	0	0	.270	6	0	0	12	3
Chalk, Dave, Calif.	.277	149	519	58	144	184	27	2	3	45	9	6	12	8	.355	52	2	5	69	13
Chambliss, Chris, N.Y.*	.287	157	600	90	172	267	32	6	17	90	0	5	4	0	.445	45	5	2	73	22
Chiles, Rich, Minn.*	.264	108	261	31	69	96	16	1	3	36	4	5	0	1	.368	23	2	2	17	5
Clleman, Dave, Bos.	.000	11	12	1	0	0	0	0	0	0	0	0	0	0	.000	1	0	0	3	0
Collins, Dave, Sea.†	.239	120	402	46	96	126	9	3	5	28	6	3	25	10	.313	33	0	3	66	2
Coluccio, Bob, Chgo.	.270	20	37	4	10	10	0	0	0	7	0	2	0	2	.270	6	0	0	2	1
Cooper, Cecil, Milw.*	.300	160	643	86	193	298	31	7	20	78	1	7	13	8	.463	28	4	0	110	13
Corcoran, Tim, Det.*	.282	55	103	13	29	41	3	0	3	15	0	2	0	1	.398	6	1	0	9	3
Cowens, Al, K.C.	.312	162	606	98	189	318	32	14	23	112	1	5	16	12	.525	41	4	8	64	14
Cox, Larry, Sea	.247	35	93	6	23	35	6	0	2	6	1	0	1	1	.376	10	0	0	12	2
Cox, Ted, Bos	.362	13	58	11	21	29	3	1	1	6	1	0	0	0	.500	3	0	0	6	0
Crawford, Willie, Oak.*	.184	59	136	7	25	37	7	1	1	16	2	1	0	0	.272	18	4	0	20	5
Criscione, Dave, Balt.	.333	7	9	1	3	6	0	0	1	1	1	0	0	0	.667	0	0	0	1	0
Crowley, Terry, Balt.*	.364	18	22	3	8	12	1	0	1	9	0	0	0	0	.545	1	0	0	3	0
Cruz, Henry, Chgo.*	.286	16	21	3	6	12	0	0	2	5	0	0	0	0	.571	1	1	0	3	0
Cruz, Julio, Sea.†	.256	60	199	25	51	59	3	1	1	7	7	0	15	6	.296	24	1	0	29	2
Cruz, Tommy, Chgo.*	.000	4	2	1	0	0	0	0	0	0	0	0	0	0	.000	0	0	0	0	0
Cubbage, Mike, Minn.*	.264	129	417	60	110	163	16	5	9	55	6	4	1	4	.391	37	6	0	49	4
Dade, Paul, Clev.	.291	134	461	65	134	164	15	3	3	45	4	9	16	8	.356	32	4	2	58	12
Darwin, Bobby, Bos.	.222	4	9	1	2	3	1	0	0	1	0	0	0	0	.333	0	0	0	4	1
Dauer, Rich, Balt.	.243	96	304	38	74	106	15	1	5	25	2	1	1	0	.349	20	0	2	28	10
Davis, Dick, Milw.	.275	22	51	7	14	16	2	0	0	6	0	2	0	0	.314	1	0	0	8	1
DeCines, Doug, Balt..	.259	150	522	63	135	226	28	3	19	69	0	5	8	8	.433	64	6	2	86	14
Delgado, Luis, Sea.	.182	13	22	4	4	4	0	0	0	2	0	0	0	0	.182	1	0	0	8	0
Dempsey, Rick, Balt.	.226	91	270	27	61	85	7	4	3	34	5	3	2	3	.315	34	1	2	34	9
Dent, Bucky, N.Y.	.247	158	477	54	118	168	18	4	8	49	14	9	1	1	.352.	39	0	1	28	9
Diaz, Bo, Bos.	.000	2	1	0	0	0	0	0	0	0	0	0	0	0	.000	0	0	0	1	0
Dillard, Steve, Bos.	.241	66	141	22	34	44	7	0	1	13	2	4	4	3	.312	7	0	0	13	1
Dimmel, Michael, Balt.	.000	25	5	8	0	0	0	0	0	0	1	0	1	0	.000	0	0	0	1	0
Downing, Brian, Chgo.	.284	69	169	28	48	68	4	2	4	15	5	4	1	2	.402	34	0	2	21	3
Doyle, Denny, Bos.*	.240	137	455	54	109	140	13	6	2	49	8	4	2	4	.308	29	3	4	50	8
Duffy, Frank, Clev.	.201	122	334	30	67	96	13	2	4	31	13	1	8	3	.287	21	0	0	47	8
Ellis, John, Tex.	.235	49	119	7	28	47	7	0	4	15	0	0	0	0	.395	8	2	0	26	1
Essian, Jim, Chgo.	.273	114	322	50	88	140	18	2	10	44	4	2	1	4	.435	52	1	1	35	9
Etchebarren, Andy, Calif.	.254	80	114	11	29	35	2	2	0	14	3	2	3	1	.307	12	0	0	19	3

*Bats Lefthanded †Switch Hitter Batter and Club	PCT	G	AB	R	H	TB	2B	3B	HR	RBI	SH	SF	SB	CS	SLG	TBB	IBB	HP	SO	GI DP
Evans, Dwight, Bos.	.287	73	230	39	66	121	8	2	14	36	6	1	4	1	.526	28	0	0	58	3
Ewing, Sam, Tor.*	.287	97	244	24	70	94	8	0	4	34	3	3	2	2	.385	19	4	0	42	8
Fahey, Bill, Tex.*	.221	37	68	3	15	19	4	0	0	5	3	0	0	0	.279	1	0	0	8	1
Fairly, Ron, Tor.*	.279	132	458	60	128	213	24	1	19	64	8	2	0	0	.465	58	11	2	58	12
Fisk, Carlton, Bos.	.315	152	536	106	169	279	26	3	26	102	0	5	7	6	.521	75	2	9	85	9
Flannery, John, Chgo.	.000	7													.000					
Flores, Gil, Calif.	.278	104	342	41	95	125	19	4	1	26	6	1	12	10	.365	23	2	0	39	0
Ford, Dan, Minn.	.267	144	453	66	121	193	25	7	11	60	1	5	6	4	.426	41	3	2	79	13
Fosse, Ray, Cl. 78, Sea. 11	.276	89	272	28	75	105	10	1	6	32	8	1	0	0	.386	9	0	3	28	12
Fregosi, Jim, Tex.	.250	13	28	4	7	11	1	0	1	5	2	1	0	0	.393	3	1	0	4	7
Fuentes, Tito, Det†	.309	151	615	83	190	244	19	0	5	51	5	1	4	2	.397	38	3	1	61	0
Gamble, Oscar, Chgo.*	.297	137	408	75	121	240	22	1	31	83	0	5	2	1	.588	54	6	1	54	11
Gantner, Jim, Milw.*	.298	14	47	4	14	18	1	0	0	5	1	0	0	0	.383	3	0	0	5	3
Garcia, Kiko, Balt.	.221	65	131	20	29	41	6	0	2	10	2	0	2	0	.313	5	0	0	31	1
Garcia, Pedro, Tor.	.221	41	130	10	27	39	10	1	0	9	2	0	2	0	.300	5	0	3	21	4
Garr, Ralph, Chgo.*	.300	134	543	78	163	236	29	7	10	54	1	3	12	7	.435	27	4	0	44	2
Gomez, Luis, Minn.	.246	32	65	6	16	24	4	2	0	11	5	1	0	2	.369	4	0	0	9	7
Goodwin, Danny, Calif.*	.209	35	91	5	19	30	3	1	2	8	0	0	0	0	.330	5	1	0	19	0
Gorinski, Bob, Minn.	.195	54	118	14	23	38	4	1	3	22	2	1	1	0	.322	5	0	0	29	2
Gray, Gary, Tex.	.000	1	2	0	0	0	0	0	0	0	0	0	0	0	.000	0	0	0	1	1
Grich, Bobby, Calif.	.243	52	181	24	44	71	6	0	7	23	3	3	6	6	.392	37	4	1	40	0
Grieve, Tom, Tex.	.225	79	236	24	53	83	9	0	7	30	0	0	1	0	.352	13	0	0	57	5
Griffin, Doug, Bos.	.000	5	6	0	0	0	0	0	0	0	1	0	0	0	.000	0	0	0	3	4
Griffin, Dave, Clev.	.146	14	41	5	6	7	1	0	0	3	0	0	2	0	.171	3	0	0	5	1
Gross, Wayne, Oak.*	.233	146	485	66	113	202	21	1	22	63	0	3	5	4	.416	86	6	5	84	7
Grubb, John, Clev.*	.301	34	93	8	28	43	3	3	2	14	2	0	3	3	.462	19	2	1	18	1
Guerrero, Mario, Calif.	.283	86	244	17	69	84	8	0	1	28	8	0	0	0	.344	4	0	0	16	3
Guidry, Ron, N.Y.*	.000	36		0	0	0	0	0	0	0	4	0	0	0	.000	0	0	0	0	0
Hairston, Jerry, Chgo.†	.308	13	26	3	8	10	2	0	0	4	0	2	0	0	.385	5	0	1	7	0
Hampton, Ike, Calif.	.295	63	122	23	36	58	7	1	9	29	3	0	1	0	.523	5	0	0	10	2
Haney, Larry, Milw.	.228	46	48	4	11	12	1	0	0	10	0	2	0	0	.244	2	0	0	30	2
Hargrove, Mike, Tex.*	.305	153	525	90	160	250	28	1	18	69	5	6	6	5	.476	103	7	0	59	13
Harlow, Larry, Balt.*	.208	46	48	4	10	12	2	0	0	4	0	0	0	1	.250	5	1	0	8	0
Harrah, Toby, Tex.	.263	159	539	90	142	258	25	5	27	87	0	9	27	5	.479	109	7	0	73	12
Healy, Fran, N.Y.	.224	27	67	10	15	20	0	0	0	7	2	0	0	0	.299	6	0	0	13	1
Hegan, Mike, Milw.*	.170	35	53	8	9	15	5	0	2	3	0	0	0	0	.283	10	1	1	17	0

Player	AVG	G	AB	R	H	2B	3B	HR	RBI	SO	SB	SLG
Heidemann, Jack, Milw.	.000	5	1	0	0	0	0	0	0	0	0	.000
Heise, Bob, K.C.	.258	54	62	5	16	2	1	0	5	7	0	.323
Helms, Tom, Bos.	.271	21	59	5	16	5	0	0	6	4	0	.356
Henderson, Ken, Tex.†	.258	75	244	23	63	6	1	7	21	56	8	.377
Hendricks, Elrod, N.Y.*	.273	10	11	0	3	1	0	1	5	2	0	.636
Hisle, Larry, Minn.	.302	141	546	95	165	36	3	28	119	106	21	.533
Hobson, Butch, Bos.	.265	159	593	77	157	33	5	30	112	162	0	.489
Horton, Willie, De. 1, Te. 139	.289	140	523	55	151	23	3	15	75	117	1	.430
Hosley, Tim, Oak.	.192	39	78	5	15	3	0	0	10	13	0	.231
Howell, Roy, Te. 7, To. 96*	.302	103	381	41	115	21	1	8	44	80	3	.430
Humphrey, Terry, Calif.	.227	123	304	17	69	12	1	1	34	58	0	.283
Hurdle, Clint, K.C.*	.308	9	26	5	8	2	0	0	7	7	1	.538
Jackson, Reggie, N.Y.*	.286	146	525	93	150	39	2	32	110	129	17	.550
Jackson, Ron, Calif	.243	106	292	38	71	11	1	10	44	42	0	.390
Johnson, Cliff, N.Y	.296	56	142	24	42	8	0	12	31	23	0	.606
Johnson, Lamar, Chgo	.302	118	374	52	113	20	1	18	65	53	0	.505
Johnson, Tim, Milw.*	.061	30	33	5	2	1	0	0	2	10	1	.091
Jones, Bob, Calif.*	.176	14	17	3	3	0	0	1	2	5	0	.353
Jones, Ruppert, Sea.*	.263	160	597	85	157	26	8	24	76	120	13	.454
Jorgensen, Mike, Oak.*	.246	66	203	18	50	13	1	5	22	44	0	.394
Joshua, Von, Milw.*	.261	144	536	58	140	20	6	4	35	44	12	.384
Jutze, Skip, Sea.	.220	42	109	10	24	7	0	0	8	12	0	.321
Kelly, Pat, Balt.*	.256	120	360	50	92	11	1	10	49	75	25	.375
Kemp, Steve, Det.*	.257	151	552	75	142	29	4	18	88	93	3	.422
Kendall, Fred, Clev.	.249	103	317	18	79	13	1	3	39	27	0	.325
Kessinger, Don, Chgo.†	.235	39	119	12	28	4	1	0	11	16	2	.294
Kimm, Bruce, Det.	.080	14	25	2	2	0	0	0	4	4	0	.080
Kingman, Dave, Ca. 10, N.Y. 8	.217	18	60	6	13	1	0	9	28	29	2	.583
Kirkpatrick, Ed, Te. 20, Mi.29*	.240	49	125	19	30	5	0	0	19	19	1	.280
Klutts, Mickey, N.Y.	.267	5	15	3	4	1	0	1	2	2	0	.533
Kuiper, Duane, Clev.*	.277	148	610	62	169	25	3	1	50	55	11	.333
Kusick, Craig, Minn.	.254	115	268	34	68	6	0	14	45	60	2	.433
Lacock, Pete, K.C.*	.303	118	218	25	66	9	1	4	29	25	1	.408
Lahoud, Joe, K.C.*	.262	34	65	6	17	5	0	2	8	16	0	.431
Landreaux, Ken, Calif.*	.250	23	76	6	19	5	0	0	5	15	1	.342
LeFlore, Ron, Det	.325	154	652	100	212	30	10	16	57	121	39	.475
Lemon, Chet, Chgo.	.273	150	553	99	151	38	4	19	67	88	8	.459
Lezcano, Sixto, Milw.	.273	109	400	50	109	21	4	21	49	78	6	.503

*Bats Lefthanded †Switch Hitter

Batter and Club	PCT	G	AB	R	H	TB	2B	3B	HR	RBI	SH	SF	SB	CS	SLG	TBB	IBB	HP	SO	GI DP
Lintz, Larry, Oak.†	.133	41	30	11	4	5	1	0	0	0	1	0	13	5	.167	8	1	1	13	0
Lis, Joe, Sea.	.231	9	13	1	3	3	0	0	0	1	0	0	0	0	.231	2	0	0	2	3
Littell, Mark, K.C.*	.000	48	1	0	0	0	0	0	0	0	1	0	0	0	.000	0	0	0	1	0
Locklear, Gene, N.Y.*	.600	1	5	0	3	3	0	0	0	2	0	0	0	0	.600	0	0	0	0	0
Lopez, Carlos, Sea.	.283	99	297	39	84	128	18	1	8	34	2	3	16	4	.431	14	1	3	61	6
Lowenstein, John, Clev.*	.242	81	149	24	36	56	6	1	4	12	3	0	0	8	.376	21	1	2	29	9
Lynn, Fred, Bos.*	.260	129	497	81	129	222	29	5	18	76	2	8	2	2	.447	51	7	3	63	6
Maddox, Elliot, Balt.	.262	49	107	14	28	33	4	0	0	5	5	1	2	1	.262	13	0	2	9	14
Mallory, Sheldon, Oak.	.214	64	126	19	27	33	4	1	0	9	2	1	12	5	.262	11	0	3	18	5
Mankowski, Phil, Det.*	.276	94	286	27	79	101	7	3	3	27	6	2	1	1	.353	16	4	0	41	2
Manning, Rick, Clev.*	.226	68	252	33	57	85	7	3	5	18	2	1	9	5	.337	21	4	0	35	4
Martinez, Buck, K.C.	.225	29	80	3	18	25	4	0	1	9	6	1	0	1	.313	3	0	0	12	4
Mason, Jim, To. 22, Te. 36*	.187	58	134	19	25	34	6	1	0	9	2	0	1	0	.254	13	0	0	20	2
May, Carlos, N.Y. 65, Ca. 11*	.236	76	199	21	47	62	7	1	2	17	5	1	0	0	.312	22	4	0	25	1
May, Dave, Tex.*	.241	120	340	46	82	119	14	1	7	42	2	3	2	3	.350	32	5	1	43	8
May, Lee, Balt.	.253	150	585	75	148	248	15	2	27	99	0	5	0	2	.424	38	2	0	119	20
May, Milt, Det.*	.249	115	397	32	99	150	15	0	12	46	8	7	0	2	.378	26	5	0	31	14
Mayberry, John, K.C.*	.230	153	543	73	125	218	22	1	23	82	1	7	1	3	.401	83	9	7	86	31
McCall, Larry, N.Y.*	.000	3	0	0	0	0	0	0	0	0	0	0	0	0	.000	0	0	0	0	0
McKay, Dave, Tor.	.177	95	274	18	54	73	4	3	3	22	2	0	1	1	.266	7	0	2	51	9
McKinney, Rich, Oak.	.177	86	198	13	35	60	7	0	6	21	0	1	0	0	.303	16	5	0	43	11
McMillan, Tom, Sea.	.000	2	5	0	0	0	0	0	0	0	0	0	0	0	.000	0	0	0	0	0
McMullen, Ken, Milw.	.228	63	136	15	31	55	7	1	5	19	2	0	0	0	.404	15	5	1	33	4
McRae, Hal, K.C.	.298	162	641	104	191	330	54	11	21	92	2	2	18	14	.515	59	13	0	43	12
Melton, Bill, Clev.	.241	50	133	17	32	43	11	4	0	14	1	1	0	1	.323	17	4	1	21	4
Meyer, Dan, Sea.†	.273	159	582	75	159	257	24	4	22	90	5	8	11	8	.442	43	4	1	51	19
Milbourne, Larry, Sea.†	.219	86	242	25	53	69	10	0	2	21	8	5	3	1	.285	6	0	2	20	4
Miller, Eddie, Tex	.333	17	6	2	2	2	0	0	0	0	0	0	11	1	.333	1	0	1	1	0
Miller, Rick, Bos.*	.254	86	189	34	48	63	9	3	0	24	6	0	11	5	.333	22	2	1	30	2
Molinaro, Bob, Det.-4, Chgo-1*	.333	3	3	0	1	2	1	0	0	0	0	0	0	0	.667	0	0	0	3	0
Money, Don, Milw.	.279	152	570	86	159	268	28	3	25	83	4	6	8	0	.470	57	0	7	70	17
Montgomery, Bob, Bos.	.300	17	40	6	12	20	2	0	2	7	9	0	0	7	.500	4	0	1	9	9
Moore, Charlie, Milw.	.248	138	375	42	93	135	15	6	5	45	8	2	1	1	.360	31	1	1	39	13
Mora, Andres, Balt.	.245	77	233	32	57	108	8	2	13	44	0	2	0	1	.464	5	1	1	53	4
Mulliniks, Rance, Calif.*	.269	78	271	36	73	99	13	2	3	21	8	2	1	1	.365	23	2	1	36	2
Munson, Thurman, N.Y.	.308	149	595	85	183	275	28	5	18	100	0	2	5	6	.462	39	8	2	55	18

Player	Pct.	G.	AB.	R.	H.	2B.	3B.	HR.	RBI.	BB.	SO.	SB.	SLG.
Murray, Eddie, Balt.†	.283	160	611	81	173	29	2	27	88	48	104	0	.470
Murray, Larry, Oak.†	.179	90	162	19	29	5	2	2	7	17	36	12	.253
Muser, Tony, Balt.*	.229	120	118	14	27	6	0	0	7	13	16	1	.280
Nahorodny, Bill, Chgo.	.261	7	23	3	6	3	0	0	1	2	3	0	.435
Nelson, Dave, K.C.	.188	27	48	8	9	1	1	0	4	7	11	1	.292
Nettles, Graig, N.Y.*	.255	158	589	99	150	23	4	37	107	68	79	2	.496
Newman, Jeff, Oak.	.222	94	162	17	36	6	0	4	15	11	24	2	.352
Nolan, Gary, Calif.	.000	6	0	0	0	0	0	0	0	0	0	0	.000
Nordbrook, Tim, Ch. 15, To. 24	.193	39	83	11	16	0	0	0	2	11	15	0	.217
Nordhagen, Wayne, Chgo.	.315	52	124	16	39	7	0	4	22	2	12	0	.516
Norris, Jim, Clev.*	.270	133	440	60	119	23	3	2	37	64	57	6	.364
Norris, Mike, Oak.	.000	17	0	0	0	0	0	0	0	0	0	0	.000
North, Billy, Oak.†	.261	133	184	32	48	6	3	3	9	32	25	17	.326
Norwood, Willie, Minn.	.229	39	83	15	19	0	3	3	9	6	17	6	.373
Nyman, Nyls, Chgo.*	.000	12	4	0	0	0	0	0	0	0	0	0	.000
Oglivie, Ben, Det.*	.262	132	450	63	118	24	2	21	61	41	80	9	.464
Oliver, Dave, Clev.*	.318	7	22	7	7	2	0	0	3	2	4	0	.409
Orta, Jorge, Chgo.*	.282	144	564	71	159	27	8	11	84	40	49	1	.417
Otis, Amos, K.C.	.251	145	478	85	120	27	8	8	78	46	88	23	.433
Page, Mitchell, Oak.*	.307	145	501	85	154	28	8	21	75	78	95	42	.521
Parrish, Lance, Det.	.196	12	46	10	9	2	0	3	7	5	12	0	.435
Pasley, Kevin, Sea.	.385	4	13	5	5	0	0	0	1	0	2	0	.385
Patek, Fred, K.C.	.262	154	497	72	130	26	6	5	60	41	84	53	.368
Perez, Marty, N.Y. 1, Oa. 115	.233	116	377	32	88	7	2	5	23	29	66	0	.313
Perlozzo, Sam, Minn.	.292	10	24	6	7	2	0	0	0	2	4	0	.458
Picciolo, Rob, Oak.	.200	148	419	35	84	12	1	2	22	9	55	3	.258
Piniella, Lou, N.Y.	.330	103	339	47	112	19	2	12	45	20	31	2	.510
Poquette, Tom, K.C.*	.292	106	342	43	100	23	3	3	33	19	21	2	.412
Porter, Darrell, K.C.*	.275	130	425	61	117	10	3	16	60	53	70	0	.452
Pruitt, Ron, Clev.	.288	78	219	29	63	12	0	2	32	28	22	3	.379
Putnam, Pat, Tex.*	.308	11	26	8	8	1	1	0	3	1	4	0	.462
Quirk, Jamie, Milw.*	.217	93	221	16	48	4	2	3	13	8	47	1	.330
Rader, Doug, Tor.	.240	96	313	47	75	18	1	13	40	38	67	1	.435
Ramirez, Orlando, Calif.	.077	25	13	6	1	0	0	0	0	1	3	0	.077
Randall, Bobby, Minn.	.239	103	306	36	73	13	0	2	22	15	25	13	.294
Randolph, Willie, N.Y.	.274	147	551	91	151	28	11	4	40	64	53	13	.387
Remy, Jerry, Calif.*	.252	154	575	74	145	19	9	4	44	59	59	41	.341
Reynolds, Craig, Sea.*	.248	135	420	41	104	12	3	4	28	15	23	6	.319

*Bats Lefthanded †Switch Hitter

Batter and Club	PCT	G	AB	R	H	TB	2B	3B	HR	RBI	SH	SF	SB	CS	SLG	TBB	IBB	HP	SO	GI DP
Rice, Jim, Bos.	.320	160	644	104	206	382	29	15	39	114	5	5	5	14	.593	53	10	8	120	21
Rivers, Mickey, N.Y.*	.326	138	565	79	184	248	18	5	12	69	5	2	22	4	.439	18	4	0	45	2
Robinson, Brooks, Balt.	.149	24	47	3	7	12	2	0	0	4	0	1	0	0	.255	4	0	0	8	2
Rodriguez, Aurelio, Det.	.219	96	306	30	67	113	14	1	10	32	1	1	0	1	.369	16	2	0	36	8
Rojas, Cookie, K.C.	.250	64	156	8	39	50	9	1	0	10	1	1	3	3	.321	8	2	0	17	5
Romero, Ed, Milw.	.280	10	25	4	7	8	1	0	0	2	0	0	0	0	.320	4	0	0	3	1
Roof, Phil, Tor.	.000	3	5	0	0	0	0	0	0	0	2	0	0	0	.000	0	0	0	1	0
Rudi, Joe, Calif.	.264	64	242	48	64	120	13	1	13	53	0	4	1	0	.496	22	4	4	48	2
Rudolph, Ken, Balt.	.286	11	14	4	4	5	1	0	0	2	0	0	0	0	.357	0	0	0	4	0
Sakata, Len, Milw.	.162	53	154	13	25	33	2	0	2	12	6	1	2	3	.214	9	0	0	22	1
Sanguillen, Manny, Oak.	.275	152	571	42	157	202	17	0	6	58	2	4	2	1	.354	22	4	4	35	13
Scott, George, Bos.	.269	157	584	103	157	292	26	5	33	95	0	2	5	5	.500	57	4	3	112	24
Scott, Rodney, Oak.†	.261	133	364	56	95	107	9	0	1	20	5	6	33	18	.294	43	0	3	50	4
Scott, John, Tor.	.240	79	233	26	56	71	9	0	2	15	6	1	10	0	.305	8	0	3	39	4
Scrivener, Chuck, Det.	.083	61	72	6	6	6	0	0	0	3	2	0	1	0	.083	5	0	0	9	1
Sexton, Jimmy, Sea.	.216	14	37	5	8	14	1	0	0	3	5	1	3	0	.378	2	0	0	9	1
Sheldon, Bob, Milw.*	.203	31	64	15	13	19	4	1	0	5	2	1	0	3	.297	6	0	0	9	0
Shopay, Tom, Balt.*	.188	67	69	13	13	19	4	0	1	3	4	0	3	0	.275	8	0	0	8	0
Singleton, Ken, Balt.†	.328	152	536	90	176	272	24	0	24	99	2	6	0	3	.507	107	13	0	101	15
Skaggs, Dave, Balt.	.287	80	216	22	62	76	9	1	1	24	8	1	0	2	.352	20	0	0	34	12
Smalley, Roy, Minn.†	.231	150	584	93	135	184	21	5	6	56	15	6	5	5	.315	74	2	1	89	11
Smith, Billy, Balt.†	.215	109	367	33	79	110	12	2	5	29	9	5	5	3	.300	33	3	1	71	3
Smith, Keith, Tex.	.239	23	67	13	16	26	2	0	2	6	6	0	2	4	.388	4	0	0	7	0
Smith, Tommy, Sea.*	.259	21	27	13	7	10	1	1	0	4	3	0	0	0	.370	4	0	2	6	0
Soderholm, Eric, Chgo.	.280	130	460	77	129	230	20	1	25	67	4	4	2	4	.500	47	5	4	47	15
Solaita, Tony, Calif.*	.241	116	324	40	78	135	15	0	14	53	2	5	1	3	.417	56	6	2	77	6
Spencer, Jim, Chgo.*	.247	128	470	56	116	188	16	1	18	69	2	5	1	2	.400	36	11	2	50	11
Spikes, Charlie, Clev.	.232	32	95	22	22	33	0	1	3	11	0	0	0	2	.347	11	0	0	17	0
Squires, Mike, Chgo.*	.000	3	3	0	0	0	0	0	0	0	0	0	0	0	.000	0	0	0	0	0
Staggs, Steve, Tor.†	.258	72	291	37	75	104	11	0	6	28	3	3	5	9	.359	36	2	0	38	2
Stanley, Mickey, Det.	.230	75	222	30	51	86	9	1	8	23	2	3	0	1	.387	18	0	1	30	2
Stanley, Fred, N.Y.	.261	48	46	6	12	15	0	0	1	7	2	0	1	1	.326	8	0	0	6	0
Stanton, Lee, Sea.	.275	133	454	56	125	232	24	3	27	90	2	3	0	1	.511	42	2	5	115	8
Staub, Rusty, Det.*	.278	158	623	84	173	279	34	5	22	101	2	6	3	3	.448	59	2	1	47	27
Stein, Bill, Sea.	.259	151	556	53	144	219	26	5	13	67	2	6	1	4	.394	29	4	1	79	14
Stillman, Royle, Chgo.*	.210	56	119	18	25	43	7	1	3	13	0	1	2	1	.361	17	1	0	21	1

Player	AVG	G	AB	R	H	TB	2B	3B	HR	RBI	BB	SO	SB
Stinson, Bob, Sea.†	.269	105	297	27	80	117	11	1	8	32	5	50	6
Sundberg, Jim, Tex.	.291	149	453	61	132	176	20	3	6	65	20	77	0
Tabb, Jerry, Oak.*	.222	51	144	8	32	52	6	0	6	19	1	26	2
Terrell, Jerry, Minn.	.224	93	214	32	48	57	9	0	0	20	7	21	1
Thomas, Dan, Milw.	.271	22	70	11	19	32	3	0	2	11	0	1	1
Thompson, Jason, Det.*	.270	158	585	87	158	285	24	2	31	105	0	91	1
Thorton, Andre, Clev.	.263	131	433	77	114	228	20	5	28	70	5	82	11
Torres, Hector, Tor.	.241	91	266	33	64	92	7	3	1	26	4	33	1
Torres, Rusty, Calif.†	.156	58	77	9	12	24	1	1	3	10	3	18	1
Trammell, Alan, Det.	.186	19	43	6	8	8	0	0	0	1	0	12	0
Tyrone, Jim, Oak.	.245	96	294	32	72	100	11	1	5	26	5	62	1
Velez, Otto, Tor.	.256	120	360	50	92	165	19	1	16	62	2	87	1
Veryzer, Tom, Det.	.197	125	350	31	69	89	12	1	1	28	4	44	0
Wagner, Mark, Det.	.146	22	48	8	7	12	1	0	1	3	1	12	1
Washington, Claudell, Tex.*	.284	129	521	63	148	219	31	2	12	68	7	112	10
Washington, U.L. K.C.	.200	10	20	0	4	4	1	0	0	1	0	4	1
Wathan, John, K.C.	.328	11	32	4	11	15	2	1	0	7	1	8	0
Whitaker, Lou, Det.*	.250	11	119	18	39	56	5	1	2	21	3	6	4
White, Frank, K.C.	.245	152	474	59	116	162	21	5	5	50	11	67	11
White, Roy, N.Y.†	.268	143	519	72	139	210	25	1	2	52	8	58	1
Whitt, Ernie, Tor.*	.171	23	41	7	7	10	1	0	1	6	3	12	1
Wilfong, Rob, Minn.*	.246	73	171	22	42	48	8	2	0	13	3	26	4
Williams, Earl, Oak.	.241	100	348	39	84	136	13	1	13	38	1	58	0
Williams, Mark, Oak.*	.000	1	2	0	0	0	0	0	0	1	0	1	0
Wills, Bump, Tex.†	.287	152	541	87	155	222	28	6	9	62	12	96	19
Wilson, Willie, K.C.†	.324	13	34	4	11	13	2	0	0	1	0	8	0
Wockenfuss, John, Det.	.274	53	164	26	45	82	8	1	3	25	3	18	1
Wohlford, Jim, Milw.	.248	129	391	41	97	125	16	3	2	36	6	49	9
Wolfe, Bob, Minn.	.240	8	25	3	6	7	1	0	0	3	0	0	0
Woods, Al, Tor.*	.284	122	440	58	125	168	17	4	6	35	7	38	11
Woods, Gary, Tor.	.216	60	227	21	49	60	9	3	3	17	3	7	5
Wynegar, Butch, Minn.†	.261	144	532	76	139	197	22	3	10	79	8	61	11
Wynn, Jim, N.Y. 30, Mi. 36	.175	66	194	17	34	46	5	1	1	13	28	49	10
Yastrzemski, Carl, Bos.*	.296	150	558	99	165	282	27	3	28	102	11	40	11
Yount, Robin, Milw.	.288	154	605	66	174	228	34	4	4	49	16	80	10
Zdeb, Joe, K.C.	.297	105	195	26	58	73	5	2	2	23	6	23	5
Zeber, George, N.Y.†	.323	25	65	8	21	33	3	1	3	10	0	11	1
Zisk, Richie, Chgo.	.290	141	531	78	154	273	17	6	30	101	9	98	15

INDIVIDUAL PITCHING

TOP FIFTEEN QUALIFIERS FOR EARNED RUN LEADERSHIP

*Pitches Lefthanded

Pitcher, Club	ERA	W	L	PCT	G	GS	CG	GF	SV	SHO	IP	H	BFP	R	ER	HR	SH	SF	TBB	IBB	HP	SO	WP	BK
Tanana, Frank, Calif. *	2.54	15	9	.625	31	31	20	0	0	5	241	201	973	72	68	19	8	1	61	1	12	205	8	1
Blyleven, Bert, Tex.	2.72	14	12	.538	30	30	15	0	0	5	235	181	935	81	71	20	10	5	69	1	7	182	8	1
Ryan, Nolan, Calif.	2.77	19	16	.543	37	37	22	0	0	4	299	198	1272	110	92	12	22	10	204	2	9	341	21	0
Guidry, Ron, N.Y.*	2.82	16	7	.696	31	25	9	4	1	5	211	174	850	72	66	12	5	5	65	2	2	176	6	0
Palmer, Jim, Balt.	2.91	20	11	.645	39	39	22	0	0	5	319	263	1289	106	103	24	10	6	99	0	8	193	7	0
Leonard, Dennis, K.C.	3.04	20	12	.625	38	37	21	1	0	5	293	246	1186	117	99	18	6	6	79	0	8	244	14	2
Rozema, Dave, Det.	3.10	15	7	.682	28	28	16	0	0	0	218	222	890	87	75	25	8	5	34	2	2	92	4	2
Goltz, Dave, Minn.	3.36	20	11	.645	39	39	19	0	0	2	303	284	1253	129	113	23	13	4	91	4	2	186	2	1
Perry, Gaylord, Tex.	3.37	15	12	.556	34	34	13	0	0	1	238	239	986	108	89	21	11	5	56	7	5	177	3	2
Eckersley, Dennis, Clev.	3.63	14	13	.519	33	33	12	0	0	3	247	214	1006	100	97	17	11	6	54	11	7	191	3	0
Bibby, Jim, Clev.	3.57	12	13	.480	41	23	6	12	2	1	207	211	976	100	82	17	7	6	73	6	4	141	12	4
Hartzell, Paul, Calif.	3.58	8	11	.500	37	23	3	6	1	1	189	200	793	92	75	18	10	7	38	6	4	79	3	1
Figueroa, Ed, N.Y.	3.58	16	11	.593	32	32	17	0	0	0	239	228	999	102	95	19	7	10	75	1	3	104	3	1
Slaton, Jim, Milw.	3.58	10	14	.417	32	31	7	1	0	1	221	223	942	104	88	25	8	9	77	5	11	104	3	1
Garland, Wayne, Clev.	3.59	13	19	.406	38	38	21	0	0	1	283	281	1184	130	113	23	11	7	88	8	2	118	12	1

(All Pitchers Listed Alphabetically)

*Pitches Lefthanded

Player and Club	ERA	W	L	PCT	G	GS	CG	GF	SV	SHO	IP	H	BFP	R	ER	HR	SH	SF	TBB	IBB	HP	SO	WP	BK
Aase, Don, Bos.	3.13	6	2	.750	13	13	4	0	0	2	92	85	373	36	32	6	2	0	49	0	0	49	0	0
Abbott, Glenn, Sea.	4.46	12	13	.480	36	34	7	0	0	0	204	212	864	111	101	32	7	4	56	2	2	100	9	0
Alexander, Doyle, Tex.	3.65	17	11	.607	34	34	12	0	0	0	237	221	995	103	96	24	9	6	82	3	4	82	4	0
Andersen, Larry, Clev.	3.21	0	1	.000	11	0	0	7	0	0	14	10	62	7	5	1	5	0	9	0	0	8	1	0
Anderson, Larry, Chgo	9.00	0	1	.250	6	0	0	4	0	0	9	10	54	10	9	1	0	0	4	0	0	7	4	0
Arroyo, Fernando, Det	4.18	8	18	.308	38	28	8	5	0	0	209	227	883	102	97	23	6	6	52	5	1	60	3	0
Augustine, Jerry, Milw.*	4.48	12	18	.400	33	33	10	0	0	0	209	222	898	119	104	23	10	11	72	5	3	68	4	0
Bacsik, Mike, Tex.	22.50	0	0	.000	2	0	0	1	0	0	2	9	16	5	5	1	0	0	5	0	1	0	1	0
Bahnsen, Stan, Oak	6.14	1	2	.333	11	2	0	3	0	0	22	24	100	16	15	5	0	0	13	5	0	21	2	0
Bair, Doug, Oak.	3.47	4	6	.400	45	0	0	28	8	0	83	78	377	39	32	11	6	0	57	9	0	68	6	0
Bare, Ray, Det	12.86	0	1	.000	6	2	0	0	0	0	14	24	71	21	20	3	1	0	7	2	0	4	0	0
Barker, Len, Tex.	2.68	4	1	.800	15	2	1	6	1	0	47	36	196	15	14	3	1	1	24	6	0	51	5	0
Barlow, Mike, Calif.	4.58	4	2	.667	30	1	0	9	4	3	59	53	250	33	30	3	0	1	27	6	4	25	1	4
Berrios, Francisco, Chgo	4.13	14	7	.667	37	31	9	1	0	1	231	241	982	117	106	22	10	8	58	1	1	119	4	0
Beare, Gary, Milw	6.41	3	3	.500	17	6	0	3	0	0	59	63	273	46	42	6	3	3	38	3	1	32	4	2
Bibby, Jim, Clev	3.57	12	13	.480	37	30	9	5	2	2	207	197	876	100	82	17	7	6	73	6	4	141	12	4
Bird, Doug, K.C.*	3.89	11	4	.733	53	5	0	31	14	0	118	120	490	52	51	14	6	7	29	4	3	83	3	4
Blue, Vida, Oak.*	3.83	14	19	.424	38	38	16	0	0	5	280	284	1184	138	119	23	12	9	86	1	1	157	11	0
Blyleven, Bert, Tex	2.72	14	12	.538	30	30	15	0	0	5	235	181	935	81	71	20	10	5	69	1	7	182	8	1
Boggs, Tommy, Tex	6.00	0	3	.000	6	6	0	0	0	0	27	40	130	30	18	1	3	0	12	0	1	15	1	0
Brett, Ken, Ch-13, C*-21*	4.52	13	14	.481	34	34	9	1	0	2	225	258	950	120	113	25	7	7	53	0	6	80	6	2
Briles, Nelson, Tx-28, Ba-2	4.18	6	4	.600	30	15	2	4	2	0	112	119	473	61	52	15	4	2	30	1	5	59	5	5

Pitcher	W	L	PCT	ERA
Bruno, Tom, Tor	0	1	.000	8.00
Burgmeier, Tom, Minn.*	6	4	.600	5.10
Burke, Steve, Sea	0	0	.000	2.81
Burton, Jim, Bos.*	0	0	.000	0.00
Buskey, Tom, Clev	0	0	.000	5.29
Butler, Bill, Minn.*	0	2	.000	6.86
Byrd, Jeff, Tor	2	13	.133	6.21
Caldwell, Mike, Milw.*	5	8	.385	4.60
Campbell, Bill, Bos	13	9	.591	2.96
Camper, Ken, Clev	0	2	.000	4.00
Caneira, John, Calif.	1	1	.500	4.03
Carrithers, Don, Minn	0	3	.000	4.91
Carroll, Clay, Chgo	1	0	1.000	7.07
Castro, Bill, Milw	8	6	.571	12.38
Clancy, Jim, Tor	2	3	.400	4.17
Clay, Ken, N.Y	2	3	.308	5.03
Cleveland, Reggie, Bos	11	9	.579	4.34
Colborn, Jim, K.C	11	4	.563	4.26
Coleman, Joe, Oak	15	14	.500	3.62
Cort, Barry, Milw	4	4	.500	2.95
Crawford, Jim, Det.*	7	8	.467	3.38
Cuellar, Mike, Calif.*	0	0	.000	4.79
Darr, Mike, Tor	0	2	.000	21.00
DeBarr, Dennis, Tor*	0	2	.000	6.00
DalCanton, Bruce, Cha.	1	0	1.000	1.29
Devine, Adrian, Tex	11	6	.647	45.00
Dobson, Pat, Clev	3	12	.200	3.57
Drago, Dick, Ca-13, Ba-36	6	4	.600	6.16
Dunning, Steve, Oak	1	1	.500	3.39
Eckersley, Dennis, Clev	14	13	.519	4.00
Ellis, Dock, Te-23, N.Y.-10	12	12	.500	3.53
Erardi, Greg, Sea	0	0	.000	3.63
Farmer, Ed, Balt.	3	2	.600	6.00
Fidrych, Mark, Det	16	11	.593	2.89
Figueroa, Ed, N.Y.	16	10	.600	3.58
Fitzmorris, Al, Clev	15	10	.375	5.41
Flanagan, Mike, Balt.	0	1	.000	3.64
Folkers, Rick, Milw.*	7	9	.500	4.50
Foucault, Steve, Det	0	6	.000	3.16
Galasso, Bob, Chgo	6	6	.500	3.00
Garland, Wayne, Clev	13	19	.406	9.59
Garvin, Jerry, Tor.*	24	34	.357	3.19
Giusti, Dave, Oak*	0	1	.500	4.19
Glynn, Ed, Det.*	3	3	.667	5.33

*Pitches Lefthanded

Player and Club	ERA	W	L	PCT	G	GS	CG	GF	SV	SHO	IP	H	BFP	R	ER	HR	SH	SF	TBB	IBB	HP	SO	WP	BK
Goltz, Dave, Minn	3.36	20	11	.645	39	39	19	0	0	2	303	284	1253	129	113	23	7	5	91	2	4	186	9	1
Grilli, Steve, Det	4.81	1	2	.333	30	2	0	13	0	0	73	71	326	42	39	19	5	1	49	2	2	44	5	1
Grimsley, Ross, Balt.	3.96	14	10	.583	34	34	11	0	0	5	218	230	923	105	96	24	8	7	74	2	4	53	2	0
Guidry, Ron, N.Y.*	2.82	16	7	.696	31	25	9	4	1	0	211	174	850	72	66	12	6	5	65	1	0	176	6	0
Gullett, Don, N.Y.*	3.59	14	4	.778	22	22	7	0	0	0	158	137	667	67	63	14	3	4	69	1	1	116	6	0
Gura, Larry, K.C.*	3.14	8	5	.615	52	6	1	24	10	0	106	108	445	43	37	8	2	4	28	4	1	46	0	1
Haas, Bryan, Milw	4.32	10	12	.455	32	32	6	0	0	0	198	195	844	104	95	21	5	7	84	4	1	113	7	0
Hall, Tom, K.C.*	3.38	0	0	.000	6	0	0	2	0	0	8	7	32	3	3	2	0	0	6	0	0	6	0	0
Hamilton, Dave, Chgo	3.63	4	5	.444	55	0	0	19	6	0	67	71	307	33	27	7	2	5	45	5	0	41	4	0
Hargan, Steve, To-6, Te-6	6.37	2	3	.400	12	5	1	2	0	0	40	58	198	30	29	8	1	4	15	0	0	21	1	0
Hartenstein, Chuck, Tor	6.67	0	2	.000	10	0	0	6	0	0	18	30	123	22	22	4	2	0	7	1	0	15	0	0
Hartzell, Paul, Calif	3.57	6	10	.400	41	23	6	12	4	0	189	200	793	92	75	14	9	4	38	6	6	79	3	1
Hassler, Andy, K.C.	4.21	9	6	.600	29	27	6	1	0	0	156	166	701	88	73	7	8	6	75	0	4	83	6	1
Hernandez, Ramon, Bos.*	5.54	0	0	.000	5	0	0	3	0	0	13	14	58	10	8	1	0	0	7	1	0	8	1	0
Hiller, John, Det.*	3.56	8	14	.364	45	8	7	21	7	0	124	120	539	59	49	15	5	7	61	3	2	115	6	0
Hinds, Sam, Milw	4.75	0	3	.000	29	1	0	11	0	0	72	77	324	42	38	5	0	3	40	3	1	46	3	0
Holdsworth, Fred, Balt	6.43	0	1	.000	18	1	0	6	0	0	48	57	207	37	34	10	2	1	32	1	2	14	2	0
Holly, Jeff, Minn.*	6.94	2	3	.400	11	4	0	1	0	0	29	45	164	27	22	7	0	1	7	3	1	11	1	1
Holtzman, Ken, N.Y.*	5.75	2	3	.400	18	11	1	4	0	0	72	105	336	55	46	7	6	2	24	2	3	14	1	0
Honeycutt, Rick, Sea.*	4.34	5	7	.417	25	15	1	5	0	0	122	126	523	66	59	16	7	4	49	3	7	62	2	1
Hood, Don, Clev*	3.00	2	1	.667	41	1	0	17	1	0	105	97	440	47	35	12	6	0	25	3	7	45	4	0
House, Tom, Bo-8, Se-26*	4.64	5	5	.500	34	0	0	9	1	0	143	137	608	83	74	16	5	5	47	4	0	52	1	2
Hughes, Jim, Minn	2.25	0	0	.000	4	0	0	2	0	0	4	4	18	1	1	0	0	0	3	0	0	2	0	0
Hunter, Catfish, N.Y.	4.72	9	9	.500	33	33	8	0	0	1	143	137	938	75	74	29	3	3	47	2	1	52	2	1
Jefferson, Jesse, Tor	4.31	9	17	.346	33	33	12	0	0	1	217	224	790	123	104	23	8	0	83	2	0	114	3	1
Jenkins, Fergie, Bos	3.68	10	10	.500	28	28	11	0	0	2	193	190	790	91	79	30	10	4	36	1	2	105	2	0
Johnson, Bart, Chgo	4.01	4	5	.444	29	6	3	11	0	0	92	86	426	48	41	9	5	4	46	3	3	33	3	0
Johnson, Dave, Minn	4.56	2	5	.286	43	3	0	16	2	0	86	91	320	50	44	7	5	2	23	4	4	54	3	0
Johnson, Jerry, Tor	4.60	2	4	.333	43	0	0	25	5	0	91	91	392	52	47	11	8	4	37	8	5	87	10	3
Johnson, Tom, Minn	3.12	16	7	.696	71	0	0	54	15	0	147	152	403	57	51	10	6	8	47	4	1	87	0	1
Jones, Rick, Sea*	5.14	1	4	.200	10	10	1	0	0	0	39	47	201	24	22	7	4	4	16	0	4	16	3	2
Kekich, Mike, Sea.	5.60	5	4	.556	41	7	0	19	0	0	90	90	401	55	56	10	8	2	55	5	6	55	5	1
Keough, Matt, Oak	4.81	1	3	.250	7	6	0	0	0	0	43	47	181	25	23	4	3	1	22	0	1	23	1	0
Kern, Jim, Clev	3.42	10	10	.444	60	0	0	46	18	0	122	99	253	53	35	13	3	4	47	6	1	91	4	0
Kirkwood, Don, Ca-13, Ch-16	5.12	4	7	.632	29	27	2	1	0	0	146	166	664	89	83	18	6	8	50	0	6	34	2	0
Knapp, Chris, Chgo	4.81	12	7	.632	27	26	4	0	0	0	146	166	664	90	78	16	6	1	61	1	7	103	5	1
Knowles, Darold, Tex.*	3.24	2	4	.333	26	0	0	27	7	0	35	35	216	22	18	1	0	2	23	0	6	14	2	0
Kravec, Ken, Chgo*	4.10	11	8	.579	26	25	7	1	0	0	167	161	718	87	76	12	11	0	57	2	6	125	4	1
Kreuger, Rick, Bos.*	—	0	1	.000	3	0	0	0	0	0	8	10	40	4	4	2	0	0	7	0	0	4	0	0
Kucek, Jack, Chgo	3.60	0	0	.000	8	3	0	1	0	0	35	35	148	20	14	4	2	0	10	0	2	25	1	0
Kuhaulua, Fred, Calif*	16.62	0	1	.000	3	0	0	3	0	0	4	15	40	8	8	1	1	1	7	0	0	7	1	0
Lacey, Bob, Oak*	2.45	6	8	.429	64	0	0	29	7	0	99	81	400	46	27	13	17	4	35	3	4	69	4	0
LaGrow, Lerrin, Chgo	2.45	7	3	.700	66	0	0	49	25	0	122	81	492	46	27	13	17	4	35	3	4	63	11	1
Langford, Rick, Oak	4.02	7	9	.296	37	31	8	2	0	0	208	223	901	107	93	18	9	3	73	3	1	141	3	0
Lance, Gary, K.C.	4.50	0	1	.000	2	0	0	1	0	0	2	2	10	1	1	0	0	0	2	0	0	0	0	0

Player	ERA	W	L	PCT	G	GS	CG	IP	H	R	ER	BB	SO
LaRoche, Dave, Cl-13, Ca-46*	3.51	8	7	.533	59	0	0	100	79	44	39	50	79
Laxton, Bill, Se-43, Cl-2*	4.92	3	2	.600	45	0	0	74	64	45	41	17	50
Lee, Bill, Bos.*	4.43	9	5	.643	27	16	2	128	155	67	63	31	87
Lemanczyk, Dave, Tor	4.25	13	16	.448	38	34	11	252	246	143	119	105	105
Leonard, Dennis, K.C.	3.04	20	12	.625	38	37	21	293	246	117	99	79	244
Lindblad, Paul, Tex.*	4.18	4	4	.500	44	0	0	99	103	50	46	27	46
Littell, Mark, K.C.	3.60	8	4	.667	48	0	0	105	73	49	42	55	106
Lyle, Sparky, N.Y.*	2.17	13	5	.722	72	0	0	137	131	41	33	33	68
MacCormack, Frank, Sea	3.86	0	2	.000	12	4	0	44	554	31	19	12	10
Marshall, Mike, Tex.	4.00	7	2	.667	42	0	0	167	159	86	64	13	4
Martinez, Dennis, Balt	4.10	14	7	.667	42	13	5	167	708	86	76	64	107
Martinez, Silvio, Chgo	5.57	0	1	.500	12	4	0	36	157	19	16	13	18
Martinez, Tippy, Balt.*	2.70	5	1	.833	40	0	0	42	199	14	14	27	10
May, Rudy, Balt.*	3.61	18	14	.563	41	37	11	252	210	114	101	78	29
McCall, Larry, N.Y	7.50	0	0	.000	2	0	0	6	33	6	5	7	105
McCatty, Steve, Oak	5.14	1	2	.000	11	2	0	12	306	8	7	5	1
McClure, Bob, Milw.*	2.54	2	1	.667	68	0	0	71	64	25	20	34	57
McGilberry, Randy, K.C.	5.14	0	0	.000	5	0	0	7	302	4	4	1	9
McGregor, Scott, Balt.*	4.42	3	5	.375	29	9	1	114	480	56	56	30	55
McLaughlin, Byron, Sea	36.00	0	0	.000	2	0	0	1	5	4	4	7	0
Medich, Doc, Oa-26, Se-3	4.55	12	0	.667	29	28	2	170	181	98	86	53	77
Miller, Dyar, Ba-12, Cr-41	3.55	6	6	.500	53	0	0	115	106	49	45	40	58
Miller, Randolph, Balt	27.00	0	0	.000	3	0	0	1	8	3	3	1	0
Mingori, Steve, K.C.*	3.09	4	2	.333	43	0	0	64	59	26	22	19	19
Mitchell, Craig, Oak	7.50	0	3	.000	3	1	0	6	9	5	5	4	4
Mitchell, Paul, Oe-5, Se-9	6.33	6	9	.250	37	12	0	53	71	42	38	23	33
Monge, Sid, Ca-4, Cl-33	5.47	4	8	.333	14	0	0	51	61	31	31	33	75
Montague, John, Sea	4.30	8	12	.400	47	16	1	182	254	95	87	10	10
Moore, Balor, Calif.*	3.91	2	3	.000	15	8	0	23	193	20	19	21	21
Moore, Tommy, Sea	4.91	3	0	.667	14	3	0	33	796	19	10	38	38
Moret, Roger, Tex.*	3.75	3	0	.500	7	1	0	72	36	47	44	23	30
Morris, Jack, Det	4.77	1	1	.500	7	6	1	46	155	30	44	20	28
Murphy, Tom, Bc-16, To-19	0.00	0	0	.000	35	1	0	83	189	38	30	1	0
Newman, Jeff, Oak	9.00	0	0	.000	1	0	0	1	374	1	1	0	0
Nolan, Gary, Calif	4.79	3	2	.000	5	5	0	18	89	10	10	4	4
Norris, Mike, Oak	6.14	2	7	.222	16	12	1	77	31	54	52	35	55
Pagan, Dave, Sea	2.91	2	1	.667	24	4	0	66	77	45	45	26	30
Palmer, Jim, Balt	2.91	20	11	.645	39	39	22	319	335	86	300	99	193
Parrott, Mike, Balt	2.25	0	0	.000	4	1	0	4	263	2	1	1	7
Patterson, Gil, N.Y	5.45	1	2	.333	10	10	4	33	1269	20	20	18	20
Pattin, Marty, K.C	3.59	8	10	.769	31	6	0	128	156	56	51	37	55
Paxton, Mike, Bos	3.83	10	5	.667	31	12	2	108	115	53	46	25	58
Pazik, Mike, Minn.*	2.50	0	2	.000	29	4	0	18	529	7	4	1	6
Perry, Gaylord, Tex.	3.37	15	12	.556	34	34	13	238	134	108	89	56	177
Pole, Dick, Sea	5.16	7	12	.368	34	25	6	122	467	70	70	57	6
Poloni, John, Tex.*	6.43	1	0	1.000	2	1	0	7	986	5	5	1	51
Redfern, Pete, Minn	5.19	6	9	.400	30	28	1	137	8	79	29	66	73

*Pitches Lefthanded

Player and Club	ERA	W	L	PCT	G	GS	CG	GF	SV	SHO	IP	H	BFP	R	ER	HR	SH	SF	TBB	IBB	HP	SO	WP	BK
Renko, Steven, Chgo	3.57	5	5	.500	11	8	0	0	0	0	53	55	223	23	21	3	2	2	17	1	1	36	0	0
Roberts, Dave, Det.*	5.16	2	5	.286	22	22	5	1	0	0	129	143	570	88	74	20	3	3	41	2	3	46	2	1
Rodriguez, Edward, Milw	4.34	5	6	.455	42	5	1	22	4	0	143	126	602	70	69	15	6	4	56	3	6	104	1	1
Romo, Enrique, Sea	2.84	8	10	.444	58	3	0	39	16	0	114	93	461	41	36	8	4	4	39	5	1	105	1	1
Ross, Gary, Calif	4.59	2	4	.333	14	12	0	1	0	0	58	83	260	41	36	10	6	2	11	1	2	30	2	2
Rozema, Dave, Det	3.10	15	7	.682	28	28	16	0	0	4	218	222	890	92	75	25	2	7	34	0	2	92	2	2
Ruhle, Vern, Det	5.73	3	5	.375	14	10	0	1	0	0	66	83	294	44	42	9	5	2	15	2	9	37	2	2
Ryan, Nolan, Calif	2.77	19	16	.543	37	37	22	0	0	4	299	198	1272	110	92	12	22	10	204	2	7	341	21	3
Schueler, Ron, Minn	4.40	8	7	.533	52	7	0	21	3	0	135	131	587	74	66	11	16	0	61	6	0	75	4	3
Scott, Mickey, Calif.*	5.63	0	0	.000	12	0	0	4	0	0	16	19	97	11	10	2	0	1	6	0	1	7	1	0
Segui, Diego, Sea.	5.68	0	7	.000	40	7	0	18	1	0	111	108	481	75	70	10	20	4	43	3	0	91	1	0
Serum, Gary, Minn	4.30	0	0	.000	8	0	0	2	0	0	23	22	97	11	11	4	1	0	10	1	1	14	0	0
Shellenback, Jim, Minn*	7.50	0	0	.000	5	0	0	1	0	0	6	10	32	5	5	1	0	0	5	0	0	3	1	0
Simpson, Wayne, Calif	5.63	6	12	.333	27	23	0	0	0	0	122	154	576	90	79	14	3	4	62	3	3	55	8	0
Singer, Bill, Tor.	6.75	2	8	.200	13	12	0	0	0	0	60	71	248	54	45	5	8	3	39	1	8	33	3	1
Slaton, Jim, Milw	3.58	10	14	.417	32	31	7	1	0	3	221	223	942	104	88	25	8	9	77	4	1	104	1	3
Sorensen, Lary, Milw	4.37	10	12	.412	37	37	9	0	0	1	229	243	984	72	69	11	4	5	36	1	1	99	5	1
Splittorff, Paul, K.C.*	3.69	16	6	.727	37	37	10	0	0	1	229	243	980	104	94	11	16	6	83	3	2	99	5	3
Stanley, Bob, Bos	3.99	8	7	.533	41	13	0	13	0	0	151	176	651	74	67	10	9	3	43	1	2	44	1	1
Stephenson, Earl, Balt.*	9.00	0	0	.000	3	0	0	3	0	0	3	5	14	4	3	0	0	0	3	0	0	2	0	0
Stone, Steve, Chgo	4.52	15	12	.556	31	31	8	0	0	0	207	228	917	115	104	25	13	6	80	3	5	124	10	1
Sykes, Bob, Det.*	4.40	5	7	.417	32	20	3	7	0	0	133	141	585	71	72	15	4	5	50	0	2	58	3	1
Tanana, Frank, Calif.*	2.54	15	9	.625	31	31	20	0	0	7	201	201	973	72	68	19	8	7	61	2	12	205	8	1
Taylor, Bruce, Det.*	3.41	0	0	1.000	19	0	0	12	0	0	29	23	118	11	11	2	0	0	15	1	0	19	4	0
Thomas, Stan, Se-13, N.Y.-3	6.19	1	3	.250	16	3	0	4	0	0	65	81	303	56	44	8	3	3	29	5	0	15	6	0
Thormodsgard, Paul, Minn	3.62	11	15	.423	37	37	8	0	0	1	218	236	926	122	112	25	8	6	65	1	1	94	6	0
Throop, Jim, K.C	3.60	0	0	.000	2	2	0	0	0	0	9	7	21	2	1	0	0	0	3	0	0	3	1	0
Tidrow, Dick, N.Y	4.32	12	4	.733	49	10	3	26	5	0	151	143	624	57	53	19	8	7	51	11	2	83	2	4
Torealba, Pablo, Oak.*	3.16	11	11	.500	35	2	0	17	0	0	92	94	507	45	34	5	8	7	38	0	1	51	3	0
Torrez, Mike, Oa-4, N.Y.-31	3.93	17	13	.567	35	35	17	0	0	2	243	235	1025	113	106	23	11	8	86	1	7	102	4	2
Travers, Bill, Milw.*	5.24	4	12	.250	15	15	0	0	0	0	122	140	558	75	71	13	7	3	57	5	3	49	11	0
Umbarger, Jim, Oa-12, Te-3*	6.32	2	6	.250	53	8	1	35	5	0	76	269	48	6	5	1	2	1	5	0	2	9	5	0
Verhoeven, John, Ca-3, Ch-6	3.00	2	0	.000	9	0	0	5	0	0	15	13	65	6	5	1	2	1	12	0	1	5	0	2
Vuckovich, Pete, Tor	3.47	7	7	.500	53	8	0	35	8	0	148	143	633	64	57	13	6	4	59	7	5	123	12	0
Waits, Rick, Clev.*	4.00	9	7	.563	37	16	5	9	0	2	135	132	581	67	60	13	11	2	64	7	0	62	6	0
Walker, Tom, Calif	9.00	0	0	.000	3	0	0	0	0	0	2	3	8	2	2	0	1	0	0	1	0	0	0	0
Wallace, Mike, Tex.*	7.88	0	0	.000	11	0	0	7	0	0	8	10	43	7	7	1	0	0	10	2	0	2	1	0
Wheelock, Gary, Sea	4.91	6	2	.750	20	17	4	0	0	0	88	94	441	48	48	13	4	2	26	6	0	47	0	0
Wilcox, Milt, Det	3.65	6	2	.750	20	13	1	4	0	0	106	96	446	46	43	11	2	5	37	1	1	82	1	0
Wiles, Randy, Chgo.*	9.00	0	0	.000	9	0	0	3	0	0	3	5	16	4	3	0	0	0	3	1	0	0	0	0
Willis, Mike, Tor.*	3.95	2	6	.250	43	9	0	16	2	0	107	105	434	48	47	15	5	0	59	2	0	59	2	0
Willoughby, Jim, Bos	4.91	6	7	.500	43	0	0	17	10	0	128	139	555	68	68	10	13	3	18	6	2	33	1	0
Wise, Rick, Bos.	4.78	11	5	.689	26	26	20	1	0	3	128	139	548	75	68	19	1	1	50	0	10	85	0	2
Wood, Wilbur, Chgo.*	4.11	7	8	.467	24	24	18	2	0	0	123	139	548	75	68	10	11	1	28	1	1	42	1	0
Zahn, Geoff, Minn.*	4.68	12	14	.462	34	32	7	0	0	1	198	234	870	116	103	20	10	7	66	4	5	88	5	0

COSELL continued from page 17

"I learned my runner-stunner from Muhammad Ali," Cosell quips.

OAKLAND, Aug. 16—Cosell knows everything except how to chew tobacco. It isn't simply a matter of how to chew, but how much to put in a Cosell mouth.

"How big's your foot?" asks Sparky Lyle, offering a chaw.

Cosell stuffs a wad in his mouth, grimaces, gulps and purpose-fully strides to the plate to present his lineup card. The sight of Cosell with his stuffed cheek convulses plate umpire Ron Luciano. "Hey, Howard, did Reggie hit you?"

Cosell gags, dribbling tobacco juice on his Yankee pinstripes.

ANAHEIM, Aug. 22—The pennant race is heating up. The Boston Red Sox and the Baltimore Orioles are pressuring the Yankees and threatening to overtake them in the standings. The 11½-game lead the Yankees had under Martin has shrunk to 1½ games. Except, Cosell hasn't noticed. He has been too busy making sure his toupee looks right under his cap and extricating his fingers from his eyes at third base.

But now even Cosell can see the ratings on the wall. He remembers all too well how his Saturday night television variety show had bombed and he isn't about to let this variety show bomb, too. He takes immediate corrective action.

First, he throws Steinbrenner out of the dugout and tells him if he, Howard, is running the team on the field, he, George, will have to return to his seat in his private box.

"I know, George," Howard says, "that in the past you have been generous enough to allow me the privilege of witnessing games from your locale, but this is war, George, and the troops have to see that there is only one leader. There is no room for Patton and MacArthur in the same foxhole."

Next, he begins taking batting practice before games.

"I want to show my men I'm with them every step of the way," Cosell explains, "from the batting cage to the bullpen. There will be no pretense here. Here, boy, throw that spheroid right in here and I'll show them how I can make the necessary contact between bat and ball to send it to the distant crevices of the edifice."

For step No. 3, he benches Reggie Jackson, the team's cleanup hitter who has the only bigger mouth on the team than his.

"There shall be only one vacuous vesicle of verbosity around here," Howard proclaims.

That is only one of Cosell's commandments. The others:

● There shall be no other manager before thee.

- Thou shalt not spit tobacco juice on my shiny black tassle loafers.
- Thou shalt listen attentively every day, before every game, to my well-chosen words of wisdom.
- There shall be periodic uplifting discussions of baseball's exemption from the anti-trust laws with me as the discussion leader, of course.
- There shall be 90-second breaks between innings so the fans can get a longer look at me on the coaching lines.
- Thou shalt not kill my ratings.
- Thou shalt carry dictionaries with thee so thou can understand that on which I discourse.
- Thou shalt talk only to television newsmen and those from ABC at that.
- Thou shalt not take the name of thy manager in vain.

NEW YORK, Sept. 15—Despite the moves with Steinbrenner and Jackson and the issuance of Cosell's commandments etched in teleprompter, the Yankees enter a three-game series with the Red Sox at Yankee Stadium in a virtual tie for first place with Boston.

It is the ninth inning and Nestor Chylak, the league's senior umpire, has called Chris Chambliss out in a close play at the plate. Cosell is enraged. He rushes toward the plate from his coaching box, floating like a butterfly, stinging like a bee. He remonstrates with Chylak, jabbing at the area above the umpire's head with his long, bony forefinger.

"I am," Howie tells Nestor, "unchanging in my objection to the anomaly we have in which baseball is exempt from the anti-trust laws. I've testified six times before Senate and House committees on that. I'm unchanging in my opposition to the carpetbagging of franchises. My objection is to baseball operations when I think they are not in the public interest. Besides that, I think he was safe."

NEW YORK, Oct. 1—Yankee Stadium is overflowing, not unlike the manager's mouth. It is the last day of the season and the Yankees must win this game against Cleveland to clinch the pennant.

"Gentlemen," Cosell addresses his troops in his 81st consecutive clubhouse meeting, "I needn't tell you the importance of this confrontation. It is the ultimate game of our season, that is, the ultimate game if we lose. If we prevail—and we must prevail—we will have additional ultimate games. But for the moment, the moment at hand, at this point in time, this is the ultimate confrontation. If any of you have any doubts about our ability to conquer today's obstreperous foe, I suggest you remove your sporting apparel, replace them with your civilian attire and hastily depart the premises. I want only those men with me out on the field of battle who will march boldly to victory evermore. Now, gentlemen, let us assemble and seek in our own way the divine leadership that will transport our aggregation to our ultimate conquest. . . . Oh, great television eye in the sky, see to it that we are not canceled here today, that we may prevail in this ratings imbroglio and proceed to a recompense infinitely greater than even an Emmy award."

Whether it was the players or Howard or divine intervention—no one, not even Nielsen, knows for sure—the Yankees won that day and then they proceeded to thrash thoroughly the Texas Rangers, their dastardly opponents in the American League pennant playoffs. Now it was time for the World Series and the Los Angeles Dodgers were back to try and win the championship they believed should be theirs. It was the classic confrontation: the great Dodger in the sky versus the great television eye in the sky.

Fans all over the country eagerly anticipated the clash. Cosell and Lasorda—no one would get a word in edgewise.

The Series would go all seven games, with each game a scintillating thriller down to the last out. The games were so titanic, in fact, that each lasted so long it seemed to run into the next. Fireball pitches. Crunching blows with the bat. Vicious slides. Diving, tumbling, rolling catches.

But was it really that way, Howard?

Cosell, you see, was a rabid Dodger fan as a younger man (yes, he once was younger). He lived, breathed and ate Dodgers. Lasorda thinks he has Dodger blue blood? He should cut Cosell; his blood is bluer.

And even though these Dodgers now played in Los Angeles, they were still Howard's Dodgers and he realized it the moment they stepped onto the field for the first game. Their names now were Garvey and Cey and Baker and Smith and Russell and Yeager and Lopes and Sutton, but when Howard gazed at them, all he could see were Brooklyn Dodgers.

Jackie, hey Jackie! Pee Wee, there's Pee Wee! And Duke, the Duker is back! And look, there's Big Newk and Campy and Carl and Coxie! They're all here, the guys are all here. And Branch must be around somewhere, too. Branch. . . .

Like Little Black Sambo's tiger, Howard dissolved into a pool of melted butter. He never knew that his Yankees lost; his Dodgers won the World Series.

OFFICIAL NATIONAL LEAGUE SCHEDULE — 1978

EAST

1978	AT CHICAGO	AT MONTREAL	AT NEW YORK	AT PHILADELPHIA	AT PITTSBURGH	AT ST. LOUIS
CHICAGO		May 29*, 30*, 31* August 11*, 12*, **13** Sept. 8, 9*, **10**	April 10, 11, 12 July 6*, 7*, 8, **9** Sept. 11*, 12*	April 24*, 25*, 26* June 23(TN),24*, **25** Sept. 13*, 14	April 7, 8, **9** June 19*, 20*, 21* Sept. 25*, 26*, 27*	May 26*, 27*, **28** July 3*, 4*, 5* Sept. 22*, 23, 24
MONTREAL	April 18, 19, 20 Aug. 4, 5, **6**, **6** Sept. 4, 5		April 7, 8, **9**, **9** June 20*, 21*, 22* Sept. 13*, 14*	April 11*, 12* July 6*, 7*, 8(TN), **9** Sept. 26*, 27*	May 26*, 27*, **28** July 3*, 4, 4 Sept. 15*, 16, **17**	May 23*, 24*, **25** June 23*, 24*, **25** Sept. 29*, 30 Oct. **1**
NEW YORK	April 21, 22, **23** June 29, 30 Sept. 29, 30 Oct. **1**	April 14, 15, **16** May 10*, 11* Aug. 8*, 9* Sept. 6*, 7*		May 5*, 6*, **7** July 31* Aug. 1*, 2 Sept. 15*, 16*, **17**	May 23*, 24*, 25* June 29*, 30* July 1*, **2** Sept. 4, 4	April 17*, 18*, 19 Aug. 4*, 5*, **6** Sept. 19*, 20*, 21*
PHILADELPHIA	May 23, 24, 25 June 29, 30 July 1, **2** Sept. 6, 7	April 21, 22, **23** June 26*, 27*, 28* Sept. 19*, 20*, 21*	April 24*, 25*, 26* June 23*, 24, **25** Sept. 8*, 9*, **10**		April 17*, 18* Aug. 4*, 5, **6** Sept. 29, 30 Oct. **1**	April 14*, 15, **16** Aug. 7*, 8(TN), 9* Sept. 4, 4
PITTSBURGH	April 14, 15, **16** Aug. 7, 8, 9 Sept. 19, 20, 21	May 19*, 20, **21**, 22 July 31* Aug. 1*, 2 Sept. 23, **24**	May 19*, 20, **21** July 3*, 4(TN) Sept. 22*, 23, **24**	May 29*, 30*, 31* Aug. 10*, 11*, 12*, **13** Sept. 11*, 12*		April 10*, 11*, 12, **13** July 6*, 7*, 8(TN), 9* Sept. 6*, 7*
ST. LOUIS	May 19, 20, **21** August 1, 2, 3 Sept. 15, 16, **17**	April 24, 25, 26 June 30* July 1, 2, **2** Sept. 11*, 12*	May 29(TN), 30*, 31* Aug. 11*, 12, **13** Sept. 25*, 26*	April 7*, 8*, **9** June 20*, 21*,22* Sept. 8*, 9*, **10**	April 20, 21*, 22, **23** June 26*, 27*, 28* Sept. 13*, 14*	

ATLANTA	June 2, 3, **4** / Aug. 14, 15, 16	May 12* 13, **14** / July 19(TN), 20*	May 16* 17* 18* / July 21* 22, **23**	June 9* 10* **11** / July 24, 25, 26*	June 5* 6* / Sept. 1(TN), 2, **3**	June 7* 8 / Aug. 17* 18* 19* **20**
CINCINNATI	June 7, 8 / Aug. 17, 18, 19, **20**	May 16* 17* 18* / July 21, 22, **23**	April 28* 29, **30** / July 24* 25* 26	May 11* 12* 13* **14** / July 19* 20*	June 9* 10, **11** / Aug. 14* 15* 16*	June 5* 6* / August 31* / Sept. 1*, 2, **3**
HOUSTON	June 5, 6 / Sept. 1, 2, **3**, **3**	May 2* 3* / July 13* 14* 15* **16**	May 12* 13, **14**, **14** / July 19* 20	May 8* 9* 10* / July 21* 22* **23**	June 7* 8* / Aug. 17* 18* 19* **20**	June 9* 10* **11** / Aug. 14* 15* 16
LOS ANGELES	May 2, 3, 4 / July **16**, **16**, 17	June 8* 9* 10* **11** / Aug. 21* 23*	June 5* 6* 7* / Aug. 18* 19* **20**	June 2* 3* **4** / Aug. 15* 16* 17*	May 5* 6, **7** / July 18* 19* 20	April 28* 29* **30** / July 13* 14* 15*
SAN DIEGO	June 9, 10, **11** / July 13, 14, 15	June 5* 6* 7* / Aug. 18* 19* **20**	June 2* 3* **4** / Aug. 15* 16* 17*	April 28* 29, **30** / Aug. 21* 22, 23	May 1* 2* 3* / July **16**, **16**, 17*	May 5* 6* **7** / July 18* 19* 20
SAN FRANCISCO	May 5, 6, **7** / July 18, 19, 20	June 2* 3* **4** / Aug. 15* 16* 17*	June 9* 10, **11** / Aug. 21* 22* 23	June 5* 6* 7* / Aug. 18* 19* 20*	April 28* 29, **30** / July 13* 14* 15	May 1* 2, 3* 4 / July **16**, 17*

*NIGHT GAME
HEAVY BLACK FIGURES DENOTE SUNDAY
NIGHT GAME: Any game starting after 5:00 P.M.

JULY 11 – ALL STAR GAME AT SAN DIEGO STADIUM

OFFICIAL NATIONAL LEAGUE SCHEDULE — 1978

WEST

1978	AT ATLANTA	AT CINCINNATI	AT HOUSTON	AT LOS ANGELES	AT SAN DIEGO	AT SAN FRANCISCO
CHICAGO	April 28*, 29*, 30 Aug. 28*, 29*, 30*	June 12*, 13*, 14 Aug. 25*, 26, 27	June 16*, 17*, 18* Aug. 21*, 22*, 23*	May 12*, 13*, 14 July 24*, 25*, 26*	May 9*, 10*, 11 July 21*, 22*, 23	May 16*, 17 July 28*, 29, 30, 30
MONTREAL	May 8*, 9* July 28(TN), 29*, 30	May 5*, 6, 7, 7 July 17*, 18*	April 28*, 29*, 30 July 24*, 25*, 26*	June 16*, 17*, 18 Aug. 28*, 29*, 30*	June 14(TN), 15 August 31 Sept. 1*, 2*	June 12, 13* Aug. 25*, 26, 27, 27
NEW YORK	May 1*, 2*, 3*, 4* July 17*, 18*	May 8*, 9* July 13* 14*, 15* 16	May 26*, 27*, 28 July 27*, 28*, 30*	June 14*, 15* Sept. 1*, 2, 2, 3	June 12*, 13* Aug. 24*, 25*, 26*, 27	June 16*, 17*, 18, 18 Aug. 29*, 30
PHILADELPHIA	May 26*, 27*, 28 July 14*, 15*, 16	May 1*, 3* July 28(TN), 29, 30	May 15*, 16*, 17*, 18* July 17*, 18*	June 12*, 13* Aug.24*, 25*, 26*, 27	June 16*, 17*, 18 Aug. 28*, 29*, 30*	June 14, 15 Sept. 1*, 2, 3, 3
PITTSBURGH	June 16*, 17*, 18 Aug. 22*, 23*, 24*	June 2*, 3*, 4 Aug. 28*, 29*, 30*	June 12*, 13*, 14* Aug. 25*, 26*, 27	May 15*, 16*, 17* July 28*, 29*, 30	May 12*, 13*, 14 July 25*, 26*, 27	May 9*, 10, 11 July 21*, 22*, 23
ST. LOUIS	June 12*, 13*, 14* Aug. 25*, 26*, 27	June 16*, 17, 18 Aug. 21*, 22*, 24*	June 2*, 3(TN), 4 Aug. 29*, 30*	May 9*, 10*, 11* July 21*, 22*, 23	May 15*, 16*, 17 July 28*, 29*, 30	May 12*, 13, 14, 14 July 25*, 26

	Atlanta	Cincinnati	Houston	Los Angeles	San Diego	San Francisco
ATLANTA		May 22*, 23*, 24 Aug. 7*, 8*, **9** Sept. 29*, 30 October **1**	May 19*, 20*, **21** Aug. 11*, 12*, **13** Sept. 19*, 20*, 21*	April 14*, 15*, **16** July 3*, 4*, 5* Sept. 15*, 16*, **17**	April 20, 21*, 22*, **23** June 20*, 21*, 22 Sept. 11*, 12*	April 17, 18*, 19 June 23*, 24*, **25, 25** Sept. 13, 14
CINCINNATI	May 29*, 30*, 31* July 31* Sept. 22*, 23*, **24**		April 14*, 15*, **16** June 26*, 27*, 28*, 29 Sept. 4*, 5*	April 17*, 18*, 19* June 23*, 24, **25** Sept. 18*, 19*, 20*	May 26*, 27*, **28** Aug. 10*, 11*, 12*, **13** Sept. 13*, 14*	April 21*, 22, **23** June 20*, 21* 22* Sept. 15*, 16, **17**
HOUSTON	May 5*, 6*, **7** Aug. 4*, 5*, **6** Sept. 26*, 27*, 28*	April 6, 7, 8, **9** July 3*, 4*, 5* Sept. 11*, 12		April 20*, 21*, 22*, **23** June 20*, 21*, 22 Sept. 13*, 14*	April 18*, 19* June 23*, 24*, **25, 25** Sept. 15*, 16*, **17**	May 23*, 24, 25 Aug. 8*, 9 Sept. 22*, 23, **24, 24**
LOS ANGELES	April 7*, 8, **9** June 26*, 27* 28*, 29* Sept. 9*, **10**	April 25*, 26* June 30 (TN) July 1*, 2 Sept. 26*, 27*, 28*	April 10*, 11*, 12* July 7*, 8 (TN), **9** Sept. 7*, 8*		May 22*, 23*, 24* July 31* Aug. 1*, 2 Sept. 29*, 30 October **1**	May 26*, 27, **28** Aug. 3*, 4*, 5, **6** Sept. 11*, 12*
SAN DIEGO	April 10*, 11*, 12* July 7*, 8*, **9** Sept. 4*, 5*, 6*	May 19*, 20* **21, 21** Aug. 4*, 5*, 6 Sept. 7*, 8*	April 24*, 25*, 26* June 30* July 1 (TN), **2** Sept. 9*, **10**	May 29*, 30*, 31* Aug. 7*, 8*, 9* Sept. 22*, 23, **24**		April 7, 8, 9 July 3, 4, 5, **6** Sept. 26*, 27
SAN FRANCISCO	April 25*, 26*, 27* June 30 (TN) July 1*, **2** Sept. 7*, 8*	April 11*, 12*, 13 July 7 (TN), 8*, **9** Sept. 9*, **10**	May 29*, 30*, 31* July 31* Aug. 1*, 2 Sept. 29*, 30 October **1**	May 19*, 20*, **21** Aug. 10*, 11*, 12*, **13** Sept. 4*, 5*	April 14*, 15*, **16** June 26*, 27*, 28* Sept. 19*, 20*, 21*	

JULY 11 – ALL STAR GAME AT SAN DIEGO STADIUM

*NIGHT GAME

HEAVY BLACK FIGURES DENOTE SUNDAY

NIGHT GAME: Any game starting after 5:00 P.M.

1978 OFFICIAL AMERICAN LEAGUE SCHEDULE

(Note: Oakland/Denver was unresolved at press time.)

*NIGHT GAMES   TN – TWI-NIGHT DOUBLEHEADERS

	AT SEATTLE	AT OAKLAND or DENVER	AT CALIFORNIA	AT TEXAS	AT KANSAS CITY	AT MINNESOTA	AT CHICAGO
SEATTLE		April 10*, 11*, 12*, 13; Aug. 4*, 5, 6	April 24*, 25*, 26*, 27*; July 7*, 8 TN, 9	May 26 TN, 27*, 28*; Sept. 22*, 23*, 24(2)	May 29*, 31*; June 1*; July 26*, 27*; Sept. 25*, 26*, 27*	April 14, 15, 16(2); Aug. 7*, 8*, 9*	June 19*, 20*, 21*; Sept. 7, 8*, 9, 10
OAKLAND or DENVER	April 21*, 22* 23; July 3*, 4*, 5*, 6*		April 7*, 8*, 9; July 31*; Aug. 1*, 2*, 3*	May 17*, 18*; June 19*, 20*, 21; Sept. 15*, 16*, 17	June 23 TN, 24*, 25; Sept. 11*, 12*, 13*, 14*	April 17, 18, 19; Aug. 11*, 12, 13(2)	May 26*, 27, 28(2); July 26*, 27*; Sept. 25, 26*
CALIFORNIA	April 17*, 18*, 19*; Aug. 11*, 12 TN, 13	April 14*, 15, 16; June 7*, 8*; Aug. 7*, 8*, 10*		June 22*, 23*, 24*, 25*; Sept. 11*, 12*, 13*, 14*	July 3*, 4*, 5*, 6*; Sept. 15*, 16*, 17	April 21*, 22, 23; June 20*, 21*; Sept. 18*, 19*	May 17*, 18, 29, 30*, 31; Sept. 22*, 23, 24
TEXAS	May 19 TN, 20*, 21; Sept. 28*, 29*, 30*; Oct. 1	June 27 TN, 28*, 29; Sept. 8*, 9, 10(2)	June 30*; July 1*, 2; Sept. 4*, 5*, 6*, 7*		June 12*, 13*; July 18*, 19*; Aug. 18*, 19, 20	May 22*, 23*, 24*, 25; Aug. 23*, 24; Sept. 22*, 23*, 24	June 14*, 15*; July 3*, 4*; July 28*, 29, 30(2)
KANSAS CITY	May 22*, 23 TN, 24*, 25; Sept. 18*, 19	June 30*; July 1, 2(2); Sept. 4*, 5*, 6	June 26*, 27*, 28*, 29*; Sept. 8*, 9 TN, 10	April 24*, 25*; June 6*, 7*, 8*; Aug. 25*, 26*, 27*		May 26*, 27, 28; Aug. 16*, 17*; Sept. 22*, 23*, 24	June 16*, 17, 18(2); Aug. 22*, 23*, 24*
MINNESOTA	April 5*, 6*, 7*, 8*, 9; Aug. 1*, 2*, 3*	April 24*, 25*, 26*, 27; July 7 TN, 8, 9	April 10*, 11*, 12*, 13; Aug. 4*, 5 TN, 6	May 29-TN, 30*; June 1*; Sept. 25*, 26*, 27*	May 18*, 19*, 20*, 21; Sept. 29*, 30*; Oct. 1		May 10*, 11*; June 23*, 24*, 25; Sept. 11*, 12*
CHICAGO	June 26*, 27*, 28*, 29*; Sept. 14*, 15*, 16*, 17	May 19*, 20, 21(2); Sept. 18*, 19 TN	May 23*, 24*, 25*; Sept. 28*, 29*, 30*; Oct. 1	June 9*, 10*, 11*; Aug. 14*, 15*, 16*, 17*	June 2*, 3*, 4; Aug. 7*, 8*, 28*, 29*, 30*	June 7*, 8*, 30*; July 1, 2; Sept. 4*, 5*, 6*	

MILWAUKEE	June 30* July 1*, 2 Sept. 11*, 12*	May 23*, 24* Sept. 29*, 30 Oct. 1	May 26*, 27*, 28 June 26*, 27*	May 15*, 16* July 21*, 22*, 23*	April 28*, 29*, 30 Sept. 20*, 21*	July 3*, 4*, 5* Sept. 8*, 9, 10	May 12*, 13*, 14 July 24*, 25*
DETROIT	April 28*, 29*, 30 July 13*, 14*	May 5*, 6, 7 July 18*, 19	May 2*, 3* July 15*, 16, 17*	April 11*, 12* July 7*, 8*, 9*	June 14*, 15* Sept. 1*, 2*, 3	June 16*, 17, 18 Aug. 21*, 22*	April 24*, 25*, 26 Aug. 11*, 12*, 13
CLEVELAND	May 2*, 3* July 15*, 16*, 17*	April 28*, 29, 30 July 13*, 14*	May 5*, 6*, 7 July 18*, 19*	April 26*, 27* Aug. 4*, 5*, 6*	April 14*, 15*, 16 June 19*, 20*, 21*	June 14*, 15* Sept. 1*, 2, 3	June 12*, 13* Aug. 25*, 26*, 27
TORONTO	May 5*, 6*, 7 July 18*, 19*	May 2*, 3* July 15, 16, 17*	April 28*, 29*, 30 July 13*, 14*	June 16 TN, 17*, 18* Aug. 28*, 29*	April 26*, 27* Aug. 4*, 5*, 6	July 26*, 27* Aug. 18*, 19, 20	April 11, 12 July 7*, 8, 9
BALTIMORE	June 2*, 3*, 4 Aug. 15*, 16*	June 9*, 10, 11 Aug. 21*, 22*, 23*	June 5*, 6* April 18*, 19*, 20	May 12*, 13*, 14 July 24*, 25*	April 10*, 12* July 7*, 8*, 9	May 15*, 16* July 21*, 22, 25	April 28*, 29*, 30 July 19*, 29*
NEW YORK	June 5*, 6*, 7* Aug. 18*, 19*, 20*	June 2*, 3, 4 Aug. 15*, 16*	June 9*, 10*, 11 Aug. 22*, 23*	April 8, 9, 10* July 5*, 6*	May 12*, 13*, 14 July 24, 25	April 28*, 29, 30 July 19*, 20*	May 15*, 16* July 21*, 22*, 23
BOSTON	June 9*, 10*, 11 Aug. 22*, 23*	June 5*, 6* Aug. 18*, 19, 20	June 2*, 3*, 4 Aug. 15*, 16*, 17*	April 28*, 29*, 30 July 26*, 27*	May 15*, 16* July 21*, 22, 23	May 12*, 13, 14 July 24*, 25*	April 7, 8, 9 July 5*, 6*

NOTE: ALL-STAR GAME AT SAN DIEGO STADIUM, JULY 11.

1978 OFFICIAL AMERICAN LEAGUE SCHEDULE

(Note: Oakland/Denver was unresolved at press time.)

*NIGHT GAMES   TN – TWI-NIGHT DOUBLEHEADERS

	AT MILWAUKEE	AT DETROIT	AT CLEVELAND	AT TORONTO	AT BALTIMORE	AT NEW YORK	AT BOSTON
SEATTLE	June 23*, 24*, 25 / Sept. 4(2)	May 15*, 16* / July 28*, 29, 30	May 9*, 10* / July 21*, 22, 23(2)	May 12*, 13, 14 / July 24*, 25*	June 12*, 13* / Aug. 25*, 26*, 27	June 14*, 15* / Sept. 1*, 2*, 3	June 16*, 17, 18¹ / Aug. 28*, 29*
OAKLAND or DENVER	May 29, 30* / Sept. 22*, 23, 24	May 12*, 13, 14 / July 24*, 25*	May 15*, 16 / July 28*, 29*, 30	May 8*, 9*, 10* / July 21*, 22*, 23	June 16*, 17*, 18 / Aug. 28*, 29*	June 12*, 13* / Aug. 25*, 26*, 27	June 14*, 15* / Sept. 1*, 2*, 3
CALIFORNIA	May 19*, 20*, 21 / July 26*, 27*	May 9*, 11* / July 21 TN, 22, 23	May 12*, 13, 14 / July 24*, 25*	May 15*, 16* / Sept. 1, 2, 3	June 14*, 15* / July 28*, 29*, 30	June 16*, 17*, 18 / Aug. 28*, 29*	June 12*, 13* / Aug. 25*, 26, 27
TEXAS	May 9*, 10* / Sept. 1*, 2*, 3	April 21, 22, 23 / Aug. 8*, 9*	April 17*, 18 / Aug. 11*, 12, 13	June 2*, 3*, 4 / Aug. 21, 22	May 3*, 4* / July 15*, 16, 17*, 18*	May 5*, 6, 7 / July 31* / Aug. 1*	April 14, 15, 16 / July 13*, 14*
KANSAS CITY	May 5*, 6*, 7 / July 13*, 14*	June 9*, 10, 11 / Aug. 14*, 15*	April 8, 9 / July 31* / Aug. 1*, 2*	April 17, 18 / Aug. 11*, 12*, 13	April 21*, 22*, 23 / Aug. 9*, 10*	May 1*, 2*, 3* / July 15*, 16, 17*	May 8*, 9* / July 28*, 29, 30
MINNESOTA	June 26*, 27* / Sept. 15*, 16*, 17	June 2*, 3, 4 / Aug. 29*, 31*	June 9*, 10*, 11 / Aug. 14*, 15*	June 12*, 13* / Aug. 25, 26, 27	May 5*, 6*, 7 / July 13*, 14*	May 8*, 9* / July 28*, 29, 30	May 3*, 4* / July 15, 16(2), 17*
CHICAGO	May 2*, 3* / July 15, 16, 17*, 18*	April 17, 18 / Aug. 4*, 5*, 6	June 5*, 6* / Aug. 18*, 19*, 20	April 21, 22, 23 / Aug. 9*, 10*	May 8 TN / Sept. 1*, 2*, 3	April 13, 15, 16 / July 13, 14*	May 5*, 6, 7 / July 31* / Aug. 1*

	MILWAUKEE	DETROIT	CLEVELAND	TORONTO	BALTIMORE	NEW YORK	BOSTON
MILWAUKEE		May 17*, 18 June 6*, 7* Aug. 18*, 19*, 20	May 31* June 1*, 12*, 13* Aug. 25*, 26, 27, 28	June 16*, 17, 18(2) June 29*, 30*, 31*	June 14 TN July 28*, 29, 30 Sept. 6*, 7*	April 14, 15, 16(2) July 2*, 3* Aug. 2*, 3*	April 21*, 22, 23 Aug. 8*, 9*, 10* Sept. 18*, 19*
DETROIT	May 2*, 3, 4(2) Aug. 22 TN, 23*, 24		April 19*, 20 June 27*, 28 TN Sept. 15*, 16, 17	April 14, 15, 16 June 20*, 21* July 31* Aug. 1*	May 23*, 24 TN, 25* Sept. 22, 23 TN, 24	June 30* July 1, 2(2), 5*, 6*	May 26*, 27, 28(2) Sept. 26*, 27*, 28*
CLEVELAND	June 9*, 10, 11(2) Aug. 15 TN, 16*, 17	July 5*, 6* Aug. 16*, 17* Sept. 8*, 9, 10		April 24, 25 June 30* July 1, 2(2) Sept. 4*, 5*	May 23*, 24 TN, 25* Sept. 29*, 30 Oct. 1	May 26*, 27 Sept. 29*, 30	April 21*, 22, 23(2) Aug. 8*, 9*, 10
TORONTO	June 9*, 10, 11(2) Aug. 15 TN, 16*, 17	April 6, 8, 9 July 3*, 4* Aug. 23 TN, 24*	June 7 TN, 23*, 24*, 25 Sept. 11*, 12*		April 24, 25 June 30* July 1, 2(2) Sept. 4*, 5*	May 17*, 18* July 5*, 6* Sept. 15*, 16, 17	May 29, 30*, 31* Aug. 30 TN Sept. 29*, 30 Oct. 1
BALTIMORE	April 6, 8, 9 June 20*, 21*, 22 Sept. 13*, 14*	May 29*, 30* July 26*, 27* Sept. 29*, 30 Oct. 1	May 19*, 20, 21(2) July 7*, 8* Sept. 18*, 19*	June 26*, 27 TN, 28* Aug. 7, 8* Sept. 8*, 9*		April 17*, 18 May 31* June 1 Aug. 4*, 5*, 6	May 1*, 2* June 23*, 24, 25 Sept. 11*, 12*
NEW YORK	April 11, 12 June 28 TN July 7*, 8*, 9	June 22*, 23*, 24*, 25 Sept. 12*, 13*, 14*	May 17*, 18*, 29*, 30* Sept. 12*, 13, 24	April 19*, 20, 21(2) May 19*, 20, 21(2) Sept. 20*, 21*	April 24*, 25* May 11*, 12*, 13, 14* Aug. 30*, 31*		June 19*, 20*, 21* July 3*, 4 Sept. 8*, 9, 10
BOSTON	April 25, 26 July 19*, 20* Aug. 4*, 5, 6	May 19*, 20, 21(2) Sept. 18*, 19*, 20* 21*	April 10, 12 July 7*, 8 TN, 9 Sept. 13*, 14*	May 22, 23*, 24*, 25* Sept. 22*, 23, 24	May 11*, 12* June 1*, 2 July 1*, 2 Sept. 4*, 5*	June 26*, 27* Aug. 2*, 3* Sept. 15*, 16, 17	

ALL-TIME MAJOR LEAGUE RECORDS

National	American

Batting (Season)
Average
.438 Hugh Duffy, Boston, 1894	.422 Napoleon Lajoie, Phila., 1901
.424 Rogers Hornsby, St. Louis, 1924	

At Bat
699 Dave Cash, Phila., 1975	692 Bobby Richardson, N.Y., 1962

Runs
196 William Hamilton, Phila., 1894	177 Babe Ruth, New York, 1921
158 Chuck Klein, Phila., 1930	

Hits
254 Frank J. O'Doul, Phila., 1929	257 George Sisler, St. Louis, 1920
254 Bill Terry, New York, 1930	

Doubles
64 Joseph M. Medwick, St. L., 1936	67 Earl W. Webb, Boston, 1931

Triples
36 J. Owen Wilson, Pitts., 1912	26 Joseph Jackson, Cleve., 1912
	26 Samuel Crawford, Detroit, 1914

Home Runs
56 Hack Wilson, Chicago, 1930	61 Roger Maris, New York, 1961
	(162-game schedule)
	60 Babe Ruth, New York, 1927

Runs Batted In
190 Hack Wilson, Chicago, 1930	184 Lou Gehrig, New York, 1931

Stolen Bases
118 Lou Brock, St. Louis, 1974	96 Ty Cobb, Detroit, 1915

Bases on Balls
148 Eddie Stanky, Brooklyn, 1945	170 Babe Ruth, New York, 1923
148 Jim Wynn, Houston, 1969	

Strikeouts
189 Bobby Bonds, S.F., 1970	175 Dave Nicholson, Chicago, 1963

Pitching (Season)
Games
106 Mike Marshall, L.A., 1974	88 Wilbur Wood, Chicago, 1968

Innings Pitched
434 Joseph J. McGinnity, N.Y., 1903	464 Edward Walsh, Chicago, 1908

Victories
41 Jack Chesbro, New York, 1904	37 Christy Mathewson, N.Y., 1908

Losses
29 Victor Willis, Boston, 1905	26 John Townsend, Wash., 1904
	26 Robert Groom, Wash,, 1909

Strikeouts
(Lefthander)
382 Sandy Koufax, Los Angeles, 1965	343 Rube Waddell, Phila., 1904

(Righthander)
289 Tom Seaver, New York, 1971	383 Nolan Ryan, Cal., 1973

Bases on Balls
185 Sam Jones, Chicago, 1955	208 Bob Feller, Cleveland, 1938

Earned-Run Average
(Minimum 200 Innings)
1.12 Bob Gibson, St. L., 1968	1.01 Hubert Leonard, Boston, 19

Shutouts
16 Grover C. Alexander, Phila., 1916	13 John W. Coombs, Phila., 1910